ver 1.0

끝장편입

독해 유형편
핵심 (Top 20)

편입, 이제 이 책으로 **끝장**내자!

▶ 추가 응용문제 다운로드 가능
올바른선생님연합 자료실 이용

▶ 끝장편입 인터넷강의
크리스선생님 영상자료 활용

▶ 인서울 Top 20위 대학
  3개년 기출유형 제시

▶ 편입 수험생들을 위한
  정답해설 정밀 분석노트

▶ 편입영어 독해 유형별
  접근방식 제시

올바른선생님연합 편입영어 연구팀

편입을 준비하는 수험생들을 위해 대학별 다양한 유형과 난이도를 분석하여, 더 나은 학습 전략 그리고 효율성의 극대화를 목표로 두고 있습니다. 연합 어학연구소의 우수한 연구진과 현장 선생님들의 최신 정보력을 바탕으로 다양한 편입영어 교재를 개발하고 있습니다.

끝장편입 독해 유형편(핵심) TOP 20

펴낸곳 올바른선생님연합 편입부 출제위원 **책임기획** 크리스선생님 **저자** 크리스선생님
검토위원 강영미, 김문경, 김정현, 박도희, 배상윤, 서은지, 송영석, 오재욱, 윤준섭, 정일호, 조원웅, Jen **영문교열** Mark Kim
디자인 이정화, Hannah(장희영) (이미지 Freepik.com) **편집** 이정화, Hannah(장희영)
물류1 류순기 **물류2** 연합지역배송 2팀 (영샘문고) **인쇄팀** 박동제(사피엔스컬쳐) **제지팀** 김경석
발행일 2022년 06월 24일 **ISBN** 979-11-89120-43-6 **교재문의** 02-1600-3474 **집필부** 070-4740-2001 **FAX** 070-7680-0049

본 교재의 독창적인 내용에 대한 일체의 무단 전재 및 모방은 법률로 금지되어 있습니다.

Edition Copyright ⓒ 2022 by 대한민국 올바른선생님연합 Inc.

All right reserved. No part of this publication may be reproduced, stored in a retreval system, or transmitted in any form or by any means, electronic, mechanical, photocopying, recording, or otherwise, without the prior permission of the copyright owner.

독해 유형편
핵심 (Top 20)

끝장 편입

편입, 이제 이 책으로 끝장내자!

TOP 20

가천대학교	상명대학교
가톨릭대학교	서울여자대학교
강남대학교	세종대학교
건국대학교	숙명여자대학교
경기대학교	인하대학교
광운대학교	한국산업기술대학교
국민대학교	한국항공대학교
단국대학교	한성대학교
덕성여자대학교	한양대학교 에리카
명지대학교	홍익대학교

머리말
PREFACE

『끝장편입 독해 유형편(핵심)』을 기획하면서

안녕하세요. 끝장편입에 크쌤입니다. 선생님이 현장에서 수업을 하면서, 인서울 상위권 대학을 위한 편입영어의 핵심은 바로 독해라고 이야기합니다. 그 이유는 상위권 편입영어로 올라갈수록 시험 유형이 문법보다는 독해 문제가 많아지고 논리 정연한 글로 가득한 지문들이 많이 등장하기 때문입니다. 그래서 가장 고난도 수업 기술이 요구되는 수업이기도 하고, 선생님이 개인적으로 제일 좋아하는 수업 이기도 하답니다.

하지만, 준비되지 않은 편입 수험생들에겐 독해는 늘 어렵기만 하고, 멀게만 느껴집니다. 마치 여태껏 해온 학창 시절 영어 독해와는 차원이 다른 것 즈음으로 받아들이는 학생들도 많습니다. 그래서 선생님이 편입영어 상위권 대학의 독해 유형 분류를 『유형편 기본』, 『유형편 핵심(top20)』, 그리고 『유형편 도전(top6)』 이렇게 3가지로 나누어 보았습니다.

이 책은 독해 기본이 잡힌 학생들이 봐야 하는 그러면서 가장 많은 학생들이 응시하는 대학교들의 독해유형들로 엮은 『끝장편입 독해 유형편 핵심(top20)』입니다. 책의 구성은 실제 출제되었던 독해 지문과 문제로만 구성하였습니다. 즉, 주로 응시하는 top 20위 대학교들의 최신 출제 유형과 정답 접근 방법을 체화하기 위한 전략서입니다.

마지막으로, 정답해설은 독학하는 학생들을 위한 그리고 상위권을 도전하는 학생들을 생각하며 제작하였습니다. 즉 선생님의 정성을 담은 손필기 방식의 정밀 분석 노트로 구현한 만큼, 편입학을 준비하는 학생들에게 큰 도움이 될 겁니다. 수험생 여러분 반드시 『끝장편입 독해 유형편』을 통해 편입영어의 최신 유형별 학습 방식과 정답 접근 전략을 자기 것으로 만들 수 있길 바랍니다. 마지막까지 '끝장편입' 크쌤이 여러분들을 응원하겠습니다.

2022년 여름이 올 때 즈음
끝장편입 크리스선생님 서재에서

Preview 끝장편입 독해 유형편 (핵심) Top 20

문제집

01 실제 유형 표시

문장삽입

forbidden federal employees

02 출제된 년도와 학교 표시

text and drive. E

2020학년도 건국대학교 인문·예체능계 A형 32번

03 가독성 있는 배치

006 글의 흐름으로 보아, 주어진 문장이 들어가기에 가장 적절한 것은?

With all the water now in the atmosphere, the intense ultraviolet radiation from the Sun split the water molecules into hydrogen and oxygen.

① A   ② B   ③ C   ④ D   ⑤ E

유형 03 문장삽입

문장삽입

President Obama has forbidden federal employees from texting while driving. A The federal Transportation Department plans to do the same for commercial-truck and Interstate-bus drivers. B And support is building in Congress for legislation that would require states to outlaw texting or e-mailing while driving. C Such distractions cause tens of thousands of deaths each year. But the way to stop people from using cellphones while driving is not to make it a crime. D A more effective way is to make it difficult or impossible to text and drive. E

2019학년도 상명대학교 인문·자연계 32번

005 아래 문장을 위 본문 중에 추가할 경우, 가장 적절한 위치를 고르시오.

Too many drivers value convenience more than safety and would assume they wouldn't get caught.

문장삽입

Do you know why Venus is so hot? A Scientists think the original atmospheres of both Venus and Earth were created from gases released by volcanoes, when both planets were very young and volcanic activity was much more intense. B But because Venus is so close to the Sun, the "greenhouse effect," in which heat is trapped within its atmosphere, results in the temperature rising so high that all the surface water evaporated. C The hydrogen escaped into space and the oxygen combined with other chemicals in the atmosphere. D In contrast, Earth cooled down, oceans formed, and life began to develop. E Earth became a living planet while Venus, despite its connection to the goddess of love and fertility, remained barren.

2019학년도 건국대학교 인문·예체능계 A형 25번

006 글의 흐름으로 보아, 주어진 문장이 들어가기에 가장 적절한 것은?

With all the water now in the atmosphere, the intense ultraviolet radiation from the Sun split the water molecules into hydrogen and oxygen.

① A   ② B   ③ C   ④ D   ⑤ E

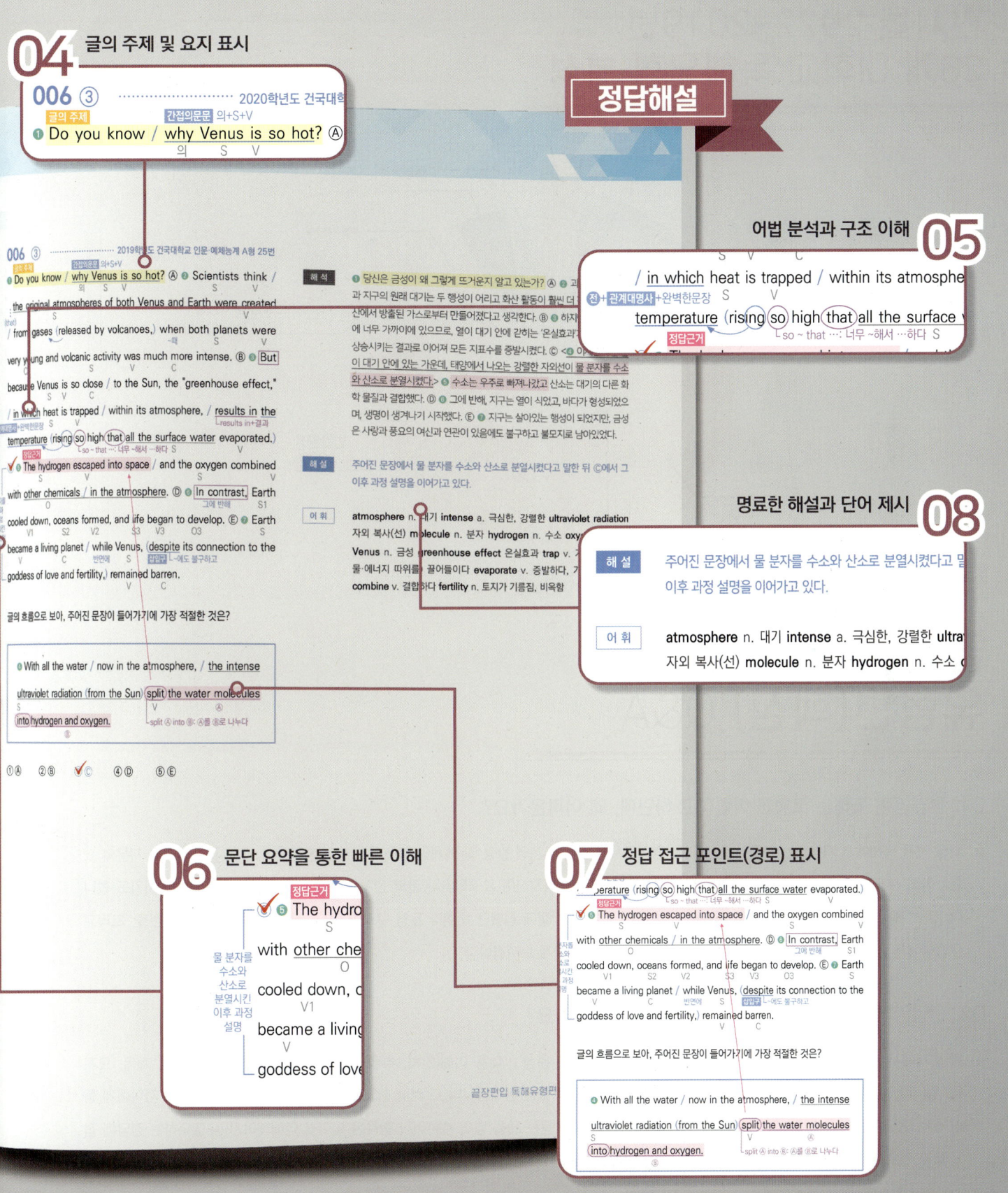

인서울 2022~2019년 26개 대학교 독해유형 분석

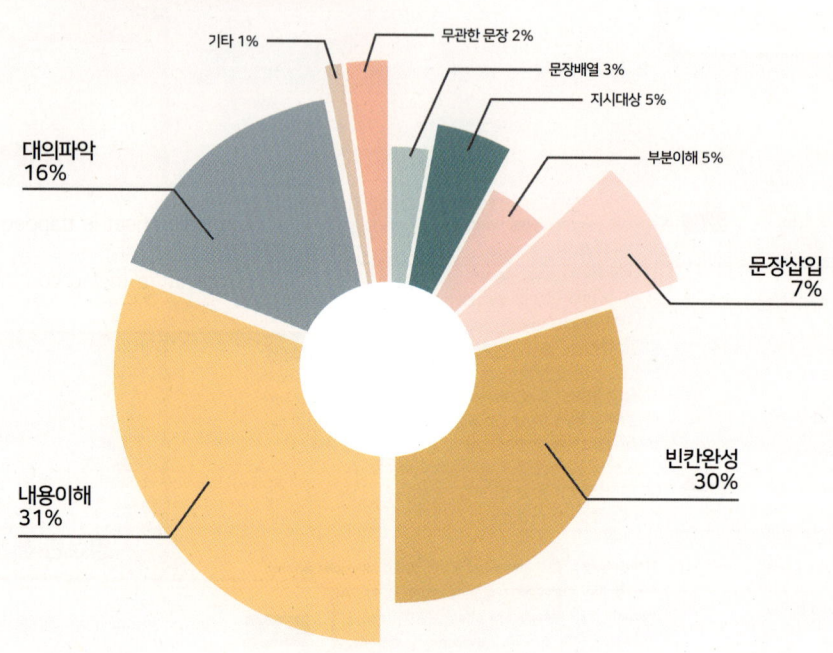

끝장편입 독해 유형편(핵심) Q&A

Q1. 편입영어 독해는 그렇게 어렵다고 하던데, 왜 어려운가요?

A. 가장 먼저 독해에서 사용되는 지문이 인문 과학 영어원서나 관련 주제의 칼럼 및 에세이 등에서 발췌된 지문들이 많습니다. 따라서 지문의 표현들이 원서 작가의 필체가 그대로 담겨있습니다. 그렇다 보니 배경지식이 요구되거나 글의 전개가 논문처럼 복잡한 논리로 이어지기도 합니다. 두 번째로는 어휘나 영어 문장의 구문들이 일반적으로 학창 시절에 접했던 어휘나 문장 구조가 아닌, 상당한 전문 용어와 표현들, 그리고 문법책에서 설명되지 않은 어법 구조들이 등장하다 보니 더욱 어렵게 느껴집니다.

Q2. 편입영어 독해는 일반 영어 시험과 유형도 다른가요?

A. 위 통계에서 보다시피 편입영어에서 가장 많은 출제 유형은 '빈칸완성', '내용 이해(일치, 추론, 파악)', 그리고 '대의 파악(주제, 제목, 요지 등)'입니다. 이런 유형 자체는 일반 여러 영어 시험에서 자주 볼 수 있는 형태입니다. 그러나 정답에 접근하는 방법이 더욱 어렵고 까다롭게 형성되어 있습니다. 예를 들면 내용 이해 유형에서는 객관적 사실을 묻는 것을 넘어 추론이나 함축된 의미를 이해해야지만, 질의하는 정답에 접근할 수 있도록 출제됩니다. 그렇다 보니 수험생들은 난해함 혹은 시간의 압박으로 당황스럽게 느껴질 수 있습니다.

Q3. 그렇다면 편입영어 독해는 어떻게 준비해야 하나요?

A. 기본적으로 글의 대의를 파악하는 능력부터 길러져야 합니다. 무작정 글을 읽는 것이 아니라 글의 소재 그리고 글쓴이가 이 글을 통해 무슨 말을 하고자 하는 것인지를 가늠하며 읽는 것을 말합니다. 그리고 난 뒤 목표하는 대학의 출제 유형들을 많이 접하고 실전 문제를 풀어봄으로써 패턴을 이해할 필요가 있습니다. 구체적 팁은 다음과 같습니다.

∴ 책을 많이 읽는 사람이 책을 잘 읽고 이해합니다.

많은 문제를 풀어봐야 합니다. 다만, 편입영어라는 특수한 시험인 만큼, 연관성 있는 책이나 문제집을 통해 집중하실 수 있길 바랍니다. 그리고 학교마다 독해의 수준 차이가 상당합니다. 따라서,『끝장편입 독해유형(기본)』과 같은 입문서 문제집을 통해 기본을 쌓은 뒤,『끝장편입 독해유형(핵심)』,『끝장편입 독해유형(도전)』등의 책으로 목표하는 대학교 문제를 많이 풀고 수준과 정답에 접근하는 방법을 체화할 수 있어야 합니다.

∴ 문제집을 한 번 풀고 난 다음에는 반드시 복습할 것

처음 『끝장편입 독해 유형편(핵심)』을 1회 풀고 난 뒤, 틀린 문제를 다시 정독하여 읽고 답을 찾아봅니다. 그리고 난 뒤에는 비록 맞춘 문제라 할지라도 해당 지문에 등장했던 몰랐던 표현이나 구문 이해가 어려웠던 문장들을 다시 한번 정리하면서, 고난도 구문 독해 능력을 계속해서 키워나가야 합니다.

∴ 정독과 다독을 할 것

문제집을 많이 풀어보는 것이 다독이라면, 1개 지문을 혹은 1개 문제집을 정확하게 독해하는 것이 정독입니다. 올바른 다독은 올바른 정독에서 비롯됩니다. 모르는 표현과 구문이 있는데도 정리하지 않고 바쁜 마음에 문제집 개수나 문제 푸는 양에만 집착하는 학생들이 있습니다. 1개 문제집을 완료하는 순간은 해당 문제집에서 몰랐던 표현을 정리 및 암기하고, 구문 해석이 어려웠던 문장들을 모두 이해한 것이라고라고 말하고 싶습니다.

∴ 어렵다고 어려운 문제만 풀지 말 것

일부 편입영어 독해 문제는 매우 어렵습니다. 그리하여 항상 어려운 문제나 지문들을 읽는 것만이 옳은 학습이라 생각하는 경우가 있습니다. 특히 독학생들이 그렇게 한다면 금방 지치거나 고통스러울 수 있습니다. 따라서 쉬운 지문이나 유형부터 잡아나가야 합니다. 예를 들면, 비전문가가 경제학 논문을 잘 이해하려면, 경제학 교양 입문서를 통한 전반적 이해와 지식 습득이 우선인 것처럼 말입니다. 그분만 아니라 인서울 편입학 영어 필답고사에서 합격점이 90점을 넘는 경우가 그리 많지 않습니다. 따라서 맞출 수 있는 문제부터 안정적인 답을 찾아간다는 목표, 그리고 집중하면 충분히 독해하고 문제를 풀 수 있는 교재를 많이 다독하길 바랍니다.

∴ 독학생들은 정답해설이 잘 되어 있는 교재로 공부할 것

혼자 공부하는 학생들은 풀이에 많은 시간이 걸립니다. 따라서 정답해설이 친절하고 가독성이 중요합니다. 고등부 교재가 일반적으로 정답해설 수준이 좋습니다. 또는『끝장편입 시리즈』처럼 분석 노트가 겸비된 편입영어 문제집이 혼자서 공부하는 학생들에겐 가장 안성맞춤입니다.

끝장편입 독해
유형편 유형분석

STEP 1 — 끝장편입 독해 유형편 (기본)
top 26개 대학교 기출 분석 후 응용한 문제 패턴으로 각 유형별 체화를 위한 기본서
(실제 기출 및 출제 가능 지문으로 구성)

STEP 2 — 끝장편입 독해 유형편 (핵심) top 20
가장 응시를 많이 하는 주요 대학교 실제 기출 지문을 유형별로 구성함.
: 가천대, 가톨릭대, 강남대, 건국대, 경기대, 광운대, 국민대, 단국대, 덕성여대, 명지대, 상명대, 서강대, 서울여대, 세종대, 숙명여대, 인하대, 한국산업기술대, 한국항공대, 한성대, 홍익대

STEP 3 — 끝장편입 독해 유형편 (도전) top 6
편입학 등급이 가장 높은 학교들의 실제 기출 지문을 유형별로 구성함.
: 서강대, 성균관, 이화여대, 중앙대, 한국외대, 한양대

1. 대의파악(제목, 주제, 요지, 목적) [중요 유형]

인서울 20개 대학 모든 독해 지문 유형에서 약 16%를 차지하고 있다. 그럴 뿐만 아니라 각 편입영어 독해 유형의 기본 틀이다. 따라서 각 글의 소재와 주제를 파악하며 글을 읽는 것, 그리고 선택지의 구성을 이해하는 것이 매우 중요하다. 주로 1개의 분명한 정답 선택지, 1~2개의 매력적인 오답 선택지, 그리고 2~3개의 완전 오답 선택지로 구성된다. 정답과 매력적인 오답 선택지들에는 공통으로 글의 '소재'의 낱말이 들어있다. 따라서 사전에 선택지의 구성을 먼저 파악함으로써 글의 소재를 가늠하며 읽는 것도 좋은 방법이다.

2. 문장배열

글의 문단을 논리적 흐름이나 순서에 따라 배열하는 유형으로서 일반적인 흐름 즉 큰 범주에서 작은 것으로 이어지거나, 『주제에서 논증』 또는 『주제 반전 후 논증』 형태의 자주 볼 수 있는 전개와 단서에 항상 유의해야 한다. 난이도가 쉬운 경우 지시어, 대명사, 연결어 등으로도 간단하게 파악할 수 있다(수능 수준과 동일).

3. 문장삽입

문장의 본래 위치를 찾는 유형이며, 출제가 빈도가 그리 높지는 않지만 비교적 난이도가 높아 오답률이 높다. 기본적으로 전후 내용의 인과 관계, 대명사, 관사 및 연결사 등을 통해 글 전개의 순서를 파악하자. 그리고 절대 답이 될 수 없는 순서를 선택지에서 먼저 소거(지우는)하는 전략을 쓰는 것도 좋다.

4. 무관한 문장

글의 전반적인 일관성을 파악하면서 내용과 맞지 않는 문장을 찾아내야 한다. 주로 『같은 소재에 다른 주제』 또는 앞뒤가 맞지 않은 글의 기조로 이어지는 형태가 정답이다.

5. 빈칸완성 중요 유형

내용 이해와 함께 가장 빈번하게 출제되는 유형으로서 약 30%를 차지했으며, 학생들이 가장 까다로워하는 유형이기도 하다. 정·오답 근거를 찾는 독해 풀이의 체화 그리고 상당한 독해의 집중력과 맥락 이해가 요구된다. 주로 글의 주제(대의) 혹은 이를 뒷받침하는 핵심 논증 구간에 빈칸으로 출제된다.

6. 내용이해(일치, 추론, 파악) 중요 유형

정독과 함께 객관적인 글의 내용 이해 뿐만 아니라 논리에 따른 사고가 요구되는 유형이다. 대부분 학교에서 가장 많이 나오는 유형으로서 세부적으로는 내용 『일치』, 『추론』, 『파악』 이렇게 나뉜다. 비슷하지만 세부 유형별로 약간의 정답 접근법의 차이가 있다. 이 유형은 시험 시간 조절에 상당한 영향을 미치며, 시간의 압박에서 집중을 흩트려 놓는 문제를 일으키기도 한다. 전략은 정독과 속독의 능력 그리고 어휘력과 추론의 능력까지 요구된다.

1. 『내용 일치』
수능 영어와 같은 형태로 객관적 사실을 빠르게 찾아 나가야 한다. 주로 선택지 순서별로 정답의 근거를 지문에서 찾을 수 있다.

2. 『내용 추론』
지문의 내용을 이해한다면 선택지와 같은 언급도 가능한 것인가를 물어보는 유형이다. 즉, 어떤 판단을 근거로 다른 판단도 끌어낼 수 있는 것을 찾는 유형이다. (가장 시간이 오래 걸리고 까다로운 유형)

3. 『내용 파악』
지문의 특정 부분의 이해나 내용을 묻는 유형이다. 예를 들면, "왜 주인공은 미국으로 갔는가?"와 같은 구체적 질문을 주고 그에 대한 답을 찾아야 하는 유형이다.

7. 부분이해

밑줄 친 부분의 이해를 묻는 유형이다. 밑줄 친 문장의 이해를 위해선 앞뒤 문장의 정확한 구문 독해가 가능해야 한다. 간단하게는 깊은 유추가 필요하지 않은 단순한 표현(낱말)을 묻기도 한다. 하지만 어렵게 출제되는 학교는 해당 부분 의미를 유추하기 위해 전후(앞뒤) 문장뿐만 아니라 전체적인 글의 흐름과 논리에 따른 추론도 요구된다.

8. 지시대상

주로 인칭대명사를 활용한 등장인물, 사건, 영향 등이 무엇인지를 묻는 유형이다. 따라서 대명사나 한정사(관사, 지시사, 소유격 대명사 등) 등 의미를 특정해주는 어구들을 분명하게 파악하는 습관이 필요하다. 흔히 대명사가 가리키는 것은 바로 앞 문장에 있음을 주목하자.

9. 기타: 태도, 분위기, 어조, 견해

출제 빈도수가 매우 드문 유형이다. 내용의 주체를 파악하고 인물이나 필자의 심경, 상황 묘사가 주는 어감 등을 종합적으로 파악하여 정답을 찾아야 한다. 정답의 접근 방법은 문체에 드러난 어휘에 근거를 두어야 한다.

크쌤 목차 구성 방법:

1~4강을 통해서 글의 전반적인 흐름 즉 전개를 이해하는 연습이 가장 선행되어야 한다. 그래서 목차 순서를 먼저 배치하였다. 그리고 난 뒤 글의 전개를 잘 이해해야만 맞힐 수 있는 빈칸완성 유형을 배치하였으며, 다음으로 세부적이고 꼼꼼한 지문 이해가 요구되는 내용이해 유형을 순서로 하였다.

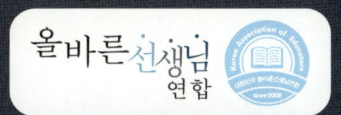

	문제	정답
유형 01. 대의파악	013	006
유형 02. 문장배열	039	046
유형 03. 문장삽입	053	066
유형 04. 무관한 문장	069	088
유형 05. 빈칸완성	081	108
유형 06. 내용이해	111	146
유형 07. 부분이해	141	194
유형 08. 지시대상	157	218
유형 09. 기타	171	240

2022학년도 올바른 책 시리즈의
다양한 교재 정보와 자료를
좌측 QR코드를 통해
확인하세요.

유형 01
대의파악
(제목, 주제, 요지, 목적)

Teacher Chris Tip

인서울 20개 대학 모든 독해 지문 유형에서 약 16%를 차지하고 있다. 그럴 뿐만 아니라 각 편입 영어 독해 유형의 기본 틀이다. 따라서 각 글의 소재와 주제를 파악하며 글을 읽는 것, 그리고 선택지의 구성을 이해하는 것이 매우 중요하다. 주로 1개의 분명한 정답 선택지, 1~2개의 매력적인 오답 선택지, 그리고 2~3개의 완전 오답 선택지로 구성된다. 정답과 매력적인 오답 선택지들에는 공통으로 글의 '소재'의 낱말이 들어있다. 따라서 사전에 선택지의 구성을 먼저 파악함으로써 글의 소재를 가늠하며 읽는 것도 좋은 방법이다.

가천대학교	상명대학교	한국항공대학교
가톨릭대학교	서울여자대학교	한양대학교 에리카
건국대학교	세종대학교	홍익대학교
경기대학교	숙명여자대학교	
광명대학교	숭실대학교	
국민대학교	아주대학교	
덕성여자대학교	인하대학교	
명지대학교	한국산업기술대학교	

유형 01 대의파악 | 제목, 주제, 요지, 목적

• 주어진 글을 읽고 물음에 답하시오.

글의 제목

There is a difference between striving for excellence and striving for perfection. The first is attainable, gratifying and healthy. The second is often unattainable, frustrating, and neurotic. It's also a terrible waste of time. The stenographer who retypes a lengthy letter because of a trivial error, or the boss who demands such retyping, might profit from examining the Declaration of Independence. When the inscriber of that document made two errors of omission, he inserted the missing letters between the lines. If this is acceptable in the document that gave birth to American freedom, surely it would be acceptable in a letter that will be briefly glanced at en route to someone's file cabinet or wastebasket!

2020학년도 가톨릭대학교 인문계 A형 28번

001 What is the best title for the passage above?
① Don't Be a Perfectionist
② Accuracy Is the Key to Success
③ The Need to Strive for Excellence
④ Lessons from the Declaration of Independence

글의 제목

I had a great-uncle of whom nothing is known. I don't even know his name, if I ever did. He came to America in the 1920s and never wrote home. Got rich, my relatives said. How do you know that? I asked. Nobody knew how they knew. They had heard rumors. Then the people who'd heard the rumors died. Today there's no one left to ask. My great-uncle was like one of those ants who, coming upon a line of marching ants, turns and goes in the opposite direction for reason of his own. Ants being ants, this is not supposed to happen, but it sometimes does, and no one knows why.

2019학년도 광운대학교 인문계 A형 27번

002 글의 제목으로 가장 적절한 것은?
① My Mythical Great-Uncle Interests Me!
② My Great-Uncle Immigrated to America!
③ My Great-Uncle Made Amazing Rumors!
④ My Great-Uncle Studied Ants' Activities!
⑤ My Successful Great-Uncle Became Insane!

Mosquitoes are without a doubt one of the biggest nuisances to endure during summer. It seems like they do us no good and only harm. Though extremely annoying, mosquitoes are actually very crucial and important to the food chain. Not all mosquitoes attack humans. It's actually only the female mosquitoes that suck blood from people in order to reproduce. The male mosquitoes, however, live on nectar from flowers. They, in fact, play a substantial role in producing flowers as the second most active pollen deliverer after the bee! If they stop spreading pollen around as much as they do, flowers will start disappearing. But it doesn't stop there; the animals that eat plants will also be affected and so on.

2019학년도 건국대학교 인문·예체능계 A형 29번

003 다음 글의 주제로 가장 적절한 것은?
① 인간에게 미치는 모기의 해악
② 모기의 성별에 따른 생태학적 차이
③ 먹이 사슬에서 모기의 역할
④ 모기가 전염시키는 질병의 위험성
⑤ 효율적인 모기 퇴치 방안

I still believe, many years after coming to Johnson University from my native Canada, that teaching is a noble calling and that professors are obligated to serve their students. Yet, no professor can be all things to all students, so one must be prepared to temper one's aspirations with practicality. For me, this balancing act has led me to focus my working life primarily on assisting my students in the development of their English as a foreign language speaking and listening skills by endeavoring to be an effective classroom teacher and a useful researcher. In the classroom, I understand the importance of motivating learners to exceed their English language limits without setting unreasonable goals for them to achieve. If I were to abandon reason and set impractical learning goals, the result would likely be failure, which would in turn negatively impact motivation. So I have sought to invoke passion in my students for learning while at the same time being practical about the expectations that I have for them.

2019학년도 경기대학교 인문·예체능계 A형 40번

004 Which of the following is the most appropriate title for this passage?
① Balance in an Academic Context
② Practicality is the Key to Effective Instruction
③ Teaching Is a Noble Profession
④ Daily Life at Johnson University

유형 01 대의파악

글의 제목

You may not always have access to a first aid kit in an emergency. Here are some suggestions for other everyday items you can use. If you don't have water to cool the burn, use juice, beer, or milk. In fact, use any cold, harmless liquid, until you have access to cold running water. The aim is to cool the area as quickly as possible, using whatever cold liquid is available. Remember: the burn should be cooled for at least ten minutes for the treatment to be effective. If you don't have cling film to cover the burn, use a clean plastic carrier bag, a freezer bag, or similar. These types of items will not stick to the burn and will create a barrier to stop infection. Plastic bags are particularly useful for covering a burned hand or foot.

2019학년도 인하대학교 인문계 04번

005 Which is the best title for the passage?
① No First Aid Kit? No Problem
② Basic Ways to Prevent Burns!
③ Why Are We Learning First Aid?
④ Who to Treat First in Emergency
⑤ Alternative Medicine to Save People

글의 제목

Some psychiatrists, such as Thomas Lewis from the University of California, hypothesize that romantic love is rooted in experiences of physical closeness in childhood — for example, how we felt in our mother's arms. These feelings of comfort and affection are written on our brain, and as adults, our constant inclination is to find them again. According to this theory, we love whom we love not so much because of the future we hope to build, but rather because of the past we hope to live again. The person who "feels right" has a certain look, smell, sound, or touch that activates very deep memories.

Evolutionary psychologists explain, however, that survival skills are inherent in our choice of a mate. According to this hypothesis, we are attracted to people who look healthy — for example, a woman with a 70 percent waist-to-hip ratio is attractive because she can likely bear children successfully. A man with rugged features probably has a strong immune system and therefore is more likely to give his partner healthy children.

2019학년도 한국산업기술대학교 인문계 33번

006 Which is the best title of the passage?
① The Relation of Love and Affection
② The Best Way to Find the Life Partner
③ Reasons to be Attracted to Someone
④ Different Types of Romantic Love

In this first decade of the twenty-first century, the world community is confronted with staggering problems. There are 6 billion people on our globe and forecasters project that the world population will reach 10 billion by 2050. Those people will need food, shelter, and an education that will allow them to lead fulfilled lives. The twentieth century saw great advances in many fields, but these advances did not come without costs. Acid rain, for example, polluted our vegetation, wild life, and the very bodies of millions of people. Together, the people of the world need to stop the systemic despoiling of our planet. Weaponry, such as nuclear devices and improvised explosive devices, daily threaten the world's peace and progress. Religious fanaticism, hunger, and poverty have bred a desperate terrorism in many corners of the world. It is no overstatement to say that we are in a race for global survival.

2019학년도 숙명여자대학교 인문계 28번

007 What would be the best title for the above passage?
① Great Advances Made in the Twentieth Century
② Global Warming, Vegetation, and Wildlife
③ Great Advances Made with Significant Costs Paid
④ How to Lead Fulfilled Religious Lives
⑤ Desperate Terrorism and Global Survival

Going to university is supposed to be a mind-broadening experience. That assertion is presumably made in contradiction to training for work straight after school, which might not be so stimulating. But is it actually true? Jessica Golle of the University of Tubingen in Germany thought she would try to find out. Her result, however, is not quite what might be expected. She found that those who have been to university do indeed seem to leave with broader and more inquiring minds than those who have spent their immediate post-school years in vocational training for work. However, it was not the case that university broadened minds. Rather, work seemed to narrow them. In the university group, changes in personalities or attitudes were not detectable. But those who had chosen the vocational route had become more conscientious but showed marked drops in interest in tasks that are investigative and enterprising in nature, and that might restrict their choice of careers.

2019학년도 한양대학교 에리카 인문계 A형 33번

008 위 글의 제목으로 가장 알맞은 것을 고르시오.
① Vocational Training in Germany
② Advantages of Early Job Training
③ Benefits of University versus Work
④ Career Choices for High School Graduates

Whereas the discovery of the double-helical structure of DNA was originally revered, it is now thought to have opened a door to an uncertain future. The scientists were able to put new DNA parts into living cells immediately, those activities were looked upon suspiciously. It was considered that human civilization could be destroyed by some disease that could be engineered into cells. People realized that calls needed to be made for strict rules to control such research. Because of this, it took a while before scientists discovered recombinant-DNA technology. The controlling rules did not get put into action, fortunately, so when the fears about DNA technology went unfounded, all attempts at regulation, even moderate, dissipated.

009 Which of the following is best for the main idea of the passage?

① Successful attempts at regulations on DNA technology
② The unreliability of biology technology
③ Groundless fear of DNA technology
④ The potential of biological advances

In most paper and pencil tests, the test-taker is presented with all the items, usually in ascending order of difficulty, and is required to respond to as many of them as possible. This is not the most economical way of collecting information on someone's ability. There is no real need for strong candidates to attempt easy items, and no need for weak candidates to attempt difficult items. Computer adaptive testing offers a potentially more efficient way of collecting information on people's ability. All test-takers are presented initially with an item of average difficulty. The computer goes on to present individual candidates with items that are appropriate for their apparent level of ability as estimated by their performance on previous items, raising or lowering the level of difficulty until a dependable estimate at their ability is achieved.

010 Choose the best title of the following passage.

① Rationale behind Test-takers' Preference for Computer Adaptive Testing
② How to Encourage Weak Candidates to Attempt Difficult Questions
③ The History of Sequencing Test Items Based on Item Difficulty
④ The Efficacy of Computer Adaptive Testing in Estimating Ability

Vigorous debates are going on today about whether our world could sustain double its present population (along with its consumption and waste), or even whether our world's economy is sustainable at its present level. Yet those aren't the biggest risks. If, through globalization, everyone living on Earth today were to achieve the standard of living of an average American, the effect on the planet would be some 10 times what it is today, and it would certainly be unsustainable.

We can't prevent people around the world from aspiring to match our way of life any more than the exporters of cultures during the first wave of globalization could expect other cultures not to embrace the farming way of life. But since the world couldn't sustain even its present population if all people lived the way that those in the First World do now, we are left with a paradox. Globalization, most analysts feel, is unstoppable. But its consequences may overtax the Earth's ability to support us. That's a paradox that needs resolving.

2019학년도 상명대학교 인문·자연계 19번

011 윗 글의 제목으로 적절한 것을 고르시오.

① Environmental Crisis Caused by Overpopulation
② Imbalance of Life Standards Between America and Farming Societies
③ Problems of Globalization
④ Increasing Living Costs in the First World
⑤ Solutions for Sustainable Development

The Egyptians were certainly the first civilization to preserve food on a large scale. Those narrow fertile strips on either bank of the Nile were their principal source of food, and a dry year in which the Nile failed to flood could be disastrous. To be prepared, Egyptians put up food in every way they could, including stockpiling grain in huge silos. This fixation on preserving a food supply led to considerable knowledge of curing and fermentation. Were it not for their aversion to pigs, the Egyptians would probably have invented ham, for they salt-cured meat and knew how to domesticate the pig. But Egyptian religious leadership pronounced pigs carriers of leprosy*, made pig farmers social outcasts, and never depicted the animal on the walls of tombs. They tried to domesticate for meat the hyenas that scavenged** the edge of villages looking for scraps and dead animals to eat, but most Egyptians were revolted by the idea of eating such an animal. Other failed Egyptian attempts at an animal husbandry include antelope and gazelle. But the Egyptians did succeed in domesticating fowl — ducks, geese, quail, pigeon, and pelican. Ancient walls show fowl being splayed, salted, and put into large earthen jars. *leprosy 나병, 한센병, **to scavenge 쓰레기를 뒤지다

2019학년도 서울여자대학교 인문·자연계 A형 35번

012 Which of the following does the passage mainly discuss?

① Preservation of food in Ancient Egypt
② Food and wall-painting in Ancient Egypt
③ Domestication of animals by the Egyptians
④ Importance of the Nile in Egyptian civilization

Ticked off, peeved, irritated, bothered, annoyed, no matter how you may say it, being angry is an emotion no one enjoys feeling. But while it's completely normal and human to experience anger, problems can come into play when we don't process our feelings in a healthy way. Anger can become a very real, chronic issue, if not handled properly and in a timely manner. You could find yourself blowing up at the smallest things, doing or saying things in the heat of the moment that you later regret.

Here are some healthy ways to process your anger. It may sound silly, but counting to ten (or, if you're really angry, 100) is a great way to immediately relieve some built up tension. Why? Because it focuses your mind on the specific task of taking care of yourself first.

Plenty of things can cause anger but those problems can also be solved if you're willing to meet them head-on. Rather than just blowing up and storming off when your teen misbehaves, your co-worker annoys you or your spouse doesn't see eye-to-eye with you on a certain issue, work on getting to the root of the problem. Discussing differences in a way that all parties involved feel respected and letting someone you care about know how you feel are things every human being is capable of doing.

013 What is the best headline for the 3rd paragraph?
① Give yourself a time out
② Address the issue
③ Hit the gym
④ Find a way to endure

> 글의 주제
>
> The "three worlds" model of geopolitics first arose in the mid-20th century as a way of mapping the various players in the Cold War. The First World included the United States and its capitalist allies in places such as Western Europe, Japan and Australia. The Second World consisted of the communist Soviet Union and its Eastern European satellites. The Third World, meanwhile, encompassed all the other countries that were not actively aligned with either side in the Cold War. These were often impoverished former European colonies, and included nearly all the nations of Africa, the Middle East, latin America and Asia. Today, the powerful economies of the West are still sometimes described as "First World," but the term "Second World" has become largely obsolete following the collapse of the Soviet Union. "Third World" remains the most common of the original designations, but its meaning has changed from "non-aligned" and become more of a blanket term for the developing world.
>
> 2019학년도 가톨릭대학교 인문계 A형 27번

014 What is the passage mainly about?

① Why the term Second World is rarely used today

② The three worlds model as a relic of the Cold War

③ The significance of the three worlds model in modern political scene

④ Original use of three worlds model terminology and its current adoption

Shawn wants to be sure that his nursing home foodservice is using environmentally sound practices. He plants a small organic garden and the residents who can do so enjoy working in the garden. Shawn carefully integrates the produce into his menu. This is an excellent practice and everyone wins. Shawn then decides to purchase beef from a local farmer. But because Shawn's operation is in a large metropolitan area, he must travel frequently to the ranch, which is 250 miles away, to ensure proper practices that meet his green requirements, and he must then go to the packing company to select his meat and the packing company is another 150 miles away. The packer must then travel in a small truck to Shawn's operation several times per week. The travel that Shawn and the small packer's truck must undertake to accomplish this green practice results in a larger carbon footprint than receiving a shipment from a large truck that was making fewer trips would. This does not mean that Shawn cannot find a more environmentally friendly source of beef – he simply must consider more than just the appearance of eco-friendliness.

015 What is the main point of the passage?

① Meat production causes more environmental harm than vegetable growing.

② Organic farming is more sustainable, but less productive than conventional farming.

③ We should consider both farming methods and food miles when assessing eco-friendliness of food.

④ When purchasing beef that meets green requirements, buying it in bulk helps reduce the environmental impact.

Thousands of people will go into the bush this summer to cut the high cost of living. A man who gets his two weeks' salary while he is on vacation should be able to put those two weeks in fishing and camping and be able to save one week's salary clear. He ought to be able to sleep comfortably every night, to eat well every day and to return to the city rested and in good condition. But if he goes into the woods with a frying pan, an ignorance of black flies and mosquitoes, and a great and abiding lack of knowledge about cookery, the chances are that his return will be very different. He will come back with enough mosquito bites to make the back of his neck look like a relief map of the Caucasus. His digestion will be wrecked after a valiant battle to assimilate half-cooked or charred grub. And he won't have had a decent night's sleep while he has been gone. He will solemnly raise his right hand and inform you that he has joined the grand army of never-agains.

2019학년도 상명대학교 인문·자연계 24번

016 위 글의 목적으로 가장 적절한 것을 고르시오.

① To inform the benefits of comfortable camping out
② To prepare men before joining military camps
③ To advocate decent camping sites
④ To warn the dangers of unprepared camping out
⑤ To describe people's responses after camping out

Whether you get car sick, sea sick or light-headed from playing interactive video games, motion sickness is seriously unpleasant. *Kinetosis*, the official term, can affect both kids and adults at varying levels. So what is the root cause of motion sickness?

According to neurologist Dr Hain, it is caused by conflict between the senses responsible for registering motion. If the eyes, inner ear and sensory nerves in the skin are all sending different signals to the brain, the cross-talk will leave you feeling ill.

Dr Rosenman says some individuals feel nauseous from reading while reading in a car or bus because their eyes are focusing on a steady (non-moving) thing, but the inner ear senses motion, so your brain gets confused and you feel sick. Drivers have an advantage over passengers because they anticipate what is coming next and are less dependent on external senses.

If you can't be the driver, the next best place to sit is the front passenger seat and keep your gaze focused on the road ahead. When the senses match, this prevents sensory conflict and motion sickness. Stop what you're doing or try looking at something outside that is still and in front of you, so that your ears and eyes get similar information.

2019학년도 국민대학교 인문계 오후 A형 20번

017 What is the passage mainly about?

① The reason for motion sickness
② The importance of reactive behaviors
③ Dangers of construction on winding roads
④ Factors to be considered in car seat designs

Today we are confronted with an expanding array of technical means for making acts of seeing themselves into objects of observation. The most advanced forms of surveillance and data analysis used by intelligence agencies are now equally indispensable to the marketing strategies of large businesses. Widely employed are screens or other forms of display that track eye movements, as well as durations and fixations of visual interest in sequences or streams of graphic information. One's casual perusal of a single web page can be minutely analyzed and quantified in terms of how the eye scans, pauses, moves, and gives attentive priority to some areas over others. Even in the ambulatory* space of big department stores, eye-tracking scanners provide detailed information about individual behavior — for example, determining how long one looked at items that one did not buy. A generously funded research field of optical ergonomics** has been in place for some time. Passively and often voluntarily, one now collaborates in one's own surveillance and data-mining.

* ambulatory 보행의 ** ergonomics 인체공학

2019학년도 서울여자대학교 인문·자연계 A형 37번

018 Which of the following does the passage mainly discuss?

① Technological innovations in the process of production
② New methodologies of data analysis in management science
③ The ways an observer is turned into an object of observation
④ The prison surveillance system utilizing inmates' optical activities

A special case of time deepening is multitasking. The term multitasking (and multiprocessing) was originally applied to a computer's ability to execute more than one task or program at the same time. In contemporary parlance it applies the concept of time deepening to work tasks. Multitasking typically involves juggling phone calls, e-mails, instant messages, and computer work all at once in order to be more productive. Several research reports, however, provide evidence that multitasking doesn't actually increase productivity. The findings of neuroscientists, psychologists and management professors suggest multitasking slows you down and increases the chances of mistakes. Doing more than one task at a time prohibits our ability to process information. The young, according to conventional wisdom, are the most adept multitaskers; e-mailing, instant messaging, listening to iPods, and studying at the same time. Yet, in one recent study of young Microsoft workers, it took them 15 minutes to be able to return to serious mental tasks, like writing reports or computer code, after responding to incoming e-mails or instant messages. It is estimated that the cost of such lost productivity to the U.S. economy is nearly $650 billion a year.

019 What does the passage mainly discuss?

① Tips for how to encourage multitasking
② Effects of multitasking on work productivity
③ Positive influence of multitasking on time saving
④ Importance of connecting multitaskers to computer work
⑤ Ways that technology-enabled communication thrives in workplace

유형 01 대의파악

글의 목적

If you were to enter the baby's room in a typical American home today, you would probably see a crib full of stuffed animals and colorful toys dangling directly over the infant. Some of these toys may light up, move, or play music. What do you suppose is the parents' reasoning behind providing infants with so much to see and do? Aside from the fact that babies seem to enjoy and respond positively to these toys, most parents believe that children need a stimulating environment for optimal brain development.

The question of whether certain experiences produce physical changes in the brain has been a topic of research among scientists for centuries. In 1785, Vincenzo Malacarne, an anatomist, studied pairs of dogs from the same litter and pairs of birds from the same batches of eggs. For each pair, he would train one participant over a long period of time while the other would be equally cared for but untrained. He discovered later, in his autopsies of the animals, that the brains of the trained animals appeared more complex, with a greater number of folds and fissures. In the 19th century, attempts were made to relate the circumference of the human head with the amount of learning a person had experienced. Although some early findings claimed such a relationship, later research determined that this was not a valid measure of brain development.

2019학년도 세종대학교 인문계 A형 48번

020 Which of the following best describes the purpose of writing the above passage?

① to introduce a line of scientific research
② to advertise a new line of toys for children
③ to advise parents about the best child-rearing practices
④ to report a problematic phenomenon in society

021 Which is the best title for the passage?

① Why Home Teams Win
② Athletes' Challenging Spirit
③ Supportive Audience: Good or Bad?
④ Why Figure Skating Gains Popularity

Heading to the 2002 Winter Olympics, a 21-year-old American figure skater Michelle Kwan was favored to win her first gold medal. An accomplished skater, she had already won four world championships and six U.S. titles. True to form, she entered the final four minutes of competition at a distinct advantage — she was in first place and in front of a home crowd rooting for her to win. She proceeded; however, she fell to the ice on her triple flip. She finished third. In sharp contrast, 16-year-old Sarah Hughes had very low expectations. As she put it, "I skated for pure enjoyment." Yet she proceeded through a highly challenging program and skated flawlessly. In the end, she won the gold.

What happened? Was Kwan feeling too pressured? Could an arena filled with supportive and expectant fans have made it worse, causing her to "choke" under pressure? A study reports that an audience of friendly faces raises the pressure — and our fear of failure (we hate to disappoint those who root for us). It also makes us more self-conscious, a state of mind that can cause athletes to stiffen up. Either way, these results seem at odds with the home-field advantage known to exist in professional sports. Across the board, statistics show that home teams tend to win. Perhaps the added pressure in these situations is offset by other advantages.

There are certain things that, so far, social media seem to do very well. The most remarkable one is coordination. Coordinating large numbers of people to do exactly the same thing at the same time is notoriously difficult. So long as the activity is relatively simple — say, show up and protest the government — the new social media drastically reduce the costs of coordination. But if social media are good at coordinating simple events, so far they have failed at building political parties on a grander scale. In Egypt and Tunisia, the tech savvy young people who facilitated anti-government protests have already begun to fall behind in the race to political organization. Ahead of them are Islamic democrats, political groups that have years of experience in attracting, organizing and mobilizing followers.

Why should Facebook and Twitter be good for social parties but not political parties? It's too soon to know definitively, and of course it is possible that, as technology changes and user culture evolves, more complex political organizations may come out of social media. For now, however, the answer seems to lie in the fact that they lack the kinds of contacts needed to create extended political cohesion. To show up at a social gathering, I don't need to have any close or repeated bonds with the other people. All of us can show up, enjoy ourselves and go our separate ways. The key is that our objective is simple rather than complex. Political organization, by contrast, is very complicated indeed. A successful political organization must generate beliefs about the way the world works and how it should be. It must reflect a shared ethos or morality. Above all, it must produce some sense of community.

022 Which of the following would be the most suitable title for the passage?

① Social Media's Limitations
② Social Media vs. Political Parties
③ Advantages of Social Media
④ Ethos of Social Media

A druid was a member of the high-ranking professional class in ancient Celtic cultures. While perhaps best remembered as religious leaders, they were also legal authorities, adjudicators, lorekeepers, medical professionals, and political advisors. While the druids are reported to have been literate, they are believed to have been prevented by doctrine from recording their knowledge in written form, thus they left no written accounts of themselves. They are however attested in some detail by their contemporaries from other cultures, such as the Romans and the Greeks.

The earliest known references to the druids date to the fourth century BC and the oldest detailed description comes from Julius Caesar's *Commentarii de Bello Gallico* (50s BC). They were also described by later Greco-Roman writers such as Cicero, Tacitus, and Pliny the Elder. Following the Roman invasion of Gaul, the druid orders were suppressed by the Roman government under the 1st century AD emperors Tiberius and Claudius, and had disappeared from the written record by the 2nd century.

In about 750 AD the word druid appears in a poem by Blathmac, who wrote about Jesus, saying that he was " ... better than a prophet, more knowledgeable than every druid, a king who was a bishop and a complete sage." The druids then also appear in some of the medieval tales from Christianized Ireland like the "Iain 86 Cuailnge," where they are largely portrayed as sorcerers who opposed the coming of Christianity. In the wake of the Celtic revival during the 18th and 19th centuries, fraternal and neopagan groups were founded based on ideas about the ancient druids, a movement known as Neo-Druidism. Many popular notions about druids, based on misconceptions of 18th century scholars, have been largely superseded by more recent study.

023 Which of the following would be best for the title?
① Roman Empire and the Druids
② Christianity and the Druidism
③ Historical Accounts on the Druids
④ Neopaganism or Neo-Druidism?

Perhaps more than any other element, the rise of commerce and consumerism as a central feature of the American economy determined the customs of Christmas charity and, more obviously, gift-giving. Earlier in the nineteenth century, especially in rural areas and along the frontier, gifts had been of necessity usually simple and homemade (although youngsters regarded "store-bought" candy with particular fondness). Commonly, children received most of them. Mothers knitted, tied, stuffed, laced, stitched, or baked special treats. Fathers whittled and carved toys.

As the nation became more market-oriented, such homey pleasures sometimes seemed inadequate. Stores and shops throughout the nation offered the consumer an ever-growing feast of choices, nearly any of which might be made a gift.

By late nineteenth century, the definition of gift had broadened to include every category of practical housewares, novelty items, greeting cards, money, extravagant oddities, and simple mementos. There was, in a phrase, something for everyone. Beginning in the 1880s and lasting for many years, cheap and useless novelties known as "gimcracks" enjoyed a vogue. Those seeking more tasteful, but still relatively inexpensive, tokens of goodwill gave Prang Christmas cards. These could be framed, displayed on Christmas trees or on special racks, or made into wallpaper appropriate for home china cabinets. Others turned their attention to more prosaic and efficient wares; household work savers became acceptable gifts for mothers and wives. Parents, aunts, and other well-meaning elders could always rely on a gold piece or a $2 bill as a gift intended to encourage a child's habit of saving.

It would be erroneous to assume, however, that the new marketplace alone determined the importance of Christmas gifts. Several studies of gift-giving in the twentieth century suggest that the custom helps chart and establish hierarchies of social relationships. Gift acts as tangible evidence of ties between and among individuals. Those who participate in a gift transaction determine the worth of an item.

024 Which of the following would be best for the title?
① A History of Christmas Gifts in America
② The Best Gifts for Your Children
③ Why You Should Make Your Own Christmas Gift
④ The Consumer Pattern in the Frontier Regions

글의 제목

[A] The first brains appeared on earth about 500 million years ago, spent a leisurely 430 million years evolving into the brains of the earliest primates and another 70 million years evolving into the brains of the first protohumans. Then, something happened and the soon-to-be-human brain experienced an unprecedented growth spurt that more than doubled its mass in a little over two million years, transforming it from the one-and-a-quarter-pound brain of Homo habilis to the nearly three-pound brain of Homo sapiens.

[B] Now if you were put on a hot-fudge diet and managed to double your mass in a very short time, we would not expect all of your various body parts to share equally in the gain. Your belly and buttocks would probably be the major recipients of newly acquired flab, while your tongue and toe would remain relatively svelte and unaffected. Similarly, the dramatic increase in the size of the human brain did not democratically double the mass of every part so that modern people ended up with new brains that were structurally identical to the old ones, only bigger. Rather a disproportionate share of the growth centered on a particular part of the brain known as the frontal lobe.

[C] Scientists noticed that although patients with frontal lobe damage often performed well on standard intelligence tests, they showed severe impairment on any test that involved planning. They even found it practically impossible to say what they would do later that afternoon. This finding helps us assume that the frontal lobe is a time machine that allows each of us to vacate the present and experience the future before it happens. No other animals have a frontal lobe quite like ours, which is why we are the only animal that thinks about the future as we do. If the story of the frontal lobe tells us how people conjure their imaginary tomorrows, it doesn't tell us why.

2019학년도 아주대학교 인문계 A형 47번

025 Which of the following is the best title for the above passage?

① The Steady Evolution of the Human Brain
② The Importance of Brain Size
③ Amazing Human Brain Power Demystified
④ Future-Planning Brain Areas
⑤ Impact of Brain Damage on Time-Concept

유형 01 대의파악

• Read the following passages and answer the questions

> 글의 목적

To go into solitude, a man needs to retire as much from his chamber as from society. I am not solitary whilst I read and write, though nobody is with me. But if a man would be alone, let him look at the stars. The rays that come from those heavenly worlds will separate between him and what he touches. One might think the atmosphere was made transparent with this design, to give man, in the heavenly bodies, the perpetual presence of the sublime. Seen in the streets of cities how great they are! If the stars should appear one night in a thousand years, how would men believe and adore; and preserve for many generations the remembrance of the city of God which had been shown! But every night come out these envoys of beauty, and light the universe with their admonishing smile.

The stars awaken a certain reverence, because though always present, they are inaccessible; but all natural objects make a kindred impression, when the mind is open to their influence. Nature never wears a mean appearance. Neither does the wisest man extort her secret, and lose his curiosity by finding out all her perfection. Nature never became a toy to a wise spirit. The flowers, the animals, the mountains, reflected the wisdom of his best hour, as much as they had delighted the simplicity of his childhood.

When we speak of nature in this manner, we have a distinct but most poetical sense in the mind. We mean the integrity of impression made by manifold natural objects. It is this which distinguishes the stick of timber of the wood-cutter from the tree of the poet. The charming landscape which I saw this morning is indubitably made up of some twenty or thirty farms. Miller owns this field, Locke that, and Manning the woodland beyond. But none of them owns the landscape. There is a property in the horizon which no man has but he whose eye can integrate all the parts, that is, the poet. This is the best part of these men's farms, yet to this their warranty-deeds give no title.

2019학년도 홍익대학교 서울 인문계 A형 37번

026 Which of the following is the purpose of the passage?

① to inform his readers of the hidden rule of the heavenly bodies
② to persuade his readers to go into a quiet retirement
③ to encourage his readers to participate in an environmental movement
④ to remind his readers of the wonderful values of nature

Astronomers all over the world were waiting In excitement as August 1993 approached. Mars Observer, the American spacecraft, was scheduled to move into orbit around Mars and begin sending new information back to Earth. In addition to mapping the planet, Mars Observer was going to study the Martian atmosphere and surface. Unfortunately, scientists lost contact with Mars Observer on August 24. The Mars Observer mission, which cost $845 million, failed. In contrast, the United States' previous mission to Mars was a great success. In 1976, two American spacecraft landed on Mars in order to search for signs of life. The tests that the Viking landers performed had negative results. However, scientists still had questions about our close neighbor in space. They wanted to investigate further into the possibility of life on Mars. This was the purpose of the Mars Observer mission.

Scientists were dissatisfied with the Viking mission. The two sites where the spacecraft landed provided safe landing places, but they were not particularly interesting locations. Scientists believe there are other areas on Mars that are similar to specific places on Earth that support life. For example, an area in Antarctica, southern Victoria Land, which is not covered by ice, resembles an area on Mars. In the dry valleys of southern Victoria Land, the temperature averages below zero, yet biologists found simple life forms in rocks and frozen lakes. Perhaps this is also true of places on Mars.

Scientists want another investigation of Mars. They want to map the planet's surface and land a spacecraft in a more promising location. They want to search for fossils, the ancient remains of life. If life ever existed on Mars, scientists believe that future missions might find records of it under sand, or in the ice. They are very disappointed in the failure of the Mars Observer mission and want to start a new mission.

027 위 글의 제목으로 가장 적절한 것은?
① Missions to Find Life on Mars
② The Disaster of Mars Observer
③ Astronomers' Challenge In Mars
④ How Earth and Mars are Similar
⑤ Future Spacecraft for Space Travel

• Read the following passages and answer the questions

글의 주제

The term normal or healthy can be defined in two ways. Firstly, from the standpoint of a functioning society, one can call a person normal or healthy if he is able to fulfill the social role he is to take in that given society. More concretely, this means that he is able to work in the fashion which is required in that particular society, and furthermore that he is able to participate in the reproduction of society that he can raise a family. Secondly, from the standpoint of the individual, we look upon health or normalcy as the optimum of growth and happiness of the individual. If the structure of a given society were such that it offered the optimum possibility for individual happiness, both viewpoints would coincide.

However, this is not the case in most societies we know, including our own. Although they differ in the degree to which they promote the aims of individual growth, there is a discrepancy between the aims of the smooth functioning of society and of the full development of the individual. This fact makes it imperative to differentiate sharply between the two concepts of health. The one is governed by social necessities, the other by values and norms concerning the aim of individual existence. Unfortunately, this differentiation is often neglected.

Most psychiatrists take the structure of their own society so much for granted that to them the person who is not well adapted assumes the stigma of being less valuable. On the other hand, the well-adapted person is supposed to be the more valuable person in terms of a scale of human values. If we differentiate the two concepts of normal and neurotic, we come to the following conclusion: the person who is normal in terms of being well adapted is often less healthy than the neurotic person in terms of human values. Often he is well adapted only at the expense of having given up his self in order to become more or less the person he believes he is expected to be. All genuine individuality and spontaneity may have been lost. On the other hand, the neurotic person can be characterized as somebody who was not ready to surrender completely in the battle for his self. To be sure, his attempt to save his individual self was not successful, and instead of expressing his self productively he sought salvation through neurotic symptoms and by withdrawing into a phantasy life. Nevertheless, from the standpoint of human values, he is less crippled than the kind of normal person who has lost his individuality altogether.

2019학년도 한국항공대학교 인문계 19번

028 Which one is the above passage mainly about?

① The discrepancy between the two definitions of health, and the significance of the neurotic.
② The malfunction of the neurotic in comparison with the healthy and the normal.
③ The harmonious relationship of the normal, the healthy, and the neurotic in a normal society.
④ The reductionism of the unhealthy and the neurotic in relation to individuality in an abnormal society.

The doctrine of original sin is the oldest manifestation of the rotten-to-the-core dogma, but such thinking has not died out in our democratic, secular state. Freud dragged this doctrine into twentieth-century psychology, defining all of civilization (including modern morality, science, religion, and technological progress) as just an elaborate defense against basic conflicts over infantile sexuality and aggression. We "repress" these conflicts because of the unbearable anxiety they cause and this anxiety is transmuted into the energy that generates civilization. So the reason I am sitting in front of my computer writing this preface — rather than running out to rape and kill — is that I am "compensated," zipped up and successfully defending myself against underlying savage impulses.

Freud's philosophy, as bizarre as it sounds when laid out so starkly, finds its way into daily psychological and psychiatric practice, wherein patients scour their past for the negative impulses and events that have formed their identities. Thus the competitiveness of Bill Gates is really his desire to outdo his father, and Princess Diana's opposition to landmines was merely the outcome of sublimating her murderous hatred for Prince Charles and the other royals. The rotten-to-the-core doctrine also pervades the understanding of human nature in the arts and social sciences.

Just one example of thousands is *No Ordinary Time*, a gripping history of Franklin and Eleanor Roosevelt written by Doris Kearns Goodwin, one of the great living political scientists. Musing on the question of why Eleanor dedicated so much of her life to helping people who were black, poor, or disabled, Goodwin decides that it was "to compensate for her mother's narcissism and her father's alcoholism." Nowhere does Goodwin consider the possibility that deep down, Eleanor Roosevelt was pursuing virtue. Motivations like exercising fairness or pursuing duty are ruled out as fundamental; there must be some covert, negative motivation that underpins goodness if the analysis is to be academically respectable.

I cannot say this too strongly: In spite of the widespread acceptance of the rotten-to-the-core dogma in the religious and secular world, there is not a shred of evidence that strength and virtue are derived from negative motivation. I believe that evolution has favored both good and bad traits, and any number of adaptive roles in the world have selected for morality, cooperation, altruism, and goodness, just as any number have also selected for murder, theft, self-seeking, and terrorism. This dual-aspect premise is the cornerstone of the second half of this book. Authentic happiness comes from identifying and cultivating your most fundamental strengths and using them every day in work, love, play, and parenting.

029 What would be the best title of the passage above?
① The hidden power of negative motivation
② Dual aspects of human nature
③ The illusion of pursuing virtuous behaviors
④ Authentic happiness derived from negative motivation

• Read each passage and answer the corresponding questions for each.

글의 제목

A At the time of the First World War the transfer of Western ideas and institutions beyond Europe's boundaries was well under way. At the height of European imperialism, aspiring young non-Western men, commonly from privileged families, went to study in Europe or the United States. Westerners themselves established Western schools in lands under their domination. There arose a non-Western intelligentsia, its members prompted by the most advanced Western ideals and equipped with Western learning. Their sense of human dignity was patterned after that of their teachers, yet stunted because the Westerns treated them as inferior. Copying their Western masters, these uprooted and inwardly divided intellectuals became nationalists. Western-educated, they wanted to be "modern" Turks, Arabs, Indians, or Africans. They wanted their nations to be respected.

B These educated nationalists soon became revolutionaries as well, because colonial officials or traditional rulers generally suppressed open resistance. As revolutionaries they turned elitist and socialist. They believed that their people did not know how to make themselves strong. Yet the Western-trained, non-Western intelligentsia also remained dedicated — at least in the abstract — to the democratic ideal. How its eliticism and pro-Western orientation could be reconciled with its faith in the common people and its attachment to indigenous culture remained an unresolved problem for the future.

C The progress of this intelligentsia varied from one non-Western country to the next. In the dying Ottoman Empire, for instance, the Western-trained young Turks seized power in 1908. After the collapse of their ramshackle state at the end of World War 1, they created a reasonably modern and stable Turkey under the leadership of Kemal Ataturk. The transformation was achieved in relatively short order and has endured to the present.

D The experience in India, though, was more representative of non-Western trends. British-educated Indians, with the help of a British civil servant, established in 1885 the Indian National Congress and made it the instrument of a moderate Indian nationalism. Radicalized by World War 1, the Indian National Congress fell under the sway of Mohandas Gandhi, one of the most remarkable of the Westernized anticolonial leaders. Under the British rule for over 150 years, India developed effective nationalist leadership and administrative, legal and economic structures suitable for nationhood. Its Westernization proceeded from both above and below: from British rule and native resistance to it. When independence came in 1947, the Indian subcontinent was split into two states: India and Pakistan. The chief flaw in Indian nationalism lay in the insurmountable religious division between Muslims and Hindus. Independence was followed by a war of communal riots that took many hundreds of thousands of lives.

2019학년도 아주대학교 인문계 A형 19번

030 Which of the following would be the best title for the above passage?

① Worldwide Westernization
② Experiments in Globalism
③ The Rise of the Industrial Age
④ Obstacles to Political Developments
⑤ Global Dominance of Western Imperialism

유형 02
문장배열

Teacher Chris Tip

글의 문단을 논리적 흐름이나 순서에 따라 배열하는 유형으로서 일반적인 흐름 즉 큰 범주에서 작은 것으로 이어지거나, 『주제에서 논증』 또는 『주제 반전 후 논증』 형태의 자주 볼 수 있는 전개와 단서에 항상 유의해야 한다. 난이도가 쉬운 경우 지시어, 대명사, 연결어 등으로도 간단하게 파악할 수 있다(수능 수준과 동일).

가톨릭대학교
건국대학교
국민대학교
명지대학교
인하대학교
한국산업기술대학교
한성대학교
한양대학교 에리카

Ⓐ In the immune system, that job is done by T-cells, which recognize the molecular signatures of threats to their owner's well-being.

Ⓑ To defeat the enemy, you must first know the enemy.

Ⓒ The technology they use merges gene therapy, synthetic biology and cell biology.

Ⓓ Recently, researchers explained how turbocharging these cells can boost the immune system's ability to fight cancer, and possibly other illnesses, too.

001 Which is the proper order of sentences Ⓐ~Ⓓ?

① Ⓐ – Ⓑ – Ⓒ – Ⓓ
② Ⓑ – Ⓐ – Ⓓ – Ⓒ
③ Ⓒ – Ⓐ – Ⓓ – Ⓑ
④ Ⓓ – Ⓒ – Ⓐ – Ⓑ

Human beings can eat many different kinds of food, but some people choose not to eat meat. Vegetarians often have more in common than just their diet. Their personalities might be similar, too.

(A) They are competitive and good at business. They are also usually in a hurry. Many fast-food eaters might not agree with this description of their personalities, but it is a common picture of them.

(B) For example, vegetarians in the United States and Canada may be creative people, and they might not enjoy competitive sports or jobs. They worry about the health of the world, and they are probably strongly opposed to war.

(C) Some people eat mostly fast food. One study shows that many fast food eaters have a lot in common with one another, but they are very different from vegetarians.

002 다음 글에 이어질 글의 순서로 가장 적절한 것은?

① (A) – (C) – (B)   ② (B) – (A) – (C)
③ (B) – (C) – (A)   ④ (C) – (A) – (B)
⑤ (C) – (B) – (A)

Navigation is the science of accurately determining one's location and then planning and following a route. The earliest form of navigation was land navigation. This relied on physical landmarks to chart the journey from one place to another. Away from land, one must use other markers in order to navigate successfully.

Ⓐ Latitude is distance north or south of Earth's equator.
Ⓑ These are two kinds of imaginary lines drawn on maps or globes representing the Earth.
Ⓒ One modern way to do this is to keep track of one's position using longitude and latitude.

Longitude is distance east or west of the Greenwich Meridian, an imaginary line that runs from the North Pole to the South Pole and through Greenwich, England.

2019학년도 한양대학교 에리카 인문계 A형 25번

003 전체 글의 의미가 통하도록 Ⓐ~Ⓒ의 순서를 알맞게 배열한 것을 고르시오.
① Ⓐ - Ⓑ - Ⓒ
② Ⓑ - Ⓒ - Ⓐ
③ Ⓒ - Ⓑ - Ⓐ
④ Ⓒ - Ⓐ - Ⓑ

[I] The exact reason is unclear, but it may be related to the effect of carotenoid levels in the blood.

[II] A study conducted by the University of Queensland's School of Pharmacy involving more than 12,000 Australians revealed that the benefits of a fresh produce-rich diet extend beyond physical health.

[III] With every added daily portion of fruits or vegetables (up to eight), the subjects' happiness levels rose slightly.

[IV] The researchers calculated that if someone were to switch from a diet free of fruit and vegetables to eight servings per day, he or she would theoretically gain as much life satisfaction as someone who transitioned from unemploymnet to a job.

2018학년도 국민대학교 인문계 오전 A형 14번

004 Which is the proper order of the four sentences [I]~[IV]?
① [I]-[III]-[II]-[IV]
② [II]-[III]-[IV]-[I]
③ [III]-[II]-[I]-[IV]
④ [IV]-[II]-[III]-[I]

유형 02 문장배열

단락배열

> Much of the appeal of soccer lies in the fact that it can be played without special equipment.

Ⓐ Understandably so, a bladder alone did not last very long, so as time passed people began to protect the bladders in a shell made of animal skin properly cured to turn it into leather.

Ⓑ Children everywhere know that a tin can, some bound-up rags, or a ball from a different sport entirely can be satisfyingly kicked around. This ingenuity was first displayed hundreds of years ago when people discovered that an animal's bladder could be inflated and knotted to provide a light, bouncy ball.

Ⓒ This design worked so well that it is still used to this day, but with modern, synthetic materials rather than animal products.

2019학년도 명지대학교 인문계 14번

005 Choose the best order after the sentence given in the box.

① Ⓐ - Ⓒ - Ⓑ   ② Ⓑ - Ⓐ - Ⓒ
③ Ⓑ - Ⓒ - Ⓐ   ④ Ⓒ - Ⓐ - Ⓑ

문장배열

> If you are not an early adopter, you almost certainly know one.

Ⓐ She was the first person in our group of friends to own a smart phone, and she couldn't wait to show you what it could do. He was the guy who talked excitedly about moving all his data to the cloud before you even knew what the cloud was.

Ⓑ While the majority of us sit back and wait for an innovation to prove itself, the early adopters jump right in.

Ⓒ Early adopters are that minority of users who adopt a new technology in its earliest days before it is widely used or even thoroughly tested. According to one widely cited piece of research, early adopters are defined as the first thirteen percent or so of people who begin using a device, game, social network, or other new product.

Ⓓ By doing so, they get the pleasure of conquering a new frontier, enhanced prestige, and even power within the tech industry.

2020학년도 인하대학교 인문계 09번

006 Which of the following is the best order for a passage starting with the given sentence in the box?

① Ⓐ - Ⓒ - Ⓑ - Ⓓ   ② Ⓐ - Ⓑ - Ⓓ - Ⓒ
③ Ⓑ - Ⓐ - Ⓓ - Ⓒ   ④ Ⓑ - Ⓓ - Ⓐ - Ⓒ
⑤ Ⓓ - Ⓐ - Ⓒ - Ⓑ

• Read the following passages and answer the questions.

Mark Twain wrote *The Adventures of Huckleberry Finn* in the late nineteenth century, but he set his novel decades earlier when slavery was still legal, making his book an extended exploration of the morality of one person owning another human being.

Ⓐ As long as the country as a whole condoned and benefitted from such an exploitative practice of labor, no black American could consider himself truly free.

Ⓑ Slavery in the American South was a brutal institution involving the physical and psychological domination of black people to serve as laborers on American cotton and tobacco plantations.

Ⓒ But the free labor that slaves were forced to perform still constituted the major force behind the American economy.

Ⓓ By 1804 all Northern states had abolished slavery within their borders.

That is why Jim's emancipation at the end of *Huckleberry Finn* is bittersweet, rather than fully triumphant. Jim's wife and children are still slaves, as are all the other enslaved characters in the story.

007 Which of the following is the best order for a passage?

① Ⓐ – Ⓑ – Ⓒ – Ⓓ
② Ⓐ – Ⓓ – Ⓒ – Ⓑ
③ Ⓑ – Ⓓ – Ⓒ – Ⓐ
④ Ⓑ – Ⓐ – Ⓓ – Ⓒ
⑤ Ⓒ – Ⓓ – Ⓐ – Ⓑ

Ⓐ At first, the Tsingy landscape forms like other karst landscapes; water begins to erode the rock and causes small holes and cracks to form. As more water flows into the caves, the process of eroding continues, making the caves larger and larger.

Ⓑ As the process continues, the tops of some of the caves collapse, creating even bigger caves. The roofs of other caves may collapse. At this point, the landscape is a series of rock pillars and deep canyons. As more rain falls, it erodes the rock pillars more and more, and forms the sharp, knifelike points that you can see now.

Ⓒ Karst landscapes form in areas where limestone is exposed to the weather. The best example is Tsingy de Bemaraha National Park located near the western coast of the island of Madagascar. The word Tsingy can be translated into English as something like "place where one cannot walk without shoes," and that's an appropriate name. The limestone peaks can be very sharp. In fact, some people call this area the Forest of Knives.

008 Choose the appropriate order of the paragraphs.

① Ⓐ – Ⓒ – Ⓑ
② Ⓑ – Ⓐ – Ⓒ
③ Ⓒ – Ⓐ – Ⓑ
④ Ⓒ – Ⓑ – Ⓐ

The diversity of plant colors and odors probably fascinated humans long before the history of writing and long before the start of modern science. It seems intuitively convincing that immobile plants can increase their fitness by attracting the animals they depend on for dispersal of pollen and seeds.

A This occurs obviously if sensory traits, such as odor and color, are fine-tuned to the sensory abilities of the animals so that they stand out from the environment.

B The adaptive framework of signaling is even more appealing because of our own inherent biases.

C Pollinators and seed dispersers in turn can forage more effectively if plant colors and odors are matched to their sensory abilities.

It is a long-standing hypothesis that color vision, the sense we humans rely upon most for evaluating our distant environment, evolved as an adaptation to locate colorful fruits against a predominantly green background.

009 Which is the proper order of A - C?
① A - B - C
② B - A - C
③ B - C - A
④ C - A - B

A Typically below unconfined aquifers are confined aquifers and are topped with an impermeable layer of stone and clay. Therefore, while there is some part that remains unconfined to allow for water recharge, most of the groundwater remains under high pressure. If a well should be drilled into the rock, the groundwater will rise to the surface.

B Deep underground are large deposits of water. These reservoirs can be found in every kind of environment including deserts. The total amount of this groundwater is significantly more than the sum of all lakes and rivers. Most of the water existing underground is found in aquifers, layers of porous rock that can store water. Scientists categorize them into two types: unconfined and confined. The unconfined aquifer lies under a layer of permeable material. As a result, it can easily receive water from the surface, and the water table surface fluctuates up and down, depending on the rate of water recharge.

C Confined and unconfined aquifers are refilled by groundwater. However, the rate for them differs. Most groundwater is the result of rain penetrating the soil. The water will then trickle down to the lower layers until it reaches the aquifer. Confined aquifers recharge at a slower rate than unconfined. This is mainly because the water has more difficulty entering them. In tropical regions, recharge occurs during the rainy seasons. In more temperate regions, it happens during the winter.

010 Choose the appropriate order of the paragraphs.
① A - C - B
② B - A - C
③ C - A - B
④ C - B - A

• Read the following passages and answer the questions.

단락배열

Ⓐ How can you stop these tiny invaders from making you sick? Your skin is the first defense against germs. One of the easiest ways to prevent some illnesses is simply by washing with soap and water. But germs can still enter the body through small cuts in the skin or through the mouth, eyes, and nose.

Ⓑ There are two types of germs: viruses and bacteria. Viruses use the cells inside animals or plants to live and multiply. Viruses cause illnesses such as influenza, or the flu. Bacteria are tiny creatures. Some bacteria are good. They can help your stomach digest food. Other bacteria aren't as good. They can cause sore throats and ear infections.

Ⓒ A germ is a bit of living matter capable of growth and development into an organism. Germs can cause many problems, including disease. The germs that make people sick are everywhere. You can't see them, but they're there. They're sitting on your desk. They're hiding on your computer's keyboard. They're even in the air that you are breathing.

2019학년도 한성대학교 인문계 A형 11번

011 Which one is the right order?
① Ⓑ - Ⓒ - Ⓐ   ② Ⓑ - Ⓐ - Ⓒ
③ Ⓒ - Ⓑ - Ⓐ   ④ Ⓒ - Ⓐ - Ⓑ

문장배열

Ⓐ They can also darken light that helps you see better. Ⓑ This superior lens technology was first discovered when NASA scientists looked to nature for a means to superior eye protection — specifically, by studying the eyes of eagles, known for their extreme visual acuity. Ⓒ But now, independent research conducted by scientists from NASA's Jet Propulsion Laborato has brought forth ground-breaking technology to help protect human eyesight from the harmful effects of solar radiation light. Ⓓ Some ordinary sunglasses can obscure our vision by exposing your eyes to harmful UV rays blue light and reflective glare.

This discovery resulted in what is now known as Eagle Eyes. Eagle Eyes features the most advanced eye protection technology ever created. It offers triple-filter polarization to block 99.9% UVA and UVB as well as the added benefit of blue-light eye protection. Eagle Eyes is the only optic technology that has qualified official recognition from the Space Certification Program for this remarkable technology.

2019학년도 한성대학교 인문계 A형 36번

012 Which one is the right order?
① Ⓓ - Ⓐ - Ⓒ - Ⓑ   ② Ⓐ - Ⓑ - Ⓒ - Ⓓ
③ Ⓓ - Ⓐ - Ⓑ - Ⓒ   ④ Ⓐ - Ⓑ - Ⓓ - Ⓒ

유형 02 문장배열

문장배열

No one really knows how many species of animal there are in the world, but one estimate puts it at just under nine million.

Ⓐ Some biologists calculate that between 0.01% and 0.1% of all species could become extinct annually. This rate would mean between 900 and 9,000 extinctions every year.

Ⓑ While this is an alarming rate, it is not inevitable that an animal will become extinct. In fact, a number of animals that were close to dying out have actually been brought back from the edge of extinction.

Ⓒ However, the majority of species have not been identified, and we are still discovering new ones at a rapid rate. Since we have identified so few animals, it is difficult to determine the rate of extinction.

Achieving such a feat may help ensure the biodiversity and health of the animal kingdom.

2019학년도 한양대학교 에리카 인문계 A형 36번

013 전체 글의 의미가 통하도록 Ⓐ~Ⓒ의 순서를 알맞게 배열한 것을 고르시오.

① Ⓐ – Ⓑ – Ⓒ ② Ⓑ – Ⓐ – Ⓒ
③ Ⓑ – Ⓒ – Ⓐ ④ Ⓒ – Ⓐ – Ⓑ

문장배열

Several studies suggest that there are gender differences in language use in children as young as 3 years old. Preschool boys tend to be more assertive and demanding in their conversational style, whereas preschool girls tend to be more polite and cooperative.

Ⓐ And, when conflict arises, boys handle it differently than girls do. Amy Sheldon (1990) videotaped same-sex triads of preschool girls and boys at a day care center.

Ⓑ Given these gender differences in preschoolers' conversational style, perhaps it is not surprising that there are more disputes when preschool boys interact than when preschool girls interact.

Ⓒ For example, it was found that boys tended to use simple imperatives in talking to their partner in pretend play. Girls in the same situation used fewer simple imperatives and instead used language that included the other child in planning.

She observed that when the boys had conflicts, they frequently issued directives and made threats. The girls, in contrast, tended more to try to negotiate a settlement.

2020학년도 국민대학교 인문계 오전 A형 34번

014 Which is the proper order of Ⓐ – Ⓒ?

① Ⓐ – Ⓑ – Ⓒ ② Ⓐ – Ⓒ – Ⓑ
③ Ⓒ – Ⓐ – Ⓑ ④ Ⓒ – Ⓑ – Ⓐ

Much of what we do as adults is based on imitative absorption during our childhood years. Frequently we imagine that we are behaving in a particular way because such behaviour accords with some abstract, lofty code of moral principles, when in reality all we are doing is obeying a deeply ingrained and long 'forgotten' set of purely imitative impressions. Ⓐ <u>This is the cross we have to bear if we are going to sail through our vital juvenile 'blotting paper' phase of rapidly mopping up the accumulated experiences of previous generations.</u> Ⓑ <u>Even when faced with exciting, brilliantly rational new ideas, based on the application of pure, objective intelligence, the community will still cling to its old home-based habits and prejudices.</u> Ⓒ <u>It is the unmodifiable obedience to these impressions that makes it so hard for societies to change their customs and their beliefs.</u> We forced to take the biased opinions along with the valuable facts.

Luckily we have evolved a powerful antidote to this weakness which is inherent in the imitative learning process. We have a sharpened curiosity, an intensified urge to explore which work against the other tendency and produce a balance that has the potential of fantastic success. Only if a culture becomes too rigid as a result of its slavery to imitative repetition, or too daring and rashly exploratory, will it flounder. Those with a good balance between the two urges will thrive. Lucky is the society that enjoys the gradual acquisition of a perfect balance between imitation and curiosity, between slavish, unthinking copying and progressive, rational experimentation.

015 Which of the following is the best order?

① Ⓐ – Ⓑ – Ⓒ   ② Ⓑ – Ⓐ – Ⓒ
③ Ⓒ – Ⓐ – Ⓑ   ④ Ⓒ – Ⓑ – Ⓐ

Shedding kilos is harder than putting on, which is why the weight-loss industry is so big. Its latest manifestation is online weight-management sites: social networks for the plump in which participants can set a target weight and monitor their progress towards it.

A As with other social networks, they can also get their help from friends — either real-life ones who sign up to the same site, or else digital ones whom they have befriended on the internet. Those friendships are likely to be important. Other studies of weight-loss programs have suggested that having the support or chivying of friends helps people stick to their diets and exercise regimes.

B But she and her colleagues are quick to point out that a study like this can establish only that two things — in this case, friends and weight-loss — are correlated. It cannot show which causes which. Working this out requires controlled experiments.

C Their results are, nonetheless, encouraging. Weight-management websites have the potential to reach many more people much more cheaply than real-world support groups do. Moreover, if it turns out that friendship networks are a magic wand for weight loss, then it may be easier to nudge people into such networks electronically than if they actually had to meet each other in a sweaty gym. Given the medical consequences of rising levels of obesity, that would be well worth doing.

D Those studies, however, have all been done with groups of people who knew each other in the real world. A team of researchers led by Julia Poncela-Casanovas of Northwestern University, in Illinois, decided to check if the same was true of groups in cyberspace. Their results suggest that it is.

2019학년도 국민대학교 인문계 오전 A형 21번

016 Which is the proper order of paragraphs A – D?

① A – B – C – D   ② A – D – B – C
③ B – D – C – A   ④ B – C – D – A

An important theme of Gordimer's novel "The Moment Before the Gun Went Off", is that of paternal inheritance.

A The fact that Marais Van der Vyver has had no volitional control over this pivotal event in his life emphasizes that responsibility for this misdeed does not reside exclusively with him and suggests that Marais may not be entirely responsible for his other inheritances.

B Marais Van der Vyver's own prehistory, then, in his father's generation — the generation that created the modern apartheid system in 1948 — may be the historical "moment before" the story's fin-de-siecle epoch. By extending the guilt for this offense transgenerationally, Gordimer implicates a whole morally corrupt society in the fate of Lucas.

C The story contains several references to Willem Van der Vyver, the late, great patriarchal figure whose presence seems to overshadow his son's life. Marais Van der Vyver's prominence in the community is directly related to his father's legacy; the son inherited the father's "best farm" and his employees are the children of those who worked for "old Van der Vyver." This suggests that the son inherited an entire network of social, economic, and psychological relationships.

D Significantly, then, we learn that it is the gun of Marais Van der Vyver's father that kills Lucas, the farmworker who is Marais's son; this legacy of violence is passed on from grandfather, to son, and finally — tragically — to grandson.

2019학년도 국민대학교 인문계 오후 A형 22번

017 Which is the proper order of paragraphs A – D?
① A – C – B – D ② B – C – A – D
③ C – D – A – B ④ D – B – C – A

Motion detectors are small electronic eyes that detect infrared waves — heat waves that radiate from moving objects. When the detector senses an object moving across its field of view — especially warmer objects such as people, animals and cars — it electronically turns on the lights. The light stays on anywhere from 1 to 20 minutes, depending on how you preset the time. Then the detector automatically shuts the light off unless it continues to sense movement. A photocell deactivates the light during daylight hours.

Ⓐ However, you can solve most unwanted switching-on by adjusting the distance-range setting and by carefully aiming the sensor to limit its field of view. You can also narrow the field of view even more by applying tape to the sensor. If nuisance trips concern you, be sure to buy a light that has an adjustable distance-range setting, and an aimable detector unit.

Ⓑ Most motion detectors have a semicircular field of view of up to 240 degrees and a distance range, adjustable on most detectors, that extends to 70 feet or more. The detector will react to the movement of your dog, an approaching person, a passing car or sometimes even wind-blown leaves.

Ⓒ Nuisance trips, such as blowing leaves or a passing car, can fool the detector and turn the lights on when you don't want them. These can be annoying to both you and your neighbors, and in fact, some homeowners won't install motion detector lights for this reason.

018 Which of the following is the best order for a passage starting with the given sentences in the box?

① Ⓐ – Ⓒ – Ⓑ   ② Ⓑ – Ⓐ – Ⓒ
③ Ⓑ – Ⓒ – Ⓐ   ④ Ⓒ – Ⓐ – Ⓑ
⑤ Ⓒ – Ⓑ – Ⓐ

If you're shopping for a live Christmas tree this year, you may have to search harder than in the past. Over the last five years Christmas tree shortages have been reported in many parts of the U.S.

A Collectively, these trends don't bode well for Christmas tree lovers, the growers, or the industry. However, there are opportunities for younger farmers to enter this market, either full- or part-time.

B One factor is that growers sold off land and planted fewer trees during and after the 2008 recession. In the lifespan of Christmas trees, the decade from 2008 to the present is roughly a single generation of plantings. However, in my research on the human dimensions of farming and food systems, I also see other factors at play.

C If new and beginning growers live in an area with appropriate environmental conditions, Christmas trees are a high-quality complementary crop that farmers can use to diversify their operations and provide off-season income.

D Christmas trees take 6 to 12 years to mature, and consumer preferences often change more quickly than farmers can adjust. Climate change is altering temperature and rainfall patterns, which severely affects growers' ability to produce high-quality trees and the varieties that customers seek.

2020학년도 인하대학교 인문계 29번

019 Which of the following is the best order for a passage starting with the given sentences in the box?

① A - C - B - D   ② B - D - A - C
③ B - C - D - A   ④ D - A - C - B
⑤ D - C - A - B

유형 02 문장배열

단락배열

In 1798 Thomas Malthus explained that the frequent famines of his era were unavoidable because "population, when unchecked, increases in a geometrical ratio while subsistence increases only in an arithmetic ratio." Where did Malthus's math go wrong? Looking at the first of his curves, we already saw that population growth needn't increase in a geometric ratio indefinitely, because when people get richer and more of their babies survive, they have fewer babies. Conversely, famines don't reduce population growth for long.

A It was only at the time of the Industrial Revolution that people figured out how to bend the curve upward. Crop rotation and improvements to plows and seed drills were followed by mechanization. In the mid-19th century it took twenty-five men a full day to harvest and thresh a ton of grain; today one person operating a combine harvester can do it in six minutes.

B So forget arithmetic ratios: over the past century, grain yields per hectare have swooped upward while real prices have plunged. The savings are mind-boggling. If the food grown today had to be grown with pre-nitrogen-farming techniques, an area the size of Russia would go under the plow.

C Looking at the second curve, we discover that the food supply can grow geometrically when knowledge is applied to increase the amount of food that can be coaxed out of a patch of land. Since the birth of agriculture ten thousand years ago, humans have been genetically engineering plants and animals by selectively breeding the ones that were the easiest to plant and harvest. Clever farmers also tinkered with irrigation, plows, and organic fertilizers, but Malthus always had the last word.

2019학년도 명지대학교 인문계 17번

020 Choose the best order after the paragraph in the box.

① C - A - B ② A - C - B
③ C - B - A ④ A - B - C

유형 03
문장삽입

Teacher Chris Tip

문장의 본래 위치를 찾는 유형이며, 출제가 빈도가 그리 높지는 않지만 비교적 난이도가 높아 오답률이 높다. 기본적으로 전후 내용의 인과 관계, 대명사, 관사 및 연결사 등을 통해 글 전개의 순서를 파악하자. 그리고 절대 답이 될 수 없는 순서를 선택지에서 먼저 소거(지우는)하는 전략을 쓰는 것도 좋다.

가톨릭대학교	아주대학교
건국대학교	인하대학교
광운대학교	한국산업기술대학교
국민대학교	홍익대학교
덕성여자대학교	
명지대학교	
상명대학교	
세종대학교	

• Read the following and answer the questions.

> The first thing that DNA molecules do is to replicate, that is to say they make copies of themselves. Ⓐ This has gone on non-stop ever since the beginning of life, and the DNA molecules are now very good at it indeed. Ⓑ As an adult, you consist of a thousand million million cells, but when you were first conceived you were just a single cell, endowed with one master copy of the plans to build your body. Ⓒ Successive divisions took the number of cells up to 4, 8, 16, 32, and so on into the billions. Ⓓ At every division the DNA plans were faithfully copied, with scarcely any mistakes.
>
> 2019학년 국민대학교 인문계 오전 A형 30번

001 Which is the best place for the following?

> This cell divided into two, and each of the two cells received its own copy of the plans.

① Ⓐ ② Ⓑ ③ Ⓒ ④ Ⓓ

• Read the following passages and answer the questions.

> Ⓐ Many supermarket chains discount food at regular intervals — for example, a certain ice cream might be half price once every four weeks. Ⓑ Other staple foods that are discounted regularly include bread, juice, pasta sauce, coffee, biscuits, yoghurt and cereals. Ⓒ Also, think about doing your shopping in the last hour before your local supermarket closes. Ⓓ That's when you can find big discounts on perishable products such as bread, meat, fish and dairy products.
>
> 2019학년도 국민대학교 인문계 오후 A형 14번

002 Which is the best place for the following?

> Once you're aware of the pattern, you need never buy these products at full price again.

① Ⓐ ② Ⓑ ③ Ⓒ ④ Ⓓ

Influenza is a constantly evolving virus. Ⓐ It quickly goes through mutations that slightly alter the properties of its H and N antigens. Ⓑ Due to these changes, acquiring immunity (either by getting sick or vaccinated) to an influenza subtype such as H1N1 one year will not necessarily mean a person is immune to a slightly different virus circulating in subsequent years. Ⓒ In other cases, however, the virus can undergo major changes to the antigens such that most people don't have an immunity to the new virus, resulting in pandemics. Ⓓ This antigenic shift can occur if an influenza A subtype in an animal jumps directly into humans.

2019학년도 가톨릭대학교 인문계 A형 22번

003 Choose the best place for the following sentence.

> But since the strain produced by this antigenic drift is still similar to older strains, the immune systems of some people will still recognize and properly respond to the virus.

① Ⓐ　② Ⓑ　③ Ⓒ　④ Ⓓ

Icy water is soaking my backside, my hands are freezing and the waves are breaking over our kayak's bow. Ⓐ I'm starting to consider the wisdom of what we're doing. But there's a penguin squawking as it swims past the kayak and then an iceberg — AN ICEBERG! Ⓑ Shockingly, it floats past and there's a huge grin on my dad's face. Ⓒ Dad and I have kicked around an Antarctic trip for years, but the timing was never quite right. Ⓓ And both of us were skeptical of spending so much time aboard a cruise ship to get there. Ⓔ But commercial cruise ships are generally the only option for most people, unless you can sneak into one of the government-run research bases or have a friend with a boat big enough to confront the Drake Passage.

2019학년도 광운대학교 인문계 A형 30번

004 다음 주어진 표현이 들어갈 가장 적절한 위치는?

> And it hits me: This is why we're here in Antarctica.

① Ⓐ　② Ⓑ　③ Ⓒ　④ Ⓓ　⑤ Ⓔ

유형 03 문장삽입

President Obama has forbidden federal employees from texting while driving. Ⓐ The federal Transportation Department plans to do the same for commercial-truck and Interstate-bus drivers. Ⓑ And support is building in Congress for legislation that would require states to outlaw texting or e-mailing while driving. Ⓒ Such distractions cause tens of thousands of deaths each year. But the way to stop people from using cellphones while driving is not to make it a crime. Ⓓ A more. effective way is to make it difficult or impossible to text and drive. Ⓔ

2019학년도 상명대학교 인문·자연계 32번

005 아래 문장을 위 본문 중에 추가할 경우, 가장 적절한 위치를 고르시오.

> Too many drivers value convenience more than safety and would assume they wouldn't get caught.

① Ⓐ   ② Ⓑ   ③ Ⓒ   ④ Ⓓ   ⑤ Ⓔ

Do you know why Venus is so hot? Ⓐ Scientists think the original atmospheres of both Venus and Earth were created from gases released by volcanoes, when both planets were very young and volcanic activity was much more intense. Ⓑ But because Venus is so close to the Sun, the "greenhouse effect," in which heat is trapped within its atmosphere, results in the temperature rising so high that all the surface water evaporated. Ⓒ The hydrogen escaped into space and the oxygen combined with other chemicals in the atmosphere. Ⓓ In contrast, Earth cooled down, oceans formed, and life began to develop. Ⓔ Earth became ·a living planet while Venus, despite its connection to the goddess of love and fertility, remained barren.

2019학년도 건국대학교 인문·예체능계 A형 25번

006 글의 흐름으로 보아, 주어진 문장이 들어가기에 가장 적절한 것은?

> With all the water now in the atmosphere, the intense ultraviolet radiation from the Sun split the water molecules into hydrogen and oxygen.

① Ⓐ   ② Ⓑ   ③ Ⓒ   ④ Ⓓ   ⑤ Ⓔ

• Read the following passages and answer the questions.

War is a howling, baying jackal. Or is it the animating storm? Suicidal madness or the purifying fire? An imperialist travesty? Or the glorious explosion of a virile nation made manifest upon the planet? Ⓐ In all recorded history, this debate is recent, as is the idea of peace to describe an active state happier than a mere interregnum between fisticuffs. Ⓑ In fact, it never had serious competition — not until 1898, anyway, when Czar Nicholas II of Russia called for an international conference specifically to discuss "the most effectual means" to "a real and durable peace." Ⓒ That was the first time nations would gather without a war at their backs to discuss how war might be prevented systematically. Ⓓ Nicholas II was successful. His first Peace Conference was held in 1899. It was followed by a second, in 1907. These meetings gave rise to a process in which the world gained a common code of international laws.

2019학년도 국민대학교 인문계 오후 A형 24번

007 Which is the best place for the following?

> Astounding as it may seem, war has consistently won the debate.

① Ⓐ   ② Ⓑ   ③ Ⓒ   ④ Ⓓ

Stoicism was one of the many philosophical movements which originated in Athens during its golden age. First formulated by Zeno of Citium in 301 BC, stoicism stresses indifference to both pleasure and pain, whether in a physical or emotional form. Stoics hold that reason should be the sole guide of one's actions, and that passions, such as pleasure and pain, cloud one's reason. Ⓐ Stoics train themselves to lead a materially simple life. Ⓑ Luxuries are to be avoided. Ⓒ Similarly, stoics seek to lead an emotionally simple life, free of emotional entanglements. Ⓓ Stoics taught themselves to live apart from their society, at least in an emotional sense.

2019학년도 덕성여자대학교 오후 26번

008 Where should the following sentence be inserted to make the paragraph complete?

> To a stoic, the ability to think clearly is the greatest of all virtues, and anything that impairs this ability should be avoided.

① Ⓐ   ② Ⓑ   ③ Ⓒ   ④ Ⓓ

유형 03 문장삽입

문장삽입

Parents have different social expectations of daughters and sons. Ⓐ Daughters, more than sons, are socialized to think more about the family, for example, to remember birthdays, to spend time with the family on holidays, and, when they get older, to provide care for sick family members and relatives. Ⓑ Sons are not expected to do these things. They are expected to be more interested in the world outside the family and more independent of the family in social activities. Ⓒ For example, parents may make their daughters come home earlier at night and forbid them to go to places that they might let their sons go to. Ⓓ Such protectiveness often encourages girls to be less active in exploring their environment.

2019학년도 한국산업기술대학교 인문계 30번

문장삽입

I was born among the working classes and brought up among them. My father was a coal miner, and only a coal miner, nothing praiseworthy about him. He wasn't even respectable, in so far as he got drunk rather frequently, never went near chapel, and was usually rather rude to his little immediate bosses at the pit. Ⓐ He was always saying tiresome and foolish things about the men just above him in control at the mine. Ⓑ He offended them all, almost on purpose, so how could he expect them to favour him? Ⓒ My mother was, I suppose, superior. She came from town, and belonged really to the lower bourgeoisie. Ⓓ She spoke King's English, without an accent, and never in her life could even imitate a sentence of the dialect which my father spoke, and which we children spoke out of doors. Ⓔ

2019학년도 인하대학교 인문계 11번

009 Choose the most suitable position of the sentence below in the above passage.

> Daughters are also taught to need more protection than sons.

① Ⓐ   ② Ⓑ   ③ Ⓒ   ④ Ⓓ

010 Choose the best place for the sentence(s) in the box.

> Yet he grumbled when they didn't.

① Ⓐ   ② Ⓑ   ③ Ⓒ   ④ Ⓓ   ⑤ Ⓔ

Acrophobia is an intense, unreasonable fear of high places. People with acrophobia exhibit emotional and physical symptoms in response to being at great heights. Ⓐ For instance, one sufferer of extreme acrophobia, Sally Maxwell, is unable to go above the third floor of any building without feeling enormous anxiety. Ⓑ Suddenly she was struck with terror by the idea that she might jump or fall out the open window. Ⓒ She crouched behind a steel filing cabinet, trembling, unable to move. Ⓓ When she finally gathered her belongings and left the building, she was sweating, her breathing was rapid, and her heart was pounding. Ⓔ Yet she had no rational explanation for her fears.

2019학년도 인하대학교 인문계 30번

011 Which is the best place in the passage for the sentence in the box?

> Her acrophobia began one evening when she was working alone in her office on the eighth floor of a large building.

① Ⓐ   ② Ⓑ   ③ Ⓒ   ④ Ⓓ   ⑤ Ⓔ

Ⓐ Discovering the basic neural circuitry turned out to be a key breakthrough in understanding anxiety. Ⓑ Just as a car can go out of control due to either a stuck accelerator or failed brakes, it's not always clear which part of the brain is at fault. Ⓒ It may turn out that some anxiety disorders are caused by an overactive amygdala (the accelerator) while others are caused by an underactive prefrontal cortex (call it the brake). Ⓓ It may also be that an entirely different part of the brain holds the key to understanding anxiety. Ⓔ A behavioral neuroscientist at Emory University has spent six years studying a pea-size knot of neurons located near the amygdala with an impossible name: the bed nucleus of the stria terminalis.

2019학년도 인하대학교 인문계 10번

012 Choose the best place for the sentence(s) in the box.

> It showed that the anxiety response isn't necessarily caused by an external threat; rather, it may be traced to a breakdown in the mechanism that signals the brain to stop responding.

① Ⓐ   ② Ⓑ   ③ Ⓒ   ④ Ⓓ   ⑤ Ⓔ

유형 03 문장삽입

• Read the following passages and answer the questions.

문장배열

Historically, people believed that the best way to predict whether a horse will succeed has been to analyze his or her pedigree. Being a horse expert means being able to rattle off everything anybody could possibly want to know about a horse's father, mother, grandfathers, grandmothers, brothers, and sisters. (①) Agents announce, for instance, that a big horse "came to her size legitimately" if her mother's line has lots of big horses. (②) While pedigree does matter, it can only explain a small part of a horse's success. (③) Consider the track record of siblings of all the horses named Horse of the Year, racing's most prestigious annual award. (④) These horses have the best possible pedigrees — the identical family history as world-historical horses. Still, more than three-fourths do not win a major race. The traditional way of predicting horse success, the data tells us, leaves plenty of room for improvement.

2019학년도 명지대학교 인문계 13번

013 Choose the best place for the sentence given in the box.

> There is one problem, however.

단락배열

The most important thing you need when applying for a job is a resume — a list of your achievements and qualifications. ⒶThe resume should give all the essential facts about the position you seek, the date of your availability, your education, your work experience, your extra-curricular activities, and your special interests. ⒷYou may include personal data, but you do not have to. The resume should also list the names and addresses of your references — persons who can write to a prospective employer on your behalf. ⒸWith the resume you must send what a hiring officer expects to see first: a covering letter. ⒹSince the resume will list all the essential facts about you, the covering letter may be brief. But it should nonetheless be carefully written. If the letter makes a bad first impression, you will have one strike against you even before your resume is seen. With some company offices getting over a thousand applications a month, you need to give yourself the best possible chance, and your covering letter can make a difference in the way your resume is read.

2019학년도 국민대학교 인문계 오후 A형 34번

014 Which is the best place for the following?

> The resume alone, however, will seldom get you a job or even an interview.

① Ⓐ ② Ⓑ ③ Ⓒ ④ Ⓓ

The wage gap is a statistical indicator often used as an index of the status of women's earnings relative to men's. It is also used to compare the earnings of other races and ethnicities to those of white males, a group generally not subject to race- or sex-based discrimination. The wage gap is expressed as a percentage (e.g., in 2012, women earned 80.9% as much as men aged 1.6 and over) and is calculated by dividing the median annual earnings for women by the median annual earnings for men.

The Equal Pay Act (EPA), which aims to promote gender equality in the workplace, was signed in 1963, making it illegal for employers to pay unequal wages to men and women who hold the same job and do the same work. Ⓐ At the time of the EPA's passage, women earned just 58 cents for every dollar earned by men. Ⓑ By 2011, that rate had increased to 82 cents. Ⓒ African-American women earn just 69 cents to every dollar earned by white men, and for Hispanic women that figure drops to merely 60 cents per dollar. Ⓓ Asian women are the exception, earning 87 cents for every dollar earned by white men — a sum higher than women of all other races/ethnicities as well as African-American and Hispanic men.

015 Choose the best place for the following sentence.

Minority women fare the worst.

① Ⓐ　② Ⓑ　③ Ⓒ　④ Ⓓ

After traveling 300 million miles through the solar system, NASA's InSight spacecraft descended through the Martian sky and touched down safely on the smooth surface of Elysium Planitia. [A]

Using a robotic arm, the lander will first install a super-sensitive seismometer on the Martian surface, where it will listen for meteorite impacts and Marsquakes. [B] The seismic waves from these events will give scientists a clearer picture of the planet's internal structure. InSight will then release its heat probe, a self-hammering 16-inch nail that will burrow down as deep as 16 feet over the course of several weeks. The instrument will measure how much heat escapes from Mars' interior, which will reveal the amount of heat-producing radioactive elements it contains and how geologically active the planet is today. [C] The spacecraft also has two X-band antennas on its deck that make up a third instrument, called RISE. [D] Radio signals from RISE will be used to track the wobble of Mars' orbit. This will help researchers understand the size and state of the Martian core. Together, these experiments will crack open Mars and spill the planetary secrets scientists have sought for decades.

016 Which is the most appropriate place for the sentence below?

> Unlike the space agency's rovers, InSight is a lander designed to study an entire planet from just one spot.

① [A] ② [B] ③ [C] ④ [D]

• Read the following and answer the questions.

In 1874 Francis Galton, a British polymath, analyzed a sample of English scientists and found the vast majority to be first-born sons. This led him to speculate that first-born children enjoyed a special level of attention from their parents that allowed them to thrive intellectually. Half a century later, Alfred Adler, an Austrian psychologist, made a similar argument relating to personality. First-born children, he thought, were more conscientious, while the later-born were more extrovert and emotionally stable. A Many subsequent studies have explored these ideas, but their findings have been equivocal — some supporting and some rejecting them. Now a team led by Stefan Schmukle of the University of Leipzig, in Germany, has collected the most comprehensive evidence on the matter yet. Its conclusion is that Adler was wrong, but Galton may have been right.

Birth order, they found, had no effect on personality: first-borns were no more, no less, likely than their younger sibs to be conscientious, extrovert or neurotic. But it did affect intelligence. B In a family with two children, the first child was more intelligent than the second 60% of the time, rather than the 50% that would be expected by chance. On average, this translated to a difference of 1.5 IQ points between first and second siblings. C That figure agrees with the consensus from previous studies, and thus looks confirmed. It is, nevertheless, quite a small difference — and whether it is enough to account for Galton's original observation is moot. In any event, it is clearly not deterministic. D

2019학년도 국민대학교 인문계 오전 A형 24번

017 Which is the best place for the following?

> Galton was the youngest of nine.

① A   ② B   ③ C   ④ D

유형 03 문장삽입

The format of the Sun Dance, a traditional Native American ceremonial dance, has always varied from community to community. Nevertheless, there are certain features of the dance that many tribes share. Often, the dance must be initiated by a sponsor, someone who takes a vow in the hope of being relieved of a worry, or being blessed in the coming year. [A] It is almost always performed near the time of summer solstice. Most Sun Dances begin with the erection of a circular lodge around a solemnly chosen and cut central pole. During the next three or four days, periods of dancing, accompanied by singing and drumming, are interspersed with periods of rest and meditation. Dancers do not eat or drink during the entire period of the dance, although some do chew on bear root to keep their mouths moist. Toward the end of the dance, participants experience visions and receive blessings. [B]

Early Europeans were repulsed by some tribes' practice of self-mortification in the ceremony. [C] Dancing and straining against the ropes, they eventually tore loose from the skewers. Through this ritual, participants literally suffer on behalf of their community and call upon the Creator to pity and assist them in the fulfillment of their vows. [D] This aspect of the ritual was the main reason federal officials prohibited it between the late 1870s and 1935. Despite the ban, however, many tribes continued to hold the Sun Dance surreptitiously in remote areas of their reservations or to enact it without its objectionable features.

2019학년도 세종대학교 인문계 A형 50번

018 Which is the most appropriate place for the sentence below?

> Male dancers had their breasts or backs skewered and tied to a central lodge pole.

① [A] ② [B] ③ [C] ④ [D]

The fashion industry is a product of the modern age. Prior to the mid-19th century, virtually all clothing was handmade for individuals, either as home production or on order from dressmakers and tailors. Ⓐ By the beginning of the 20th century — with the rise of new technologies such as the sewing machine, the rise of global capitalism and the development of the factory system of production, and the proliferation of retail outlets such as department stores — clothing had increasingly come to be mass-produced in standard sizes and sold at fixed prices. Ⓑ Although the fashion industry developed first in Europe and America, today it is an international and highly globalized industry, with clothing often designed in one country, manufactured in another, and sold in a third. Ⓒ The fashion industry has long been one of the largest employers in the United States, and it remains so in the 21st century. However, employment declined considerably as production increasingly moved overseas, especially to China. Because data on the fashion industry typically are reported for national economies and expressed in terms of the industry's many separate sectors, aggregate figures for world production of textiles and clothing are difficult to obtain. However, by any measure, the industry inarguably accounts for a significant share of world economic output. Ⓓ The fashion industry consists of four levels: the production of raw materials, principally fibres and textiles but also leather and fur; the production of fashion goods by designers, manufacturers, contractors, and others; retail sales; and various forms of advertising and promotion. These levels consist of many separate but interdependent sectors, all of which are devoted to the goal of satisfying consumer demand for apparel under conditions that enable participants in the industry to operate at a profit.

019 Where should the following sentence be added?

For example, an American fashion company might source fabric in China and have the clothes manufactured in Vietnam, finished in Italy, and shipped to a warehouse in the United States for distribution to retail outlets internationally.

① Ⓐ ② Ⓑ ③ Ⓒ ④ Ⓓ

[A] The object called the Möbius strip has fascinated environmentalists, artists, engineers, mathematicians and many others ever since its discovery in 1858 by August Möbius, a German mathematician. Möbius seems to have encountered the Möbius strip while working on the geometric theory of polyhedra, solid figures composed of vertices, edges, and flat faces. ① A Möbius strip can be created by taking a strip of paper, giving it an odd number of half-twists, then taping the ends back together to form a loop. If you take a pencil and draw a line along the center of the strip, you'll see that the line runs along both sides of the loop.

[B] The concept of a one-sided object inspired artists like Dutch graphic designer M.C. Escher, whose woodcut "Möbius Strip II" shows red ants crawling one after another along a Möbius strip. ② The Möbius strip has more than just one surprising property. For instance, try taking a pair of scissors and cutting the strip in half along the line you just drew. You may be astonished to find that you are left not with two smaller one-sided Möbius strips, but instead with one long two-sided loop.

[C] ③ A topologist studies properties of objects that are preserved when moved, bent, stretched or twisted, without cutting or gluing parts together. For example, a tangled pair of earbuds is in a topological sense the same as an untangled pair of earbuds, because changing one into the other requires only moving, bending and twisting. Another pair of objects that are topologically the same are a coffee cup and a doughnut. ④ Because both objects have just one hole, one can be deformed into the other through just stretching and bending. The number of holes in an object is a property which can be changed only through cutting or gluing. This property — called the "genus" of an object — allows us to say that a pair of earbuds and a doughnut are topologically different, since a doughnut has one hole, whereas a pair of earbuds has no holes.

[D] Unfortunately, a Möbius strip and a two-sided loop, like a typical silicone awareness wristband, both seem to have one hole, so this property is insufficient to tell them apart — at least from a topologist's point of view. Instead, the property that distinguishes a Möbius strip from a two-sided loop is called orientability. Like its number of holes, an object's orientability can only be changed through cutting or gluing. ⑤ Imagine writing yourself a note on a see-through surface, then taking a walk around on that surface. The surface is orientable if, when you come back from your walk, you can always read the note. On a nonorientable surface, you may come back from your walk only to find that the words you wrote have apparently turned into their mirror image and can be read only from right to left. On the two-sided loop, the note will always read the same, no matter where your journey took you. Since the Möbius strip is nonorientable, whereas the two-sided loop is orientable, the Möbius strip and the two-sided loop are topologically different.

020 The following paragraph is removed from the passage. In which part may it be inserted to support the argument made by the author?

> While the strip certainly has visual appeal, its greatest impact has been in mathematics, where it helped to spur on the development of an entire field called topology.

① ② ③ ④ ⑤

유형 04
무관한 문장

Teacher Chris Tip

글의 전반적인 일관성을 파악하면서 내용과 맞지 않는 문장을 찾아내야 한다. 주로 『같은 소재에 다른 주제』 또는 앞뒤가 맞지 않은 글의 기조로 이어지는 형태가 정답이다.

가톨릭대학교
강남대학교
건국대학교
숭실대학교
인하대학교

It would be a great comfort to terminally ill patients to end their lives if their suffering became unbearable. ① Not all pain can be controlled, and it's arrogant to insist it can. ② Quality of life decisions are the sole right of the individual. ③ It is nonsense to say death shouldn't be part of a doctor's mission. ④ Doctors are healers, not killers.

001 Choose the sentence that does NOT fit.
① ② ③ ④

There are few problems more annoying than hiccups, which can last for hours or even days. Ⓐ Acoording to one doctor who has studied them, hiccups are usually caused by eating or drinking too quickly. Ⓑ People do some pretty strange things to remedy this ridiculous problem. Ⓒ Some common remedies include holding your breath, eating a teaspoon of sugar, and putting a paper bag over your head. Ⓓ The best exercise for a healthy heart is walking. Ⓔ Undoubtedly, that last one is the strangest one of all.

003 Choose the one that does not fit in the passage.
① Ⓐ ② Ⓑ ③ Ⓒ ④ Ⓓ ⑤ Ⓔ

Christopher Columbus is said to have discovered America in 1492. ① History says, however, the Vikings came to the New World earlier, in the 10th Century A.D. ② Leif Erikson, a Norwegian Viking, and his crew got lost on the way to Greenland, and landed on North America. ③ He called his discovery Vinland, "land of the vines", which is today Labrador in eastern Canada. ④ Vintand Saga, a heroic report of Erikson's expedition, eloquently supports the idea that Columbus was the first European to visit America.

002 Choose the sentence that does NOT fit.
① ② ③ ④

Why do people choose to home educate their child? Some families make a carefully considered decision to home educate long before their child reaches "school age." Ⓐ There may be philosophical, religious or various other reasons for their choice and ultimately they feel that in some way they can offer a more suitable education for their child at home. Ⓑ It is also a natural choice for parents who have enjoyed participating in their child's early learning and see no reason to give up this responsibility when the child reaches the age of five. Ⓒ Other parents send their child into the school system, but later find that school does not work for their child. Ⓓ In school, students can get comparatively high marks by remembering what teachers have said. Ⓔ School does not suit everyone. Sometimes children may find it hard to "fit in" so their parents may also decide to home educate.

2019학년도 건국대학교 인문·예체능계 A형 27번

004 글의 흐름으로 보아, Ⓐ~Ⓔ 가운데 어색한 것은?

① Ⓐ ② Ⓑ ③ Ⓒ ④ Ⓓ ⑤ Ⓔ

The close relationship between language and religious belief pervades cultural history. Often, a divine being is said to have invented speech, or writing, and given it as a gift to mankind. One of the first things Adam has to do, according to the Book of Genesis, is to name the acts of creation. Many other cultures have a similar story. Ⓐ In Egyptian mythology, the god Thoth is the creator of speech and writing. Ⓑ It is Brahma who gives the knowledge of writing to the Hindu people. Ⓒ Odin is the inventor of runic script, according to the Icelandic sagas. Ⓓ Literacy is often introduced into a community by the spread of a religion. Ⓔ A heaven-sent water turtle, with marks on its back, brings writing to the Chinese. All over the world, the supernatural provides a powerful set of beliefs about the origins of language.

2019학년도 인하대학교 인문계 33번

005 Choose the one that does not fit in the passage.

① Ⓐ ② Ⓑ ③ Ⓒ ④ Ⓓ ⑤ Ⓔ

유형 04 무관한 문장

글의 흐름상 적절하지 않은 문장 고르기

Soon after an infant is born, many mothers hold their infants in such a way that they are face-to-face and gaze at them. [A] Mothers have been observed to address their infants, vocalize to them, ask questions, and greet them. [B] In other words, from birth on, the infant is treated as a social being and as an addressee in social interaction. [C] The infant's vocalizations, and physical movements and states are often interpreted as meaningful and are responded to verbally by the mother or other care-giver. [D] The cultural dispreference for saying what another might be thinking or feeling has important consequences for the organization of exchanges between care-giver and child. [E] In this way, protoconversations are established and sustained along a two-party, turn-taking model. Throughout this period and the subsequent language-acquiring years, care-givers treat very young children as communicative partners.

2018학년도 인하대학교 인문계 10번

글의 흐름상 적절하지 않은 문장 고르기

Why don't we "think something different" more often? There are several main reasons. The first is that we don't need to be creative for most of what we do. Ⓐ For example, we don't need to be creative when we're driving on the freeway, or riding in an elevator, or waiting in line at a grocery store. Ⓑ We are creatures of habit when it comes to the business of living — from doing paperwork to tying our shoes. For most of our activities, these routines are indispensable. Without them, our lives would be in chaos, and we wouldn't get much accomplished. Ⓒ If you got up this morning and started contemplating the bristles on your toothbrush or questioning the meaning of toast, you probably wouldn't make it to work. Ⓓ These attitudes are necessary for most of what we do, but they can get in the way when we're trying to be creative. Ⓔ Staying on routine thought paths enables us to do the many things we need to do without having to think about them.

2018학년도 건국대학교 인문·예체능계 B형 32번

006 Which of the following does not fit in the passage?
① [A] ② [B] ③ [C] ④ [D] ⑤ [E]

007 글의 흐름으로 보아, Ⓐ~Ⓔ 가운데 어색한 것은?
① Ⓐ ② Ⓑ ③ Ⓒ ④ Ⓓ ⑤ Ⓔ

The natural surveillance provided by passers-by or by windows and balconies overlooking streets is enough to deter most crime and vandalism. Ⓐ Well-designed neighborhoods promote this casual policing, which can work alongside more formal schemes for watching over one another's homes. Ⓑ Homes should be flexible to adapt to a household's changing needs over time. Ⓒ Thoughtfully sited car parking and bicycle storage, as well as well-integrated recycling bins, contribute not only to a sense of order but also to reducing litter, vandalism and theft. Ⓓ To encourage these changes, police services award Secured by Design certificates to homes and developments whose design deters crime. It considers the materials and design of entry points such as doors and windows, the deployment of burglar alarms and video entry systems, and the natural surveillance offered by windows to open spaces.

2017학년도 가톨릭대학교 일반·학사편입 A형 24번

Before the Industrial Revolution, most goods were produced by hand in rural homes or urban workshops. [A] Merchants, known as entrepreneurs, distributed the raw materials to workers, collected the finished products, paid for the work, then sold them. [B] Growing demand for consumer products, together with a shortage of labour, placed pressure on entrepreneurs to find new, more efficient methods of production. [C] The great era of European exploration that began in the 15th century arose primarily out of a desire to seek out new trade routes and partners. [D] With the development of power-driven machines, it made economic sense to bring workers, materials and machines together in one place, giving rise to the first factories. [E] For added efficiency, the production process was broken down into basic individual tasks that a worker could specialize in, a system known as the division of labour.

2018학년도 인하대학교 인문계 32번

008 Choose one that is <u>unnecessary</u> for the flow of the passage.

① Ⓐ   ② Ⓑ   ③ Ⓒ   ④ Ⓓ

009 Which of the following does <u>not</u> fit in the passage?

① [A]   ② [B]   ③ [C]   ④ [D]   ⑤ [E]

유형 04 무관한 문장

글의 흐름상 적절하지 않은 문장 고르기

Vigorous activity is usually a healthful pursuit but it can become maladaptive when carried to extremes. [A] There are runners and body builders, for instance, who use their obsessive workouts to avoid taking responsibility for other aspects of their lives, allowing little time for family, friends, or additional interests. [B] Rather than enjoying their fitness endeavors, they feel powerless to make any adjustments in their routines except to try to do more. [C] Pursuing pleasurable fitness endeavors can be a great coping strategy for lessening daily pressures. [D] Unfortunately, the exercise patterns of some adolescents and adults reflect deep-seated psychological problems. [E] They become dangerously fixated on trying to change their bodies by a combination of exhausting exercise and dieting, increasing their risk of serious health problems including substance abuse and eating disorders.

2017학년도 인하대학교 일반·학사편입 인문계 22번

010 Choose the sentence that does <u>not</u> fit in each passage.

① [A] ② [B] ③ [C] ④ [D] ⑤ [E]

글의 흐름상 적절하지 않은 문장 고르기

John Henry was an ex-slave who went to work on the railroad as a steel-driver for the Chesapeake & Ohio (C&O) Railroad. His job was hitting steel spikes into rocks, and he was the fastest and strongest worker on the line. [A] When the owners of the C&O decided to drill right through Big Bend Mountain in West Virginia instead of building the railroad around it, many workers lost their lives because of the dangerous work. But not John Henry. [B] Thousands of African-Americans worked on the railroad, with hundreds perishing during the drilling of the Great Bend Tunnel. He drove spike after spike, digging his way through the mountain. [C] One day a salesman appeared, touting the efficiency and speed of a new steam-powered drill. The workers arranged a contest: John Henry versus the machine. [D] When the dust settled, John Henry dug a 14-foot (4-meter) hole, but the machine made it only 9 feet (nearly 3 meters). [E] As the rail workers celebrated, John Henry toppled over and died from exhaustion.

2017학년도 인하대학교 일반·학사편입 인문계 21번

011 Choose the sentence that does <u>not</u> fit in each passage.

① [A] ② [B] ③ [C] ④ [D] ⑤ [E]

The 2012-13 flu season took a serious toll on families: 158 children — most of them younger than 11 — died. Sadly, about 90 percent of those who died missed out on the one thing that could have saved them: a flu vaccination. Ⓐ Despite studies proving that flu vaccinations are a lifesaver, less than half of all children in the U.S. are immunized each year. Ⓑ One recent survey from a social-research company found that 16 percent of Americans consider the vaccine to be unsafe and 35 percent believe the vaccine causes the flu. Ⓒ "The tragedy is that children continue to die from an illness that is largely preventable," says Dr. Blumberg. Ⓓ Doctors want moms and dads to understand that children ages 6 months to 5 years are at a high risk of serious diseases like diarrhea and dehydration. Ⓔ Because awareness and education are key to making smart decisions about your family's health, it's of primary importance for parents with children to get clear-cut information about the flu and the vaccine.

2017학년도 인하대학교 일반·학사편입 인문계 20번

012 Choose the sentence that does not fit in each passage.

① Ⓐ   ② Ⓑ   ③ Ⓒ   ④ Ⓓ   ⑤ Ⓔ

Abraham Lincoln's election to the presidency in 1860 brought to a climax the long festering debate about the relative powers of the federal and the state government. Ⓐ By the time of his inauguration, six Southern states had seceded from the Union and formed the Confederate States of America, soon to be followed by five more. Ⓑ The war that followed between North and South put constitutional government to its severest test. Ⓒ After four bloody years of war, the Union was preserved, four million African American slaves were freed, and an entire nation was released from the oppressive weight of slavery. Ⓓ The war can be viewed in several different ways: as the final, violent phase in a conflict of two regional subcultures; as the breakdown of a democratic political system: as the climax of several decades of social reform: or as a pivotal chapter in American racial history. Ⓔ As important as the war itself was the tangled problem of how to reconstruct the defeated South. However interpreted, the Civil War stands as a story of great heroism, sacrifice, triumph, and tragedy.

2020학년도 건국대학교 인문·예체능계 A형 27번

013 글의 흐름으로 보아, Ⓐ~Ⓔ 가운데 어색한 것은?

① Ⓐ   ② Ⓑ   ③ Ⓒ   ④ Ⓓ   ⑤ Ⓔ

Differences in values, culture, experience, and perceptions may well lead parties to disagree about the relative merits of different standards. [A] If it were necessary to agree on which standard was "best" settling a negotiation might not be possible. [B] But agreement on criteria is not necessary. [C] A well-established reputation for fair dealing can be an extraordinary asset. [D] Criteria are just one tool that may help the parties find an agreement better for both than no agreement. [E] Using external standards often helps narrow the range of disagreement and may help expand the area of potential agreement. When standards have been refined to the point that it is difficult to argue persuasively that one standard is more applicable than another, the parties can explore tradeoffs or resort to fair procedures to settle the remaining differences. They can flip a coin, use an arbitrator, or even split the difference.

014 Which of the following does not fit in the passage?

① A   ② B   ③ C   ④ D   ⑤ E

During adolescence, people become increasingly involved with their peer group, a group whose members are about the same age and have similar interests. The peer group, along with the family and the school, is one of the three main agents of socialization. However, the peer group is very different from the family and the school. [A] Whereas parents and teachers have more power than children and students, the peer group is made up of equals. [B] Peer groups develop among all age groups, but they are particularly important for adolescents' development. [C] There may be differences across cultures in how adolescents behave. [D] The adolescent peer group teaches its members social skills, the values of friendship among equals, and to be independent from adult authorities. [E] Sometimes this means that a peer group encourages its members to go against authorities and adults. It is important to remember, however, that this kind of rebellious behavior is partly cultural and not universal.

015 Choose the one that does not fit in the passage.

① A   ② B   ③ C   ④ D   ⑤ E

글의 흐름상 적절하지 않은 문장 고르기

Three musical instruments played an important role in eighteenth-century warfare. One of them was the snare drum. Often played by boys between 12 and 16 years old, snare drums were used to set the marching rhythm for soldiers. Ⓐ With a skilled drummer playing 96 beats per minute, a commander could march his troops three miles in fifty minutes allowing ten minutes each hour for a breather and a drink. Ⓑ A second is chordophones or stringed instruments like zithers, which consist of sets of string stretched in parallel fashion along a board. Ⓒ Another important instrument was a small flute called a fife. Ⓓ The fife's role in an army was to entertain soldiers and communicate orders. Ⓔ For example the son "Pioneer's March" was the signal for road-clearing crews to get started ahead of the infantry. Fifes were also used to give orders to soldiers during battle since they could be heard above the roar of firearms. The third instrument used in warfare was the trumpet. Requiring just one hand to play, it was used by soldiers on horsebacks to send messages to soldiers in battle and on the march.

2019학년도 인하대학교 인문계 14번

016 Choose the one that does not fit in the passage.

① Ⓐ ② Ⓑ ③ Ⓒ ④ Ⓓ ⑤ Ⓔ

글의 흐름상 적절하지 않은 문장 고르기

The art of camping includes the ability to set up a safe and comfortable camp and to provide food that is tasty and nutritious. Because mountaineering is such a strenuous and demanding activity, your body will need a variety of foods to provide sufficient carbohydrates, protein, and fats. Ⓐ With planning, it's not hard to choose foods that keep well, are lightweight, meet your nutritional needs, and are appropriately geared to your objective. Ⓑ For example. monotonous prepared foods might work best for a short climb, whereas a week-long trip requires more variety and complexity. Ⓒ In general mountaineering, the loss of body salts that accompanies heavy sweating is normally not a major problem, as most electrolytes are replaced naturally in a well-balanced diet. Ⓓ And don't forget the other requirement of camping food: it must taste good, or you simply won't eat it. Ⓔ If fueling your body quickly and simply is the first aim of alpine cuisine, the enjoyment of doing so is a worthy secondary goal.

2020학년도 인하대학교 인문계 07번

017 Choose the one that does not fit in the passage.

① Ⓐ ② Ⓑ ③ Ⓒ ④ Ⓓ ⑤ Ⓔ

In today's youth-obsessed culture, getting older is often seen as something to fear. Ⓐ But a new study says at least one thing gets better with age: self-esteem. Age 60 seems to be best for self-esteem, according to Ulrich Orth, a professor of psychology at the University of Bern in Switzerland. Self-esteem first begins to rise between ages 4 and 11, as children develop socially and cognitively and gain some sense of independence. Ⓑ Levels then seem to plateau — but not decline — as the teenage years be in from ages 11 to 15, the data show. That's somewhat surprising, given that many people assume that self-esteem takes a hit during the traditionally awkward early teenage years, "possibly because of pubertal changes and increased emphasis on social comparison at school," Orth says. "However, our findings show that this is not the case." Ⓒ Instead, self-esteem appears to hold stead until mid-adolescence. After that lull, self-esteem seems to increase substantially until age 30, then more gradually throughout middle adulthood, before peaking around age 60 and remaining stable until age 70. Ⓓ Old age frequently involves loss of social roles as a result of retirement and the empty nest which lower self-esteem. Ⓔ "Many people," Orth says, "are able to maintain a relatively high level of self-esteem even during old age."

2019학년도 인하대학교 인문계 13번

018 Choose the one that does not fit in the passage.

① Ⓐ ② Ⓑ ③ Ⓒ ④ Ⓓ ⑤ Ⓔ

Although scattered local airline companies began offering flights to passengers as early as 1913, scheduled domestic flights did not become widely available in the United States until the 1920s. Ⓐ During the early years of commercial aviation, U.S. airline travel was limited to a small population of business travelers and wealthy individuals who could afford the high ticket prices. Ⓑ The majority of travelers relied instead on more affordable train services for their intercity transportation needs. Ⓒ Over ninety-five years later, the airlines have grown to be one of the most important and heavily used transportation options for American business and leisure travelers. Ⓓ Following deregulation of the airline industry by the U.S. government in 1978, airline routes increased, ticket fares decreased, and discount carriers prospered, thus making airline travel accessible to a much broader segment of the U.S. population. Ⓔ Plane tickets were generally prepared by hand using carbon paper and were given to passengers upon their arrival at the airports. In 2008 alone, 649.9 million passengers traveled on domestic flights on U.S. airlines.

2017학년도 인하대학교 일반·학사편입 인문계 19번

019 Choose the sentence that does not fit in each passage.

① Ⓐ ② Ⓑ ③ Ⓒ ④ Ⓓ ⑤ Ⓔ

• Read the following passages and answer the questions.

문맥상 적절하지 않은 문장 고르기

In the last days of 2019, as millions of Americans were contemplating their resolutions for the year ahead, the moving-and-storage company U-Haul set one for all of its future employees. The company announced that starting February 1, it will stop hiring people who use nicotine in the 21 states where such a prohibition is legal, including Texas, Florida, and Massachusetts. Seventeen of those states allow employers to administer drug test for nicotine.

While a new policy for U-Haul, this move is part of a larger trend toward "workplace wellness" programs, which encourage employees to pursue dietary changes and hit daily activity goals. Over the past decade, companies have become far more coercive in their insistence that employees optimize their bodies and behavior on their own time. Ⓐ This cuts costs and, at least in theory, helps employees live healthier lives.

In a press release, U-Haul's chief of staff, Jessica Lopez, repeated some of the supposedly inspirational words that have embedded themselves into the workplace-wellness vernacular. "Ⓑ We are deeply invested in the well-being of our team members. Nicotine products are addictive and pose a variety of serious health risks," she said. Lopez characterized the move as "a responsible step in fostering a culture of wellness at U-Haul, with the goal of helping our team members on their health journey."

According to U-Haul's announcement, the company plans to note its policy on job applications, question applicants about their nicotine usage in interviews, and require them to consent to nicotine testing in the seventeen states that allow it. The policy will apply to any nicotine use, which means that vapers and other users of smokeless tobacco will be excluded from the hiring pool, in addition to smokers. The policy won't apply to people already employed with the company. Ⓒ People believe that the fundamental interests of employees and employers are necessarily hostile to each other.

Nicotine is, indeed, tied to some serious health risks. Globally, smoking cigarettes kills about 8 million people each year. But employers seeking to control ever more aspects of their employees' lives is already a troubling trend. Ⓓ It's bleak when anyone's health is regarded as malfunctioning workplace machinery, but the problem becomes even worse when these expectations are foisted on the workers least equipped to fight back.

2020학년도 숭실대학교 인문계 49번

020 Which of the following is NOT appropriate?

① Ⓐ ② Ⓑ ③ Ⓒ ④ Ⓓ

유형 05
빈칸완성

Teacher Chris Tip

내용 이해와 함께 가장 빈번하게 출제되는 유형으로서 약 30%를 차지했으며, 학생들이 가장 까다로워하는 유형이기도 하다. 정·오답 근거를 찾는 독해 풀이의 체화 그리고 상당한 독해의 집중력과 맥락 이해가 요구된다. 주로 글의 주제(대의) 혹은 이를 뒷받침하는 핵심 논증 구간에 빈칸으로 출제된다.

가천대학교	덕성여자대학교	한국항공대학교
가톨릭대학교	상명대학교	한성대학교
경기대학교	숙명여자대학교	한양대학교 에리카
건국대학교	숭실대학교	
광운대학교	아주대학교	
국민대학교	인하대학교	
단국대학교	한국산업기술대학교	

빈칸완성

In pre-colonial times, New York City's Coney Island was known for its beach bunnies — the seaside was teeming with rabbits. Later, this part of the city became known for its amusement park, which has quickly become run-down over the years. But recently, land developers are hoping to transform the area into one with upscale beach resorts and hotels. They hope Coney Island will be known for _____ _____.

2019학년도 덕성여자대학교 오후 23번

001 Which of the following is the most suitable for the blank?
① exciting nightlife along with natural beauty
② chic accommodations as opposed to urban blight
③ local wildlife together with improved facilities
④ its extensive history instead of the recent renovations

빈칸완성

All my life I've been registering exceptional scores with tests, so that I have the complacent feeling that I'm highly intelligent. Actually, though, don't such scores simply mean that I am good at answering the type of academic questions that are considered worthy of answers by the people making up the intelligence tests — people with an intellectual bent similar to mine?

In a world where I could not use my academic training and my verbal talents, I would do poorly. My intelligence, then, is not absolute but is a function of the society I live in and of the fact that a small subsection of that society has managed to foist itself on the rest as a Ⓑ_____ of matters of intelligence.

2019학년도 가천대학교 인문계 1교시 C형 33번

002 Which of the following is most appropriate for the blank Ⓑ?
① layman   ② judge
③ dissenter   ④ recluse

• Read the following passage and answer the questions.

It took Europe some 300 years to modernize, and the process was wrenching and traumatic, involving bloody revolutions, often succeeded by reigns of terror, brutal holy wars, dictatorships, cruel exploitation of the workforce, and widespread alienation and anomie. We are now witnessing the same kind of Ⓐ_____ in developing countries presently undergoing modernization. But some of these countries have had to attempt this difficult process far too rapidly and are forced to follow a western programme, rather than their own. Ⓑ_____ created deep divisions in developing nations. Only an elite has a western education that enables them to understand the new modern institutions. The vast majority remains trapped in the premodern ethos.

2019학년도 가천대학교 인문계 2교시 A형 28,29번

003
(A) Which of the following is most appropriate for the blank Ⓐ?
① upheaval   ② languor
③ seclusion   ④ transcendence

003
(B) Which of the following is most appropriate for the blank Ⓑ?
① The regression of modernity
② This accelerated modernization
③ This intermittent modernization
④ The resistance against modernity

Although a high birthrate typified most preindustrial cultures, it was the low death rate and long average life span that pushed up American population numbers. With no huge urban centers, colonial epidemics proved less devastating than in Europe. Food was plentiful, and housing improved steadily. Newborns who survived infancy could live a long life. Ⓐ_____, the 1720s and 1730s proved peaceful compared to earlier decades, so soldiering did not endanger lives among men of military age. For women, death related to pregnancy and childbirth still loomed as a constant threat. Ⓑ_____ women still outnumbered men among people living into their 60s, 70s, and 80s.

2019학년도 인하대학교 인문계 22번

004 Choose the most appropriate one for each blank.

	Ⓐ		Ⓑ
①	However	–	Thus
②	Moreover	–	Also
③	Similarly	–	So
④	However	–	But
⑤	Moreover	–	Yet

유형 05 빈칸완성

빈칸완성

Social networking sites are ruining our lives. I know that might sound drastic, but we seem to have lost the art of talking to each other. Last week, I was sitting in a cafe and was taken aback by how many people were using their cell phones rather than chatting to the people they were with. People seem to have stopped _____ to each other — all they do is "chatting" on Facebook. I've even seen waiters stop _____ their cell phones when taking orders! I find that unbelievable. Does that make me old-fashioned? I don't know, but I'd rather be labeled as boring and out of touch than spend my life hooked to a screen. When I tried explaining this to my girlfriend, she just laughed.

2019학년도 한국산업기술대학교 인문계 29번

005 Choose the one that best fills in the blanks.

① to tell – to look
② telling – checking
③ talking – to check
④ to talk – looking

빈칸완성

As the solar system condensed out of gas and dust, Jupiter acquired most of the matter that was not ejected into interstellar space and did not fall inward to form the Sun. Had Jupiter been several dozen times more massive, the matter in its interior would have undergone thermonuclear reactions, and Jupiter would have begun to shine by its own light. The largest planet is a star that failed. Even so, its interior temperatures are sufficiently high that it gives off about twice as much energy as it receives from the Sun. In the infrared part of the spectrum, it might even be correct to consider Jupiter a star. Had it become a star in visible light, we would today inhabit _____, and the night would come more rarely – a commonplace, I believe, in countless solar systems throughout the Milky Way Galaxy. We would doubtless think the circumstances natural and lovely.

2019학년도 한국항공대학교 인문계 21번

006 Choose the most appropriate one for the blank.

① a single-star system
② a substantial human presence
③ a weaker magnetic field
④ a binary system

The only way to really know whether an idea is reasonable is to test it. Build a quick prototype or mock-up of each potential solution. In the early stages of this process, the mock-ups can be pencil sketches, foam and cardboard models, or simple images made with simple drawing tools. I have made mock-ups with spreadsheets, PowerPoint slides, and with sketches on index cards or sticky notes. Sometimes ideas are best conveyed by skits, especially if you're developing services or automated systems that are difficult to prototype. One popular prototype technique is called "Wizard of Oz," after the wizard in L Frank Baum's classic book *The Wonderful Wizard of Oz*. The wizard was actually just an ordinary person but, through the use of smoke and mirrors, he managed to appear mysterious and omnipotent. In other words, it was all a fake: the wizard had no special powers. The Wizard of Oz method can be used to mimic a huge, powerful system _____.

2019학년도 한국항공대학교 인문계 22번

007 Choose the phrase that best fills in the blank.
① as soon as it is built
② without consideration of its building time
③ after it is built
④ before it can be built

The Fertile Crescent's biological diversity over small distances contributed to the region's wealth in ancestors not only of valuable crops but also of domesticated big mammals. There were few or no wild mammal species suitable for domestication in the other Mediterranean zones of California, Chile, southwestern Australia, and South Africa. Ⓐ_____ four species of big mammals — the goat, sheep, pig, and cow — were domesticated very early in the Fertile Crescent, possibly earlier than any other animal except the dog anywhere else in the world. Those species remain today four of the world's five most important domesticated mammals. But their wild ancestors were commonest in slightly different parts of the Fertile Crescent, with the result that the four species were domesticated in different places. Ⓑ_____, even though the areas of abundance of these four wild progenitors thus differed, all four lived in sufficiently close proximity that they were readily transferred after domestication from one part of the Fertile Crescent to another and the whole region ended up with all four species.

2019학년도 가톨릭대학교 인문계 A형 28번

008 Choose the best expressions for the blanks.

	Ⓐ		Ⓑ
①	In fact	–	Instead
②	As a result	–	However
③	In contrast	–	Nevertheless
④	For example	–	Consequently

유형 05 빈칸완성

Optimists get the last laugh and their hearts stay healthy longer than those of the grump.

People who described themselves a highly Ⓐ_____ a decade ago had lower rates of death from cardiovascular disease and lower overall death rates than strong pessimists. Nine years ago a study group — 999 men and women aged 65 to 85 — completed a questionnaire on health, self-respect, morale, optimism and relationships. Since then, 397 of them have died. Ⓑ_____ participants had a 55 percent lower risk of death from all causes and 23 percent lower risk of death from heart failure. The study notes that Ⓒ_____ people may be more prone to developing habits and problems that cut life short, such as smoking, obesity and hypertension. A predisposition toward optimism seemed to provide a survival benefit in subjects with relatively short life expectancies otherwise.

2019학년 건국대학교 인문·예체능계 A형 28번

009 다음 글의 빈칸 Ⓐ,Ⓑ,Ⓒ에 들어갈 말로 가장 적절한 것은?

	Ⓐ	Ⓑ	Ⓒ
①	optimistic	Optimistic	pessimistic
②	optimistic	Pessimistic	pessimistic
③	pessimistic	Optimistic	optimistic
④	pessimistic	Optimistic	pessimistic
⑤	optimistic	Pessimistic	optimistic

The effects of an earthquake are strongest in a broad zone surrounding the epicenter. Surface ground cracking often occurs, with horizontal and vertical displacements of several yards. Such movement does not usually occur during a major earthquake: slight periodic movements called 'fault creep' can be accompanied by micro-earthquakes, too small to be felt. The extent of earthquake vibration and subsequent damage to a region is partly dependent on characteristics of the ground. For example, earthquake vibrations last longer and are of greater wave amplitudes in unconsolidated surface material, Ⓐ_____ poorly compacted fill or river deposits; bedrock areas receive fewer effects. The worst damage occurs in Ⓑ_____ populated urban areas where structures are not built to withstand intense shaking.

2019학년도 숙명여자대학교 인문계 24번

010 Which would be the most appropriate pair for the blank Ⓐ and Ⓑ?

	Ⓐ	Ⓑ
①	such as	clearly
②	such as	rarely
③	as for	scarcely
④	for instance	scarcely
⑤	such as	densely

유형 05 빈칸완성

빈칸완성

Why would people make an adventurous journey across thousands of kilometers of ocean? Why did the pioneers cross the Great Plains, the Rocky Mountains, or the Mojave Desert to reach the American West? Why do people continue to migrate by the millions today? The hazards that many migrants have faced are a measure of the strong lure of new locations and the desperate conditions in their former homelands. A permanent move to a new location disrupts traditional cultural ties and economic patterns in one region. At the same time, when people migrate, they take with them to their new home their language, religion, ethnicity, and other cultural traits. Most people migrate for economic reasons. People think about emigrating from places that have few job opportunities, and they immigrate to places where jobs seem to be available. Because of economic restructuring, job prospects often vary from one country to another and within regions of the same country. The United States and Canada have been especially promising ⓑ_____ for economic migrants. Cultural factor can be especially a compelling push factor that forces people to move out of their present location.

2019학년도 상명대학교 인문·자연계 30번

빈칸완성

Most of the electricity in the United States is produced in steam turbines. There are many discrete steps in this process. In a steam turbine, combustion of coal, petroleum, or natural gas heats water to make steam. The steam rotates a shaft that is connected to a generator that produces electricity. Finally, that electricity is converted by a transformer and conveyed from the turbine to its place of use. Many sources can provide energy to heat the water in a steam turbine. Coal is a Ⓐ_____ source, producing 51 percent of the country's electricity. Another common way to heat water for steam turbines is through nuclear power. In nuclear fission, atoms of uranium fuel are hit by neutrons, triggering a continuous chain of fission that releases heat. In 2001, nuclear power generated 21 percent of the electricity in the United States. Solar power meets less than 1 percent of the United States' electricity needs, because it is not regularly available and harnessing it is more expensive than using fossil fuels. Dependence on electricity permeates daily life in the United States. Still, few people are aware of the many components of electricity production.

2019학년도 경기대학교 인문·예체능계 A형 35번

011 문맥상 밑줄 친 ⓑ에 들어갈 가장 적절한 것을 고르시오.
① stopovers ② storages ③ destinations
④ refuge ⑤ starting points

012 Which of the following is most appropriate for blank Ⓐ?
① cost-effective ② demanding
③ primary ④ manageable

Ramadan is the ninth month of the Islamic calendar, and is observed by Muslims worldwide as a month of fasting Ⓐ_____ the first revelation of the Quran to Muhammad according to Islamic belief. This annual observance is regarded as one of the Five Pillars of Islam. The month lasts 29-30 days based on the visual sightings of the crescent moon, according to numerous biographical accounts compiled in the hadiths. The word, Ramadan, means scorching heat or dryness. Fasting is obligatory for adult Muslims, except those who are suffering from an illness, travelling, elderly, pregnant, breastfeeding, diabetic, chronically ill or menstruating. Muslims who live in regions with a natural phenomenon such as the midnight sun or polar night should follow the timetable of Mecca, but the more commonly accepted opinion is that Muslims in those areas should follow the timetable of the closest country to them in which night can be distinguished from day. While fasting from dawn until sunset, Muslims refrain from consuming food, drinking liquids, smoking, and engaging in sexual relations. Muslims are also instructed Ⓑ_____ sinful behavior that may negate the reward of fasting, such as false speech (insulting, cursing, lying, etc.) and fighting except in self-defense.

013 빈칸 Ⓐ와 Ⓑ에 들어가기에 가장 적절한 표현의 쌍은?

	Ⓐ	Ⓑ
①	to observe	to reflect on
②	to overlook	to leave off
③	to celebrate	to stand for
④	to disregard	to get around
⑤	to commemorate	to refrain from

Read the following passage and answer the questions.

Recently it has been claimed that the struggle against childhood dependency and for becoming oneself in fairy tales is frequently described differently for the girl than for the boy, and that this is the result of sexual Ⓐ_____. Fairy tales do not render such one-sided pictures. Even when a girl is depicted as turning inward in her struggle to become herself, and a boy as aggressively dealing with the external world, these two together symbolize the two ways in which one has to gain selfhood: through learning to understand and master the inner as well as the outer world. In this sense the male and female heroes are again projections onto two different figures of two (artificially) separated aspects of one and the same process which everybody has to undergo in growing up. While some literal-minded parents do not realize it, children know that, whatever the sex of the hero, the story Ⓑ_____ their own problems.

In "The Sleeping Beauty," the harmonious meeting of prince and princess, their awakening to each other, is a symbol of what maturity implies: not just harmony within oneself, but also with the other. It depends on the listener whether the arrival of the prince at the right time is interpreted as the event which causes sexual awakening or the birth of a higher ego: the child probably comprehends both these meanings.

2019학년도 가천대학교 인문계 1교시 C형 38,39번

014 (A) Which of the following is most appropriate for the blank Ⓐ?

① initiation ② orientation
③ reproduction ④ stereotyping

014 (B) Which of the following is most appropriate for the blank Ⓑ?

① contradicts ② pertains to
③ subverts ④ competes with

유형 05 빈칸완성

• Read the following passages and answer the questions.

By studying instinctive and learned fear in people and in experimental animals, we have gained much insight into both the behavioral and the biological mechanisms of instinctive and learned fear in people. One of the first behavioral insights was stimulated by the theories of Freud and the American philosopher William James, who realized that fear has both conscious and unconscious components. What was not clear was how the two components interact.

Traditionally, fear in people was thought to begin with conscious perception of an important event, such as seeing one's house on fire. This recognition produces in the cerebral cortex an emotional experience — fear — that triggers signals to the heart, blood vessels, adrenal glands, and sweat glands to mobilize the body in preparation for defense or escape. Thus, according to this view, a conscious, emotional event initiates the later Ⓐ_____ defensive responses in the body.

James rejected this view. In a highly influential article published in 1884 and entitled "What is Emotion?" he proposed that the cognitive experience of emotion is secondary to the physiological expression of emotion. He suggested that when we encounter a potentially dangerous situation — for example, a bear sitting in the middle of our path — our evaluation of the bear's ferocity does not generate a consciously experienced emotional state. We do not experience fear Ⓑ_____ we have run away from the bear.

2019학년도 국민대학교 인문계 오후 A형 36,37번

015 (A) Which does NOT fit in the blank Ⓐ?
① cognitive   ② reflexive
③ biological   ④ physiological

015 (B) Which does NOT fit in the blank Ⓑ?
① because   ② so that
③ until after ④ irrespective of

The scientific consensus on global warming comes from the Intergovernmental Panel on Climate Change (IPCC). It was established in 1988 by the World Meteorological Organization and the United Nations Environment Program to assess the science of climate change, determine its impacts on the environment and society, and formulate strategies to respond. More than 900 scientists from 40 countries have participated as authors or expert reviewers in the IPCC's latest report, published in 1995.

"It's a look at the state of the art — what we know about the climate system," says Gerald Meehl of the National Center for Atmospheric Research, a lead author for one of the report's chapters. "Literally thousands of people wind up reading these things.... It's the consensus view of just about everyone who's chosen to become involved." In June, some 2,400 scientists signed a letter saying they _____ the findings.

The basics of global warming are simple. So-called greenhouse gases — including carbon dioxide and methane — build up in the atmosphere. Carbon dioxide is the most important of the greenhouse gases generated by human activity. The gases trap the sun's heat, like a car parked in the sun with the windows closed. Couple that with a basic fact: The amount of carbon dioxide in the atmosphere has risen by 30% since pre-industrial times (about 1750). The implication is that temperatures are rising, and that's what the IPCC was charged with studying.

2019학년도 단국대학교 자연계 A형 25번

016 Which is the most appropriate for the blank?
① endorsed ② disputed
③ rebuked ④ denounced

유형 05 빈칸완성

• 주어진 글을 읽고 물음에 답하시오.

빈칸완성

Not everyone consumes news. The time has come to better understand the segment of people who are not the news audience but who are the news un-audience. Several years ago, I estimated that about 20 percent of the U.S. adults were what I described as "News Avoiders." More recently, I found the habit of news avoidance predates adulthood, with 50 percent of U.S. teenagers reporting very low exposure to any type of news.

Why is studying the news un-audience important? One answer is that news organizations need news audiences. If half of U.S. teenagers are News Avoiders, and that doesn't change when they reach adulthood, it's problematic for the long-term survival of the news industry. A second answer is that democracy needs news consumers. News avoidance is related to several negative democratic outcomes. I found that it was News Avoiders who exhibited Ⓐ_____ across a variety of political and community-based activities. It was their voices, their concerns, and their help that was largely absent. For all the important differences in the types of news that people do consume, the fact remains that being a news consumer is related to civic and political participation.

How can we better understand the un-audience? It requires reframing the question. In addition to asking "Why do people consume news?" we need to ask Ⓑ"_____" These are different questions that yield different insights. What drives people toward news is not the same as what drives them away. Understanding the un-audience requires going beyond demographics.

2019학년도 광운대학교 인문계 A형 38,39번

017 빈칸 Ⓐ에 들어가기에 가장 적절한 것은?
(A)
① the importance of news organizations
② the lowest level of participation
③ the absence of concerns about global issues
④ the change in audience growth
⑤ the good understanding of current issues

017 빈칸 Ⓑ에 들어가기에 가장 적절한 것은?
(B)
① What drives people toward news?
② Why don't people consume news?
③ Why are teenagers different from adults?
④ What do people have to learn to reframe questions?
⑤ Why is demographics important to understand the news un-audience?

Ⓐ_____ kilos is harder than putting on, which is why the weight-loss industry is so big. Its latest manifestation is online weight-management sites: social networks for the plump in which participants can set a target weight and monitor their progress towards it.

As with other social networks, they can also get their help from friends — either real-life ones who sign up to the same site, or else digital ones whom they have befriended on the internet. Those friendships are likely to be important. Other studies of weight-loss programs have suggested that having the support or chivying of friends helps people stick to their diets and exercise regimes.

Those studies, however, have all been done with groups of people who knew each other in the real world. A team of researchers led by Julia Poncela-Casanovas of Northwestern University, in Illinois, decided to check if the same was true of groups in cyberspace. Their results suggest that it is.

But she and her colleagues are quick to point out that a study like this can establish only that two things — in this case, friends and weight-loss — are correlated. It cannot show which causes which. Working this out requires controlled experiments.

Their results are, nonetheless, encouraging. Weight-management websites have the potential to reach many more people much more cheaply than real-world support groups do. Moreover, if it turns out that friendship networks are a magic wand for weight loss, then it may be easier to nudge people into such networks electronically than if they actually had to meet each other in a sweaty gym. Given the medical consequences of rising levels of obesity, that would be well worth doing.

018 Which best fits in the blank Ⓐ?
① Shedding   ② Controlling
③ Increasing ④ Calculating

Ethics may be profoundly affected by an adoption of the scientific point of view; that is to say, the attitude that men of science, in their professional capacity, adopt towards the world. This attitude includes a high (perhaps an unduly high) regard for the truth, and a refusal to come to unjustifiable conclusions which expresses itself on the plane of religion as agnosticism. And along with this is found a deliberate suppression of emotion until the last possible moment, on the ground that emotion is stumbling-block on the road to truth. So a rose and a tape-worm must be studied by the same methods and viewed from the same angle, even if the work is ultimately to lead to the killing of the tape-worms and the propagations of roses. Again, the scientific point of view involves the cultivation of a scientific esthetic which rejoices in the peculiar forms of beauty which characterize scientific esthetic theory. Those who find an intimate relation between the good and the beautiful will realize the importance of the fact that a group of men so influential as scientific workers are pursuing a particular kind of beauty. _____, since the scientist, as such, is contributing to an intellectual structure that belongs to humanity as a whole, his influence will inevitably fall in favour of ethical principles and practices which transcend the limits of nation, colour, and class.

019 Which is the most appropriate for the blank?

① Instead
② Finally
③ Nevertheless
④ Intriguingly

Egypt has recovered a stolen ancient artifact that was listed for sale at a London auction house, the country's Ministry of Antiquities has confirmed. The section of tablet — engraved with the cartouche, or royal symbol, of King Amenhotep I — was stolen from the Karnak Open Air Museum in Luxor, Egypt, in 1988. It was smuggled out of the country, and ultimately put up for auction in London.

Raed Khoury, director of repatriation at the Ministry of Antiquities, said that the organization worked to track down the stolen relief. They monitored the websites of international auction houses before eventually finding the artifact for sale in the UK. The ancient tablet was subsequently removed from sale and delivered to the London embassy. The ministry officially announced its return to Egypt on January 4.

The tablet's recovery comes as a dispute brews around another ancient Egyptian artifact: a casing stone from the Great Pyramid of Giza. This block of limestone will go on display at the National Museum of Scotland in Edinburgh from February. However, Egypt's Ministry of Antiquities has contested the legitimacy of the stone's Ⓐ_____, asking the museum to produce documents of ownership. The museum says the stone was extracted from Giza in the 19th century by engineer Waynman Dixon and given to Scotland's Astronomer Royal, Charles Smyth, who kept it in his Edinburgh home. If it transpires that the stone was Ⓒ_____ removed from Egypt, Khoury said, the ministry will take "all the necessary steps" to bring it back.

2019학년도 한성대학교 인문계 A형 08번

020 Choose the best word for Ⓐ and Ⓒ.

	Ⓐ		Ⓒ
①	export	–	illegally
②	imposter	–	illegally
③	export	–	lawfully
④	imposter	–	lawfully

As you get older, little growths called skin tags might start popping up on your body. You'll recognize them because they're thinner at the base and get wider at the top. They aren't painful or dangerous like cancerous moles, but there's a very good reason you'll want them removed. People have used all kinds of crazy methods to try removing skin tags on their own, says Dr. Rossi, MD, dermatologic surgeon. He's heard of people tying strings around them, burning them, trying to pick them off with their fingers, and even slamming books against them. A dermatologist, on the other hand, can snip away skin tags quickly and cleanly.

For one thing, dermatologists have sterile instruments, but using your own could lead to an infection. Plus, while dermatologists can use local anesthesia and have supplies to stop the blood, you could bleed uncontrollably with at-home methods. Even hospital medications claiming to dissolve the skin tags could be bad news, says Dr. Rossi. "You could burn the skin or make marks," he says. "There could be unintended consequences."

But there's an even bigger reason you should visit an expert. After dermatologists remove a growth, they'll look at it under a microscope. "There are things that look like skin tags but are cancerous," says Dr. Rossi. That doesn't mean you should freak out if you do find a skin tag. Most will just be benign, but you won't know for sure until you've asked. Plus, checking a skin tag is a "Ⓔ_____" to get your doctor to check the rest of your body for skin cancer and atypical or malignant growths, says Dr. Rossi.

2019학년도 한성대학교 인문계 A형 50번

021 Choose the best expression for Ⓔ.
① good excuse   ② dangerous process
③ useless method   ④ necessary evil

Dave Balter worked in advertising, and he knew that most people don't like ads. They avoid watching them, reading them, or listening to them. He also knew that people do pay attention when they hear about goods and services from people they know. So he said to himself, "If no one pays attention to advertising, but they do pay attention to the opinions of their friends and family, let's focus our attention there."

What Balter came up with was a website where consumers could sign up to receive free products. _____, they promised that if they liked the products, they would tell their friends. In most cases, the volunteers also got coupons to give to their friends. All Balter asked was that they report back on two questions: what did you think of the product, and who did you talk to about it?

After four years, Balter had 65,000 volunteers trying products and telling people about the ones they liked. Then a reporter heard about Balter's idea and wrote a story on it for a major magazine. Free advertising! Within a year after that story appeared, Balter had 130,000 volunteers. Today, the company he started has over one million people spreading the word about a wide variety of products. They are doing word-of-mouth advertising, perhaps the best kind of advertising there is.

There may be a risk to advertising by word of mouth, however, according to George Silverman, the author of *The Secrets of Word-of-Mouth Marketing*. What's the danger? Studies have shown that a customer who likes a product or service will tell an average of three people about it. But when customers don't like it, on average they'll tell eleven.

2019학년도 한양대학교 에리카 인문계 A형 37번

022 빈칸에 들어갈 가장 알맞은 것을 고르시오.

① Similarly   ② In return
③ Consequently   ④ In fact

So what's the right way to be wrong? Are there techniques that allow organizations and individuals to embrace the necessary connection between small failures and big successes? Smith College, the all-women's school in western Massachusetts, has created a program called "Falling Well" to teach its students what all of us could stand to learn. "What we're trying to teach is that failure is not a bug of learning; it's the feature," explained Rachel Simmons, who runs the initiative, in a recent *New York Times* article. Indeed, when students enroll in her program, they receive a Certificate of Failure that declares they are "hereby authorized to screw up, bomb, or fail" at a relationship, a project, a test, or any other initiative that seems hugely important and "still be a totally worthy, utterly excellent human being." Students who are prepared to handle failure are less fragile and more daring than those who expect perfection and flawless performance. That's a lesson worth applying to business as well. Patrick Doyle, CEO of Domino's Pizza since 2010, has had one of the most successful seven-year runs of any business leader in any field. But all of his company's triumphs, he insists, are based on its willingness to face up to the likelihood of mistakes and missteps. In a presentation to other CEOs, Doyle described two great challenges that stand Ⓐ_____ the way of companies and individuals being more honest about failure. The first challenge, he says, is what he calls "omission bias" — the reality that most people with a new idea choose not to pursue the idea because if they try something and it doesn't work, the setback might damage their career. The second challenge is to overcome what he calls "loss aversion" — the tendency for people to play not to lose rather than play to win, because for most of us, "The pain of loss is double the pleasure of winning."

2019학년도 숭실대학교 인문계 A형 39번

023 Which of the following best fits in Ⓐ?
① with   ② for
③ on   ④ in

In 1923 the *New York Times* published an article about a Danish man who had recently visited Germany. He had arrived sporting a large up-turned moustache, which he soon shaved off upon discovering that "the Kaiser Wilhelm brand of upper lip decoration is not popular in the very modern commercial city of Hamburg." However, the Dane encountered a problem when, at the completion of his visit, he attempted to leave Germany. According to the article, "The heavily moustached chap on his passport photograph did not in the least resemble the smooth-faced modern appearing Dane. Passport officials turned him back and detectives gave him the third degree. In his changed appearance they found resemblance to a famous international swindler." Apparently "ashamed" of his failure to resemble himself, the unnamed Dane did not seek the assistance of Danish officials. Instead he chose to grow a new moustache, which the article confidently predicted, "[would] enable him to measure up to his passport photograph." This article, one of a handful from the period that recounts the problems shaving purportedly created for male passport bearers, reads today as somewhat Ⓐ_____, if not perhaps a little preposterous. While it may indeed be out of step with our contemporary understanding of official identification practices, and even if the events did not occur exactly as reported, the article accurately captures some of the cultural and social tensions that existed around the documentation of individual identity in the early decades of the twentieth century when travelers and immigrants first encountered universal demands for a passport. The informal introduction of official attempts to systematically use documents to verify identity pushes the beginnings of this history back to the mid-nineteenth century; the apparent general acceptance of the necessity and accuracy of the passport as an identification document a decade after the story of the clean-shaven Dane and his passport photograph brings this history to an end in the 1930s.

024 Which of the following best fits in Ⓐ?

① emotional   ② reasonable
③ bizarre   ④ serious

유형 05 빈칸완성

[A] In the global resource wars, the environmentalism of the poor is frequently triggered when an official landscape is forcibly imposed on a vernacular one. A vernacular landscape is shaped by the affective, historically textured maps that communities have devised over generations, maps replete with names and routes, maps alive to significant ecological and surface geological features. A vernacular landscape, although neither monolithic nor undisputed, is integral to the socio-environmental dynamics of community rather than being wholly externalized – treated as out there, as a separate nonrenewable resource.

[B] By contrast, an official landscape — whether government, NGO, corporate or some combination of those — is typically oblivious to such earlier maps; instead, it writes the land in a bureaucratic, externalizing, and extraction-driven manner that is often pitilessly instrumental. Lawrence Summers' scheme to export rich nation garbage and toxicity to Africa, for example, stands as a grandiose (though hardly exceptional) instance of a highly rationalized official landscape that, whether in terms of elite capture of resources and toxic disposal, has often been projected onto ecosystems inhabited by those "disposable citizens."

[C] The exponential upsurge in indigenous resource rebellion across the globe has resulted largely from a clash of temporal perspectives between the short-termers who arrive with their Ⓐ_____ landscape maps to extract, despoil, and depart and the long-termers who must live inside the ecological aftermath and must therefore weigh wealth differently in time's scale. More than material wealth is here at stake: imposed Ⓑ_____ landscapers typically discount spiritualized Ⓒ_____ landscape, severing webs of accumulated cultural meaning and treating the landscape as if it were uninhabited by the living, the unborn, and the animate deceased.

2019학년도 아주대학교 인문계 A형 44번

025 Which of the following can best fill in the blanks Ⓐ, Ⓑ and Ⓒ in the paragraph [C]?

	Ⓐ	Ⓑ	Ⓒ
①	official	– official	– vernacular
②	vernacular	– official	– vernacular
③	vernacular	– vernacular	– official
④	official	– vernacular	– official
⑤	official	– official	– official

Ground beef has likely been served on some form of bread since time immemorial, but that does not make a hamburger. A hamburger is defined as much by the use of a purposefully baked bread — universally called a "hamburger bun" — as by the beef patty. You can add as many toppings as you like to this combination or cook the beef in a myriad of ways and you will still have a hamburger. But replace the bread or use a different type of meat and you have something other than a hamburger.

The modern hamburger, as we enjoy it today was first conceived in 1916 in Wichita, Kansas when Walter A. Anderson combined a beef patty with a custom-made bun designed to encapsulate it. In fact, it was just another type of sandwich until 1921 when Anderson partnered with Edgar Waldo Ingram and founded White Castle.

In this restaurant, the hamburger was commoditized and standardized for a defined universally recognizable American dish. In addition to creating the modern hamburger, White Castle also set up the first fast food "system," creating the blueprint for all fast food chains to come. The hamburger existed on restaurant menus before White Castle, but it was listed within the sandwich section. After White Castle, the hamburger became separate and distinct from other sandwiches, with its own section on the menu.

The first hamburgers were small in size — about two to three ounces of beef. But it did not remain stagnant. Innovations came quick and fast. The first cheeseburger was reputedly created in 1926 at the Rite Spot in Pasadena, CA as a "cheese hamburger."

In the post World War II era, the nation enjoyed an explosion of cheap beef and cheap steel, as well as a burgeoning interstate highway system. This allowed the hamburger to move out of the industrial park and onto Main Street. The hamburger that emerged after the war spoke to America's rapid rise — they became _____.

026 Which of the following is most appropriate for the blank?

① out of fashion
② more European
③ local and isolated
④ bigger and more diverse
⑤ something other than a hamburger

유형 05 빈칸완성

• Read the following passage and answer the questions.

Nearly every night of our lives, we undergo a startling metamorphosis. Our brain profoundly alters its behavior and purpose, dimming our consciousness. Around 350 BC, Aristotle wrote an essay, "On Sleep and Sleeplessness," wondering just what we were doing and why during sleep. For the next 2,300 years no one had a good answer. In 1924 German psychiatrist Hans Berger invented the electroencephalograph, which records electrical activity in the brain, and the study of sleep shifted from philosophy to Ⓐ_____. It's only in the past few decades, though, as imaging machines have allowed ever deeper glimpses of the brain's inner workings, that we've approached a convincing answer to Aristotle.

Everything we've learned about sleep has emphasized its importance to our mental and physical health. Our sleep-wake pattern is a central feature of human biology — an adaptation to life on a spinning planet, with its endless wheel of day and night. The 2017 Nobel Prize in medicine was awarded to three scientists who, in the 1980s and 1990s, identified the molecular clock inside our cells that aims to keep us in sync with the sun. When this circadian rhythm breaks down, recent research has shown, we are at increased risk for illnesses such as diabetes, heart disease, and dementia.

Yet an imbalance between lifestyle and sun cycle has become epidemic. "It seems as if we are now living in a worldwide test of the negative consequences of sleep deprivation," says Robert Stickgold, director of the Center for Sleep and Cognition at Harvard Medical School. The average American today sleeps less than seven hours a night, about two hours less than a century ago. This is chiefly due to the proliferation of electric lights, followed by televisions, computers, and smartphones. In our restless, floodlit society, we often think of sleep as an Ⓑ_____, a state depriving us of productivity and play. Thomas Edison, who gave us light bulbs, said that "sleep is an absurdity, a bad habit." He believed we'd eventually dispense with it entirely.

2019학년도 숭실대학교 인문계 A형 30,31번

027 (A) Which of the following best fits in Ⓐ?
① myth ② art
③ logic ④ science

027 (B) Which of the following best fits in Ⓑ?
① adversary ② assistance
③ equipment ④ image

A The textbook genre, irrespective of the discipline it is associated with, serves a common purpose in academic contexts, which is reflected in a number of typical features of textbook genres. Textbooks disseminate discipline-based knowledge and, at the same time, display a somewhat unequal writer-reader relationship, with the writer as the specialist and the reader as the non-initiated novice in the discipline. However, this effort to disseminate introductory uncontested knowledge is sometimes compromised by an attempt to offer what is claimed to be the 'cutting edge' theories. Textbooks nevertheless are seen as 'repositories of codified knowledge' made accessible to large audiences by the frequent use of a variety of rhetorical devices such as reporting, questioning, advance labelling and enumeration.

B However, Ⓐ_____, disciplinary cultures differ on several dimensions, some of which include constraints on patterns of membership, variation in knowledge structure and norms of inquiry, typical patterns of rhetorical intimacy associated with typical modes of expressions, specialist lexis and discourses, and distinct approaches to the teaching of these disciplines.

C Let me begin with two disciplines, i.e. those of economics and law, in an attempt to compare the way disciplinary knowledge is structured and communicated in instructional contexts. On the face of it, the two disciplines appear to be similar in that both of them tend to reinforce the relationship between rhetorical aspects, processes, and outcomes. Similarly, they may also create and formulate a complexity of integrated concepts and use grammatical metaphors to pack disciplinary knowledge for their specific audiences. They may also share the way they need to explain the interrelationship between various concepts by referring to facts and figures, though it is likely that in business such facts and figures have numerical values, whereas in law they consist of human acts entangled in socio-legal relations.

D In a number of other ways, the two disciplines appear to be very different, especially in terms of the rhetorical strategies they employ to construct knowledge. Business studies, in general, depends on aggressive innovation in the way it constructs its discourses. In fact, much of innovation in communicative practices in many other professional contexts, in the last few decades, has been inspired by changes in communicative patterns in the field of business, which is also reflected in economics textbooks. Law, on the other hand, relies on extreme conservatism in the way it constructs its discourses. This has also influenced other forms of expressions in the field. Textbook writing in law is no exception in this respect.

2019학년도 아주대학교 인문계 A형 24번

028 Which of the following best fits in the blank Ⓐ in paragraph Ⓑ.

① in spite of these shared characteristics of textbooks across disciplines
② regardless of definitions and clarifications of technical concepts
③ with reference to a number of common disciplinary variations
④ by means of similar discursive practices in different disciplines
⑤ apart from the universal relationship between genres and specialist disciplines

Many parents grew up with punishments, and it's understandable that they rely on them. But punishments tend to escalate conflict and shut down learning. They elicit a fight or flight response, which means that sophisticated thinking in the frontal cortex goes dark and basic defense mechanisms kick in. Punishments make us either rebel, feel shamed or angry, repress our feelings, or figure out how not to get caught. In this case, full-fledged 4-year-old resistance would be at its peak.

So rewards are the positive choice then, right? Not so fast. Over decades, psychologists have suggested that rewards can decrease our natural motivation and enjoyment. For example, kids who like to draw and are, under experimental conditions, paid to do so, draw less than those who aren't paid. This is what psychologists call the "overjustification effect" — the external reward overshadows the child's internal motivation.

_____. In one classic series of studies, people were given a set of materials (a box of pins, a candle, and a book of matches) and asked to figure out how to attach the candle to the wall. The solution requires innovative thinking — seeing the materials in a way unrelated to their purpose (the box as a candle holder). People who were told they'd be rewarded to solve this dilemma took longer, on average, to figure it out. Rewards narrow our field of view. Our brains stop puzzling freely. We stop thinking deeply and seeing the possibilities.

The whole concept of punishments and rewards is based on negative assumptions about children — that they need to be controlled and shaped by us, and that they don't have good intentions. But we can flip this around to see kids as capable, wired for empathy, cooperation, team spirit and hard work. That perspective changes how we talk to children in powerful ways. Rewards and punishments are conditional, but our love and positive regard for our kids should be unconditional. In fact, when we lead with empathy and truly listen to our kids, they're more likely to listen to us.

2019학년도 인하대학교 인문계 17번

029 Which of the following is most appropriate for the blank?

① Rewards have also been associated with lowering creativity
② However, rewards make kids more attentive to the parents
③ Rewards have also been associated with enhancing creativity
④ Rewards and punishments are vital to enhancing creativity
⑤ Rewards were more effective than punishments in enhancing creativity

After running a plastic comb through your hair, you will find that the comb attracts bits of paper. The attractive force is often strong enough to suspend the paper from the comb, defying the gravitational pull of the entire Earth. The same effect occurs with other rubbed materials, such as glass and hard rubber. Another simple experiment is to rub an inflated balloon against wool. On a dry day, the rubbed balloon will then stick to the wall of a room, often for hours. These materials have become electrically charged. You can give your body an electric charge by vigorously rubbing your shoes on a wool rug or by sliding across a car seat. You can then surprise and annoy a friend or co-worker with a light touch on the arm, delivering a slight shock to both yourself and your victim.

These experiments work best on a dry day because excessive moisture can facilitate a leaking away of the charge. Experiments also demonstrate that there are two kinds of electric charge, which Benjamin Franklin named positive and negative. A hard rubber or a plastic rod that has been rubbed with fur is suspended by a piece of string. When a glass rod that has been rubbed with silk is brought near the rubber rod, the rubber rod is attracted toward the glass rod. If two charged rubber rods or two charged glass rods are brought near each other, the force between them is repulsive. These observations may be explained by assuming that the rubber and glass rods have acquired different kinds of excess charge. We use the convention suggested by Franklin, where the excess electric charge on the glass rod is called positive and that on the rubber rod is called negative. On the basis of observations such as these, we conclude that like charges repel one another and unlike charges attract one another.

Objects usually contain equal amounts of positive and gative charge — electrical forces between objects arise when those objects have net negative or positive charges. Nature's basic carriers of positive charge are protons, which, along with neutrons, are located in the nuclei of atoms. The nucleus is surrounded by a cloud of negatively charged electrons about ten thousand times larger in extent. An electron has the same magnitude charge as a proton, but the opposite sign. In a gram of matter there are approximately 10^{23} positively charged protons and just as many negatively charged electrons, so the net charge is zero. Because the nucleus of an atom is held firmly in place inside a solid, protons never move from one material to another. Electrons are far lighter than protons and hence more easily accelerated by forces.

Furthermore, they occupy the outer regions of the atom. _____, objects become charged by gaining or losing electrons. Charge transfers readily from one type of material to another. Rubbing the two materials together serves to increase the area of contact, facilitating the transfer process. An important characteristic of charge is that electric charge is always conserved. Charge isn't created when two neutral objects are rubbed together; rather, the objects become charged because negative charge is transferred from one object to the other. One object gains a negative charge while the other loses an equal amount of negative charge and hence is left with a net positive charge. When a glass rod is rubbed with silk, electrons are transferred from the rod to the silk. As a result, the glass rod carries a net positive charge, the silk a net negative charge. Likewise, when rubber is rubbed with fur, electrons are transferred from the fur to the rubber.

030 Choose the most appropriate one for the blank.
① In contrast ② Consequently
③ However   ④ Nevertheless

유형 06
내용이해
(일치, 추론, 파악)

Teacher Chris Tip

정독과 함께 객관적인 글의 내용 이해 뿐만 아니라 논리에 따른 사고가 요구되는 유형이다. 대부분 학교에서 가장 많이 나오는 유형으로서 세부적으로는 내용 『일치』, 『추론』, 『파악』 이렇게 나뉜다. 비슷하지만 세부 유형별로 약간의 정답 접근법의 차이가 있다. 이 유형은 시험 시간 조절에 상당한 영향을 미치며, 시간의 압박에서 집중을 흩트려 놓는 문제를 일으키기도 한다. 전략은 정독과 속독의 능력 그리고 어휘력과 추론의 능력까지 요구된다.

1. 『내용 일치』
수능 영어와 같은 형태로 객관적 사실을 빠르게 찾아 나가야 한다. 주로 선택지 순서별로 정답의 근거를 지문에서 찾을 수 있다.

2. 『내용 추론』
지문의 내용을 이해한다면 선택지와 같은 언급도 가능한 것인가를 물어보는 유형이다. 즉, 어떤 판단을 근거로 다른 판단도 끌어낼 수 있는 것을 찾는 유형이다. (가장 시간이 오래 걸리고 까다로운 유형)

3. 『내용 파악』
지문의 특정 부분의 이해나 내용을 묻는 유형이다. 예를 들면, "왜 주인공은 미국으로 갔는가?"와 같은 구체적 질문을 주고 그에 대한 답을 찾아야 하는 유형이다.

가톨릭대학교	세종대학교	한국항공대학교
건국대학교	숙명여자대학교	한성대학교
경기대학교	숭실대학교	한양대학교 에리카
국민대학교	명지대학교	홍익대학교
단국대학교	아주대학교	
덕성여자대학교	인하대학교	
서울여자대학교	한국산업기술대학교	

유형 06 내용이해 | 일치, 추론, 파악

내용일치

Lee Child, the author of the perennially best-selling *Jack Reacher* series, sits down to write each day unsure of what's about to happen. "I get the same shock the reader gets," Mr. Child says, "at the end of a chapter. 'Wow, I definitely did not see that coming.' And the really funny thing for me is when, afterward, a reader will say, 'Oh, I had it all figured out by Page 50,' and I think, 'Really? I didn't.'"

2019학년도 인하대학교 인문계 05번

001 Which of the following is true about Mr. Child?

① He is famous for romance novels.
② He does not plan the ending in advance.
③ He usually begins his chapter with a surprise.
④ He intends to shock readers as late as possible.
⑤ He fails to solve the mystery in his own novel.

내용추론

The 200 signatories to the historic Paris climate accord may have agreed to a "rulebook" on tracking efforts to curb emissions at the COP24 meet last week in Poland. But there was little talk on countries actually ratcheting up emissions control. Global temperatures are headed for a 3 degree Celsius rise from pre-industrial levels although scientists have warned that anything above 1.5 degrees would be disastrous.

2019학년도 숙명여자대학교 인문계 21번

002 What can be inferred from the above passage?

① All the signatories to the historic Paris climate accord had made actual policies for curbing emissions.
② All the signatories to the historic Paris climate accord did not make a practical policy for curbing emissions.
③ Global temperatures rise for a 1.5 degree Celsius from pre-industrial levels.
④ The 200 signatories took the warning of scientists very seriously.
⑤ Scientists warned that Global temperatures are going to be headed for a 3 degree Celsius rise.

내용파악

Cubism was a modern art movement that began in Paris around 1907. Its original founders were Pablo Picasso and Georges Braque. Most of the early cubist art revolved around geometric shapes, planes, and fragmentation. Cubists were more concerned with representing a complete or whole view of the subject matter. Space and volume played important roles in their art. Furthermore, cubists avoided realistic or accurate painting. Instead, they focused on representing an object from multiple perspectives on the canvas. Reducing the natural form into the abstract was also a trait of cubist artists. The imitation of nature was no longer as important as it was in previous art movements. Paul Cezanne is considered a major influence of the early cubists.

2019학년도 한국산업기술대학교 인문계 28번

003 Which of the following is a characteristic of cubism?

① the use of geometric shapes
② the details of the subject matter
③ the adoption of a single perspective
④ the depiction of natural objects

내용일치

Gum disease is common among adults. In fact, the loss of teeth after forty is attributed more often to gum disease than to cavities. Gum disease comes as bacteria builds up in plaque, affecting the bone that surrounds and supports teeth. Then the teeth become loose, and sometimes fall out eventually. The gum becomes red and puffy and it sometimes bleeds. However, it is often not recognized until it becomes too late. Tips for healthy gum are similar to those for healthy teeth. Brushing teeth well is the first to be kept in mind. We have bacteria that live on carbohydrates in sugars and starches. And dentists advise to avoid sweet or starchy foods and to brush teeth right after meal or snack. Flossing once a day to remove plaque from between teeth and below the gum line is also important, according to dentists.

2019학년도 건국대학교 인문·예체능계 A형 30번

004 잇몸병(gum disease)에 관한 다음 글의 내용과 일치하지 않는 것은?

① 성인들한테서 흔히 발생한다.
② 40세 이후의 치아 손실은 주로 잇몸병 때문에 생긴다.
③ 종종 너무 늦게 발견되기도 한다.
④ 건강한 잇몸을 유지하는 방법과 건치를 유지하는 방법은 다르다.
⑤ 달고 딱딱한 음식은 피하는 것이 좋다.

유형 06 내용이해

추론 가능한 문장 고르기

The transportation revolution and the market revolution would have come much more slowly if the Americans of the early republic had followed the *laissez-faire* (non-interference) notions of political economy that are often mistakenly ascribed to them. Instead, the people demanded that their governments ally themselves with private enterprise to speed the march of progress.

Ⓐ The most notable alliance of public and private enterprise was in the field of politics.
Ⓑ The Americans of the early republic are frequently misunderstood to have followed the policy of *laissez-faire*.
Ⓒ The people of the early republic asked their governments to work with private businesses.
Ⓓ Because the Americans of the early republic did not adopt the non-inference policy, the transportation and market revolutions were achieved more rapidly.

2019학년도 아주대학교 인문계 15번

005 Choose the number with a correct set of statements that can be restated or inferred from the original text.

① Ⓐ & Ⓑ   ② Ⓑ & Ⓒ
③ Ⓑ & Ⓓ   ④ Ⓐ,Ⓒ & Ⓓ
⑤ Ⓑ,Ⓒ & Ⓓ

내용일치

Macroeconomics is the study of the whole market economy. Like other parts of economics, macroeconomics uses the central idea that people make purposeful decisions with scarce resources. However, instead of focusing on the workings of one market — whether the market for peanuts or the market for bicycles — macroeconomics focuses on the economy as a whole. Macroeconomics looks at the big picture: Economic growth, recessions, unemployment, and inflation are among its subject matter. Macroeconomics is important to you and your future since you will have a much better chance of finding a desirable job after you graduate from college during a period of economic expansion than a period of recession. Strong economic growth can help alleviate poverty, free up resources to clean up the environment, and lead to a brighter future for your generation.

2019학년도 숙명여자대학교 인문계 27번

006 Which of the following is TRUE for the above passage?

① Macroeconomics uses the idea that people use enough data to reach decisions.
② Macroeconomics is selective in the sense that it focuses on a critical area.
③ Macroeconomics helps us to understand the future economic directions better.
④ Macroeconomics could result in economic recession and poverty.
⑤ Macroeconomics always provides a blue print for the bright future.

The nature of acquiring languages is still quite mysterious. Children seem to have a natural inclination toward learning to speak from birth, and they are capable of quickly speaking intelligently. Three theories have been developed by researchers as to why children are able to learn a language with ease. These theories attempt to clarify some of the unfamiliar aspects of language acquisition. Specifically, they examine the behavior children exhibit during the various stages of speech development. The conditioning theory, the imitation theory, and the innateness theory all concentrate on the distinctive characteristics of this development.

No single theory is sufficient to completely explain the various characteristics of language acquisition, despite the fact that research on the subject is expanding. However, when taken together, the conditioning, imitation, and innateness theories can provide some assistance in comprehending the subtleties of language development in children.

007 Which one CANNOT be inferred from the passage?
① One theory is enough to expound the acquisition of languages.
② Children learn languages effortlessly.
③ Researchers have not ceased studying language acquisition.
④ The ability to acquire languages is still enigmatic.

유형 06 내용이해

내용일치

The movie, "Deadpool," which has so far taken more than $500 million in cinemas worldwide, is an atypical blockbuster, a foul-mouthed anti-hero film with a mature "R" audience rating. But in one important respect, it is typical of many of Hollywood's recent successful movies: it does not bank on a world-famous star to sell it. In contrast, two recent "star vehicle" films struggled in vain to attract audiences despite heavy promotion and high-profile openings. Much of the film industry's recent success, at home and abroad, comes from the rise of the big special-effects event film. Such productions are more likely to make stars than to be made by them.

Yet there is one arena where stars are as relevant as ever: the international market. Foreign cinemas like to exhibit films with known names in the lead roles. Some old-school stars are still big draws in the international market, even if the movies in which they appear are flops at home. Even if big names have lost some of their luster at home, abroad they can be "sort of like supernovas," a studio executive says. "They have flamed out a long time ago, but the light shines on past their death.

2019학년도 국민대학교 인문계 오전 A형 18번

008 According to the passage, which is NOT true?

① "Deadpool" is one of the "R"-rated movies.
② Many Hollywood's recent successful movies are "star vehicle" films.
③ There is no appearance of world-famous stars in "Deadpool."
④ Big names still have influence in drawing audiences in the international market.

Doctors Without Borders (Medecins Sans Frontieres, or MSF) is an international medical humanitarian organization. The doctors, nurses, and other medical specialists who work with MSF are dedicated to helping people in crisis situations regardless of their race, religion, or political affiliation. Since 1971, MSF teams have been responsible for providing quality medical care in nearly 60 countries. The teams have well-qualified specialists who are familiar with working in difficult, even dangerous, circumstances and the majority of MSF's aid workers are from the communities where the crises are occurring. The work of MSF teams is not limited to offering direct medical care; they also share a commitment about serving as witnesses to the crises of the people they assist. However, as an organization, MSF is neutral. It has a reputation for not taking sides in armed conflicts and for being concerned with providing care on the basis of need alone. This belief in operating independently of government or other parties and obtaining independent funding is the key to MSF's ability to conduct its aid efforts.

2019학년도 한양대학교 에리카 인문계 A형 32번

009 위 글의 내용과 맞지 <u>않는</u> 것을 고르시오.

① MSF aims to provide qualified medical care to people in crisis.
② Most MSF members are volunteers from communities in peaceful situations.
③ MSF aims to obtain funding independently of government or other parties.
④ MSF offers direct medical care but stays away from political matters.

Stress is inevitable. No one can prevent it. But we can try to minimize its harmful effects on our health. To understand how some people keep their composure while others crumble under the pressure, it is useful to examine the coping process and ask the question: What are some adaptive ways to cope with stress?

Researchers distinguished two general types of coping strategies. The first is problem-focused coping, designed to reduce stress by overcoming the source of the problem. Difficulties in school? Study harder or hire a tutor. The goal is to attack the source of your stress. A second-approach is emotion-focused coping, in which one tries to manage the emotional turmoil, perhaps by learning to live with the problem. If you're struggling at school, at work, or in a relationship, you can keep a stiff upper lip and ignore the situation or make the best of it. People probably take an active problem-focused approach when they think they can overcome a stressor but fall back on an emotion-focused approach when they see the problem as out of their control.

010 Which can be inferred as an example of emotion-focused coping?

① Talking to parents when you have problems with them
② Asking a stranger for a cell phone when you lost your phone
③ Trying to keep calm when you are in stressful situations
④ Studying extra time when you have academic difficulties at school

- Read the following passages and choose the one best answer for each question.

Nature challenges humans in many ways, through disease, weather, and famine. For those living along the coast, one unusual phenomenon capable of catastrophic destruction is the tsunami. A tsunami is a series of waves generated in a body of water by an impulsive disturbance. Earthquakes, landslides, volcanic eruptions, explosions, and even the impact of meteorites can generate tsunamis. Starting at sea, a tsunami slowly approaches land, growing in height and losing energy through bottom friction and turbulence. Still, just like any other water waves, tsunamis unleash tremendous energy as they plunge onto the shore. They have great erosion potential, stripping beaches of sand, undermining trees, and flooding hundreds of meters inland. They can easily crush cars, homes, vegetation, and anything they collide with. To minimize the devastation of a tsunami, scientists are constantly trying to anticipate them more accurately and more quickly. Because many factors come together to produce a life-threatening tsunami, foreseeing them is not easy. Despite this, researchers in meteorology persevere in studying and predicting tsunami behavior.

2019학년도 경기대학교 인문·예체능계 A형 31,34번

011 (A) In the first sentence, why does the author mention weather?

① because tsunamis are caused by bad weather
② because tsunamis are more destructive than weather phenomena
③ as an example of a destructive natural force
④ as an introduction to the topic of coastal storms

011 (B) Which sentence best expresses the essential information of this passage?

① Tsunamis could become a new source of usable energy in the near future.
② Tsunamis do more damage to the land than flooding.
③ Tsunamis can have an especially catastrophic impact on coastal communities.
④ Scientists can predict and track tsunamis with a fair degree of accuracy, reducing their potential impact.

Most of us are good at spotting overtly aggressive people. While it doesn't feel good when someone insults, criticizes, or belittles you, at least you know why you are hurting. But sometimes the people around us, including our close family, friends, and colleagues, make us feel uncomfortable, but we cannot quite put a finger on why. For example, your friend may fail to greet you in the hallway for the third time in a week. You make yourself believe that it is probably a slip, yet you feel that something is amiss.

If this happens frequently with one or more people in your life, you may be dealing with passive-aggressive behavior, which is much harder to detect than overtly aggressive behavior. Passive aggression is a tendency to engage in implicit expression of hostility through acts such as subtle insults, sullen behavior, stubbornness, or a deliberate failure to accomplish required tasks. Because passive-aggressive behavior is implicit, it can be hard to spot, even when you're feeling the psychological consequences. To help you identify this type of behavior, I describe five instances of it below. These are not all of the ways a person can be passive-aggressive, but they are the most common.

012 What will be discussed right after the passage?

① Comparison of aggressive behaviors
② Causes of passive aggression
③ Ways to deal with passive aggression
④ Effects of passive aggression
⑤ Examples of passive-aggressive behavior

- Read the following passages and choose the best answers to the questions.

The variety of life on Earth, its biological diversity, is commonly referred to as biodiversity. The number of species of plants, animals, and microorganisms, the enormous diversity of genes in these species, the different ecosystems on the planet, such as deserts, rainforests and coral reefs are all part of a biologically diverse Earth. Appropriate conservation and sustainable development strategies attempt to recognize this as being integral to any approach. In some way or form, almost all cultures have recognized the importance of nature and its biological diversity for their societies and have therefore understood the need to maintain it. Yet, power, greed and politics have affected the precarious balance.

Why is Biodiversity important? Does it really matter if there aren't so many species? Biodiversity boosts ecosystem productivity where each species, no matter how small, all have an important role to play. For example, a larger number of plant species means a greater variety of crops; greater species diversity ensures natural sustainability for all life forms; and healthy ecosystems can better withstand and recover from a variety of disasters. And so, while we dominate this planet, we still need to preserve the diversity in wildlife.

013 According to the author of this passage, why is biodiversity so important?
① because all cultures have recognized its importance
② because all species no matter how big or small play an important part in ecosystem productivity
③ because a diverse wildlife means a more beautiful world
④ because a greater variety of crops means a larger number of animal species

In 2006, researchers at Cornell University released results of a long-term study containing some hypotheses about the reorganization of television in the 1980s. The research project assembled data to suggest a correlation between television viewing by very young children and autism. One of the most urgent problems in autism studies has been to explain the extraordinary and anomalous rise in its frequency beginning in the mid to late 1980s. From the late 1970s, when autism occurred in one out of 2,500 children, the rate of incidence has risen so fast that, as of a few years ago, it affected approximately one in 150 children, and showed no sign of leveling off. Obviously, television had been pervasive in North American homes since the 1950s: Why then might it have markedly different consequences beginning in the 1980s? The study proposes that a new coalescence of factors occurred in that decade — in particular, the widespread availability of cable TV, the growth of dedicated children's channels and video cassettes, and the popularity of VCRs, as well as huge increases in households with two or more television sets. Thus conditions were, and continue to be, in place for the exposure of very young children to television for extended periods of time on a daily basis. Their specific conclusions were relatively cautious: that extended television viewing before the age of three can trigger the onset of the disorder in "at risk" children.

2019학년도 서울여자대학교 인문·자연계 A형 30번

014 According to the passage, which of the following is true?

① In North America, dedicated children's channels were already popular in the 1950s.
② In the late 1970s, the rate of child autism incidence was no higher than one in 2,500 children.
③ Watching TV for an extended period of time tends to cause autism in adults as well as in children.
④ A few years ago, the rate of child autism incidence stabilized with approximately one in 150 children affected.

• Read the following passages and answer the questions

내용일치

In the eighteenth century, Linnaeus classed human beings as primates, placing them in the same genus as apes, monkeys, and lemurs. Then in 1859 Charles Darwin proclaimed his theory of evolution in *The Origin of Species*, suggesting (at first, he did not dare say it outright) that humanity evolved from something like an ape. There were passionate debates and embarrassed snickers people joked about having gorillas for grandfathers. Racists depicted those from other cultures — Africans, Irish, Jews, and Japanese — as being like apes. The targeted people were drawn as slouched over with dangling arms and receding foreheads.

But modern people have feared above all the "animal" in themselves. The metaphor of "the beast within" was used in the Victorian era to explain all sorts of vices, from lechery to gluttony. Physiognomists looked for animal features in the faces of human beings. Sigmund Freud and his disciples divided human character into the "id," which represented the beast (or instinct) in human beings, and the "ego," or self — the two of which were in constant conflict.

Today anthropomorphic animals are everywhere we look: tigers sell cornflakes and gasoline talking cows sell milk; bulls and ducks represent sports teams. Centerfolds of undressed women in *Playboy* are called "bunnies," while in *Penthouse*, a rival magazine, they are called "pets." The cartoon character Joe Camel was so effective in selling cigarettes to teenagers that massive protests forced the tobacco company to discontinue ads with him in 1997.

2019학년도 홍익대학교 인문계 A형 32번

015 According to the passage, which of the following is NOT true?

① Both Linnaeus and Darwin were concerned with the animal classification.
② Animals have often been used for the purpose of profit motivation.
③ Negative sentiments toward animals have "humanized" them.
④ It was Freud who discovered the missing link between humans and animals.

유형 06 내용이해

• Read the following passages and answer the questions.

> **내용일치**
>
> For Marxism, an ideology is a belief system, and all belief systems are products of cultural conditioning. For example, capitalism, communism, Marxism, patriotism, religion, ethical systems, humanism, environmentalism, astrology, and karate are all ideologies. Even our assumption that nature behaves according to the laws of science is an ideology. However, although almost any experience or field of study we can think of has an ideological component, not all ideologies are equally productive or desirable. Undesirable ideologies promote repressive political agendas and, in order to ensure their acceptance among the citizenry, pass themselves off as natural ways of seeing the world instead of acknowledging themselves as ideologies. "It's natural for men to hold leadership positions because their biological superiority renders them more physically, intellectually, and emotionally capable than women" is a sexist that sells itself as a function of nature, rather than as a product of cultural belief. "Every family wants to own its own home on its own land" is a capitalist ideology that sells itself as natural by pointing, for example, to the fact that almost all Americans want to own their own property, without acknowledging that this desire is created in us by the capitalist culture in which we live. By posing as natural ways of seeing the world, repressive ideologies prevent us from understanding the material/historical conditions in which we live because they refuse to acknowledge that those conditions have any bearing on the way we see the world.
>
> 2020학년도 숭실대학교 인문계 26번

016 Which of the following is true?

① Ideologies depend for their base on nature's operation.

② Repressive ideologies tend to reveal the material conditions people live in.

③ All ideologies are equally desirable.

④ Human desires reflect certain aspects of cultures in which people live.

The posthuman subject is an amalgam, a collection of heterogeneous components, a material-informational entity whose boundaries undergo continuous construction and reconstruction. Consider the six-million-dollar man, a paradigmatic citizen of the posthuman regime. As his name implies, the parts of the self are indeed owned, but they are owned precisely because they were purchased, not because ownership is a natural condition preexisting market relations. Similarly, the presumption that there is an agency, desire, or will belonging to the self and clearly distinguished from the wills of others is undercut in the posthuman, for the posthuman's collective heterogenous quality implies a distributed cognition located in disparate parts. We have only to recall Robocop's memory flashes that interfere with his programmed directives to understand how the distributed cognition of the posthuman complicates individual agency. If human essence is freedom from the wills of others, the posthuman is "post" not because it is necessarily unfree but because there is no a priori way to identify a self-will that can be clearly distinguished from an other-will. Although these examples foreground the cybernetic aspect of the posthuman, it is important to recognize that the construction of the posthuman does not require the subject to be a literal cyborg. Whether or not interventions have been made on the body, new models of subjectivity emerging from such fields as cognitive science and artificial life imply that even a biologically unaltered *Homo sapiens* count as posthuman. The defining characteristics involve the construction of subjectivity, not the presence of nonbiological components.

017 Which of the following can be inferred from the passage?

① There is a humanist presumption that is never weakened in the posthuman.
② The posthuman is represented only through bodily interventions.
③ The construction of the posthuman subjectivity is not altogether artificial.
④ The posthuman gives way to the biological aspect of *Homo sapiens*.

Over millennia, prolonged seasonal freezing of Lake Baikal has caused most of the lake's flora and fauna to adapt to life on and under the ice. Phytoplankton, microscopic organisms that live in fresh- or saltwater environments, are the basis of the lake's food web. Lake Baikal is the only lake in the world in which both the dominant primary producers (phytoplankton) and the top predator (the Baikal seal) require ice for reproduction.

Baikal's phytoplankton include green algae, which can grow explosively in "blooms" that may last days and weeks. Ice thickness and transparency determine the amount of light reaching the water, a critical factor for phytoplankton growth. Because these unique algae have adapted to specific under-ice conditions, recent changes in the ice, which was caused by warming air temperature, have decreased algae growth rates and slowed spring algal blooms. The effects of this decrease then move up the food chain, from the enormous quantities of tiny crustaceans that eat the algae to the fish that eat the crustaceans to the seals that depend on fish as their main food source.

The Baikal seal, smallest of the world's seals and the only species exclusively living in freshwater, mates and gives birth on the lake ice. The seals require ice in early spring for shelter. If ice melt occurs early, the seals are forced into the water, and the extra energy expended affects female fertility and nurturing ability.

2019학년도 가톨릭대학교 인문계 A형 39번

018 According to the passage above, what is the best expression for the blank in the following sentence?

> Recent changes in water temperature and ice over at Lake Baikal exemplify _____ _____.

① that global warming may lead to beneficial changes in some areas around the globe
② that living things display remarkable resilience in the face of environmental changes
③ how flora and fauna can protect the freshwater environment from climate change
④ how changes in the atmosphere link to changes in the hydrosphere and biosphere

• Read the following passages and answer the questions.

If you ask any man in America, or any man in business in England, what it is that most interferes with his enjoyment of existence, he will say: "The struggle for life." He will say this in all sincerity; he will believe it. In a certain sense, it is true; yet in another very important sense, it is profoundly false. The struggle for life is a thing which does, of course, occur. It may occur to any of us if we are unfortunate. It occurred, for example, to Conrad's hero Falk, who found himself on a derelict ship, one of the two men among the crew who were possessed of firearms, with nothing to eat but the other men. When the two men had finished the meals upon which they could agree, a true struggle for life began. Falk won, but was ever after a vegetarian. Now that is not what the businessman means when he speaks of the "struggle for life." It is an inaccurate phrase which he has picked up in order to give dignity to something essentially trivial. Ask him how many men he has known in his class of life who have died of hunger. Ask him what happened to his friends after they had been ruined. Everybody knows that a businessman who has been ruined is better off far as material comforts are concerned than a man who has never been rich enough to have the chance of being ruined. What people mean, therefore, by the struggle for life is really the struggle for success. What people fear when they engage in the struggle is not that they will fail to get their breakfast next morning, but that they will fail to outshine their neighbors.

2019학년도 국민대학교 인문계 오후 A형 16번

019 According to the passage, which is true of Conrad's hero Falk?

① He had a weapon on the derelict ship.
② He found himself on a deserted island.
③ He and other crew members survived in the end.
④ He was chasing after a vegetarian who was on the ship.

PRE-CONFERENCE EVENT
FIBERS FOR HIGH PERFORMANCE TEXTILES TUTORIAL
2:00-5:15pm Tuesday, March 6
Presenter: Dr. Seshardri Ramkumar, Professor of Advanced Materials, Nonwovens & Advanced Materials Laboratory, Texas Tech University

 High performance textiles are basically functional textiles that provide added value to the textiles in addition to common attributes of clothing materials. The functionality is achieved due to the starting material, i.e., fibers, structural aspects and finishing imparted to the final product.

 This tutorial will focus on the first pillar, which is the raw material for advanced textile products. The seminar is aimed at beginners in this field as well as those who have the basic understanding of textiles and industrial textiles in particular. Subject areas covered will include: an outline of high performance textiles, classification of fibers, fibers that provide different functionality, functionality provided by 3-dimensional and structural fibers such as bi-component, sustainability aspects, micro and nano structural fibers, and what's next?

 The tutorial is not included with the conference registration. A discounted tutorial registration fee will be available to individuals attending the conference.

020 Who is most likely to have interest in this information?
① accountants of clothing companies
② researchers in fiber materials
③ laborers working at energy plants
④ teachers engaging in kindergartens

• 주어진 글을 읽고 물음에 가장 알맞은 답을 고르시오.

내용추론

Dr. Pickett, a Canadian entomologist, and his associates struck out on a new road instead of going along with other entomologists who continued to pursue the will-o'-the-wisp of the ever more toxic chemical. Recognizing that they had a strong ally in nature, they devised a program that makes maximum use of natural controls and minimum use of insecticides. Whenever insecticides are applied only minimum dosages are used — barely enough to control the pest without avoidable harm to beneficial species. Proper timing also enters in. Thus, if nicotine sulphate is applied before rather than after the apple blossoms turn pink one of the important predators is spared, probably because it is still in the egg stage.

How well has this program worked? Nova Scotia orchardists who are following Dr. Pickett's modified spray program are producing as high a share proportion of first-grade fruit as are those who are using intense chemical applications. They are also getting as good production. They are getting these results, moreover, at a substantially lower cost.

More important than even these excellent results is the fact that Dr. Pickett's program is not doing violence to nature's balance. It is well on the way to realizing the philosophy stated by G. C. Ullyett a decade ago: "We must change our philosophy, abandon our attitude of human superiority and admit that in many cases in natural environments we find ways of limiting populations of organisms in a more economical way than we can do it ourselves."

2020학년도 세종대학교 인문계 A형 49번

021 Which of the following can NOT be inferred from the passage?

① Dr. Pickett and his associates believed that they had a strong ally in nature.

② One of the advantages of the Dr. Pickett's program was that it produced positive results at a lower cost.

③ G. C. Ullyett and Dr. Pickett saw eye to eye about ways to use nature.

④ Dr. Pickett and his associates did not believe in the need to limit populations of organisms.

• Read the following passages and answer the questions.

내용추론

1) Strokes cause almost twice as many deaths as all accidents combined, but 80% of respondents judged accidental death to be more likely.

2) Tornadoes were seen as more frequent killers than asthma, although the latter cause 20 times more deaths.

3) Death by lightning was judged less likely than death from botulism even though it is 52 times more frequent.

4) Death by disease is 18 times as likely as accidental death, but the two were judged about equally likely.

5) Death by accidents was judged to be more than 300 times more likely than death by diabetes, but the true ratio is 4:1.

The media do not just shape what the public is interested in, but also are shaped by it. Editors cannot ignore the public's demands that certain topics and viewpoints receive extensive coverage. The world in our heads is not a precise replica of reality; our expectations about the frequency of events are distorted by the prevalence and emotional intensity of the messages to which we are exposed. The estimates of causes of death are an almost direct representation of the activation of ideas in associative memory, and are a good example of substitution. But Slovic and his colleagues were led to a deeper insight: they saw that the ease with which ideas of various risks come to mind and the emotional reactions to these risks are inextricably linked. Frightening thoughts and images occur to us with particular ease, and thoughts of danger that are fluent and vivid exacerbate fear.

2019학년 한국항공대학교 인문계 32번

022 It can be inferred from the passage that _____.

① unusual events get less attention and are consequently perceived as more unusual than they really are

② unusual events get less attention and are consequently perceived as less unusual than they really are

③ unusual events attract disproportionate attention and are consequently perceived as more unusual than they really are

④ unusual events attract disproportionate attention and are consequently perceived as less unusual than they really are

In a study by some social psychologists participants were asked to take part in two tasks. In the first task, they were asked to make sentences out of sets of provided words. Next, as part of what was supposedly a different study, participants played an economic game in which they were given ten $1 coins and asked to divide them up between themselves and the next participant. Only the next participant would know what they decided, and that participant wouldn't know who the givers were. Think for a moment what you would do in this situation. Here's an opportunity to make a quick 10 bucks, and there is a definite temptation to pocket all the coins. But you might feel a little guilty hoarding all the money and leaving nothing for the next person. This is one of those situations in which there is a devil on one of our shoulders ("Don't be a fool, take it all!") and an angel on the other ("Do unto others as you would have them do unto you"). In short, people want the money but this conflicts with their goal to be nice to others. Which goal wins out?

It depends in part on which goal has been recently primed. Remember the sentence completion task people did first? In the task, half of the participants were given the words that had to do with God (spirit, divine, God, sacred, and prophet), which were designed to set the goal of acting kindly to one's neighbor. The other half got neutral words. An important detail is that the participants did not make a connection between the sentence-making task and the economic game — they thought the two tasks were completely unrelated. Even so, the people who made sentences out of words having to do with God left significantly more money for the next participant ($4.56 on average) than did people who got the neutral words ($2.56 on average).

023 Which of the following is true according to the passage?

① All the participants were given the same set of words.
② Who left money to the next participant remained unknown to the recipient.
③ The participants were well aware of the connection between the two given tasks.
④ The participants were given two options — taking all the money or giving half of it to the next person.

Medicine is as old as humankind. More than 50,000 years ago, stone-age, cave-dwelling humans first crushed and infused herbs for their curative properties. Traditional forms of medicine — few of which, sadly, are known to written history — evolved on all continents, from the deserts and jungles of Africa to North American plains, South American rain forests, and balmy Pacific islands. Earliest records in West Asia, the Middle East, North Africa, China, and India document myriad diseases, healing plants, and surgical procedures. Ancient Egyptians had complex, hierarchical methods of medicine integrated into their religious beliefs. Gods and spirits were in charge of mortal disease, and priest-physicians — Imhotep is one of the first great names in medical history — mediated with the supernatural realm to ease human suffering. The civilizations of Greece and Rome had their respective medical giants in Hippocrates and Galen. Hippocrates set standards for patient care and the physician's attitudes and philosophy that persist today. Galen wrote so extensively and authoritatively that his theories and practices attained quasi-religious status and effectively stalled medical progress in Europe for 1,400 years. After the Roman Empire ended, the murky arts of alchemy, sorcery, exorcism, and miracle cures flourished in Western Europe. Ancient India and China also developed sophisticated medical systems with outstanding contributors. In India, in the centuries before and after Hippocrates, Susruta and Chakara produced encyclopedic founding works of Ayurvedic medicine. Chinese physician Zhang Zhongjing, a contemporary of Galen, also compiled works that described hundreds of diseases and prescribed thousands of remedies.

024 Choose the one that is <u>not</u> true according to the passage.

① Ancient Egyptian priest-physicians are recognized in medical history.
② Galen's practices advanced medicine after the fall of the Roman Empire.
③ In the past, medicine was thought to be tied to matters of faith.
④ Europe and China developed medical systems around the same time.

- Read the following passages and answer the questions.

Human error is defined as any deviance from "appropriate" behavior. The word appropriate is in quotes because in many circumstances, the appropriate behavior is not known or is only determined after the fact. But still, error is defined as deviance from the generally accepted correct or appropriate behavior. Error is the general term for all wrong actions. There are two major classes of error: slips and mistakes. Slips are further divided into two major classes and mistakes into three. These categories of errors all have different implications for design. I now turn to a more detailed look at these classes of errors and their design implications. A slip occurs when a person intends to do one action and ends up doing something else. With a slip, the action performed is not the same as the action that was intended. There are two major classes of slips: action-based and memory-lapse. In action-based slips, the wrong action is performed. In lapses, memory fails, so the intended action is not done or its results not evaluated. Action-based slips and memory lapses can be further classified according to their causes. A mistake occurs when the wrong goal is established or the wrong plan is formed. From that point on, even if the actions are executed properly they are part of the error, because the actions themselves are inappropriate; they are part of the wrong plan. With a mistake, the action that is performed matches the plan: it is the plan that is wrong.

Mistakes have three major classes: rule-based, knowledge-based, and memory-lapse. In a rule-based mistake, the person has appropriately diagnosed the situation, but then decided upon an erroneous course of action: the wrong rule is being followed. In a knowledge-based mistake, the problem is misdiagnosed because of erroneous or incomplete knowledge. Memory-lapse mistakes take place when there is forgetting at the stages of goals, plans, or evaluation.

025 It can be inferred from the passage that to pour some milk into coffee and then put the coffee cup into the refrigerator is an example of _____.

① knowledge-based mistake
② memory-lapse mistake
③ action-based slip
④ memory-lapse slip

There are several pro tips for long and healthy life. First, diet. Weight loss likely explains many of the positive changes, such as lower blood pressure and better blood-sugar levels. But some experts speculate that fasting also makes the body more resistant to stress, which can have beneficial effects at the cellular level. One expert says, "Diet is by far the most powerful intervention to delay aging and age-related diseases."

In the past couple of years, scientists have shown that sedentary behavior, like sitting all day, is a risk factor for earlier death. They found that hours spent sitting are linked to increased risks of Type 2 diabetes and nonalcoholic fatty liver disease. You can't exercise away all the bad effects of sitting too much. But the good news is that doing anything but sitting still — even fidgeting counts — can add up. People who logged the least physical activity had the highest risk of a heart event in the next ten years, which isn't shocking. But to the surprise of the researchers, moving just a little bit more during the day — like doing chores around the house — was enough to lower the risk of a heart event.

By now it's clear to scientists that our emotions affect our biology. Studies have shown for years that anger and stress can release stress hormones like adrenaline into our blood, which trigger the heart to beat faster and harder. Stress may even have an effect on how well our brains hold up against Alzheimer's disease. The researchers found that people who held more negative views of aging earlier in life had greater loss in the volume of their hippocampus, a region of the brain whose loss is linked to Alzheimer's disease. This is not the first time research has suggested that how we feel about aging can affect how we age.

026 According to the passage, which is NOT one of the pro tips for long and healthy life?
① not sitting still for long
② doing excessive exercise
③ keeping to a regimen of diet
④ having an optimistic attitude

• Read the following passage and answer the questions.

The New Negro: An Interpretation (1925) is an anthology of fiction, poetry, and essays on African and African-American art and literature edited by Alain Locke, who lived In Washington, DC and taught at Howard University during the Harlem Renaissance. As a collection of the creative efforts coming out of the burgeoning New Negro Movement or Harlem Renaissance, the book is considered by literary scholars and critics to be the definitive text of the movement. This book included Locke's title essay "The New Negro," as well as nonfiction essays, poetry, and fiction by many of the African American writers.

The New Negro dives into how the African Americans sought social, political, and artistic change. Instead of accepting their position in society, Locke saw the New Negro as championing and demanding civil rights. In addition, his anthology sought to change old stereotypes and replaced them with new visions of black identity that resisted simplification. The essays and poems in the anthology mirror real life events and experiences. The anthology reflects the voice of middle class African American citizens that wanted to have equal civil rights like the white, middle class counterparts.

A theme used by Locke commonly is this idea of the Old vs the New Negro. The Old Negro according to Locke was a product of stereotypes and judgments that were put on them, not ones that they created. They were forced to live in a shadow of themselves and others' actions. The New Negro is a Negro that now has an understanding of oneself. They at one point lacked self-respect and self-dependence which has created a new dynamic and allowed the birth of the New Negro. They have become the Negro of today which is also the changed Negro. Locke speaks about the migration having an effect on the Negro leveling the playing field and increasing the realm of how the Negro is viewed because they were moved out of the southern parts of U.S. and into other areas where they could start over. The migration in a sense transformed the Negro and fused them together as they all came from all over the world, all walks of life, and all different backgrounds.

027 (A) Which of the following is NOT true about the book *The New Negro*?

① It was written by Alain Locke alone.
② It includes works from a variety of literary genre.
③ It deals with African Americans' effort for a new identity.
④ It reflects the real life experiences well.

027 (B) Which of the following is NOT a feature of the New Negro?

① crave for a new identity
② quest for black supremacy
③ knowledge of oneself
④ demand for civil rights

유형 06 내용이해

• Read the following and answer the questions.

내용파악

For the past 48 hours the 280-foot vessel *Knorr*, temporary if not harmonious home to some 30 engineers, scientists, and academics, as well as a rotating roster of friends and financial supporters, has been lashed to a pier in the northern Turkish city of Sinop, kept from its appointed mission by the lack of research visas. The American ship and crew have come to the Black Sea to investigate ancient shipwrecks, but the local media are skeptical. During the day packs of journalists scramble up and down the stone dock, aiming their cameras and questions at anyone on the deck within earshot.

"Why are you really here? Are you searching for oil? Are you on a secret mission for the U.S. military? Are you looking for Noah's ark?"

Hundreds of residents, curious to see for themselves, stroll arm in arm to the waterfront in the lovely late July evenings to marvel at the great ship stuffed with high-tech wizardry bobbing in the bay of their historic walled city.

But for expedition leader Robert D. Ballard, who is spending $40,000 a day on the project and is losing priceless research time — having invested millions in a state-of-the-art remotely controlled submersible, deep-sea high-definition cameras, and a futuristic high-bandwidth satellite communications system — there's nothing magical about the nightly carnival on the dock.

"We're bleeding to death," he says. "We're hemorrhaging money."

Nor has this latest delay been the only setback of the summer. Ballard's original itinerary called for testing his machines on a series of Greek and Byzantine wrecks off Bulgaria and Turkey before moving on to a pair of 2,700-year-old Phoenician wrecks off Egypt. But weeks earlier, just before the *Knorr* left its home port at Woods Hole, Massachusetts, complications in his negotiations with the Bulgarian Academy of Sciences forced Ballard to cancel that part of the cruise for now. Later, after the expedition was under way, Ballard also got words that Egyptian security had denied him permission to explore the Phoenician ships.

2019학년도 인하대학교 인문계 39번

028 According to the passage, why did the ship *Knorr* come to Turkey?

① To search for oil
② To accomplish a military mission
③ To investigate ancient shipwrecks
④ To look for the remains of Noah's ark
⑤ To rescue the crew from a sunken ship

- Read each passage and answer the corresponding questions for each.

[A] *Cinderella* causes me a feeling of urgency. What is unsettling about that fairy tale is that it is essentially the story of household — a world, if you please — of women gathered together and held together in order to abuse another woman. There is a rather vague absent father and a nick-of-time prince with a foot fetish. However, neither has much personality. There are also the surrogate "mothers," of course (god- and step-), who contribute both to Cinderella's grief and to her release and happiness. In fact, it is her step-sisters who interest me. How crippling it must be for those girls to grow up with a mother, to watch and imitate that mother, enslaving another girl.

[B] I am curious about their fortunes after the story ends. For contrary to recent adaptations, the step-sisters were not ugly, clumsy, stupid girls with outsize feet. The Grimm collection describes them as "beautiful and fair in appearance." Having watched and participated in the violent dominion of another woman, will they be any less cruel when it comes their turn to enslave other children, or even when they are required to take care of their own mother?

[C] It is not a wholly medieval problem. It is quite a contemporary one: feminine power when directed at other women has historically been wielded in what has been described as a masculine manner. I am alarmed by the violence that women do to each other: professional violence, competitive violence, and emotional violence. I am alarmed by the willingness of women to enslave other women.

[D] I want not to ask you but to tell you not to participate in the oppression of your sisters. I am suggesting that we pay as much attention to our nurturing sensibilities as to our ambition. You are moving in the direction of freedom and the function of freedom is to free somebody else. You are moving toward self-fulfillment and the consequences of that fulfillment should be to discover that there is something just as important as you are.

029 Which of the following CANNOT be inferred from the passage above?

① The surrogate "mothers" in *Cinderella* abused Cinderella.

② The portrayal of Cinderella's step-sisters in our contemporary movies is different from that in the original story.

③ In a way, Cinderella's step-sisters are also victims, having been exposed to the abuse of another girl at a tender age.

④ Women shouldn't trade feminine sensibilities for success.

⑤ You cannot liberate yourself by enslaving others.

Kant rejects maximizing welfare and promoting virtue. Neither, he thinks, respects human freedom. So Kant is a powerful advocate for freedom. But the idea of freedom he puts forth is demanding — more demanding than the freedom of choice we exercise when buying and selling goods on the market. What we commonly think of as market freedom or consumer choice is not true freedom, Kant argues, because it simply involves satisfying desires we haven't chosen in the first place. So, if we're capable of freedom, we must be capable of acting not according to a law that is given or imposed on us, but according to a law we give ourselves. But where could such a law come from?

Kant's answer: from reason. We're not only sentient beings, governed by the pleasure and pain delivered by our senses; we are also rational beings, capable of reason. If reason determines my will, then the will becomes the power to choose independent of the dictates of nature or inclination. (Notice that Kant isn't asserting that reason always does govern my will; he's only saying that, insofar as I'm capable of acting freely, according to a law I give myself, then it must be the case that reason can govern my will.)

Of course, Kant isn't the first philosopher to suggest that human beings are capable of reason. But his idea of reason, like his conceptions of freedom and morality, is especially demanding. Thomas Hobbes called reason the "scout for the desires." David Hume called reason the "slave of the passions." Reason's work, for the utilitarians, is not to determine what ends are worth pursuing. Its job is to figure out how to maximize utility by satisfying the desires we happen to have.

Kant rejects this subordinate role for reason. For him, reason is not just the slave of the passions. If that were all reason amounted to, Kant says, we'd be better off with instinct. Kant's idea of reason — of practical reason, the kind involved in morality — is not instrumental reason but "pure practical reason, which legislates a priori, regardless of all empirical ends." But how can reason do this? Kant distinguishes two ways that reason can command the will, two different kinds of imperative. One kind of imperative, perhaps the most familiar kind, is a hypothetical imperative. Hypothetical imperatives use instrumental reason: If you want X, then do Y. If you want a good business reputation, then treat your customers honestly. Kant contrasts hypothetical imperatives, which are always conditional, with a kind of imperative that is unconditional: a categorical imperative. "If the action would be good solely as a means to something else," Kant writes, "the imperative is hypothetical. If the action is represented as good in itself, and therefore as necessary for a will which of itself accords with reason, then the imperative is categorical."

The term categorical may seem like jargon, but it's not that distant from our ordinary use of the term. By "categorical," Kant means unconditional. So, for example, when a politician issues a categorical denial of an alleged scandal, the denial is not merely emphatic; it's unconditional — without any loophole or exception. Similarly, a categorical duty or categorical right is one that applies regardless of the circumstances.

2019학년도 한국항공대학교 인문계 40번

030 Which of the following statement is true?

① Kant's exalted idea of freedom incorporates the principles of the greatest happiness.
② Kant's notion of practical reason is based upon a practical aspect of empirical truth.
③ Maximizing utility is the ultimate goal of both Kant and utilitarians, though they pursued it in different ways.
④ A categorical imperative is founded upon the good itself rather than its consequences.

유형 07
부분이해

Teacher Chris Tip

밑줄 친 부분의 이해를 묻는 유형이다. 밑줄 친 문장의 이해를 위해선 앞뒤 문장의 정확한 구문 독해가 가능해야 한다. 간단하게는 깊은 유추가 필요하지 않은 단순한 표현(낱말)을 묻기도 한다. 하지만 어렵게 출제되는 학교는 해당 부분 의미를 유추하기 위해 전후(앞뒤) 문장뿐만 아니라 전체적인 글의 흐름과 논리에 따른 추론도 요구된다.

강남대학교 숭실대학교
광운대학교 한국산업기술대학교
단국대학교 한성대학교
덕성여자대학교
명지대학교
서울여자대학교
숙명여자대학교

- Read the following passages and answer the questions.

Who am I? I am your greatest helper or worst enemy. I will lift you up or drag you down. You can control me 100%. Show me exactly how you want something, and after a little practice, I will do it every time. All great people, I made great. All failures, I made fail. Train and guide me, and ⒶI will put the world at our feet. Be careless with me, and I will destroy you. Who am I?

2019학년도 강남대학교 인문·자연계 28번

001 What do the underlined words Ⓐ mean?

① I will make you very happy.

② I will make you a great failure.

③ I will make you a great success.

④ I will make you very comfortable.

House cats act like their wild ancestors in several ways. Although most house cats do not have to catch their own food, they show hunting behavior such as being active at dawn and dusk, and chasing and jumping on Ⓐ pretend prey. Long legs, strong muscles and flexible joints give cats great jumping skill. Much of this behavior is inborn, and does not have to be trained. A cat raised away from all other cats still acts this way.

2019학년도 강남대학교 인문·자연계 30번

002 What does the underlined part Ⓐ mean?

① canned food   ② cat toys

③ wild cats   ④ mice

• Read the following passages and answer the questions.

While many countries have endured the rise and fall of diverse forms of government, few have changed as extensively, suddenly, and repeatedly as Japan. Once an international trading destination and home to hundreds of thousands of Christians, Japan closed itself to foreign commerce and religion seemingly overnight. Ⓐ In doing so, it may be argued that it laid the thematic foundation for a significant degree of indigenous development beyond the influence of the West.

2019학년도 덕성여자대학교 오후 29번

003 Which of the following best summarizes the information in the underlined sentence Ⓐ?

① Japanese culture developed over time without significant influences from the Western world.
② Japan's modern culture is based on a combination of foreign Western influences and native traditional practices.
③ The cultural foundations of Japanese society are considered to be native rather than Western in nature.
④ By rejecting foreign institutions, Japan was able to develop on its own in several important ways without Western influences.

Karl Mannheim is one of the most important figures in the history of society, founding a branch of the science commonly known as the sociology of knowledge. Ⓐ The field deals with the relationships between ideas and societies, exploring how societal structures can affect the creation of new ideas and how ideas themselves can affect societies in their own right. The three phases of Mannheim's career each led to an increasingly sophisticated understanding of the complex interaction between theoretical concepts and the communities that produce them.

2019학년도 덕성여자대학교 오후 30번

004 Which of the following best summarizes the information in the underlined sentence Ⓐ?

① The sociology of knowledge is primarily interested in how new ideas develop within societies.
② The sociology of knowledge deals with the way social structure affects ideas present in the culture.
③ The sociology of knowledge looks at how ideas and societal structures affect each other.
④ The sociology of knowledge is mainly concerned with the way ideas affect and shape societies.

The idea of neurodiversity is really a paradigm shift in how we think about kids in special education. Instead of regarding these students as suffering from deficit, disease, or dysfunction, neurodiversity suggests that we speak about their strengths. <u>Neruodiversity urges us to discuss brain diversity using the same kind of discourse that we employ when we talk about biodiversity and cultural diversity.</u> We don't pathologize a colla lily by saying that it has a "petal deficit disorder." We simply appreciate its unique beauty. We don't diagnose individuals who have skin color that is different from our own as suffering from "pigmentation dysfunction." That would be racist. Similarly, we ought not to pathologize children who have different kinds of brains and different ways of thinking and learning.

005 What does the underlined sentence mean best?

① The common principle that we use for biodiversity and cultural diversity should be applied to the area of brain diversity.
② Discourse analysis is a helpful tool that can be used in common in all those three areas.
③ Neurodiversity brings our attention back to the areas of biodiversity and cultural diversity.
④ Biodiversity and cultural diversity are more advanced areas of knowledge.
⑤ Biodiversity and cultural diversity are used as models for a psychological treatment.

The movie industry is obviously affected by personal recommendations. Even though well over a billion dollars is spent every year on promoting new movies, people talking to people is <u>what really counts</u>. According to Marvin Antonowsky, head of marketing for Universal Pictures, "Word of mouth is like wildfire". This point is well illustrated by the number of low budget movies that have succeeded with little or no advertising — and by the number of big budget flops. Like the movies, book publishing is another industry where lots of money is traditionally spent on advertising but can't begin to compete with the power of friends telling friends about their discoveries. Twenty five years ago, *The Road Less Traveled*, by psychiatrist M. Scott Peck, was just another psychology book lying unnoticed on bookstore shelves. Then a few people read it, told their friends, and started a chain reaction that is still going on. Today, there are well over two million copies in print.

006 Which of the following is closest in meaning to the underlined part?

① what people don't like
② what is really important
③ what people can't trust
④ what is accounted for

- Read paragraph Ⓐ and answer the questions.

Ⓐ The Taklimakan Desert, at Asia's heart, keeps an ancient secret. Here, long ago, two great civilizations — the East and the West — made forgotten contact. Here, hints of long-gone life raise the question: was early Chinese culture born alone, or was there a lost link with the West? Ⓐ <u>Silent voices now speak</u>: a woman, and others like her up to 4,000 years old, amazingly preserved. Surprisingly, the mummies are clearly not Chinese. They help answer how distant cultures met and exchanged precious goods and ideas.

Ⓑ The Silk Road, 6,000 kilometers long, crossed the whole known world. At one end were the great civilizations of Rome and Greece, and at the other, China's borderlands. It was thought that the ruins at the Silk Road's eastern end were Chinese. Now, it seems the builders were a little-known people called Tocharians, who came over 4,000 years ago. The mummies show that people of European origins lived on China's frontier as early as 2,000 B.C.

2019학년도 강남대학교 인문·자연계 33번

007 What does the underlined part Ⓐ mean?

① The desert people spoke no Chinese.
② Lost voices have been restored by modern technology.
③ The desert people used body language to communicate.
④ Archeological finds provide evidence of a long-forgotten culture.

"Beauty is difficult," says Cacciari, former mayor of Venice and professor of philosophy, sounding as if he were addressing a graduate seminar in aesthetics rather than answering a question about municipal regulations. The preceding day, heavy rains had flooded Mestre in Venice again. Rain caused the flood, not acqua alta, Cacciari says, "High tide is not a problem for me. It's a problem for foreigners. " End of discussion on flooding! No, he stresses, however, the problem lies elsewhere. There is tourism. Of that, Cacciari says, "Venice is not a sentimental place of honeymoon. It's a strong, contradictory, overpowering place. It is not a city for tourists. Ⓐ <u>It cannot be reduced to a postcard.</u>" Tourism has been part of the Venetian landscape since the 14th century, when pilgrims stopped en route to the Holy Land. So, what's so different about tourism now? "Now, Venice gets giant cruise ships. The ship is ten stories high. You can't understand Venice from ten stories up. You might as well be in a helicopter."

2020학년도 광운대학교 인문계 A형 35번

008 밑줄 친 Ⓐ의 의미는?

① Tourists should not use a postcard.
② Venice has so many places to visit.
③ Honeymooners send many postcards.
④ Venice is a big place to fit into a postcard.
⑤ Venice shouldn't be known only for tourism

유형 07 부분이해

• Read the following passages and answer the questions.

빈칸완성

Like other industries in 2008, plastic surgery suffered a drop in revenues when the recession began to worsen. Recently, however, people have begun investing in cosmetic surgery to increase their value in the job market. For example, 56-year-old Max Seddon is aware that the weakening music industry will likely force him to begin seeking work elsewhere. He spent $17,000 on a facelift to make his appearance more youthful and to bolster his confidence when he goes job-hunting. Other middle-aged men and women have found it necessary to turn to cosmetic surgery because they are competing with younger job applicants who look young and fresh.

Plastic surgeons have noted that people now have cosmetic surgery done not just so they can enjoy life more, but also because they know skills are often not enough in a competitive job market. Surgeons are now offering cheaper face-lifts that use only local anesthesia to reduce the price and the recovery time. A plastic surgeon in Manhattan has considered the fact that the older yet more qualified people ⓒ <u>are being passed over for</u> their younger, better-looking counterparts and has offered a "job-fighter package" that makes use of cosmetic surgery methods that are less invasive and much cheaper.

2019학년도 한성대학교 인문계 A형 16번

009 Which one can best replace ⓒ <u>are being passed over for</u>?

① are being preferred to
② are being less preferred to
③ are getting closer to
④ are getting less close to

부분이해

The idea that you can't buy happiness has been exposed as a myth, over and over. Richer countries are happier than poor countries. Richer people within richer countries are happier, too. The evidence is unequivocal: Money makes you happy. You just have to know what to do with it. Stop buying so much stuff, psychologist Daniel Gilbert said in an interview a few years ago, and try to spend more money on experiences. We think that experiences can be fun but leave us with nothing to show for them. But that turns out to be a good thing. Happiness, for most people, comes from sharing experiences with other people; experiences are usually shared – first when they happen and then again and again when we tell our friends.

On the other hand, <u>objects wear out their welcome</u>. If you really love a rug, you might buy it. The first few times you see, you might admire it, and feel happy. But over time, it will probably reveal itself to be just a rug. Try to remember the last time an old piece of furniture made you ecstatic.

2020학년도 서울여자대학교 인문·자연계 A형 32번

010 What does the underlined sentence imply?

① We can shop our way out of a bad mood.
② Objects are usually preferred to experiences.
③ Our happiness from buying things declines with time.
④ We usually buy what we want rather than what we need.

Genus Homo's position in the food chain was, until recently, solidly in the middle. For millions of years, humans hunted smaller creatures and gathered what they could, all the while being hunted by larger predators. It was only 400,000 years ago that several species of man began to hunt large game on a regular basis, and only In the last 100,000 years — with the rise of Homo sapiens — that man jumped to the top of the food chain.

That spectacular leap from the middle to the top had enormous consequences. Other animals at the top of the pyramid, such as lions and sharks, evolved into that position very gradually, over millions of years. This enabled the ecosystem to develop checks and balances that prevent lions and sharks from wreaking too much havoc. As lions became deadlier, so gazelles evolved to run faster, hyenas to cooperate better, and rhinoceroses to be more bad-tempered. In contrast, humankind ascended to the top so quickly that the ecosystem was not given enough time to adjust. Moreover, humans themselves failed to adjust. Most top predators of the planet are majestic creatures. Millions of years of domination have filled them with confidence. <u>Sapiens by contrast is more like a banana-republic dictator.</u>

011 According to the passage, which best explains the underlined part?

① Sapiens first evolved from the apes, being dependent on staple food crops, bananas.
② Homo sapiens accomplished immense power based on unique political structures.
③ Humans are anxious about their position, which makes them brutal and dangerous.
④ Humankind accomplished agricultural revolution to make the original affluent society.

One key question for the United States in the 21st century is whether noncoastal towns and rural communities will be able to participate in the digital revolution. We know that almost all Americans are avid consumers of technology, but many lack the opportunity to do the creative work that fuels our digital economy. Ⓐ At stake is the dignity of millions of people.

Within the next 10 years, nearly 60 percent of jobs could have a third of their tasks automated by artificial intelligence. Many traditional industries are becoming digital. Recently, a senior hotel executive described his business as essentially a digital one, explaining that his profit margins were contingent on the effectiveness of his software architects. Today's hospitality vendors, precision farmers and electricians spend significant time on digital work. Economists keep telling those left out of our digital future to move to the tech hubs. If they visit places like Lincoln, NE or Tacoma, WA, they will realize that many people there are not looking to move. They are proud of their small-town values and enjoy being close to family. They brag that their town doesn't need many traffic lights. Ⓑ The choice facing small towns should not be binary — it should not be "adopt the Silicon name or miss out on the tech future."

012 (A) 밑줄 친 Ⓐ의 원인은?

① A great number of people in the rural areas have become unemployed although the economy started to recover.
② Americans spend way too much money to purchase the latest technologies with artificial intelligence.
③ Although America undergoes technological development, many people fail to be productive with such a change.
④ Companies started to replace traditional human labors avidly with modern technologies with artificial intelligence.
⑤ As companies in the United States relocate to other areas, many people who can't move may lose their jobs.

012 (B) 밑줄 친 Ⓑ의 내용과 가장 잘 부합하는 것은?

① Small towns should adopt the Silicone name or miss out on the tech future.
② Small towns must delimit the growth to protect the populations to move out.
③ Small towns may move toward the digital future as changing to tech hubs.
④ Small towns can protect their community value as creating various tech jobs there.
⑤ Small towns need to encourage their people to be more aware of the digital economy.

• Read the following passages and choose the best answers to the questions.

As globalization in its current form expands, so too does the inequality that accompanies it. Rising inequality can result in an increase in racial bias which advances xenophobic and isolationist tendencies. During the days of British and French Imperialism, for example, racial bias was Ingrained within culture itself. However, an element of this is still seen in today's period of globalization, with the increasing "xenophobic culture of Globalization" seen in some parts of the world.

With expanding globalization, the demand for more skilled workers, especially in North America, has led to increased efforts to attract foreign workers — but filtered, based on skill. On the other hand, it is harder to Immigrate to the wealthier nations unless these citizens are part of the chosen few: highly-skilled computer wizards, doctors and nurses trained at Third World expense. Global migration management strategy saps the Third World and the former Soviet bloc of its economic lifeblood, by creaming off their most skilled and educated workforces. From the perspective of globalization the skills pool, not the genes pool, is key.

2019학년도 덕성여자대학교 사회·자연·예술대학 29번

013 Which phrase is closest in meaning to the phrase "xenophobic culture of globalization" in this passage?

① isolation of foreign culture by globalization
② excessive fear of foreign people within globalized societies
③ cultures which resist globalization
④ imported cultures through globalization

- Read the following passages and answer the questions.

These days most people around the world dress in much the same way: the same jeans, the same sneakers, the same T-shirts. There are just a few places Ⓐ where people hold out against the giant sartorial* blending machine. One of them is rural Peru. In the mountains of the Andes, the Quechua women still wear their brightly coloured dresses and shawls and their little felt hats, pinned at jaunty angles and decorated with their tribal insignia. Except that these are not traditional Quechua clothes at all. The dresses, shawls and hats are in fact of Andalusian origin and were imposed by the Spanish Viceroy Francisco de Toledo in 1572, in the wake of Tupac Amaru's defeat. Authentically traditional Andean female attire consisted of a tunic, secured at the waist by a sash, over which was worn a mantle, which was fastened with a *tupu* pin. What Quechua women wear nowadays is a combination of these earlier garments with the clothes they were ordered to wear by their Spanish masters. The bowler hats popular among Bolivian women came later, when British workers arrived to build that country's first railways. The current fashion among Andean men for American casual clothing is thus merely the latest chapter in a long history of sartorial Westernization.

* sartorial 의복의

2019학년도 서울여자대학교 인문·자연계 A형 31번

014 What does the underlined Ⓐ imply?

① where people wear cheap clothes
② where people dislike baggy clothes
③ where people refuse mass-produced clothes
④ where people follow a current fashion trend

Democracy has another merit. It allows criticism, and if there isn't public criticism there are bound to be hushed-up scandals. That is why I believe in the press, despite all its lies and vulgarity, and why I believe in Parliament. The British Parliament is often sneered at because it's <u>a talking shop.</u> Well, I believe in it because it is a talking shop. I believe in the private member who makes himself nuisance. He gets snubbed and is told that he is cranky or ill-formed, but he exposes abuses which would otherwise never have been mentioned, and very often an abuse gets put right just by being mentioned. Occasionally, too, in my country, a well-meaning public official loses his head in the cause of efficiency, and thinks himself God Almighty. Such officials are particularly frequent in the Home Office. Well, there will be questions about them in Parliament sooner or later, and then they'll have to mend their steps. Whether Parliament is either a representative body or an efficient one is very doubtful, but I value it because it criticizes and talks, and because its chatter get widely reported. So two cheers for democracy: one because it admits variety and two because it permits criticism. Two cheers are quite enough: there is no occasion to give three.

2019학년도 단군대학교 자연계 A형 29번

015 Which has the closest meaning to the underlined part?

① A space for diplomatic meetings
② A place for genuine and serious discussion
③ A space for healthy arguments
④ A noisy and boisterous place

• Read the following passages and answer the questions.

We talk about food in the negative: What we shouldn't eat, what we'll regret later, what's evil, dangerously tempting, unhealthy. Ⓐ The effects are more insidious than any overindulgent amount of "bad food" can ever be. By fretting about food, we turn occasions for comfort and joy into sources of fear and anxiety. And when we avoid certain foods, we usually compensate by consuming too much of others. All of this happens under the guise of science. But a closer look at the research behind our food fears shows that many of our most demonized foods are actually fine for us. Consider salt. It's true that, if people with high blood pressure consume a lot of salt, it can lead to cardiovascular events like heart attacks. It's also true that salt is overused in processed foods. But the average American consumes just over three grams of sodium per day, which is actually in the sweet spot for health. Eating too little salt may be just as dangerous as eating too much. This is especially true for the majority of people who don't have high blood pressure. Regardless, experts continue to push for lower recommendations. Many of the doctors and nutritionists who recommend avoiding certain foods fail to properly explain the magnitude of their risks. In some studies, processed red meat in large amounts is associated with an increased relative risk of developing cancer. The absolute risk, however, is often quite small.

016 What does the underlined Ⓐ mean?

① The effects of food fears
② The effects of "bad food"
③ The effects of eating too much
④ The effects of eating processed food

Recently, as the British doctor Lord Robert Winston took a train from London to Manchester, he found himself becoming steadily enraged. A woman had picked up the phone and begun a loud conversation, which would last an unbelievable hour. Furious, Winston began to tweet about the woman, taking her picture and sending it to his more than 40,000 followers. When the train arrived at its destination, Winston bolted. The press were waiting for the woman and showed her the Lord's messages. She used just one word to describe Winston's actions: *rude*.

Studies have shown that rudeness spreads quickly and virally, almost like the common cold. Just witnessing rudeness makes it far more likely that we, in turn, will be rude later on. Once infected, we are more aggressive, less creative and worse at our jobs. The only way to end a strain is to make a ⓑ conscious decision to do so. We must have the guts to call it out, face to face. We must say, "Just stop." For Winston, that would have meant approaching the woman, politely asking her to speak more quietly or make the call at another time.

The rage and injustice we feel at the rude behavior of a stranger can drive us to do odd things. In one research, surveying 2,000 adults, the acts of revenge people had taken ranged from the ridiculous ("I rubbed fries on their windshield") to the disturbing ("I sabotaged them at work").

We must combat rudeness head on. When we see it occur in a store, we must step up and say something. If it happens to a colleague, we must point it out. We must defend strangers in the same way we'd defend our best friends. But we can do it with grace, by handling it without a trace of aggression and without being rude ourselves. Because once rude people can see their actions through the eyes of others, they are far more likely to end that strain themselves. As this tide of rudeness rises, civilization needs civility.

017 Which is implied by the underlined ⓑ?
① aggressive tweeting
② outrageous injustice
③ ludicrous behavior
④ decent appeal

• Read the following passage and answer the questions.

Environmentalists say that clean coal is a myth. Of course it is. Just look at West Virginia, where whole Appalachian peaks have been knocked into valleys to get at the coal underneath and streams run orange with acidic water. Or look at downtown Beijing, where the air these days is often thicker than in an airport smoking lounge. Air pollution in China, much of it from burning coal, is blamed for more than a million premature deaths a year. That's on top of the thousands who die in mining accidents, in China and elsewhere.

These problems aren't new. In the late 17th century, when coal from Wales and Northumberland was lighting the first fires of the industrial revolution in Britain, the English writer John Evelyn was already complaining about the "stink and darkness" of the smoke that wreathed London. Three centuries later, in December 1952, a thick layer of coal-laden smog descended on London and lingered for a long weekend, provoking an epidemic of respiratory ailments that killed as many as 12,000 people in the ensuing months.

Coal, to use the economists' euphemism, is fraught with ⓑ "externalities" — the heavy costs it imposes on society. It's the dirtiest, most lethal energy source we have. But by most measures it's also the cheapest, and we depend on it. So the big question today isn't whether coal can ever be "clean." It can't. It's whether coal can ever be clean enough — to prevent not only local disasters but also a radical change in global climate.

In 2012 the world emitted a record 34.5 billion metric tons of carbon dioxide from fossil fuels. Coal was the largest contributor. Cheap natural gas has lately reduced the demand for coal in the U.S., but everywhere else, especially in China, demand is surging. During the next two decades several hundred million people worldwide will get electricity for the first time, and if current trends continue, most will use power produced by coal. Even the most aggressive push for alternative energy sources and conservation could not replace coal — at least not right away.

018 Which of the following is closest in meaning to ⓑ "externalities"?

① the direct costs in producing coal
② the costs that coal miners pay to society
③ the indirect costs that society has to pay
④ the costs that consumers do not have to pay

• Read the following passage and answer the questions.

American football draws as much attention lately for the knocks that players take as it does for their drives down the field. The emergence of research linking head collisions with behavioral and cognitive changes similar to those seen in Alzheimer's patients puts the colliding in a new context. Whether ramming opponents head-on or butting helmets, athletes may face the risk of long-term brain injury from hits accumulated over time.

Brain degeneration from repeated blows to the head had been known in boxers since the 1920s as dementia pugilistica, or punch-drunk syndrome. Recent research indicates that small impacts can cause damage as much as big ones, widening the field of concern to young athletes, hockey players, and soldiers subject to head-rattling blasts.

At the University of North Carolina, where football players receive an average of 950 hits to the head each season, neuroscientist Kevin Guskiewics and colleagues have spent six years analyzing impact data from video recordings and helmets equipped with accelerometers. They note that there are plans to test similar technologies on various football teams starting soon. Guskiewics believes that on-field monitoring and education are paths to progress. Already the spotlight on football-related brain trauma has resulted in new football practices, state laws, and congressional hearings on ways to protect young athletes.

On the medical side, there is hope for advanced brain-imaging techniques, experimental blood or spinal fluid tests, and even a genetic marker that would enable doctors to identify chronic traumatic encephalopathy (CTE, the same as punch-drunk syndrome, but not limited to boxers) early on. At the moment, the definitive mark of the disease — clumps of abnormal tau protein in the brain — can be seen only when the brain is sliced, stained, and studied under a microscope. CTE typically appears years after head traumas, and "we don't want to diagnose a disease after death," says Ann McKee, co-director of Boston University's Center for the Study of Traumatic Encephalopathy.

Guskiewics envisions databases that track all the hits athletes take throughout their playing years to help explain neurologic changes later in life. But, he says, ⒷB "it'll probably be my grandchildren who are analyzing that data."

019 Which of the following is closest in meaning to Ⓑ?
① Data collection was finished long ago.
② Analysis of data is not possible right now.
③ Guskiewics cannot have access to data now.
④ Accumulating data will be grandchildren's job.

Read the passage below and answer the questions that follow.

Even the zone of cultural memory from the last century has relics that feel like they belong to a foreign country. Take the decline of martial culture. The older cities in Europe are dotted with public works that flaunt the nation's military might. Pedestrians can behold statues of commanders on horseback and victory arches crowned by chariots. Photos from a century ago show men in gaudy military dress uniforms parading on national holidays. But in the West today, public places are no longer named after military victories. Our war memorials depict not proud commanders on horseback but weeping mothers, or weary soldiers. Military men are inconspicuous in public life, with drab uniforms and little prestige among the hoi polloi. Another major change we have lived through in the 20th century is an intolerance of displays of force in everyday life. In earlier decades a man's willingness to use his fists in response to an insult was the sign of respectability. Today it is the sign of a boor, a symptom of impulse control disorder. An incident from 1950 illustrates the change. President Harry Truman had seen an unkind review in The Washington Post of a performance by his daughter, Margaret, an aspiring singer. Truman wrote to the critic: "Some day I hope to meet you. When that happens you'll need a new nose and a lot of beefsteak for black eyes." Though every writer can sympathize with the impulse, today a public threat to commit aggravated assault against a critic would seem buffoonish, indeed sinister, if it came from a person in power. But at the time Truman was widely admired for his paternal chivalry. Even more revolutionary than the scorn for violence between men is the scorn for violence against women. Many baby boomers are nostalgic for The Honeymooners, a 1950s sitcom featuring Jackie Gleason as Ralph, a burly bus driver. In one of the show's recurring laugh lines, an enraged Ralph shakes his fist at his wife and bellows, "One of these days, Alice, POW, right in the kisser!" Nowadays our sensitivity to violence against women makes this kind of comedy in a mainstream television program unthinkable.

020 Which of the following best explains the underlined the impulse?

① Truman's desire to physically attack the critic
② Truman's desire to protest to the newspaper
③ Truman's desire to invite the critic to dinner
④ Truman's desire to sue the critic

유형 08
지시대상

Teacher Chris Tip

주로 인칭대명사를 활용한 등장인물, 사건, 영향 등이 무엇인지를 묻는 유형이다. 따라서 대명사나 한정사(관사, 지시사, 소유격 대명사 등) 등 의미를 특정해주는 어구들을 분명하게 파악하는 습관이 필요하다. 흔히 대명사가 가리키는 것은 바로 앞 문장에 있음을 주목하자.

가천대학교	인하대학교
건국대학교	한국산업기술대학교
국민대학교	한성대학교
상명대학교	
서울여자대학교	
세종대학교	
명지대학교	

Since the advent of the automobile, over 20 million fatalities have been recorded. Even as late as the 1950's, car manufacturers stood by the claim that it was impossible to make vehicles any safer than they were because the physical forces of a crash were too great to overcome. At the same time, after testing with cadavers, the first crash test dummy was unveiled. A crash test dummy is a full-scale anthropomorphic test device (ATD) that resembles the body in weight, proportions, and movement. Today's dummies are equipped with sensitive high-tech sensors that provide vital crash test data. Thanks to these Ⓐ silent heroes, humans have the greatest chances of surviving fatal accidents than they have ever had.

2019학년도 가천대학교 인문계 2교시 A형 26번

We continue to test products rigorously so you can make the best decision for your family. Our New York City-based team methodically evaluates all the latest appliances, beauty essentials, clothing, and more for safety, quality, and value, using state-of-the-art consumer testing methods. First, we put products to the test in our labs by evaluating safety and quality claims. We'll stretch, drop, pull, and even heat up products to make sure they can stand up to any conditions you and your family might put them through. Then, we send the items out to select readers to understand how they actually work in the real world. Only after all that do we deliver our recommendations to you.

2019학년도 인하대학교 인문계 31번

001 Which of the following does the underlined Ⓐ silent heroes refer to?

① fatalities ② manufactures
③ cadavers ④ dummies

002 What does the underlined they refer to?

① products ② select readers
③ consumers ④ testing methods
⑤ safety and quality claims

• Read the following passages and answer the questions.

Invasive plants are introduced species that can thrive in areas beyond Ⓐ their natural range of dispersal. These plants are characteristically adaptable, aggressive, and have a high capacity to propagate. Because Ⓑ they evolved over long periods of time in completely different habitats elsewhere in the world, these exotics often have few natural enemies and contribute little to the support of native wildlife. Ⓒ Their vigor combined with a lack of natural enemies often leads to outbreaks in populations. Invasive plants can totally overwhelm and devastate established native plants and their habitats by out-competing Ⓓ them for nutrients, water, and light — and because they offer so little food value to native wildlife, Ⓔ they are destructive of biodiversity on every level.

2019학년도 인하대학교 인문계 08번

003 Which of the following refers to a different thing from the others?

① Ⓐ ② Ⓑ ③ Ⓒ ④ Ⓓ ⑤ Ⓔ

What is consciousness? This may sound like a simple question but it is not. Consciousness is at once the most obvious and the most difficult thing we can investigate. We seem either to have to use consciousness to investigate itself, which is Ⓐ a slightly weird idea, or to have to extricate ourselves from Ⓑ the very thing we want to study. No wonder that philosophers and scientists have struggled for millennia with Ⓒ the concept, and that scientists rejected Ⓓ the whole idea for long periods and refused even to study it. The good news is that, at the start of the 21st century, 'consciousness studies' is thriving. Psychology, biology, and neuroscience have reached the point when they are ready to confront some tricky questions: What does consciousness do? Could we have evolved without it? What is consciousness, anyway?

2020학년도 국민대학교 인문계 오전 A형 27번

004 Which is different from the others in its meaning?

① Ⓐ ② Ⓑ ③ Ⓒ ④ Ⓓ

유형 08 지시대상

• Read the following passages and answer the questions.

지시대상

A large genetic study looked at nearly 1,000 people in 51 places around the world and found the most genetic diversity in Africa and less farther away from Africa. How could this happen? When small groups of people moved away, they took only a small amount of all the possible genetic information with them. People in the small groups reproduced. Their offspring inherited their parents' more limited set of genes. Therefore, their traits were very similar to those of their parents. This process continues as small groups of people moved farther and farther from Africa.

2020학년도 한국산업기술대학교 인문계 27번

005 According to the passage, This process most likely refers to the fact that _____.

① children inherited their ancestors' traits
② transmittable genetic information grew bigger
③ small groups survived when moving out of Africa
④ offsprings have fewer sets of genes than their ancestors

• Read the following passages and answer the questions.

지시대상이 같지 않은 것 고르기

It was not until the War of 1812 with Britain that US officials realized the country was in desperate need of roads. Troops stationed in the West were needed at the battlefront, but because of the lack of adequate transportation networks, military leaders found moving Ⓐ them to be a painfully slow process. A solution came in the form of privately built roadways called turnpikes, Ⓑ which were maintained by private companies hoping to earn big profits by charging a toll for Ⓒ their use. These early toll roads, often established along stagecoach routes, were predecessors to modem highways and interstate systems, and Ⓓ most were eventually taken over by state highway departments in the twentieth century.

2020학년도 가천대학교 인문계 1교시 B형 26번

006 Which of the following underlined Ⓐ, Ⓑ, Ⓒ and Ⓓ does NOT refer to the same thing?

① Ⓐ   ② Ⓑ   ③ Ⓒ   ④ Ⓓ

Asian Americans have been described in the media as "excessively, even provocatively" successful in gaining admission to universities. Asian American shopkeepers have been congratulated, as well as criticized, for their ubiquity and entrepreneurial effectiveness. If Asian Americans can make it, many politicians and pundits ask, why can't African Americans? Such comparisons pit minorities against each other and generate African American resentment toward Asian Americans. The Ⓑ victims are blamed for their plight, rather than racism and an economy that has made many young African American workers superfluous. The celebration of Asian Americans has obscured reality. For example, figures on the high earnings of Asian Americans relative to Caucasians are misleading. Most Asian Americans live in California, Hawaii, and New York — states with higher incomes and higher costs of living than the national average.

2019학년도 상명대학교 인문·자연계 26번

007 밑줄 친 Ⓑ의 victims는 누구를 가리키는가?

① African Americans
② Asian Americans
③ Minorities
④ Unknown
⑤ Caucasians

Thousands of years ago, people used ancient types of wheat and other grains to make flat bread on the hot rocks of their campfires. At some point in time, early cooks started putting other kinds of food on the bread — using the bread as a plate. It was the world's first pizza crust!

Over time, pizza began to look more like the food we know today. When European explorers arrived in the Americas, they saw Native American people eating tomatoes. When they brought Ⓑ them back to Europe, however, people there wouldn't eat Ⓒ them. They thought eating tomatoes could make Ⓓ them ill.

Slowly, however, Europeans discovered that tomatoes were delicious and safe to eat. Cooks in Naples, an Italian city, began putting Ⓔ them on their flat bread. The world's first true pizza shop opened in Naples in 1830. People there ate for lunch and dinner. They even ate it for breakfast!

2019학년도 한성대학교 인문계 A형 03번

008 Which refers to a **different** one?

① Ⓑ ② Ⓒ ③ Ⓓ ④ Ⓔ

유형 08 지시대상

• Read the following passages and answer the questions.

Sometime in the nineteenth century, philosophy was replaced by literature in the quest for national identity. For one thing, after Immanuel Kant, the sciences were philosophy's chief preoccupation, and in the process of their incorporation, philosophy, excepting ethics, lost its taste for speculation. Novels and poems came to typify what Matthew Arnold called the "best that has been thought and said," at least in the West. What the state and most educators wanted was to imbue the student's imagination with Ⓐ <u>what it was to be English, American, or French.</u> Literature was best suited to this task because, unlike philosophy and history, which were international in scope and were assimilated into the sciences, literature was essentially national. You can read the works of, say, Dostoevsky, Flaubert, or Mann in translation, but as everyone knows, something is always missing — chiefly, the sense of place, that is, the specificity of the vernacular of which particular cultures are made.

2020학년도 국민대학교 인문계 오후 A형 17번

009 Which does the underlined Ⓐ refer to?

① national identity
② taste for speculation
③ western perspectives
④ philosophical preoccupation

Of all the horrors Louis Zamperini endured during World War II — a plane crash into the Pacific, 47 days stranded at sea, two years in a prisoner-of-war camp — the one experience that truly haunted him was when a Japanese guard tortured and killed an injured duck. The episode, recounted in Laura Hillenbrand's best seller "Unbroken," also traumatized many readers. So when she was writing a new edition aimed at young adults, she left that scene out. "I know that if I were 12 and reading it, Ⓐ <u>that</u> would upset me," Ms. Hillenbrand said. Inspired by the booming market for young adult novels, a growing number of biographers and historians are retrofitting their works to make them palatable for younger readers. Prominent nonfiction writers like Ms. Hillenbrand are now grappling with how to handle unsettling or controversial material in their books as they try to win over this impressionable new audience. These slim-down, simplified and sometimes sanitized editions of popular nonfiction titles are fast becoming a vibrant, growing and lucrative niche.

2019학년도 서울여자대학교 인문·자연계 A형 40번

010 What does the underlined Ⓐ refer to?

① A writer modifying her or his original works
② A guard torturing an injured animal to death
③ A child being inspired by a novel at the age of 12
④ A man being in a prisoner-of-war camp for two years

Every girl I met is amazing. I feel honored to share their stories and images — and their strength — with you: the look on Alice's face after she conquered the big hill on her bike and Aris's proud smile when she achieved her goal of becoming a pilot at just 16. It is my goal with these images to inspire girls and women to be their best selves, to challenge and test their limits. We all are constantly bombarded with ⓐ <u>societal messages</u> about how women and girls should act, look, or be, and processing ⓑ <u>them</u> in a healthy way can be hard even for a 40-year-old mother of two who knows better. I worry about what my girls and their friends are exposed to and how their opinions of their bodies and selves are being shaped by the internet, TV, and magazines. I want these images to combat ⓒ <u>those</u> negative voices that tell us we are not good enough, thin enough, or whatever enough; because we are far more than enough! I want these girls to be able to hear their own voices through these images, and to inspire them to use ⓓ <u>them</u> and continue to use them. Loudly.

011 The following refer to a similar idea except _____.

① ⓐ ② ⓑ ③ ⓒ ④ ⓓ

People ask how I do <u>it</u>. Well, I love clover: the sweet smell, the common variant with its cute trio of leaves. I look at it more than most people do. I expect that's the first reason I find so many. I have a habit of dragging my fingers or toes across a patch, momentarily separating the individuals, which brings irregularities into focus. That's part of finding them: not a hardening of focus, but a softening. The other reason is artful. Do you remember those posters from the 1980s made up of thick dots? If you looked too hard, all you'd see was the pattern. But if you let your eyes slip out of focus, scenes would appear: dinosaurs, landscapes, butterflies — a trick of the eye. It's the same with four-leaf clovers. If you try too hard, you will only ever see the patch. Instead, slip into a lazy, soft-focus, summer state of mind. Drift your hand across a thick patch, letting the clovers reveal themselves. Appreciate the ones that have only three leaves. Common things are beautiful too. And a four-leaf clover may show itself to you.

012 What does the underlined it refer to?

① To soften the focus

② To find four-leaf clovers

③ To savor the smell of clovers

④ To separate individual clovers quickly

⑤ To appreciate the beauty of three-leaf clovers

유형 08 지시대상

It now seems a curiously innocent time, though not that long ago, when the lack of information appeared to be one of society's fundamental problems. Theorists talked about humanity's "bounded rationality" and the difficulty of making decisions in conditions of limited or imperfect information. Chronic information shortages threatened work, education, research, innovation, and economic decision making — whether at the level of government policy, business strategy, or household shopping. The one thing we all apparently needed was more information.

So it's not surprising that 'infoenthusiasts' exult in the simple volume of information that technology now makes available. They count the bits, bytes, and packets enthusiastically. They cheer the disaggregation of knowledge into data (and provide a new word, *datafication*, to describe it). As ⓐ the lumps break down and the bits pile up, words like *quadrillion*, *terabyte*, and *megaflop* have become the measure of value.

2020학년도 상명대학교 인문·자연계 30번

Prague Castle is not only a beautiful complex of historical monuments, but also a place that is closely connected with the political and legal developments of our country. Within these walls are reflected both great and tragic events. Since Ⓐ it was built, the castle has fulfilled a number of functions — Ⓑ it was the monarch's residence, a military fortification, a tribal sanctuary, a centre of Christianity, the seat of provincial councils and the hub of courts and administrative offices. Not least is Ⓒ its function as the burial place of Czech kings and the repository of the Czech Crown Jewels, which are still a symbol of Czech statehood. Since 1918, Ⓓ it has been the seat of the President of the Republic, together with his office, and continues the tradition of Prague Castle as the seat of the head of the country, which has lasted for more than 1,000 years. The symbol of the presidential seat is the flag of the President of the Republic flying over Prague Castle, one of the state symbols of the Czech Republic with a great state coat of arms in Ⓔ its centre and the motto Pravda vitezi, which means "Truth prevails."

2020학년도 건국대학교 인문·예체능계 A형 31번

013 What does ⓐthe lumps above refer to?

① the '*infoenthusiasts*'
② knowledge
③ technology
④ datafication
⑤ measurements

014 밑줄 친 Ⓐ~Ⓔ 가운데 가리키는 것이 다른 하나는?

① Ⓐ ② Ⓑ ③ Ⓒ ④ Ⓓ ⑤ Ⓔ

One morning, after I had been hanging the washing out to dry, something glistened in front of me. With the morning sun shining in my eyes, I squinted to find the most glorious masterpiece in our garden.

ⓐ The mini architect had meticulously spun its web across the path, from the roof to the fence. I stared in awe at the fine artistry of ⓒ our garden resident. Spanning about two metres, it was truly a magical sight. The web gently danced in the morning breeze, reflecting light from the sun. It was as if the spider had spun a fine web from rays of sunlight itself.

How did it weave its web from the roof to the fence? It's almost as if it built a house while enjoying extreme sports at the same time. Very carefully, I ducked my head under the web, taking great care not to ruin ⓓ the spider's creation.

Later that day I went back to the web to take another look. My heart sank. The beautiful web was now broken and swaying aimlessly in the breeze. It was nothing more than a few pitiful strands hanging loose. I almost choked on emotion. "Sorry, ⓔ little fella. It was such a splendid structure."

But the very next morning to my amazement, there was another castle floating in the air. The mini architect had come back to work.

2020학년도 국민대학교 인문계 오전 A형 30번

The Celts were the first Indo-European occupants of Britain. The southern British Celts had been first subdued and thereafter ruled and sheltered by the Romans. Julius Caesar's attempt at an early invasion in 55-54 BC did not result in occupation, unlike the results elsewhere in the Roman Empire, in particular Gaul (where the Latin spoken by Caesar's legions became, ultimately, Modern French). It was during the rule of the emperor Claudius (from AD 43) that the Roman invasion was followed by a more permanent occupation and military control. For about 400 years thereafter, Britain was a province of the Roman Empire. By the beginning of the fifth century, however, maintaining occupation forces in that outlying territory became too costly for the Romans, who were constantly subjected to the attacks of the Germanic tribes on the Continent. A highly simplified version of the events that followed is that when the Romans pulled out, with all of them gone by AD 410, the Celts in the south of the island were relatively defenseless. It was then that they invited Germanic mercenary soldiers to come over from northern Europe and protect them from invading Vikings, as well as from the Celts from the north and from Ireland (the Scots and the Picts).

2019학년도 인하대학교 인문계 36번

016 What does the underlined that outlying territory refer to?

① Britain ② Gaul
③ Germany ④ Europe
⑤ Ireland

015 Which is different from the others in its meaning?

①   ②   ③   ④

017 밑줄 친 Ⓐ~Ⓔ 가운데 의미하는 바가 다른 것 하나를 고르시오.

① Ⓐ ② Ⓑ ③ Ⓒ ④ Ⓓ ⑤ Ⓔ

Five score years ago, a great American, in whose symbolic shadow we stand, signed the Emancipation Proclamation. This momentous Ⓐ decree came as a great beacon light of hope to millions of Negro slaves who had been seared in the flames of withering injustice. It came as Ⓑ a joyous daybreak to end the long night of captivity. But one hundred years later, we must face the tragic fact that the Negro is still not free. One hundred years later, the life of the Negro is still sadly crippled by the manacles of segregation and the chains of discrimination. One hundred years later, the Negro lives on a lonely island of poverty in the midst of a vast ocean of material prosperity. One hundred years later, the Negro is still languishing in the corners of American society and finds himself an exile in his own land. So we have come here today to dramatize Ⓒ an appalling condition. In a sense we have come to our nation's capital to cash Ⓓ a check. When the architects of our republic wrote the magnificent words of the Constitution and the Declaration of Independence, they were signing Ⓔ a promissory note to which every American was to fall heir. This note was a promise that all men would be guaranteed the unalienable rights of life, liberty, and the pursuit of happiness.

2019학년도 상명대학교 인문·자연계 34번

The material culture of the Paleo-Indians differed little from that of other Stone Age people found in Asia, Africa, and Europe. In terms of human health, however, something occured on the Beringian tundra that forever altered the history of Native Americans. For reasons that remain obscure, the members of these small migrating groups stopped hosting a number of communicable diseases — smallpox and measles being the deadliest — and although Native Americans experienced illnesses such as tuberculosis, they no longer suffered the major epidemics* that under normal conditions would have killed a large percentage of their population every year. The physical isolation of the various bands may have protected them from the spread of contagious diseases. Another theory notes that epidemics* have frequently been associated with prolonged contact with domestic animals such as cattle and pigs. Since the Paleo-Indians did not domesticate animals, not even horses, they may have avoided the microbes that caused virulent European and African diseases.

Whatever the explanation for this curious epidemiological** record, Native Americans lost inherited immunities that later might have protected them from many contagious germs. Thus, when they first came into contact with Europeans and Africans, Native Americans had no defense against Ⓐ the great killers of the Early Modern world.

*epidemics 전염병 **epidemiological 역학

018 밑줄 친 Ⓐ가 의미하는 바는 무엇인가?
① soldiers
② immunities
③ migrants
④ microbes
⑤ livestock

유형 08 지시대상

• Read the passage below and answer the questions that follow.

지시대상

Diseases represent evolution in progress, and microbes adapt by natural selection to new hosts and vectors. But compared with cows' bodies, ours offer different immune defenses, lice, feces, and chemistries. In that new environment, a microbe must evolve new ways to live and to propagate itself. In several instructive cases doctors or veterinarians have actually been able to observe microbes evolving those new ways.

The best-studied case involves what happened when myxomatosis hit Australian rabbits. The myxo virus, native to a wild species of Brazilian rabbit, had been observed to cause a lethal infectious disease in European domestic rabbits, which are a different species. Hence the virus was intentionally introduced to Australia in 1950 in the hopes of ridding the continent of <u>its plague</u>, foolishly introduced in the nineteenth century. In the first year, myxo produced a gratifying 99.8 percent mortality rate in infected rabbits. Unfortunately for the farmers, the death rate then dropped in the second year to 90 percent and eventually to 25 percent, frustrating hopes of eradicating rabbits completely from Australia. The problem was that the myxo virus evolved to serve its own interests, which differed from ours as well as from those of the rabbits. The virus changed so as to kill fewer rabbits and to permit lethally infected ones to live longer before dying. As a result, a less lethal myxo virus spreads baby viruses to more rabbits than did the original, highly virulent myxo.

2020학년도 명지대학교 인문계 26번

019 What does the underlined <u>its plague</u> refer to?

① European domestic rabbits
② infected rabbits
③ the myxo virus
④ a lethal infectious disease in European domestic rabbits

- Read the following passages and answer the questions.

> 지시대상
>
> Originally, election days varied by state, but in 1845 a law was passed to set a single election day for the entire country. At first, it applied only to presidential elections, but it was later extended to congressional elections as well. At that time, the United States was still a largely agrarian society. For farmers, who made up a majority of the labor force, much of the year was taken up by the planting, tending, and harvesting of crops. Early November was a good time to vote because the harvest was over but the weather was still relatively mild.
>
> Still, some days of the week were better than others. <u>Two days</u> were definitely out of the question. Most Americans were devout Christians and thus set aside Sunday as a day of rest and worship. Wednesday in many areas was a market day, when farmers sold their crops in town. In addition, a travel day was sometimes required. In rural areas, the nearest polling place might have been several miles away, and, in an era before automobiles, getting there could take a while. If people couldn't use Sunday or Wednesday as their travel day, then that meant election day couldn't be on Monday or Thursday, either. And so Tuesday was perceived as the best option.
>
> The reason that election day was specified as the Tuesday "after the first Monday" was to prevent it from falling on November 1. That day was considered unfavorable because some Christians observed it as All Saints' Day and also because merchants typically took the first day of the month to settle their books for the previous month.
>
> 2020학년도 서울여자대학교 인문·자연계 A형 37번

020 What does the underlined <u>Two days</u> refer to?

① Sunday and Wednesday

② Monday and Thursday

③ Friday and Saturday

④ Tuesday and Thursday

유형 09
기타
(기타, 분위기, 어조, 견해)

Teacher Chris Tip

출제 빈도수가 매우 드문 유형이다. 내용의 주체를 파악하고 인물이나 필자의 심경, 상황 묘사가 주는 어감 등을 종합적으로 파악하여 정답을 찾아야 한다. 정답의 접근 방법은 문체에 드러난 어휘에 근거를 두어야 한다.

광운대학교
단국대학교
덕성여자대학교
명지대학교
숭실대학교

A: Our assignment is actually easier than I thought.
B: Really? Then, can you finish it on time, Peter?
A: Yes! _____

2020학년도 광운대학교 인문계 A형 01번

001 빈칸에 들어가기에 가장 적절한 것은?

① I bet you will do that.
② You can count on me
③ Take your time, though.
④ Are you supposed to do that?
⑤ What do you think I should do?

• Read the following passages and choose the best answers to the questions.

Use your frequent flyer programs to donate to charity. Your frequent flyer points may be used to help people with life-threatening medical conditions travel by plane to obtain the treatment they need, or to transport emergency relief personnel to the site of natural disasters, or simply to enable seriously ill children and their families to enjoy a trip to Jeju Island. You will be glad you helped others.

2020학년도 덕성여자대학교 오전(사회·자연·예술 대학) 26번

002 Which adjective best describes the author's tone in this passage?

① Angry
② Sympathetic
③ Persuasive
④ Impersonal

• Read the following passages and choose the best answers to the questions.

> 저자의 견해

The Ebola virus causes an acute, serious illness which is often fatal if untreated. Ebola virus disease (EVD) first appeared in 1976 in 2 simultaneous outbreaks, one in Nzara, Sudan, and the other in Yambuku, Democratic Republic of Congo. The latter occurred in a village near the Ebola River, from which the disease takes its name. Ebola is introduced into the human population through close contact with the blood, secretions, organs or other bodily fluids of infected animals such as fruit bats, monkeys and porcupines found ill or dead.

Ebola then spreads through human-to-human transmission via direct contact with the blood, secretions, organs or other bodily fluids of infected people, and with surfaces and materials contaminated with these fluids. Health-care workers have frequently been infected while treating patients with suspected or confirmed EVD. This has occurred through close contact with patients when infection control precautions are not strictly practiced. People remain infectious as long as their blood and body fluids, including semen and breast milk, contain the virus.

2019학년도 덕성여자대학교 사회·자연·예술대학 25번

003 Which of the following best expresses the author's opinions about the Ebola virus in this passage?

① Ebola is a disease which just started to appear in the past year.
② People contract the Ebola virus only with direct contact with other victims.
③ Few health-care workers are willing to take care of patients with the Ebola virus since Ebola is very contagious through human contact.
④ Medical researchers have warned that close contact with people who have been infected by the Ebola virus is very dangerous, and therefore such people should take special precautions.

유형 09 기타

• Read the following passages and choose the best answers to the questions.

The American Revolution symbolized the connection between the rights of the citizen and the rights of the state. The free citizen had a right to govern himself; therefore the whole community of the free citizens had a right to govern itself. This was not yet modern nationalism. The American people did not see themselves as a national group but as a community of free men dedicated to a proposition. But within two decades, the identification had been made.

The French Revolution, proclaiming the Rights of Man, formed the new style of nation. The levee-en-messe which defeated the old dynastic armies of Europe was the first expression of total nation unity as the basis of the sovereign state. Men and nations had equally the right to self-determination. Men could not be free if their national community was not.

The same revolution quickly proved that the reverse might not be true. The nation could become completely unfettered in its dealings with other states while enslaving its own citizens. In fact, over-glorification of the nation might lead inevitably to the extinction of individual rights. The citizen could become just a tool of the national will. But in the first explosion of revolutionary ardour, the idea of the Rights of Man and of the Rights of the Nation went together. And, formally, that is where they have remained.

004 Which of the following can be the key words of the passage?

① Individualism and nationalism
② Individual rights and national prosperity
③ Revolution and free citizens
④ Sovereign states and nationalism

In Jamaica, most British and American people encounter tourism as consumers — of culture, good weather, beautiful buildings, or any of the other things that people travel in search of. During my year as a student living in Jamaica and traveling around the Caribbean, I have seen tourism through the eyes of people who live with it, and witnessed the corrupting effects of tourism on the cultures that depend on it for economic survival.

When I tell people that I was living in Jamaica on scholarship, they roll their eyes and marvel at my luck, because they have seen the ads for Jamaican tourism, showing empty beaches, clear blue skies, and the occasional smiling black face. I don't know how to respond, because the Jamaica that I lived in, and that only some tourists are privileged to see, is a poor, crowded, violent place where most people, from police officers to ganja (marijuana) peddlers, resent tourists for their leisure and their money — money that goes almost exclusively to a small elite of hotel owners and government officials.

Among the rest, who must bow, beg, sell, or steal to capture the visitors' money, tourism creates pickpockets and impostors.

It might be different if the tourists weren't so obvious in their appearance. Many things — dress, language, looks — can distinguish tourists from the native population. In Jamaica, it is skin color that sets the tourists apart, as 95 percent of Jamaicans are black, and most tourists are white. A white stranger in the streets of Jamaica is assumed to be a tourist, and therefore interested in buying trinkets, souvenirs, or drugs.

2019학년도 단국대학교 인문계 A형 22번

005 Which is the tone of the passage?
① excited ② optimistic
③ analytic ④ aesthetic

Read the following passages and answer the questions.

Technical flaws can result in surprising and charming effects that you can only dream of achieving with Instagram filters. For example, some of our favorite analog photos are tinted green or purple from film used past its expiration date. In fact, many photographers actually seek out expired film to experience the excitement of not knowing what the shot will end up looking like.

Sometimes a film photograph looks like it has a fabric overlay, a gritty surface, or even a dreamy smoothness. The depth of this texture is a delicate feature that is often overlooked. However, once you start paying attention it simply becomes a key factor in appreciating the true beauty of a photo.

Film photography aims to grab all the color in your shot and hand paint it. The amazing variety of film choices available allows you to choose the best characteristics for each shooting — whether it's cooler or warmer tones, more or less light, or natural or vibrant colors.

Monochromatic film is a classic. The deep blacks, contrast and dark shadows are any photographer's dream. Some shots are just meant to be taken in black and white, and film manages to capture this in the moodiest of ways. The feeling of holding an old film camera and carrying around rolls of film brings us back to a different era and reminds us of cherished memories. This heartwarming feeling is believed to be one of the main reasons behind the growing trend of photographers going back to film over the last few years. Yet it's about so much more than just reminiscing about past experiences. Film also makes us miss a time when the world moved slower.

006 Which of the following best summarizes the first paragraph?
① the flawless rendering of the analog world
② the use of recycled film
③ the unexpected imperfections
④ the vibrant character of creativity

• Read the following passages and answer the questions.

저자의 태도

My aunt Marti calls me at home tonight and asks what I am doing. "Just hitting the books," I say. That doesn't go over so well. She scolds me for the violent metaphor — no need to use the word "hit." "Okay, I'm performing gentle acupressure on the books," I say. She seems to like that better. I love Marti, but a conversation with her always includes a list of what I'm doing and saying wrong, and how it supports the phallocentric power structure. She's got some opinions, my aunt. There's liberal, there's really liberal, then there's Marti, a few miles farther to the left. She lives out near Berkeley, appropriately enough — though even Berkeley is a bit too fascist for her.

I haven't talked to Marti since Julie got pregnant. I break the news to her as gently as I can, and apologize to her for contributing to the overpopulation problem. "That's okay," she says. She'll forgive me. But, she points out, I can help minimize the damage to the environment by raising the child vegan.

Marti herself is beyond vegan. Animal rights are her passion (even if she thinks the concept of rights is too Western), and she spends a good part of the year flying around the country attending vegetarian conferences. I could take up quite a bit of space listing the things that Marti doesn't eat meat, of course, and chicken, fish, eggs, dairy (she likes to call ice cream "solidified mucus"), but also honey — she won't eat honey because the bees are oppressed, not paid union scale or something.

You'd think she'd like soy, but she believes the soy industry is corrupt. She recently took her diet to a new level by becoming a raw foodist, meaning she eats only food that's uncooked, because it's more natural.

2019학년도 명지대학교 인문계 29번

007 Choose the one that best describes the author's demeanor.

① enraged and flabbergasted
② calm and nonchalant
③ excited but critical
④ humorous but candid

• Read the following passage and answer the questions.

Much of the criticism leveled against globalization today is related to the idea that it enriches the few, leaving the many behind. The people making this argument frequently advocate for the wholesale abandonment of globalization.

If the world takes the isolationist path, three major shifts will happen. First, a more isolated world will force businesses to adopt increasingly local and decreasingly global models. In essence, they will be more likely to rely on local and regional capital — and less likely to be centrally run from leading financial centers such as New York City, Tokyo and London. This change will significantly alter how businesses fund themselves, how they structure costs and how they view the proposition of long-term growth. They will be less able to access to fund investments and grow companies — reducing their opportunities to hire people and invest in communities.

Second, there will be short-term deflation and then long-term inflation. We've already begun to observe the former. Low energy costs, low wages and indeed the low price of money itself indicate a prevailing deflationary world, though they all have notably risen recently. As for the latter, the persistence of low inflation has defied warnings of a sharp uptick that date as far back as 2009, right after the financial crisis. Beyond that, rising trade tariffs and protectionism will decrease rices of imported products. This will undercut the actual value of wages' being forced higher by a relatively closed economy with reduced movement of labor.

The final shift is that governments will likely favor national champions — companies that enjoy regulatory protections, tax breaks and subsidies that offer an advantage in their home markets against foreign competitors. What results are corporate monopolies rather than competitive markets, where the government becomes a bigger arbiter of who wins and who loses. Ultimately, these companies gain outsize pricing power, which promotes larger and less efficient companies while disadvantaging consumers.

008 What is the tone of the passage?
① persuasive   ② sympathetic
③ humorous   ④ investigative

• Read the following passages and answer the questions.

> 필자의 태도

Americans are among the most ignorant people in the world when it comes to history. Opinion surveys have shown that large percentages of them do not know the difference between World War I and World War II. Many believe that Germany and the Soviet Union were allies in the latter conflict. Many never heard of Hiroshima and have no idea that the United States dropped an atomic bomb on that city. Many could not tell you what issues were involved in the Vietnam war or other armed conflicts in which the United States has participated. Nor could they say much about the history of aggression perpetrated against Native Americans and the slavery inflicted upon Africans in America.

Americans themselves are not totally to blame for this. They are taught almost nothing of these things in primary and secondary school nor even at the university level. And what they are taught is usually devoid of the urgent political economic realities that allow both past and present to inform each other, making history meaningful to us. Nor do U.S. political leaders, news pundits, and other opinion makers find much reason to place current developments in a historical context, especially one that might raise troublesome questions about the existing social order. Popular ignorance is not without its functions. Those at the top prefer that people know little about history's potentially troublesome lessons except those parts of history that have been specially packaged with superpatriotic, system-supporting messages.

When portrayed in movies and television dramas, history is usually stood on its head or reduced to personal heroics. In this regard, the make-believe media reinforce the kind of history taught in the schools, mouthed by political leaders, and recorded by the news media. One can present almost any subject in the U.S. news and entertainment media: sex and scandal, deviancy and depravity, and sometimes even racial oppression and gender discrimination. What cannot be touched is the taboo subject of class, specifically the importance of class power and class struggle.

2020학년도 숭실대학교 인문계 20번

009 Which of the following is the author's attitude toward Americans' ignorance of history?

① nostalgic   ② humorous
③ critical   ④ timid

Read the following passages and answer the questions.

Rafael Nadal, one of the world's top tennis players, now has twelve French Open championships. A bit of perspective: until Roger Federer, Novak Djokovic, and Nadal came along, Pete Sampras led the list of Grand Slam championship winners, with an all-time total of fourteen. On Sunday afternoon, with the wind and rain that had marred play at Roland-Garros for days yielding to comfortable Paris-in-springtime weather, Nadal defeated Dominic Thiem 6-3, 5-7, 6-1, 6-1. A bit more perspective: it was not as lopsided as the scoring line suggests. The first hour or so was as good — with lengthy rallies, barefooted scrambles, keen variations of pace and placement — as clay-court tennis gets. In the hour that followed, Thiem managed to take a set from Nadal, something he'd never before done at Roland-Garros, despite being, arguably, the second-best men's clay-surface player at the moment. Even in the final two sets, Thiem reached balls and struck shots that should have earned him points, but didn't — not against Nadal. Which is to say that Thiem played championship-level tennis, but not Nadal-on-Chatrier-level tennis.

There are particular aspects of Thiem's game that make it difficult for him to beat Nadal, though he had beaten him four times on clay, and lost eight times, before this match. Thiem requires time to set up his groundstrokes — he takes his racquet way back, especially when getting ready to deliver his one-handed drive backhand. He has to get his adjustment steps just right and his feet firmly planted. This buys Nadal that extra second to reestablish court position after he's been yanked to the corner by, say, a deep, sharply angled shot. A player like Djokovic can deny Nadal that time by taking the ball early, on the rise, or by hitting big balance-defying down-the-line shots at full stretch. But that's not Thiem. And Thiem, like Federer in years past, struggles with Nadal's serve to his backhand, especially in the ad court. The lefty's slice skids out wide on him; more than once on Sunday, Thiem's feet got tangled in pursuit of it. And Nadal kept showing him that serve, unceasingly as the match wore on.

010 What is the tone of the passage?
① ironic   ② analytic
③ sarcastic   ④ emphatic

memo

독해 유형편
핵심 (Top 20)

정답 및 해설

빠른정답 모음 끝장편입(독해편) 유형편 TOP 20

유형1) 대의파악

01	①	02	①	03	③	04	②	05	①
06	③	07	③	08	③	09	③	10	④
11	③	12	①	13	②	14	④	15	③
16	④	17	①	18	②	19	②	20	①
21	③	22	①	23	③	24	①	25	④
26	④	27	①	28	①	29	②	30	①

유형 2) 문장배열

01	②	02	③	03	③	04	②	05	②
06	①	07	③	08	③	09	④	10	②
11	③	12	①	13	④	14	④	15	④
16	②	17	③	18	③	19	②	20	①

유형 3) 문장삽입

01	③	02	③	03	③	04	③	05	④
06	③	07	②	08	①	09	②	10	②
11	②	12	③	13	②	14	③	15	②
16	①	17	④	18	③	19	③	20	③

유형 4) 무관한 문장

01	④	02	④	03	④	04	④	05	④
06	④	07	④	08	②	09	④	10	③
11	②	12	④	13	⑤	14	④	15	④
16	②	17	④	18	④	19	⑤	20	③

유형 5) 빈칸완성

01	②	02	②	03 A)	①	03 B)	②	04	⑤
05	③	06	④	07	④	08	③	09	①
10	⑤	11	③	12	③	13	⑤	14 A)	④
14 B)	②	15 A)	①	15 B)	③	16	①	17 A)	②
17 B)	②	18	①	19	②	20	①	21	①
22	②	23	④	24	③	25	①	26	④
27 A)	④	27 B)	①	28	①	29	①	30	②

유형6) 내용이해

01	②	02	②	03	①	04	④	05	⑤
06	③	07	①	08	②	09	②	10	③
11 A)	③	11 B)	③	12	⑤	13	②	14	②
15	④	16	④	17	③	18	④	19	①
20	②	21	④	22	④	23	②	24	②
25	③	26	②	27 A)	①	27 B)	②	28	③
29	③	30	④						

유형 7) 부분이해

01	③	02	②	03	④	04	③	05	①
06	②	07	④	08	⑤	09	②	10	③
11	③	12 A)	③	12 B)	④	13	②	14	③
15	④	16	①	17	④	18	③	19	②
20	①								

유형 8) 지시대상

01	④	02	①	03	④	04	①	05	④
06	①	07	①	08	③	09	①	10	②
11	④	12	②	13	②	14	⑤	15	③
16	①	17	③	18	④	19	①	20	①

유형 9) 기타

01	②	02	③	03	④	04	①	05	③
06	③	07	④	08	①	09	③	10	②

정답 및 해설

유형 01. 대의파악	006
유형 02. 문장배열	046
유형 03. 문장삽입	066
유형 04. 무관한 문장	088
유형 05. 빈칸완성	108
유형 06. 내용이해	146
유형 07. 부분이해	194
유형 08. 지시대상	218
유형 09. 기타	240

2022학년도 올바른 책 시리즈의
다양한 교재 정보와 자료를
좌측 QR코드를 통해
확인하세요.

Preview 끝장편입 독해 유형편 (핵심) Top 20

정답해설

01 빠른 이해를 위한 문장별 해석 번호 제시

해석 ❶ 당신은 금성이 왜 그렇게 뜨거운지 알고 있는가? Ⓐ ❷ 과학자들은 금성과 지구의 원래 대기는 두 행성이 어리고 화산 활동이 훨씬 더 강력했을 때 화산에서 방출된 가스로부터 만들어졌다고 생각한다. Ⓑ ❸ 하지만 금성은 태양에 너무 가까이에 있으므로, 열이 대기 안에 갇히는 '온실효과'가 기온을 너무 상승시키는 결과로 이어져 모든 지표수를 증발시켰다. Ⓒ <❹ 이제는 모든 물이 대기 안에 있는 가운데, 태양에서 나오는 강렬한 자외선이 물 분자를 수소와 산소로 분열시켰다.> ❺ 수소는 우주로 빠져나갔고 산소는 대기의 다른 화학 물질과 결합했다. Ⓓ ❻ 그에 반해, 지구는 열이 식었고, 바다가 형성되었으며, 생명이 생겨나기 시작했다. Ⓔ ❼ 지구는 살아있는 행성이 되었지만, 금성은 사랑과 풍요의 여신과 연관이 있음에도 불구하고 불모지로 남아있었다.

02 명료한 해설과 단어 제시

해설 주어진 문장에서 물 분자를 수소와 산소로 분열시켰다고 말한 뒤 Ⓒ에서 그 이후 과정 설명을 이어가고 있다.

어휘 atmosphere n. 대기 intense a. 극심한, 강렬한 ultraviolet radiation 자외 복사(선) molecule n. 분자 hydrogen n. 수소 oxygen n. 산소 Venus n. 금성 greenhouse effect 온실효과 trap v. 가두다; (가스·물·에너지 따위를) 끌어들이다 evaporate v. 증발하다, 기화(氣化)하다 combine v. 결합하다 fertility n. 토지가 기름짐, 비옥함

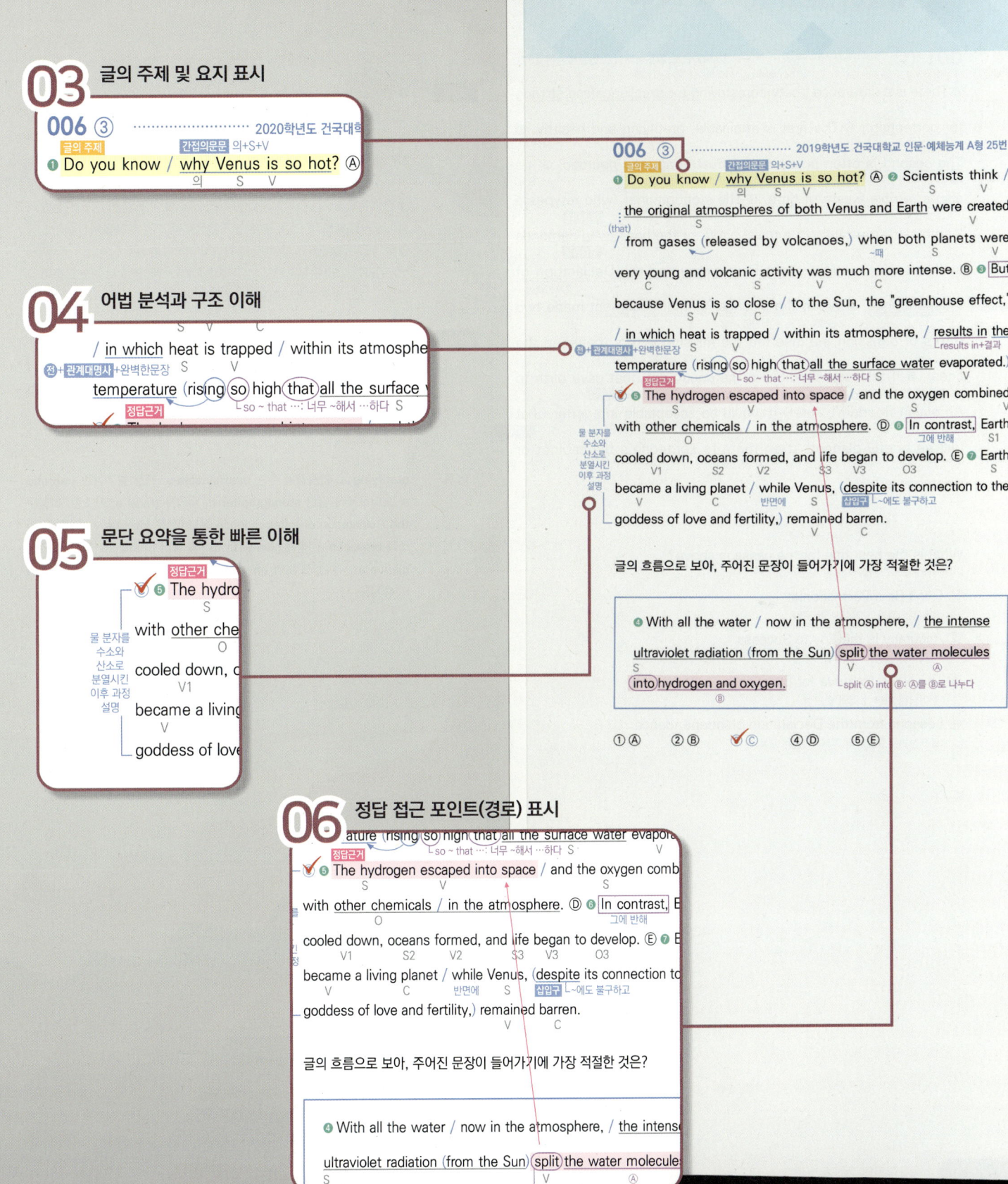

유형 01 대의파악 | 제목, 주제, 요지, 목적

001 ①   2020학년도 가톨릭대학교 인문계 A형 28번

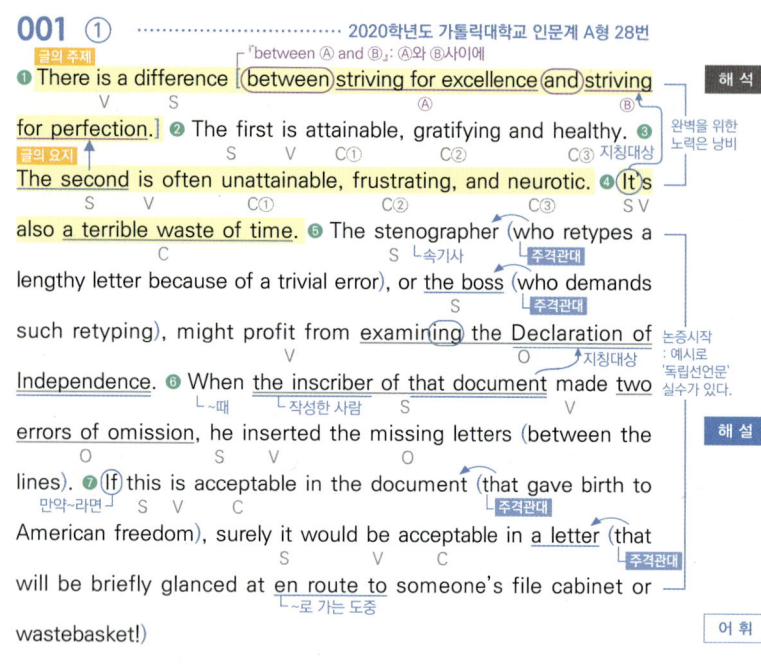

What is the best title for the passage above?
이 글의 제목으로 가장 적절한 것은?

✓ ① Don't Be a Perfectionist
   완벽주의자가 되어서는 안 된다.

② Accuracy Is the Key to Success
   정확성이 성공의 열쇠다.

③ The Need to Strive for Excellence
   뛰어남을 위한 노력의 필요성

④ Lessons from the Declaration of Independence
   독립선언문으로부터 얻을 수 있는 교훈

해석
❶ 뛰어나기 위해 노력하는 것과 완벽하기 위해 노력하는 것 사이에는 차이가 있다. ❷ 전자는 달성할 수 있고, 만족감을 주며, 건강하다. ❸ 후자는 종종 달성할 수 없고, 좌절감을 주며, 노이로제에 걸리게 한다. ❹ 이것은 또한 엄청난 시간낭비이기도 하다. ❺ 사소한 오류 때문에 긴 편지를 다시 타이핑하는 속기사나 그렇게 다시 타이핑하도록 요구하는 직장 상사가 있다면, 독립선언문을 한번 검토해보는 것이 도움이 될 수도 있다. ❻ 이 독립선언문을 작성한 사람이 글자를 빠뜨리는 실수를 두 번 저질렀을 때, 그는 행간에 빠진 글자를 삽입해 넣었다. ❼ 만약 이러한 글자 삽입이 미국의 자유를 만들어낸 문서에서 허용된다면, 그것은 누군가의 서류 캐비닛이나 쓰레기통으로 가는 도중에 잠깐 힐끗 보고 말 편지에도 허용되는 것일 것이다!

해설
논증이 시작되기 전 첫 번째와 두 번째 문장에서 글의 주제와 요지를 확인할 수 있다. 완벽하기 위해 노력하는 것은 종종 성취할 수 없고, 좌절감을 주며, 노이로제에 걸리게 한다고 주장한다. 독립선언문 작성은 그에 대한 논증이다. 따라서 ①이 가장 적절하다.

*주장→논증

어휘
gratifying a. 만족감을 주는 unattainable a. 도달 불가능한 neurotic a. 노이로제에 걸린 stenographer n. 속기사 trivial a. 사소한, 하찮은 the Declaration of Independence 독립선언문 inscribe v. (이름 등을) 쓰다 omission n. 생략 give birth to ~을 낳다 briefly ad. 잠시, 간단히 glance at ~을 힐끗 보다 en route to ~로 가는 도중에 wastebasket n. 휴지통

002 ①
2019학년도 광운대학교 인문계 A형 27번

❶ I had a great-uncle (of whom nothing is known.) ❷ I don't even know his name, if I ever did. ❸ He came to America in the 1920s and never wrote home. ❹ Got rich, my relatives said. ❺ How do you know that? I asked. ❻ Nobody knew [how they knew.] ❼ They had heard rumors. ❽ Then the people (who'd heard the rumors) died. ❾ Today there's no one (left to ask.) ❿ My great-uncle was like one of those ants [who, (coming upon a line of marching ants,) turns and goes in the opposite direction for reason of his own.] ⓫ Ants being ants, this is not supposed to happen, but it sometimes does, and no one knows why.

글의 제목으로 가장 적절한 것은?

✓ ① My Mythical Great-Uncle Interests Me!
  신비한 나의 종조부가 나의 관심을 끈다!
② My Great-Uncle Immigrated to America!
  나의 종조부가 미국에 이민 가셨다!
③ My Great-Uncle Made Amazing Rumors!
  나의 종조부가 놀라운 소문을 만들어냈다!
④ My Great-Uncle Studied Ants' Activities!
  나의 종조부가 개미의 활동을 연구하셨다!
⑤ My Successful Great-Uncle Became Insane!
  성공한 나의 종조부는 제정신이 아니셨다!

해석 ❶ 나에겐 알려진 것이 아무것도 없는 종조부 한 분이 계셨다. ❷ 전에 안 적이 있었을지라도, 나는 그의 이름조차 지금은 모른다. ❸ 그는 1920년대에 미국에 오셨고, 한 번도 고향에 편지를 쓴 적이 없으셨다. ❹ 친척들 말로는 부자가 되셨다고 한다. ❺ 그걸 어떻게 아냐고 내가 물어보았다. ❻ 어떻게 알고 있는지는 아무도 몰랐다. ❼ 그들은 소문으로만 들었던 것이다. ❽ 그리고 그 소문을 들었던 사람들이 돌아가셨다. ❾ 이제 물어볼 사람이 아무도 안 계신다. ❿ 나의 종조부는 마치 일렬로 행진하는 개미들과 마주치면 자신만의 이유로 몸을 돌려 반대 방향으로 가는 개미 같았다. ⓫ 개미는 개미이기 때문에, 이런 일이 꼭 일어나기로 되어있는 것은 아니지만 때때로 일어나며, 아무도 그 이유를 모른다.

해설 내용 일치 유형처럼 보이는 선택지로 인해 접근 시 유의해야 한다. 윗글의 사실을 파악하는 것이 아니라, 전체 내용을 한 문장으로 담아내는 제목을 선택해야 한다. 따라서 잘 몰랐던 '종조부(great-uncle: 할아버지의 남자 형제)'의 이야기로, 그의 베일에 싸인 내용을 풀어나가며 이야기하는 부분에서 흥미롭다고 볼 수 있다. 그래서 ①이 가장 적절하다.

어휘 great-uncle n. 종조부(조부모의 형제) come upon ~을 우연히 만나다 march v. 행진하다, 걸어가다 be not supposed to V ~해서는 안 된다 mythical a. 신화의; 상상의 immigrate v. 이민하다, 이주하다 amazing a. 놀라운, 흥미로운 insane a. 미친, 제정신이 아닌

정답 및 해설

003 ③ 2019학년도 건국대학교 인문·예체능계 A형 29번

❶ Mosquitoes are without a doubt one of the biggest nuisances (to endure during summer.) ❷ It seems like / they do us no good and only harm. ❸ Though extremely annoying, / mosquitoes are actually very crucial and important / to the food chain. ❹ Not all mosquitoes attack humans. ❺ It's actually only the female mosquitoes that suck blood / from people in order to reproduce. ❻ The male mosquitoes, however, live / on nectar / from flowers. ❼ They, (in fact), play a substantial role / in producing flowers / as the second most active pollen deliverer / after the bee! ❽ If they stop spreading pollen around / as much as they do, / flowers will start disappearing. ❾ But it doesn't stop there; / ❿ the animals (that eat plants) will also be affected and so on.

다음 글의 주제로 가장 적절한 것은?
① 인간에게 미치는 모기의 해악
② 모기의 성별에 따른 생태학적 차이
☑ ③ 먹이 사슬에서 모기의 역할
④ 모기가 전염시키는 질병의 위험성
⑤ 효율적인 모기 퇴치 방안

해석 ❶ 모기는 틀림없이 여름에 견뎌내야 하는 가장 큰 성가신 것들 중에 하나이다. ❷ 모기는 우리에게 이로운 점은 없고 오직 해만 입히는 것 같다. ❸ 모기는 극도로 짜증나지만, 실제로는 먹이 사슬에서 아주 중대하고 중요한 존재이다. ❹ 모든 모기들이 사람들을 공격하지는 않는다. ❺ 실제로 번식을 위해 사람들의 피를 빨아먹는 것은 오직 암컷 모기들 뿐이다. ❻ 그러나, 수컷 모기들은 꽃의 꿀을 먹고 산다. ❼ 그들은, 사실, 벌 다음으로 두 번째로 가장 활발한 꽃가루 전달자이며, 꽃을 생산하는 데 상당히 중요한 역할을 한다! ❽ 만약 그들이 지금처럼 꽃가루를 많이 퍼뜨리지 않는다면, 꽃들은 사라지기 시작할 것이다. ❾ 그러나 그것은 거기서 그치지 않는다; ❿ 식물을 먹는 동물들도 영향을 받는 등의 일이 일어날 것이다.

해설 모기는 골칫거리 중 하나라고 시작한다. 하지만 이어서 상반된 내용인 '실제로는 먹이 사슬에서 매우 필수적이고 중요한 존재이다'라고 언급한다. 그리고 이어서 왜 그러한지에 대한 논증이 시작된다.
*주장→역접→논증

어휘 nuisance n. 성가신[귀찮은] 사람[것,일], 골칫거리 endure v. 견디다, 참다, 인내하다 crucial a. 중대한, 결정적인 reproduce v. 생식하다, 번식하다 nectar n. (꽃의) 꿀 substantial a. 실질적인; 실제의; 상당한 pollen n. 꽃가루, 화분

004 ② · 2019학년도 경기대학교 인문·예체능계 A형 40번

해석

❶ 나는 모국인 캐나다를 떠나 존슨대학교에 온 지 여러 해가 지난 지금도 여전히 가르치는 것은 고귀한 소명이고 교수들은 그들의 학생들에게 봉사할 의무가 있다고 생각한다. ❷ 그러나 모든 학생들의 마음에 다 들 수 있는 교수는 없기 때문에, 자신의 포부를 현실성과 조화시킬 준비가 돼 있어야 한다. ❸ 나의 경우에, 이러한 균형을 잡는 행동을 통해, 나는 유능한 선생님이자 유용한 연구원이 되기 위해 노력함으로써 주로 학생들이 외국어인 영어 말하기와 듣기 능력을 개발하는 돕는 데 내 직장 생활을 집중하게 만들었다. ❹ 교실에서, 나는 지나친 성취 목표를 정하지 않고 학생들이 자신들의 영어 실력의 한계를 넘어서도록 동기를 부여하는 것이 중요하다고 생각한다. ❺ 만약 내가 이성을 버리고 터무니없는 학습 목표를 세운다면, 그 결과는 실패가 될 가능성이 높고, 이는 다시 동기부여에 부정적인 영향을 미칠 것이다. ❻ 그래서 나는 학생들에게 배움에 대한 열정을 불러일으키면서, ❼ 그와 동시에, 내가 그들에게 가지는 기대에 대해 현실적인 태도를 가졌다.

해설

보편적인 교수의 역할 언급 이후 이와 대립하는 내용을 언급할 수 있는 Yet(그렇지만) 다음에서 주제문이 나온다. 그리고 for me 이하부터는 이에 대한 논증이 시작되며 본인의 사례 속에서 여러 차례 주제가 반복되고 있다. 안정적으로 글을 파악할 수 있는 전개이다.

*주장→논증

어휘

noble a. 고귀한; 고상한, 숭고한 calling n. 소명; 천직, 직업 be obligated to ~해야 한다 temper v. 완화하다, 진정시키다; 조화시키다, 조절하다 aspiration n. 열망; 포부 practicality n. 실현 가능성, 현실성, 실질적인 측면, 실제 형편 assist v. 돕다, 조력하다 endeavor v. ~하려고 노력하다, 애쓰다 effective a. 유효한; 인상적인; 실제의, 사실상의; 유능한 motivate v. ~에게 동기를 부여하다, 자극하다 exceed v. (수량·정도·한도·범위를) 넘다, 초과하다; (역량 등이) ~보다 뛰어나다 unreasonable a. 비합리적인, 비현실적인 abandon v. 버리다, 단념하다 impractical a. 비현실적인, 비실용적인 negatively ad. 부정적으로 impact n. 충돌, 충격; 영향 invoke v. 기원하다, 호소하다, 야기하다

Which of the following is the most appropriate title for this passage?
다음 중 위 글의 제목으로 가장 적절한 것은?

① Balance in an Academic Context
학문적 맥락에서의 균형

✓② Practicality is the Key to Effective Instruction
현실적인 태도가 효과적인 교육의 핵심이다

③ Teaching Is a Noble Profession
가르치는 일은 고귀한 직업이다

④ Daily Life at Johnson University
존슨 대학교의 일상

정답 및 해설

005 ①   2019학년도 인하대학교 인문계 04번

글의 주제

❶ You may not always have access to a first aid kit / in an emergency. ❷ Here are some suggestions / for other everyday items you can use. ❸ If you don't have water (to cool the burn), / use juice, beer, or milk. ❹ In fact, / use any cold, harmless liquid, / until you have access to cold running water. ❺ The aim is to cool the area as quickly as possible, / using whatever cold liquid is available. ❻ Remember: the burn should be cooled / for at least ten minutes / for the treatment / to be effective. ❼ If you don't have cling film (to cover the burn), use a clean plastic carrier bag, a freezer bag, or similar. ❽ These types of items will not stick to the burn and will create a barrier to stop infection. ❾ Plastic bags are particularly useful / for covering a burned hand or foot.

Which is the best title for the passage?
위 글의 제목으로 가장 적절한 것은?

✓ No First Aid Kit? No Problem
  구급상자가 없는가? 전혀 문제없다.
② Basic Ways to Prevent Burns!
  화상을 예방하는 기본적인 방법들!
③ Why Are We Learning First Aid?
  우리는 왜 응급처치를 배우는가?
④ Who to Treat First in Emergency
  응급상황에서 누구를 먼저 치료해야 하는가?
⑤ Alternative Medicine to Save People
  사람들을 살리는 대체 의학

해석

❶ 응급상황이 발생했을 때 항상 구급상자를 이용할 수 있는 것은 아닐 수 있다. ❷ 다음은 당신이 사용할 수 있는 다른 일상용품에 대한 몇 가지 제안이다. ❸ 화상을 식힐 물이 없다면 주스, 맥주 또는 우유를 사용해라. ❹ 사실, 차갑고 무해한 액체라면 흐르는 차가운 물을 사용할 수 있을 때까지 어떤것이든 사용해도 좋다. ❺ 구할 수 있는 차가운 액체라면 무엇이든 사용하여 가능한 빨리 화상 부위를 식히는 것이 목적이다. ❻ 화상 부위는 최소 10분 동안 냉각되어야 치료가 효과적이라는 것을 명심해라. ❼ 화상 부위를 덮을 수 있는 랩이 없다면, 깨끗한 쇼핑용 비닐봉지, 냉동용 봉지, 또는 그 비슷한 것들을 이용해라. ❽ 이런 종류의 물건들은 화상 부위에 달라붙지 않고 감염을 막기 위한 보호막을 만들 것이다. ❾ 특히 비닐봉지는 화상을 입은 손이나 발을 덮는 데 유용하다.

해설

두괄식 구조의 가장 일반적 패턴으로 첫 문장(문단)에서 주제가 언급된다(응급상황 발생 시 사용할 수 있는 일상 용품 제안). 그리고 이어서 구체적인 사안을 소개하며 세부 내용으로 이어진다.

*주장→논증

어휘

have access to ~에게 접근[출입] 할 수 있다 first aid kit 구급상자, 구급함 emergency n. 비상사태, 돌발사태 suggestion n. 암시, 시사; 제안 harmless a. 해가 없는, 무해한 liquid n. 액체, 유동체 treatment n. 취급, 대우; 치료, 치료법 cling firm (식품포장용) 랩 freezer n. 결빙시키는 것, 냉동장치 barrier n. 울타리, 방벽; 장애물, 장벽 infection n. 전염, 감염; 전염병

006 ③ — 2019학년도 한국산업기술대학교 인문계 33번

▶ 낭만적 사랑은 어린시절 경험한 신체적 친밀감

글의 주제

❶ Some psychiatrists, (such as Thomas Lewis from the University of California), hypothesize / that romantic love is rooted in / experiences of physical closeness / in childhood / — for example, (how we felt / in our mother's arms). ❷ These feelings of comfort and affection / are written / on our brain, / and (as) adults, / our constant inclination is to find them again. ❸ According to this theory, / we love / whom we love (not) so much / because of the future (we hope to build), / (but) rather because of the past; (we hope to live again). ❹ The person (who "feels right") has a certain look, smell, sound, or touch (that activates very deep memories).

❺ Evolutionary psychologists explain, however, / that survival skills are inherent / in our choice of a mate. ❻ According to this hypothesis, / we are attracted to people (who look healthy) — (for example), a woman (with a 70 percent waist-to-hip ratio) is attractive / because she can likely bear children successfully. ❼ A man (with rugged features) probably has a strong immune system and therefore is more likely to / give his partner healthy children.

Which is the best title of the passage?
다음 중 이 글의 가장 적절한 제목은 무엇인가?

① The Relation of Love and Affection
　사랑과 애정의 관계
② The Best Way to Find the Life Partner
　인생의 동반자를 찾는 가장 좋은 방법
③ **Reasons to be Attracted to Someone** ✓
　누군가에게 끌리는 이유
④ Different Types of Romantic Love
　낭만적인 사랑의 서로 다른 유형

[해석]

❶ 캘리포니아 대학교의 토마스 루이스(Thomas Lewis)와 같은 몇몇 정신과 의사들은 낭만적인 사랑이, 예를 들어, 우리가 어머니의 품에서 느꼈던 감정처럼 어린 시절에 경험한 신체적 친밀감으로부터 비롯된다는 가설을 세웠다. ❷ 이런 편안함과 애정은 우리의 뇌에 기록되고, 어른이 되면 우리의 끊임없는 성향이 그러한 느낌을 다시 찾으려고 한다는 것이다. ❸ 이 이론에 따르면, 우리가 사랑하는 사람을 사랑하는 것은 우리가 만들려는 미래 때문이라기보다 오히려 우리가 다시 살고자 하는 과거 때문이라고 한다. ❹ "딱 맞다고 느끼는" 사람은 매우 깊은 기억을 활성화하는 특정한 외모, 냄새, 소리 또는 촉감을 가지고 있다.

❺ 그러나 진화심리학자들은 생존 기술이 우리가 짝을 선택하는 데 내재해 있다고 설명한다. ❻ 이 가설에 따르면, 우리는 건강하게 보이는 사람들에게 끌리는데, 예를 들면, 허리둘레가 엉덩이 둘레의 70%인 여성은 아마도 아이를 성공적으로 낳을 수 있을 것이기 때문에 매력적이다. ❼ 강인하게 생긴 남자는 강한 면역체계를 가지고 있어서 그의 파트너에게 건강한 아이들 줄 가능성이 더 높다.

[해설]

어떤 주장을 할 때 공신력 있는 인물(의사, 박사, 교수, 기관의 수장들)을 등장시키는 것은 편입영어 지문의 일반적인 패턴이다. 그래서 글의 말의 인용이나 설명에 유의해서 읽어야 한다. 따라서 토마스 루이스 박사가 말하는 신체적 친밀감 그리고 배우자의 선택으로 이어지는 글이다. 이어서 두 번째 단락에서는 신체적 친밀감이 아닌 생존 기술로서 건강하게 보이는 사람이 배우자의 선택으로 이어진다고 언급한다. 단락이 나뉠 때는 글의 기조가 바뀔 수 있음에 유의해야 하며, 제목은 전체 글을 가장 잘 아우러야 한다. 따라서 배우자 선택의 두 가지 설명을 모두 포괄할 수 있는 ③ '누군가에게 매력을 느끼는 이유'가 가장 적절하다.

*주장→논증

[어휘] psychiatrist n. 정신과 의사 hypothesize v. 가설을 세우다[제기하다] be rooted in ~에 원인이 있다; ~에 뿌리박고 있다 inclination n. 의향[뜻]; 성향 evolutionary a. 진화의, 진화론에 의한 inherent a. 내재하는 rugged a. (매력적으로) 강인하게[다부지게] 생긴 immune system 면역체계

정답 및 해설

007 ③ 2019학년도 숙명여자대학교 인문계 28번

① In this first decade of the twenty-first century, / the world community is confronted with / staggering problems. ② There are 6 billion people / on our globe / and forecasters project / that the world population / will reach / 10 billion / by 2050. ③ Those people will need food, shelter, and an education (that will allow them to lead fulfilled lives). ④ The twentieth century saw great advances in many fields, / but these advances did not come / without costs. ⑤ Acid rain, (for example), polluted our vegetation, wild life, and the very bodies of millions of people. ⑥ (Together), the people of the world / need to stop / the systemic despoiling of our planet. ⑦ Weaponry, (such as nuclear devices and improvised explosive devices), daily threaten the world's peace and progress. ⑧ Religious fanaticism, hunger, and poverty have bred a desperate terrorism / in many corners of the world. ⑨ It is no overstatement / to say / that we are in a race for global survival.

해석

① 21세기의 첫 10년 동안, 세계 사회는 엄청난 문제에 직면해 있다. ② 지구에는 60억 명의 인구가 있으며, 예보가들은 2050년에 세계 인구가 100억 명이 될 거라고 예측한다. ③ 그 사람들은 만족된 삶을 살게 해줄 음식, 쉼터, 교육을 필요로 할 것이다. ④ 20세기에는 많은 분야에서 큰 발전을 보였지만, 이러한 발전이 대가 없이 이루어진 것이 아니었다. ⑤ 예를 들어, 산성비는 우리의 식물, 야생 생물, 그리고 수많은 사람들의 몸을 오염시켰다. ⑥ 전 세계 사람들이 협력해서 지구에 대한 체계적인 약탈을 막아야 한다. ⑦ 핵무기와 급조 폭발물 같은 무기는 날마다 세계의 평화와 발전을 위협한다. ⑧ 종교적 광신주의, 굶주림, 가난은 세계 곳곳에서 절망적인 테러를 낳았다. ⑨ 우리가 지금 전 인류의 생존을 위한 경쟁 중에 있다 해도 과언이 아니다.

해설

처음 지구상의 문제점에 대한 소재를 언급한 뒤 ④번 문장부터 지문의 끝까지 지난 20세기의 직면한 문제점과 사례를 언급하고 있다.

*추상→논증

어휘

confront v. 직면하다, 맞서다 **staggering** a. 충격적인, 믿기 어려운 **forecaster** n. 예측자; (일비) 예보관 **project** v. 예상[추정]하다 **shelter** n. 주거지, 대피처 **fulfill** v. 이행하다, 수행하다, 만족시키다 **acid rain** 산성비 **pollute** v. 오염시키다, 더럽히다 **despoil** v. 약탈하다, 빼앗다 **improvised** a. 즉흥[즉석]의, 임시변통의 **explosive device** 폭파 장치 **desperate** a. 필사적인, 무모한 **overstatement** n. 과장한 말, 허풍

What would be the best title for the above passage?
윗글의 가장 적절한 제목은 무엇인가?

① Great Advances Made in the Twentieth Century
  20세기에 이루어진 위대한 발전
② Global Warming, Vegetation, and Wildlife
  지구 온난화, 초목, 그리고 야생 생물
✓③ Great Advances Made with Significant Costs Paid
  상당한 비용을 들인 위대한 발전
④ How to Lead Fulfilled Religious Lives
  충만한 종교적인 삶을 사는 방법
⑤ Desperate Terrorism and Global Survival
  무모한 테러와 전 세계의 생존

008 ③ 2019학년도 한양대학교 에리카 인문계 A형 33번

글의 소재: 대학 → 사고의 폭 확장

❶ Going to university is supposed to be a mind-broadening experience. ❷ That assertion is presumably made in contradiction to training for work / straight after school /, which might not be so stimulating. ❸ But is it actually true? ❹ Jessica Golle of the University of Tubingen in Germany thought / : she would try to find out. ❺ Her result, however, is not quite what might be expected. ❻ She found that / those (who have been to university) do indeed seem to leave / with broader and more inquiring minds / than those (who have spent their immediate post-school years / in vocational training for work). ❼ However, it was not the case (that university broadened minds). ❽ Rather, work seemed to narrow them. ❾ In the university group, / changes (in personalities or attitudes) were not detectable. ❿ But those (who had chosen the vocational route) had become more conscientious / but showed marked drops / in interest in tasks (that are investigative and enterprising / in nature), ⓫ and (that might restrict their choice of careers).

위 글의 제목으로 가장 알맞은 것을 고르시오.

① Vocational Training in Germany
　독일의 직업 교육
② Advantages of Early Job Training
　조기 직업 교육의 장점
✓③ Benefits of University versus Work
　직장에 비해 대학의 장점
④ Career Choices for High School Graduates
　고등학교 졸업생을 위한 진로 선택

해석

❶ 대학에 가는 것은 사고의 폭을 넓히는 경험이 되어야 한다. ❷ 그 주장은 아마도 그다지 자극이 되는 일이 아닐지 모르는 고등학교 졸업 후 곧바로 이어지는 직업 교육에 상반되는 주장일 것이다. ❸ 하지만 그게 정말로 사실일까? ❹ 독일 튜빙겐(Tübingen) 대학의 제시카 골레(Jessica Golle)는 자신이 알아내겠다고 마음먹었다. ❺ 그러나 그녀의 연구결과는 예상했던 것과는 다르다. ❻ 그녀는 대학을 다닌 사람들이 대학 졸업 때 고등학교 졸업하자마자 일을 위한 직업 훈련을 받은 사람들보다 실제로 사고의 폭이 넓고 더 탐구적인 사고방식을 가지고 있는 것처럼 보인다는 사실을 발견했다. ❼ 그러나 대학이 사고의 폭을 넓혀준 것이 아니다. ❽ 오히려 일이 사고의 폭을 좁히는 것 같았다. ❾ 대학을 다닌 사람들에게서 성격이나 태도의 변화가 감지되지 않았다. ❿ 그러나 취업으로 진로를 선택한 사람들은 더 양심적이게 되었지만 탐구적이고 진취적인 성격의 일에 대한 관심은 현저히 떨어졌고, ⓫ 그것이 그들의 직업 선택을 제한할 수도 있다.

해설

시작은 대학이 사고의 폭을 넓혀준다는 내용이며, ❹번 문장부터 공신력 있는 전문가 등장 이후 오해와 진실을 말해주고 있다. 연구의 결과는 대학이 사고의 폭을 반드시 넓혀준다는 것은 아니지만, 직장 일은 사고의 폭을 좁혀 놓는다는 것이다. 그뿐만 아니라 직장으로의 취업은 탐구적이고 진취적 성격의 업무에 관심을 줄여준다고 말한다. 따라서 전반적으로 직장 일과 비교한 대학의 장점이 전체 내용을 포괄하기에 가장 적절하다.

어휘

assertion n. 주장, 단언 **presumably** ad. 추측하건대, 아마도 **in contradiction to** ~에 상반되는, ~와 모순되는 **stimulating** a. 자극하는, 격려하는 **inquiring** a. 캐묻기 좋아하는; 탐구적인 **vocational** a. 직업의, 직업상의 **broaden** v. 넓히다, 확장하다 **personality** n. 개성, 성격, 인성 **attitude** n. 태도, 마음가짐 **detectable** a. 찾아낼 수 있는, 탐지할 수 있는 **conscientious** a. 양심적인; 성실한, 꼼꼼한 **marked** a. 현저한, 두드러진; 명료한 **investigative** a. 조사의, 조사에 종사하는, 연구적인 **enterprising** a. 진취적인, 모험적인 **restrict** v. 제한하다, 한정하다 **career** n. (직업상의) 경력, 이력, 생애; (일생의) 직업

009 ③
2019학년도 가천대학교 인문계 2교시 A형 31번

상반된 내용시사 (역접)

❶ Whereas the discovery of the double-helical structure of DNA was originally revered, / ❷ it is now thought / to have opened a door / to an uncertain future. ❸ The scientists were able to put new DNA parts into living cells immediately, / those activities were looked upon suspiciously. ❹ It was considered / that human civilization could be destroyed / by some disease (that could be engineered into cells). ❺ People realized / that calls needed to be made / for strict rules / to control such research. ❻ Because of this, / it took a while / before scientists discovered recombinant-DNA technology. ❼ The controlling rules did not get put into action, fortunately, ❽ so when the fears (about DNA technology) went unfounded, all attempts (at regulation), (even moderate), dissipated.

Which of the following is best for the main idea of the passage?
다음 중 위 글의 주제로 가장 적절한 것은?

① Successful attempts at regulations on DNA technology
   DNA 기술에 대한 성공적인 규제 시도
② The unreliability of biology technology
   신뢰할 수 없는 생물학 기술
✓ Groundless fear of DNA technology
   DNA 기술에 대한 근거 없는 두려움
④ The potential of biological advances
   생물학적 진보의 가능성

해석 ❶ DNA의 이중 나선 구조의 발견은 처음에는 존경받았지만, ❷ 지금은 불확실한 미래의 문을 연 것으로 여겨진다. ❸ 과학자들은 살아있는 세포 속에 새로운 DNA의 일부를 즉시 주입할 수 있었고, 그런 활동들은 의심쩍은 듯이 보였다. ❹ 인류 문명이 세포 속에 넣을 수 있는 어떤 질병에 의해 파괴될 수도 있다고 여겨졌다. ❺ 사람들은 그러한 연구를 통제하기 위해 엄격한 규칙을 요청해야 한다는 것을 깨달았다. ❻ 이 때문에, 과학자들이 재조합 DNA 기술을 발견하기까지 오랜 시간이 걸렸다. ❼ 다행히도 통제하는 규칙은 시행되지 않았고, ❽ 그래서 DNA 기술에 대한 두려움이 근거 없는 것으로 밝혀졌을 때, 규제하려는 시도, 심지어 온건한 시도까지도 모두 사라졌다.

해설 DNA의 이중 나선 구조의 발견은 높은 평가를 받았고, DNA 조작을 통해 문명 파괴의 두려움이 있었다. 하지만 그런 두려움이 근거가 없는 것으로 밝혀지자 실험 규제 등은 사라지게 되었다. 따라서 글의 주제는 ③이 가장 적절하다.

주장 → 역접

어휘 double-helical structure (DNA의) 이중 나선 구조 originally ad. 원래, 최초에 revere v. 존경하다, 숭배하다 civilization n. 문명, 문화 strict a. 엄격한, 엄한 recombinant a. 재조합형의 put ~ into action ~을 행동에 옮기다 unfounded a. 근거가 없는, 사실무근의 regulation n. 규칙, 규정 moderate a. 삼가는, 절제하는, 온건한 dissipate v. 사라지다, 흩어져 없어지다

010 ④　　　　2019학년도 명지대학교 인문계 12번

❶ In most paper and pencil tests, / the test-taker is presented with all the items, / usually in ascending order of difficulty, / and is required to respond to / as many of them as possible. ❷ This is not the most economical way / of collecting information / on someone's ability. ❸ There is no real need / for strong candidates / to attempt easy items, / and no need for weak candidates / to attempt difficult items. ❹ Computer adaptive testing offers a potentially more efficient way / of collecting information / on people's ability. ❺ All test-takers are presented initially with an item of average difficulty. ❻ The computer goes on to present individual candidates / with items / that are appropriate / for their apparent level of ability / as estimated / by their performance / on previous items, ❼ [raising or lowering the level of difficulty / until a dependable estimate / at their ability / is achieved].

Choose the best title of the following passage.
이 글에 대한 가장 적절한 제목을 고르시오.

① Rationale behind Test-takers' Preference for Computer Adaptive Testing
　수험생들의 컴퓨터 적응형 시험 선호에 대한 논리적 근거
② How to Encourage Weak Candidates to Attempt Difficult Questions
　실력이 떨어지는 수험생들이 어려운 문제를 풀도록 용기를 북돋우는 방법
③ The History of Sequencing Test Items Based on Item Difficulty
　문항 난이도에 따른 시험 문항을 차례로 배열하는 역사
✓④ The Efficacy of Computer Adaptive Testing in Estimating Ability
　(수험생의) 능력 평가에 있어서 컴퓨터 적응형 시험의 효율성

❶ 대부분의 지필시험에서는 보통 모든 항목을 난이도가 쉬운 문제부터 어려운 문제 순으로 수험생에게 문항이 제시되며, 수험생은 가능한 많은 항목에 응답해야 한다. ❷ 이것은 누군가의 능력에 관한 정보를 수집하는 가장 경제적인 방법이 아니다. ❸ 강력한 후보가 쉬운 문제를 풀 필요가 없고, 약한 후보가 어려운 문제를 시도할 필요도 없기 때문이다. ❹ 컴퓨터 적응형 시험은 잠재적으로 사람들의 능력에 대한 정보를 수집하는데 더욱 효율적인 방법을 제공한다. ❺ 모든 수험생들은 처음에 평균 난이도의 문제를 받는다. ❻ 컴퓨터는 이전에 풀었던 문제들의 성적에 의해 추정되는 수험생들의 표면적인 수준에 알맞은 문항들을 계속해서 수험생 개인에게 제시하며, ❼ 수험생의 능력에 대해 신뢰할 만한 평가가 완성될 때까지 난이도를 계속 높이거나 낮춘다.

지필시험에 문제점 지적에 이어 해결책으로 컴퓨터 적응형 시험(CAT)를 언급하며 논증으로 효율적인 이유를 구체적으로 설명하고 있다. 따라서 ④이 가장 적절하다.

paper and pencil test 지필시험(紙筆試驗), 연필이나 펜으로 종이에 답을 쓰는 형식의 시험 **test-taker** n. 수험생 **be presented with** ~이 주어지다 **item** n. 항목, 안건; 문항 **in ascending order** 오름차순으로 **candidate** n. (자격 취득 시험의) 수험생 **computer adaptive testing** 컴퓨터 적응형 시험(응시자의 실력에 따라 난이도가 컴퓨터 내에서 조절되는 시험) **potentially** 가능성 있게, 잠재적으로; 어쩌면 **rationale** n. 논리적 근거 **sequence** v. 차례로 배열하다 **efficacy** n. 효능, 능률

정답 및 해설

011 ③   2019학년도 상명대학교 인문·자연계 19번

❶ Vigorous debates are going on today / about [whether our world could sustain double / its present population / (along with its consumption and waste),] or even [whether our world's economy is sustainable / at its present level.] ❷ Yet those aren't the biggest risks. ❸ If, (through globalization), everyone (living on Earth today) were to achieve the standard of living of an average American, the effect (on the planet) would be some 10 times (what it is today), and it would certainly be unsustainable. ❹ We can't prevent people (around the world) / from aspiring / to match our way of life any more / than the exporters of cultures / (during the first wave of globalization) / could expect other cultures not to embrace the farming way of life. ❺ But since the world couldn't sustain / even its present population / if all people lived the way (that those in the First World do now), we are left with a paradox. ❻ Globalization, (most analysts feel), is unstoppable. ❼ But its consequences may overtax the Earth's ability (to support us). That's a paradox (that needs resolving).

윗 글의 제목으로 적절한 것을 고르시오.
① Environmental Crisis Caused by Overpopulation
   인구 과잉으로 인한 환경 위기
② Imbalance of Life Standards Between America and Farming Societies
   미국과 농업 사회 사이의 생활수준의 불균형
✓ Problems of Globalization
   세계화의 문제
④ Increasing Living Costs in the First World
   제 1 세계의 생활비 증가
⑤ Solutions for Sustainable Development
   지속 가능한 개발을 위한 해결책

해석
❶ 오늘날 세계가 (소비와 낭비와 함께) 현재 인구의 두 배를 유지할 수 있는지, 혹은 심지어 우리 세계의 경제가 현재 수준에서 지속 가능한지에 대한 격렬한 논쟁이 벌어지고 있다. ❷ 그러나 그것은 가장 큰 위험은 아니다. ❸ 만약 세계화를 통해, 오늘날 지구에 살고 있는 모든 사람이 평균적인 미국인의 생활수준에 도달한다면, 지구에 미치는 영향은 현재의 10배가 될 것이고, 그렇다면 분명히 지속 가능하지 않을 것이다. ❹ 첫 번째의 세계화 물결 동안 문화 수출국들이 다른 문화권들이 농업 생활방식을 용납하지 않을 것으로 기대할 수는 없었던 것처럼, 지금 우리는 전 세계 사람들이 우리의 생활 방식에 맞추기를 열망하는 것을 못하게 막을 수 없다. ❺ 그러나 모든 사람들이 제1세계(서구 선진국 세계)의 사람들이 지금처럼 살았다면, 세계는 현재의 인구조차 지탱할 수 없기 때문에, 우리는 한가지 역설에 직면해있다. ❻ 대부분의 분석가들은 세계화는 막을 수 없다고 생각한다. ❼ 그러나 그 결과는 우리를 지탱하는 지구의 능력에 과도한 부담을 지울 수도 있다. 그것은 해결해야 할 역설이다.

해설
세계화에 따른 인구 수용력이 지속되지 못함을 지적하고 있다. 즉 증가하는 인구와 생활 수준의 지속성을 지적한다. 두 번째 단락에서는 세계화 물결로 인해 생활 수준이 제 1세계(선진국)와 같아지는 위험성을 언급하며, 문제를 인식하면서도 마주할 수밖에 없는 역설을 지적한다. 따라서 ③이 가장 적절하다.

*문제제기 → 경각심(경종의 글)

어휘
vigorous a. 활발한, 격렬한; 강력한 **debate** v. 논의하다, 숙고하다 **sustain** v. 유지하다, 지속하다 **sustainable** a. 유지[지속]할 수 있는, 환경을 파괴하지 않고 지속될 수 있는 **unsustainable** a. 지속 불가능한; 입증[확증] 할 수 없는 **aspire** v. 열망하다, 갈망하다 **match** v. ~에 필적하다, ~에 미치다, ~와 비슷해지다 **embrace** v. 받아들이다, 포용하다 **paradox** n. 역설, 모순 **unstoppable** a. 막을 수 없는, 제지할 수 없는 **overtax** v. 지나치게 과세하다, 과도한 부담을 지우다, 혹사하다

012 ①   2019학년도 서울여자대학교 인문·자연계 A형 35번

❶ The Egyptians were certainly the first civilization (to preserve food / on a large scale.) ❷ Those narrow fertile strips (on either bank of the Nile) were their principal source of food, and a dry year (in which the Nile failed to flood) could be disastrous. ❸ To be prepared, / Egyptians put up food / in every way (they could), including stockpiling grain / in huge silos. ❹ This fixation (on preserving a food supply) led to considerable knowledge of curing and fermentation. ❺ Were it not for their aversion to pigs, the Egyptians would probably have invented ham, for they salt-cured meat and knew how to domesticate the pig. ❻ But Egyptian religious leadership pronounced pigs carriers of leprosy*, ❼ made pig farmers social outcasts, and never depicted the animal on the walls of tombs. ❽ They tried to domesticate for meat the hyenas [that scavenged** the edge of villages (looking for scraps and dead animals to eat)], ❾ but most Egyptians were revolted / by the idea of eating / such an animal. ❿ Other failed Egyptian attempts (at an animal husbandry) include antelope and gazelle. ⓫ But the Egyptians did succeed in domesticating fowl — ducks, geese, quail, pigeon, and pelican. ⓬ Ancient walls show fowl being splayed, salted, and put into large earthen jars.

* leprosy 나병, 한센병, ** to scavenge 쓰레기를 뒤지다

Which of the following does the passage mainly discuss?
위 글은 주로 무엇에 관해 논하고 있는가?

☑ ① Preservation of food in Ancient Egypt
   고대 이집트의 식량 보존
② Food and wall-painting in Ancient Egypt
   고대 이집트의 식량과 벽화
③ Domestication of animals by the Egyptians
   이집트인의 동물 사육
④ Importance of the Nile in Egyptian civilization
   이집트 문명에서 나일강의 중요성

해석

❶ 이집트인들은 확실히 음식을 대규모로 보존한 최초의 문명이었다. ❷ 나일(Nile)강의 양쪽 둑에 형성된 비옥한 길쭉한 땅은 주요 식량 공급원이어서, 나일강이 범람하지 못한 건조한 해는 재앙이 될 수 있었다. ❸ 이에 대비하기 위해, 이집트인들은 거대한 곡식 저장고에 곡식을 저장하는 것을 포함하여 그들이 할 수 있는 모든 방법으로 음식을 저장했다. ❹ 이러한 식량 저장에 대한 집착은 절임과 발효에 관한 상당한 지식으로 이어졌다. ❺ 이집트인들의 돼지에 대한 혐오만 아니었더라면, 아마도 이집트인들이 햄을 발명했을 것인데, 이집트인들은 고기를 소금에 절였고, 돼지를 사육하는 방법을 알고 있었기 때문이다. ❻ 그러나 이집트의 종교 지도자들은 돼지를 나병 보균자로 선언했고, ❼ 양돈업자를 사회적으로 버림받은 사람으로 만들었으며, 무덤 벽화에 절대 돼지를 그려 넣지 않았다. ❽ 그들은 먹다 남은 음식과 죽은 동물들을 찾아 먹으려고 마을 변두리의 쓰레기를 뒤지는 하이에나를 식용으로 길들이려고 노력했지만, ❾ 대부분의 이집트인들은 그러한 동물을 먹는다는 생각에 혐오감을 보였다. ❿ 이집트인들이 축산에 실패한 다른 동물에는 영양과 가젤이 있다. ⓫ 그러나 이집트인들은 오리, 거위, 메추라기, 비둘기, 펠리컨 등의 가금류를 길들이는데에는 성공했다. ⓬ 고대 무덤의 벽화는 가금류의 속을 벌리고 소금에 절인 다음 큰 토기에 넣는 것을 보여준다.

해설

첫 번째 문장에서 글의 소재인 이집트인들의 음식 보전을 확인할 수 있으며, 이어서 주제문이 언급되고 있다. ❺번 문장부터는 구체적인 사례, 특징, 방법이 언급되고 있다. 따라서 ①이 가장 적절하다.

주장 → 논증

어휘

preserve v. 보존 가공하다; 설탕 조림[소금 절임]하여 저장하다 **fertile** a. 비옥한 **strip** n. (좁고) 길쭉한 땅 **bank** n. (하천·호수·바다의) 둑, 제방 **flood** v. 범람하다 **disastrous** a. 처참한, 형편없는 **stockpile** v. 저장하다 **silo** n. 사일로, (곡식 등의 저장용) 지하실 **cure** v. (육류·어류를 말리거나 절여서) 보존하다, 저장하다 **fermentation** n. 발효 **were it not for** 만약 ~이 없다면 **aversion** n. 싫음, 반감, 혐오 **domesticate** v. (동물을) 사육하다 **pronounce** v. (공개적으로) 선언하다 **carrier** n. (병원체의) 매개체 **leprosy** n. 나병, 문둥병 **social outcast** 사회에서 추방된 자 **tomb** n. 무덤, 묘지 **hyena** n. 하이애나 **scavenge** v. (이용할 수 있는 것을 찾아) 쓰레기 더미를 뒤지다 **scraps** n. 쓰레기; 먹다 남은 음식 **revolt** v. 혐오감을 느끼게 하다 **animal husbandry** 축산업 **antelope** n. 영양 **fowl** n. 가금류 **quail** n. 메추라기 **splay** v. ~을 펼치다, 벌리다 **earthen jar** 옹기 항아리

013 ②   2019학년도 세종대학교 인문계 A형 59번

① Ticked off, peeved, irritated, bothered, annoyed, / no matter how you may say it), being angry is an emotion : no one enjoys feeling). ② But while it's completely normal and human to experience anger, / ③ problems can come into play / when we don't process our feelings in a healthy way. ④ Anger can become a very real, chronic issue, / if not handled properly / and in a timely manner. ⑤ You could find yourself blowing up at the smallest things, doing or saying things / in the heat of the moment (that you later regret).

⑥ Here are some healthy ways (to process your anger). ⑦ It may sound silly, but counting to ten (or, if you're really angry, 100) is a great way (to immediately relieve some built up tension). ⑧ Why? Because it focuses your mind on the specific task of taking care of yourself first.

⑨ Plenty of things can cause anger / but those problems can also be solved / if you're willing to meet them head-on. ⑩ Rather than just blowing up and storming off / when your teen misbehaves, / your co-worker annoys you or your spouse doesn't see eye-to-eye with you / on a certain issue, / work on getting to the root of the problem. ⑪ Discussing differences / in a way that all parties (involved) feel respected and letting someone (you care about) know / how you feel) / are things (every human being is capable of doing).

What is the best headline for the 3rd paragraph?
다음 중 세 번째 문단의 제목으로 가장 적절한 것은?

① Give yourself a time out
   자신에게 시간을 내도록 하라
✓ Address the issue
   문제를 중점적으로 다루어라
③ Hit the gym
   헬스클럽에 다녀라
④ Find a way to endure
   견디는 방법을 찾아라

해석

❶ 화나다, 울화가 치밀다, 짜증나다, 귀찮다, 언짢다 등, 여러분이 어떻게 말하든 화나는 것은 아무도 느끼고 싶지 않은 감정이다. ❷ 그러나 분노를 경험하는 것이 지극히 정상적이고 인간적인 것이지만, ❸ 우리가 건강한 방법으로 감정을 처리하지 않을 때는 문제가 발생할 수도 있다. ❹ 분노가 시기적절하고 제대로 다뤄지지 않는다면, 그것은 매우 현실적이고 고질적인 문제가 될 수 있다. ❺ 당신은 사소한 일에도 화를 낼 수 있고, 순간적으로 욱해서 나중에 후회할 말이나 행동을 할 수도 있다.

❻ 다음은 당신의 분노를 처리하는 건강한 방법들이다. ❼ 어리석게 들릴 수도 있지만, 10까지 (또는 정말 화가 많이 났다면 100까지) 세는 것은 쌓인 긴장을 즉시 풀어줄 수 있는 좋은 방법이다. ❽ 왜 그럴까? 왜냐하면 그것은 특정한 일, 즉 스스로의 마음을 먼저 돌보는 일에 집중시키기 때문이다.

❾ 아주 많은 것들이 분노를 일으킬 수 있지만, 그런 문제들도 당신이 기꺼이 정면으로 맞닥뜨리고자 한다면 해결할 수 있다. ❿ 여러분의 십대 자녀들이 잘못된 행동을 하고, 동료가 당신을 짜증나게 하거나, 배우자가 특정 문제에 대해 여러분과 의견이 같지 않을 때, 화를 내고 자리를 뜨기보다 문제의 근원에 다가갈 수 있도록 노력해라. ⓫ 모든 관련 당사자들이 존중받는다고 느끼는 방식으로 차이점을 토론하는 것과 당신이 아끼는 누군가에게 당신이 어떻게 느끼는지를 알게 하는 것은 모든 인간이 할 수 있는 일이다.

해설

세 번째 문단의 첫 번째 문장에서 주제를 확인할 수 있으며, 십대 자녀들의 예시에서 '문제의 근본에 다가갈 수 있도록 노력'이라는 글에서 주제를 다시 재확인할 수 있다. 따라서 정답은 ②이 가장 적절하다.

어휘

tick off 성나게 하다 peeve v. 약올리다, 성나게 하다 irritate v. 초조하게 하다; 노하게 하다 bother v. 괴롭히다, 성가시게 하다 annoy v. 괴롭히다, 화나게 하다 come into play 작동[활동]하기 시작하다 chronic a. 만성적인, 고질적인 properly ad. 올바르게, 적당하게 blow up 화를 내다, 분통을 터뜨리다 relieve v. (고통·부담 따위를) 경감하다, 덜다; (고통·공포 따위로부터) 해방하다 plenty n. 풍부한 양 ad. 많이, 충분히 head-on ad. 정면으로 storm off 화가 나서 떠나버리다 misbehave v. 나쁜 짓을 하다, 행실이 나쁘다 spouse n. 배우자 see eye-to-eye 의견을 같이 하다

014 ④   2019학년도 가톨릭대학교 인문계 A형 27번

글의 소재: 3대 세계

❶ The "three worlds" model (of geopolitics) first arose / in the mid-20th century / as a way of mapping the various players / in the Cold War. ❷ The First World included the United States and its capitalist allies in places / such as Western Europe, Japan and Australia. ❸ The Second World consisted of the communist Soviet Union and its Eastern European satellites. ❹ The Third World, meanwhile, encompassed all the other countries (that were not actively aligned with / either side in the Cold War). ❺ These were often impoverished former European colonies, and included nearly all the nations of Africa, the Middle East, Latin America and Asia. ❻ Today, / the powerful economies of the West are still sometimes described as "First World," / ❼ but the term "Second World" has become largely obsolete / following the collapse of the Soviet Union. ❽ "Third World" remains the most common of the original designations, ❾ but its meaning has changed from "non-aligned" / and become more of a blanket term / for the developing world.

What is the passage mainly about?
위 글은 주로 무엇에 관한 내용인가?

① Why the term Second World is rarely used today
오늘날 제 2세계라는 용어가 거의 사용되지 않는 이유

② The three worlds model as a relic of the Cold War
냉전의 유물로서의 3세계 모델

③ The significance of the three worlds model in modern political scene
현대 정치 현장에서 3세계 모델이 가진 중요성

✓ Original use of three worlds model terminology and its current adoption
3세계 모델 용어의 원래 사용과 오늘날의 사용

해석

❶ 지정학의 "3대 세계" 모델은 냉전시대의 다양한 참여 국가들을 지도화하는 방법으로 20세기 중반에 처음 등장했다. ❷ 제 1세계는 미국과 미국의 자본주의 동맹국들인 서유럽, 일본, 호주 등지의 국가들이 포함됐다. ❸ 제 2세계는 공산주의 소비에트 연방과 그것의 동유럽 위성국가들로 이루어져 있었다. ❹ 한편, 제 3세계는 냉전에서 어느 한쪽과도 적극적으로 협력하지 않았던 다른 모든 나라들이 포함됐다. ❺ 이들은 종종 가난한 옛 유럽의 식민지였으며, 아프리카, 중동, 라틴 아메리카, 아시아의 거의 모든 나라들이 포함됐다. ❻ 오늘날, 강력한 경제를 가진 서구의 국가들은 여전히 때때로 "제 1세계"로 묘사되고 있지만, ❼ "제 2세계"라는 용어는 소련의 붕괴 이후 대부분 쓰이지 않았다. ❽ "제 3세계"는 처음 정해졌던 명칭들 가운데 가장 흔하게 사용되고 있지만, ❾ 그 의미는 "비동맹"에서 바뀌어서 개발도상국들을 위한 포괄적인 용어가 되었다.

해설

20세기 중반에 등장한 '세 세계(3개 분류)'의 정의와 오늘날 용어의 차이와 정의를 말하는 글이다. 따라서 ④가 가장 적절하다.
- 설명문: 세 세계 20세기 정의 → 세 세계 오늘날(21세기) 정의

어휘

geopolitics n. 지정학 **arise** v. 생기다, 발생하다, 유발하다 **map** v. 지도를 만들다, 지도에 나타내다; ~을 정확히 나타내다 **various** a. 여러 가지의, 가지각색의 **include** v. 포함하다 **capitalist** a. 자본주의의 **ally** n. 동맹국, 연합국 **consist of** ~으로 구성돼 있다 **communist** a. 공산주의의 **satellite** n. 위성; 위성국가 **encompass** v. 에워싸다, 포위하다; 포함하다 **align** v. 정렬시키다; 같은 태도를 취하게 하다, (정치적으로) 제휴시키다 **impoverish** v. 가난하게 하다, 곤궁하게 하다 **colony** n. 식민지 **term** n. 기간, 학기; 용어; 임기 **obsolete** a. 쓸모없이 된, 폐물이 된; 시대에 뒤진, 구식의 **collapse** n. 붕괴, 와해 **designation** n. 지시; 지정; 지명; 명칭 **blanket** a. 총괄적인, 포괄적인, 전면적인 **relic** n. 유물, 유적 **terminology** n. 전문 용어, 용어들

정답 및 해설

015 ③   2019학년도 가톨릭대학교 인문계 A형 29번

❶ Shawn wants to be sure that his nursing home foodservice is using environmentally sound practices. ❷ He plants a small organic garden and the residents who can do so enjoy working in the garden. ❸ Shawn carefully integrates the produce into his menu. ❹ This is an excellent practice and everyone wins. ❺ Shawn then decides to purchase beef from a local farmer. ❻ But because Shawn's operation is in a large metropolitan area, ❼ he must travel frequently to the ranch, which is 250 miles away, to ensure proper practices that meet his green requirements, ❽ and he must then go to the packing company to select his meat and the packing company is another 150 miles away. ❾ The packer must then travel in a small truck to Shawn's operation several times per week. ❿ The travel that Shawn and the small packer's truck must undertake to accomplish this green practice results in a larger carbon footprint than receiving a shipment from a large truck that was making fewer trips would. ⓫ This does not mean that Shawn cannot find a more environmentally friendly source of beef — ⓬ he simply must consider more than just the appearance of eco-friendliness.

What is the main point of the passage?
위 글의 요지는 무엇인가?

① Meat production causes more environmental harm than vegetable growing.
  육류 생산은 채소 재배보다 환경에 더 많은 피해를 줍니다.

② Organic farming is more sustainable, but less productive than conventional farming.
  유기농법은 재래식 농법보다 더 지속 가능하지만 생산성이 더 떨어진다.

✓③ We should consider both farming methods and food miles when assessing eco-friendliness of food.
  식품의 친환경성을 평가할 때, 영농 방법과 푸드 마일리지(식품이 생산된 이후 최종 소비자에게 도달할 때까지 이동한 거리)를 모두 고려해야 한다.

④ When purchasing beef that meets green requirements, buying it in bulk helps reduce the environmental impact.
  친환경 요건을 충족하는 쇠고기를 구매할 때, 대량으로 구매하는 것이 환경에 미치는 영향을 줄이는 데 도움이 된다.

해석

❶ 숀(Shawn)은 자신이 운영하는 요양원의 급식이 확실히 환경적으로 건전한 방식을 사용하고 있다는 것을 확신하기를 원한다. ❷ 그는 작은 유기농 정원을 가꾸고 일할 수 있는 요양원 거주자들은 정원에서 일하는 것을 즐긴다. ❸ 숀은 조심스럽게 그의 메뉴에 정원에서 생산된 농산물을 포함시킨다. ❹ 이것은 모든 사람이 이득을 볼 수 있는 훌륭한 방식이다. ❺ 그리고 숀은 지역 농부로부터 소고기를 구입하기로 결심한다. ❻ 하지만, 숀의 요양원 운영은 대도시 지역에서 이루어지기 때문에, ❼ 자신의 친환경적인 조건을 충족시키는 적절한 방식을 확실하게 지키기 위해서는 250마일 떨어진 목장으로 자주 가야하고, ❽ 그 다음에는 고기를 고르기 위해 도매업체에 가야 하는데, 이 업체는 150마일 더 떨어진 곳에 있다. ❾ 그러면 도매업자는 작은 트럭을 타고 숀의 요양원으로 일주일에 여러 번 이동해야 한다. ❿ 이렇게 친환경적인 방식을 이루기 위해 숀과 도매업체의 소형트럭의 이동은 이동을 더 적게 하는 대형 트럭으로 물건을 받는 것보다 더 많은 탄소 발자국을 발생시키는 결과를 초래한다. ⓫ 이것이 숀이 더 환경 친화적인 소고기 공급원을 찾을 수 없다는 것을 뜻하는 것은 아니다 — ⓬ 그가 단지 친환경의 겉모습 이상의 것들을 고려해야 한다는 것이다.

해설

스토리 텔링 글은 주인공에 결부된 중심사건 그리고 그로인한 교훈을 찾아가는 패턴을 참고하자. 친환경 유기농 농원을 운영하는 숀에게 배송을 위한 장거리 이동이 많은 탄소를 발생시키는 결과를 초래한다는 이야기다. 이야기의 결론은 환경 친화 이상의 것을 고려해야 한다는 것이다.

*주인공 → 중심사건 → 교훈

어휘

nursing home 양로원 environmentally ad. 환경적으로 sound a. 건전한, 안전한 organic a. 유기농의, 유기의 resident n. 거주자, 거주민 integrate v. 통합하다; 완전하게 하다; 결합시키다 produce n. 농산물 purchase v. 사다, 구입하다 ensure v. 보장하다, 확실하게 하다 metropolitan a. 대도시[수도]의 requirement n. 요구, 필요; 필요조건 packing n. 식료품(특히 쇠고기·돼지고기)을 포장하여 시장에 내는 도매업 undertake v. 떠맡다, 책임을 지다; 착수하다 carbon footprint 탄소발자국(온실 효과를 유발하는 이산화탄소의 배출량) shipment n. 수송, 선적, 수송품 appearance n. 출현; 외관, 겉보기

20 끝장편입 독해유형편 Top 20

016 ④ 2019학년도 상명대학교 인문·자연계 24번

❶ Thousands of people will go into the bush this summer / to cut the high cost of living. ❷ A man (who gets his two weeks' salary while he is on vacation) should be able to put those two weeks in fishing and camping and be able to save one week's salary clear. ❸ He ought to be able to sleep comfortably every night, / to eat well every day and to return to the city / rested and in good condition. ❹ But if he goes into the woods / with a frying pan, an ignorance of black flies and mosquitoes, and a great and abiding lack of knowledge about cookery, the chances are that / his return will be very different. ❺ He will come back / with enough mosquito bites / to make the back of his neck / look like a relief map of the Caucasus. ❻ His digestion will be wrecked / after a valiant battle to assimilate half-cooked or charred grub. ❼ And he won't have had a decent night's sleep / while he has been gone. ❽ He will solemnly raise his right hand and inform you / that he has joined the grand army of never-agains.

위 글의 목적으로 가장 적절한 것을 고르시오.

① To inform the benefits of comfortable camping out
   편안한 캠핑의 장점을 알리기 위해
② To prepare men before joining military camps
   군사 캠프에 참가하기 전에 사람들을 준비시키기 위해
③ To advocate decent camping sites
   괜찮은 캠핑장을 지지하기 위해
④ ✓ To warn the dangers of unprepared camping out
   준비되지 않은 캠핑의 위험성을 경고하기 위해
⑤ To describe people's responses after camping out
   캠핑 후에 사람들의 반응을 설명하기 위해

해석

❶ 이번 여름에 수천 명의 사람들이 높은 생활비를 줄이기 위해 숲 속으로 들어갈 것이다. ❷ 휴가 중에 2주치 급여를 받는 사람은 그 2주 동안 낚시와 캠핑을 할 수 있을 것이고 일주일의 급여를 완전히 절약할 수 있을 것이다. ❸ 그는 매일 밤에 편하게 잠을 자고, 매일 잘 먹고, 피로가 풀려 좋은 상태로 도시로 돌아올 수 있을 것이다. ❹ 하지만 만약 그가 프라이팬을 들고, 검은 파리와 모기에 대해 무지한 상태로, 요리에 대한 지식이 대단히 그리고 지속적으로 부족한 상태로 숲에 들어간다면, 그의 복귀는 매우 달라질 것이다. ❺ 그는 목 뒤에 코카서스의 입체지도처럼 보이는 모기에 물린 상처를 가지고 돌아올 것이다. ❻ 그의 소화력은 덜 익거나 까맣게 탄 음식을 소화하기 위해 용감한 전투를 벌인 후에 망가질 것이다. ❼ 그리고 그는 숲에 있는 동안 제대로 잠을 못 잘 것이다. ❽ 그는 엄숙하게 오른손을 들고 다시는 가고 싶지 않은 휴가의 대군에 그가 합류했음을 당신에게 알려줄 것이다.

해설

캠핑의 장점을 소개한 뒤 ❹번 문장부터 기조가 전환되어 부정적 측면으로 준비가 안 된 상태에서의 캠핑의 문제점을 말해주고 있는 글이다.

*주장 → 역접

어휘

bush n. 관목, 덤불, 숲 **salary** n. 급여, 봉급, 월급 **clear** ad. 완전히, 모조리, 줄곧 **ought to** ~해야 하다 **rested** a. 원기를 회복한, 피로가 풀린 **ignorance** n. 무지, 무식 **abiding** a. 지속적인, 영속적인 **cookery** n. 요리, 요리법 **relief map** 입체 지도 **digestion** n. 소화, 소화력 **wreck** v. 파괴하다, 망가뜨리다 **valiant** a. 용감한 **assimilate** v. 동화시키다, (음식물을) 소화 흡수하다 **half-cooked** a. 설익은, 설구운 **charred** a. 새까맣게 탄, 숯이 된 **grub** n. 유충, 구더기, 음식 **decent** a. (수준·질이) 괜찮은, 제대로 된 **solemnity** ad. 엄숙하게, 진지하게

017 ① 2019학년도 국민대학교 인문계 오후 A형 20번

❶ Whether you get car sick, sea sick or light-headed / from playing interactive video games, / motion sickness is seriously unpleasant. **❷** *Kinetosis*, (the official term), can affect both kids and adults / at varying levels. **❸** So what is the root cause of motion sickness? **❹** According to neurologist Dr Hain, / it is caused / by conflict [between the senses responsible for registering motion.] **❺** If the eyes, inner ear and sensory nerves in the skin are all sending different signals / to the brain, / the cross-talk will leave you feeling ill. **❻** Dr Rosenman says : some individuals feel nauseous / from reading / while reading in a car or bus / **❼** because their eyes are focusing on a steady (non-moving) thing, / but the inner ear senses motion, so your brain gets confused and you feel sick. **❽** Drivers have an advantage / over passengers / because they anticipate (what is coming next) and are less dependent on external senses. **❾** If you can't be the driver, / the next best place (to sit) is the front passenger seat / and keep your gaze focused on the road ahead. **❿** When the senses match, / this prevents sensory conflict and motion sickness. **⓫** Stop (what you're doing) or try looking at something outside (that is still and in front of you), so that your ears and eyes get similar information.

What is the passage mainly about?
본문은 주로 무엇에 대한 내용인가?

✓ ① The reason for motion sickness
  멀미하는 이유
② The importance of reactive behaviors
  반응 행동의 중요성
③ Dangers of construction on winding roads
  구불구불한 도로 공사의 위험성
④ Factors to be considered in car seat designs
  자동차 좌석을 설계할 때 고려해야 할 요소들

해석

❶ 당신이 차멀미를 하든, 뱃멀미를 하든, 쌍방향 비디오 게임을 하면서 현기증이 나든, 멀미는 심각할 정도로 불쾌하다. ❷ 전문 용어로 '가속도병'이라고 하는데, 다양한 수준에서 아이와 어른 모두에게 영향을 미친다. ❸ 그렇다면 멀미의 근본적인 원인은 무엇일까? ❹ 신경학자인 헤인(Hain) 박사에 따르면, 멀미는 움직임의 기록을 담당하는 감각들 사이의 충돌에 의해 발생한다고 한다. ❺ 만약 피부의 눈, 내이, 피부의 감각신경이 모두 뇌에 다른 신호를 보낸다면, 혼선으로 인해 당신이 불편하다는 느낌을 받을 것이다. ❻ 로젠만(Rosenman) 박사는 어떤 사람들은 경우 차나 버스에서 책을 읽으면 메스꺼움을 느낀다는데, ❼ 사람의 눈은 일정한(움직이지 않는) 것에 초점을 맞추는 반면에, 내이는 움직임을 감지하기 때문에 당신의 뇌가 (두 감각의 차이로 인해) 혼란을 느끼기 때문에 멀미를 한다고 주장한다. ❽ 운전자들은 다음에 무엇이 다가올지를 예측해서 외부 감각에 덜 의존하기 때문에 운전자가 동승객보다 유리하다. ❾ 만약 당신이 운전할 수 없다면, 그 다음으로 앉기 좋은 자리는 조수석이고, 전방 도로를 계속 주시해라. ❿ 그렇게 여러 감각들이 일치하면, 감각의 충돌과 멀미를 예방해 줄 것이다. ⓫ 하고 있는 일을 멈추거나 차 밖에 당신 앞에 정지한 것을 봐서 귀와 눈이 비슷한 정보를 얻도록 해라.

해설

첫 번째 문장에서 '멀미'라는 소재를 확인할 수 있으며 첫 단락 마지막 문장인 ❸번 문장에서 멀미의 근본적 원인을 질문하고 있다. 그다음 단락부터 지문의 끝까지 멀미의 원인 그리고 해결 방안에 관해 설명하는 글이다. 따라서 정답은 ①이 가장 적절하다.

*질문 → 답변

어휘

carsick a. 차멀미하는 **seasick** a. 뱃멀미하는 **light-headed** a. 현기증이 나는 **interactive** a. 쌍방향의 **motion sickness** 멀미 **Kinetosis** n. 가속도병(뱃멀미·기차 멀미·항공병 따위와 같이 교통 기관의 동요에 의한 병적 상태) **neurologist** n. 신경학자, 신경과 의사 **register** v. 등록하다, 신고하다 **inner ear** 내이(內耳) **cross-talk** n. (통신 상의) 혼선 **nauseous** a. 구역질나는, 메스꺼운 **steady** a. 안정된, 불변의

018 ③ 2019학년도 서울여자대학교 인문·자연계 A형 37번

글의 주제
① Today we are confronted with an expanding array of technical means / for making acts of seeing themselves into objects of observation. ② The most advanced forms of surveillance and data analysis (used by intelligence agencies) are now equally indispensable / to the marketing strategies of large businesses. ③ Widely employed are screens or other forms of display (that track eye movements), as well as durations and fixations of visual interest / in sequences or streams of graphic information. ④ One's casual perusal of a single web page can be minutely analyzed and quantified in terms of (how the eye scans, pauses, moves, and gives attentive priority / to some areas / over others). ⑤ Even in the ambulatory* space of big department stores, / eye-tracking scanners provide detailed information / about individual behavior / — for example, determining how long one looked at items (that one did not buy.)] ⑥ A generously funded research field of optical ergonomics** has been in place / for some time. ⑦ Passively and often voluntarily, / one now collaborates in one's own surveillance and data-mining.

*ambulatory 보행의 ** ergonomics 인체공학

Which of the following does the passage mainly discuss?
위 글은 주로 무엇에 관해 논하고 있는가?
① Technological innovations in the process of production
생산 과정에서의 기술 혁신
② New methodologies of data analysis in management science
경영 과학에 있어 새로운 데이터 분석 방법론
✓③ The ways an observer is turned into an object of observation
관찰자가 관찰 대상이 되는 방법들
④ The prison surveillance system utilizing inmates' optical activities
수감자의 광학 활동을 활용한 교도소 감시 시스템

해석

① 오늘날 우리는 보는 행동 자체를 관찰 대상으로 만들기 위한 확장된 기술적 수단에 직면해 있다. ② 정보기관들이 사용하는 가장 선진화된 형태의 감시 및 데이터 분석이 이제는 대기업의 마케팅 전략에 있어서도 마찬가지로 필수적인 것이 되었다. ③ 그래픽 정보의 순서나 흐름 속에서 시각적 관심의 지속 시간과 고정뿐만 아니라 눈길의 움직임도 추적하는 스크린이나 다른 형태의 디스플레이들이 널리 사용된다. ④ 하나의 웹페이지를 정독하는 것은 눈이 어떻게 훑어보고, 멈추고, 움직이고, 어떤 부분에 다른 부분들보다 더 주의를 기울이는가 하는 측면에서 세밀하게 분석되고 수량화될 수 있다. ⑤ 심지어 대형 백화점의 보행 공간에서도, 눈길을 추적하는 스캐너들은 개인의 행동에 대한 상세한 정보를 제공해주는데, 예를 들어, 구매하지 않은 상품을 얼마나 오랫동안 봤는지를 확인시켜준다. ⑥ 연구 자금이 후하게 주어지는 시각적 인체공학이라는 연구 분야가 한동안 자리를 지켜왔다. ⑦ 사람들은 이제 수동적으로 그리고 종종 자발적으로 저마다의 감시와 데이터 마이닝에서 협력한다.

해설

보는 행동 자체가 관찰 대상이 되었으며, 가장 선진화된 형태의 감시 데이터 분석이 사용되는 사례를 언급하고 있다. 따라서 ③이 가장 적절하다.

*주장 → 논증

어휘

be confronted with ~에 직면하다 **an array of** 여러 가지의, 다수의 **surveillance** n. 감시 **intelligence agency** 정보국, 첩보 기관 **indispensable to** ~에 없어서는 안 되는, 필수적인 **duration** n. 지속기간 **sequence** n. 연속 **stream** n. 흐름; (사람·일·사건 등의) 끊임없는 움직임, 연속 **casual** a. 우연한, 일시적인, 그때그때의 **perusal** n. 숙독, 정독 **minutely** ad. 자세하게, 상세하게 **quantify** v. 양을 나타내다, 수량화하다 **give priority to** ~을 우선시하다 **attentive** a. 주의[귀]를 기울이는, 섬세한 **department store** 백화점 **detailed** a. 상세한, 정밀한 **optical** a. 시각적인, 광학의 **in place** 제자리의, 준비가 다 된 **passively** ad. 수동적으로, 소극적으로 **voluntarily** ad. 자발적으로, 자진해서 **collaborate in** ~에 (대해) 협력[협동]하다 **data-mining** n. 데이터 마이닝(데이터를 캐낸다는 뜻으로 겉으로는 보이지 않는 데이터들 간의 상호 관계를 분석함으로써 데이터 속에 숨어 있던 새로운 정보를 추출해 내는 작업) **methodology** n. 방법론, 방안 **inmate** n. 수감자, 재소자; (정신 병원) 입원 환자[피수용자] **optical activity** 광학 활성(도), 선광성(旋光性)

정답 및 해설

019 ②   2019학년도 인하대학교 인문계 37번

글의 소재
❶ A special case of time deepening is multitasking. ❷ The term multitasking (and multiprocessing) was originally applied to a computer's ability (to execute more than one task or program / at the same time). ❸ In contemporary parlance / it applies the concept of time deepening to work tasks. ❹ Multitasking typically involves juggling phone calls, e-mails, instant messages, and computer work all at once / in order to be more productive. ❺ **Several research reports, / however, provide evidence (that multitasking doesn't actually increase productivity.)** ❻ The findings (of neuroscientists, psychologists and management professors) suggest / multitasking slows you down and increases the chances of mistakes. ❼ Doing more than one task at a time prohibits our ability to process information. ❽ The young, (according to conventional wisdom), are the most adept multitaskers; e-mailing, instant messaging, listening to iPods, and studying at the same time. ❾ Yet, in one recent study of young Microsoft workers, / it took them 15 minutes / to be able to return to serious mental tasks, / like writing reports or computer code, / after responding to incoming e-mails or instant messages. ❿ It is estimated that / the cost (of such lost productivity / to the U.S. economy) is nearly $650 billion a year.

What does the passage mainly discuss?
위 글은 주로 무엇에 대해 논하고 있는가?
① Tips for how to encourage multitasking
　멀티태스킹을 독려하는 요령
✓ ② **Effects of multitasking on work productivity**
　멀티태스킹이 업무 생산성에 미치는 영향
③ Positive influence of multitasking on time saving
　멀티태스킹이 시간 절약에 미치는 긍정적인 영향
④ Importance of connecting multitaskers to computer work
　멀티태스킹을 하는 사람들을 컴퓨터 업무에 연결시키는 것의 중요성
⑤ Ways that technology-enabled communication thrives in workplace
　기술을 기반으로 한 통신이 직장에서 잘 쓰이게 되는 방법

해석

❶ 시간 심화의 한 특별한 사례는 멀티태스킹이다. ❷ 멀티태스킹(또한 멀티프로세스)이라는 용어는 원래 두 개 이상의 과제나 프로그램을 동시에 실행할 수 있는 컴퓨터의 기능에 적용되었다. ❸ 현대적인 용어로, 멀티태스킹은 시간 심화 개념을 업무 수행에 적용한다. ❹ 멀티태스킹은 보통 생산성을 더 높이기 위해 전화, 이메일, 온라인 메시지와 컴퓨터 작업 모두를 동시에 처리하는 것을 포함한다. ❺ 몇몇 연구보고서들은, 그러나, 멀티태스킹이 실제로 생산성을 증가시키지 않는다는 증거를 제공한다. ❻ 신경과학자, 심리학자, 경영학 교수들의 연구 결과는 멀티태스킹이 당신이 일하는 속도를 늦추고 실수할 확률을 높인다고 주장한다. ❼ 한 번에 두 가지 이상의 일을 하는 것은 우리의 정보 처리 능력을 방해한다. ❽ 사회적 통념에 따르면, 젊은 사람들이 멀티태스킹에 가장 능숙하다. 그들은 이메일 보내기, 온라인 메신저 보내기, 아이팟 듣기, 공부하기를 동시에 한다. ❾ 하지만 최근 마이크로소프트의 젊은 직원들을 대상으로 한 연구에서, 그 직원들이 들어오는 이메일이나 온라인 실시간 메시지에 대답한 후에 보고서나 컴퓨터 코드를 쓰는 진지한 정신적인 업무로 돌아오는 데 15분이 걸렸다. ❿ 이러한 생산성 낭비가 미국 경제에 미치는 손실 비용은 연간 6,500억 달러에 이를 것으로 추정된다.

해설

'다중작업(멀티 테스킹)'의 긍정적 정의를 설명한 뒤 ❺번 문장부터 기조가 바뀌어 사실은 효율성이 없으며 손실이 됨을 설명하는 글이다. 따라서 정답은 ②이 가장 적절하다.

*주장 → 역접 → 논증

어휘

time deepening 시간 심화, 시간의 효율적 사용(현대인의 시간 부족을 나타내는 표현) **multitasking** n. 다중 작업, 멀티태스킹 **term** n. 용어; 학기, 기간 **originally** ad. 원래; 독창적으로 **apply to** ~에 적합하다, 적용되다 **execute** v. (계획 따위를) 실행하다, 실시하다; (목적·직무 따위를) 수행하다 **task** n. 일, 임무, 작업, 과업 **contemporary** a. 동시대의; 당대의, 현대의, 최신의 **parlance** n. 말투, 어조, 전문 용어 **typically** ad. 전형적으로, 일반적으로 **involve** v. 수반하다, 필요로 하다 **juggle** v.(곡예 등에서) (공·접시 따위를) 절묘하게 다루다; (두 가지 일 따위를) 기술적으로 잘 처리하다, 솜씨 있게 해내다 **neuroscientist** n. 신경과학자 **psychologist** n. 심리학자 **prohibit** v. 금지하다, 방해하다, ~에게 지장을 가져오다 **process** v. 처리하다 **conventional wisdom** (대부분의 사람들이 가지고 있는) 사회적 통념 **adept** a. 숙련된, 정통한 **incoming** a. 들어오는, 다음에 오는 **estimate** v. 견적하다, 어림잡다; 판단하다

020 ①
2019학년도 세종대학교 인문계 A형 48번

❶ If you were to enter the baby's room / in a typical American home today, / you would probably see a crib full of stuffed animals and colorful toys dangling directly over the infant. ❷ Some of these toys may light up, move, or play music. ❸ What do you suppose / is the parents' reasoning / behind providing infants with so much to see and do? ❹ Aside from the fact that babies seem to enjoy and respond positively / to these toys, / most parents believe that / children need a stimulating environment / for optimal brain development.

❺ The question of whether certain experiences produce physical changes in the brain has been a topic of research / among scientists / for centuries. ❻ In 1785, / Vincenzo Malacarne, (an anatomist), studied pairs of dogs / from the same litter and pairs of birds / from the same batches of eggs. ❼ For each pair, / he would train one participant / over a long period of time / while the other would be equally cared for / but untrained. ❽ He discovered later, / (in his autopsies of the animals), that the brains of the trained animals appeared more complex, / with a greater number of folds and fissures. ❾ In the 19th century, / attempts were made / to relate the circumference of the human head with the amount of learning (a person had experienced). ❿ Although some early findings claimed such a relationship, / later research determined / that this was not a valid measure of brain development.

Which of the following best describes the purpose of writing the above passage?
다음 중 위 글을 쓴 목적을 가장 잘 나타내고 있는 것은?

① ✓ to introduce a line of scientific research
   과학 연구 한 가지를 소개하기 위해
② to advertise a new line of toys for children
   어린이들을 위한 새로운 종류의 장난감을 광고하기 위해
③ to advise parents about the best child-rearing practices
   부모들에게 최고의 육아 방법에 대해 조언하기 위해
④ to report a problematic phenomenon in society
   사회에서 문제가 되는 현상을 이야기하기 위해

해석

❶ 만약 여러분이 오늘날 전형적인 미국 가정의 아기 방에 들어간다면, 아마도 봉제 동물인형과 아기 바로 위에 매달려 있는 다채로운 장난감들로 가득 차 있는 아기침대를 볼 수 있을 것이다. ❷ 이런 장난감들 중 일부는 불이 들어오거나, 움직이거나, 음악이 나올 수도 있다. ❸ 아기한테 그렇게 많은 볼거리와 놀거리를 제공하는 행동의 이면에 있는 부모들의 논리가 무엇이라고 생각하는가? ❹ 아기들이 이런 장난감을 즐기고 긍정적으로 반응하는 것 같다는 사실과는 별개로, 대부분의 부모들은 최적의 두뇌 발달을 위해 아이들에게 자극적인 환경이 필요하다고 믿는다.

❺ 특정 경험이 뇌에 물리적인 변화를 일으키는지에 관한 문제는 수세기 동안 과학자들 사이에서 연구 주제가 되어왔다. ❻ 1785년에, 해부학자 빈첸초 말라카르네(Vincenzo Malacarne)는 한 배에서 태어난 여러 쌍의 강아지와 한 알 묶음에서 태어난 여러 쌍의 새들을 연구했다. ❼ 각각의 쌍에 대해, 하나는 장기간에 걸쳐 훈련을 시킨 반면에, 나머지 하나는 동등하게 보살펴 주었지만 훈련은 시키지 않았다. ❽ 그는 나중에 그 동물들의 부검을 하여 훈련을 받은 동물의 뇌가 주름과 균열의 수가 훨씬 더 많아서 더 복잡하게 보인다는 것을 발견했다. ❾ 19세기에는, 인간의 머리 둘레와 사람이 경험하여 알게 된 지식의 양을 연관시키려는 시도가 있었다. ❿ 비록 몇몇 초기 연구결과들이 그러한 연관성을 주장했지만, 이후의 연구에서 이것은 뇌 발달에 대한 타당한 척도가 아니라고 결론 냈다.

해설

두 번째 문단의 내용, 즉 '특정 경험이 뇌에 물리적인 변화를 일으키는 지에 관한 연구 내용'을 소개하려는 목적의 글이다.
글의 목적이 상당히 포괄적이다. 첫 단락에서는 아이들의 장난감 경험과 이에 대한 부모들의 논리를 설명하지만, 두 번째 단락부터는 특정 경험에 관한 뇌의 연구 역사와 결론을 말한다. 앞 단락과 개연성이 떨어져 보이지만 ❸번 문장에서 아기들의 장난감 경험도 영향을 받을 수 있음을 추측해 볼 수 있다. ❾번 문장 부터는 다시 뇌에 대한 또 다른 연구가 있었음을 언급하고 있다. 따라서 ①번 가장 적절하다.

크쌤 첨언

글의 전개와 논리가 그렇게 좋아 보이지는 않지만, 선택지 ②~④번은 많이 소재도 일치하지 않은 선택지임으로 ①번 선택지가 그나마 나은 정답이라 여겨진다.

어휘

crib n. 구유, 마구간; (소아용) 테두리 난간이 있는 침대, 베이비 베드 **stuffed animals** 봉제 동물인형, 솜으로 만든 동물인형 **dangle** v. 매달리다, 흔들흔들하다 **infant** n. 유아 **reasoning** n. 추론, 추리 **respond** v. 반응하다; 응답하다, 대답하다 **positively** ad. 확실히; 적극적으로; 긍정적으로 **stimulating** a. 자극적인, 격려하는 **optimal** a. 최선의, 최적의 **physical** a. 육체적인, 물리적인, 유형의 **litter** n. 잡동사니, 쓰레기; (동물의) 한 배 새끼 **batch** n. 한 벌, 한 묶음; 한 떼, 일단(一團) **participant** n. 참여자, 참가자 **autopsy** n. 시체해부, 부검 **complex** a. 복잡한, 어려운 **fold** n. 주름 **fissure** n. 갈라진 자리, 틈, 균열 **circumference** n. 원주(圓周), 원둘레 **claim** v. 요구하다, 청구하다, 주장하다 **valid** a. 근거가 확실한, 확실한, 정당한 **measure** n. (평가·판단 등의) 기준, 척도

정답 및 해설

021 ③
2019학년도 국민대학교 인문계 오후 A형 40번

Heading to the 2002 Winter Olympics, / a 21-year-old American figure skater Michelle Kwan was favored to win her first gold medal. ② An accomplished skater, she had already won four world championships and six U.S. titles. ③ True to form, she entered the final four minutes of competition / at a distinct advantage — she was in first place / and in front of a home crowd (rooting for her to win.) ④ She proceeded; however, she fell to the ice / on her triple flip. She finished third. ⑤ In sharp contrast, 16-year-old Sarah Hughes had very low expectations. ⑥ As she put it, / "I skated for pure enjoyment." ⑦ Yet she proceeded through a highly challenging program and skated flawlessly. ⑧ In the end, she won the gold. ⑨ What happened? ⑩ Was Kwan feeling too pressured? ⑪ Could an arena (filled with supportive and expectant fans) have made it worse, causing her to "choke" / under pressure? ⑫ A study reports / that an audience of friendly faces raises the pressure — and our fear of failure (we hate to disappoint those who root for us). ⑬ It also makes us more self-conscious, a state of mind (that can cause athletes to stiffen up.) ⑭ Either way, these results seem at odds with the home-field advantage (known to exist / in professional sports.) ⑮ Across the board, statistics show / that home teams tend to win. ⑯ (Perhaps) the added pressure / in these situations / is offset / by other advantages.

해석

❶ 2002년 동계올림픽을 앞두고, 21세의 미국 피겨스케이팅 선수 미셸 콴(Michelle Kwan)은 그녀의 첫 금메달을 딸 수 있는 기회를 얻었다. ❷ 뛰어난 피겨스케이팅 선수였던 그녀는 이미 세계 피겨스케이팅 선수권대회에서 네 번 우승했고, 미국 피겨스케이팅 선수권대회에서 여섯 번 우승했다. ❸ 여느 때처럼 이번에도, 다른 사람들보다 훨씬 유리한 상태로 - 그녀가 이기기를 응원하는 홈팀 관중들 앞에서 예선 1위로 - 4분 동안의 결승전에 올랐다. ❹ 그러나 그녀는 프로그램을 진행하다가, 트리플 플립 점프에서 빙판에서 넘어졌고 3위를 차지했다. ❺ 이와 아주 대조적으로, 열여섯 살의 사라 휴즈(Sarah Hughes)경기에 큰 기대가 없었다. ❻ 그녀는 "순수한 즐거움을 위해 스케이트를 탔다." 라고 말했다. ❼ 그러나 그녀는 매우 고난도의 프로그램을 잘 진행해 나갔고, 흠잡을 데 없이 스케이트를 탔다. 결국, 그녀가 금메달을 땄다. ❾ 무슨 일일까? ❿ 미셸 콴이 과도한 스트레스를 받고 있었을까? ⓫ 응원하고 기대하는 팬들로 가득한 경기장이 상황을 더 나빠지게 하여, 그녀가 압박감으로 숨막혀 실수한 것일까? ⓬ 한 연구에 따르면, 친절한 얼굴의 관중이 압박감과 실패에 대한 두려움을 증가시킨다고 한다(우리는 우리를 응원하는 사람을 실망시키는 것을 매우 싫어한다). ⓭ 그것은 또한 우리 스스로를 더욱 의식하게 만드는데, 이것은 운동선수를 경직되게 할 수 있다. ⓮ 어느 쪽이든, 이런 결과는 프로 스포츠에 존재한다고 알려진 홈경기장의 이점과 상충하는 것처럼 보인다. ⓯ 전반적으로, 통계자료는 홈팀이 승리하는 경향이 있다. ⓰ 아마도 이런 상황에 더해지는 압박감은 다른 이점들에 의해 상쇄될 것이다.

어휘

head to ~으로 나아가다, 향하다 **favor** v. 편애하다, 총애하다; 지지하다 **accomplished** a. 성취한, 기량이 뛰어난, 노련한, 익숙한 **championship** n. 선수권대회 **true to form** 예상대로 **distinct** a. 뚜렷한, 별개의 **in sharp contrast** 이와 매우 대조적으로 **flawlessly** ad. 흠 하나 없이, 완벽하게 **arena** n. 경기장 **make a person self-conscious** ~을 겸연쩍게 만들다 **stiffen up** (몸 등이) 뻣뻣해지다, 경직되다 **at odds with** ~와 반목하는 [사이가 안 좋은] **home-field advantage** 홈 경기장 이점(본거지에서 경기를 하는 경우의 이점) **across the board** 전반적으로 **statistics** n. 통계자료 **offset** v. 상쇄하다 **defiant** a. 반항적인

Which is the best title for the passage?
본문의 제목으로 가장 적절한 것은?
① Why Home Teams Win
왜 홈팀이 우승하는가?
② Athletes' Challenging Spirit
선수들의 도전 정신
✓ Supportive Audience: Good or Bad?
응원하는 관중: 약인가 독인가?
④ Why Figure Skating Gains Popularity
왜 피겨스케이팅이 인기를 끄는가?

해설 동계 올림픽 피겨 스케이팅 경기에서 기대가 높았던 미셸 콴 선수의 부진에 이어서, 오히려 기대가 없었던 사라 휴즈가 금메달을 획득한 이야기다. 그리고 ❾번 문장부터는 이에 대한 원인을 분석하고 있다. 즉, 관중들의 많은 기대와 응원이 오히려 부정적 영향이 될 수도 있음을 설명한다. 정답은 ③이 가장 적절하다.

*주인공 → 중심사건 → 교훈

크쌤 첨언 스토리텔링 형식의 글에서는 주인공을 포착한 뒤 중심사건에 주목해야 한다. 여기서 중심사건은 기대가 없었던 사라 휴즈의 금메달 이야기가 된다.

어휘 head to ~으로 나아가다, 향하다 favor v. 편애하다, 총애하다; 지지하다 accomplished a. 성취한, 기량이 뛰어난, 노련한, 익숙한 championship n. 선수권대회 true to form 예상대로 distinct a. 뚜렷한, 별개의 in sharp contrast 이와 매우 대조적으로 flawlessly ad. 흠 하나 없이, 완벽하게 arena n. 경기장 make a person self-conscious ~을 겸연쩍게 만들다 stiffen up (몸 등이) 뻣뻣해지다, 경직되다 at odds with ~와 반목하는[사이가 안 좋은] home-field advantage 홈 경기장 이점(본거지에서 경기를 하는 경우의 이점) across the board 전반적으로 statistics n. 통계자료 offset v. 상쇄하다 defiant a. 반항적인

정답 및 해설

022 ① 2019학년도 덕성여자대학교 오전(사회·자연·예술대학) 22번

❶ There are certain things [that, (so far), social media seem to do very well.] ❷ The most remarkable one is coordination. ❸ Coordinating large numbers of people / to do exactly the same thing / at the same time / is notoriously difficult. ❹ So long as the activity is relatively simple / — say, show up and protest the government — the new social media drastically reduce the costs of coordination. ❺ But if social media are good at coordinating simple events, (so far) they have failed at building political parties / on a grander scale. ❻ In Egypt and Tunisia, / the tech savvy young people (who facilitated anti-government protests) have already begun to fall behind / in the race to political organization. ❼ Ahead of them are Islamic democrats, political groups (that have years of experience / in attracting, organizing and mobilizing followers.) ❽ Why should Facebook and Twitter be good for social parties / but not political parties? ❾ It's too soon to know definitively, / and of course / it is possible that, / as technology changes and user culture evolves, / more complex political organizations / may come out of social media. ❿ (For now), however, the answer seems to lie / in the fact [that they lack the kinds of contacts needed to create extended political cohesion.] ⓫ To show up at a social gathering, / I don't need to have any close or repeated bonds with the other people. ⓬ All of us can show up, enjoy ourselves and go our separate ways. ⓭ The key is [that our objective is simple rather than complex.] ⓮ Political organization, by contrast, is very complicated indeed. ⓯ A successful political organization must generate beliefs / about the way (the world works) and (how it should be.) ⓰ It must reflect a shared ethos or morality. ⓱ Above all, it must produce some sense of community.

해 석

❶ 지금까지 소셜 미디어가 아주 잘 하는 것처럼 여겨지는 것이 몇 가지 있다. ❷ 가장 주목할 만한 것은 협동이다. ❸ 같은 시간에 정확히 똑같은 일을 하도록 다수의 사람들을 협동시키는 것은 어렵기로 악명 높다. ❹ 이러한 활동이, 예를 들어, 함께 모여서 반정부 시위를 하는 것처럼- 비교적 간단한 일이기만 한다면, 새로운 소셜 미디어가 통합의 비용을 크게 줄일 수 있다. ❺ 그러나 만일 소셜 미디어가 간단한 이벤트들을 협동시키는 것을 잘한다 하더라도, 더 큰 규모로 정치적 단체를 만드는 것은 지금까지 실패해왔다. ❻ 이집트와 튀니지에서, 반(反)정부 시위들을 가능하게 했던 첨단기술에 밝은 젊은이들이 정치 조직을 만들려는 경쟁에서 이미 뒤처지기 시작했다. ❼ 그들 이전엔 이슬람 민주주의자들로, 이들은 오랜 세월에 걸쳐 추종자들을 끌어들이고, 조직하고, 동원한 경험이 있는 정치 집단들이다. ❽ 페이스북과 트위터가 사회적인 단체를 만드는 데는 유용하지만 정치적인 단체를 만드는 데는 그렇지 않은 이유는 무엇일까? ❾ 이를 확실히 알기는 이르며, 기술이 변하고 사용자 문화가 발전하면서 소셜 미디어에서 복잡한 정치 조직들이 생겨날 수 있다. ❿ 그러나 현재로선 답은 페이스북과 트위터에는 확대된 정치적 응집을 만드는 데 필요한 종류의 접촉이 부족하다는데 있는 것 같다. ⓫ 사교모임에 나가기 위해 나는 다른 친밀하거나 반복적인 유대관계를 사람들과 형성할 필요가 없다. ⓬ 우리들 모두는 모임에 나와서 즐기고, 각자의 길을 갈 수 있다. ⓭ 핵심은 사교 모임에서는 우리가 가진 목적이 복잡하기 보단 간단하다는 것이다. ⓮ 이와는 대조적으로, 정치 조직은 매우 복잡하다. ⓯ 성공적인 정치 조직은 세상이 돌아가는 방식과 바람직한 세상에 대한 믿음을 만들어내야 한다. ⓰ 그리고 그것은 공유된 사회 기풍이나 도덕성을 반영해야 한다. ⓱ 무엇보다도, 그것은 반드시 어떤 공동체 의식을 만들어내야 한다.

어 휘

remarkable a. 주목할 만한, 현저한, 뛰어난 **coordination** n. 조화, 일치, 조정, 통합 **coordinate** v. 대등하게 하다; 통합하다; 조정하다 **notoriously** ad. 악명 높게 **relatively** ad. 상대적으로, 비교적 **show up** (예정된 곳에) 나타나다 **protest** n. 항의, 시위 v. 항의하다, 이의를 제기하다 **drastically** ad. 격렬하게, 맹렬하게, 과감하게, 철저하게 **reduce** v. (양·정도·액수를) 줄이다, 감소시키다 **savvy** a. 사리를 이해한, 정통한, 요령 있는, 경험 있고 박식한 **facilitate** v. 손쉽게 하다; (행위 따위를) 돕다; 촉진[조장]하다 **attract** v. (주의·흥미를) 끌다; (사람을) 끌어들이다 **organize** v. (단체 따위를) 조직하다, 편제[편성]하다 **mobilize** v. (군대·함대를) 동원하다 **evolve** v. 서서히 발전시키다, 진화하다 **complex** a. 복잡한 **contact** n. 접촉 **extended** a. 장기간의; 광범위한 **cohesion** n. 결합; 단결; 유대, 응집력 **gathering** n. 모임, 회합, 집회 **bond** n. 유대, 결속 **separate** a. 분리된, 개별적인 **objective** n. 목적, 목표 **generate** v. 산출하다; (전기·열 등을) 발생시키다; (결과·상태 등을) 야기[초래]하다 **reflect** v. 반영하다, 나타내다 **ethos** n. 사회 사조, 기풍, 풍조 **morality** n. 도덕성, 윤리성

Which of the following would be the most suitable title for the passage?
다음 중 위 글의 제목으로 가장 적절한 것은?

① **Social Media's Limitations**
  소셜 미디어의 한계
② Social Media vs. Political Parties
  소셜 미디어 vs. 정치적 단체
③ Advantages of Social Media
  소셜 미디어의 장점
④ Ethos of Social Media
  소셜 미디어의 사회 기풍

해설 소셜 미디어라는 소재로 이점을 언급하며 글을 시작한다. ⑤번 문장부터 기조가 바뀌어 사회적 단체 결성은 가능한데, 정치적 단체 결성이 실패한 이유를 질문하고 이에 대한 답변을 논리적으로 이어가는 글이다. 따라서 ①이 가장 적절하다.

*주장 → 역접 → 논증

023 ③ 2019학년도 숭실대학교 인문계 A형 21번

① A druid was a member of the high-ranking professional class in ancient Celtic cultures. ② While (perhaps) best remembered as religious leaders, they were also legal authorities, adjudicators, lorekeepers, medical professionals, and political advisors. ③ While the druids are reported to have been literate, they are believed to have been prevented by doctrine from recording their knowledge in written form, thus they left no written accounts of themselves. ④ They are however attested in some detail by their contemporaries from other cultures, such as the Romans and the Greeks.

⑤ The earliest known references to the druids date to the fourth century BC, and the oldest detailed description comes from Julius Caesar's *Commentarii de Bello Gallico* (50s BC). ⑥ They were also described by later Greco-Roman writers such as Cicero, Tacitus, and Pliny the Elder. ⑦ Following the Roman invasion of Gaul, the druid orders were suppressed by the Roman government under the 1st century AD emperors Tiberius and Claudius, ⑧ and had disappeared from the written record by the 2nd century.

⑨ In about 750 AD, the word druid appears in a poem by Blathmac, (who wrote about Jesus), saying that he was " ... better than a prophet, more knowledgeable than every druid, a king who was a bishop and a complete sage.)" ⑩ The druids (then) also appear in some of the medieval tales from Christianized Ireland, like the "Iain 86 Cuailnge," where they are largely portrayed as sorcerers who opposed the coming of Christianity. ⑪ In the wake of the Celtic revival (during the 18th and 19th centuries), fraternal and neopagan groups were founded based on ideas about the ancient druids, a movement known as Neo-Druidism. ⑫ Many popular notions (about druids), (based on misconceptions of 18th century scholars), have been largely superseded by more recent study.

해석

① 드루이드는 고대 켈트 문화에서 상위 전문직 계층의 일원이었다. ② 아마 종교 지도자로 가장 잘 기억될 수도 있지만, 그들은 또한 법의 권위자, 재판관, 현자(賢者), 의료 전문가, 정치 고문이기도 했다. ③ 드루이드는 글을 읽고 쓸 줄 아는 것으로 알려져 있지만, 교리에 의해 그들의 지식을 글로 기록하는 것을 금지했던 것으로 믿어지기 때문에 그들은 그들 자신들에 대한 어떠한 기록도 남기지 않았다. ④ 그러나 그들은 로마인이나 그리스인처럼 다른 문화권에 살던 동시대인들에 의해서 어느 정도 상세히 증명되었다.

⑤ 드루이드에 관한 최초의 알려진 언급은 기원전 4세기로 거슬러 올라가며, 가장 오래된 상세한 설명은 율리우스 시저의 '갈리아 전기'(Commentarii de Bello Gallieo)(기원전 50년대)에 나온다. ⑥ 그들은 또한 키케로, 타키투스, 플리니와 같은 후기 그리스 로마 작가들에 의해 묘사되었다. ⑦ 로마의 갈리아 침공 이후 드루이드 왕조는 서기 1세기 티베리우스(Tiberius) 황제와 클라우디우스(Claudius) 황제 통치하의 로마 정부에 의해 억압되었고, ⑧ 2세기경에는 문서 기록에서 사라졌다.

⑨ 서기 750년경에 드루이드라는 단어는 블라드맥(Blathmac)이 쓴 시에서 나왔는데 그는 예수 그리스도에 대해 "예언자보다 낫고, 주교이자 완전한 현자(賢者)인 왕은 모든 드루이드보다 더 박식하다."라고 썼다. ⑩ 또한 드루이드는 '탄 보 후알케녀'(Táin Bó Cúailinge, 쿨리의 가축 약탈)처럼 기독교화된 아일랜드의 중세 이야기에서 등장하는데, 그들은 대체로 기독교의 도래에 반대하는 마법사들로 묘사된다. ⑪ 18세기와 19세기 켈트족 부흥 운동의 결과로서 고대 드루이드 사상에 바탕을 둔 형제적이고 신 이교주의적인 단체들이 설립되었고, 이는 신드루이디즘으로 알려진 운동이었다. ⑫ 드루이드에 대한 많은 대중적인 개념들은 18세기 학자들의 잘못된 인식에 기초를 두고 있으며, 보다 최근의 연구로 대부분 대체되었다.

어휘

druid n. 드루이드(고대 켈트족 종교였던 드루이드교의 성직자) **high-ranking** a. 고위의, 중요한 **authority** n. 권한, 권위 **adjudicator** n. 재판자, 심판자 **lore** n. 지식, 민간 전승, 학문, 지식 **literate** a. 글을 읽고 쓸 줄 아는, 박식한 **doctrine** n. 교리; 신조; 정책, 주의 **attest** v. 증명[입증]하다 **detail** n. 세부, 세목, 사소한 일 **contemporary** n. 같은 시대[시기]의 사람 **reference** n. 말하기, 언급 **Gual** n. 갈리아(고대 켈트 사람의 땅, 지금의 북이탈리아·프랑스·벨기에 등을 포함함) **prophet** n. 예언자, 선지자 **bishop** n. 주교 **sage** n. 현자, 철인; 경험이 풍부한 현자 **medieval** a. 중세의 **sorcerer** n. 마법사 **in the wake of** ~에 뒤이어 **fraternal** a. 형제의, 형제다운 **neopagan** a. 신이교주의의 **supersede** v. 대체[대신]하다

Which of the following would be best for the title?
다음 중 이 글의 제목으로 가장 적절한 것은 무엇인가?

① Roman Empire and the Druids
  로마 황제와 드루이드
② Christianity and the Druidism
  기독교와 드루이드교
✓ Historical Accounts on the Druids
  드루이드에 대한 역사적 기록
④ Neopaganism or Neo-Druidism?
  신이교도주의냐 아니면 신드루이디즘이냐?

해설 드루이드 계층의 설명과 직업적 역할에 대한 설명 이후 그들의 기록이 역사에 남아 있지 않다고 말하고 있다. ❹번 문장부터는 기조가 바뀌어 로마와 그리스 시대에 남아 있는 그들(드루이드)의 역사를 말하며 10번 문장까지 각 시기마다 존재하는 그들의 역사적 기록을 설명하고 있다. 따라서 정답은 ③이 가장 적절하다.

*주장 → 역접 → 논증

정답 및 해설

024 ①
2019학년도 숭실대학교 인문계 A형 42번

해석

❶ (Perhaps more than any other element), / the rise of commerce and consumerism / as a central feature of the American economy / determined the customs of Christmas charity and, (more obviously), gift-giving. ❷ Earlier in the nineteenth century, / (especially in rural areas and along the frontier), gifts had been of necessity usually simple and homemade (although youngsters regarded "store-bought" candy with particular fondness). ❸ Commonly, / children received most of them. ❹ Mothers knitted, tied, stuffed, laced, stitched, or baked special treats. ❺ Fathers whittled and carved toys.
❻ As the nation became more market-oriented, / such homey pleasures sometimes seemed inadequate. ❼ Stores and shops (throughout the nation) offered the consumer an ever-growing feast of choices, nearly any of which might be made a gift.
❽ By late nineteenth century, / the definition of gift had broadened / to include every category of practical housewares, novelty items, greeting cards, money, extravagant oddities, and simple mementos. ❾ There was, (in a phrase), something for everyone.
❿ Beginning in the 1880s and lasting for many years, / cheap and useless novelties (known as "gimcracks") enjoyed a vogue. ⓫ Those seeking more tasteful, / but still relatively inexpensive, tokens of goodwill gave Prang Christmas cards. ⓬ These could be framed, displayed / on Christmas trees / or on special racks, / or made into wallpaper (appropriate for home china cabinets.) ⓭ Others turned their attention to more prosaic and efficient wares; / household work savers became acceptable gifts / for mothers and wives. ⓮ Parents, aunts, and other well-meaning elders could always rely on a gold piece or a $2 bill / as a gift (intended to encourage a child's habit of saving.)
⓯ It would be erroneous to assume, however, / that the new

❶ 아마도 다른 어떤 요소보다, 미국 경제의 중심적인 특징인 무역과 소비주의의 증가가 크리스마스 자선 행사, 더 분명하게는 선물 주기의 관습을 결정했을 것이다. ❷ 19세기 초, 특히 시골 지역과 변경(邊境)지역에서, 선물은 당연히 대개 간단하고 집에서 만든 것들이었다(비록 젊은이들은 '상점에서 산' 캔디를 특히 좋아했지만 말이다). ❸ 일반적으로, 아이들은 그것들 대부분을 받았다. ❹ 엄마들은 뜨개질을 하거나, 끈을 매거나, 인형을 솜으로 채우거나, 레이스로 장식하거나, 바느질하거나, 특별한 간식을 구웠다. ❺ 아버지들은 깎고 조각해서 장난감을 만들었다.
❻ 미국이 더욱 시장 중심이 되면서, 그런 가정적인 즐거움은 때때로 불충분해 보였다. ❼ 전국의 가게와 상점은 소비자에게 계속 증가하는 선택의 향연을 제공했는데, 그 중 거의 모든 것들이 선물이 될 수 있었다.
❽ 19세기 후반에 선물에 대한 정의가 모든 범주의 실용적인 가정용품, 새로 나온 상품, 연하장, 돈, 사치품, 단순한 기념품까지 포함하도록 확대되었다. ❾ 한 마디로, 모든 사람들을 위한 무언가가 있었다. ❿ 1880년대부터 수 년 동안, 값이 싸고 실용성이 없는 새로운 "싸구려"로 알려진 물건들이 유행했다. ⓫ 좀 더 고상하지만 여전히 비교적 저렴하고 의의 징표를 찾는 사람들은 프랑 크리스마스 카드를 주었다. ⓬ 이것을 액자로 만들거나, 크리스마스 트리 또는 특별한 받침대에 진열하고, 가정의 찬장에 어울리는 벽지로 만들기도 했다. ⓭ 다른 사람들은 조금 더 평범하고 효율적인 상품으로 그들의 관심을 돌렸고, 집안일을 줄여주는 편리한 가정용품들은 엄마들과 아내들에게 받아들여질 만한 상품이 되었다. ⓮ 부모님, 이모들, 그리고 다른 친절한 어른들은 아이의 저축습관을 장려하기 위한 선물로 금 조각 또는 2달러 지폐에 항상 의지할 수 있었다.
⓯ 그러나 새로운 시장만이 크리스마스 선물의 중요성을 결정지었다고 생각하는 것은 잘못된 일일 것이다.

어휘

commerce n. 통상, 무역 **consumerism** n. 소비자 중심주의, 컨슈머리즘 (건전한 경제의 기초로서 소비의 확대를 주장함) **charity** n. 자선(행위) **frontier** n. (특히 19세기 미국 서부 개척지의) 변경(邊境) **of necessity** 필연적으로, 당연히 **store-bought** a. 상점에서 산, 기성품의 **fondness** n. 아주 좋아함, 애호; 기호, 취미 **knit** v. 뜨개질을 하다, 뜨다 **stuff** v. 채워 넣다 **lace** v. 끈으로 묶다 **stiched** v. 바느질하다, 꿰매다 **whittle** v. (나무 등을) 깎아서 만들다 **carve** v. 조각하다, 깎아서 만들다 **market-oriented** a. 시장 지향의 **homey** a. 가정과 같은; 마음 편한, 즐거운 **feast** n. 향연, 잔치; 기쁨, 즐거움 **broadan** v. 넓히다 **extravagant** a. 낭비하는, 사치스러운 **oddity** n. 별난 물건, 이상한 일 **memento** n. (사람·장소를 기억하기 위한) 기념품 **gimcrack** a. n. 값싸고 번지르르한 (물건), 허울만 좋은(물건) **vogue** n. 유행 **token** n. 표시, 징표 **goodwill** n. 친선, 호의 **rack** n. 받침대, 선반 **prosaic** a. 평범한, 단조로운; 상상력이 없는 **well-meaning** a. 선의의, 사람이 좋은 **erroneous** a. 잘못된, 틀린

32 끝장편입 독해유형편 Top 20

marketplace alone determined the importance of Christmas gifts. ⓰ Several studies of gift-giving in the twentieth century suggest that the custom helps chart and establish hierarchies of social relationships. ⓱ Gift acts as tangible evidence of ties between and among individuals. ⓲ Those who participate in a gift transaction determine the worth of an item.

Which of the following would be best for the title?
다음 중 이 글의 제목으로 가장 적절한 것은 무엇인가?

✓ ① A History of Christmas Gifts in America
  미국의 크리스마스 선물의 역사
② The Best Gifts for Your Children
  자녀를 위한 최고의 선물
③ Why You Should Make Your Own Christmas Gift
  크리스마스 선물을 직접 만들어야 하는 이유
④ The Consumer Pattern in the Frontier Regions
  변경 지역의 소비자 패턴

해석 ⓰ 20세기에 선물 증여에 대한 몇몇 연구들은 그 관습이 사회적 관계의 위계 질서를 세우고 확립하는 데 도움이 된다는 것을 보여준다. ⓱ 선물은 개인 사이의 유대를 보여주는 명백한 증거로 작용한다. ⓲ 선물을 주고받는데 참여하는 사람들이 물건의 가치를 결정한다.

해설 첫 문장에서 미국 경제 특징으로 크리스마스 선물의 관행을 결정지었을 것이란 주제문 언급 이후 19세기 초부터 20세기까지 선물을 주는 것에 대한 개념의 변화를 설명하고 있다. 따라서 글의 제목은 ①이 가장 적절하다.

어휘 **hierarchy** n. 계층, 체계 **tangible** a. 분명히 실재하는, 유형의 **transaction** n. 거래, 매매, 처리

정답 및 해설

025 ④   2019학년도 아주대학교 인문계 A형 47번

A ❶ The first brains appeared / on earth / about 500 million years ago, / spent (a leisurely 430 million years) evolving into the brains of the earliest primates and ❷ (another 70 million years) evolving into the brains of the first protohumans. ❸ Then, / something happened and the soon-to-be-human brain experienced an unprecedented growth spurt (that more than doubled its mass / in a little over two million years), ❹ transforming it / from the one-and-a-quarter-pound brain of Homo habilis to the nearly three-pound brain of Homo sapiens.

B ❺ Now if you were put on a hot-fudge diet and managed to double your mass / in a very short time, / we would not expect all of your various body parts to share equally in the gain. Your belly and buttocks would probably be the major recipients / of newly acquired flab, / while your tongue and toe would remain relatively svelte and unaffected. ❼ Similarly, the dramatic increase (in the size of the human brain) did not democratically double / the mass of every part / so that modern people ended up with new brains (that were structurally identical / to the old ones, only bigger). ❽ Rather a disproportionate share of the growth / centered on a particular part of the brain : (known as the frontal lobe).

C ❾ Scientists noticed / that although patients (with frontal lobe damage) often performed well on standard intelligence tests, / they showed severe impairment / on any test (that involved planning). ❿ They even found it practically impossible / to say what they would do later that afternoon. ⓫ This finding helps us assume / that the frontal lobe is a time machine (that allows each of us to vacate the present and : experience the future / before it happens). ⓬ No other animals have a frontal lobe / quite like ours,

해석

A ❶ 최초의 뇌는 약 5억 년 전에 지구에 나타났고, 4억 3천만 년 동안 서서히 초기 영장류의 뇌로 진화했으며, ❷ 그로부터 7천만 년을 더 진화하여 최초의 원인(原人)의 뇌로 진화했다. ❸ 그 뒤에, 어떤 일이 일어났고, 곧 인류의 뇌가 될 원인의 뇌는 200만년이 조금 넘는 시간 동안 전례 없는 급격한 성장을 경험하면서 부피가 두 배 이상 늘어났는데, ❹ 이것은 1.25파운드였던 호모 하빌리스의 뇌에서 거의 3파운드인 호모 사피엔스의 뇌로 변화시켰다.

B ❺ 만약 핫퍼지를 주식으로 하면서 매우 짧은 시간 안에 몸의 질량 두 배 늘린다면, 우리는 당신의 다양한 신체 기관의 부피가 똑같이 늘어날 거라고 예측하지 않을 것이다. ❻ 새로 얻은 군살은 아마도 배와 엉덩이에 주로 몰릴 것인 반면에, 혀와 발가락은 상대적으로 날씬한 상태 그대로 있을 것이다. ❼ 마찬가지로, 인간의 뇌 크기가 급격하게 커졌다고 해서 현대인들의 새로운 뇌가 구조적으로는 이전의 뇌와 완전히 똑같고 크기만 커지도록 모든 부분의 부피가 평등하게 두 배로 늘어난 것은 아니었다. ❽ 오히려 전두엽으로 알려진 뇌의 특정 부분에 집중된 불균형적인 성장을 했다.

C ❾ 과학자들은 전두엽 손상이 있는 환자들이 종종 표준 지능 검사에서는 좋은 결과를 보이지만 계획을 세우는 것과 관련된 검사에서는 심각한 장애를 보였다는 사실을 발견했다. ❿ 그들은 심지어 그 환자들이 그날 오후 늦게 무엇을 할 것인지 말하는 것도 사실상 불가능하다는 것도 알았다. ⓫ 이러한 발견은 우리가 전두엽을 우리들 각자가 현재로부터 떠나 미래를 미리 경험할 수 있게 해주는 타임머신이라고 추측하게 한다. ⓬ 다른 어떤 동물도 인간과 비슷한 전두엽을 갖고 있지 않으며, 인간이 미래를 생각하는 유일한 동물인 것도 이러한 이유 때문이다.

어휘

leisurely a. 한가한, 느긋한, 여유 있는 **evolve** v. 서서히 발전하다, 진화하다 **primate** n. 영장류의 동물 **protohuman** n. 원인(原人) **unprecedented** a. 전례 없는, 미증유의, 새로운 **spurt** n. 분출, 뿜어 나옴; 급등 **mass** n. 부피, 크기, 질량 **transform** v. 변형시키다, (성질·기능·구조 등을) 바꾸다 **fudge** n. 퍼지(설탕, 버터, 우유로 만든 연한 사탕), 임시방편 **various** a. 가지가지의, 여러 가지의 **buttock** n. 둔부 **recipient** n. 어떤 것을 받는 사람, 수령인 **flab** n. 군살 **structurally** ad. 구조상, 구조적으로 **identical** a. 아주 동일한, 같은, 일치하는 **disproportionate** a. 불균형의 **frontal lobe** (대뇌의) 전두엽(前頭葉) **notice** v. 알아채다, 인지하다 **impairment** n. 장애 **involve** v. 수반하다, 포함하다, 연루시키다 **assume** v. 추정하다, 추측하다, 가정하다 **vacate** v. 비우다, 퇴거하다, 떠나가다 **conjure** v. (마음에) 그려내다, 생각해 내다

/ which is why [we are the only animal (that thinks about the future
as we do.)] ⑱ If the story of the frontal lobe tells us (how people
conjure their imaginary tomorrows), / it doesn't tell us why.

Which of the following is the best title for the above passage?
다음 중 위 글의 제목으로 가장 적절한 것은?

① The Steady Evolution of the Human Brain
   인간의 뇌의 꾸준한 진화
② The Importance of Brain Size
   뇌의 크기의 중요성
③ Amazing Human Brain Power Demystified
   놀라운 인간 두뇌의 신비화
✓ Future-Planning Brain Areas
   미래를 계획하는 뇌의 영역
⑤ Impact of Brain Damage on Time-Concept
   뇌 손상이 시간개념에 미치는 영향

해석 ⑱ 전두엽에 관한 이야기는 우리에게 사람들이 상상 속의 내일을 어떻게 떠올리는지를 말해주지만, 그 이유는 말해주지 않는다.

해설 A 단락에서는 인류의 변화와 뇌 부피의 변화로 글을 설명하며 B 단락에서는 몸무게처럼 뇌도 비례하여 커지지 않았으며 전두엽이 비대하게 커졌음을 말한다. 여기서 글의 핵심 소재가 나온 것이며 마지막 C 단락에서는 전두엽이 미래를 생각하는 역할론을 설명하고 있다. 따라서 정답은 ④이 가장 적절하다.

*주장 → 논증

어휘 conjure v. (마음에) 그려내다, 생각해 내다

정답 및 해설

026 ④ 2019학년도 홍익대학교 서울 인문계 A형 37번

❶ To go into solitude, a man needs to retire as much from his chamber as from society. ❷ I am not solitary whilst I read and write, though nobody is with me. ❸ But if a man would be alone, let him look at the stars. ❹ The rays that come from those heavenly worlds will separate between him and what he touches. ❺ One might think the atmosphere was made transparent with this design, to give man, in the heavenly bodies, the perpetual presence of the sublime. ❻ Seen in the streets of cities, how great they are! ❼ If the stars should appear one night in a thousand years, how would men believe and adore; and preserve for many generations the remembrance of the city of God which had been shown! ❽ But every night come out these envoys of beauty, and light the universe with their admonishing smile. ❾ The stars awaken a certain reverence, because though always present, they are inaccessible; **but all natural objects make a kindred impression, when the mind is open to their influence.** ❿ Nature never wears a mean appearance. ⓫ Neither does the wisest man extort her secret, and lose his curiosity by finding out all her perfection. ⓬ Nature never became a toy to a wise spirit. ⓭ The flowers, the animals, the mountains, reflected the wisdom of his best hour, as much as they had delighted the simplicity of his childhood. ⓮ When we speak of nature in this manner, we have a distinct but most poetical sense in the mind. ⓯ We mean the integrity of impression made by manifold natural objects. ⓰ It is this which distinguishes the stick of timber of the wood-cutter from the tree of the poet. ⓱ The charming landscape which I saw this morning is indubitably made up of some twenty or thirty farms. ⓲ Miller owns this field, Locke that, and Manning the woodland beyond. ⓳ But none of them owns the landscape. ⓴ There is a property in

해석

❶ 고독에 빠지기 위해 인간은 사회에서 은퇴하는 것만큼 자신의 방에서도 은퇴할 필요가 있다. ❷ 비록 내가 책을 읽고 쓰는 동안 내 곁에 아무도 없어도 고독하지 않다. ❸ 그러나 만약 어떤 사람이 혼자 있다면, 그 사람에게 별을 보게 하라. ❹ 천국에서 나오는 그 빛은 그 사람과 그 사람이 만지는 것들 사이를 갈라놓을 것이다. ❺ 사람들은 천체들 속에서 영원한 존재의 숭고함을 인간에게 주려는 이러한 의도로 공기가 투명해졌다고 생각할 수도 있다. ❻ 도시의 거리에서 바라보면 별들은 얼마나 멋있는가! ❼ 만약 그 별들이 천년 만에 하룻밤만 나타난다면 사람들은 어떻게 믿음과 동경심을 갖고 신이 보여준 신의 도시에 대한 기억을 수세대 동안 보존하겠는가! ❽ 그러나 이 미(美)의 특사들은 매일 밤 세상에 나와서 꾸짖는 미소를 지으며 우주를 비추고 있다. ❾ 별들은 언제나 존재하지만 접근할 수 없어서 어떠한 경외감을 불러일으킨다. ❿ **그러나 모든 자연의 사물들도 그것들이 주는 영향력에 마음을 열면 비슷한 감동을 준다.** ⓫ 자연은 결코 인색한 모습을 보이지 않는다. ⓬ 현자도 또한 자연의 비밀을 억지로 알아내지 않고, 자연의 모든 완벽함을 다 발견해 호기심을 잃지도 않는다. ⓭ 자연은 한 번도 현자(賢者)의 장난감이 된 적이 없었다. ⓮ 꽃과 동물, 그리고 산이 현자의 유년기의 순박함을 기쁘게 했듯이, 현자의 전성기 때의 지혜를 반영했다. ⓯ 우리가 이런 식으로 자연에 대해 말할 때, 우리는 뚜렷하지만 가장 시적인 감각을 가지고 있다. ⓰ 다양 자연의 물체들이 주는 깊은 인상의 완전무결함을 뜻하는 것이다. ⓱ 이것이 바로 나무꾼의 나뭇가지와 시인의 나뭇가지를 구분해준다. ⓲ 오늘 아침 내가 보았던 매력적인 풍경은 의심할 여지없이 20~30개의 농장으로 이루어져 있다. ⓳ 이 밭은 밀러(Miller) 소유이고, 저 밭은 로크(Locke) 소유이고, 그 너머의 삼림지대는 매닝(Manning)이 소유하고 있다. ⓴ 그러나 그들 중 누구도 이 풍경을 소유하지 않는다. ㉑ 지평선에는 자신의 눈으로 모든 부분을 통합할 수 있는 사람, 즉 시인 외에는 어느 누구도 가질 수 없는 땅이 있다.

어휘

solitude n. 고독, 외로움 retire v. 은퇴하다; 물러나다 chamber n. (집의) 방, (특히) 침실 solitary a. 고독한, 혼자의 ray n. 광선, 빛 atmosphere n. (지구의) 대기 transparent a. 투명한 heavenly body 천체 perpetual a. (오래 동안) 끊임없이 계속되는 sublime a. 숭고[장엄, 웅장, 장대]한 adore v. 숭배하다; 흠모하다, 몹시 좋아하다 remembrance 추모, 추도 envoy n. 사절, 사신, 특사 admonish v. 타이르다, 훈계하다 reverence n. 숭상, 존경 inaccessible a. 접근하기 어려운, 이용할 수 없는 make an impression 느낌을 주다, 깊은 인상을 남기다 kindred n. 일가친척 a. 비슷한, 동의의, 관련된 mean a. 비열한, 상스러운 extort v. (남으로부터) 빼앗다, 강탈하다 simplicity n. 천진난만 distinct a. 뚜렷한; 독특한 poetical a. 시적인, 이상화된 integrity n. 완전무결한 상태, 흠 없는 상태 manifold a. 다양한, 많은, 다수의 wood-cutter n. 나무꾼; 목판화가 indubitably ad. 확실하게, 의심할 여지없이

the horizon [which no man has / but he (whose eye can integrate all the parts), that is, the poet]. ② This is the best part of these men's farms, / yet to this / their warranty-deeds give no title.

Which of the following is the purpose of the passage?
다음 중 이 글의 목적은 무엇인가?

① to inform his readers of the hidden rule of the heavenly bodies
   독자들에게 천체의 숨겨진 법칙을 알리기 위해
② to persuade his readers to go into a quiet retirement
   독자들을 조용히 은퇴하라고 설득하기 위해
③ to encourage his readers to participate in an environmental movement
   독자들에게 환경운동에 참여하라고 권하기 위해
✓ to remind his readers of the wonderful values of nature
   독자들에게 자연이 지닌 놀라운 가치를 상기시키기 위해

해석 ② 이 땅은 이 사람들의 밭들 중 가장 좋은 부분이지만, 그들의 토지보증서는 이 땅에 대한 어떤 권리도 그들에게 주지 않는다.

해설 고독을 위해 혼자 있으려 하는 사람에게 자연의 별을 볼 것을 권장하며 예찬을 시작한다. ⑩번 문장부터는 별 이외 다른 자연들의 예찬을 이어나가고 있다. 따라서 ④이 목적으로 가장 적절하다.

어휘 horizon n. 지평선, 수평선; 한계, 범위 integrate v. 통합하다, 합치다
warranty-deed n. 하자 담보 증서

027 ①

2019학년도 건국대학교 인문·예체능계 A형 40번

❶ Astronomers / all over the world / were waiting / in excitement / as August 1993 approached. ❷ Mars Observer, (the American spacecraft), was scheduled to move into orbit / around Mars / and begin sending new information / back to Earth. ❸ In addition to mapping the planet / , Mars Observer was going to study / the Martian atmosphere and surface. ❹ Unfortunately, / scientists lost contact with Mars Observer / on August 24. ❺ The Mars Observer mission, (which cost $845 million), failed.

❻ In contrast, / the United States' previous mission to Mars was a great success. ❼ In 1976, two American spacecraft landed on Mars / in order to search for signs of life. ❽ The tests (that the Viking landers performed) had negative results. ❾ However, scientists still had questions / about our close neighbor / in space. ❿ They wanted to investigate further / into the possibility of life on Mars. ⓫ This was the purpose of the Mars Observer mission.

⓬ Scientists were satisfied with the Viking mission. ⓭ The two sites (where the spacecraft landed) provided safe landing places, but they were not particularly interesting locations. ⓮ Scientists believe : there are other areas on Mars [that are similar to specific places on Earth (that support life)]. ⓯ For example, an area in Antarctica, southern Victoria Land, (which is not covered by ice), resembles an area on Mars. ⓰ In the dry valleys of southern Victoria Land, / the temperature averages / below zero, / yet biologists found simple life forms / in rocks and frozen lakes. ⓱ Perhaps this is also true of places on Mars.

⓲ Scientists want another investigation of Mars. ⓳ They want to map the planet's surface and : land a spacecraft / in a more promising location. ⓴ They want to search for fossils, / the ancient remains of life. ㉑ If life ever existed on Mars, scientists believe / that future missions might find records of it / under sand, / or in

해석

❶ 전 세계의 천문학자들은 1993년 8월이 다가오자 흥분한 마음으로 기다리고 있었다. ❷ 미국의 우주선인 마스 옵서버(Mars Observer)가 화성의 주위 궤도로 이동해서 새로운 지구에 정보를 보내기 시작할 예정이었다. ❸ 화성의 지도를 제작하는 것 이외에도, 마스 옵서버는 화성의 대기와 표면을 연구할 예정이었다. ❹ 안타깝게도 과학자들은 8월 24일에 마스 옵서버와의 연락이 끊기고 말았다. ❺ 8억 4천 5백만 달러의 비용이 들었던 마스 옵서버의 미션은 결국 실패해 버렸다.

❻ 대조적으로, 이전의 미국의 화성 탐사는 아주 성공적이었다. ❼ 1976년, 두 대의 미국 우주선이 생명의 흔적을 찾기 위해 화성에 착륙했다. ❽ 바이킹 착륙선들이 수행한 실험은 부정적인 결과를 가져왔다. ❾ 하지만, 과학자들은 여전히 우리와 가까이 있는 이웃 행성에 대해 의문을 가지고 있었다. ❿ 그들은 화성에서 생명체가 존재할 가능성에 대한 좀 더 자세히 조사하기를 원했다. ⓫ 이것이 마스 옵서버 임무의 목적이었다.

⓬ 과학자들은 바이킹호의 미션에 불만족했다. ⓭ 우주선이 착륙했던 두 장소는 안전한 착륙지를 제공했지만, 특별히 흥미로운 장소는 아니었다. ⓮ 과학자들은 생명체를 지탱하는 지구의 특정한 장소와 유사한 다른 지역들이 화성에 있다고 믿는다. ⓯ 예를 들어, 얼음으로 뒤덮여 있지 않은 남극의 한 지역인 남부 빅토리아랜드는 화성의 한 지역과 유사하다. ⓰ 남부 빅토리아랜드의 건조한 계곡에서는 평균기온이 영하이지만, 생물학자들은 바위와 얼어붙은 호수에서 단순한 생명체들을 발견했다. ⓱ 아마도 화성에 있는 지역도 이와 같을 것이다.

⓲ 과학자들은 화성에 대한 또 다른 조사를 원한다. ⓳ 그들은 화성 표면의 지도를 제작하고 더 가능성 있는 장소에 우주선을 착륙시키길 원한다. ⓴ 그들은 생명의 오래된 유해인 화석을 연구하기를 원한다. ㉑ 생명이 화성에 존재했었다면, 과학자들은 미래의 화성탐사가 모래 아래에서 또는 얼음에서 그것의 기록을 찾을지도 모른다고 생각한다.

어휘

astronomer n. 천문학자 spacecraft n. 우주선 be scheduled to ~할 예정이다 orbit n. 궤도 lander n. 상륙자; (달 등에의) 착륙선 in order to ~하기 위해서 investigate v. 조사하다, 살피다 Antarctica n. 남극대륙 valley n. 계곡, 골짜기 promising a. 유망한, 촉망되는 fossil n. 화석

the ice. ㉒ They are very disappointed / in the failure of the Mars
           S   V   C
Observer mission / and want to start a new mission.
                      V   O

위 글의 제목으로 가장 적절한 것은?

☑ Missions to Find Life on Mars
   화성에서 생명체를 찾기 위한 탐사
② The Disaster of Mars Observer
   화성 관찰자의 재난
③ Astronomers' Challenge In Mars
   화성에서의 천문학자들의 도전
④ How Earth and Mars are Similar
   지구와 화성의 유사한 점
⑤ Future Spacecraft for Space Travel
   우주여행을 위한 미래의 우주선

해석 ㉒ 과학자들은 마스 옵서버의 탐사 실패에 대해서 매우 실망했지만 새로운 탐사를 시작하기를 원한다.

해설 미국 화성 탐사선 마스 옵서버의 실패 소식과 함께 과거 화성 탐사의 성공과 실패 사례를 설명하고 있다. 마지막 분단에서는 지속해서 화성 탐사를 기대하고 있다고 말하고 있다. 따라서 ①이 가장 적절하다.

028 ① 2019학년도 한국항공대학교 인문계 19번

글의 주제 1
① The term normal or healthy / can be defined / in two ways. ② Firstly, [from the standpoint of a functioning society], one can call a person normal or healthy / if he is able to fulfill the social role / (he is to take / in that given society). ③ More concretely, / this means that [he is able to work / in the fashion (which is required / in that particular society)], and furthermore / [that he is able to participate in the reproduction of society (that he can raise a family)]. ④ Secondly, / from the standpoint of the individual, / we look upon health or normalcy (as) the optimum of growth and happiness of the individual. ⑤ If the structure of a given society were / such that it offered the optimum possibility / for individual happiness, / both viewpoints would coincide.

글의 주제 2
⑥ However, this is not the case / in most societies (we know), / including our own. ⑦ Although they differ / in the degree (to which they promote the aims of individual growth), there is a discrepancy (between the aims of the smooth functioning of society and of the full development of the individual.) ⑧ This fact makes it imperative to differentiate sharply / between the two concepts of health. ⑨ The one is governed / by social necessities, the other / by values and norms (concerning the aim of individual existence). ⑩ Unfortunately, this differentiation is often neglected. ⑪ Most psychiatrists take the structure of their own society / (so) much (for granted) (that) to them / the person (who is not well adapted) assumes / the stigma of being less valuable. ⑫ On the other hand, / the well-adapted person / is supposed to be the more valuable person / in terms of a scale of human values. ⑬ If we differentiate the two concepts of normal and neurotic, we come to the following conclusion: ⑭ the person (who is normal in terms of being well adapted) is often less healthy / than the neurotic person / in terms of human values.

해석

❶ '정상적인'이나 '건강한'이라는 용어는 두 가지 방법으로 정의될 수 있다. ❷ 첫번째로, 기능적 사회의 관점에서, 어떤 사람이 주어진 그 사회에서 해야 하는 사회적인 역할을 수행할 수 있다면 그 사람 '정상적이다' 또는 '건강하다'고 부를 수 있다. ❸ 좀 더 구체적으로 말하면 이것은 그가 그 특정한 사회에서 요구되는 방식으로 일할 수 있고 더 나아가 그가 가족을 부양할 수 있는 사회를 재생산하는 데 참여할 수 있다는 것을 뜻한다. ❹ 둘째로, 개인의 관점에서, 우리는 건강이나 정상성을 개인의 성장과 행복이 최적화되어 있는 상태라고 본다. ❺ 만약 주어진 사회의 구조가 개인의 행복을 위한 최적의 가능성을 제공한다면, 이 두 가지 관점은 일치할 것이다.

❻ 하지만, 이것은 우리 사회를 포함해 우리가 알고 있는 대부분의 사회에서는 해당되지 않는다. ❼ 개인의 성장이라는 목표를 촉진하는 정도가 사회마다 다르긴 해도, 사회의 원활한 기능이라는 목표와 개인의 완전한 발달이라는 목표 사이에는 차이가 존재한다. ❽ 이러한 사실로부터 건강의 두 개념을 명확하게 구별해야 한다는 것이 분명해진다. ❾ 하나는 사회적 필요에 의해 지배되고, 다른 하나는 개인의 존재 목적과 관련된 가치와 규범을 따른다. ❿ 안타깝게도, 이러한 구별은 종종 무시된다. ⓫ 대부분의 정신과 의사들은 그들 자신의 사회적 구조를 너무나 당연하게 여기기 때문에, 그 구조에 잘 적응하지 못한 사람은 가치가 떨어진다는 오명을 쓰게 되는 반면에, ⓬ 잘 적응한 사람은 인간 가치의 척도에서 볼 때 더 가치 있는 사람으로 여겨진다. ⓭ 만약 우리가 정상적인 것과 신경증적인 것의 두 개념을 구별한다면, 우리는 다음과 같은 결론에 도달한다. ⓮ 잘 적응했다는 측면에서 볼 때 정상적인 사람이 인간적 가치의 관점에서 보면 신경질적인 사람보다 종종 덜 건강하다는 것이다.

어휘

standpoint n. 견지, 관점 **concretely** ad. 구체적으로, 명확하게 **normalcy** n. 정상임, 정상 상태 **optimum** n. 최적, 조건, 최적도 **coincide** v. 일치하다 **promote** v. 촉진하다, 증진하다, 장려하다 **discrepancy** n. 불일치, 모순 **imperative** a. 피할 수 없는, 절대 필요한 **differentiate** v. 구별하다, 구별짓다 **psychiatrist** n. 정신과 의사 **stigma** n. 낙인 **neurotic** a. 신경증에 걸린

⑮ Often he is well adapted / only at the expense of having given up his self / in order to become more or less the person / (he believes) he is expected to be. ⑯ All genuine individuality and spontaneity may have been lost. ⑰ On the other hand, the neurotic person can be characterized / as somebody (who was not ready to surrender completely / in the battle for his self). ⑱ To be sure, / his attempt (to save his individual self) was not successful, and instead of expressing his self productively / he sought salvation / through neurotic symptoms and / by withdrawing into a phantasy life. ⑲ Nevertheless, from the standpoint of human values, / he is less crippled / than the kind of normal person (who has lost his individuality altogether).

Which one is the above passage mainly about?
위 글의 주제로 가장 적절한 것은?

☑ ① The discrepancy between the two definitions of health, and the significance of the neurotic.
건강에 대한 두 정의의 불일치와 신경증 환자의 의의

② The malfunction of the neurotic in comparison with the healthy and the normal.
건강한 사람들 및 정상적인 사람들과 비교했을 때의 신경증 환자들의 기능부전

③ The harmonious relationship of the normal, the healthy, and the neurotic in a normal society.
정상적 사회에서 정상적인 사람들, 건강한 사람들, 신경증 환자들 간의 조화로운 관계

④ The reductionism of the unhealthy and the neurotic in relation to individuality in an abnormal society.
비정상적 사회의 개성과 관련된 건강하지 못한 사람들과 신경증 환자들의 환원주의

해석
⑮ 종종, 그는 자신에게 기대되는 바라고 자신이 믿는 그런 사람이 되고자, 자기를 포기하는 대가를 치르고서 비로소 잘 적응하고 있는 것이다. ⑯ 모든 진정한 개성과 자발성을 잃어버렸을지도 모른다. ⑰ 반면에, 신경증적인 사람은 자신을 위한 전투에서 완전히 항복할 준비가 되지 않은 사람이라고 특징지어질 수 있다. ⑱ 확실히, 자신의 개인적인 자아를 구하려는 그의 시도는 성공하지 못했고, 그는 그의 자아를 생산적으로 표현하는 대신에 신경증 증세들을 통해 그리고 환상 속의 삶으로 빠져들면서 구원을 얻으려고 했다. ⑲ 그럼에도 불구하고, 인간적 가치의 관점에서 볼 때 그는 자신의 개성을 완전히 상실해 버린 그런 종류의 정상적인 사람보다 덜 불구이다.

해설
건강의 두 가지 관점을 소개하고 사회의 구조가 개인 행복을 위한 최적의 가능성을 제공하는 구조라면 관점은 일치한다고 말한다. 하지만 ⑥번 문장부터 대부분의 사회에서는 그렇지 않으며 '개인 성장'과 '사회의 원활한 기능'이라는 목표 사이 불일치가 존재함을 말하고 있다. 이런 관점에서 정신병리학에서 말하는 '건강한' 사람과 '그렇지 못한' 사람 사이의 개념도 설명을 이어가는 글이다. 따라서 정답은 ①이 가장 적절하다.

*주장 → 역접 → 논증

어휘
at the expense of ~을 희생하면서, ~을 잃어가면서 genuine a. 참된, 진짜의 spontaneity n. 자발성 salvation n. 구조, 구원 withdraw v. 움츠리다, 물러나다 crippled a. 불구의

029 ② 2019학년도 한국항공대학교 인문계 34번

글의 주제

❶ The doctrine of original sin is the oldest manifestation of the rotten-to-the-core dogma, but such thinking has not died out in our democratic, secular state. ❷ Freud dragged this doctrine into twentieth-century psychology, defining all of civilization (including modern morality, science, religion, and technological progress) as just an elaborate defense against basic conflicts over infantile sexuality and aggression. ❸ We "repress" these conflicts because of the unbearable anxiety they cause and this anxiety is transmuted into the energy that generates civilization. ❹ So the reason I am sitting in front of my computer writing this preface — rather than running out to rape and kill — is that I am "compensated," zipped up and successfully defending myself against underlying savage impulses. ❺ Freud's philosophy, as bizarre as it sounds when laid out so starkly, finds its way into daily psychological and psychiatric practice, wherein patients scour their past for the negative impulses and events that have formed their identities. ❻ Thus the competitiveness of Bill Gates is really his desire to outdo his father, ❼ and Princess Diana's opposition to landmines was merely the outcome of sublimating her murderous hatred for Prince Charles and the other royals. ❽ The rotten-to-the-core doctrine also pervades the understanding of human nature in the arts and social sciences.

❾ Just one example of thousands is *No Ordinary Time*, a gripping history of Franklin and Eleanor Roosevelt written by Doris Kearns Goodwin, one of the great living political scientists. ❿ Musing on the question of why Eleanor dedicated so much of her life to helping people who were black, poor, or disabled, Goodwin decides that it was "to compensate for her mother's narcissism and her father's alcoholism." ⓫ Nowhere does Goodwin consider

해석

❶ 원죄설은 부패한 교리의 가장 오래된 표현이지만, 그러한 생각은 민주적이고 세속적인 우리 국가에서 완전히 사라지지 않았다. ❷ 프로이트(Freud)는 이 원죄설을 20세기 심리학으로 끌어들여 모든 문명(현대의 도덕, 과학, 종교, 그리고 기술적 진보를 포함한)을 유아기의 성욕과 공격성에 관한 기본적 갈등들에 대한 정교한 방어기제라고 정의하였다. ❸ 우리는 이러한 갈등들이 유발하는 견딜 수 없는 불안으로 인해 우리는 이 갈등들을 "억제"하고, 이 불안은 문명을 발생시키는 에너지로 바뀐다. ❹ 그러므로 내가 지금 밖으로 뛰어나가 약탈과 살인을 하기보다 컴퓨터 앞에 앉아 서문을 쓰고 있는 이유는, 바깥세상에 대해서는 깜깜한 채 마음 밑바닥의 야만적 충동들로부터 맞서 나 자신을 지켜냄으로써 "보상받고" 있기 때문이다.

❺ 프로이트의 철학은, 너무 적나라하게 보여지면 이상하게 들리지만, 일상적인 심리학 및 정신의학적인 실천으로 길을 찾아가고, 그 일상적 실제에서 환자들은 그들의 과거를 샅샅이 파헤쳐서 그들의 정체성을 형성한 부정적인 충동들과 사건들을 찾아낸다. ❻ 그러므로 빌 게이츠(Bill Gates)의 경쟁력은 바로 자신의 아버지를 능가하려는 그의 욕망이고, ❼ 다이애나 왕세자비(Princess Diana)의 지뢰에 대한 반대는 단지 찰스(Charles) 왕세자와 다른 왕족들에 대한 그녀의 살인적인 증오를 승화시킨 결과일 뿐이다. ❽ 속까지 부패한 원죄설은 예술과 사회과학에서도 인간의 본성에 대한 이해에 만연하다.

❾ 수천개의 예시들 중의 하나는 현존하는 위대한 정치학자 중 한 명인 도리스 컨스 굿윈(Doris Kearns Goodwin)이 쓴 프랭클린 루즈벨트(Franklin Roosevelt)와 엘리너 프랭클린(Eleanor Roosevelt) 부부에 관한 흥미로운 역사인 『비범한 시간(No Ordinary Time)』이다. ❿ 엘리너가 왜 흑인, 가난한 사람들, 장애인을 돕는 데 인생의 많은 부분을 헌신했는지에 대해 깊게 생각하다 굿윈은 그것은 "어머니의 나르시시즘과 아버지의 알코올 중독을 보상하기 위한 것"이었다고 결론냈다. ⓫ 책의 어떤 부분에서도 굿윈은 엘리너 루즈벨트가 마음 속으로 미덕을 추구했을 가능성을 고려하지 않는다.

어휘

doctrine n. 교리; 신조 manifestation n. 징후, 발현, 표현, 명시 rotten-to-the-core a. 속속들이 썩은; 완전히 타락한 dogma n. 교의, 교조 secular a. 비종교적인, 세속의 infantile a. 유아기의 aggression n. 공격성 repress v. 억압하다 transmute v. 바꾸다, 변화시키다 zip up 지퍼로 잠그다 rape v. 약탈하다 starkly ad. 적나라하게 bizarre a. 기괴한 psychiatric a. 정신과의, 정신의학의 scour v. 샅샅이 뒤지다 outdo v. ~를 능가하다 landmine n. 지뢰 sublimate v. 승화하다 pervade v. 널리 퍼지다 gripping a. 주의를 끄는, 시선을 사로잡는 muse on ~을 회상하다

정답 및 해설

해석

⑪ the possibility (that deep down,) / Eleanor Roosevelt was pursuing virtue.) ⑫ Motivations (like exercising fairness or pursuing duty) are ruled out / (as) fundamental; / ⑬ there must be some covert, negative motivation (that underpins goodness / if the analysis is to be academically respectable.)
⑭ I cannot say this too strongly: / ⑮ In spite of the widespread acceptance / of the rotten-to-the-core dogma / in the religious and secular world, / ⑯ there is not a shred of evidence (that strength and virtue are derived from negative motivation.) ⑰ I believe / that evolution has favored both good and bad traits, and any number of adaptive roles in the world have selected / for morality, cooperation, altruism, and goodness, / just as any number have also selected for murder, theft, self-seeking, and terrorism. ⑱ This dual-aspect premise is the cornerstone / of the second half of this book. ⑲ Authentic happiness comes / from identifying and cultivating your most fundamental strengths and using them every day / in work, love, play, and parenting.

What would be the best title of the passage above?
본문의 제목으로 가장 적절한 것은?

① The hidden power of negative motivation
부정적 동기의 숨겨진 힘
✓ Dual aspects of human nature
인간 본성의 이중적 측면
③ The illusion of pursuing virtuous behaviors
고결한 행동을 추구한다는 환상
④ Authentic happiness derived from negative motivation
부정적인 동기에서 유래하는 참된 행복

해석

⑫ 공정함을 실천하고 의무를 다하려는 동기들은 근본적인 동기로서는 배제되어 있다. ⑬ 만약 그 분석이 학문적으로 존경받으려면 선함을 뒷받침하는 어떤 은밀하고 부정적인 동기가 반드시 있어야 한다.
⑭ 나는 다음과 같이 아무리 강조해도 지나치지 않다. ⑮ 속까지 부패한 원죄설의 교리가 종교 세계와 세속적인 세계에서 널리 받아들여지고 있음에도 불구하고, ⑯ 강점과 미덕이 부정적 동기에서 나온다는 증거는 조금도 없다. ⑰ 나는 진화가 선한 특성과 악한 특성 모두에 유리하게 작용해왔으며, 이 세상에는 살인, 절도, 이기주의, 테러리즘 등을 선택해온 적응적인 역할들도 그만큼 존재한다고 믿는다. ⑱ 이 이중적인 전제가 이 책 후반부의 초석이다. ⑲ 진정한 행복은 여러분의 가장 근본적인 강점들을 찾아내고 함양하는 것과 그것들을 매일 일, 사랑, 놀이, 자녀양육에 활용하는 것에서 생겨난다.

해설

글의 시작에서부터 속속들이 썩은 교리인 원죄설이 우리 사회에서 완전히 사멸하지 않았다고 말하는 부분에서 비판적 시각을 알 수 있다. 그리고 그 원죄설을 이어받은 프로이트 이론을 통해 인간의 본성적 측면(행동의 동기)을 설명하고 있다. ⑧번 문장에서 예술과 사회과학에서도 잘못된 원죄설(프로이트 이론도 마찬가지)이 널리 스며들어 있음을 비판하며, 이어지는 ⑨번 문장에서 여러 예시를 소개하며 수용되고 있는 인간 행동의 동기를 파악하는데 오류를 지적한다. 따라서 정답은 ② '인간 본성의 이중적 측면'이 가장 적절하다.

*주장 → 논증

어휘

deep down 마음속으로는, 내심 rule out 배제하다 covert a. 비밀스러운, 은밀한 underpin v. 뒷받침하다, 근거를 대다 shred n. 소량 altruism n. 이타주의 self-seeking n. 이기주의 premise n. 전제, 가정 cornerstone n. 초석, 토대 authentic a. 진정한, 참된

정답 및 해설

030 ① 2019학년도 아주대학교 인문계 A형 19번

A ❶ At the time of the First World War / the transfer (of Western ideas and institutions / beyond Europe's boundaries) was well under way. ❷ [At the height of European imperialism,] / aspiring young non-Western men, (commonly from privileged families), went to study in Europe or the United States. ❸ Westerners (themselves) established Western schools / in lands / under their domination. ❹ There arose a non-Western intelligentsia, [its members (prompted / by the most advanced Western ideals and equipped with Western learning.)] ❺ Their sense of human dignity was patterned / after that of their teachers, / yet stunted / because the Westerns treated them as inferior. ❻ Copying their Western masters, / these uprooted and inwardly divided intellectuals became nationalists. ❼ Western-educated, they wanted to be "modern" Turks, Arabs, Indians, or Africans. ❽ They wanted their nations to be respected.

B ❾ These educated nationalists soon became revolutionaries as well, / because colonial officials or traditional rulers generally suppressed open resistance. ❿ [As] revolutionaries / they turned elitist and socialist. ⓫ They believed / that their people did not know how to make themselves strong. ⓬ Yet the Western-trained, non-Western intelligentsia also remained dedicated — at least / in the abstract — to the democratic ideal. ⓭ [How its eliticism and pro-Western orientation could be reconciled with its faith / in the common people and its attachment to indigenous culture] remained an unresolved problem / for the future.

C ⓮ The progress of this intelligentsia varied / from one non-Western country to the next. ⓯ [In the dying Ottoman Empire], [for instance], the Western-trained young Turks seized power / in 1908. ⓰ After the collapse of their ramshackle state / at the end of World War 1, / they created a reasonably modern and stable Turkey / under the leadership of Kemal Ataturk.

해석

A ❶ 제1차 세계대전 당시에 유럽의 경계 너머로 서구의 사상과 제도는 순조롭게 잘 진행되고 있었다. ❷ 유럽 제국주의가 절정에 달했을 때, 야망 있는 비(非)서구권 청년들은, 대부분 특권층 가정 출신으로서, 유럽이나 미국으로 유학을 떠났다. ❸ 서양인들은 그들이 지배하고 있던 땅에 서양식 학교를 설립했다. ❹ 거기서 비서구권 출신의 지식인 계층이 생겨났는데, 이들은 서구의 가장 진보된 사상에 자극을 받았고 서양의 학문을 갖추고 있었다. ❺ 그들은 그들의 선생들처럼 인간 존엄성에 대한 의식을 가지고 있었으나, 서양인들이 그들을 열등하다고 여겼기 때문에 좌절되었다. ❻ 자신이 살던 곳을 떠나 내적으로 분열돼 있던 이 지식인들은 서양인 선생들을 따라 민족주의자가 되었다. ❼ 서양식 교육을 받은 그들은 "현대적인" 터키인, 아랍인, 인도인, 아프리카인이 되기를 원했다. ❽ 그들은 자신들의 조국이 존중받기를 원했다.

B ❾ 식민지의 관리들이나 전통적인 통치자들이 일반적으로 공개적인 저항을 억압했기 때문에 교육을 받은 이 민족주의자들 또한 얼마 지나지 않아 혁명가가 되었다. ❿ 혁명가들이었던 그들은 엘리트 주의자와 사회주의자가 되었다. ⓫ 그들은 자기 국민들이 스스로를 강하게 만드는 법을 알지 못한다고 생각했다. ⓬ 그러나 서양식 교육을 받은 비서구권 지식인 계급은 -적어도 추상적으로는- 민주주의적 이상에도 전념하고 있었다. ⓭ 그 지식인 계급의 엘리트주의와 친서구적 경향이 민중에 대한 믿음과 토착문화에 대한 애착과 조화를 어떻게 이룰 수 있을 것인가는 향후에 해결되지 않은 문제로 남아 있었다.

C ⓮ 이 지식인 계의 발전은 비서구 국가들마다 달랐다. ⓯ 예를 들어, 죽어가는 오스만 제국에서는 1908년에 서구식 교육을 받은 젊은 터키인들이 권력을 잡았다. ⓰ 제1차 세계대전 말에 금방이라도 무너질 듯한 그들의 국가가 붕괴된 후에, 그들은 케말 아타튀르크(Kemal Atatirk)의 리더십 아래에 상당히 현대적이고 안정적인 터키를 만들었다.

어휘

transfer n. 이동, 이전; 양도 **institution** n. 제도, 관습 **boundary** n. 경계, 경계선 **be well under way** 잘 되어가다 **imperialism** n. 제국주의 **aspiring** a. 포부가 있는, 야심이 있는 **privileged** a. 특권이 있는, 특전이 있는 **establish** v. 설립하다, 창립하다, 수립하다 **domination** n. 지배; 우월 **intelligentsia** n. 지식 계급 **prompt** v. 자극하다, 격려하다, 고무하다 **dignity** n. 존엄, 위엄 **stunt** v. 성장을 방해하다, 저지하다 **inferior** a. 하위의, 하층의, 〈품질·정도 등이〉 열등한 **uproot** v. 뿌리째 뽑다, 근절시키다, (정든 땅·집 따위에서) 몰아내다 **intellectual** n. 지식인, 인텔리 **revolutionary** n. 혁명가 **resistance** n. 저항, 반대 **dedicated** a. (이상·주의(主義)등에) 일신을 바친, 헌신적인 **in the abstract** 개략적으로 **reconcile** v. 화해시키다; 조화시키다, 일치시키다 **attachment** n. 애착, 사모애착, 집착 **indigenous** a. 토착의, 원산의 **collapse** n. 붕괴, 와해 **ramshackle** a. (당장이라도) 넘어질 듯한; 흔들거리는, 덜컥거리는 **reasonably** ad. 상당히, 꽤; 합리적으로; 타당하게 **stable** a. 안정된, 견고한

⑰ The transformation was achieved in relatively short order / and has endured / to the present. D ⑱ The experience in India, though, was more representative of non-Western trends. ⑲ British-educated Indians, (with the help of a British civil servant), established (in 1885) the Indian National Congress and made it the instrument of a moderate Indian nationalism. ⑳ Radicalized / by World War 1, / the Indian National Congress fell / under the sway of Mohandas Gandhi, / one of the most remarkable of the Westernized anticolonial leaders. ㉑ Under the British rule / for over 150 years, / India developed effective nationalist leadership and administrative, legal and economic structures (suitable for nationhood). ㉒ Its Westernization proceeded from both above and below: / from British rule and native resistance to it. ㉓ When independence came in 1947, / the Indian subcontinent was split into two states: / India and Pakistan. ㉔ The chief flaw (in Indian nationalism) lay / in the insurmountable religious division / between Muslims and Hindus. ㉕ Independence was followed by a war of communal riots (that took / many hundreds of thousands of lives.)

Which of the following would be the best title for the above passage?
다음 중 위 글의 제목으로 가장 적절한 것은?

✓ ① Worldwide Westernization
  세계적인 서구화
② Experiments in Globalism
  세계화에서의 실험
③ The Rise of the Industrial Age
  산업 시대의 도래
④ Obstacles to Political Developments
  정치적 발전에 대한 장애물들
⑤ Global Dominance of Western Imperialism
  서구 제국주의의 세계적 지배

해석

⑰ 그런 변화는 비교적 짧은 기간 안에 이루어졌고 지금까지 지속되고 있다.

D ⑱ 그러나 인도에서의 경험은 비서구적 경향을 더 잘 나타낸다. ⑲ 영국 교육을 받은 인도인들은 영국 공무원들의 도움을 받아 1885년에 인도국민회의를 설립했고 그것을 온건한 인도 민족주의의 도구로 만들었다. ⑳ 1차 세계대전을 겪으면서 급진주의가 된 인도국민회의는 서양식 사고방식을 가진 가장 주목할 만한 반식민지 지도자 중의 한 사람인 모한다스 간디(Mohandas Gandhi)의 지배하에 들어갔다. ㉑ 150년 이상의 영국의 통치 아래에서, 인도는 효과적인 민족주의 리더십과 국민성에 적합한 행정, 법률, 경제 구조를 발전시켰다. ㉒ 인도의 서구화는 위와 아래 모두에서부터 진행되었고, 영국의 지배와 그것에 대한 원주민의 저항이었다. ㉓ 1947년에 독립을 했을 때, 인도 아대륙은 인도와 파키스탄 두 나라로 나누어졌다. ㉔ 인도 민족주의의 가장 큰 결함은 이슬람교도와 힌두교도간의 극복할 수 없는 종교적 분열에 있었다. ㉕ 독립 후에 서로 대립하는 종교단체들 간에 폭동 전쟁이 이어졌고, 수십만 명이 목숨을 잃었다.

해설

1차 세계대전 당시 비서구권 젊은이들이 유학을 떠나 서구권 교육을 받게 되는 시대적 상황 설명 그리고 서구권 교육을 받은 그들의 변화를 설명하고 있다. 따라서 정답은 ① '전 세계의 서구화'가 가장 적절하다.

어휘

transformation n. 변형, 변화 moderate a. 삼가는, 절제하는, 온건한 radicalize v. 급진적으로 하다, 과격하게 되다 sway n. 동요, 흔들림, 지배, 통치 remarkable a. 주목할 만한, 현저한 suitable a. 적당한, 알맞은, 어울리는

유형 02 문장배열

001 ② 2019학년도 국민대학교 인문계 오전 A형 16번

Ⓑ ❶ To defeat the enemy, / you must first know the enemy.
  ~하기 위해서   S   V   O

Ⓐ ❷ In the immune system, / that job is done / by T-cells, / which
          S   V   = and they
  recognize the molecular signatures of threats / to their owner's
       V   O   분자적 특징   위협하는 것들의
  well-being.

Ⓓ ❸ Recently, / researchers explained / [how turbocharging (these
              S   V   간접의문문 터보차지(강화시키다)
  cells) can boost the immune system's ability (to fight cancer, and
           V   O
  possibly other illnesses, too.)]

Ⓒ ❹ (The technology) : (they use) merges gene therapy, synthetic
          S   목적격관대 that 생략 V   O①   O②
  biology and cell biology.
                O③

Which is the proper order of sentences Ⓐ~Ⓓ?
Ⓐ~Ⓓ에 들어갈 문장의 순서로 적절한 것은?

① Ⓐ - Ⓑ - Ⓒ - Ⓓ   ✓② Ⓑ - Ⓐ - Ⓓ - Ⓒ
③ Ⓒ - Ⓐ - Ⓓ - Ⓑ   ④ Ⓓ - Ⓒ - Ⓐ - Ⓑ

해석
Ⓑ 적을 물리치려면 먼저 적을 알아야 한다.
Ⓐ 면역 체계에서 그 일은 T세포에 의해 이루어지는데, T세포는 주인의 건강을 위협하는 것들의 분자적 특징을 인식한다.
Ⓓ 최근에, 과학자들은 이 세포들을 강화시키는 것이 면역계가 암과 다른 질병들과 싸우는 능력을 어떻게 향상시킬 수 있는지 설명했다.
Ⓒ 그들이 사용하는 기술은 유전자 치료, 합성 생물학, 세포 생물학을 융합한다.

해설 면역 체계를 설명하기 전 일반론으로 '적을 물리치려면 먼저 적을 알아야 한다'는 Ⓑ가 첫 문장으로 적절하다. 이어서 'you must first know the enemy'를 Ⓐ에서 that job이 받아준다. Ⓐ에서 말한 T-cells를 Ⓓ에서 these cell가 받아주고 있으며 마지막으로 Ⓒ에서 말하는 they가 Ⓓ에서 언급한 researchers가 된다.

어휘 **immune system** 면역체계 **recognize** v. 알아보다, 인지하다; 인정하다 **molecular** a. 분자의, 분자로 된 **signature** n. 서명, 사인; 특징 **thread** n. 실, 섬유, 가닥 **merge** v. 합병하다, 합체시키다; 서서히 ~을 하나로 만들다 **gene** n. 유전자 **therapy** n. 치료, 치료법 **synthetic** a. 종합적인; 합성의, 인조의 **boos** v. (뒤·밑에서) 밀어 올리다, (생산량을) 증대[증가]시키다

002 ③ 2018학년도 건국대학교 인문·예체능계 B형 26번

❶ Human beings can eat many different kinds of food, but some people choose not to eat meat. ❷ Vegetarians often have more in common / than just their diet. ❸ Their personalities might be similar, too.

(B) ❹ For example, vegetarians (in the United States and Canada) may be creative people, ❺ and they might not enjoy competitive sports or jobs. ❻ They worry about the health of the world, and they are probably strongly opposed to war.

(C) ❼ Some people eat mostly fast food. ❽ One study shows / that many fast food eaters have a lot in common with one another, / ❾ but they are very different from vegetarians.

(A) ❿ They are competitive and good at business. ⓫ They are also usually in a hurry. ⓬ Many fast-food eaters might not agree with this description of their personalities, but it is a common picture of them.

다음 글에 이어질 글의 순서로 가장 적절한 것은?

① (A) - (C) - (B)
② (B) - (A) - (C)
③ (B) - (C) - (A) ✓
④ (C) - (A) - (B)
⑤ (C) - (B) - (A)

해 석

❶ 인간은 많은 다른 종류의 음식들을 먹을 수 있지만, 어떤 사람들은 고기를 먹지 않기로 선택한다. ❷ 채식주의자들은 종종 그들의 식단 외에도 더 많은 공통점을 가지고 있다. ❸ 그들의 성격 또한 비슷할 수도 있다.
(B) ❹ 예를 들어, 미국과 캐나다의 채식주의자들은 창의적인 사람들일 수 있고, ❺ 그들은 경쟁적인 운동이나 직업을 즐기지 않을 수도 있다. ❻ 그들은 세계의 건강에 대해 걱정하며 아마도 전쟁에 강하게 반대할 것이다.
(C) ❼ 어떤 사람들은 패스트푸드를 주로 먹는다. ❽ 한 연구는 패스트푸드를 많이 먹는 사람들은 서로 공통점이 많지만, ❾ 채식주의자들과는 아주 다르다는 것을 보여준다.
(A) ❿ 그들은 경쟁적이고 사업에 능숙하다. ⓫ 또한 일반적으로 성격이 급하다. ⓬ 패스트푸드를 먹는 사람들은 그들의 성격에 대한 이러한 설명에 동의하지 않을 수도 있지만, 그것은 그들의 공통적인 모습이다.

해 설

주어진 문장에서 채식주의자들은 공통점을 갖고 있다고 말하는데 ⓑ에서 채식주의자들의 공통점이 언급되며 ⓒ에서 말하는 패스트푸드 섭취자들의 공통은 ⓐ에서 언급하고 있다.

어 휘

vegetarian n. 채식주의자 personality n. 성격, 인격 competitive a. 경쟁적인, 경쟁심이 강한 description n. 기술, 설명 creative a. 창조적인, 독창적인 oppose v. 반대하다 have something in common (관심사·생각 등을) 공통적으로 지니다

정답 및 해설

003 ③
2019학년도 한양대학교 에리카 인문계 오전 A형 25번

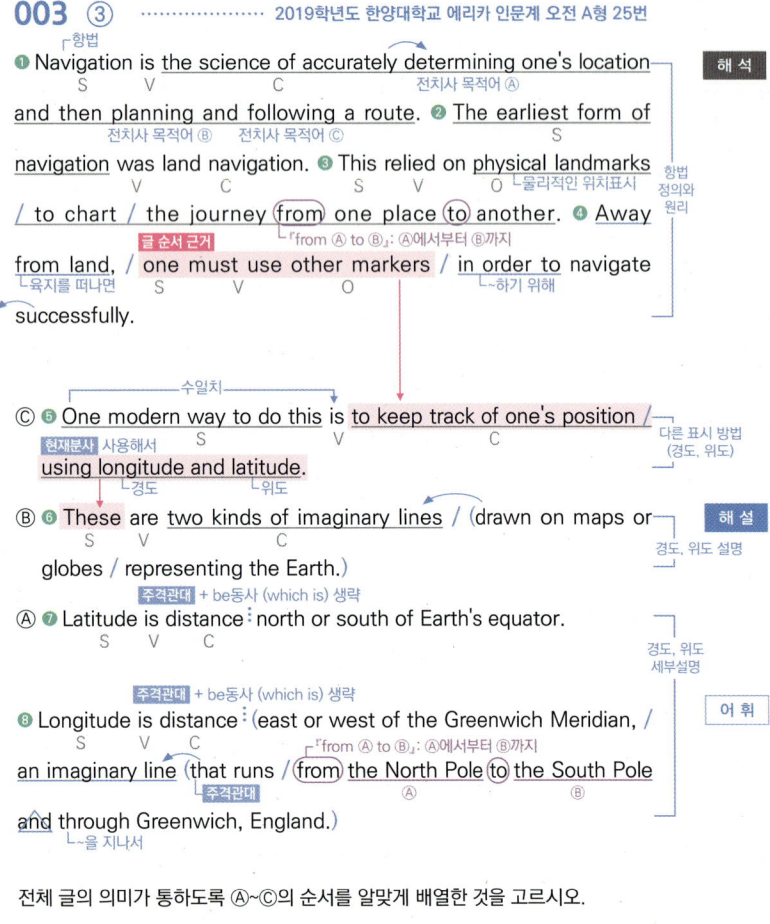

전체 글의 의미가 통하도록 Ⓐ~Ⓒ의 순서를 알맞게 배열한 것을 고르시오.

① Ⓐ - Ⓑ - Ⓒ
② Ⓑ - Ⓒ - Ⓐ
③ ✓ Ⓒ - Ⓑ - Ⓐ
④ Ⓒ - Ⓐ - Ⓑ

해석

❶ 항해술은 자신의 위치를 정확하게 파악한 뒤 경로를 계획하고 따라가는 과학이다. ❷ 항해술의 초기 형태는 육상 항해였다. ❸ 이것은 육지에 있는 물리적인 위치표시에 의지해서 한 곳에서 다른 곳으로의 여정을 지도에 나타냈다. ❹ 육지에서 벗어나면, 성공적인 항법을 위해 다른 표지들을 사용해야 한다.
Ⓒ 이렇게 하는 현대적인 한 가지 방법은 경도와 위도를 이용해서 자신의 위치를 추적하는 것이다.
Ⓑ 이것들은 지구를 나타내는 지도나 지구본 위에 그려진 두 종류의 가상의 선이다.
Ⓐ 위도는 지구의 적도에서 북쪽 또는 남쪽으로 떨어진 거리이다. ❽ 경도는 그리니치 자오선(Greenwich Meridian)에서 동쪽이나 서쪽으로 떨어진 거리인데, 그리니치 자오선은 북극에서 남극으로 영국 그리니치를 지나는 가상의 선이다.

해설

주어진 문장에서 항법의 정의와 원리를 설명하고 설명한다. 주어진 단락 마지막 문장에서 육지를 떠나면 다른 표지들을 이용해야 한다고 하는데, 이것은 Ⓒ에서 말하는 경도와 위도를 이용하는 것을 가리킨다. 그리고 Ⓑ에서 경도와 위도의 개괄적인 설명 이후 Ⓐ에서 위도의 세부적 정의 그리고 마지막 문단에서 경도의 세부적 정의와 함께 글을 마무리하는 것이 적절하다.

어휘

navigation n. 운항, 항해; 항법 determine v. 결정하다, 확정하다 physical a. 물리적인; 실제의, 눈에 보이는 landmark n. 경계표; 육상지표 latitude n. 위도 equator n. 적도 represent v. 나타내다 longitude 경도

004 ② — 2018학년도 국민대학교 인문계 오전 A형 14번

[II] ❶ A study (conducted by the University of Queensland's School of Pharmacy / involving more than 12,000 Australians) revealed / that the benefits of a fresh produce-rich diet extend / beyond physical health.

[III] ❷ With every added daily portion of fruits or vegetables (up to eight), / the subjects' happiness levels rose slightly.

[IV] ❸ The researchers calculated / that if someone were to switch / from a diet free of fruit and vegetables to eight servings per day, he or she would theoretically gain as much life satisfaction as someone (who transitioned from unemployment / to a job).

[I] ❹ The exact reason is unclear, / but it may be related to the effect of carotenoid levels / in the blood.

Which is the proper order of the four sentences [I]~[IV]?
[I]~[IV]에 들어갈 문장으로 적절한 것은?

① [I]-[III]-[II]-[IV]　　✓② [II]-[III]-[IV]-[I]
③ [III]-[II]-[I]-[IV]　　④ [IV]-[II]-[III]-[I]

해석

[II] 퀸즐랜드 대학의 약학대학에서 12,000명 이상의 호주 사람들을 대상으로 실시한 한 연구에 따르면, 신선한 농산물이 풍부한 식단의 이점은 신체 건강 이상으로 나타났다.

[III] 하루에 과일이나 채소를 먹는 비중이 늘어날 때마다 (최대 8회까지), 피실험자의 행복도는 약간씩 상승했다.

[IV] 연구원들은 만약 누군가가 과일과 채소가 전혀 없는 식단에서 하루 8차례 과일과 채소를 먹는 것으로 바꾼다면, 이론적으로 그 사람은 실직상태에서 일자리를 얻은 사람만큼 삶의 만족도를 얻게 될 것이라고 추정했다.

[I] 정확한 이유는 분명하지 않지만, 혈중 카로티노이드 수치가 미치는 영향과 관련이 있을 수 있다.

해설

연구의 소개와 결론 [II]가 먼저 와야 하며, [II]의 마지막 문장에서 언급한 '신체 건강상의 이득'에 대해 구체적으로 설명하는 [III]이 이어지고 이에 대한 부연설명인 [IV]와 [I]가 이어지는 것이 적절하다.

어휘

carotenoid a. 카로티노이드의 pharmacy n. 약학, 약국 reveal v. 드러내다, 나오다 benefit n. 이익, 이득 produce-rich a. 농산물이 풍부한, 천연산물이 풍부한 extend v. 퍼지다, 연장되다; 미치다 portion n. 일부, 부분 slightly ad. 약간, 조금 calculate v. 계산하다, 산정하다, 추산하다 theoretically ad. 이론상, 이론적으로 transition v. 이행하다, 변천하다

005 ② · 2019학년도 명지대학교 인문계 14번

❶ Much of the appeal of soccer lies in the fact that it can be played without special equipment.

Ⓑ ❷ Children everywhere know that a tin can, some bound-up rags, or a ball (from a different sport entirely) can be satisfyingly kicked around. ❸ This ingenuity was first displayed hundreds of years ago when people discovered that an animal's bladder could be inflated and knotted to provide a light, bouncy ball.

Ⓐ ❹ Understandably so, a bladder alone did not last very long, so as time passed people began to protect the bladders in a shell made of animal skin properly cured to turn it into leather.

Ⓒ ❺ This design worked so well that it is still used to this day, but with modern, synthetic materials rather than animal products.

Choose the best order after the sentence given in the box.
주어진 문장 다음에 이어질 말로 가장 적절한 순서는?

① Ⓐ - Ⓒ - Ⓑ　　　☑ Ⓑ - Ⓐ - Ⓒ
③ Ⓑ - Ⓒ - Ⓐ　　　④ Ⓒ - Ⓐ - Ⓑ

해 석
❶ 축구의 큰 매력은 특별한 장비 없이도 경기를 할 수 있다는 사실에 있다.
Ⓑ ❷ 모든 아이들은 깡통, 붕대로 묶은 천 조각, 그리고 다른 스포츠에 쓰이는 공들을 만족스럽게 찰 수 있다는 것을 알고 있다. ❸ 이 발명품은 동물들의 방광에 바람을 넣어 매듭을 지으면 가볍고 탱탱한 공이 될 수 있다는 것을 수백 년 전에 사람들이 발견했을 때 처음 보여졌다.
Ⓐ ❹ 당연하게도 방광만으로는 오래 가지 못했기 때문에, ❺ 시간이 지나면서 사람들은 적절히 가공하여 가죽으로 만든 동물 가죽으로 된 껍데기에 방광을 넣어 보호하기 시작했다.
Ⓒ ❻ 이 디자인은 매우 잘 작동하여 오늘날까지 사용이 되고 있지만, 동물성 제품이 아닌 현대의 합성소재가 사용된다.

해 설
주어진 문장에서 특별한 장비 없이 할 수 있는 구체적인 방법을 Ⓑ에서 설명하고 있으며, 그 방법이 동물의 오줌보인데 그것의 한계와 극복을 담고 있는 Ⓐ가 다음에 와야 하며, Ⓒ에서는 그것이 발전되어 오늘날의 축구공 설명으로 이어지는 것이 적절하다.

어 휘
appeal n. 매력 lie in ~에 있다 turn A into B A가 B로 변하다 tin can 깡통 bind up 붕대로 묶다 rag n. (속에 채워 넣는) 천 조각 ingenuity n. (정교한) 발명품 bladder n. 방광, 오줌보 inflate v. (공기나 가스로) 부풀리다 knot v. 매듭을 묶다 bouncy a. 탱탱한 last v. 지속되다 cure v. 가공하다, 경화시키다 synthetic material 합성물질

006 ①　　2020학년도 인하대학교 인문계 09번

❶ If you are not an early adopter, / you almost certainly know one.

❷ She was the first person in our group of friends / to own a smart phone, / and she couldn't wait to show you what it could do. ❸ He was the guy who talked excitedly / about moving all his data / to the cloud (before you even knew what the cloud was).

❹ Early adopters are that minority of users who adopt a new technology in its earliest days / before it is widely used or even thoroughly tested. ❺ According to one widely cited piece of research, / early adopters are defined as the first thirteen percent or so of people who begin using a device, game, social network, or other new product.

❻ While the majority of us sit back and wait for an innovation / to prove itself, / the early adopters jump right in.

❼ By doing so, / they get the pleasure of conquering a new frontier, enhanced prestige, and even power within the tech industry.

Which of the following is the best order for a passage starting with the given sentence in the box?
주어진 문장 다음에 이어질 순서로 가장 적절한 것은?

✓① A - C - B - D　　② A - B - D - C
③ B - A - D - C　　④ B - D - A - C
⑤ D - A - C - B

해석
❶ 만약 당신이 얼리어답터가 아니라고 해도, 분명히 얼리어답터 한 명쯤은 알고 있을 것이다.
A ❷ 그녀는 우리 친구 무리 중에서 스마트폰을 가장 먼저 소유한 사람이었고, 그녀는 스마트폰으로 무엇을 할 수 있는지 당신에게 몹시 보여주고 싶어 했다. ❸ 그는 당신이 클라우드가 무엇인지를 알기도 전에 자신의 모든 데이터를 클라우드로 옮기는 것에 대해 신나게 얘기한 남자였다.
C ❹ 얼리어답터란 새로운 기술이 널리 이용되거나 심지어 철저하게 테스트되기도 전에 그것을 가장 먼저 받아들이는 소수의 사용자들을 말한다. ❺ 널리 인용되는 한 연구에 따르면, 얼리어답터는 기기, 게임, 소셜 네트워크 또는 다른 신제품 사용을 일찍 시작하는 13% 정도 이내에 드는 사람들로 정의된다.
B ❻ 우리 대부분이 가만히 앉아서 혁신이 증명되기를 기다리는 동안, 얼리어답터들은 곧바로 뛰어든다.
D ❼ 그렇게 함으로써, 그들은 새로운 개척지를 정복하고, 위신을 높이며, 그리고 심지어는 기술 산업 내에서의 힘까지도 얻는 기쁨을 누린다.

해설
얼리어답터를 알고 있을 것이라는 주어진 문장 다음에 그들의 특징을 설명하는 A, C가 이어진다. 그리고 B에서 말하는 얼리어답터의 특징인 새로운 기술의 시계 구매에 바로 뛰어 든다고 말하고 있는데, 이런 행동의 원인을 D에서 설명하고 있다.

크쌤 첨언
A~D 순서를 파악하다 보면 각 순서의 연관성이 모호하여 서로 순서를 바꾸어 보더라도 말이 그럴듯하여 혼란스러울 때가 있다. 그럴 때는 A와 B의 연관성에 집착하기보다는 C 다음에 D가 이어져야 하는 논리 전개를 확인하고 선택지의 정답을 추론하는 자세가 필요하다.

어휘
early adopter 얼리어답터(남들보다 먼저 신제품을 사서 써보는 사람) majority n. 대부분, 대다수 innovation n. 기술혁신, 쇄신 minority n. 소수파, 소수의 무리 thoroughly ad. 완전히, 충분히, 철저히 cite v. 인용하다; 예증하다 define v. (말의) 정의를 내리다, 뜻을 밝히다 device n. 장치, 설비 conquer v. 정복하다, 이기다, 물리치다 frontier n. 국경, 국경지방; (지식·학문 등의) 미개척 영역 enhance v. 향상하다; (가치·능력·매력 따위를) 높이다, 늘리다, 더하다 prestige n. 위신, 명성

정답 및 해설

007 ③   2019학년도 인하대학교 인문계 29번

❶ Mark Twain wrote *The Adventures of Huckleberry Finn* in the late nineteenth century, / ❷ but he set his novel / decades earlier / when slavery was still legal, making his book an extended exploration of the morality / of one person (owning another human being).

Ⓑ ❸ Slavery (in the American South) was a brutal institution (involving the physical and psychological domination of black people / to serve as laborers / on American cotton and tobacco plantations).

Ⓓ ❹ By 1804 / all Northern states had abolished slavery / within their borders.

Ⓒ ❺ But the free labor (that slaves were forced to perform) still constituted the major force / behind the American economy.

Ⓐ ❻ As long as the country as a whole condoned and benefitted from / (such an) exploitative practice of labor, no black American could consider himself truly free.

❼ That is why Jim's emancipation (at the end of Huckleberry Finn) is bittersweet, / rather than fully triumphant. ❽ Jim's wife and children are still slaves, as are all the other enslaved characters / in the story.

Which of the following is the best order for a passage?
주어진 문장 다음에 이어질 말로 가장 적절한 것은?
① Ⓐ-Ⓑ-Ⓒ-Ⓓ
② Ⓐ-Ⓓ-Ⓒ-Ⓑ
✓③ Ⓑ-Ⓓ-Ⓒ-Ⓐ
④ Ⓑ-Ⓐ-Ⓓ-Ⓒ
⑤ Ⓒ-Ⓓ-Ⓐ-Ⓑ

해석
❶ 마크 트웨인(Mark Twain)은 19세기 후반에 '허클베리 핀의 모험(The Adventures of Huckleberry Finn)'을 썼지만, ❷ 노예제도가 여전히 합법이었던 수십 년 전을 소설의 배경으로 삼음으로써, 그의 책은 한 사람이 다른 사람을 소유하는 것의 도덕성에 대해 확장된 탐구를 한 책이 되었다.
Ⓑ ❸ 미국 남부의 노예제도는 흑인들을 신체적·정신적으로 지배하여 미국의 면화 농장과 담배 농장에서 노동자로 일하도록 하는 잔인한 제도였다.
Ⓓ ❹ 1804년에 이미 모든 북부의 주(州)들은 주 경계 안에서 노예제도를 폐지한 상태였다.
Ⓒ ❺ 그러나 노예들에게 강요된 무보수 노동이 여전히 미국 경제를 떠받치는 주된 힘이었다.
Ⓐ ❻ 온 나라가 그와 같은 착취적 노동 관행을 묵인하고 혜택을 받는 한, 그 어떤 흑인 미국인도 자신이 진정으로 자유롭다고 생각할 수 없었다.
❼ '허클베리 핀의 모험'의 마지막 부분에서 짐(Jim)이 해방된 것이 완전한 승리라기보다 달콤 씁쓸한 느낌을 주는 것은 이 때문이다. ❽ 이야기 속의 다른 모든 노예가 된 인물들처럼 짐의 아내와 아이들은 여전히 노예로 남아 있었다.

해설
주어진 문장에서 『허클베리 핀의 모험』 책을 소개하며 노예제도라는 소재를 확인한다. 주어진 단락 마지막 문장에서 노예 제도에 대한 도덕성 고찰을 언급하고 있으며 Ⓑ에서 자세한 설명과 비판을 이어간다. 그리고 잔인한 제도인 만큼 Ⓓ에서 폐지하였다고 말하지만 Ⓒ에서는 노예제도가 경제에 이익이 된다고 언급한다. Ⓐ에서는 이러한 잘못된 점을 묵인하는 형태를 비판한다.

어휘
legal a. 합법적인, 적법한 extended a. 광대한, 광범위한; 더욱 자세한 exploration n. 탐구, 조사 morality n. 도덕, 도덕성, 윤리 own v. 소유하다 condone v. 용서하다, 너그럽게 봐주다 benefit v. 이익을 얻다 exploitative a. 착취적인 slavery n. 노예상태, 노예의 신분 brutal a. 잔인한, 사나운 institution n. 학회, 협회; 제도, 관례 involve v. 연루시키다; 수반하다 domination n. 지배; 우월 plantation n. 농원, 농장 constitute v. 구성하다, 조직하다; ~의 구성요소가 되다 abolish v. 폐지하다, 철폐하다 border n. 경계, 국경 emancipation n. (노예) 해방 bittersweet a. 달콤 씁쓸한; 괴로움도 있고 즐거움도 있는 triumphant a. 승리를 거둔, 성공한 enslave v. 노예로 만들다, 예속시키다

008 ③ 2020학년도 한국산업기술대학교 인문계 38번

C ❶ Karst landscapes form / in areas (where limestone is exposed to the weather). ❷ The best example is Tsingy de Bemaraha National Park (located near the western coast of the island of Madagascar). ❸ The word Tsingy can be translated into English / as something like / "place (where one cannot walk / without shoes)," / and that's an appropriate name. ❹ The limestone peaks can be very sharp. ❺ In fact, / some people call this area the Forest of Knives.

A ❻ At first, the Tsingy landscape forms / like other karst landscapes; / ❼ water begins to erode the rock and causes small holes and cracks to form. ❽ As more water flows into the caves, the process of eroding continues, making the caves larger and larger.

B ❾ As the process continues, / the tops of some of the caves collapse, / creating even bigger caves. ❿ The roofs of other caves may collapse. ⓫ At this point, / the landscape is a series of rock pillars and deep canyons. ⓬ As more rain falls, / it erodes the rock pillars more and more, and forms the sharp, knifelike points (that you can see now).

Choose the appropriate order of the paragraphs.
단락의 순서로 적절한 것은?
① A - C - B　　② B - A - C
✓③ C - A - B　　④ C - B - A

해석

C ❶ 카르스트 경관은 석회암이 날씨에 노출되는 지역에서 만들어진다. ❷ 가장 좋은 예는 마다가스카르섬 서쪽 해안 근처에 위치한 베마라하 칭기(Tsingy de Bemaraha) 국립공원이다. ❸ 칭기라는 단어는 "신발 없이 걸을 수 없는 곳"이라는 의미인데, 이는 적절한 이름이다. ❹ 그 석회암 봉우리는 아주 날카롭다. ❺ 사실, 어떤 사람들은 이 지역을 '칼의 숲(Forest of knives)'이라 부른다.

A ❻ 처음에, 칭기의 경관은 다른 카르스트 지형과 마찬가지로 ❼ 물이 바위를 침식시켜 작은 구멍들과 균열들이 생기기 시작한다. ❽ 더 많은 물이 동굴 속으로 흘러들면서, 침식 과정은 계속되고, 동굴들은 점점 더 커진다.

B ❾ 이 과정이 계속되면서 일부 동굴들의 꼭대기가 붕괴해 더 큰 동굴들이 만들어진다. ❿ 다른 동굴들의 지붕들이 무너질 것이다. ⓫ 이 시점에서, 일련의 암석 기둥들과 깊은 협곡들로 이루어진 지형이 만들어진다. ⓬ 더 많은 비가 내릴수록, 그것이 바위 기둥을 점점 침식시키고, 당신이 지금 보는 것처럼 날카롭고, 뾰족한 지점이 형성된다.

해설

카르스트 경관 소개와 함께 날카로운 느낌의 칼의 숲이라 불린다는 설명이 가장 먼저 위치해야 한다. 이어서 A와 C에서는 그렇게 생기는 과정을 설명하고 있다.

어휘

karst n. 카르스트 지형(침식된 석회암 대지) limestone n. 석회석 erode v. 침식하다 collapse v. 붕괴하다 pillar n. 기둥 canyon n. 협곡

정답 및 해설

009 ④   2020학년도 국민대학교 인문계 오후 A형 32번

❶ The diversity (of plant colors and odors) probably fascinated humans / long before the history of writing / and long before the start of modern science. ❷ It seems intuitively convincing [that immobile plants can increase their fitness / by attracting the animals (they depend on) / for dispersal of pollen and seeds].

C ❸ Pollinators and seed dispersers in turn can forage more effectively / if plant colors and odors are matched to their sensory abilities.

A ❹ This occurs obviously / if sensory traits, (such as odor and color), are fine-tuned / to the sensory abilities of the animals / so that they stand out from the environment.

B ❺ The adaptive framework of signaling is even more appealing / because of our own inherent biases.

❻ It is a long-standing hypothesis [that color vision, the sense : (we humans rely upon most / for evaluating our distant environment), evolved (as) an adaptation / to locate colorful fruits / against a predominantly green background].

Which is the proper order of A – C?
A – C의 적절한 순서는?
① A – B – C
② B – A – C
③ B – C – A
✓④ C – A – B

해석

❶ 식물의 색깔과 냄새의 다양성은 아마도 문자의 역사와 현대의 과학이 시작되기 훨씬 전에 인간을 매혹시켰을 것이다. ❷ 움직일 수 없는 식물들이 꽃가루와 씨앗의 확산을 위해 그들이 의존하는 동물들을 유인함으로써 그들의 적응력을 증진할 수 있다는 것은 직관적으로 설득력이 있어 보인다.
C ❸ 꽃가루 매개자와 씨앗 배포자들(동물) 또한 식물의 색깔과 냄새가 그들의 감각 능력과 일치한다면 더 효과적으로 식량(식물)을 찾아다닐 수 있다.
A ❹ 이것은 냄새와 색깔과 같은 감각적 특성이 환경에서 두드러져 보이도록 동물의 감각 능력에 맞게 미세조정되면 분명히 일어난다.
B ❺ 신호 전달의 적응적 구조는 우리 고유의 편견 때문에 훨씬 더 매력적이다.
❻ 우리 인간이 멀리 있는 환경을 평가하기 위해 가장 많이 의존하는 감각인 색채 지각이 대부분 초록색 배경에서 다채로운 열매를 찾기 위한 적응으로 진화했다는 것은 오래된 가설이다.

해설

주어진 문장에서 식물의 색과 냄새로 생존 전략을 가지고 있다고 말한다. 즉 번식을 위한 동물의 유인인데, 이러한 구체적인 방법을 C와 A에서 설명을 이어가고 있다. 그리고 B에서 이런 색에 의존하는 것을 우리의 고유 편견이라고 말하는데, 마지막 문단에서 말하는 우리 인간이 녹색 배경의 다양한 색깔 열매를 찾기 위해 진화한 가설을 말하고 있다.

어휘

diversity n. 다양성, 포괄성 odor n. 냄새, 김새, 평판 fascinate v. 마음을 사로잡다, 매혹(매료)하다 intuitively ad. 직관[직각]적으로 convincing a. 설득력 있는, 납득이 가는 immobile a. 움직일 수 없는, 고정된 fitness n. 〈생물〉 적응도 depend on ~에 의존하다 dispersal n. 확산, 분산 pollen n. 꽃가루, 화분(花粉) seed n. 씨앗, 종자 forage v. (식량을) 찾아 돌아다니다 fine-tune v. 미세 조정을 하다 stand out from ~중에 두드러지다 framework n. 뼈대, 틀, 체계 inherent a. 내재하는 long-standing a. 오래된 color vision 색채 지각 rely upon ~에 의지하다 evaluate v. 평가하다 evolve v. 발달하다, 진화하다 adaptation n. 적응, 적합 predominantly ad. 대개, 대부분

010 ② 2019학년도 한국산업기술대학교 인문계 38번

B ❶ Deep underground are large deposits of water. ❷ These reservoirs can be found in every kind of environment including deserts. ❸ The total amount of this groundwater is significantly more than the sum of all lakes and rivers. ❹ Most of the water (existing underground) is found in aquifers, layers of porous rock that can store water. ❺ Scientists categorize them into two types: unconfined and confined. ❻ The unconfined aquifer lies under a layer of permeable material. ❼ As a result, it can easily receive water from the surface, and the water table surface fluctuates up and down, depending on the rate of water recharge.

A ❽ Typically below unconfined aquifers are confined aquifers and are topped with an impermeable layer of stone and clay. ❾ Therefore, while there is some part that remains unconfined to allow for water recharge, most of the groundwater remains under high pressure. ❿ If a well should be drilled into the rock, the groundwater will rise to the surface.

C ⓫ Confined and unconfined aquifers are refilled by groundwater. ⓬ However, the rate for them differs. ⓭ Most groundwater is the result of rain penetrating the soil. ⓮ The water will then trickle down to the lower layers until it reaches the aquifer. ⓯ Confined aquifers recharge at a slower rate than unconfined. ⓰ This is mainly because the water has more difficulty entering them. ⓱ In tropical regions, recharge occurs during the rainy seasons. ⓲ In more temperate regions, it happens during the winter.

Choose the appropriate order of the paragraphs.
단락의 적절한 순서를 고르시오.
① Ⓐ-Ⓒ-Ⓑ ✓② Ⓑ-Ⓐ-Ⓒ
③ Ⓒ-Ⓐ-Ⓑ ④ Ⓒ-Ⓑ-Ⓐ

해석

B ❶ 지하 깊은 곳에 많은 양의 물이 매장되어 있다. ❷ 이런 저수지들은 사막을 포함한 모든 종류의 환경에서 발견될 수 있다. ❸ 지하수의 총량은 모든 호수와 강을 합친 것보다 훨씬 많다. ❹ 지하에 존재하는 대부분의 물은 물을 저장할 수 있는 다공성 암석층인 대수층에서 발견된다. ❺ 과학자들은 대수층을 비피압(非被壓) 대수층(unconfined aquifer)과 피압 대수층(confined aquifer) 두 가지 유형으로 분류했다. ❻ 비피압 대수층은 투과성 물질의 층 아래에 있다. ❼ 그 결과, 비피압 대수층은 지표면으로부터 물을 쉽게 받을 수 있고, 물이 재충전되는 속도에 따라 수면이 위아래로 오르내린다.

A ❽ 일반적으로 비피압 대수층 아래에는 피압 대수층이 있으며 이 대수층은 돌과 점토로 이루어진 불투성층(不透水層)으로 덮여있다. ❾ 따라서 비피압 상태에 있어서 물의 재충전을 허용하는 지하수도 일부 있긴 하지만, 대부분의 지하수는 여전히 큰 압력을 받는다. ❿ 만약 바위를 뚫어 우물을 판다면, 지하수는 표면 위로 올라올 것이다.

C ⓫ 피압 대수층과 비피압 대수층은 지하수로 다시 채워진다. ⓬ 하지만 피압 대수층과 비피압 대수층에 지하수가 채워지는 속도는 다르다. ⓭ 대부분의 지하수는 비가 땅을 투과해서 들어간 것의 결과물이다. ⓮ 이 물이 대수층에 도착할 때까지 점점 더 낮은 층으로 조금씩 흘러들어갈 것이다. ⓯ 비피압 대수층보다 피압 대수층이 더 느린 속도로 물이 채워진다. ⓰ 이것은 주로 물이 피압 대수층으로 들어가기가 더 어렵기 때문이다. ⓱ 열대 지방에서는 물의 재충전이 우기(雨期) 동안 일어나고, ⓲ 더 온화한 지역에서는 겨울에 일어난다.

해설

지하수는 암석층인 대수층에서 발견된다고 말하며, 이 대수층은 두 가지 유형 즉 '비피압'과 '피압' 대수층이 있다고 한다. 여기서 Ⓑ의 마지막 부분에서 비피압 대수층을 설명하고 이어서 Ⓐ에서 피압 대수층의 설명이 이어지는 것이 적절하다. 그렇게 비피압과 피압 대수층의 설명 이후 이 두 가지의 차이를 설명하는 Ⓒ가 이어지는 것이 적절하다.

크쌤 첨언 소재가 어려울수록 글 전개의 개연성은 분명하다. 본 지문에서는 처음 2가지 타입이 있다고 말한 뒤 각각의 타입을 설명하는 글의 전개는 상당히 흔한 편입영어 독해 패턴이다.

어휘 unconfined a. 제한을 받지 않는, 무한정의 aquifer n. 대수층(帶水層:지하수를 품고 있는 지층) impermeable a. 통과시키지 않는, 불침투성의 clay n. 점토, 찰흙 groundwater n. 지하수 well n. 우물; (유전 등의) 정(井) drill v. (드릴로) 구멍을 뚫다 deposit n. 퇴적물, 침적물, 침전물 reservoir n. 저수지, 급수장 significantly ad. 중요하게, 의미가 있게, 상당히 sum n. 합계, 총계 porous a. (구멍이 많은) 다공성[투과성]의 store v. 저장하다, 보관하다 categorize v. 분류하다 permeable a. 침투할[스며들] 수 있는, 투과성[투기성]의 water table 지하수면 fluctuate v. 변동[등락]을 거듭하다 refill v. 다시 채우다, 리필하다 penetrate v. ~을 관통하다, 꿰뚫다, 투과하다 trickle down (조금씩) 흘러내리다

011 ③   2019학년도 한성대학교 인문계 A형 11번

[C] ❶ A germ is a bit of living matter (capable of growth and development into an organism). ❷ Germs can cause many problems, including disease. ❸ The germs (that make people sick) are everywhere. ❹ You can't see them, / but they're there. ❺ They're sitting / on your desk. ❻ They're hiding / on your computer's keyboard. ❼ They're even / in the air (that you are breathing).

[B] ❽ There are two types of germs: viruses and bacteria. ❾ Viruses use the cells / inside animals or plants / to live and multiply. ❿ Viruses cause illnesses such as influenza, or the flu. ⓫ Bacteria are tiny creatures. ⓬ Some bacteria are good. ⓭ They can help your stomach digest food. ⓮ Other bacteria aren't as good. ⓯ They can cause sore throats and ear infections.

[A] ⓰ How can you stop these tiny invaders from making you sick? ⓱ Your skin is the first defense / against germs. ⓲ One of the easiest ways / to prevent some illnesses is simply by washing with soap and water. ⓳ But germs can still enter the body / through small cuts in the skin / or through the mouth, eyes, and nose.

[해석]
[C] ❶ 세균은 유기체로 성장하고 발달할 수 있는 작은 생명체이다. ❷ 세균은 질병을 포함한 많은 문제를 일으킬 수 있다. ❸ 사람들을 아프게 하는 세균은 어디에나 있다. ❹ 당신은 그것들을 볼 수 없지만, 그것들은 거기에 있다. ❺ 그것들은 책상 위에 앉아있다. ❻ 그것들은 당신의 컴퓨터 키보드에 숨어 있다. ❼ 그것들은 심지어 당신이 숨 쉬는 공기에도 있다.
[B] ❽ 세균에는 바이러스와 박테리아 두 종류가 있다. ❾ 바이러스는 생존하고 증식하기 위해 동물 또는 식물 안에 있는 세포를 사용한다. ❿ 바이러스는 인플루엔자나 독감 같은 질병을 유발한다. ⓫ 박테리아는 아주 작은 생물이다. ⓬ 어떤 박테리아는 유익하다. ⓭ 이 박테리아는 당신의 위가 음식을 소화하는 것을 도울 수 있다. ⓮ 다른 박테리아는 그렇게 좋지 않다. ⓯ 그것들은 인후염과 귓병을 일으킬 수 있다.
[A] ⓰ 이런 작은 침략자가 당신을 아프게 하는 것을 어떻게 막을 수 있을까? ⓱ 당신의 피부는 세균에 대한 첫 번째 방어 수단이다. ⓲ 몇몇 질병을 예방하는 가장 쉬운 방법 중 하나는 그냥 비누와 물로 씻는 것이다. ⓳ 하지만 세균은 여전히 피부의 작은 상처나 입, 눈, 코를 통해 몸속으로 들어갈 수 있다.

[해설] 세균을 정의하는 [C]가 먼저 오고 난 뒤, 세균의 종류가 2가지 있다는 설명인 [B]가 이어지는 것이 바람직하다. 그리고 [B] 마지막 문장에서 언급하는 좋지 않은 박테리아를 예방하는 방법이 [A]에서 이어지고 있다.

[어휘] **invader** n. 침략자[군], 침입자 **cut** n. (베인[긁힌]) 상처, 자상 **germ** n. 세균, 미생물 **cell** n. 세포 **multiply** v. 증식[번식]하다 **stomach** n. 위(胃); 복부 **digest** v. (음식을) 소화하다 **capable** a. ~을 할 수 있는 **organism** n. 유기체, 생물

Which one is the right order?
올바른 순서는 무엇인가?
① ⓑ - ⓒ - ⓐ
② ⓑ - ⓐ - ⓒ
✓③ ⓒ - ⓑ - ⓐ
④ ⓒ - ⓐ - ⓑ

012 ①   2019학년도 한성대학교 인문계 A형 36번

❶ ⒟ Some ordinary sunglasses can obscure our vision / by exposing your eyes to harmful UV rays blue light and reflective glare. ❷ ⒜ They can also darken light (that helps you see better). ❸ ⒞ But now, independent research (conducted by scientists / from NASA's Jet Propulsion Laborato) has brought forth ground-breaking technology / to help protect human eyesight from the harmful effects of solar radiation light. ❹ ⒝ This superior lens technology was first discovered / when NASA scientists looked to nature / for a means / to superior eye protection — specifically, / by studying the eyes of eagles, / known for their extreme visual acuity.

❺ This discovery resulted in what is now known as Eagle Eyes. ❻ Eagle Eyes features the most advanced eye protection technology ever created. ❼ It offers triple-filter polarization / to block 99.9% UVA and UVB as well as the added benefit of blue-light eye protection.

❽ Eagle Eyes is the only optic technology (that has qualified official recognition / from the Space Certification Program / for this remarkable technology).

Which one is the right order?
올바른 순서는 무엇인가?

✓① ⒟ - ⒜ - ⒞ - ⒝   ② ⒜ - ⒝ - ⒞ - ⒟
③ ⒟ - ⒜ - ⒝ - ⒞   ④ ⒜ - ⒝ - ⒟ - ⒞

해석

❶ ⒟ 몇몇 평범한 선글라스는 해로운 자외선과 블루라이트 그리고 눈부신 반사광에 당신의 눈을 노출시킴으로써 당신의 시야를 흐리게 할 수 있다. ❷ ⒜ 그것들은 또한 당신이 더 잘 볼 수 있게 도와주는 빛을 어둡게 할 수 있다. ❸ ⒞ 그러나 이제, NASA의 제트추진연구소의 과학자들에 의해 수행된 독립적인 연구는 태양 방사선의 해로운 영향으로부터 인간의 시력을 보호하는 것을 도와주는 획기적인 기술을 내놓았다. ❹ ⒝ 이 뛰어난 렌즈 기술은 NASA의 과학자들이 우수한 시력 보호의 수단을 자연에서 찾았을 때, 특히, 최고의 시력을 가진 것으로 유명한 독수리의 눈을 연구함으로써 처음 발견되었다.

❺ 이 발견은 지금 Eagle Eyes로 알려진 것을 만들어 냈다. ❻ Eagle Eyes는 이때까지 만들어진 것 중 가장 진보된 눈 보호 기술을 특징으로 한다. ❼ Eagle Eyes는 UVA와 UVB를 99.9% 차단하는 삼중 필터 편광 뿐만 아니라 블루라이트로부터 눈을 보호하는 부가적 혜택을 제공한다. ❽ Eagle Eyes는 이런 놀라운 기술로 우주 인증 프로그램으로부터 공식적인 인정을 받은 유일한 광학기술이다.

해설

⒟ 문장에서 선글라스의 문제점을 지적하고 이어서 ⒜에서 추가적인 문제점 언급을 한다. 그리고 ⒞부터 해결책 제시 그리고 ⒝에서는 해결책의 세부적인 내용을 이어간다.

*문제 지적→해결책

어휘

darken v. 어둡게[캄캄하게] 만들다 superior a. 우수한, 뛰어난 visual acuity n. 시력(視力) bring forth ~을 낳다, 생산하다 ground-breaking a. 신기원을 이룬, 획기적인 eyesight n. 시력 obscure v. 어둡게 하다, 흐리게 하다 expose v. 노출시키다 blue light n. 블루라이트(모니터에서 나오는 파란색 계열의 빛) reflective a. 빛[열]을 반사하는 glare n. 반짝거리는 빛, 눈부신 빛, 섬광 acuity n. 예리함, 명민함 result in ~을 낳다, 야기하다 feature v. 특징으로 삼다 polarization n. 편의(偏倚), 편광(偏光) optic a. 눈의; 시력의; 시각의 recognition n. 인식, 지각, 인정 remarkable a. 놀라운, 주목할 만한

013 ④ 2019학년도 한양대학교 에리카 인문계 A형 26번

글의 주제

① No one / really knows / how many species of animal there are in the world, / but one estimate puts it / at just under nine million.

ⓒ ② However, the majority of species have not been identified, and we are still discovering new ones / at a rapid rate. ③ Since we have identified so few animals, / it is difficult [to determine / the rate of extinction.]

ⓐ ④ Some biologists calculate / that between 0.01% and 0.1% of all species could become extinct annually. ⑤ This rate would mean between 900 and 9,000 extinctions every year.

ⓑ ⑥ While this is an alarming rate, / it is not inevitable [that an animal will become extinct.] ⑦ In fact, a number of animals (that were close to dying out) have actually been brought back / from the edge of extinction.

⑧ Achieving such a feat / may help ensure / the biodiversity / and health of the animal kingdom.

해석

① 이 세상에 얼마나 많은 종(種)의 동물이 있는지는 아무도 모르지만, 한 추정치는 900만 종에 조금 못 미친다고 본다.
ⓒ ② 그러나 대부분의 종은 확인되지 않았고, 우리는 여전히 빠른 속도로 새로운 종을 발견하고 있다. ③ 우리는 극히 적은 수의 동물들을 확인했기 때문에, 멸종 속도를 판단하는 것은 어려운 일이다.
ⓐ ④ 일부 생물학자들은 모든 종의 0.01에서 0.1%가 매년 멸종될 수 있다고 추정한다. ⑤ 이 비율은 매년 900에서 9,000종의 멸종을 의미한다.
ⓑ ⑥ 이 비율은 놀라운 것이지만, 동물이 멸종되는 것이 피할 수 없는 것은 아니다. ⑦ 사실, 거의 멸종할 뻔했던 많은 동물이 실제로 멸종 위기에서 벗어난 적도 있다.
⑧ 그러한 위업을 달성하는 것은 동물계의 생물 다양성과 건강을 보장하는 데 도움이 될 수 있다.

해설

주어진 문장에서 생존하는 동물 종의 추정치를 언급하고 ⓒ에서 추정치가 정확하지 않음을 부연 설명하며 멸종 속도 판단도 어렵다고 말한다. 그리고 ⓐ에서 멸종 속도의 구체적인 추정치가 나오고 마지막 ⓑ에서는 이러한 멸종 위기를 벗어난 적도 있음을 말하고 있다.

어휘

species n. (공통된 특성을 가진) 종류; 종(種) **estimate** n. 평가, 견적; 판단, 의견 **calculate** v. 계산하다; 추정하다 **extinct** a. 멸종한, 절멸한 **annually** ad. 해마다, 매년 **alarming** a. 놀라운 **rate** n. 속도; 비율 **inevitable** a. 피할 수 없는, 부득이한 **die out** 멸종되다, 자취를 감추다 **bring back** 상기시키다 **majority** n. 대부분, 대다수 **identify** v. 확인하다; 인지하다; 동일시하다 **determine** v. 결정하다, 확정하다 **feat** n. 위업, 공훈 **ensure** v. 보장[보증]하다; (지위 등을) 확보하다 **biodiversity** n. 생물 다양성 **animal kingdom** 동물계

전체 글의 의미가 통하도록 ⓐ~ⓒ의 순서를 알맞게 배열한 것을 고르시오.

① ⓐ-ⓑ-ⓒ ② ⓑ-ⓐ-ⓒ
③ ⓑ-ⓒ-ⓐ ✓④ ⓒ-ⓐ-ⓑ

014 ④ 2020학년도 국민대학교 인문계 오전 A형 34번

글의 주제

❶ Several studies suggest / that there are gender differences / in language use in children / as young as 3 years old. ❷ Preschool boys tend to be more assertive and demanding / in their conversational style, / whereas preschool girls tend to be more polite and cooperative.

C ❸ For example, it was found [that boys tended to use simple imperatives / in talking to their partner / in pretend play.] ❹ Girls (in the same situation) used fewer simple imperatives / and instead used language (that included the other child / in planning.)

B ❺ Given these gender differences in preschoolers' conversational style, / perhaps it is not surprising [that there are more disputes / when preschool boys interact / than when preschool girls interact.]

A ❻ And, when conflict arises, / boys handle it differently than girls do. ❼ Amy Sheldon (1990) videotaped same-sex triads of preschool girls and boys / at a day care center.

❽ She observed / that when the boys had conflicts, / they frequently issued directives and made threats. ❾ The girls, in contrast, tended more to try to negotiate a settlement.

Which is the proper order of A – C?
A – C 의 적절한 순서는?
① A – B – C   ② A – C – B
③ C – A – B   ✓ ④ C – B – A

해석

❶ 몇몇 연구들에 따르면 3살 정도의 아이들의 언어 사용에 성별 차이가 있다고 한다. ❷ 미취학 남자아이들은 대화 스타일에 있어 더 적극적이고 요구가 많은 경향이 있는 반면에, 미취학 여자아이들은 더 예의 바르고 협조적인 경향이 있다.

C ❸ 예를 들어, 남자아이들은 가상(假想)놀이에서 파트너와 대화할 때 단순 명령문을 사용하는 경향이 있음이 밝혀졌다. ❹ 여자아이들은 같은 상황에서 단순 명령문을 덜 사용했으며, 대신 다른 아이를 계획에 끌어들이는 언어를 사용했다.

B ❺ 이러한 미취학 아이들의 대화 스타일에 있어서 성별 차이를 고려할 때, 미취학 여자아이들이 상호 작용할 때 보다 미취학 남자아이들이 상호 작용할 때 더 많은 분쟁이 있다는 것은 놀라운 일이 아니다.

A ❻ 그리고 갈등이 생겼을 때, 남자아이들은 여자아이들과 다르게 상황을 다룬다. ❼ 에이미 셸던(Amy Sheldon)(1990)은 탁아소에서 같은 성별로만 이루어진 3인조들을 각각 비디오로 촬영했다.

❽ 그녀는 남자아이들이 갈등을 있을 때, 자주 지시를 내리고 위협을 가한다는 것을 관찰했다. ❾ 대조적으로, 여자아이들은 협의로 해결하려는 경향이 더 컸다.

해설

연구 결과 미취학 여자 아이들이 남자 아이들 보다 예의 있고 협조적이라는 내용으로 첫 단락이 끝이 난다. 그리고 C에서 구체적으로 어떻게 여자 아이들이 협조적인지 설명하고 있다. 그리고 B에서 남자 아이들이 여자 보다 더 많은 분쟁 가능성을 언급하고 있으며, 이에 대한 구체적인 남녀 아이들의 태도가 A와 이어지는 마지막 단락에서 설명되고 있다.

어휘

assertive a. 단정적인 **demanding** a. 요구가 많은 **conversational** a. 대화의 **cooperative** a. 협력하는, 협조하는 **pretend play** 가상놀이, 역할놀이 **dispute** n. 분쟁 **imperative** n. 명령 **directive** n. 지시, 명령 **negotiate** v. 협상하다 **settlement** n. 합의, 해결

정답 및 해설

015 ④ 2019학년도 가톨릭대학교 인문계 A형 33번

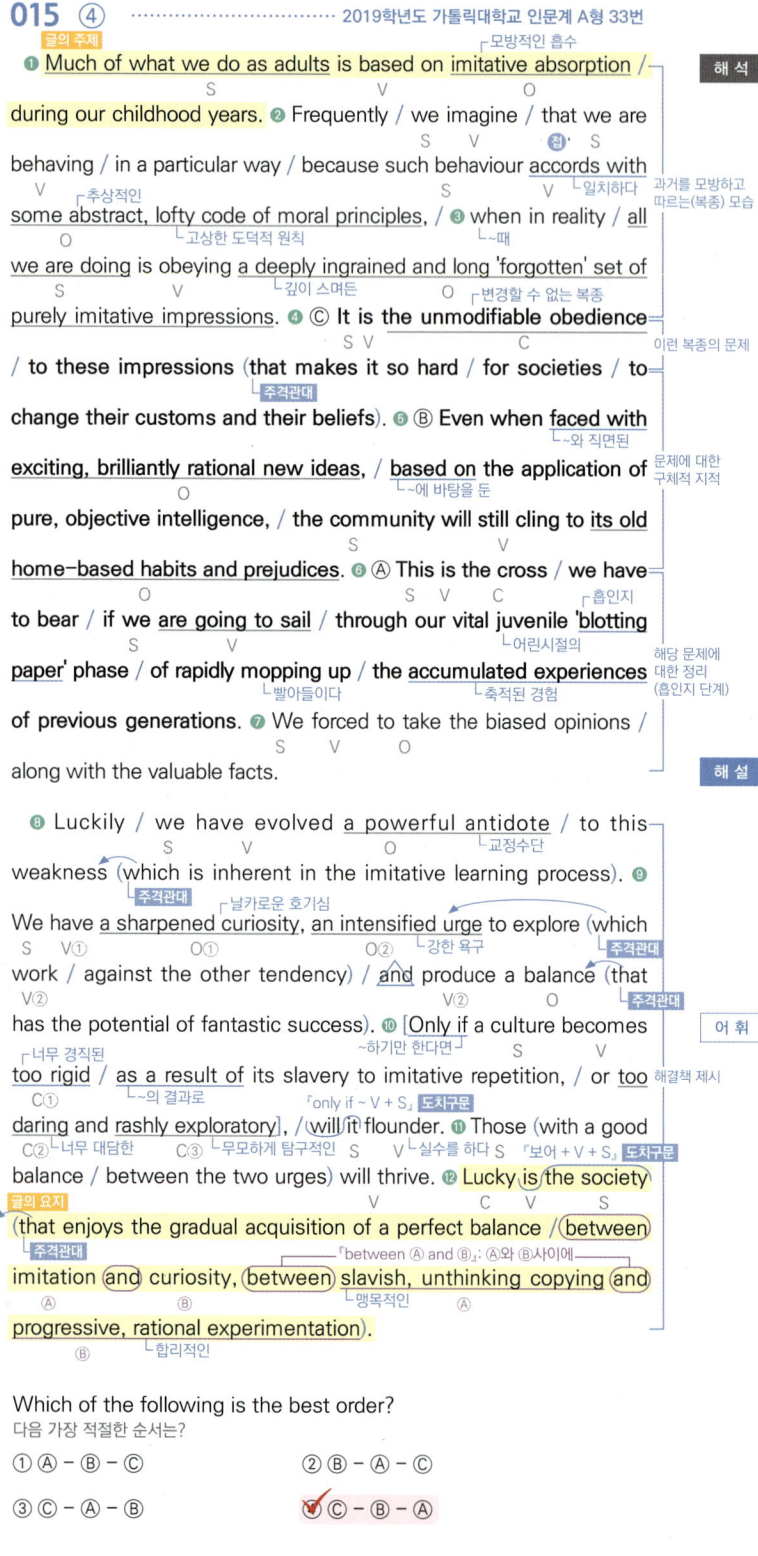

❶ 성인으로서 우리가 하는 일의 대부분은 우리의 어린 시절 동안 했던 모방적인 흡수를 바탕으로 한다. ❷ 우리는 종종 우리가 특정한 방식으로 행동하고 있는 이유가 그러한 행동이 어떤 추상적이고 고상한 도덕 원칙의 체계와 일치하기 때문이라고 생각하지만, ❸ 실제로 우리는 깊이 뿌리 박혀있고 오래도록 '잊고 있었던' 대단히 모방적인 일련의 인상들을 따르고 있을 뿐이다. ❹ ⓒ 바로 이러한 인상들에 대한 변경할 수 없는 복종이 사회가 그들의 관습과 믿음을 바꾸기 어렵게 만든다. ❺ Ⓑ 순수하고 객관적인 지성의 적용에 바탕을 둔 흥미롭고, 뛰어나게 합리적인 새로운 아이디어에 직면하더라도, 공동체는 가정에 기반을 둔 오래된 관습과 편견을 계속 고수할 것이다. ❻ Ⓐ 이것은 이전 세대들의 축적된 경험을 빠르게 흡수하는 유년의 매우 중요한 '흡인지(吸引紙)' 단계를 순조롭게 지나가기 위해 우리가 견뎌야 하는 십자가이다. ❼ 우리는 귀중한 사실들과 편향된 의견도 함께 받아들이도록 강요했다.

❽ 다행히도 우리는 모방적인 학습 과정에 내재된 이런 약점에 대해 강력한 해독제를 발전시켜 왔다. ❾ 우리는 날카로운 호기심과 탐구하고자 하는 강한 욕구를 가지고 있는데, 이것들이 다른 하나의 경향에 대해 반작용하여 엄청난 성공 잠재력을 가진 균형을 만들어 낸다. ❿ 한 문화가 모방을 통한 반복에 속박돼서 지나치게 경직돼 있거나 혹은 너무 대담하고 무모하게 탐구적이지만 않다면, 그 문화가 허우적거릴 일은 없을 것이다. ⓫ 두 욕구 사이에 균형이 잘 잡혀 있는 문화들은 번영할 것이다. ⓬ 모방과 호기심, 맹목적이고 분별없는 모방과 발전적이고 합리적인 실험 사이의 완벽한 균형을 점진적으로 획득하는 사회는 운이 좋은 사회이다.

ⓒ에서 말하는 '이러한 인상들(these impressions)'은 앞 문장에서 '따르고 있는 깊이 뿌리 박혀있고 오래도록 잊고 있었던 모방적 인상들'을 말한다. 그리고 이러한 복종이 사회가 그러한 관습과 믿음을 바꾸기 어렵다고 말한다. 그리고 Ⓑ에서 심지어 합리적인 새로운 개념과 마주할 때도 그런 인습을 고수할 것이라고 부연 설명을 이어가고 있다. 그리고 마지막 Ⓐ에서는 이러한 행태가 어린 시절 흡인지 단계를 지나가기 위해 견뎌내야 하는 십자가라고 말하고 있다.

imitative a. 모방의, 모방적인 **absorption** n. 흡수, 열중, 몰두, 전념 **behave** v. 행동하다 **accord with** ~와 일치하다, 조화하다 **abstract** a. 추상적인 **lofty** a. 고상한, 고결한 **moral** a. 도덕적인, 윤리적인 **principle** n. 원리, 원칙, 법칙 **obey** v. 따르다, 복종하다 **ingrained** a. (사상이나 이론이) 깊이 스며든, 뿌리 깊은; 상습적인, 철저한 **impression** n. 인상, 감명; 느낌 **juvenile** a. 젊은, 어린, 소년소녀의 **blotting paper** (잉크 글씨의 잉크를 닦아내는) 압지, 흡인지 **phase** n. 단계, 국면 **mop up** (엎지른 물을) 씻어[닦아]내다, 빨아들이다 **accumulate** v. (조금씩) 모으다, 축적하다 **rational** a. 이성적인, 합리적인 **application** n. 적용, 응용 **objective** a. 객관적인 **cling to** 고수하다, 집착하다 **prejudice** n. 선입견 **unmodifiable** a. 변경할 수 없는, 수정할 수 없는 **obedience** n. 복종; 순종 **biased** a. 치우친, 편견을 가진, 편향된 **evolve** v. 서서히 발전[전개]시키다 **antidote** n. 해독제; (해악 따위의) 교정수단, 대책 **inherent** a. 본래부터 가지고 있는, 본래의, 타고난 **intensify** v. 강렬하게 하다, 증강하다 **urge** n. (강한) 욕구, 충동; 자극, 압박 **tendency** n. 경향, 풍조, 추세 **potential** n. 잠재력, 가능성 **rigid** a. 굳은, 단단한; 엄격한 **exploratory** a. 탐험의; 탐험을 좋아하는; 탐구적인, 시험적인 **flounder** v. 당황하다, 허둥대다, 실수를 하다 **gradual** a. 점차적인, 단계적인 **acquisition** n. 취득, 획득, 습득 **curiosity** n. 호기심 **slavish** a. 노예의, 노예근성의 **unthinking** a. 생각이 없는, 경솔한

Which of the following is the best order?
다음 가장 적절한 순서는?

① Ⓐ - Ⓑ - ⓒ
② Ⓑ - Ⓐ - ⓒ
③ ⓒ - Ⓐ - Ⓑ
④ ⓒ - Ⓑ - Ⓐ ✓

016 ② 2019학년도 국민대학교 인문계 오전 A형 21번

❶ Shedding kilos is harder / than putting on, which is / why the weight-loss industry is so big. ❷ Its latest manifestation is online weight-management sites: social networks for the plump (in which participants can set a target weight and monitor their progress / towards it).

A ❸ As with other social networks, / they can also get their help / from friends / — either real-life ones (who sign up to the same site), or else digital ones (whom they have befriended / on the internet). ❹ Those friendships are likely to be important. ❺ Other studies of weight-loss programs have suggested / that having the support or chivying of friends helps people stick to their diets and exercise regimes.

D ❻ Those studies, however, have all been done / with groups of people (who knew each other / in the real world). ❼ A team of researchers (led by Julia Poncela-Casanovas of Northwestern University, in Illinois), decided to check / if the same was true of groups in cyberspace. ❽ Their results suggest / that it is.

B ❾ But she and her colleagues are quick / to point out / that a study like this can establish only that two things / — in this case, / friends and weight-loss — are correlated. ❿ It cannot show which causes which. Working this out requires controlled experiments.

C ⓫ Their results are, nonetheless, encouraging. ⓬ Weight-management websites have the potential / to reach many more people / much more cheaply / than real-world support groups do. ⓭ Moreover, / if it turns out / that friendship networks are a magic wand / for weight loss, / then it may be easier / [to nudge people / into such networks electronically / than if they actually had to meet each other / in a sweaty gym]. ⓮ Given the medical consequences of rising levels of obesity, / that would be well worth doing.

Which is the proper order of paragraphs A~D?
① A-B-C-D
✓② A-D-B-C
③ B-D-C-A
④ B-C-D-A

해석

❶ 살을 빼는 것이 찌우는 것보다 더 어려우며, 이것이 체중감량 산업이 크게 성장한 이유이다. ❷ 최근 그것은 온라인 체중 관리 사이트로 나타났는데, 이것은 통통한 사람들을 위한 소셜 네트워크로, 이 안에서 참여자들은 자신의 목표 체중을 설정하고 그 진행 상황을 지켜볼 수 있다.

A ❸ 다른 소셜 네트워크와 마찬가지로, 이들은 친구 - 같은 사이트에 가입하는 실제 친구, 또는 그렇지 않은 경우에는 인터넷상에서 친구가 된 온라인 친구 - 에게도 도움을 받을 수 있다. ❹ 그런 우정은 중요할 것 같다. ❺ 체중감량 프로그램에 관한 다른 연구들에서는 친구들이 응원하거나 (살을 빼라고) 재촉하는 것이 식이요법과 운동요법을 계속하는 데 도움이 됨을 시사했다.

D ❻ 그러나 그 연구들은 모두 현실 세계에서 서로 알고 있던 사람들을 대상으로 이루어졌다. ❼ 일리노이주 노스웨스턴대학의 줄리아 폰셀라-카사노바스(Julia Poncella-Casanovas)가 이끄는 연구팀은 사이버 공간 속의 사람들의 경우도 그런지를 확인해보기로 했다. ❽ 그들의 연구결과는 그 경우도 마찬가지라는 것을 보여준다.

B ❾ 그러나 그녀와 그녀의 동료들은 이와 같은 연구가 입증하는 것은 오직 두 가지 — 이 경우에는 친구와 체중감량 — 가 상관관계가 있다는 사실밖에 없다고 재빨리 지적한다. ❿ 그런 연구는 둘 중 어떤 것이 원인이 되는지를 보여주지 못하고, 이 문제를 해결하려면 대조 실험이 필요하다.

C ⓫ 그럼에도 불구하고, 그들의 연구결과는 고무적이다. ⓬ 체중 관리 웹사이트는 실제 지원 그룹(공통의 고민을 가진 사람들이 모여 서로 정신적으로 지원하는 그룹)보다 훨씬 저렴하게 더 많은 사람에게 다가갈 수 있는 잠재력을 가지고 있다. ⓭ 게다가, 만약 우정 네트워크로 연결된 친구들이 체중감량을 위한 마법 지팡이라는 것이 밝혀진다면, 땀에 젖은 체육관에서 그들이 실제로 만나기보다 온라인을 통해 사람들을 그러한 네트워크로 밀어 넣는 것이 더 쉬울 수도 있다. ⓮ 비만 수치의 증가로 인한 의학적 중요성을 고려하면, 그것은 충분히 할 가치가 있을 것이다.

해설

주어진 문장에서 체중감량 산업의 성장과 함께 소셜 네트워크를 통해 감량할 수 있음을 말한다. 이어서 A에서 구체적으로 감량 온라인 사이트를 통해 어떻게 도움이 되는지에 대해 말한 뒤, D에서는 사실 온라인 친구들이 아닌 현실 친구들에 의해서 연구가 이루어졌기에 새로운 연구를 통해서, 온라인 친구들도 도움이 되는지 실험을 한다. 하지만 B에서는 그 연구의 입증의 한계를 말하고 있으며 마지막으로 C에서는 그런데도 연구의 결과는 고무적이고 온라인을 통한 감량이 가치가 있다고 말하고 있다.

어휘

manifestation n. 징후, 나타남 **plump** a. 살찐, 포동포동한, 통통한 **participant** n. 참여자, 관계자 **real-life** a. 현실의, 실재하는 **befriend** v. ~의 친구가 되다, 사귀다, 편들다 **chivy** v. 몰다, 쫓다 **regime** n. 식이 요법 **correlate** v. 서로 관련시키다 **potential** n. 잠재력, 가능성 **wand** n. 막대기, (마술사의) 지팡이 **nudge** v. (~을 특정 방향으로) 조금씩 밀다[몰고 가다] **sweaty** a. 땀에 젖은; 땀을 빼게 만드는, 힘이 드는 **given** prep. ~라고 가정하면 **consequence** n. 결과; 중요성 **obesity** n. 비만

정답 및 해설

017 ③
2019학년도 국민대학교 인문계 오후 A형 22번

❶ An important theme of Gordimer's novel "The Moment Before the Gun Went Off", is that of paternal inheritance.

C ❷ The story contains several references to Willem Van der Vyver, the late, great patriarchal figure whose presence seems to overshadow his son's life. ❸ Marais Van der Vyver's prominence in the community is directly related to his father's legacy; ❹ the son inherited the father's "best farm" and his employees are the children of those who worked for "old Van der Vyver." ❺ This suggests that the son inherited an entire network of social, economic, and psychological relationships.

D ❻ Significantly, then, we learn that it is the gun of Marais Van der Vyver's father that kills Lucas, the farmworker who is Marais's son; this legacy of violence is passed on from grandfather, to son, and finally — tragically — to grandson.

A ❼ The fact that Marais Van der Vyver has had no volitional control over this pivotal event in his life emphasizes that responsibility for this misdeed does not reside exclusively with him ❽ and suggests that Marais may not be entirely responsible for his other inheritances.

B ❾ Marais Van der Vyver's own prehistory, then, in his father's generation — the generation that created the modern apartheid system in 1948 — may be the historical "moment" before" the story's fin-de-siecle epoch. ❿ By extending the guilt for this offense transgenerationally, Gordimer implicates a whole morally corrupt society in the fate of Lucas.

Which is the proper order of paragraphs A~D?
① A - C - B - D
② B - C - A - D
✓③ C - D - A - B
④ D - B - C - A

해석

❶ 나딘 고디머(Nadine Godimer)의 소설 '총알이 발사되기 직전(The Moment Before the Gun Went Off)'의 중요한 주제는 부계유전(父系遺傳)이다.

C ❷ 이 소설은 빌럼 반 더 비버(Willem Van der Vyver)라는 인물에 대한 언급을 여러번 포함하는데, 그는 현재 고인이 된 가부장적인 인물로, 그의 존재만으로도 그의 아들의 삶이 빛을 잃는 것처럼 보인다. ❸ 마음에서 마레 반 더 비버(Marais Van der Vyver)의 명성은 그의 아버지의 유산과 직접적으로 관련이 있다. ❹ 아들인 마레 반 더 비버는 아버지의 '최고의 농장'을 물려받았고, 그의 직원들은 '선대의 반 더 비버'를 위해 일했던 사람들의 자녀들이다. ❺ 이것은 그 아들이 아버지의 사회적, 경제적, 심리적 인간관계 네트워크를 전부 물려받았음을 암시한다.

D ❻ 그런데, 중요하게도, 마레 반 더 비버의 아들인 농장 노동자 루카스(Lucas)를 죽이는 것은 다름 아닌 마레 반 더 비버의 아버지의 총이라는 것을, 그래서 이 폭력의 유산이 할아버지에서 아들로, 그리고 마침내 비극적이게도 손자로 전해진다는 것을 우리는 알게 된다.

A ❼ 마레 반 더 비버가 자신의 삶에서 이렇게 중요한 사건에 대해 어떤 자발적인 통제력도 갖지 못했다는 사실은 이러한 범죄에 대한 책임이 오직 그에게만 있지는 않다는 것을 강조하며, ❽ 마레가 물려받은 다른 것들에 대해서도 그에게 전적으로 책임이 있는 것은 아닐수도 있다는 것을 시사한다.

B ❾ 그렇다면 1948년에 오늘날의 인종차별정책을 만든 세대인 그의 아버지 세대 때의 마레 반 더 비버 자신의 선험(미경험) 역사는 이 소설의 세기말 시대(아들 루카스 세대) 전의 (기경험) 역사적인 순간일지도 모른다. ❿ 이러한 범죄에 대한 죄의식을 초세대적으로 확장함으로써, 고디머는 루카스의 운명에 도덕적으로 부패한 (모든 세대의) 전체 사회를 연루시킨다.

해설

주어진 문장에서 고단의 소설의 주제인 '부계유전'을 언급한다. 그리고 C 에서 주인공인 마레 반 더 비버가 부계유전으로 아버지로부터 물려받은 것이 무엇인지에 대해 설명을 하고 있다. D 에서는 물려받은 중 아들 루카스를 총으로 죽이는 비극적 사건을 폭력의 유산이라고 말한다. 이어서 A 에서는 이 비극의 책임이 전적으로 마레 개인에게만 있는 것은 아니라고 말한다. 마지막으로 B 에서는 그 책임 사회 전체에 있음을 연루시킨다.

어휘

go off (화기가) 발사되다 **paternal** a. 아버지의, 아버지로부터 물려받은 **inheritance** n. 상속 재산 **volitional control** 의지적 통제, 자발적 통제 **pivotal event** 중대사건 **misdeed** n. 나쁜 짓, 범죄 행위 **exclusively** ad. 배타적으로, 독점적으로 **reside with** ~에 있다, ~에 속하다 **prehistory** n. 선사시대사; (어떤 상황에 이르는) 과정, 경위, 전(前)단계 **apartheid** n. 아파르트헤이트 (남아프리카 공화국의 인종 차별 정책) **fin-de-siècle** n. 세기말(世紀末) a. 세기말적인 **epoch** n. (중요한 사건·변화들이 일어난) 시대 **guilt** n. 죄책감, 죄의식 **offense** n. 위법행위, 범죄 **transgenerationally** ad. 시대를 망라하게 **the late** (최근에) 사망한, 고(故) **patriarchal** a. 가부장제의, 가부장적인 **overshadow** v. (~의 그늘에 가려) 빛을 잃게 만들다, ~을 볼품없게 보이게 하다 **prominence** n. 명성, 유명함 **legacy** n. (죽은 사람이 남긴) 유산 **pass on** ~에게 물려주다 **tragically** ad. 비극적으로, 비참하게 **implore** v. ~을 애원[탄원]하다 **articulate** v. (생각·감정을) 분명히 표현하다, 설명하다 **consensus** n. 의견 일치, 합의

018 ③ 2019학년도 인하대학교 인문계 09번

글의 주제
❶ Motion detectors are small electronic eyes (that detect infrared waves) — heat waves (that radiate from moving objects). ❷ When the detector senses an object moving across its field of view / — especially warmer objects / such as people, animals and cars — / it electronically turns on the lights. ❸ The light stays on anywhere / from 1 to 20 minutes, / depending on / how you preset the time. Then the detector automatically shuts the light off / (unless it continues to sense movement). ❹ A photocell deactivates the light / during daylight hours.

Ⓑ ❺ Most motion detectors have a semicircular field of view / of up to 240 degrees and a distance range, (adjustable on most detectors), / (that extends to 70 feet or more). ❻ The detector will react to the movement of your dog, an approaching person, a passing car or sometimes even wind-blown leaves.

Ⓒ ❼ Nuisance trips, (such as blowing leaves or a passing car), can fool / the detector and turn / the lights on / when you don't want them. ❽ These can be annoying / to both you and your neighbors, / and in fact, / some homeowners won't install motion detector lights / for this reason.

Ⓐ ❾ However, you can solve most unwanted switching-on / by adjusting the distance-range setting and by carefully aiming the sensor to limit its field of view. ❿ You can also narrow the field of view even more / by applying tape / to the sensor. ⓫ If nuisance trips concern you, / be sure to buy a light (that has an adjustable distance-range setting, and an aimable detector unit).

Which of the following is the best order for a passage starting with the given sentences in the box?
주어진 문장 다음에 이어질 순서로 가장 적절한 것은?

① Ⓐ - Ⓒ - Ⓑ
② Ⓑ - Ⓐ - Ⓒ
✓③ Ⓑ - Ⓒ - Ⓐ
④ Ⓒ - Ⓐ - Ⓑ
⑤ Ⓒ - Ⓑ - Ⓐ

해석
❶ 동작 감지기는 움직이는 물체에서 발산하는 열의 파장인 적외선을 감지하는 작은 전자 눈이다. ❷ 시야를 가로질러 움직이는 물체를 감지하면 ~특히 사람, 동물, 자동차 등과 같이 주변보다 더 따뜻한 열을 가진 물체- 그것은 전자적으로(컴퓨터를 통해) 조명을 킨다. ❸ 그 조명은 당신이 사전에 맞춘 시간에 따라 1분에서 20분까지 얼마 동안이든지 켜져 있게 된다. 그 다음에 움직임을 계속해서 감지하지 못하는 경우, 동작 감지기는 자동으로 조명을 끈다. ❹ 광전지는 낮 동안에는 조명을 비활성화시킨다.
Ⓑ ❺ 대부분의 동작 감지기는 최대 240도에 이르는 반원(半圓) 시야와 70피트 이상까지 확장되는, 대부분의 감지기에서 조정이 가능한 거리 범위를 가지고 있다. ❻ 동작 감지기는 당신의 강아지의 움직임, 다가오는 사람, 지나가는 차, 때로는 바람에 날리는 나뭇잎에도 반응할 것이다.
Ⓒ ❼ 날리는 나뭇잎이나 지나가는 자동차 같은 귀찮은 움직임은 동작 감지기를 속여 당신이 원하지 않는 경우에도 조명이 켜지게 할 수 있다. ❽ 이것은 당신과 당신의 이웃 모두를 짜증나게 할 수 있으며, 사실 일부 집주인들은 이러한 이유로 동작 감지기를 설치하지 않고 싶어 한다.
Ⓐ ❾ 그러나 원치 않는 상황에서 조명이 켜지는 것은 거리 범위 설정을 조정하고 센서를 잘 조준하여 시야의 범위를 제한하여 대부분 해결할 수 있다. ❿ 또한 센서에 테이프를 붙여서 시야의 범위를 더욱 좁힐 수도 있다. ⓫ 다른 물체의 성가신 움직임이 걱정되면 반드시 거리 범위 설정 조정이 가능한 전구와 조준 방향을 변경할 수 있는 동작 감지기를 구입해라.

해설 주어진 문장에서 동작 감지기에 대한 개념을 설명하고 Ⓑ에서는 거리 범위와 반응의 한계를 이어서 설명한다. 그리고 Ⓒ에서는 반응의 한계를 성가신 것으로 언급하며 불편함을 구체적으로 설명하며, 마지막 Ⓐ에서는 이에 대한 해결책을 제시하고 있는 글이다.

어휘 motion detector 동작 감지기 detect v. 발견하다; 간파하다, 탐지하다 infrared a. 적외선의 radiate v. (빛·열 등을) 방사하다, 발하다 preset v. 미리 설치하다 photocell n. 광전지 deactivate v. (어떤 장치의 작동을) 정지시키다 unwanted a. 불필요한, 쓸모없는 adjust v. 조정하다, 맞추다 narrow v. 좁게 하다, 좁히다 nuisance n. 난처한 것, 성가신 것 semicircular a. 반원형의 extend v. 늘어나다; 달하다, 미치다 react v. 반응을 나타내다, 감응하다 annoying a. 성가신, 귀찮은 neighbor n. 이웃사람, 이웃집 install v. 설치하다

정답 및 해설

019 ②
2020학년도 인하대학교 인문계 29번

❶ If you're shopping / for a live Christmas tree / this year, / you may have to search harder / than in the past. ❷ Over the last five years / Christmas tree shortages have been reported / in many parts of the U.S.

[B] ❸ One factor is / that growers sold off land and planted fewer trees / during and after the 2008 recession. ❹ In the lifespan of Christmas trees, / the decade (from 2008 to the present) / is roughly a single generation of plantings. ❺ However, in my research (on the human dimensions of farming and food systems), / I also see other factors / at play.

[D] ❻ Christmas trees take 6 to 12 years to mature, / and consumer preferences often change more quickly / than farmers can adjust. ❼ Climate change is altering temperature and rainfall patterns, which severely affects growers' ability [to produce high-quality trees and the varieties (that customers seek)].

[A] ❽ Collectively, / these trends don't bode well for Christmas tree lovers, the growers, or the industry. ❾ However, there are opportunities / for younger farmers / to enter this market, either full- or part-time.

[C] ❿ If new and beginning growers live / in an area / with appropriate environmental conditions, / ⓫ Christmas trees are a high-quality complementary crop (that farmers can use / to diversify their operations and provide off-season income.)

Which of the following is the best order for a passage starting with the given sentences in the box?
주어진 문장 다음에 이어질 순서로 가장 적절한 것은?

① Ⓐ – Ⓒ – Ⓑ – Ⓓ   ✓② Ⓑ – Ⓓ – Ⓐ – Ⓒ
③ Ⓑ – Ⓒ – Ⓓ – Ⓐ   ④ Ⓓ – Ⓐ – Ⓒ – Ⓑ
⑤ Ⓓ – Ⓒ – Ⓐ – Ⓑ

해석 ❶ 만약 올해 생목(生木) 크리스마스트리를 구입하려 하고 있다면, 과거보다 더 열심히 검색해야 할 수도 있다. ❷ 지난 5년 동안 미국의 많은 지역에서 크리스마스트리 부족이 보고되었다.
[B] ❸ 2008년의 불경기와 그 이후에 재배업자들이 땅을 매각하고 나무를 더 적게 심은 것이 한 요인이다. ❹ 크리스마스트리의 수명에서 볼 때, 2008년부터 현재까지 10년 동안 심은 나무들이 약 한 세대에 해당한다. ❺ 그러나 농업과 식품 시스템의 인간적인 차원에 관한 연구에서 오는 다른 요소들도 작용하고 있음을 알게 된다.
[D] ❻ 크리스마스트리는 다 자라기까지 6년에서 12년이 걸리며, 소비자의 선호도는 종종 농부들이 적응할 수 있는 것보다 더 빨리 바뀐다. ❼ 기후 변화는 기온과 강수 패턴을 변화시키고 있으며, 이것은 재배업자들이 양질의 나무와 고객들이 찾는 품종을 생산해내는 데 심각한 영향을 미친다.
[A] ❽ 전체적으로, 이러한 경향은 크리스마스트리를 사랑하는 사람, 재배업자, 혹은 해당 산업에 좋은 징조가 아니다. ❾ 그러나 보다 젊은 농부들이 풀타임이나 파트타임으로 이 시장에 진출할 기회는 있다.
[C] ❿ 처음 시작하는 재배업자들이 적절한 환경 조건을 갖춘 지역에 산다면, ⓫ 크리스마스트리는 농사 운영을 다양화하고 비수기 수입을 올리기 위해 농민들이 활용할 수 있는 양질의 보완작물이다.

해설 주어진 문장에서 크리스마스 트리가 지난 5년 간 미국에서 부족했음을 언급하고 있다. [B]에서는 그에 대한 원인을 말하고 있으며 [D]에서는 또 다른 원인을 언급한다. 그리고 [A]과 [C]에서는 이러한 경향의 부정과 긍정적 측면을 말하고 있다.

어휘 shortage n. 부족, 결핍 collectively ad. 집합적으로; 공동으로 bode well for ~에게 좋은 조짐이다 sold off 매각 recession n. 후퇴; 불경기 lifespan n. (생물체의) 수명 roughly ad. 대충, 개략적으로 generation n. 세대; 자손, 일족 planting n. (나무 등을) 심기; (갓) 심은 것 dimension n. 차원; 관점 environmental a. 주위의; 환경의 complementary a. 보충하는, 상보적인 crop n. 수확; 농작물, 곡물 diversify v. 다양화하다, 다채롭게 하다; (사업을) 다각화하다 income n. 수입, 소득 mature v. 성숙하다 consumer preference 소비자 선호 adjust v. 맞추다, 조정하다 alter v. 바꾸다, 변경하다 affect v. ~에 영향을 주다; 악영향을 끼치다

020 ① 2020학년도 명지대학교 인문계 17번

❶ In 1798 / Thomas Malthus explained / that the frequent famines (of his era) were unavoidable / because "population, (when unchecked), increases / in a geometrical ratio / while subsistence increases / only in an arithmetic ratio." ❷ Where did Malthus's math go wrong? ❸ Looking at the first of his curves, / we already saw / that population growth needn't increase / in a geometric ratio / indefinitely, / ❹ (because when people get richer and more of their babies / survive), / they have fewer babies. ❺ Conversely, famines don't reduce population growth / for long.

C ❻ Looking at the second curve, / we discover / that the food supply can grow geometrically / when knowledge is applied to increase / the amount of food (that can be coaxed / out of a patch of land). ❼ (Since the birth of agriculture / ten thousand years ago), / humans / have been genetically engineering / plants and animals / (by selectively breeding the ones [that were the easiest (to plant and harvest)]. ❽ Clever farmers also tinkered with irrigation, plows, and organic fertilizers, / ❾ but Malthus always had the last word.

A ❿ (It was) only at the time of the Industrial Revolution (that) people figured out how to bend the curve upward. ⓫ Crop rotation and improvements (to plows and seed drills) were followed / by mechanization. ⓬ In the mid-19th century / it took twenty-five men / a full day / to harvest and thresh a ton of grain; ⓭ today / one person (operating a combine harvester) can do it / in six minutes.

B ⓮ So / forget arithmetic ratios: over the past century, / grain yields per hectare have swooped upward / (while real prices have plunged). ⓯ The savings are mind-boggling. ⓰ (If the food (grown today) had to be grown / with pre-nitrogen-farming techniques], / an area the size of Russia would go / under the plow.

Choose the best order after the paragraph in the box
주어진 단락 다음에 이어질 가장 적절한 순서는?

✓① C - A - B ② A - C - B
③ C - B - A ④ A - B - C

해석 ❶ 1798년 토머스 맬서스(Thomas Malthus)는 "인구는 억제되지 않을 경우 기하급수적인 비율로 증가하는 반면에 식량은 단지 산술급수적인 비율로 증가한다" 때문에 그가 살던 시대의 잦은 기근은 피할 수 없었다고 설명했다. ❷ 맬서스의 계산은 어디서 틀렸을까? ❸ 그가 제시한 곡선들 중 첫 번째 곡선(인구증가 곡선)을 보면, 인구증가가 기하급수적인 비율로 무한하게 증가할 필요가 없다는 것을 우리는 이미 알게 되는데, ❹ 왜냐하면 사람들이 부유해지고 그들의 아기들이 대부분 생존하기 때문에, 아이를 덜 낳기 때문이다. ❺ 반대로, 기근은 인구증가를 오랫동안 감소시키지 않는다.

C ❻ 그의 두 번째 곡선(식량 공급곡선)을 보면, 우리는 작은 땅에서 얻을 수 있는 식량의 수확량을 증가시키기 위해 지식이 적용될 때 식량 공급이 기하급수적으로 증가할 수 있다는 것을 발견한다. ❼ 10,000년 전 농업이 탄생한 이래로, 인간은 심고 수확하기가 가장 쉬운 작물들을 선택적으로 교배하는 방법으로 식물과 동물을 유전적으로 조작해왔다. ❽ 또한, 손재주가 있는 농부들은 관개, 쟁기질, 그리고 유기질 비료 살포도 했다. ❾ 그러나 맬서스는 항상 결정적인 발언을 했었다.

A ❿ 산업혁명 시기에 비로소 사람들이 이 곡선(식량 공급곡선)을 어떻게 위쪽으로 구부리는지 알아냈다. ⓫ 윤작, 향상된 쟁기질, 그리고 파종기는 (농업의) 기계화로 이어졌다. ⓬ (그래서) 19세기 중반에 1톤의 곡식을 수확하고 탈곡하기 위해서는 25명의 사람들이 하루 종일 일해야 했는데, ⓭ 오늘날에는 복식수확기를 작동하는 한 사람이 6분이면 그 일을 끝낼 수 있다.

B ⓮ 따라서 산술급수적인 증가율은 이제 잊자. 지난 세기 동안 실질적인 가격 폭락에도 1헥타르 당 곡물 수확량은 급증했다. ⓯ (식량의) 비축량은 믿기 어려울 정도이다. ⓰ 만일 오늘날 재배되는 식량을 질소비료 이전 농법으로 재배해야 한다면, 러시아 정도 되는 땅을 경작해야 할 것이다.

해설 주어진 문장에서 토머스 맬서스의 논리인 기하급수적 인구 증가와 산술급수적인 식량 증가가 잘못되었음을 말한다. 그리고 이어서 주어진 문장 중반 부터는 인구 증가가 기하급수적 비율로 증가할 필요가 없다는 것을 말하고, C에서는 두 번째 논리인 산술급수적인 식량 증가를 반박하기 시작한다. 이에 대한 논증으로 시간 순서로 농업혁명 그리고 A에서 산업혁명을 차례로 언급하며 B에서는 농작물 생산의 산술급수적 증가가 결론적으로 잘못되었음을 나타내고 있다.

어휘 frequent a. 잦은, 빈번한 famine n. 기근 geometrical a. 기하급수적인 subsistence n. 생활비, 생존, 생계 arithmetic a. 산술급수적인 indefinitely ad. 무기한으로 coax v. (물건을) 잘 다루어 뜻대로 되게 하다 patch n. 부분, 조각 engineer v. 유전자를 조작하다 breed v. 재배하다 harvest v. 수확하다 tinker with ~에 손을 대다 irrigation n. 관개 plow n. (경작용) 쟁기 have the last word 최종결정권을 가지다, 최종적인[결론적인] 의견을 말하다 crop rotation 윤작 seed drill 파종기 thresh v. (곡물을) 탈곡하다 hectare n. 헥타르(면적의 단위, 1ha=10,000㎡) swoop up 훽 들어 올리다 plunge v. (가격이) 급락하다 mind-boggling a. 믿기 어려운

유형 03 문장삽입

001 ③   2019학년도 국민대학교 인문계 오전 A형 30번

❶ The first thing that DNA molecules do is to replicate, that is to say: they make copies of themselves. Ⓐ ❷ This has gone on non-stop ever since the beginning of life, and the DNA molecules are now very good at it indeed. Ⓑ ❸ As an adult, you consist of a thousand million million cells, but when you were first conceived you were just a single cell, endowed with one master copy of the plans to build your body. Ⓒ ❺ Successive divisions took the number of cells up to 4, 8, 16, 32, and so on into the billions. Ⓓ ❻ At every division the DNA plans were faithfully copied, with scarcely any mistakes.

Which is the best place for the following?
주어진 단락 다음에 이어질 가장 적절한 순서는?

> ❹ This cell divided into two, and each of the two cells received its own copy of the plans.

① Ⓐ   ② Ⓑ   ③ Ⓒ   ④ Ⓓ

해석

❶ DNA 분자가 가장 먼저 하는 일은 복제, 즉, 자신과 똑같은 것을 만들어내는 것이다. Ⓐ ❷ 이것은 생명이 시작된 이래 한 번도 멈추지 않고 계속되어 왔으며, DNA 분자는 정말로 그 일에 능숙하다. Ⓑ ❸ 성인의 몸은 1천조 개의 세포로 이루어져 있지만, 처음 임신이 이루어졌을 때, 그것은 몸을 만들어나갈 설계도의 원본을 가지고 있는 단 하나의 세포일 뿐이었다. Ⓒ <❹ 이 세포는 둘로 나뉘었고, 그 각각의 두 세포는 그 설계도의 복사본을 받았다.> ❺ 잇따른 분열은 세포의 수를 4, 8, 16, 32개로, 그리고 이어서 수십억 개가 되게 했다. Ⓓ ❻ 분열이 이루어질 때마다 DNA 설계도는 실수가 거의 없이 충실히 복제되었다.

해설

❸번 문장 마지막에서 단 하나의 세포였다고 말한 뒤 주어진 문장에서 '이 세포는 둘로 나뉘었고,'라고 말하는 것이 적절하게 연결된다.

어휘

molecule n. 분자 **replicate** v. 복제하다, 복사하다 **consist of** ~로 구성돼 있다, ~로 이루어져 있다 **conceive** v. (감정·의견 따위를) 마음에 품다; (아이를) 임신하다 **endow** v. ~에게 주다, 부여하다 **successive** a. 잇따른, 계속되는 **division** n. 분할; 분배 **faithfully** ad. 충실히, 충직하게, 정확히 **scarcely** ad. 겨우, 간신히, 결코 ~이 아닌

002 ③ 2019학년도 국민대학교 인문계 오후 A형 14번

Ⓐ ❶ Many supermarket chains discount food / at regular intervals — ❷ for example, a certain ice cream might be half price / once every four weeks. Ⓑ ❸ Other staple foods (that are discounted regularly) include bread, juice, pasta sauce, coffee, biscuits, yoghurt and cereals. Ⓒ ❺ Also, think about doing your shopping / in the last hour / before your local supermarket closes. Ⓓ ❻ That's (when you can find big discounts / on perishable products / such as bread, meat, fish and dairy products.)

Which is the best place for the following?
다음 문장이 들어갈 가장 적절한 곳은?

> ❹ Once you're aware of the pattern, you need never buy these products at full price again.

① Ⓐ ② Ⓑ ③ Ⓒ ✓ ④ Ⓓ

해석
Ⓐ ❶ 많은 슈퍼마켓 체인점들은 일정한 시간 간격을 두고 식품 가격을 할인해 준다. ❷ 예를 들어, 어떤 아이스크림은 4주에 한 번씩 반값에 판매될 수도 있다. Ⓑ ❸ 정기적으로 가격을 할인해 주는 다른 주요 식품들에는 빵, 주스, 파스타 소스, 커피, 비스킷, 요구르트, 시리얼이 있다. Ⓒ <❹ 일단 당신이 이런 패턴을 알게 된다면, 당신은 이들 제품을 다시는 정가에 살 필요가 없다.> ❺ 또한 동네 슈퍼마켓이 문을 닫기 직전에 쇼핑하는 것도 한번 생각해 보라. Ⓓ ❻ 이 시간에는 빵, 육류, 생선, 유제품과 같이 상하기 쉬운 제품에 대해 큰 할인받을 수 있다.

해설
첫 문장 'at regular intervals(일정 간격)'와 '~are discounted regularly(정기적으로 할인되다)'라는 표현에서 주어진 문장에서 말하는 '패턴 (the pattern)'을 알 수 있다. 그리고 ❸번 문장에서 구체적인 할인 상품들 예시가 주어진 문장 'these products (이런 상품들)'를 가리킨다.

어휘
at regular intervals 일정한 시간간격을 두고 staple food 주식(主食), 주요 식품 perishable a. (식품이) 잘 상하는, 상하기 쉬운 dairy product 유제품

003 ③ 2019학년도 가톨릭대학교 인문계 A형 22번

❶ Influenza is a constantly evolving virus. Ⓐ ❷ It quickly goes through mutations (that slightly alter the properties of its H and N antigens.) Ⓑ ❸ Due to these changes, acquiring immunity (either by getting sick or vaccinated) to an influenza subtype such as H1N1 one year will not necessarily mean a person is immune to a slightly different virus (circulating in subsequent years.) Ⓒ ❺ In other cases, however, the virus can undergo major changes to the antigens such that most people don't have an immunity to the new virus, resulting in pandemics. Ⓓ ❻ This antigenic shift can occur if an influenza A subtype in an animal jumps directly into humans.

Choose the best place for the following sentence.
다음 문장이 들어갈 가장 적절한 곳을 고르시오.

❹ But (since the strain produced by this antigenic drift is still similar to older strains), the immune systems of some people will still recognize and properly respond to the virus.

① Ⓐ   ② Ⓑ   ✓③ Ⓒ   ④ Ⓓ

해석

❶ 독감은 끊임없이 진화하는 바이러스이다. Ⓐ ❷ 그것은 자신의 H항원과 N항원의 성질을 조금씩 바꾸는 돌연변이를 빠르게 거친다. Ⓑ ❸ 이러한 변화 때문에, 어느 해에 H1N1과 같은 인플루엔자의 아류형(亞流形)에 관한 (병에 걸려서 혹은 백신 접종을 통해) 면역력을 얻었다는 것이 다음 여러 해에 퍼지는 약간 다른 바이러스에 대해 반드시 면역된다는 것을 의미하지는 않는다. Ⓒ <❹ 그러나, 이러한 항원 변이에 의해 생성되는 변종은 여전히 원래의 변종과 유사하므로, 몇몇 사람들의 면역체계는 여전히 그 바이러스를 인식하고 적절하게 반응할 것이다.> ❺ 하지만 다른 경우에는, 그 바이러스는 대부분 사람들이 새로운 바이러스에 면역력을 갖지 못할 정도로 항원에 주요한 변화를 겪고, 그 결과 전 세계적인 유행병이 된다. Ⓓ ❻ 이러한 항원 변이는 동물의 아류형 인플루엔자 A가 사람에게 직접 침투할 경우 발생할 수 있다.

해설

❸번 문장에서 '인플루엔자의 아류형에 관한 면역력을 얻었다는 것이 다음 해에 퍼지는 약간 다른 바이러스에 대한 면역이 된다는 것을 의미하지 않는다'고 말한 뒤 역접 'But(그러나)' 이후 이 바이러스는 원래 변종과 유사하므로, 적절하게 반응할 것이라고 말하는 것이 주어진 문장 위치로 가장 적절하다.

어휘

influenza n. 인플루엔자, 독감 constantly ad. 변함없이, 항상 evolve v. 서서히 발전하다, 진화하다 mutation n. 변화; 돌연변이, 변종 slightly ad. 약간, 조금 alter v. (모양·성질 등을) 바꾸다, 변경하다 property n. 재산, 자산; 성질, 특성 antigen n. 항원(抗原) acquire v. 획득하다; (버릇·기호 따위를) 얻다, 배우다, 습득하다 immunity n. 면역; (책임·의무의) 면제 vaccinate v. ~에게 예방 접종을 하다, ~에게 백신 주사를 놓다 subtype n. 아류형, 특수형 immune a. 면역성의; (의무 등을) 면한 circulate v. 돌다, 순환하다 subsequent a. 차후의, 다음의; 계속해서 일어나는 strain n. (동식물·질병 등의) 종류[유형]; 변종(變種) antigenic drift 항원 변이 undergo v. (영향·변화·조치·검사 따위를) 받다, 입다; (시련 등을) 경험하다, 겪다 pandemic n. 전국적[세계적]으로 유행하는 질병

004 ③ 2019학년도 광운대학교 인문계 A형 30번

❶ Icy water is soaking my backside, / my hands are freezing and the waves are breaking / over our kayak's bow. Ⓐ ❷ I'm starting to consider the wisdom / of what we're doing. ❸ But there's a penguin (squawking / as it swims past the kayak and then an iceberg — AN ICEBERG!) Ⓑ ❹ Shockingly, / it floats past and there's a huge grin / on my dad's face. Ⓒ ❺ Dad and I have kicked / around an Antarctic trip / for years, / but the timing was never quite right. Ⓓ ❻ And both of us were skeptical / of spending so much time / aboard a cruise ship / to get there. Ⓔ ❼ But commercial cruise ships are generally the only option / for most people, unless you can sneak into one of the government-run research bases or have a friend / with a boat (big enough to confront the Drake Passage.)

다음 주어진 표현이 들어갈 가장 적절한 위치는?

❺ And it hits me: This is why we're here in Antarctica.

① Ⓐ   ② Ⓑ   ✓③ Ⓒ   ④ Ⓓ   ⑤ Ⓔ

해석

❶ 얼음처럼 차가운 물이 나의 엉덩이를 적시고 있고, 나의 손은 꽁꽁 얼고 있으며, 파도는 우리가 타고 있는 카약의 뱃머리에 부딪혀 부서지고 있다 Ⓐ ❷ 나는 우리가 하고 있는 일이 현명한 건지 생각하기 시작한다. ❸ 하지만 펭귄 한 마리가 꽥꽥 울며 카약 옆을 헤엄쳐 지나가고 있으며, 그 다음에는 빙산, 바로 빙산이 보인다! Ⓑ ❹ 충격적이게도, 그것이 떠다니며 우리 곁을 지나가고 있으며, 아빠는 얼굴에 커다란 미소를 띠고 있다. Ⓒ <❺ 그리고 나에게는 '그래서 우리가 남극대륙에 다 온 거구나.'라는 생각이 든다.> ❻ 아빠와 나는 수년 동안 남극 여행을 생각해 보았지만, 매년 타이밍이 적절하지 않았다. Ⓓ ❼ 그리고 우리 두 사람 모두 그곳에 가기 위해 유람선을 타고 그렇게 많은 시간을 보내는 것에 회의적이었다. Ⓔ ❽ 하지만 일반적으로 대부분 사람들에게는 민간 유람선이 유일한 선택이다. 만약 당신이 정부가 운영하는 연구 기지들 중 한 곳에 몰래 들어갈 수 없거나 드레이크 해협(Drake Passage)에 맞설 정도로 충분히 큰 배를 갖고 있는 친구도 없다면 말이다.

해설 남극대륙 도착 시 표현할 수 있는 묘사 이후 남극대륙에 우리가 도착했음을 알아차리는 문장이 오는 것이 가장 적절하다.

어휘 soak v. 적시다, 담그다 backside n. 엉덩이 freeze v. 꽁꽁 얼다 break over (파도가) 부딪쳐 ~를 씻다 bow n. 뱃머리 squawk v. 꽥꽥 울다 iceberg n. 빙산 grin n. 밝은 웃음 Antarctica n. 남극 skeptical a. 의심 많은, 회의적인 kick around (제안·계획·문제 등을) 생각해 보다 get there 도착하다 sneak into ~로 몰래 들어가다 government-run a. 정부가 운영하는 Drake Passage 드레이크 해협

005 ④   2019학년도 상명대학교 인문·자연계 32번

글의 주제

❶ President Obama has forbidden federal employees from texting while driving. [A] ❷ The federal Transportation Department plans to do the same for commercial-truck and Interstate-bus drivers. [B] ❸ And support is building in Congress for legislation that would require states to outlaw texting or e-mailing while driving. [C] ❹ Such distractions cause tens of thousands of deaths each year. [D] But the way to stop people from using cellphones while driving is not to make it a crime. ❼ A more effective way is to make it difficult or impossible to text and drive. [E]

아래 문장을 위 본문 중에 추가할 경우, 가장 적절한 위치를 고르시오.

❻ Too many drivers value convenience more than safety and would assume they wouldn't get caught.

① [A]   ② [B]   ③ [C]   ✓ ④ [D]   ⑤ [E]

해석

❶ 오바마(Obama) 대통령은 연방 정부 직원들이 운전 중에 문자메시지를 보내는 것을 금지했다. [A] ❷ 연방 교통부는 영업용 트럭과 장거리 버스의 운전자에게도 똑같은 조치를 취할 계획이다. [B] ❸ 또한 주(州) 당국으로 하여금 운전 중에 문자메시지나 이메일을 보내는 것을 불법으로 규정하는 법의 제정이 의회 내에서 지지를 얻어가고 있다. [C] ❹ 그와 같은 (운전 중에 문자메시지나 이메일을 보내는 것과 같은) 주의 산만으로 매년 수만 명이 사망한다. ❺ 하지만 그러한 행동을 범죄로 만드는 것이 사람들로 하여금 운전 중에 휴대전화를 사용하지 못하도록 하는 방법은 되지 못한다. [D] <❻ 너무 많은 운전자들이 안전보다 편의를 중요하게 생각하며, 그들은 적발되지 않을 거라고 생각할 것이다.> ❼ 더욱 효과적인 방법은 운전 중에 문자메시지를 보내는 것을 어렵거나 불가능하게 만드는 것이다. [E]

해설

운전 중 문자메시지나 이메일 전송을 불법으로 하는 법을 규정하지만, 그들을 막지 못한다고 말한 ❺번 문장 이후로, 그러지 못하는 이유를 언급하는 주어진 문장이 위치하는 것이 가장 적절하다.

어휘

forbid v. 금하다, 금지하다 **federal** a. 연방의, 연방정부의 **text** v. 문자를 보내다 **commercial** a. 상업의 **interstate** a. 주와 주 사이의(미국의) **congress** n. 회의, 의회 **legislation** n. 법률의 제정, 입법 **distraction** n. 주의 산만, 정신을 산란하게 만드는 것 **outlaw** v. 불법화하다, 금지하다 **value** v. 높이 평가하다, 중시하다 **convenience** n. 편의, 편리 **assume** v. 당연한 것으로 여기다, 가정하다

006 ③ — 2019학년도 건국대학교 인문·예체능계 A형 25번

❶ Do you know / why Venus is so hot? Ⓐ ❷ Scientists think / the original atmospheres of both Venus and Earth were created / from gases (released by volcanoes,) when both planets were very young and volcanic activity was much more intense. Ⓑ ❸ But because Venus is so close / to the Sun, the "greenhouse effect," / in which heat is trapped / within its atmosphere, results in the temperature (rising so high that all the surface water evaporated.) Ⓒ ❺ The hydrogen escaped into space / and the oxygen combined with other chemicals / in the atmosphere. Ⓓ ❻ In contrast, Earth cooled down, oceans formed, and life began to develop. Ⓔ ❼ Earth became a living planet / while Venus, (despite its connection to the goddess of love and fertility,) remained barren.

글의 흐름으로 보아, 주어진 문장이 들어가기에 가장 적절한 것은?

❹ With all the water / now in the atmosphere, / the intense ultraviolet radiation (from the Sun) split the water molecules into hydrogen and oxygen.

① Ⓐ ② Ⓑ ✓③ Ⓒ ④ Ⓓ ⑤ Ⓔ

해석

❶ 당신은 금성이 왜 그렇게 뜨거운지 알고 있는가? Ⓐ ❷ 과학자들은 금성과 지구의 원래 대기는 두 행성이 어리고 화산 활동이 훨씬 더 강력했을 때 화산에서 방출된 가스로부터 만들어졌다고 생각한다. Ⓑ ❸ 하지만 금성은 태양에 너무 가까이에 있으므로, 열이 대기 안에 갇히는 '온실효과'가 기온을 너무 상승시키는 결과로 이어져 모든 지표수를 증발시켰다. Ⓒ <❹ 이제는 모든 물이 대기 안에 있는 가운데, 태양에서 나오는 강렬한 자외선이 물 분자를 수소와 산소로 분열시켰다.> ❺ 수소는 우주로 빠져나갔고 산소는 대기의 다른 화학 물질과 결합했다. Ⓓ ❻ 그에 반해, 지구는 열이 식었고, 바다가 형성되었으며, 생명이 생겨나기 시작했다. Ⓔ ❼ 지구는 살아있는 행성이 되었지만, 금성은 사랑과 풍요의 여신과 연관이 있음에도 불구하고 불모지로 남아있었다.

해설

주어진 문장에서 물 분자를 수소와 산소로 분열시켰다고 말한 뒤 Ⓒ에서 그 이후 과정 설명을 이어가고 있다.

어휘

atmosphere n. 대기 intense a. 극심한, 강렬한 ultraviolet radiation 자외 복사(선) molecule n. 분자 hydrogen n. 수소 oxygen n. 산소 Venus n. 금성 greenhouse effect 온실효과 trap v. 가두다; (가스·물·에너지 따위를) 끌어들이다 evaporate v. 증발하다, 기화(氣化)하다 combine v. 결합하다 fertility n. 토지가 기름짐, 비옥함

007 ② 2019학년도 국민대학교 인문계 오후 A형 24번

❶ War is a howling, baying jackal. ❷ Or is it the animating storm? ❸ Suicidal madness or the purifying fire? ❹ An imperialist travesty? ❺ Or the glorious explosion (of a virile nation) made manifest / upon the planet? Ⓐ ❻ In all recorded history, / this debate is recent, / as is the idea of peace / to describe an active state happier / than a mere interrogation (between fisticuffs). Ⓑ ❽ In fact, it never had serious competition — not until 1898, / anyway, / (when Czar Nicholas II of Russia called for an international conference / specifically to discuss "the most effectual means" / to "a real and durable peace.") Ⓒ ❾ That was the first time : nations would gather / without a war / at their backs / to discuss [how war might be prevented systematically.] Ⓓ ❿ Nicholas II was successful. ⓫ His first Peace Conference was held / in 1899. It was followed / by a second, in 1907. ⓬ These meetings gave rise to a process (in which the world gained a common code of international laws.)

Which is the best place for the following?
다음 문장이 들어갈 가장 적절한 곳은?

❼ (Astounding as it may seem), war has consistently won the debate.

① Ⓐ ✓② Ⓑ ③ Ⓒ ④ Ⓓ

해 석

❶ 전쟁은 울부짖으면서 으르렁거리는 자칼이다. ❷ 아니면 생기를 주는 폭풍인가? ❸ 자살의 광기인가 아니면 정화시키는 불인가? ❹ 제국주의적인 억지 해석인가? ❺ 아니면 지구에서 어떤 박력 있는 민족의 영광스러운 폭발이 명백하게 나타난 것인가? Ⓐ ❻ 기록된 모든 역사에서, 평화는 주먹 싸움 사이의 단순한 휴지기(休止期)보다 더 행복한 능동적인 상태를 설명하기 위한 것이라는 생각이 최근에 나온 것처럼, 이 논쟁 역시 최근에 나온 것이다. Ⓑ <❼ 놀랍게 보일지도 모르지만, 전쟁은 언제나 논쟁에서 승리를 거두어왔다. (말로 하는 논쟁으로 전쟁이 미연에 방지된 적은 없었다.)> ❽ 어쨌든 러시아 황제 니콜라이(Nicholas) 2세가 '진실되고 영속적인 평화'를 가져올 수 있는 '가장 효과적인 수단'을 논의하기 위해 국제회의를 열자고 제안했던 1898년까지는 전쟁에 대해 한번도 진지한 경쟁이 일어나지 않았다. Ⓒ ❾ 그것은 어떻게 하면 전쟁을 체계적으로 예방할 수 있는지를 논의하기 위해 전쟁이 일어나고 있지 않은 상황에서 처음으로 국가들이 모인 것이다. Ⓓ ❿ 니콜라이 2세는 성공적이었다. ⓫ 그의 첫 번째 강화 회의가 1899년에 열렸고, 1907년에는 두 번째 강화 회의가 열렸다. ⓬ 이 강화 회의는 세계가 국제법이라는 공통된 법규를 만드는 과정을 야기했다.

해 설

주어진 문장에서 '전쟁은 늘 그 논쟁을 이겨왔다'고 말하는데, Ⓐ문장에서 말하고 있는 최근에 나온 그 논쟁을 가리키는 만큼, 주어진 문장은 Ⓑ에 위치하는 것이 가장 적절하다.

어 휘

howling a. 울부짖는 baying a. 으르렁거리는 jackal n. 자칼(동물) animating a. 생기를 불어넣는 suicidal a. 자살 충동을 느끼는, 죽음을 초래하는 imperialist a. 제국주의자의 travesty n. 졸렬한 모방, 억지 해석 virile a. 박력 있는, 남성미 넘치는 manifest a. 명백한, 분명한 mere a. 겨우~의, ~에 불과한 interregnum n. 군주[원수] 부재 기간; (일반적으로) 공백 (기간) fisticuffs n. 주먹 싸움 astounding a. 몹시 놀라운 Czar n. 러시아 황제, 차르 durable a. 내구성 있는, 오래 가는 Peace Conference 평화 회의, 강화(講和) 회의 give rise to ~을 초래하다 code n. (조직·국가의) 법규[규정] ongoing a. 진행중인, 전진하는

008 ①
2019학년도 덕성여자대학교 오후 26번

❶ Stoicism was one of the many philosophical movements which originated in Athens during its golden age. ❷ First formulated by Zeno of Citium in 301 BC, stoicism stresses indifference to both pleasure and pain, whether in a physical or emotional form. ❸ Stoics hold that reason should be the sole guide of one's actions, and that passions, such as pleasure and pain, cloud one's reason. ❺ Stoics train themselves to lead a materially simple life. ⓑ ❻ Luxuries are to be avoided. ⓒ ❼ Similarly, stoics seek to lead an emotionally simple life, free of emotional entanglements. ⓓ ❽ Stoics taught themselves to live apart from their society, at least in an emotional sense.

Where should the following sentence be inserted to make the paragraph complete?
단락을 완성하기 위해 주어진 문장이 들어가야 할 곳은 어디인가?

> ❹ To a stoic, the ability to think clearly is the greatest of all virtues, and anything that impairs this ability should be avoided.

✓① Ⓐ ② Ⓑ ③ Ⓒ ④ Ⓓ

해석
❶ 스토아 철학은 황금기에 아테네에서 발생한 많은 철학 운동들 중 하나였다. ❷ 기원전 301년에 키프로스의 제논(Zeno)이 최초로 정립한 스토아 철학은 물질적 형태든 정신적 형태든 쾌락과 고통 모두에 대한 무관심함을 강조한다. ❸ 스토아학파의 철학자들은 이성이 사람의 행동의 유일한 지침이 되어야 하고, 쾌락과 고통 같은 열정은 사람의 이성을 흐리게 한다고 주장한다. Ⓐ <❹ 스토아학파의 철학자에게는 명확하게 생각하는 능력이 최고의 미덕이며, 이런 능력을 해치는 것은 무엇이든 피해야 한다.> ❺ 스토아학파의 철학자들은 물질적으로 단순한 생활을 영위할 수 있도록 스스로를 훈련한다. Ⓑ ❻ 사치는 피해야 한다. Ⓒ ❼ 마찬가지로, 스토아학파의 철학자들은 감정적인 혼란에서 벗어나 정서적으로 단순한 인생을 영위하고자 한다. Ⓓ ❽ 스토아학파의 철학자들은 그들이 적어도 감정적인 면에서는 사회에서 떨어져 살 수 있도록 스스로를 가르쳤다.

해설
주어진 문장에서 '이런 능력을 해치는 것은 무엇이든 피해야 한다'고 말하고 있는데, 이에 대한 구체적인 행동을 Ⓐ문장부터 지문 마지막까지 설명하고 있다.

어휘
Stoicism n. 스토아 철학 philosophical a. 철학의, 냉철한 formulate v. 공식화하다; 만들어 내다 stress v. 강조하다 indifference n. 무관심, 냉담 Stoic n. 스토아학파의 철학자 guide n. 지침, 지표 passion n. 열정, 정념 cloud v. (기억·판단 등을) 흐리게 하다 materially ad. 실질적으로, 구체적으로, 대단히 luxury n. 사치; 사치품 쾌락 entanglement n. 얽힘, 얽히게 함, 혼란 impair v. 손상시키다, 해치다

009 ③ 2019학년도 한국산업기술대학교 인문계 30번

글의 주제

❶ Parents have different social expectations of daughters and sons. Ⓐ ❷ Daughters, (more than sons,) are socialized / to think more about the family, for example, to remember birthdays, / to spend time with the family on holidays, / and, when they get older, / to provide care for sick family members and relatives. Ⓑ ❸ Sons are not expected / to do these things. ❹ They are expected / to be more interested in the world outside the family / and more independent of the family / in social activities. Ⓒ ✓ ❻ For example, parents may make their daughters come home earlier at night and forbid them to go to places (that they might let their sons go to). Ⓓ ❼ Such protectiveness often encourages girls to be less active / in exploring their environment.

Choose the most suitable position of the sentence below in the above passage.
위 단락에서 아래 문장이 들어가기에 가장 적절한 곳을 고르시오.

> ❺ Daughters / are also taught / to need more protection than sons.
> 딸들은 / 정답근거 / 더 보호 받아야 한다

① Ⓐ ② Ⓑ ✓③ Ⓒ ④ Ⓓ

해석 ❶ 부모들은 딸과 아들에 대해 서로 다른 사회적 기대를 하고 있다. Ⓐ ❷ 예를 들어, 아들보다 딸들이 가족에 관해서 더 많이 생각하고, 생일을 기억하고, 휴일에 가족들과 시간을 보내며, 그들이 나이가 들면, 병든 가족이나 친척들을 돌보도록 사회화된다. Ⓑ ❸ 아들이 이러한 일들을 할 것으로 기대하지는 않는다. ❹ 그들은 가족 밖의 외부세계에 더 많은 관심을 가지며 가족으로부터 더 독립하여 사회 활동에 더 많은 관심을 가질 것으로 기대된다. Ⓒ <❺ 딸은 또한 아들보다 더 보호받아야 한다고 배움을 받는다.> ❻ 예를 들어, 부모들은 딸이 밤에 더 일찍 귀가하게 하고, 아들은 가게 하는 곳에 딸은 가는 것을 금지할지도 모른다. Ⓓ ❼ 그러한 보호는 종종 소녀들이 주위의 환경을 탐험하는 일에 덜 적극적이도록 만든다.

해설 주어진 문장에서 말하는 딸들이 더 보호받아야 한다는 구체적 예시가 Ⓒ에서 이어지고 있다.

어휘 expectation n. 예상, 기대 socialize v. 사귀다, 어울리다; 사회화시키다 relative n. 친척, 친족, 인척 forbid v. 금하다, 허락하지 않다

010 ③ 2019학년도 인하대학교 인문계 11번

❶ I was born / among the working classes and brought up / among them. ❷ My father was a coal miner, and only a coal miner, (nothing praiseworthy) about him. ❸ He wasn't even respectable, in so far as he got drunk rather frequently, / never went near chapel, and was usually rather rude / to his little immediate bosses / at the pit. Ⓐ ❹ He was always saying tiresome and foolish things / about the men / just above him in control / at the mine. Ⓑ ❺ He offended them all, / almost on purpose, / so how could he expect them to favour him? Ⓒ ❼ My mother was, (I suppose,) superior. ❽ She came from town, and belonged really / to the lower bourgeoisie. Ⓓ ❾ She spoke King's English, / without an accent, / and never in her life / could even imitate a sentence [of the dialect (which my father spoke)], and (which we children spoke out of doors.) Ⓔ

Choose the best place for the sentence(s) in the box.
다음 문장이 들어갈 가장 적절한 곳을 고르시오.

❻ Yet he grumbled / when they didn't.

① Ⓐ   ② Ⓑ   ✓③ Ⓒ   ④ Ⓓ   ⑤ Ⓔ

해 석

❶ 나는 노동자 계급에서 태어나 그들 사이에서 자랐다. ❷ 나의 아버지는 석탄 광부였으며, 칭찬할 만한 것이라고는 하나도 없는 석탄 광부에 불과했다. ❸ 꽤 자주 술에 취하셨고, 예배당은 근처에도 가지 않았으며, 탄광에서 대개 나이가 어렸던 직속 상사들에게 상당히 무례한 행동을 하신 것에 있어서는, 그는 심지어 존경할만한 분도 아니셨다. Ⓐ ❹ 아버지는 광산에서 감독을 맡고 있던 바로 윗사람들에 대해서 짜증스럽고 바보 같은 말들을 했다. Ⓑ ❺ 거의 의도적으로 그들 모두를 불쾌하게 만드셨는데, 아버지는 어떻게 그들이 자신에게 호의를 보이길 기대하겠는가? Ⓒ <❻ 하지만 그들이 불평하지 않을 때도 아버지는 불평을 쏟아내셨다.> ❼ 짐작하건대, 어머니는 아버지보다 나은 분이셨다. ❽ 어머니는 도시 출신이셨고, 실제로 하급 부르주아 계급에 속하셨다. Ⓓ ❾ 어머니는 사투리 억양이 없는 순수 영국 영어를 말했고, 아버지와 우리 형제들이 집 밖에서 썼던 사투리는 평생 한 문장도 흉내조차 낼 수 없으셨다. Ⓔ

해 설

주어진 문장은 '그들이 불평하지 않았을 때도 아버지는 불평했다'라는 뜻이다. 윗글의 ❸~❺번 문장 모두 직장에서 타인들에게 불평을 들을 만한 아버지의 부정적 모습이 언급되고 난 뒤, 역접을 시사하는 Yet과 함께 Ⓒ에 주어진 문장이 들어가는 것이 가장 적절하다.

어 휘

grumble v. 불평하다, 투덜거리다 bring up 기르다, 양육하다, 가르치다 praiseworthy a. 칭찬할 만한, 기특한 respectable a. 존경할만한, 훌륭한 frequently ad. 자주, 빈번하게 chapel n. 예배당 rude a. 버릇없는, 무례한 immediate a. 직접의, 바로 이웃의, 인접한 pit n. 구덩이, 구멍; 채굴장, 갱(坑) tiresome a. 성가신, 짜증스러운 mine n. 광산 offend v. 성나게 하다, 기분을 상하게 하다 on purpose 고의로, 의도적으로 favour v. ~에게 호의를 베풀다, ~에게 친절히 대하다 superior a. 우수한, 보다 나은 bourgeoisie n. 중산계급, 부르주아 계급 King's English 순수 영국 영어 accent n. 악센트, 강세; 지방 사투리 imitate v. 모방하다, 흉내 내다 dialect n. 방언, 지방사투리

011 ②   2019학년도 인하대학교 인문계 30번

❶ Acrophobia is an intense, unreasonable fear of high places. ❷ People (with acrophobia) exhibit emotional and physical symptoms in response to being at great heights. Ⓐ ❸ For instance, one sufferer of extreme acrophobia, Sally Maxwell, is unable to go above the third floor of any building / without feeling enormous anxiety. Ⓑ ❺ Suddenly / she was struck / with terror / by the idea (that she might jump or fall out the open window.) Ⓒ ❻ She crouched / behind a steel filing cabinet, / trembling, / unable to move. Ⓓ ❼ When she finally gathered her belongings and left the building, / she was sweating, her breathing was rapid, and her heart was pounding. Ⓔ ❽ Yet she had no rational explanation / for her fears.

Which is the best place in the passage for the sentence in the box?
다음 문장이 들어갈 가장 적절한 곳은?

> ❹ Her acrophobia began / one evening (when she was working alone / in her office / on the eighth floor of a large building.)

① Ⓐ   ✓ ② Ⓑ   ③ Ⓒ   ④ Ⓓ   ⑤ Ⓔ

해석
❶ 고소공포증은 높은 곳에 대한 강하고 불합리한 두려움이다. ❷ 고소공포증이 있는 사람들은 매우 높은 곳에 있는 것에 대한 반응으로 감정적이고 신체적인 증상을 보인다. Ⓐ ❸ 예를 들어, 극심한 고소공포증을 앓고 있는 샐리 맥스웰(Sally Maxwell)은 엄청난 불안감을 느끼지 않고는 어떤 건물이든 3층 위로 올라가지 못한다. Ⓑ <❹ 그녀의 고소공포증은 어느 날 저녁 대형 빌딩의 8층에 있던 그녀의 사무실에서 혼자 일하고 있을 때 시작되었다.> ❺ 갑자기 그녀는 자신이 열린 창문으로 뛰어내리거나 떨어질지도 모른다는 생각에 공포감에 휩싸였다. Ⓒ ❻ 그녀는 철제 서류 캐비닛 뒤에서 몸을 웅크리고 앉아 움직이지 못하고 떨고 있었다. Ⓓ ❼ 마침내 소지품을 챙겨 건물 밖으로 나왔을 때, 그녀는 땀을 흘리고 있었고, 호흡이 빨랐고, 심장은 심하게 두근거리고 있었다. Ⓔ ❽ 하지만 그녀는 자신이 두려움을 느낀 이유에 대해 합리적으로 설명하지 못했다.

해설
Ⓑ이하부터 샐리 맥스웰이 고소공포증을 느끼기 시작 이후 내용이 구체적으로 기술되어 있으므로, 주어진 문장 즉 고소공포증이 갑작스레 시작된 문장이 위치하는 것이 가장 적절하다.

어휘
acrophobia n. 고소공포증 intense a. 격렬한, 강렬한 unreasonable a. 불합리한, 비합리적인, 비현실적인 exhibit v. 나타내다, 보이다, 드러내다 emotional a. 감정의, 감정적인 physical a. 육체적인; 물질적인 symptom n. 증상 height n. 높은 장소 extreme a. 극도의, 심한; 최대의 enormous a. 거대한, 막대한 terror n. 공포, 두려움 crouch v. 쭈그리다; 웅크리다 tremble v. 떨다, 전율하다 belonging n. (pl.) 소유물, 소지품 sweat v. 땀을 흘리다, 식은땀을 흘리다 pound v. 둥둥 울리다; (심장이) 두근거리다 rational a. 이성적인; 합리적인

012 ② 2019학년도 인하대학교 인문계 10번

Ⓐ ❶ Discovering the basic neural circuitry turned out to be a key breakthrough in understanding anxiety. Ⓑ ❸ Just as a car can go out of control due to either a stuck accelerator or failed brakes, it's not always clear which part of the brain is at fault. Ⓒ ❹ It may turn out that some anxiety disorders are caused by an overactive amygdala (the accelerator) while others are caused by an underactive prefrontal cortex (call it the brake). Ⓓ ❺ It may also be that an entirely different part of the brain holds the key to understanding anxiety. Ⓔ ❻ A behavioral neuroscientist at Emory University has spent six years studying a pea-size knot of neurons (located near the amygdala) with an impossible name: the bed nucleus of the stria terminalis.

Choose the best place for the sentence(s) in the box.
다음 문장이 들어갈 가장 적절한 곳은?

> ❷ It showed that the anxiety response isn't necessarily caused by an external threat; rather, it may be traced to a breakdown in the mechanism that signals the brain to stop responding.

① Ⓐ   ② Ⓑ ✓   ③ Ⓒ   ④ Ⓓ   ⑤ Ⓔ

해석 Ⓐ ❶ 기본적인 신경회로의 발견이 불안감을 이해하는 데 있어 중요한 돌파구인 것으로 드러났다. Ⓑ <❷ 그것은 불안감이라는 반응이 반드시 외부의 위협으로부터 야기되는 것은 아니라는 것을 보여주었다. 오히려, 그것은 반응을 멈추라는 신호를 뇌에 보내는 메커니즘의 고장으로 인한 것일 수도 있다는 것을 보여주었다.> ❸ 자동차가 제어 불능 상태가 되는 것이 엑셀이 움직이지 않아서일 수도 있고 브레이크가 듣지 않아서일 수도 있는 것과 같이, 뇌의 어느 부분이 이상이 있는지가 항상 명확한 것은 아니다. Ⓒ ❹ 일부 불안장애는 과활성 편도체(엑셀)에 의해 유발되는 반면에, 다른 불안장애는 저활성 전두엽 전부(前部) 피질(브레이크)에 의해 유발될 수도 있다. Ⓓ ❺ 또한, 뇌의 완전히 다른 부분이 불안감을 이해하는 열쇠를 가지고 있을 수도 있다. Ⓔ ❻ 에모리(Emory) 대학의 한 행동신경과학자는 편도체 근처에 위치한 콩알 크기의 뉴런 무리를 연구하는 데 6년을 보냈는데, 이것은 있음직하지 않은 분계선 조침대핵이라는 이름을 갖고 있다.

해설 첫 문장에서 '기본적 신경회로의 발견이 불안감을 이해하는데 돌파구인 것으로 드러났다'는 말 다음에 주어진 문장이 부연 설명으로 위치하는 것이 가장 적절하다.

어휘 anxiety n. 걱정, 근심, 불안 external a. 외부의; 밖으로부터의 threat n. 위협, 협박 be traced to ~로 거슬러 올라가다, ~에 귀착하다 breakdown n. 고장, 파손; 쇠약 neural a. 신경의, 신경계의 circuitry n. 회로, 회로 설계 breakthrough n. 돌파구, (과학 혹은 기술의) 획기적인 약진 stuck a. 움직이지 않게 된 accelerator n. (자동차의) 가속 페달, 엑셀러레이터 disorder n. 혼란; 장애, 질환 overactive a. 과민성의, 과도한 amygdala n. 편도선 prefrontal cortex 전두엽 전부(前部) 피질 behavioral a. 행동의, 행동에 관한 neuroscientist n. 신경과학자 neuron n. 신경 단위, 뉴런 bed nucleus of the stria terminalis 분계선조침대핵(스트레스, 불안 등에 관여하는 뇌의 부위)

013 ②   2019학년도 명지대학교 인문계 13번

❶ Historically, people believed that the best way (to predict whether a horse will succeed) has been to analyze his or her pedigree. ❷ Being a horse expert means being able to rattle off everything (anybody could possibly want to know) about a horse's father, mother, grandfathers, grandmothers, brothers, and sisters. (①) ❸ Agents announce, for instance, that a big horse "came to her size legitimately" if her mother's line has lots of big horses. (✓) ❺ While pedigree does matter, it can only explain a small part of a horse's success. (③) ❻ Consider the track record of siblings of all the horses (named Horse of the Year,) racing's most prestigious annual award. (④) ❼ These horses have the best possible pedigrees — the identical family history — as world-historical horses. ❽ Still, more than three-fourths do not win a major race. ❾ The traditional way (of predicting horse success,) (the data tells us,) leaves plenty of room for improvement.

Choose the best place for the sentence given in the box.
다음 문장이 들어갈 가장 적절한 곳은?

❹ There is one problem, however.

해석 ❶ 역사적으로, 말의 성공 여부를 예측하는 가장 좋은 방법은 그 말의 혈통을 분석하는 것이라고 사람들은 믿었다. ❷ (그래서) 말 전문가가 된다는 것은 어떤 말의 아버지, 어머니, 할아버지, 할머니, 형제자매에 대한 누구나 궁금해할 수 있는 모든 것들을 줄줄 말할 수 있다는 것을 의미한다. ① ❸ 예를 들어, 말 중개인들은 어떤 큰 말의 모계혈통에 큰 말들이 많은 경우, 그 말들은 "적출로(적법한 혈통으로) 큰 말이 되었다"고 공표한다. ② <❹ 그러나 여기에는 하나의 문제가 있다.> ❺ 혈통이 중요하긴 하지만, 혈통은 말의 성공에서 작은 부분을 설명할 뿐이다. ③ ❻ (예를 들어) 경마에서 가장 명망 있는 상으로 매년 수여되는 '올해의 말'로 지명된 모든 말의 형제자매의 경마 성적을 검토해 보자. ④ ❼ 이들 말들은 아마도 최고로 좋은 혈통을 갖고 있을지도 모른다. 즉, 세계사에 빛나는 말들과 같은 가족 혈통을 가진 것이다. ❽ 그럼에도 불구하고, 이 말들 중에서 3/4 이상은 주요 경기에서 우승한 적이 없다. ❾ 말의 성공을 예측하는 전통적인 방법은 좀 더 개선할 여지가 많다는 것을 데이터는 말해주고 있다.

해설 말의 혈통 분석의 중요성과 의미를 설명하는 문장 다음에 문제를 제기하는 주어진 문장이 ②에 들어오는 것이 가장 적절하다. ② 다음 문제점들을 구체적으로 설명하고 있다.

어휘 pedigree n. 혈통, 족보 rattle off ~을 (줄줄) 늘어놓다 legitimately ad. 합법적으로, 진짜로 matter v. 중요하다 track record 육상경기의 성적, 실적 sibling n. 형제자매 prestigious a. 명망 있는 leave room for ~의 여지가 있다

014 ③ 2019학년도 국민대학교 인문계 오후 A형 34번

❶ The most important thing you need when applying for a job is a resume — a list of your achievements and qualifications. ⒶGroup ❷ The resume should give all the essential facts about the position you seek, the date of your availability, your education, your work experience, your extra-curricular activities, and your special interests. ⒷGroup ❸ You may include personal data, but you do not have to. ❹ The resume should also list the names and addresses of your references — persons who can write to a prospective employer on your behalf. ⒸGroup ❻ With the resume you must send what a hiring officer expects to see first: a covering letter. ⒹGroup ❼ Since the resume will list all the essential facts about you, the covering letter may be brief. ❽ But it should nonetheless be carefully written. ❾ If the letter makes a bad first impression, you will have one strike against you even before your resume is seen. ❿ With some company offices getting over a thousand applications a month, you need to give yourself the best possible chance, ⓫ and your covering letter can make a difference in the way your resume is read.

Which is the best place for the following?
다음 문장이 들어갈 가장 적절한 곳은?

> ❺ The resume alone, however, will seldom get you a job or even an interview.

① Ⓐ   ② Ⓑ   ✓③ Ⓒ   ④ Ⓓ

[해석]
❶ 입사 지원을 할 때 당신에게 필요한 가장 중요한 것은 성취와 자격에 관한 목록인 이력서이다. Ⓐ ❷ 이력서에는 지원할 부서, 근무 가능 날짜, 학력, 근무한 경력, 과외활동, 그리고 당신의 관심사에 대한 필수사항이 들어가야 한다. Ⓑ ❸ 이력서에 당신의 개인신상자료를 넣어도 되지만, 반드시 해야 하는 것은 아니다. ❹ 이력서에는 추천인의 이름과 주소가 기재되어야 하는데, 이 추천인은 당신을 위해 예비 고용주에게 추천서를 쓸 수 있는 사람을 가리킨다. Ⓒ <❺ 하지만 이력서만으로는 취직이나 심지어 면접 기회조차 거의 얻을 수 없을 것이다.> ❻ 이력서와 함께 인사담당자가 가장 처음 볼 것으로 예상되는 것인 자기소개서를 보내야 한다. Ⓓ ❼ 이력서에 당신에 대해 모든 필수 기재사항이 목록별로 기재돼 있을 것이기 때문에, 자기소개서는 간결하게 써도 된다. ❽ 하지만 자기소개서는 그럼에도 불구하고 신중하게 작성되어야 한다. ❾ 만일 자기소개서가 좋지 않은 첫인상을 준다면, 인사담당자가 당신의 이력서를 보기도 전에 당신은 불리한 감점을 하나 받게 될 것이다. ❿ 일부 기업의 경우 한 달에 1,000건이 넘는 지원서를 받기 때문에, 당신은 가능한 좋은 구직기회를 얻기 위해 최선을 다해야 하며, ⓫ 인사담당자가 이력서를 읽는 방식에 있어서 당신의 자기소개서가 큰 변화를 줄 수 있다.

[해설]
지문 시작부터 Ⓑ번 문장까지 입사 지원 시 이력서의 의미에 대해서 말하고 있다. 그리고 Ⓒ에서부터 이력서 이외 필요한 사항들을 언급하는 만큼, 주어진 문장은 Ⓒ에 위치하는 것이 가장 적절하다. 주어진 문장의 접속사 'however(하지만)'에서 상반된 내용이 시작됨을 쉽게 추측해 볼 수 있다.

[어휘]
apply for 지원하다 **resume** n. 이력서 **qualification** n. 자격증, 자격취득 **essential** a. 필수의 **extra-curricular** a. 정식 과목 이외의, 과외의 **reference** n. (취업 등을 위한) 추천인[신원 보증인] **prospective** a. 미래의, 예비의 **on a person's behalf** ~을 위하여, ~을 대신해서 **covering letter** 자기소개서 **brief** a. 간결한, 간명한 **first impression** 첫인상

015 ③

2019학년도 가톨릭대학교 인문계 A형 32번

글의 주제

❶ The wage gap is a statistical indicator often used as an index of the status of women's earnings relative to men's. ❷ It is also used to compare the earnings of other races and ethnicities to those of white males, a group generally not subject to race- or sex-based discrimination. ❸ The wage gap is expressed as a percentage (e.g., in 2012, women earned 80.9% as much as men aged 16 and over) and is calculated by dividing the median annual earnings for women by the median annual earnings for men. ❹ The Equal Pay Act (EPA), which aims to promote gender equality in the workplace, was signed in 1963, making it illegal for employers to pay unequal wages to men and women who hold the same job and do the same work. Ⓐ ❺ At the time of the EPA's passage, women earned just 58 cents for every dollar earned by men. Ⓑ ❻ By 2011, that rate had increased to 82 cents. Ⓒ ❽ African-American women earn just 69 cents to every dollar earned by white men, and for Hispanic women that figure drops to merely 60 cents per dollar. Ⓓ ❾ Asian women are the exception, earning 87 cents for every dollar earned by white men — a sum higher than women of all other races/ethnicities as well as African-American and Hispanic men.

Choose the best place for the following sentence.
다음 문장이 들어갈 가장 적절한 곳을 고르시오.

> ❼ Minority women fare the worst.

① Ⓐ ② Ⓑ ③ Ⓒ ✓ ④ Ⓓ

해석

❶ 임금 격차는 남성 소득 대비 여성 소득의 현황을 나타내는 지수로 흔히 사용되는 통계지표다. ❷ 그것은 또한 다른 인종과 민족의 소득을 일반적으로 인종차별이나 성차별을 받지 않는 집단인 백인 남성의 소득과 비교하기 위해서도 쓰인다. ❸ 임금 격차는 백분율(예를 들어, 2012년에, 여성은 16세 이상 남성의 80.9%에 해당하는 소득을 벌었다.)로 나타내지며, 여성의 연간 소득의 중앙값을 남성의 연간 소득의 중앙값으로 나누어 계산된다. ❹ 직장 내 양성평등의 촉진을 목표로 하는 평등임금법(EPA)이 1963년에 발효되어, 같은 직업을 갖고서 동일한 일을 하는 남성과 여성에게 고용주들이 불평등한 임금을 지불하는 것을 불법으로 만들었다. Ⓐ ❺ 평등임금법이 통과될 당시에, 남성이 1달러를 벌 때 여성은 58센트밖에 벌지 못했다. Ⓑ ❻ 2011년에, 이 비율은 82센트까지 늘어났다. Ⓒ <❼ 소수집단의 여성이 가장 힘들게 살아가고 있다.> 백인 남성이 1달러를 벌 때 흑인 여성은 69센트를 벌고, 라틴 아메리카계 여성의 경우, 그 수치는 1달러 당 겨우 60센트로 떨어진다. Ⓓ ❾ 백인 남성이 1달러를 버는 동안 87센트를 버는 아시아 여성은 예외인데, 이는 흑인이나 라틴아메리카 남성뿐만 아니라 다른 모든 인종/민족 출신 여성보다 높은 액수이다.

해설

두 번째 단락에서 평등임금법을 이야기한 뒤 Ⓒ 다음부터 구체적인 소수 여성의 임금 불평등 사례를 소개하고 있다. 따라서 '소수집단의 여성이 힘들게 살아가고 있다'는 내용은 Ⓒ에 들어가는 것이 가장 적절하다.

어휘

wage gap 임금 격차 statistical indicator 통계지표 index n. 색인; 지침, 지표 status n. 상태; 지위, 자격 relative a. 비교상의, 상대적인; 비례하는, 관계있는, 적절한 ethnicity n. 민족성, 민족적 배경 discrimination n. 차별, 차별대우 express v. 표현하다, 나타내다 calculate v. 계산하다, 산정하다, 추계하다 median a. 중앙의, 중간의 promote v. 진전[진척]시키다, 조장하다, 장려하다, 촉진하다 gender equality 양성 평등 illegal a. 불법의, 위법의 passage n. (의안의) 통과, 가결 fare v. 지내다, 살아가다, (일이) 되어가다 sum n. 총계, 총액, 금액 minority n. 소수, 소수자

016 ①   2019학년도 세종대학교 인문계 A형 54번

❶ After traveling 300 million miles / through the solar system, / NASA's InSight spacecraft / descended / through the Martian sky / and touched down safely on the smooth surface of Elysium Planitia. ⒜

❸ Using a robotic arm, / the lander will first install a super-sensitive seismometer / on the Martian surface, / where it will listen / for meteorite impacts and Marsquakes. ⒝ ❹ The seismic waves (from these events) will give scientists a clearer picture of the planet's internal structure. ❺ InSight will then release its heat probe, a self-hammering 16-inch nail (that will burrow down / as deep as 16 feet / over the course of several weeks.) ❻ The instrument will measure how much heat escapes from Mars' interior, ❼ which will reveal [the amount of heat-producing radioactive elements (: it contains)] and (how geologically active / the planet is today.) ⒞ ❽ The spacecraft also has two X-band antennas / on its deck (that make up / a third instrument, / called RISE.) ⒟ ❾ Radio signals (from RISE) will be used to track the wobble of Mars' orbit. ❿ This will help researchers understand the size and state of the Martian core. ⓫ Together, / these experiments will crack open Mars and spill the planetary secrets (scientists have sought for decades.)

Which is the most appropriate place for the sentence below?
다음 문장이 들어갈 가장 적절한 곳은?

❷ Unlike the space agency's rovers, InSight is a lander (designed to study an entire planet / from just one spot).

✓① Ⓐ   ② Ⓑ   ③ Ⓒ   ④ Ⓓ

해 석

❶ NASA의 인사이트(InSight) 우주선은 태양계를 가로질러 3억 마일을 여행한 후에, 화성의 하늘을 내려와 엘리시움 평원(Elysium Planitia)의 매끄러운 표면에 안전하게 착륙했다. Ⓐ <❷ 그 항공우주국의 탐사로봇들과는 달리, 인사이트는 오직 한 장소에서 행성 전체를 연구하도록 설계된 착륙선이다.> ❸ 이 착륙선은 로봇 팔을 이용하여 가장 먼저 화성 표면에 고감도 지진계를 설치할 것이며, 그곳에서 지진계는 운석 충돌과 화성지진을 감지하기 위해 귀 기울일 것이다. Ⓑ ❹ 이런 사건들(운석 충돌과 화성지진)로 인해 발생하는 지진파는 과학자들에게 화성의 보다 분명한 내부 구조의 그림을 줄 것이다. ❺ 인사이트는 그런 후에 열(熱) 탐사선을 내보낼 것인데, 이것은 스스로 땅을 쳐서 땅속으로 들어가는 16인치 못 모양의 장비로, 몇 주간의 과정을 거쳐 16피트까지 땅을 파서 내려갈 것이다. ❻ 이 기구는 화성의 내부로부터 얼마나 많은 열이 빠져나가는지를 측정할 것인데, ❼ 이를 통해 화성의 내부에 열을 발생시키는 방사성 원소가 얼마나 있는지와 현재 화성이 지질학적으로 얼마나 활동적인지 밝혀낼 것이다. Ⓒ ❽ 또한, 그 우주선의 지붕 위에는 RISE라고 불리는 X-밴드 안테나가 두 개 있으며, 이것이 세 번째 기구를 구성한다. Ⓓ ❾ RISE의 전파 신호는 화성 궤도의 흔들림을 추적하는 데 사용될 것이다. ❿ 이것은 과학자들이 화성의 중심핵의 크기와 상태를 이해하는 데 도움을 줄 것이다. ⓫ 이 실험들이 모두 합쳐져 화성을 파헤치고 과학자들이 수십 년 동안 찾아온 화성의 비밀을 밝힐 것이다.

해 설

주어진 문장에서 말하는 'the space agency(그 항공 우주국)'이 가리키는 대상이 첫 문장의 NASA인 만큼 Ⓐ가 적절한 위치가 된다.

어 휘

the solar system 태양계 descend v. 내려가다, 내려오다 touch down (우주선, 비행기 등이) 착륙하다 lander n. (달 표면에서의) 착륙선 install v. 설치하다, 가설하다, 장치하다 seismometer n. 지진계 Martian a. 화성의 meteorite n. 운석, 유성 impact n. 충돌, 충격 Marsquake n. 화성의 지진 seismic wave 지진파 planet n. 행성 internal a. 내부의 structure n. 구조 release v. 방출하다, 투하하다 probe n. 무인 우주탐사선, 탐사용 로켓, 탐사기 burrow v. 굴을 파다 instrument n. 기계, 기구, 도구 reveal v. (알려지지 않은 것을) 드러내다, 알리다 amount n. 총계, 총액; 양(量) radioactive a. 방사성의, 방사능의 element n. 요소, 원소 contain v. 내포하다, 포함하다 wobble n. 비틀거림, 흔들림, 동요 orbit n. 궤도 core n. 핵심; 중심 crack v. (호두 따위를) 까다, 부수다; ~의 비밀을 밝히다 spill v. (액체 따위를) 엎지르다; (정보·비밀을) 누설하다

017 ④   2019학년도 국민대학교 인문계 오전 A형 24번

❶ In 1874 / Francis Galton, (a British polymath,) analyzed a sample of English scientists and found the vast majority to be first-born sons. ❷ This led him to speculate / that first-born children enjoyed a special level of attention / from their parents that allowed them to thrive intellectually. ❸ Half a century later, / Alfred Adler, (an Austrian psychologist,) made a similar argument (relating to personality.) ❹ First-born children, (he thought,) were more conscientious, / while the later-born were more extrovert and emotionally stable. Ⓐ ❺ Many subsequent studies have explored these ideas, but their findings have been equivocal — ❻ some supporting and some rejecting them. ❼ Now / a team (led by Stefan Schmukle of the University of Leipzig, in Germany,) has collected the most comprehensive evidence on the matter yet. ❽ Its conclusion is / that Adler was wrong, / but Galton may have been right. ❾ Birth order, (they found,) had no effect on personality: ❿ first-borns were no more, no less, likely / than their younger sibs to be conscientious, extrovert or neurotic. ⓫ But it did affect intelligence. Ⓑ ⓬ In a family (with two children,) / the first child was more intelligent / than the second 60% of the time, / rather than the 50% (that would be expected / by chance.) ⓭ On average, / this translated / to a difference of 1.5 IQ points / between first and second siblings. Ⓒ ⓮ That figure agrees with the consensus from previous studies, and thus looks confirmed. ⓯ It is, nevertheless, quite a small difference — and whether it is enough to account for Galton's original observation is moot. ⓰ In any case, / it is clearly not deterministic. Ⓓ

Which is the best place for the following?
다음 문장이 들어갈 가장 적절한 곳은?

⓱ Galton was the youngest of nine.

① Ⓐ   ② Ⓑ   ③ Ⓒ   ✓④ Ⓓ

해석

❶ 1874년, 영국의 박식가(博識家) 프랜시스 골턴(Francis Galton)은 영국 과학자들의 표본을 분석하여 그들 중 대다수가 첫째 아들이라는 것을 발견했다. ❷ 이것은 그가 첫째 아이들이 부모로부터 특별한 수준의 관심을 받았고, 이 관심이 첫째 아이들이 지적으로 잘 자랄 수 있게 했을 것으로 추측했다. ❸ 반세기 후에, 오스트리아의 심리학자 알프레드 애들러(Alfred Adler)는 성격과 관련해서 비슷한 주장을 했다. ❹ 그는 첫째 아이들이 더 양심적이지만, 나중에 태어난 아이들은 더 외향적이고 정서적으로 안정돼 있다고 생각했다. Ⓐ ❺ 많은 후속 연구에서 이와 같은 생각들을 분석했지만, 그들의 연구결과는 애매모호했다. ❻ 일부 연구는 이 생각을 지지했고 일부 연구에서는 받아들이지 않았다. ❼ 독일 라이프치히 대학의 스테판 슈무클(Stefan Schmukle) 교수가 이끄는 연구팀은 이 문제에 대해 그때까지 가장 포괄적인 증거를 수집했다. ❽ 그 연구팀의 결론은 애들러는 틀렸지만, 골턴은 옳았을지도 모른다는 것이었다. ❾ 그들은 출생 순서가 성격에 아무런 영향을 미치지 않는다는 것을 발견했다. ❿ 첫째들이 동생보다 양심적이거나 외향적이거나 신경질적일 가능성은 더 높지도 더 낮지도 않았다. ⓫ 그러나 출생 순서가 지능에는 영향을 미쳤다. Ⓑ ⓬ 두 자녀가 있는 가정에서, 첫째 아이가 둘째 아이보다 지능이 높은 경우는 확률적으로 기대될 50%가 아니라 60%였다. ⓭ 평균적으로, 첫째와 둘째 형제자매간 IQ 차이는 1.5로 나타났다. Ⓒ ⓮ 그 수치는 이전의 연구에서 합의된 의견과 일치하고, 따라서 확정적인 것처럼 보인다. ⓯ 그럼에도 불구하고, 1.5라는 IQ 차이는 꽤 작은 것이며, 그것이 골턴이 처음에 관찰한 내용을 설명하기에 충분한지는 미지수이다. ⓰ 어쨌든, 그것은 분명히 결정적이지는 않다. Ⓓ <⓱ 골턴은 9형제 중에서 막내였다.>

해설

마지막 부분에서 골턴의 주장이 틀렸을 수 있다는 결론을 내린다. 즉 '출생 순서가 지능에 영향을 미친다'는 주장이 잘못되었음을 반증하는 예시로 '골턴은 9형제 중에서 막내였다'는 주어진 문장을 마지막에 위치시켜 주장을 논증하는 것이 적절한 위치의 전개가 된다.

어휘

soak v. 적시다, 담그다, 흠뻑 젖다 speculate v. 사색하다; 추측하다 thrive v. 번성하다, 번영하다, 잘 자라다 intellectually ad. 지적으로 psychologist n. 심리학자 conscientious a. 양심적인, 성실한 extrovert n. 사교적인 사람, 외향적인 사람 stable a. 안정된, 견고한; 건실한 subsequent a. 차후의, 다음의 equivocal a. 애매모호한 comprehensive a. 포괄적인, 이해가 빠른 conclusion n. 결말; 결론 neurotic a. 신경과민의, 비현실적인 생각에 잠기는 sib n. 일가, 친족, 형제자매 translate v. 번역하다, (행동·말 따위를) (~로) 해석하다 sibling n. 형제, 자매 consensus n. (의견·증언 따위의) 일치, 일치된 의견, 대다수의 의견; 여론 confirm v. 확증하다, 확인하다 observation n. 관찰, 관찰결과 (관찰에 의거한) 의견 deterministic a. 결정론적인

018 ③   2019학년도 세종대학교 인문계 A형 50번

① The format of the Sun Dance, (a traditional Native American ceremonial dance,) has always varied / from community to community. ② Nevertheless, there are certain features of the dance (that many tribes share.) ③ Often, the dance must be initiated / by a sponsor, / someone (who takes a vow / in the hope of being relieved of a worry, or being blessed in the coming year.) [A] ④ It is almost always performed / near the time of summer solstice. ⑤ Most Sun Dances begin with the erection of a circular lodge / around a solemnly chosen and cut central pole. ⑥ During the next three or four days, / periods of dancing, (accompanied by singing and drumming,) are interspersed / with periods of rest and meditation. ⑦ Dancers do not eat or drink / during the entire period of the dance, / although some do chew on bear root / to keep their mouths moist. ⑧ Toward the end of the dance, / participants experience visions and receive blessings. [B] ⑨ Early Europeans were repulsed / by some tribes' practice of self-mortification / in the ceremony. ☑ ⑪ Dancing and straining against the ropes, / they eventually tore loose from the skewers. ⑫ Through this ritual, / participants literally suffer on behalf of their community / and call upon the Creator / to pity / and assist them / in the fulfillment of their vows. [D] ⑬ This aspect of the ritual was the main reason (federal officials prohibited it / between the late 1870s and 1935.) ⑭ Despite the ban, however, many tribes continued to hold the Sun Dance surreptitiously / in remote areas of their reservations / or to enact it / without its objectionable features.

Which is the most appropriate place for the sentence below?
다음 문장이 들어갈 가장 적절한 곳은?

⑩ Male dancers / had / their breasts or backs / skewered and tied to a central lodge pole.

① A   ② B   ③ C ✓   ④ D

해석

① 미국 원주민이 전통 의식에서 췄던 춤인 태양 춤의 형식은 항상 지역사회마다 달랐다. ② 그럼에도 불구하고, 많은 부족들이 공유하고 있는 그 춤의 일정한 특징들이 있다. ③ 종종, 이 춤은 종교적인 대부(代父)가 시작해야 하는데, 그는 걱정에서 벗어나거나 다음 해에 축복받기를 바라면서 서약을 하는 사람이다. [A] ④ 태양 춤은 거의 항상 하지(夏至) 무렵에 거행된다. ⑤ 대부분의 태양 춤은 종교의식에 맞게 선택하고 베어낸 중앙의 나무기둥 주위에 원형의 천막집을 세우는 것으로 시작된다. ⑥ 그 후 사나흘 동안 노래를 부르고 북을 치면서 춤을 추며, 간간이 휴식과 명상의 시간이 주어진다. ⑦ 춤추는 사람들은 춤을 추는 시간 내내 먹거나 마시지 않지만, 일부는 입을 촉촉하게 유지하려고 곰 뿌리를 씹는다. ⑧ 춤이 끝날 때쯤에, 참가자들은 환상을 경험하고 축복을 받는다. [B] ⑨ 초기 유럽인들은 그 의식에서 자진해서 고행(苦行)하는 일부 부족들의 관행에 거부감을 느꼈다. [C] <⑩ 춤을 추는 남자들은 가슴이나 등이 꼬챙이에 꿰어진 채로 중앙에 있는 오두막의 기둥에 묶여 있었다.> ⑪ 춤을 추면서 (중앙기둥과 연결된) 밧줄에 팽팽히 잡아당겨 지다가 그들은 마침내 꼬챙이에서 벗어나 자유로워졌다. ⑫ 이 의식을 통해 참가자들은 그들의 공동체를 대표하여 글자 그대로 고통을 겪고, 신(神)에게 그들을 불쌍히 여기고 그들의 서약을 완수하도록 도와줄 것을 청한다. [D] ⑬ 1870년대 후반부터 1935년 사이에 연방 관리들이 이 의식을 금지한 주된 이유가 그 의식의 이런 측면 때문이었다. ⑭ 하지만 금지에도 불구하고, 많은 부족들은 그들의 보호구역 내의 외진 구역에서 몰래 태양춤 의식을 거행하거나 불쾌한 특징들을 빼고 공연하는 것을 계속했다.

해설

[C] 앞에서 말하는 '고행'의 구체적인 예시가 주어진 문장에서 말하는 '꼬챙이에 꿰어진' 것을 말한다. 그리고 [C] 다음에서 꼬챙이에 꿰어진 몸이 기둥에서 벗어나지는 과정을 설명하는 만큼 문장 위치를 정확하게 알 수 있다.

어휘

format n. 형태, 체제 ceremonial a. 의식의, 의례상의 vary v. 가지각색이다, 다르다 feature n. 특징, 특색 tribe n. 부족, 종족 initiate v. 시작하다, 개시하다 sponsor n. 보증인, 후원인, (종교적인) 대부(代父) vow n. 맹세, 서약; (수도 생활에 들어가는, 또는 계율을 지키는) 서원(誓願) relieve v. (고통·부담 따위를) 경감하다; (고통·부담 따위를) 경감하다; (고통·공포 따위로부터) 해방하다, 구원하다 summer solstice 하지(夏至) erection n. 건설, 조립; 세움 circular a. 원형의, 둥근 lodge n. 오두막집, (북아메리카 원주민의) 천막집 solemnly ad. 근엄하게, 엄숙하게, (종교적인) 의식에 맞게 accompany v. 동반하다; (현상 따위가) ~에 수반하여 일어나다 intersperse v. 흩뿌리다, 산재시키다 meditation n. 묵상, (종교적) 명상 chew on 우물거리다, 잘근잘근 씹다 bear root 천궁과 유사한 약초, 풀 moist a. 습기 있는, 축축한 participant n. 참여자 vision n. 환상, 환영(幻影) blessing n. 축복, 신의 은총 repulse v. 구역질나게 하다, 혐오감을 주다 self-mortification n. 자진하여 고행을 함 strain v. 잡아당기다 tear loose from ~로부터 자유롭게 되다, 달아나다 skewer v. 꼬챙이에 꿰다 n. 꼬챙이 ritual a. 의식의, 제식의 on behalf of ~을 대신하여, ~을 대표하여 pity v. 불쌍히 여기다 fulfillment n. 이행, 수행, 완수, 실천 aspect n. 양상, 모습; 측면 prohibit v. 금지하다 ban n. 금지, 금지령 surreptitiously ad. 내밀하게, 은밀히, 몰래 reservation n. 인디언 보호 거주지 enact v. 법제화하다, (법률을) 제정하다, (연극을) 공연하다 objectionable a. 못마땅한, 불쾌한

019 ③ 2019학년도 홍익대학교 인문계 A형 31번

❶ The fashion industry is a product of the modern age. ❷ Prior to the mid-19th century, virtually all clothing was handmade for individuals, either as home production or on order from dressmakers and tailors. ❸ By the beginning of the 20th century — (with the rise of new technologies such as the sewing machine, the rise of global capitalism and the development of the factory system of production, and the proliferation of retail outlets such as department stores) — clothing had increasingly come to be mass-produced in standard sizes and sold at fixed prices. ❹ Although the fashion industry developed first in Europe and America, today it is an international and highly globalized industry, with clothing often designed in one country, manufactured in another, and sold in a third. ❺ The fashion industry has long been one of the largest employers in the United States, and it remains so in the 21st century. ❻ However, employment declined considerably as production increasingly moved overseas, especially to China. ❼ Because data on the fashion industry typically are reported for national economies and expressed in terms of the industry's many separate sectors, aggregate figures for world production of textiles and clothing are difficult to obtain. ❽ However, by any measure, the industry inarguably accounts for a significant share of world economic output. ❾ The fashion industry consists of four levels: ❿ the production of raw materials, principally fibres and textiles but also leather and fur; the production of fashion goods by designers, manufacturers, contractors, and others; retail sales; and various forms of advertising and promotion. ⓬ These levels consist of many separate but interdependent sectors, all of which are devoted to the goal of satisfying consumer demand for apparel under conditions that enable participants in the industry to operate at a profit.

해석

❶ 패션 산업은 현대 시대의 산물이다. ❷ 19세기 중반 이전에는, 거의 모든 의류가 개인을 위해 수작업으로 만들어졌는데, 주로 가정에서 생산하거나 양장점과 양복점에서 주문 생산되었다. ❸ 20세기 초에, 재봉틀과 같은 새로운 기술의 등장, 세계적인 자본주의의 등장과 공장제 생산방식의 발달, 그리고 백화점과 같은 소매점의 급증으로, 의류는 점차 표준규격으로 대량 생산되고 고정 가격에 팔리게 되었다. ❹ 패션 산업은 유럽과 미국에서 처음으로 발전되었지만, 오늘날엔 의류는 종종 한 국가에서 디자인되고, 다른 국가에서 제조되어 또 다른 국가에서 판매되면서, 국제화되고 고도로 세계화된 산업이 되었다. ❺ 예를 들어, 미국의 패션 회사는 중국에서 섬유를 조달하고, 베트남에서 옷을 만들며, 이탈리아에서 마감을 처리하고, 미국의 창고로 옮겨져서 전 세계의 소매점으로 유통된다. ❻ 패션 산업은 오랫동안 미국에서 고용인이 가장 많은 산업 중 하나였으며, 21세기에도 여전히 그렇다. ❼ 하지만 생산이 점차 해외, 특히 중국으로 이동함에 따라, (패션 산업에서) 고용이 상당히 감소했다. ❽ 패션 산업에 대한 데이터가 일반적으로 개별 국가경제별로 보도되고 패션 산업의 많은 개별적인 영역별로 표현되기 때문에, 전 세계 섬유와 의류 생산의 총 수치를 얻기는 어렵다. ❾ 하지만, 어떤 면에서든, 패션 산업은 명백하게 전 세계 경제 생산에서 상당한 부분을 차지한다. ❿ 패션 산업은 네 단계로 구성된다. ⓫ 주로 섬유, 직물, 가죽, 모피인 원자재 생산, 디자이너, 제조업체, 거래업체 등에 의한 패션 상품 생산, 소매 판매, 그리고 다양한 형태의 광고와 홍보로 구성된다. ⓬ 이러한 단계들은 개별적이면서도 상호의존적인 많은 부분으로 구성되고, 이 모든 부분에는 패션 업계 참여자들이 수익을 내며 영업할 수 있게 해준다는 조건 아래에 의류에 대한 소비자의 수요를 충족시킨다는 목표에 전념한다.

어휘

prior to ~전에 **virtually all** 거의 모든 **on order** (물건이) 주문중인, 발주가 끝난 **dressmake** n. (여성복) 양장점 **tailor** n. (주로 신사복을 주문을 받아 만드는) 양복점 **sewing maching** 재봉틀 **capitalism** n. 자본주의 **proliferation** n. 확산, 급증 **retail outlet** 소매점 **department store** 백화점 **mass-produce** v. 대량 생산하다 **fixed price** 정가(定價) **source** v. (부품·자료 따위를 ~에서) 조달하다 **aggregate** a. 종합한, 총 **textile** n. 직물, 옷감 **inarguably** ad. 명백하게 **account for** 차지하다 **raw material** 원료, 원자재 **fibre** n. 섬유, 섬유질 **leather** n. 가죽 **fur** n. 털, 모피 **retail sale** 소매 **interdependent** a. 서로 의지하는 **apparel** n. 의류, 의복 **outsource** v. 외주제작하다

Where should the following sentence be added?
다음 문장이 추가되어야 할 곳은?

For example, an American fashion company might source fabric in China and have the clothes manufactured in Vietnam, finished in Italy, and shipped to a warehouse in the United States for distribution to retail outlets internationally.

① Ⓐ   ② Ⓑ   ③ Ⓒ   ④ Ⓓ

해설 Ⓑ에서 패션 산업이 제조 및 판매가 국제화 되어 있다고 언급한 뒤, Ⓒ에 주어진 문장이 들어가는 것이 적절하다. 주어진 문장은 패션 산업의 생산과 유통의 국제화 사례를 설명하는 문장이다.

어휘 fabric n. 직물, 천 warehouse n. 창고 distribution n. 분배, 배급, 유통

020 ③ 2019학년도 아주대학교 인문계 A형 31번

A ❶ The object (called the Möbius strip) has fascinated environmentalists, artists, engineers, mathematicians and many others / ever since its discovery / in 1858 / by August Möbius, a German mathematician. ❷ Möbius seems to have encountered the Möbius strip / while working on the geometric theory of polyhedra, solid figures (composed of vertices, edges, and flat faces. ① ❸ A Möbius strip can be created / by taking a strip of paper, / giving it an odd number of half-twists, then taping the ends back together / to form a loop. ❹ If you take a pencil and draw a line / along the center of the strip, / you'll see that / the line runs / along both sides of the loop.

B ❺ The concept of a one-sided object inspired artists / like Dutch graphic designer M.C. Escher, [whose woodcut "Möbius Strip II" shows red ants (crawling one after another / along a Möbius strip.)] ② ❻ The Möbius strip has more than just one surprising property. ❼ For instance, try taking a pair of scissors and cutting the strip in half / along the line (: you just drew.) ❽ You may be astonished / to find that / you are left / not with two smaller one-sided Möbius strips, but instead with one long two-sided loop.

C ③ ✓ ❾ A topologist studies properties of objects (that are preserved / when moved, bent, stretched or twisted, / without cutting or gluing parts together.) ❿ For example, a tangled pair of earbuds is in a topological sense : (the same as an untangled pair of earbuds,) because changing one into the other requires only moving, bending and twisting. ⓭ Another pair of objects (that are topologically the same) are a coffee cup and a doughnut. ④ ⓮ Because both objects have just one hole, / one can be deformed into the other / through just stretching and bending. ⓯ The number of holes in an object is a property (which can be changed only through cutting or gluing.)

해 석

A ❶ 뫼비우스의 띠라고 불리는 이 물체는 1858년에 독일의 수학자 아우구스트 뫼비우스(August Möbius)에 의한 발견 후부터 환경론자, 예술가, 공학자, 수학자, 그리고 다른 많은 사람들을 매혹시켜 왔다. ❷ 뫼비우스는 꼭짓점, 테두리, 평평한 면으로 이루어져 있는 다면체의 입체도형의 기하학적 이론을 연구하던 중에 뫼비우스의 띠를 우연히 접했던 것으로 보인다. ① ❸ 뫼비우스의 띠는 종이 조각 하나를 반틈만 비트는 것을 홀수 번 한 다음에 양 끝을 테이프로 붙여 고리를 형성하도록 해서 만들 수 있다. ❹ 연필로 뫼비우스의 띠를 중심을 따라 선을 그리면, 그 선이 고리의 양쪽 면을 따라 이어진다는 것을 알 수 있다.

B ❺ 한 면으로 된 물체라는 개념은 네덜란드의 그래픽 디자이너 M.C. 에셔(M.C. Escher)와 같은 예술가들에게 영감을 주었는데, 그의 목판화 『뫼비우스의 띠 II (Möbius Strip II)』는 붉은 개미들이 뫼비우스의 띠를 따라 줄줄이 기어가는 모습을 보여준다. ② ❻ 뫼비우스의 띠가 가진 놀라운 특성은 한 가지뿐이 아니다. ❼ 예를 들어, 방금 그린 선을 따라 가위로 뫼비우스의 띠를 반으로 잘라 보아라. ❽ 당신은 한 면으로 된 더 작은 뫼비우스의 띠 두 개가 아니라 양면으로 된 하나의 긴 고리가 생기는 것을 알아내고 매우 놀랄지도 모른다.

C ③ <❾ 뫼비우스의 띠가 확실히 시각적으로 매력을 가지고 있지만, 그것이 가장 큰 영향을 준 분야는 수학이었다. ❿ 수학에서 뫼비우스의 띠는 위상학이라 불리는 분야 전체의 발전에 박차를 가했다.> ⓫ 위상학자는 부분을 자르거나 붙이지 않고 움직이거나 구부리거나 펴거나 비틀 때 보존되는 물체의 속성을 연구한다. ⓬ 예를 들어, 위상학적 의미에서 볼 때 엉켜 있는 이어폰은 엉켜 있지 않은 이어폰과 같은데, 하나를 다른 하나로 바꾸기 위해서는 움직이고, 구부리고, 뒤틀기만 하면 되기 때문이다. ⓭ 위상학적으로 똑같은 또 다른 물체의 쌍은 커피 컵과 도넛이다. ④ ⓮ 두 물체는 모두 하나의 구멍이 있으므로, 잡아서 늘리고 구부리기만 하면 하나는 다른 하나로 변형될 수 있다. ⓯ 물체에 있는 구멍의 수는 자르거나 붙이는 것에 의해서만 바꿀 수 있는 속성이다.

어 휘

fascinate v. 황홀하게 하다, 매혹시키다 **environmentalist** n. 환경보호론자, 환경예술가 **mathematician** n. 수학자 **encounter** v. 우연히 만나다, 조우하다 **geometric** a. 기하학의, 기하학상의 **polyhedra** n. 다면체 **solid figure** 입체도형 **vertices** n. (vertex의 복수) 꼭짓점 **strip** n. 조각 **odd** a. 홀수의 **loop** n. 고리 **concept** n. 개념, 생각 **inspire** v. 고무하다, 격려하다, 영감을 주다 **woodcut** n. 목판화 **crawl** v. 포복하다, 기다 **property** n. 성질, 특성 **astonish** v. 깜짝 놀라게 하다 **topologist** n. 위상학자(位相學者), 위상수학자 **preserve** v. 보전하다, 유지하다, 보존하다 **bend** v. 구부리다 **stretch** v. 펴다, 뻗치다 **glue** v. 접착시키다, 꼭 붙이다 **tangled** a. 엉킨, 얽힌 **earbud** n. 이어폰, 헤드폰 **topological** a. 위상학적인 **require** v. 요구하다, 규정하다, 필요로 하다

⑯ This property (— called the "genus" of an object —) allows us to say / that a pair of earbuds and a doughnut are topologically different, / since a doughnut has one hole, whereas a pair of earbuds has no holes.

D ⑰ Unfortunately, a Möbius strip and a two-sided loop, (like a typical silicone awareness wristband,) both seem to have one hole, ⑱ so this property is insufficient / to tell them apart / — at least from a topologist's point of view. ⑲ Instead, the property (that distinguishes a Möbius strip from a two-sided loop) is called orientability. ⑳ Like its number of holes, / an object's orientability can only be changed / through cutting or gluing. ㉑ Imagine writing yourself a note / on a see-through surface, / then taking a walk / around on that surface. ㉒ The surface is orientable / if, (when you come back / from your walk,) you can always read the note. ㉓ On a nonorientable surface, / you may come back / from your walk / only to find / that the words (you wrote) have apparently turned into their mirror image and can be read / only from right to left. ㉔ On the two-sided loop, / the note will always read the same, / no matter where your journey took you. ㉕ Since the Möbius strip is nonorientable, / whereas the two-sided loop is orientable, / the Möbius strip and the two-sided loop are topologically different.

The following paragraph is removed from the passage. In which part may it be inserted to support the argument made by the author?
다음 단락은 윗글에서 제외되었다. 글쓴이가 말한 주장을 뒷받침하기 위해 어느 부분에 위치해야 할 것인가?

> ❾ While the strip certainly has visual appeal, its greatest impact has been in mathematics, ❿ where it helped to spur on the development of an entire field called topology.

    ⑤

해석
⑯ 물체의 "유(類)개념"이라 불리는 이 속성이 우리는 이어폰과 도넛이 위상학적으로 서로 다르며 그 이유는 도넛에는 한 개의 구멍이 있는 반면에 이어폰에는 구멍이 없기 때문이라고 말할 수 있게 해준다.

D ⑰ 불행히도, 뫼비우스의 띠와 실리콘 재질의 일반적인 인식용 손목밴드처럼 양면으로 된 고리는 둘 다 구멍이 하나인 것처럼 보이며, ⑱ 따라서 적어도 위상학자의 관점에서는 -이 속성은 그 둘을 구별하기에 충분하지 않다. ⑲ 대신, 뫼비우스의 띠를 양면으로 된 고리를 구별하는 속성은 방향성이라고 한다. ⑳ 그것의 구멍 개수처럼, 물체의 방향성도 자르거나 붙이는 것에 의해서만 바뀔 수 있다. ⑤ ㉑ 속이 비치는 표면에 메모한 뒤에 그 표면 위를 산책한다고 상상해 보라. ㉒ 만약 당신이 산책에서 돌아왔을 때, 그 메모를 항상 읽을 수 있다면, 그 표면은 방향성이 있는 것이다. ㉓ 방향성이 없는 표면에서는, 산책에서 돌아오면 당신이 쓴 글들이 분명히 거울에 비친 모습으로 바뀌어서 오른쪽에서 왼쪽으로만 읽을 수 있다는 것을 알아낼 것이다. ㉔ 양면으로 된 고리 위에서는, 당신이 어디로 가든지 메모는 항상 동일하게 적혀 있을 것이다. ㉕ 뫼비우스의 띠는 방향성이 없는 반면 양면으로 된 고리는 방향성이 있으므로 뫼비우스의 띠와 양면으로 된 고리는 위상학적으로 서로 다른 것이다.

해설
C에서 뫼비우스의 띠의 위상학적 측면에서 설명을 시작하고 있다. 따라서 주어진 문장에서 '위상학 분야에 발전과 원동력이 되었다'는 주어진 문장은 ❸에 들어가는 것이 가장 적절하다.

어휘
genus n. 종류, 부류, 유개념 typical a. 전형적인, 대표적인 insufficient a. 불충분한, 부족한 tell ~ apart ~을 구별하다, 분간하다 distinguish v. 구별하다, 식별하다 orientability n. 향(다양체)

끝장편입 정답 및 해설

유형 04 무관한 문장

001 ④
2019학년도 강남대학교 인문·자연계 15번

Choose the sentence that does NOT fit.

❶ It would be a great comfort / to terminally ill patients / to end their lives / if their suffering became unbearable. ❷ ① Not all pain can be controlled, / and it's arrogant / to insist / it can. ❸ ② Quality of life decisions are the sole right of the individual. ❹ ③ It is nonsense / to say / death shouldn't be part of a doctor's mission. ❺ ④ Doctors are healers, not killers.

[해석] ❶ 말기 환자들의 고통이 견딜 수 없을 정도라면 그들의 삶을 마감하는 것이 그들에게는 큰 위안이 될 것이다. ❷ ①모든 고통을 조절할 수 있는 것은 아니며, 그럴 수 있다고 주장하는 것은 오만하다. ❸ ②삶의 질에 관한 결정은 개인의 고유한 권리이다. ❹ ③죽음이 의사의 임무의 일부가 되어서는 안 된다는 주장은 말이 되지 않는다. <❺ ④의사들은 치유자이지, 살인자가 아니다.>

[해설] 윗글은 환자의 연명치료 거부 권리를 주장하는 글이다. 하지만 ④문장은 글 기조의 반대 진술로, 그런 의사를 '살인자(killer)'라고 말하고 있기에 적절하지 않은 문장이다.

[어휘] terminally ill 말기의 unbearable a. 참을 수 없는 arrogant a. 거만한, 교만한 mission n. 임무, 직무

002 ④
2019학년도 강남대학교 인문·자연계 16번

Choose the sentence that does NOT fit.

❶ Christopher Columbus is said to have discovered America / in 1492. ❷ ① History says, however, the Vikings came / to the New World earlier, / in the 10th Century A.D. ❸ ② Leif Erikson, (a Norwegian Viking), and his crew got lost / on the way to Greenland, / and landed / on North America. ❹ ③ He called his discovery Vinland, "land of the vines", / which is today Labrador in eastern Canada. ❺ ④ Vintand Saga (a heroic report of Erikson's expedition), eloquently supports the idea (that Columbus was the first European / to visit America).

[해석] ❶ 크리스토퍼 콜럼버스(Christopher Columbus)가 1492년에 아메리카 대륙을 발견했다고 한다. ❷ ①하지만 역사는 기원후 10세기에 바이킹들이 신대륙에 더 먼저 도착했다고 말한다. ❸ ②노르웨이 출신 바이킹이었던 레이프 에릭슨(Lief Erikson)과 그의 선원들은 그린란드(Greenland)로 가던 중에 길을 잃고 북아메리카 대륙에 상륙했다. ❹ ③그는 자신의 발견을 빈랜드 즉 "덩굴의 땅"이라고 불렀는데, 이곳은 오늘날 캐나다 동부의 래브라도(Labrador)에 해당한다. <❺ ④에릭슨의 탐험을 영웅적인 보고서인 "빈랜드 영웅 전설"은 콜럼버스가 아메리카에 도착한 최초의 유럽인이었다는 것을 웅변적으로 뒷받침한다.>

[해설] 윗글은 콜럼버스가 북미 도착의 최초의 유럽인이 아니라 바이킹 레이프 에릭슨과 그의 동료가 먼저 도착했다는 것이 이 글의 요지다. 하지만 ④는 반대로 콜럼버스가 아메리카 도착의 최초 유럽인이라는 기조로 말하는 문장이기에 전체 내용에 적절하지 않다.

[어휘] crew n. 승무원, 선원 vine n. 덩굴 saga n. 영웅 전설 expedition n. 탐험 여행 eloquently ad. 도도히, 웅변적으로

003 ④   2019학년도 인하대학교 인문계 34번

글의 주제

❶ There are few problems / (more annoying than hiccups), which can last / for hours or even days. ❷ Ⓐ Acoording to one doctor (who has studied them), hiccups are usually caused / by eating or drinking too quickly. ❸ Ⓑ People do some pretty strange things / to remedy this ridiculous problem. ❹ Ⓒ Some common remedies include holding your breath, eating a teaspoon of sugar, and putting a paper bag over your head. ❺ Ⓓ The best exercise (for a healthy heart) is walking. ❻ Ⓔ Undoubtedly, / that last one is the strangest one of all.

Choose the one that does not fit in the passage.

① Ⓐ   ② Ⓑ   ③ Ⓒ   ✓④ Ⓓ   ⑤ Ⓔ

해석

❶ 딸꾹질보다 더 성가신 문제는 거의 없는데, 딸꾹질은 몇 시간 또는 심지어 며칠 동안 지속될 수도 있기 때문이다. ❷ Ⓐ딸꾹질을 연구해 온 한 의사에 따르면, 딸꾹질은 대개 너무 빨리 먹거나 마시는 것 때문에 발생한다고 한다. ❸ Ⓑ사람들은 이 우스꽝스러운 문제를 치료하기 위해 상당히 이상한 일들을 한다. ❹ Ⓒ흔히 하는 치료법들에는 숨을 참는 것, 설탕을 한 숟가락을 먹는 것, 종이가방을 머리에 덮어씌우는 것 등이 있다. <❺ Ⓓ건강한 심장을 위한 가장 좋은 운동은 걷기이다.> ❻ Ⓔ의심할 여지없이, 마지막에 가장 언급한 것이 가장 이상한 것이다.

해설

윗글은 딸꾹질 그리고 딸꾹질을 멈추기 위한 치료법을 적은 글인데, Ⓓ는 건강한 심장에 대한 글로 전체 내용과 어울리지 않는다.

어휘

annoying a. 성가신, 귀찮은 hiccup n. 딸꾹질 last v. 지속하다, 오래가다 remedy n. 치료; 치료약 v. 고치다, 치료하다 ridiculous a. 우스운, 엉뚱한 include v. 포함하다 undoubtedly ad. 틀림없이, 확실히

정답 및 해설

004 ④   2019학년도 건국대학교 인문·예체능계 A형 27번

Why do people choose to home educate their child? Some families make a carefully considered decision to home educate long before their child reaches "school age." Ⓐ There may be philosophical, religious or various other reasons for their choice and ultimately they feel that in some way they can offer a more suitable education for their child at home. Ⓑ It is also a natural choice for parents who have enjoyed participating in their child's early learning and see no reason to give up this responsibility when the child reaches the age of five. Ⓒ Other parents send their child into the school system, but later find that school does not work for their child. Ⓓ In schools, students can get comparatively high marks by remembering what teachers have said. Ⓔ School does not suit everyone. Sometimes children may find it hard to "fit in" so their parents may also decide to home educate.

글의 흐름으로 보아, Ⓐ~Ⓔ 가운데 어색한 것은?

① Ⓐ   ② Ⓑ   ③ Ⓒ   ✓ ④ Ⓓ   ⑤ Ⓔ

해석
❶ 왜 사람들은 자신의 아이를 재택 교육하기로 선택할까? ❷ 어떤 가정들은 그들의 아이가 '취학 연령'에 이르기 훨씬 전에 신중하게 고려하여 재택 교육을 결정한다. ❸ Ⓐ그들의 선택에는 철학적, 종교적이거나 다양한 다른 이유들이 있을 수 있으며, ❹ 궁극적으로 그들은 어떤 면에서 집에서 자녀를 위해 더 적절한 교육을 제공할 수 있다고 느낀다. ❺ Ⓑ그것은 또한 자녀의 조기 학습에 참여하는 것을 즐겼으며 아이가 5살이 되었을 때 이 책임을 포기할 이유를 찾지 못하는 부모들에게는 자연스러운 선택이다. ❻ Ⓒ다른 부모들은 그들의 아이를 학교에 보내지만, ❼ 나중에 학교가 자신의 아이에게 효과가 없다는 것을 알게 된다. ❽ <Ⓓ학교에서 학생들은 선생님들이 말한 것을 기억함으로써 비교적 높은 점수를 받을 수 있다.> ❾ Ⓔ학교가 모든 사람들에게 적합한 것은 아니다. ❿ 때때로 아이들은 '(다른 아이들과) 어울리는 것'이 어렵게 느낄 수 있으므로 또한 그들의 부모들이 재택 교육을 결정할 수도 있다.

해설
윗글은 왜 부모들이 자녀들을 재택 교육을 선택하는지 질문하고 그에 대한 답변을 이어가는 글이다. 하지만 Ⓓ에서는 학교에서 학생들이 점수를 잘 받는 방법을 설명함으로써, 전체 글의 기조와 어울리지 않는다.

어휘   considered a. 깊이 생각한 school age 취학 연령 philosophical a. 철학의, 냉철한 religious a. 종교의, 신앙심이 깊은 comparatively ad. 비교적(으로) fit in (자연스럽게 ~와) 어울리다

005 ④ 2019학년도 인하대학교 인문계 33번

❶ The close relationship (between language and religious belief) pervades cultural history. ❷ Often, / a divine being is said to have invented speech, or writing, and given it / as a gift to mankind. ❸ One of the first things : (Adam has to do), (according to the Book of Genesis), is to name the acts of creation. ❹ Many other cultures have a similar story. ❺ Ⓐ In Egyptian mythology, / the god Thoth is the creator of speech and writing. ❻ Ⓑ It is Brahma who gives the knowledge of writing / to the Hindu people. ❼ Ⓒ Odin is the inventor of runic script, / according to the Icelandic sagas. ❽ Ⓓ Literacy is often introduced / into a community / by the spread of a religion. ❾ Ⓔ A heaven-sent water turtle, (with marks on its back), brings writing / to the Chinese. ❿ All over the world, / the supernatural provides a powerful set of beliefs / about the origins of language.

Choose the one that does not fit in the passage.

① Ⓐ ② Ⓑ ③ Ⓒ ✓④ Ⓓ ⑤ Ⓔ

해석
❶ 언어와 종교적 신앙 사이의 밀접한 관계는 문화 역사에 널리 퍼져 있다. ❷ 종종, 신성한 존재가 말이나 글을 발명하여 그것을 인류에게 선물로 주었다고 한다. ❸ 창세기에 따르면, 아담(Adam)이 가장 먼저 해야 할 일 중의 하나는 창조의 행위들에 이름을 붙이는 것이었다. ❹ 많은 다른 문화들에도 비슷한 이야기가 있다. ❺ Ⓐ이집트 신화에서, 토트(Thoth) 신은 말과 글의 창조자이다. ❻ Ⓑ힌두(Hindu) 사람들에게 글에 대한 지식을 주는 사람은 브라마(Brama)다. ❼ Ⓒ아이슬란드 전설에 따르면, 룬 문자를 만든 이는 오딘(Odin)이었다. <❽ Ⓓ읽고 쓰는 능력은 흔히 종교의 확산에 의해 사회에 도입된다.> ❾ Ⓔ하늘에서 등에 기호를 새겨서 보낸 바다거북이 중국인들에게 글을 가져다준다. ❿ 전 세계적으로, 초자연적인 것들이 언어의 기원에 대한 일련의 강력한 믿음을 제공한다.

해설
윗글은 신성한 존재가 말이나 글을 만들어 인류에게 선물로 주었다고 말한 뒤 그 예시로 '창조의 행위에 이름을 붙이는 것'을 언급한다. 그리고 마지막 문장까지 그와 관련된 각 문화의 예시를 들고 있다. 하지만 Ⓓ '읽고 쓰는 능력이 종교 확산으로 사회에 도입되었다'라는 내용은 전체 내용과 무관하다.

어휘
close a. (시간·공간·정도가) 가까운; (관계가) 밀접한, 친밀한 relationship n. 관계, 관련 pervade v. ~에 널리 퍼지다, 고루 미치다 divine a. 신(新)의, 신성한 being n. 존재, 생명 invent v. 발명하다, 고안하다; 상상력으로 만들다 mankind n. 인류, 인간 the Genensis 창세기 name v. ~에 이름을 붙이다, 명명하다 mythology n. 신화, 신화집 runic a. 룬 문자(rune)의; 고대 북유럽 사람의 script n. 대본, 원고, 글씨체; 문자 saga n. 무용담, 영웅담, 전설 literacy n. 읽고 쓸 줄 아는 능력, 교양 supernatural a. 초자연적인, 불가사의한 n. 초자연적인 것[현상] provide v. 주다, 제공하다 origin n. 기원, 발단, 원천

006 ④ 2018학년도 인하대학교 인문계 10번

① Soon after / an infant is born, / many mothers hold their infants / in such a way (that they are face-to-face and gaze at them). ② [A] Mothers have been observed / to address their infants, / vocalize to them, / ask questions, / and greet them. ③ [B] In other words, from birth on, / the infant is treated as a social being / and as an addressee / in social interaction. ④ [C] The infant's vocalizations, and physical movements and states are often interpreted as meaningful / ⑤ and are responded to verbally / by the mother or other care-giver. ⑥ [D] The cultural dispreference (for saying / what another might be thinking or feeling) has important consequences / for the organization of exchanges (between care-giver and child). ⑦ [E] In this way, / protoconversations are established and sustained along / a two-party, turn-taking model. ⑧ Throughout this period and the subsequent language-acquiring years, / care-givers treat very young children as communicative partners.

Which of the following does not fit in the passage?

① [A] ② [B] ③ [C] ✓ ④ [D] ⑤ [E]

해석
① 아기가 태어난 직후, 많은 엄마들은 얼굴을 마주 바라보는 식으로 아기를 안는다. ② [A]우리는 엄마가 아기에게 말을 걸고, 아기에게 소리를 들려주고, 질문하고, 아기에게 인사를 하는 것을 보아왔다. ③ [B]다시 말해, 태어날 때부터 아기는 사회적 존재로 그리고 사회적 상호작용에서 메시지를 듣는 대상으로 여겨진다. ④ [C]아기의 발성, 그리고 신체의 움직임과 상태는 종종 의미 있는 것으로 해석되고, ⑤ 엄마나 다른 보호자가 이에 구두로 응답한다. <⑥ [D]다른 사람이 생각하거나 느끼고 있는 것을 말하는 것에 대한 문화적인 비선호는 보호자와 아이 사이에 이뤄지는 교류의 구조에 중대한 영향을 미친다.> ⑦ [E]이런 방식으로 원시 대화가 확립되고 이것은 양자가 의사소통을 주고받는 형태로 유지된다. ⑧ 이 시기와 이후의 언어 습득 시기 동안, 보호자는 매우 어린 아이들을 의사소통의 상대로 대한다.

해설
윗글은 아이의 사회적 존재로서 태어났을 때부터의 상호작용에 관해 설명하는 글이다. 하지만 [D]는 문화적 개인 사이의 대화 중 비선호가 보호자와 아이에게 영향을 미친다는 말로서 전체 내용과 어울리지 못한다.

어휘
infant n. 유아 face to face 얼굴을 맞대고 gaze v. 응시하다 address v. ~에게 말을 걸다 vocalize v. 목소리를 내다, 말하다 addressee n. (우편물이나 메시지의) 수신인 interaction n. 상호작용 interpret v. 해석하다, 설명하다, 판단하다 respond to ~에 대답하다, 응답하다 verbally ad. 말로, 구두로 dispreference n. 선호하지 않음, 비선호 protoconversation n. 원시 대화 (엄마와 아기 사이에서의 음성적 상호작용) establish v. 확립하다, 제정하다 sustain v. 유지하다, 부양하다; (손해 따위를) 입다 subsequent a. 차후의; 다음의; 결과로서 일어나는 communicative a. 말하기 좋아하는, 수다스러운; 전달의

007 ④ — 2018학년도 건국대학교 인문·예체능계 B형 32번

Why don't we "think something different" more often? There are several main reasons. The first is that we don't need to be creative for most of (what we do). ⒶFor example, we don't need to be creative when we're driving on the freeway, or riding in an elevator, or waiting in line at a grocery store. ⒷWe are creatures of habit when it comes to the business of living — from doing paperwork to tying our shoes. For most of our activities, these routines are indispensable. Without them, our lives would be in chaos, and we wouldn't get much accomplished. ⒸIf you got up this morning and started contemplating the bristles on your toothbrush or questioning the meaning of toast, you probably wouldn't make it to work. ⒹThese attitudes are necessary for most of what we do, but they can get in the way when we're trying to be creative. ⒺStaying on routine thought paths enables us to do the many things (we need to do) without having to think about them.

글의 흐름으로 보아, Ⓐ~Ⓔ 가운데 어색한 것은?
① Ⓐ ② Ⓑ ③ Ⓒ ✓④ Ⓓ ⑤ Ⓔ

해석

❶ 우리는 왜 "다른 생각"을 좀 더 자주 하지 않는가? ❷ 여기에는 몇 가지 중요한 이유들이 있다. ❸ 첫 번째는 우리가 하는 대부분의 일은 창의적일 필요가 없기 때문이다. ❹ Ⓐ예를 들어, 고속도로에서 운전하거나, 엘리베이터를 타거나, 식료품점에서 줄을 서서 기다릴 때 우리는 창의적일 필요가 없다. ❺ Ⓑ서류작업에서부터 신발 끈을 매는 것까지 우리는 일상적인 일에 있어서 습관의 산물이다. ❻ 대부분의 활동에서 이러한 판에 박힌 행동의 틀은 필수적이다. ❼ 그것들이 없다면 우리의 삶은 혼란스러워질 것이고, 우리는 많은 것을 이루지 못할 것이다. ❽ Ⓒ만약 아침에 일어나서 칫솔모에 대해 생각하거나 토스트의 의미에 대해 의문을 갖기 시작한다면, 당신은 아마도 출근하지 못할 것이다. <❾ Ⓓ이러한 태도는 우리가 하는 대부분의 일에서 반드시 필요하지만, 우리가 창의적인 사람이 되고자 노력할 때 방해가 될 수 있다.> ❿ Ⓔ판에 박힌 사고 과정을 유지하는 것은 우리가 해야하는 많은 일을 생각할 필요 없이 할 수 있게 해준다.

해설

Ⓓ에서 말하는 these attitudes는 앞 문장에서 언급한 '칫솔모에 대해 생각하거나, 토스트의 의미에 대해 의문을 갖기 시작한다면'을 가리킨다. 따라서 이런 태도가 대부분의 일에서 반드시 필요하다는 말은 전체 내용과 어울리지 않는다. 전체 글은 오히려 그런 생각들은 오히려 할 필요 없다는 글이다.

어휘

creative a. 창조적인, 창의적인 freeway n. 고속도로 grocery store n. 식료품점 routine n. 판에 박힌 일, 일상의 일[과정] indispensable a. 없어서는 안 될, 필수적인 chaos n. 혼돈; 혼란 accomplish v. 완수하다, 성취하다 contemplate v. 고려하다, 심사숙고하다 bristle n. 빳빳한 털, 강모 attitude n. 태도[자세], 사고방식 get in the way 방해되다

008 ② 2017학년도 가톨릭대학교 일반 학사편입 A형 24번

❶ The natural surveillance [provided by passers-by or by windows and balconies (overlooking streets)] is enough / to deter most crime and vandalism. ❷ Ⓐ Well-designed neighborhoods promote this casual policing, / which can work / alongside more formal schemes / for watching over one another's homes. ❸ Ⓑ Homes should be flexible / to adapt to a household's changing needs / over time. ❹ Ⓒ Thoughtfully sited car parking and bicycle storage, as well as well-integrated recycling bins, contribute not only to a sense of order but also to reducing litter, vandalism and theft. ❺ Ⓓ To encourage these changes, / police services award Secured by Design certificates to homes and developments (whose design deters crime). ❻ It considers the materials and design of entry points / such as doors and windows, the deployment of burglar alarms and video entry systems, and the natural surveillance (offered by windows / to open spaces).

Choose one that is unnecessary for the flow of the passage.
① Ⓐ ✓② Ⓑ ③ Ⓒ ④ Ⓓ

해석 ❶ 지나가는 행인이나 거리가 내다보이는 창문과 발코니에 의해서 제공되는 자연적인 감시는 대부분 범죄와 공공기물 파손을 막기에 충분하다. ❷ Ⓐ잘 설계된 동네는 이런 비정기적인 치안 유지 활동을 촉진시키며, 이 활동은 서로 다른 가정을 감시하기 위한 보다 정규적인 계획과 함께 하여 효과를 거둘 수 있다. <❸ Ⓑ가정은 시간이 지나면서 가정의 변화하는 필요성에 적응할 수 있도록 유연해야 한다.> ❹ Ⓒ잘 통합된 재활용 쓰레기통들뿐만 아니라 신중하게 위치가 정해진 주차장과 자전거 보관소는 질서의식에 기여할 뿐 아니라 쓰레기 버리기, 기물파손, 그리고 도둑질 줄이는 데도 기여한다. ❺ Ⓓ이러한 변화를 장려하기 위해, 경찰은 범죄를 막을 수 있도록 설계된 주택과 주택단지에 '방범환경 설계(SBD: Secured By Design)' 인증을 준다. ❻ 이 인증 제도는 문과 창문 같은 입구의 재료와 설계, 도난 경보기와 비디오 출입 시스템의 배치 그리고 열린 공간으로 나 있는 창문에 의해 제공되는 자연적인 감시도 고려한다.

해설 윗글은 방범환경 조성에 대해 가정의 환경의 역할에 대해 말하고 있는 글이다. 하지만 Ⓑ에서는 '가정은 시간이 지나면서 가정의 변화하는 필요성에 적응할 수 있도록 유연해야 한다'고 말한다. 따라서 방범환경 조성이라는 전체 맥락과 어울리지 않는다.

어휘 surveillance n. 감시 passer-by n. 행인(특히 예상 밖의 일이 일어나던 순간에 지나던 사람) overlook v. ~을 조사하다, ~을 내려다보는 위치에 있다 deter v. 단념시키다, 저지하다 vandalism n. 예술, 문화, 파괴; 공공시설[자연 경관] 파손 policing n. (경찰의) 치안 유지 활동 scheme n. 계획, 제도, 책략 flexible a. 유연한, 융통성 있는 integrated a. 통합된, 통합적인 litter n. 쓰레기; 난잡 deployment n. 전개, 배치 burglar n. (주거 침입) 강도 entry n. 입장, 출입, 등장

009 ③   2018학년도 인하대학교 인문계 32번

❶ Before the Industrial Revolution, / most goods were produced / by hand / in rural homes or urban workshops. ❷ [A] Merchants, (known as entrepreneurs), distributed the raw materials to workers, / collected the finished products, paid for the work, then sold them. ❸ [B] Growing demand for consumer products, / together with a shortage of labour, placed pressure on entrepreneurs / to find new, more efficient methods of production. ❹ [C] The great era of European exploration (that be an in the 15th century) arose primarily out of a desire (to seek out new trade routes and partners). ❺ [D] With the development of power-driven machines, / it made economic sense / to bring workers, materials and machines together in one place, giving rise to the first factories. ❻ [E] For added efficiency, / the production process was broken down / into basic individual tasks (that a worker could specialize in), a system (known as the division of labour).

Which of the following does not fit in the passage?

① [A]   ② [B]   ③ [C]   ④ [D]   ⑤ [E]

해석 ❶ 산업혁명 이전에는 대부분 상품이 시골의 가정이나 도시의 작업장에서 수작업으로 생산됐다. ❷ [A]기업가로 알려진 상인은 원자재를 노동자들에게 나누어 주고 완제품을 모은 다음, 그 일에 관한 돈을 지불한 후에 그 완제품들을 판매하였다. ❸ [B]소비재에 대한 수요가 점점 커지고 이와 함께 노동력이 부족해짐에 따라, 기업가들은 새롭고 보다 효율적인 생산 방법을 찾아야 한다는 압박을 받았다. <❹ [C]15세기에 시작된 유럽의 위대한 탐험 시대는 주로 새로운 교역로와 파트너를 찾고자 하는 욕구에서 비롯되었다.> ❺ [D]동력 기계가 개발되면서, 노동자, 자재, 기계를 한 곳에서 모으는 것이 경제적으로 타당하게 되었고, 최초의 공장이 생겨나게 되었다. ❻ [E]효율성을 더 높이기 위해, 생산과정은 노동자가 전문적으로 할 수 있었던 기본적인 개별 업무들로 나누어졌는데, 이것은 분업으로 알려진 시스템이다.

해설 윗글은 산업혁명 이전과 이후 과정을 설명하는 글이다. 하지만 [C]는 '15세기에 시작된 지리상의 발전의 배경'에 관한 내용이므로 전체 글의 흐름상 적절하지 않다.

어휘 Industrial Revolution 산업혁명 goods n. 물건, 물품, 상품, 물자 rural a. 시골의, 지방의 workshop n. 일터, 작업장, 직장 merchant n. 상인 entrepreneur n. 실업가, 기업가 distribute v. 분배하다, 배급하다 raw material 원료 finished product 완제품 consumer product 소비재 efficient a. 능률적인, 효과적인 era n. 시대, 시기 exploration n. 실지답사, 탐험; (문제 등의) 탐구 trade n. 거래, 무역 specialize in ~을 전문으로 하다, 전공하다 division of labor 분업

정답 및 해설

010 ③
2017학년도 인하대학교 일반 학사편입 인문계 22번

❶ Vigorous activity is usually a healthful pursuit but it can become maladaptive when carried to extremes. ❷ [A] There are runners and body builders, for instance, who use their obsessive workouts to avoid taking responsibility for other aspects of their lives, allowing little time for family, friends, or additional interests. ❸ [B] Rather than enjoying their fitness endeavors, they feel powerless to make any adjustments in their routines except to try to do more. ❹ [C] Pursuing pleasurable fitness endeavors can be a great coping strategy for lessening daily pressures. ❺ [D] Unfortunately, the exercise patterns of some adolescents and adults reflect deep-seated psychological problems. ❻ [E] They become dangerously fixated on trying to change their bodies by a combination of exhausting exercise and dieting, ❼ increasing their risk of serious health problems including substance abuse and eating disorders.

Choose the sentence that does not fit in each passage.
① [A]   ② [B]   ③ [C]   ④ [D]   ⑤ [E]

해석
❶ 활기차게 움직이는 것은 보통 건강에 좋은 일이지만, 극단으로 치닫게 되면 부적응 상태가 될 수도 있다. ❷ [A]예를 들어, 운동을 강박적으로 하는 것을 이용해서 생활의 다른 측면들에 관해 책임을 회피하고, 그 결과 가족, 친구 또는 추가적인 관심사에는 시간을 거의 쓰지 않는 달리기 선수나 보디빌더들이 있다. ❸ [B]몸을 단련시키는 노력들을 즐기기보다, 그들은 자신들의 정해진 일상에 다른 조정을 하는 데에는 무기력함을 느끼고 오직 더 많은 운동을 하려고만 한다. <❹ [C]즐겁게 신체 단련을 추구하는 것은 일상에서 겪는 압박감들을 완화시키는데 훌륭한 대응 전략이 될 수 있다.> ❺ [D]불행히도, 일부 청소년들과 어른들이 운동을 하는 방식은 뿌리 깊은 심리적 문제들을 나타내 보이고 있다. ❻ [E]그들은 몸을 지치게 만드는 운동과 다이어트 병행하여 몸을 변화시키는 데에 위험할 정도로 사로잡혀서, ❼ 약물 남용과 섭식장애 등 심각한 건강상의 문제를 겪을 위험을 높이고 있다.

해설
윗글은 과한 운동에 집착하는 것을 문제 지적하는 글인데, [C]는 즐거운 신체 단련의 이점을 말하는 글로써 전체 내용과 어울리지 않는다.

어휘
vigorous a. 원기 왕성한, 강건한 pursuit n. 추적, 추격, 추구; 속행, 수행 maladaptive a. 부적응의, 순응성이 없는 extreme n. 극단, 극치; 극단적인 행위 obsessive a. (관념 따위가) 붙어서 떨어지지 않는, 강박관념을 일으키는 workout n. 연습, 트레이닝; 격한 운동 resposibility n. 책임, 책무, 의무 aspect n. 양상, 모습; 국면; 견지 additional a. 부가적인, 추가적인 fitness n. 신체 단련, (신체적인) 건강 endeavor n. 노력; 시도 adjustment n. 조정, 조절 routine n. 판에 박힌 일, 일상의 과정; 기계적인 순서 cope v. 대처하다, 극복하다; 대응하다 strategy n. 전략, 작전, 책략 lessen v. 적게 하다, 줄이다, 감하다 ressure v. 안심시키다 adolescent n. 청년, 젊은이 fixate v. 고정하다, 고착하다 exhausting a. 소모적인, (심신을) 지치게 하는 substance abuse 약물남용 eating disorder 섭식상애, 식이장애

011 ② 2017학년도 인하대학교 일반 학사편입 인문계 21번

❶ John Henry was an ex-slave who went to work on the railroad / as a steel-driver / for the Chesapeake & Ohio (C&O) Railroad). ❷ His job was hitting steel spikes into rocks, and he was the fastest and strongest worker / on the line. ❸ [A] When the owners of the C&O decided to drill / right through Big Bend Mountain in West Virginia / instead of building the railroad around it, / many workers lost their lives / because of the dangerous work. ❹ But not John Henry. ❺ [B] Thousands of African-Americans worked on the railroad, with hundreds perishing / during the drilling of the Great Bend Tunnel. ❻ He drove spike after spike, / digging his way through the mountain. ❼ [C] One day / a salesman appeared, / touting the efficiency and speed of a new steam-powered drill. ❽ The workers arranged a contest: John Henry versus the machine. ❾ [D] When the dust settled, / John Henry dug a 14-foot (4-meter) hole, / but the machine made it only 9 feet (nearly 3 meters). ❿ [E] As the rail workers celebrated, / John Henry toppled over and died from exhaustion.

Choose the sentence that does not fit in each passage.
① [A]   [B]   ③ [C]   ④ [D]   ⑤ [E]

해 석

❶ 노예 출신의 존 헨리는 체사피크&오하이오(C&O) 철도회사의 선로 부설자로서 철도 건설 현장에서 일했다. ❷ 그의 일은 강철 대못을 바위 속에 박아 넣는 것이었는데, 그는 자신이 속한 조에서 가장 빠르게 일을 하고 힘센 일꾼이었다. ❸ [A] C&O 철도회사의 소유주들이 웨스트버지니아 주의 빅 밴드 산을 둘러 가는 대신 그 산을 곧바로 관통하는 철도를 건설하기로 결정했을 때, 위험한 작업 때문에 많은 노동자들이 목숨을 잃었다. ❹ 하지만 존 헨리는 아니었다. <❺ [B] 수천 명의 흑인들이 철도 건설 현장에서 일을 했는데, 수백 명이 그레이트 밴드 터널을 뚫는 과정에서 목숨을 잃었다.> ❻ 그는 계속해서 못을 박아 나갔고, 마침내 산을 파헤쳐 뚫었다. ❼ [C] 하루는 한 세일즈맨이 와서 새로 나온 증기 동력 드릴의 효율성과 속도를 내세웠다. ❽ 노동자들은 존 헨리 그 기계의 대결을 주선했다. ❾ [D] 먼지가 가라앉았을 때, 존 헨리는 14피트(4미터)의 구멍을 파냈지만, 기계는 9피트(거의 3미터)의 구멍을 파내는 데 그쳤다. ❿ [E] 철도 건설 노동자들이 축하하는 가운데, 존 헨리는 쓰러져 기진맥진하여 사망했다.

해 설

윗글은 존 헨리의 작업 능력에 관한 이야기다. [A]에서 C&O 철도 회사가 철도 건설 결정이후 위험한 작업 때문에 많은 노동자들이 목숨을 잃었지만, 존 헨리는 아니었다고 말한다. 그리고 [C]에서 부터는 존 헨리가 어떻게 일을 효율적으로 했는지에 관한 이야기가 이어지고 있다. 따라서 [B]에서 다시 '수천 명의 흑인의 해당 건설 과정에서 목숨을 잃었다'는 내용은 앞서 이미 끝난 이야기로서 어울리지 않는다.

어 휘

spike n. 긴 못, (야구화 등의) 스파이크, 철도용의 대못 perish v. 멸망하다, 비명에 죽다, 썩어 없어지다, 사라지다 dig v. 땅 따위를 파다, 파헤치다, 발굴하다 tout v. ~에게 끈덕지게 권하다, 졸라대다, 극구 칭찬(선전)하다 efficiency n. 능률, 효율 steam-powered a. 증기기관의, 증기동력의 arrange v. 배열하다, 정리하다; ~을 정하다; ~의 준비를 하다 settle v. 내려앉다, 자리 잡다, 침전하다 celebrate v. (식을 올려) 경축하다; (의식을) 거행하다; (훈공 따위를) 기리다 topple over 비틀거리다, 쓰러지다 exhaustion n. 소모, 고갈; 극도의 피로, 기진맥진

정답 및 해설

012 ④   2017학년도 인하대학교 일반 학사편입 인문계 20번

❶ The 2012-13 flu season took a serious toll on families: ❷ 158 children — most of them younger than 11 — died. ❸ Sadly, about 90 percent of those who died missed out on the one thing that could have saved them: a flu vaccination. ❹ [A] Despite studies proving that flu vaccinations are a lifesaver, less than half of all children in the U.S. are immunized each year. ❺ [B] One recent survey from a social-research company found that 16 percent of Americans consider the vaccine to be unsafe ❻ and 35 percent believe the vaccine causes the flu. ❼ [C] "The tragedy is that children continue to die from an illness that is largely preventable," says Dr. Blumberg. ❽ [D] Doctors want moms and dads to understand that children (ages 6 months to 5 years) are at a high risk of serious diseases like diarrhea and dehydration. ❾ [E] Because awareness and education are key to making smart decisions about your family's health, ❿ it's of primary importance for parents with children to get clear-cut information about the flu and the vaccine.

Choose the sentence that does not fit in each passage.
① [A]   ② [B]   ③ [C]   ✓④ [D]   ⑤ [E]

해석

❶ 2012~2013년 독감 유행 철에 가정에서 많은 희생자가 나왔다. ❷ 158명의 어린이 — 대부분이 11세 이하였다 — 가 목숨을 잃었다. ❸ 슬픈 것은 숨진 아이들 가운데 약 90%가 자신들을 살릴 수도 있었을 하나를 하지 않았다는 사실이다. 그것은 바로 독감 예방접종이었다. ❹ [A]독감 예방접종이 생명을 구한다는 사실을 증명하는 연구결과들에도 불구하고, 미국의 모든 어린이들 중에 매년 예방주사를 맞는 것은 절반도 되지 않는다. ❺ [B]한 사회조사 회사에서 최근 실시한 조사에 의하면, 16%의 미국인들이 예방접종이 안전하지 않다고 여기고 있으며 ❻ 35%는 예방접종을 하면 독감에 걸린다고 믿고 있었다. ❼ [C]블룸버그 박사는 "충분히 예방할 수 있는 질병으로 인해 아이들이 계속 죽는 것은 비극입니다." 라고 말했다. <❽ [D]의사들은 생후 6개월에서 5세까지의 아이들은 설사나 탈수증 같이 심각한 질병에 걸릴 위험성이 높다는 것을 부모가 이해하길 바란다.> ❾ [E]가족의 건강에 대해 현명한 결정을 내리는 비결은 인식과 교육에 있으므로, ❿ 아이와 함께 있는 부모들이 독감과 백신 접종에 대해 명확한 정보를 얻는 것이 가장 중요하다.

해설

윗글은 아이들의 예방접종의 중요성을 알리는 글인데, [D]에서 언급하는 탈수증과 같은 다른 질병에 관한 내용은 글의 흐름 상 어울리지 않는다.

어휘

miss out on 좋은 기회를 놓치다, 실패하다; 놓치다 flue n. 인플루엔자, 유행성 독감 vaccination n. 백신 주사; 예방 접종 immunize v. ~에 대한 면역성을 주다, 예방 주사를 놓다 tragedy n. 비극, 비극적인 사건 largely ad. 대부분, 주로; 크게, 충분히 preventable a. 예방할 수 있는, 막을 수 있는 disease n. 병, 질병 diarrhea n. 설사 dehydration n. 탈수현상 clear-cut a. 분명한, 명확한

013 ⑤ 2020학년도 건국대학교 인문·예체능계 A형 27번

❶ Abraham Lincoln's election to the presidency in 1860 brought to a climax (the long festering debate / about the relative powers of the federal and the state government.) ❷ ⓐ By the time of his inauguration, / six Southern states had seceded from the Union and formed the Confederate States of America, soon / to be followed by five more. ❸ ⓑ The war (that followed between North and South) put constitutional government / to its severest test. ❹ ⓒ After four bloody years of war, / the Union was preserved, ❺ four million African American slaves were freed, ❻ and an entire nation was released from / the oppressive weight of slavery. ❼ ⓓ The war can be viewed / in several different ways: / as the final, violent phase / in a conflict of two regional subcultures; / as the breakdown of a democratic political system; / as the climax of several decades of social reform; / or as a pivotal chapter / in American racial history. ❽ [ⓔ As important as the war itself was the tangled problem of how to reconstruct the defeated South.] ❾ However interpreted, / the Civil War stands / as a story of great heroism, sacrifice, triumph, and tragedy.

글의 흐름으로 보아, ⓐ~ⓔ 가운데 어색한 것은?
① ⓐ ② ⓑ ③ ⓒ ④ ⓓ ✓⑤ ⓔ

해석 ❶ 1860년 에이브러햄 링컨(Abraham Lincoln)의 대통령 당선은 연방정부와 주정부의 상대적인 권력에 관해 오래되고 지겨운 논쟁을 절정에 이르게 했다. ❷ ⓐ그가 취임했을 때는 이미 남부의 여섯 개 주들이 미합중국에서 탈퇴하여 남부 연방을 만들었고 곧 다섯 개의 주가 더 합류했다. ❸ ⓑ뒤이은 북부와 남부 사이의 전쟁은 입헌 정부를 가장 가혹한 시험대에 올려놓았다. ❹ ⓒ 4년간 이어진 피비린내 나는 전쟁 후에 미합중국은 유지되었고, ❺ 400만 명의 미국 흑인 노예가 해방되었으며, ❻ 국가 전체가 노예제도의 억압적인 무게에서 벗어나게 되었다. ❼ ⓓ이 전쟁은 다양한 방식으로 바라볼 수 있는데, 두 지역 하위문화의 충돌의 폭력적인 최종 단계로, 민주적인 정치 체제의 몰락으로, 수십 년의 사회 개혁의 절정으로, 미국 인종 역사의 중심적인 장으로도 볼 수 있는 것이다. <❽ ⓔ전쟁 그 자체만큼 중요한 것은 패배한 남부를 어떻게 재건할 것인가에 대한 뒤얽힌 문제였다.> ❾ 하지만 어떻게 해석하든지, 남북전쟁은 위대한 영웅주의, 희생, 승리, 그리고 비극의 이야기이다.

해설 남북전쟁을 소재로 한 글로서 ⓓ 구간 부터는 남북전쟁을 바라보는 관점을 제시하는 구간인데 ⓔ에서는 패배한 남부 연합을 어떻게 재건할 것인지에 대한 언급이 나와서 뒤에 이어지는 남북전쟁의 해석의 관점의 내용과 어울리지 않는다.

어휘 festering a. 지겨운, 싫증이 나는 debate n. 토론, 논쟁 federal a. 연방의 inauguration n. (대통령·교수 등의) 취임(식) secede from ~에서 탈퇴[분리]하다 the Union 미합중국, (남북 전쟁 때 연방정부를 지지한) 북부의 여러 주, 북부 연합 Confederate States (of America) (the~) 남부 연방(=the Confederacy) constitutional a. 헌법의, 합헌적인 bloody a. 피비린내 나는 preserve v. 보전하다, 유지하다 oppressive a. 압제적인, 압박하는 subculture n. 하위문화 pivotal a. 중심(축)이 되는 racial a. 인종의, 민족의 tangled a. 헝클어진; 복잡한; 뒤얽힌 reconstruct v. 재건[복원]하다 interpret v. 설명[해석]하다, 이해[해석]하다 triumph n. 대 승리

014 ③   2020학년도 인하대학교 인문계 28번

❶ Differences (in values, culture, experience, and perceptions) may well lead parties to disagree about the relative merits of different standards. ❷ A [If it were necessary to agree on which standard was "best" settling a negotiation might not be possible.] ❸ B But agreement on criteria is not necessary. ❹ C A well-established reputation (for fair dealing) can be an extraordinary asset. ❺ D Criteria are just one tool (that may help the parties find an agreement / better for both / than no agreement). ❻ E Using external standards often helps narrow the range of disagreement ❼ and may help expand the area (of potential agreement). ❽ When standards have been refined / to the point (that it is difficult to argue persuasively / that one standard is more applicable than another), ❾ the parties can explore tradeoffs or resort to fair procedures (to settle the remaining differences). ❿ They can flip a coin, use an arbitrator, or even split the difference.

Which of the following does not fit in the passage?
① A   ② B   ✓③ C   ④ D   ⑤ E

해석
❶ 가치관, 문화, 경험과 인식의 차이로 인해 당사자들이 서로 다른 표준을 가진 상대적인 장점에 대해 동의하지 않게 되는 것은 당연한 일이다. ❷ A 어떤 표준이 "가장 좋은가"에 대해 반드시 의견이 일치해야 한다면, 협상의 타결은 불가능할 수도 있다. ❸ B 하지만 기준에 대한 의견 일치는 필요하지 않다. <❹ C 공정거래에 대해 확실히 자리를 잡은 명성은 엄청난 자산이 될 수 있다.> ❺ D 기준은 의견의 일치를 보지 못하는 것보다는 양자에게 더 이로운 합의점을 당사자들이 찾을 수 있게 도와줄 하나의 수단에 불과하다. ❻ E 외부 표준을 사용하는 것은 종종 의견 불일치의 범위를 좁히는 데 도움이 되며 ❼ 잠재적으로는 의견이 일치되는 영역을 넓히는 데 도움이 될 수도 있다. ❽ 한 표준이 다른 표준보다 더 적절하다고 설득력 있게 주장하기 어려울 정도로 표준이 정비되고 나면, ❾ 당사자들은 상호절충을 모색하거나 공정한 절차에 의존해서 나머지 차이를 해결할 수 있다. ❿ 그들은 동전을 던지거나, 중재자를 사용하거나, 심지어 타협하여 합의를 볼 수도 있다.

해설
윗글은 당사자들이 서로 다른 기준에 대해 의견 일치가 필요한 것인가에 대한 내용이다. 하지만 주어진 C 는 공정한 거래에 대한 내용으로 글의 전체 맥락 및 소재와 어울리지 않는다.

어휘
perception n. 지각 작용, 인식 merit n. 우수함, 가치; 장점 standard n. 표준, 기준 settle v. (분쟁을) 수습하다, 조정하다; (문제·곤란 따위를) 결말짓다, 해결하다 negotiation n. 협상, 교섭, 절충 criterion n. 표준, 기준 well-established a. 확고부동한, 안정된, 정착된 reputation n. 평판; 명성, 신망 extraordinary a. 비범한, 엄청난; 터무니없는 asset n. 자산, 재산 agreement n. 협정, 합의; 동의 narrow v. 좁게 하다, 좁히다 expand v. 넓히다, 확장하다, 확대하다 potential a. 잠재적인, 가능한 refine v. 정제하다; 세련되게 하다 persuasively ad. 설득력 있게 applicable a. 적용할 수 있는, 들어맞는, 적절한 tradeoff n. (특히 타협을 위한) 교환, 거래; (바람직하게 하기 위한 양자의) 균형 resort to ~에 의지하다 procedure n. 순서, 수순; 절차 flip v. (손톱·손가락으로) 튀기다, 휙 던지다 arbitrator n. 중재인 split the difference (가격 등을 논의할 때) 차액을 등분하다, 절반씩 절충해서 합의를 보다

정답 및 해설

015 ③   2020학년도 인하대학교 인문계 06번

❶ During adolescence, people become increasingly involved with their peer group, a group whose members are about the same age and have similar interests). ❷ The peer group, (along with the family and the school), is one of the three main agents of socialization. ❸ However, the peer group is very different from the family and the school. ❹ [A] Whereas parents and teachers have more power than children and students, / the peer group is made up of equals. ❺ [B] Peer groups develop / among all age groups, / but they are particularly important / for adolescents' development. ❻ [C] There may be differences / across cultures / in how adolescents behave. ❼ [D] The adolescent peer group teaches its members social skills, (the values of friendship among equals), and to be independent / from adult authorities. ❽ [E] Sometimes / this means that / a peer group encourages its members to go against authorities and adults. ❾ It is important to remember, however, / that this kind of rebellious behavior is partly cultural and not universal.

Choose the one that does not fit in the passage.

① [A]　② [B]　③ [C] ✓　④ [D]　⑤ [E]

해 석

❶ 청소년기 동안, 사람들은 구성원의 나이가 거의 같고 관심사가 유사한 집단인 또래 집단과 점점 더 밀접한 관계를 맺게 된다. ❷ 또래 집단은 가족, 학교와 함께 사회화를 담당하고 있는 세 가지 주된 주체 중 하나이다. ❸ 그러나, 또래 집단은 가족이나 학교와는 매우 다르다. ❹ [A]부모와 교사가 자녀들과 학생들보다 더 많은 지배력을 가지고 있지만, 또래 집단은 동등하게 구성되어 있다. ❺ [B]또래 집단은 모든 연령 집단에서 생겨나지만, 청소년들의 발달에 특히 중요하다. <❻ [C]청소년들의 행동 방식은 문화마다 차이점이 있을 수 있다.> ❼ [D]청소년 또래 집단은 구성원들에게 사교 기술, 동등한 자들 사이의 우정의 가치, 권위적인 어른으로부터 독립하는 것 등을 가르친다. ❽ [E]때로는 이것은 또래 집단이 구성원들에게 권위적인 어른들에게 저항하도록 부추긴다는 뜻이다. ❾ 하지만 이런 종류의 반항적인 행동은 부분적인 문화이며 보편적인 것은 아니라는 점을 기억하는 것이 중요하다.

해 설

윗글은 또래 집단이 청소년 시기에 미치는 영향과 배경에 대한 글이다. 하지만 [C]는 청소년 행동 방식은 문화마다 차이가 있을 수 있다는 내용으로 전체 맥락과 어울리지 않는다.

어 휘

adolescence n. 청년기, 사춘기 along with ~와 함께, ~와 마찬가지로 socialization n. 사회화 be made up of ~로 구성돼 있다, ~로 이루어져 있다 equal n. 대등한 사람, 동배 behave v. 행동하다, 처신하다 authority n. 권한, 권위 encourage v. 격려하다, 고무하다; 조장하다 rebellious a. 반항적인 universal a. 보편적인, 일반적인

정답 및 해설

016 ②   2019학년도 인하대학교 인문계 14번

글의 주제 전쟁시 3개 악기의 중요한 역할

❶ Three musical instruments played an important role / in eighteenth-century warfare. ❷ One of them was the snare drum. ❸ [Often played by boys between 12 and 16 years old,] / snare drums were used to set the marching rhythm for soldiers.] ❹ Ⓐ With a skilled drummer playing 96 beats per minute, / a commander could march his troops three miles / in fifty minutes / allowing ten minutes each hour / for a breather and a drink. ❺ Ⓑ A second is chordophones or stringed instruments like zithers, / which consist of sets of string (stretched in parallel fashion / along a board). ❻ Ⓒ Another important instrument was a small flute (called a fife). ❼ Ⓓ The fife's role in an army was to entertain soldiers and communicate orders. ❽ Ⓔ For example the son "Pioneer's March" was the signal for road-clearing crews / to get started ahead of the infantry. ❾ Fifes were also used to give orders / to soldiers / during battle / since they could be heard / above the roar of firearms. ❿ The third instrument (used in warfare) was the trumpet. ⓫ Requiring just one hand to play, / it was used by soldiers / on horsebacks / to send messages to soldiers in battle and on the march.

Choose the one that does not fit in the passage.
① Ⓐ ✓② Ⓑ ③ Ⓒ ④ Ⓓ ⑤ Ⓔ

해 석
❶ 18세기 전쟁에서 세 개의 악기가 중요한 역할을 했다. ❷ 그중 하나가 작은 북이었다. ❸ 12세에서 16세 사이의 소년들이 종종 작은북을 쳤고, 군인들의 행군 리듬을 맞추는 데 사용되었다. ❹ Ⓐ1분에 북을 96번 치는 숙련된 드러머가 있다면, 지휘관은 1시간마다 잠시 휴식을 취하면서 10분을 음료를 마실 수 있는 시간으로 주면서도 자신의 부대를 50분 만에 3마일을 행군시킬 수 있었다. <❺ Ⓑ두 번째는 현명(絃鳴)악기, 즉 치터(zithers)처럼 현이 있는 악기인데, 이런 악기들은 판을 따라 여러 개의 현들이 평행하게 잡아 당겨져 있다.> ❻ Ⓒ또 다른 중요한 악기는 파이프라 불리는 작은 피리였다. ❼ Ⓓ군대에서 파이프가 하는 역할은 군인들을 즐겁게 해주고 명령을 전달하는 것이었다. ❽ Ⓔ예를 들어, "개척자의 행군"이라는 노래는 도로 정비반이 보병에 앞서 출발하라는 신호였다. ❾ 파이프는 전투가 벌어지는 동안 군인들에게 명령을 내리는 데도 사용되었는데, 파이프의 소리는 포성이 울릴 때도 들을 수 있었기 때문이다. ❿ 전쟁에서 사용된 세 번째 악기는 트럼펫이었다. ⓫ 한 손만으로 소리를 낼 수 있었기 때문에, 트럼펫은 말을 타고 있는 군인들이 전투하고 있는 군인들과 행군하고 있는 군인들에게 메시지를 보내기 위해 사용되었다.

해 설 윗글은 전쟁에서 3가지 악기의 중요한 역할을 말하는 글인데, Ⓑ에서는 악기의 소개만 있으며 전쟁 시 해당 악기의 역할에 대한 설명이 없기에 전체 내용과 어울리지 못한다.

어 휘 musical instrument 악기 warfare n. 전투, 교전, 전쟁 snare drum 작은 북, 스네어 드럼 skilled a. 숙련된, 능숙한 commander n. 지휘관, 사령관; 명령자 march v. 행진시키다, 행군시키다 troop n. 군대, 병력 chordophone n. (하프 따위의) 현명(絃鳴) 악기 zither n. 치터(기타와 비슷한 현악기로, 30-40개 현(絃)이 있다.) stretch v. 뻗치다, 펴다, 잡아당기다 parallel a. 평행한; 대응하는 fife n. 파이프(작은 플루트같이 생긴 악기) entertain v. 대접하다; 즐겁게 하다 communicate v. 전달하다, 통보하다 pioneer n. 공병 infantry n. 보병, 보병대 roar n. 으르렁거리는 소리, 포효소리 firearm n. 화기(火器)

017 ③ 2020학년도 인하대학교 인문계 07번

❶ The art of camping includes the ability to set up a safe and comfortable camp and to provide food that is tasty and nutritious. ❷ Because mountaineering is such a strenuous and demanding activity, your body will need a variety of foods to provide sufficient carbohydrates, protein, and fats. ❸ [A] With planning, it's not hard to choose foods that keep well, are lightweight, meet your nutritional needs, and are appropriately geared to your objective. ❹ [B] For example, monotonous prepared foods might work best for a short climb, ❺ whereas a week-long trip requires more variety and complexity. ❻ [C] In general mountaineering, the loss of body salts that accompanies heavy sweating is normally not a major problem, as most electrolytes are replaced naturally in a well-balanced diet. ❼ [D] And don't forget the other requirement of camping food: ❽ it must taste good, ❾ or you simply won't eat it. ❿ [E] If fueling your body quickly and simply is the first aim of alpine cuisine, the enjoyment of doing so is a worthy secondary goal.

Choose the one that does not fit in the passage.
① A ② B ✓③ C ④ D ⑤ E

해석 ❶ 캠핑의 기술에는 안전하고 편안한 캠프를 꾸리고 맛있고 영양이 풍부한 음식을 제공하는 능력이 포함된다. ❷ 등산은 매우 격렬하고 힘든 활동이기 때문에, 여러분의 몸은 충분한 탄수화물, 단백질, 지방을 공급해 줄 다양한 음식을 필요로 할 것이다. ❸ [A]계획을 잘 세우면, 보존이 잘 되면서 무게도 가볍고 필요한 영양분을 충족시키면서도 여러분의 목적에 적절하게 맞춰진 음식을 선택하는 것은 어렵지 않다. ❹ [B]예를 들어, 짧은 등산에는 단순한 조리식품이 가장 효과적일 수 있는 반면에, ❺ 일주일간의 여행은 더 다양하고 복잡한 음식이 필요하다. <❻ [C]일반적인 등산의 경우, 대부분의 전해질이 균형 식사로 자연적으로 보충되기 때문에 땀을 많이 흘리는 데 다른 체내 염분 손실이 보통 큰 문제가 되지 않는다.> ❼ [D]그리고 캠핑 음식의 나머지 필요조건도 잊지 마라. ❽ 캠핑 음식은 맛있어야 한다. ❾ 만약 그렇지 않으면 여러분은 그것을 그냥 먹지 않을 것이다. ❿ [E]몸의 에너지를 빠르고 간편하게 공급하는 것이 등산 요리의 첫 번째 목적이라면, 그렇게 하는 즐거움도 가치 있는 부차적인 목표이다.

해설 윗글은 캠핑의 기술에서 영양이 풍부한 음식을 제공하는 능력의 중요성과 어떻게 음식을 준비하는가에 관한 내용이다. 하지만 [C]는 등산으로 인한 체내 염분 손실에 대한 내용으로 전체 맥락과 어울리지 않는다.

어휘 tasty a. 맛있는, 재미있는 nutritious a. 영양분이 많은, 영양가가 높은 mountaineering n. 등산 strenuous a. 힘이 많이 드는, 몹시 힘든, 격렬한 demanding a. (일이) 힘든, 벅찬 carbohydrate n. 탄수화물 protein n. 단백질 fat n. 지방 nutritional a. 영양의, 영양분의 gear v. (계획·요구 따위에) 맞게 하다 objective n. 목적, 목표 monotonous a. 단조로운 prepared food 조리식품 mountaineering n. 등산 accompany v. ~에 동반하다; (현상 따위가) ~에 수반하여 일어나다 electrolyte n. 전해질 replace v. ~에 대신하다, 대체하다 requirement n. 요구, 필요; 요구조건 fuel v. ~에 연료를 공급하다 alpine a. 높은 산의 cuisine n. 요리, 요리법

018 ④

2019학년도 인하대학교 인문계 13번

❶ In today's youth-obsessed culture, / getting older is often seen as something to fear. ❷ ⒶBut a new study says / at least one thing gets better / with age: self-esteem. ❸ Age 60 seems to be best / for self-esteem, / according to Ulrich Orth, a professor of psychology at the University of Bern in Switzerland. ❹ Self-esteem first begins to rise / between ages 4 and 11, / as children develop socially and cognitively and gain some sense of independence. ❺ ⒷLevels then seem to plateau / — but not decline / — as the teenage years be in / from ages 11 to 15, / the data show. ❻ That's somewhat surprising, / given that many people assume / that self-esteem takes a hit / during the traditionally awkward early teenage years, / "possibly because of pubertal changes and increased emphasis on social comparison at school," Orth says. ❼ "However, our findings show / that this is not the case." ❽ ⒸInstead, self-esteem appears to hold stead / until mid-adolescence. ❾ After that lull, / self-esteem seems to increase substantially / until age 30, / ❿ then more gradually throughout middle adulthood, / before peaking around age 60 / and remaining stable until age 70. ⓫ Old age frequently involves loss of social roles as a result of retirement and the empty nest (which lower self-esteem). ⓬ Ⓔ"Many people." (Orth says), "are able to maintain a relatively high level of self-esteem / even during old age."

Choose the one that does not fit in the passage.
① Ⓐ ② Ⓑ ③ Ⓒ ✓④ Ⓓ ⑤ Ⓔ

해석

❶ 오늘날처럼 젊음에 집착하는 문화에서, 나이를 먹는 것은 종종 두려워해야 하는 것으로 여겨진다. ❷ Ⓐ하지만 새로운 연구에 따르면, 적어도 한 가지는 나이가 들수록 좋아진다고 한다. 바로 자존감이다. ❸ 스위스 베른 대학의 심리학과 교수인 울리히 오르스(Ulrich Orth)에 따르면, 자존감은 60세에 최고조에 이르는 것처럼 보인다. ❹ 자존감은 아이들이 4세에서 11세 사이에 사회적·인지적으로 발달하고 어느 정도의 자립심을 가지면서 처음으로 높아지기 시작한다. ❺ Ⓑ자료에 따르면, 자존감의 수준은 11세에서 15세까지의 십 대 시절이 시작되면서 안정 상태를 유지하는 -그러나 줄어들지는 않는- 것으로 보인다. ❻ "아마도 사춘기에 따른 변화를 겪고 학교에서 다른 이들과의 비교를 통한 자기평가가 점점 더 강조될 것이기 때문에, 서투른 모습을 보이기 마련인 십 대 초기에 자존감이 타격을 입는 것으로 많은 사람들이 추측하고 있음을 고려하면, 그것은 다소 놀라운 사실입니다."라고 오르스 교수는 말한다. ❼ "하지만, 우리의 연구결과는 그렇지 않다는 것을 보여줍니다. ❽ Ⓒ대신에, 자존감은 청소년기 중반까지 한결같은 상태로 유지되는 것으로 보입니다. ❾ 그러한 소강상태를 보인 후에 30세까지 상당히 증가하고, ❿ 그런 다음 중장년기에 걸쳐서 더욱 서서히 증가하다가, 60세 무렵에 최고조에 달하고, 70세가 될 때까지는 안정된 모습을 보이는 것 같습니다." <⓫ Ⓓ자신은 퇴직을 하고 자녀들은 성장해 집을 떠나면서, 노년에는 종종 사회적 역할을 상실하며, 이것이 자존감을 낮추게 한다.> ⓬ Ⓔ오르스는 "많은 사람들이 노년기에도 비교적 높은 수준의 자존감을 유지할 수 있습니다."라고 말한다.

해설

윗글은 나이가 들면서 자존감이 올라간다는 내용으로 특히 노년인 60세 때 최고조에 이른다는 것이 요지다. 하지만 Ⓓ는 오히려 반대로 노년에 자존감이 줄어든다는 내용으로 전체 기조와 어울리지 않는다.

어휘

youth-obsessed a. 젊음에 집착하는 self-esteem n. 자존감, 자부심 cognitively ad. 인식적으로 plateau v. 안정수준에 달하다; 상승이 멈추다 awkward a. 서투른, 어색한 steady a. 확고한; 안정된; 한결같은 adolescence n. 청년기, 사춘기 lull n. (비·바람·폭풍우 등의) 진정, 잠잠함; 일시적인 고요함; 진정상태 substantially ad. 상당히, 많이; 대체로 gradually ad. 차차로, 서서히 adulthood n. 성인기 peak v. 최고점[한도]에 달하다, 절정이 되다 stable a. 안정된, 견고한 involve v. (필연적으로) 수반하다, 포함하다 retirement n. 은퇴; 퇴직 empty nest 빈 둥지(자녀가 장성하여 집을 떠나고 부모만 남은 상황) lower v. 낮추다, 내리다 maintain v. 지속하다, 유지하다 relatively ad. 상대적으로, 비교적

019 ⑤   2017학년도 인하대학교 일반 학사편입 인문계 19번

❶ Although scattered local airline companies began offering flights to passengers / as early as 1913, / ❷ scheduled domestic flights did not become widely available in the United States / until the 1920s. ❸ ⒶDuring the early years of commercial aviation, / U.S. airline travel was limited to a small population of business travelers and wealthy individuals (who could afford the high ticket prices). ❹ ⒷThe majority of travelers relied (instead on) more affordable train services / for their intercity transportation needs. ❺ ⒸOver ninety-five years later, / the airlines have grown /(to be) one of the most important and heavily used transportation options / for American business and leisure travelers. ❻ ⒹFollowing deregulation of the airline industry by the U.S. government in 1978, / airline routes increased, ❼ ticket fares decreased, and discount carriers prospered, thus making airline travel accessible / to a much broader segment of the U.S. population. ❽ ⒺPlane tickets were generally prepared by hand / using carbon paper and were given to passengers / upon their arrival at the airports. ❾ In 2008 alone, / 649.9 million passengers traveled / on domestic flights / on U.S. airlines.

Choose the sentence that does not fit in each passage.
① Ⓐ   ② Ⓑ   ③ Ⓒ   ④ Ⓓ   ☑ Ⓔ

해석

❶ 곳곳에 흩어져 있던 지방의 항공사들이 일찍이 1913년에 승객들에게 항공편을 제공하기 시작했지만, ❷ 미국에서 국내선 정기 항공편을 널리 이용할 수 있게 된 것은 1920년대에 접어들면서부터였다. ❸ Ⓐ상업 항공이 이뤄지던 초창기 동안, 미국의 항공 여행은 비싼 항공요금을 지불할 여유가 있던 소수의 비즈니스 여행객과 부유한 개인들로 제한되어 있었다. ❹ Ⓑ도시간 교통의 경우, 대부분 여행객들은 비행기 대신에 보다 저렴한 가격의 기차에 의존하고 있었다. ❺ Ⓒ95년이 넘는 시간이 지난 뒤에, 미국의 비즈니스와 레저 여행객들에게 항공편은 가장 중요하고 또 가장 많이 이용하는 운송 수단 중 하나로 성장했다. ❻ Ⓓ1978년에 미국 정부의 항공 산업 규제 완화 후에, 항공 노선은 늘어났고, ❼ 항공요금은 감소했으며, 저가 항공사가 번성했다. 이로 인해 더 광범위한 계층의 미국인들이 항공 여행을 할 수 있게 되었다. <❽ Ⓔ비행기 티켓은 대체로 먹지를 이용해서 손으로 써서 준비했고 승객이 공항에 도착하는 즉시 주었다.> ❾ 2008년 한 해에만도, 6억 4,990만 명의 승객들이 미국 항공사의 국내선을 통해 여행했다.

해설

윗글은 미국 항공 산업의 시작과 2008년까지 항공 산업의 성장 과정을 설명하는 글이다. 하지만 Ⓔ는 비행기 티켓의 용지 설명과 지급 방법은 전체 주제와 어울리지 않는다.

어휘

scatter v. 뿔뿔이 흩어버리다, 쫓아버리다, 흩뿌리다 passenger n. 승객, 여객, 선객 domestic a. 가정의, 가사의, 국내의, 자국의 commercial a. 상업의, 무역의; 영리적인 aviation n. 비행, 항공; 항공 산업 afford v. ~할 여유가 있다, ~할 수 있다; 주다, 제공하다 majority n. 대부분, 대다수, 과반수 intercity 도시 간의 transportation n. 운송, 수송; 수송기관 deregulation n. 규제 철폐 fare n. 운임, 통행료 prosper v. 번영하다, 성공하다; 잘 자라다 accessible a. 접근(가까이) 하기 쉬운; 입수하기 쉬운, 이용할 수 있는 segment n. 단편, 조각, 부분, 구획 carbon paper (복사용의) 먹지

정답 및 해설

020 ③   2020학년도 숭실대학교 인문계 49번

해 석

❶ In the last days of 2019, as millions of Americans were contemplating their resolutions for the year ahead, the moving-and-storage company U-Haul set one for all of its future employees. ❷ The company announced that starting February 1, it will stop hiring people who use nicotine in the 21 states where such a prohibition is legal, including Texas, Florida, and Massachusetts. ❸ Seventeen of those states allow employers to administer drug test for nicotine.

❹ While a new policy for U-Haul, this move is part of a larger trend toward "workplace wellness" programs, which encourage employees to pursue dietary changes and hit daily activity goals. ❺ Over the past decade, companies have become far more coercive in their insistence that employees optimize their bodies and behavior on their own time. ❻ ⒶThis cuts costs and, at least in theory, helps employees live healthier lives.

❼ In a press release, U-Haul's chief of staff, Jessica Lopez, repeated some of the supposedly inspirational words that have embedded themselves into the workplace-wellness vernacular. ❽ ⒷWe are deeply invested in the well-being of our team members. ❾ Nicotine products are addictive and pose a variety of serious health risks," she said. ❿ Lopez characterized the move as "a responsible step in fostering a culture of wellness at U-Haul, with the goal of helping our team members on their health journey."

⓫ According to U-Haul's announcement, the company plans to note its policy on job applications, question applicants about their nicotine usage in interviews, and require them to consent to nicotine testing in the seventeen states that allow it. ⓬ The policy will apply to any nicotine use, which means that vapers and other users of smokeless tobacco will be excluded from the hiring

❶ 2019년 연말에, 수백만 명의 미국인들이 새해의 결심을 고민하고 있었을 때, 이사 및 보관 회사인 U-Haul은 미래의 모든 직원들을 위해 한 가지 목표를 설정했다. ❷ 그 회사는 2월 1일부터 21개 주에서 니코틴을 사용하는 사람들을 고용하지 않을 것이라고 발표했는데, 텍사스, 플로리다, 매사추세츠 등을 포함한 21개 주에서는 이러한 금지 규정이 합법이다. ❸ 이 주들 중에서 17개의 주에서는 고용주들이 니코틴에 대한 약물검사를 실시할 수 있도록 허용하고 있다.

❹ U-Haul에게 이러한 조치가 새로운 정책이지만, 이러한 조치는 직원들이 식생활 변화를 추구하고 일상 활동의 목표를 달성하도록 장려하는 '직장 건강' 프로그램을 향한 더 큰 추세의 일부이다. ❺ 지난 수십 년 동안 기업들은 직원들이 스스로 시간을 내서 몸과 행동을 최적화해야 한다고 주장함에 있어 훨씬 더 강압적이게 되었다. ❻ Ⓐ적어도 이론상으로, 이것은 비용을 절감하고, 직원들이 더 건강한 삶을 살 수 있도록 도와준다.

❼ 보도 자료에서 U-Haul의 인사부장인 제시카 로페즈(Jessical Lopez)는 이제는 직장에서의 건강과 관련된 전문어가 되어버린 몇 마디 영감을 주는 말을 반복했다. ❽ Ⓑ"저희는 우리 팀원들의 건강에 관해 깊이 관심을 두고 있습니다. ❾ 니코틴 제품은 중독성이 있으며 여러 가지 심각한 건강상의 위험이 됩니다."라고 그녀는 말했다. ❿ 로페즈는 이 움직임 "우리 팀원들이 건강해지도록 돕는 것을 목표로 하여 U-Haul의 웰빙 문화를 육성하기 위한 중요한 조치"라고 설명했다.

⓫ U-Haul의 발표에 따르면, 회사는 입사 지원서에 회사의 방침을 공지하고, 면접에서 지원자의 니코틴 사용량에 대해 질문하며, 니코틴 테스트를 허용하는 17개 주에서는 니코틴 검사에 동의하도록 요구할 계획이다. ⓬ 그 정책은 모든 형태의 니코틴 사용에 적용될 것인데, 이는 흡연자들뿐만 아니라 전자담배 흡연자들 또 다른 무연담배 사용자들도 고용 이용 대상에서 제외될 것이라는 것을 의미한다.

어 휘

contemplate v. 고려하다, 생각하다 resolution n. (굳은) 다짐, 결심 hire v. 고용하다 nicotine n. 니코틴 prohibition n. 금지법, 금지 규정 coercive a. 강압[강제]적인 insistence n. 고집, 주장, 강조 optimize v. ~을 최대한 좋게[적합하게] 만들다[활용하다] press release 보도 자료 supposedly ad. 추정상, 아마 inspirational a. 영감을 주는 embed v. (마음·기억 등에) 깊이 새겨 두다 vernacular n. 말, 토착어, 전문어, 은어 be invested in ~에 관심이 있다 addictive a. 중독성의, 중독성이 있는 announcement n. 발표, 공표 note v. 언급하다 job application 구직 vaper n. 전자담배를 피우는 사람 smokeless tobacco 씹는 담배

정답 및 해설

pool, / in addition to smokers. ⑬ The policy won't apply to people (already employed with the company). ⑭ ✓ People believe / that the fundamental interests of employees and employers are necessarily hostile / to each other.

⑮ Nicotine is, (indeed), tied to some serious health risks. ⑯ Globally, / smoking cigarettes kills about 8 million people / each year. ⑰ But employers (seeking to control ever more aspects of their employees' lives) is already a troubling trend. ⑱ ⒹIt's bleak / when anyone's health is regarded as malfunctioning workplace machinery, ⑲ but the problem becomes even worse / when these expectations are foisted on the workers (least equipped to fight back).

Which of the following is NOT appropriate?

① Ⓐ   ② Ⓑ   ③✓Ⓒ   ④ Ⓓ

해석

⑬ 그 정책은 회사에 이미 고용된 사람들에게는 적용되지 않을 것이다. <⑭ ⒸPeople들은 직원과 고용주의 근본적인 이해관계가 서로 적대적일 수밖에 없다고 생각한다.>
⑮ 니코틴은, 사실, 심각한 건강상의 위험과 관련이 있다. ⑯ 전 세계적으로 담배를 피우는 것은 매년 약 8백만 명의 사람들을 죽게 한다. ⑰ 하지만 고용주들이 직원들 삶의 더 많은 측면을 통제하려고 하는 것은 이미 골치 아픈 추세이다. ⑱ Ⓓ누구든 건강이 직장의 고장 난 기계로 여겨질 때는 암울하지만, ⑲ 이러한 기대들을 대항할 준비가 가장 덜 된 근로자들에게 강요되면 문제는 더욱 심각해진다.

해설

윗글은 U-Haul 회사가 니코틴 사용자(흡연자)를 고용하지 않겠다는 방침, 그리고 Ⓒ가 있는 단락에서는 이런 법규가 적용되는 사람들의 범위가 규정되고 있는 글이며, 이어지는 마지막 단락에서는 해당 회사의 앞으로의 입사 지원서의 방침까지 설명하고 있다. 따라서 Ⓒ에서 말하는 직원과 고용주의 이해관계에 혹은 서로 간 적대적인 관계는 전체 글의 소재나 주제와 어울리지 않는다.

어휘

pool n. 이용 가능 인력 in addition to ~에 더하여, ~일 뿐 아니라 fundamental a. 기본적인, 근본적인, 핵심적인 hostile a. 적의 있는 troubling a. 골치 아픈, 귀찮은, 성가신, 다루기 힘든 bleak a. 암울한, 절망적인 malfunctioning a. 제대로 움직이지 않는; 제대로 기능하지 못하는 foist v. 억지로 떠맡기다, 속여 팔다 equip v. 갖추게 하다, 수여하다 fight back 저항하다, 가로막다

유형 05 빈칸완성

001 ② — 2019학년도 덕성여자대학교 오후 23번

In pre-colonial times, / New York City's Coney Island was known for its beach bunnies / — the seaside was teeming with rabbits. Later, / this part of the city became known for its amusement park, which has quickly become run-down / over the years. But recently, / land developers are hoping to transform the area into one with upscale beach resorts and hotels. They hope / Coney Island will be known for chic accommodations as opposed to urban blight.

Which of the following is the most suitable for the blank?
다음 중 중 빈칸에 가장 적절한 것은?

① exciting nightlife along with natural beauty
자연의 아름다움과 함께 신나는 밤 문화

☑ chic accommodations as opposed to urban blight
도시의 황폐와 반대되는 세련된 숙박 시설

③ local wildlife together with improved facilities
향상된 시설과 함께 지역의 야생동물

④ its extensive history instead of the recent renovations
최근의 개조 대신에 그것의 광범위한 역사

해석
① 식민지 시대 이전에, 뉴욕시의 코니아일랜드(Coney Island)는 해변의 토끼들로 유명했다. ② 그 해변은 토끼들로 가득 차 있었다. ③ 나중에, 도시의 이 지역은 놀이공원으로 알려지게 되었고, 여러 해에 걸쳐 빠르게 황폐해졌다. ④ 하지만 최근에, 토지 개발업자들은 이 지역을 고급 해변 리조트와 호텔이 있는 곳으로 바꾸기를 희망하고 있다. ⑤ 그들은 코니아일랜드가 도시의 황폐와 반대되는 세련된 숙박 시설로 알려지기를 바란다.

해설
빈칸 앞 문장에서 토지 개발업자들이 이 지역을 리조트와 호텔이 있는 곳으로 개발하는 희망을 말하고 있다. 따라서 세련된 숙박 시설의 뜻인 'chic accommodations'가 있는 ②가 가장 적절하다. 선택지의 urban blight는 본문에 run-down(황폐한)을 가리킨다. 나머지 선택지는 본문과의 소재가 일치하지 않는다.

어휘
pre-colonial a. 식민지 시대 전의 bunny n. 토끼 seaside n. 해변, 바닷가 teem with ~로 가득 차다, 많이 있다, 풍부하다 amusement park 놀이공원, 유원지 run-down a. 황폐한 upscale a. (수입.교육.사회적 지위가) 평균 이상의, 고급의 transform v. (외형을) 변형시키다; (성질.기능.구조 등을) 바꾸다 nightlife n. (환락가 등에서의) 밤의 유흥[생활] blight n. (식물의) 마름병; 어두운 그림자; (도시의) 황폐 chic a. 멋진, 세련된 accommodation n. 숙박 시설 facility n. (보통 -ies) 시설, 설비 renovation n. 혁신, 쇄신, 수선

002 ②　　2019학년도 가천대학교 인문계 1교시 C형 33번

❶ All my life / I've been registering exceptional scores with tests, / ❷ so that I have the complacent feeling (that I'm highly intelligent). ❸ Actually, though, don't such scores simply mean / that I am good at answering the type of academic questions (that are considered / worthy of answers / by the people (making up the intelligence tests) — people (with an intellectual bent / similar to mine)? ❹ In a world (where I could not use my academic training and my verbal talents), I would do poorly. ❺ My intelligence, then, is not absolute / but is a function of the society : (I live in) and of the fact (that a small subsection of that society has managed to foist itself / on the rest / as a Ⓑ judge of matters of intelligence).

Which of the following is most appropriate for the blank Ⓑ?
다음 중 빈칸 Ⓑ에 들어가기에 가장 적절한 것은?

① layman (평신도)
✓② judge (심판관)
③ dissenter (반대자)
④ recluse (은둔자)

해석
❶ 나는 평생 시험 특별히 뛰어난 성적을 받았기 때문에, ❷ 나는 내가 매우 똑똑하다는 자기 만족감을 갖고 있다. ❸ 하지만, 사실 그 점수들은 단지 학문적인 질문들에 답하는 것에 능숙하다는, 다시 말해 지능 검사를 만드는 사람들, 즉 나와 유사한 지적 성향을 가진 사람들이 가치 있다고 여길만한 답을 하는 데 능숙하다는 것을 의미하는 것에 불과하는 것은 아닐까? ❹ 나의 학문적 훈련과 나의 언어적 재능을 활용할 수 없는 세상에서라면, 나의 성적은 형편없을 것이다. ❺ 그렇다면, 나의 지능은 절대적인 것이 아니라 내가 사는 사회의 작용일 뿐이며, 사회의 작은 한 부분이 나머지 사회 전체에 스스로를 지능 문제의 Ⓑ심판관으로 속여 넘겼다는 사실이 작용한 것일 뿐이다.

해설
뛰어나고 자존감이 높은 사람이 테스트라는 것을 회의적으로 보고 있는 글이다. 즉 테스트는 지적 성향을 지닌 사람들이 가치 있다고 여길 만한 답을 다는 것에 불과하다고 말하고 있다. 그래서 특정 사회의 작용할 뿐이며 절대적인 척도가 아님을 말하는 글이다. 따라서 사회의 작은 한 부분이 나머지 사회 전체에 스스로를 지능 문제의 심판관으로 속여 넘겼다는 사실일 뿐이라고 말하는 것이 가장 적절하다.

*테스트 → 그들이 만든 척도일 뿐(절대적 척도 아님) → 그들 소수가 다수들에게 마치 지식의 심판관으로 있는 것에 불과함

어휘
register v. 등록하다, 표명하다, 나타내다　exceptional a. 특출한　complacent a. 자기만족의　bent n. 경향, 성향, 소질, 자질　verbal a. 언어의, 말의　function n. 기능, 작용, 함수　subsection n. 세부 항목　foist v. 억지로 떠안기다, 속여서 팔다　layman n. 비전문가　dissenter n. 반대자　recluse n. 은둔자

정답 및 해설

003 A) ① B) ② … 2019학년도 가천대학교 인문계 2교시 A형 28,29번

「It takes 시간 to부정사」: to ~하는데 ~만큼의 시간이 걸리다

❶ It took Europe some 300 years to modernize, and the process was wrenching and traumatic, involving bloody revolutions, / ❷ often succeeded by reigns of terror, brutal holy wars, dictatorships, cruel exploitation of the workforce, and widespread alienation and anomie. ❸ We are now witnessing the same kind of Ⓐ upheaval / in developing countries (presently undergoing modernization). ❹ But some of these countries have had to attempt this difficult process far too rapidly ❺ and are forced to follow a western programme, / rather than their own. ❻ Ⓑ This accelerated modernization created deep divisions / in developing nations. ❼ Only an elite has a western education (that enables them to understand the new modern institutions. ❽ The vast majority remains trapped / in the premodern ethos.

A) Which of the following is most appropriate for the blank Ⓐ?
다음 중 빈칸 Ⓐ에 들어가기에 가장 적절한 것은?

✓ ① upheaval 격변
② languor 무기력
③ seclusion 격리
④ transcendence 초월

B) Which of the following is most appropriate for the blank Ⓑ?
다음 중 빈칸 Ⓑ에 들어가기에 가장 적절한 것은?

① The regression of modernity 극대성의 퇴보
✓ ② This accelerated modernization 가속화된 근대화
③ This intermittent modernization 간헐적인 근대화
④ The resistance against modernity 근대성에 대한 저항

해석

❶ 유럽이 근대화되는 데 약 300년이 걸렸는데, 그것은 고통스럽고 충격적인 과정으로 피비린내 나는 혁명을 수반했으며, ❷ 종종 공포정치, 잔인한 성전(聖戰), 독재, 무자비한 노동력 착취, 광범위한 소외와 아노미 현상이 이어졌다. ❸ 우리는 현재 근대화를 겪고 있는 개발도상국에서 똑같은 종류의 Ⓐ격변을 목격하고 있다. ❹ 하지만 이들 국가들 중 일부는 이 어려운 과정을 너무 빠른 속도로 시도해야만 했고, ❺ 그들 자신의 프로그램이 아니라 서양의 프로그램을 따라야 했다. ❻ 이 Ⓑ가속화된 근대화는 개발도상국에 깊은 분열을 만들어냈다. ❼ 새로운 근대 제도를 이해할 수 있게 해주는 서양식 교육을 엘리트들만이 받고 있다. ❽ 대다수 사람들은 여전히 전근대적인 정신에 갇혀 있다

해설

A) 바로 앞 ❷번 문장에서 말하는 공포정치, 잔인한 성전 등의 의미를 포괄하는 단어가 '격변(upheaval)'이 A)에 가장 적절하다.

B) 앞 문장에서 근대화가 빠른 속도로 시도해야만 했음을 말하고 있으므로 ②의 '가속화의 근대화(This accelerated modernization)'가 B)에 가장 적절하다.

어휘

modernize v. 현대화하다 process n. 진행, 경과; 과정 wrenching a. 비통한, 고통스러운 traumatic a. 상처 깊은; 정신적 쇼크의 involve v. 관련시키다; (필연적으로) 수반하다 bloody a. 피를 흘리는, 유혈의 revolution n. 혁명, 변혁 reigns of terror 공포정치, 공포시대 brutal a. 잔인한, 사나운 dictatorship n. 독재, 독재정권 cruel a. 잔인한, 잔혹한 exploitation n. 이용; 개척, 착취 workforce n. (국가·지역·산업체 등의) 총 노동력, 노동 인구 alienation n. 소외 anomie n. 아노미 현상, 사회[도덕]적 무질서 witness v. 목격하다, 눈앞에 보다; 증언하다 presently ad. 이내, 곧; 목하, 현재 undergo v. (영양·변화·조처·검사 따위를) 받다, 입다 division n. 불일치, 분열 institution n. 학회; 기관; 제도 majority n. 대부분, 대다수 premodern a. 근대 이전의, 전근대적인 ethos n. 사회사조, 기풍, 풍조 upheaval n. 격변, 대변동 languor n. 나른함 seclusion n. 호젓함 transcendence n. 초월, 탁월 regression n. 퇴행, 퇴보, 회귀 modernity n. 현대성, 현대적임 accelerate v. 가속화하다, 속도를 높이다 intermittent a. 간헐적인

004 ⑤
2019학년도 인하대학교 인문계 22번

❶ Although a high birthrate typified most preindustrial cultures, ❷ it was the low death rate and long average life span that pushed up American population numbers. ❸ With no huge urban centers, colonial epidemics proved less devastating than in Europe. ❹ Food was plentiful, and housing improved steadily. ❺ Newborns who survived infancy could live a long life. ❻ Ⓐ Moreover, the 1720s and 1730s proved peaceful compared to earlier decades, ❼ so soldiering did not endanger lives among men of military age. ❽ For women, death related to pregnancy and childbirth still loomed as a constant threat. ❾ Ⓑ Yet women still outnumbered men among people living into their 60s, 70s, and 80s.

Choose the most appropriate one for each blank.
각 빈칸에 가장 적절한 것을 고르시오.

	Ⓐ	Ⓑ
①	However 하지만	Thus 따라서
②	Moreover 게다가	Also 또한
③	Similarly 마찬가지로	So 그래서
④	However 하지만	But 그러나
✓⑤	Moreover 게다가	Yet 그러나

해석
❶ 비록 높은 출산율은 산업화 이전의 문화 대부분에 나타난 특징이었지만, ❷ 아메리카 대륙의 인구수를 끌어올린 것은 바로 낮은 사망률과 긴 평균수명이었다. ❸ 거대한 도시 중심지가 없었기 때문에, 식민지의 전염병은 유럽에서보다 덜 파괴적인 것으로 판명됐다. ❹ 음식은 풍부했고, 주택은 꾸준히 개선되었다. ❺ 유아기에 죽지 않고 살아남은 신생아들은 장수할 수 있었다. ❻ Ⓐ게다가, 1720년대와 1730년대는 이전 수십 년에 비해 평화로웠기 때문에, ❼ 군복무를 하는 것이 징집 연령에 있는 남성들의 목숨을 위태롭게 하지 않았다. ❽ 여성들에게 임신 및 출산과 관련된 죽음은 여전히 지속적인 위협으로 다가왔다. ❾ Ⓑ하지만 60대, 70대, 80대 중에는 여전히 여성의 수가 남성보다 더 많았다.

해설
Ⓐ) 인구가 늘어나게 된 요인을 설명하는 과정이다. 같은 기조의 심화된 내용을 끌어내는 'Moreover(게다가)'이 Ⓐ에 가장 적절하다.
Ⓑ) 빈칸 바로 앞인 ❽번 문장에서 여성들에게 임신 및 출산과 관련된 죽음은 지속적 위협이라고 말하지만, 이어서는 상반된 내용으로 여전히 여성의 수가 남성보다 더 많았다고 말하고 있다. 따라서 역접을 이끄는 Yet이 Ⓑ에 가장 적절하다.

어휘
birthrate n. 출산율 typify v. 대표하다, ~의 특징이 되다 preindustrial a. 산업화 이전의, 산업혁명 전의 life span 수명 huge a. 거대한, 막대한 urban a. 도시의 colonial a. 식민지의 epidemic n. 유행병, 전염병 devastating a. 황폐시키는, 파괴적인 plentiful a. 많은, 충분한, 풍부한 steadily ad. 착실하게; 꾸준히 newborn n. 신생아 infancy n. 유년기 soldier v. 군인이 되다, 병역에 복무하다 endanger v. 위태롭게 하다, 위험에 빠뜨리다 pregnancy n. 임신 childbirth n. 분만, 해산 loom v. 어렴풋이 보이다, 아련히 나타나다; 중대하게 느껴지다 constant a. 끊임없는, 변함없는 threat n. 위협, 협박 outnumber v. ~보다 수가 많다, 수적으로 우세하다

정답 및 해설

005 ③ — 2019학년도 한국산업기술대학교 인문계 29번

[글의 주제]
❶ Social networking sites are ruining our lives. ❷ I know / that might sound drastic, ❸ but we seem to have lost the art of talking to each other. ❹ Last week, / I was sitting / in a cafe and was taken aback / by how many people / were using / their cell phones rather than / chatting to the people (they were with). ❺ People seem to have stopped talking to each other / — all (they do) is "chatting" on Facebook. ❻ I've even seen / waiters / stop to check their cell phones / when taking orders! ❼ I find that unbelievable. ❽ Does that make me old-fashioned? ❾ I don't know, but I'd rather be labeled as boring and out of touch / than spend my life / hooked to a screen. ❿ When I tried explaining this / to my girlfriend, / she just laughed.

Choose the one that best fills in the blanks.
다음 빈칸에 들어갈 적절한 말을 고르시오.

① to tell … to look
② telling … checking
③ talking … to check ✓
④ to talk … looking

[해석]
❶ 소셜 네트워크 사이트가 우리의 삶을 망치고 있다. ❷ 나는 이 말이 과격하게 들릴 수도 있다는 것을 알고 있지만, ❸ 우리는 서로 대화하는 기술을 잃어버린 것 같다. ❹ 지난주에 나는 한 카페에 앉아 있었는데, 많은 사람들이 함께 있는 사람들과 대화하지 않고 휴대폰을 사용하고 있는 것에 깜짝 놀랐다. ❺ 사람들은 서로 이야기 나누기를 멈춘 것처럼 보인다. 그들이 하는 것이라고는 페이스북에서 '대화'하는 것뿐이다. ❻ 나는 심지어 종업원들이 주문을 받을 때도 잠깐 멈추고는 자신의 휴대폰을 확인하는 모습도 보았다. ❼ 그것은 나에겐 믿을 수 없는 일이다. ❽ 그것은 나를 구식으로 만드는가? ❾ 잘 모르겠지만, 나는 휴대폰 화면에 빠져 평생을 보내기보다는 차라리 지루하고 세상 물정 모르는 사람으로 딱지가 붙는 것이 낫다. ❿ 내가 이것을 여자 친구에게 설명하자, 그녀는 그저 웃기만 했다.

[해설]
소셜 네트워크가 우리 삶을 망치고 있다는 글이다. 따라서 ❸번 문장에서 사람들이 카페에서 대화가 아니라 휴대전화를 사용하는 것에 놀랐다고 말하고 있다. 따라서 첫 빈칸에는 '~하던 것을 멈춘다'의 의미인 『stop + 동명사』가 적절하다.
두 번째 빈칸에서는 심지어 종업원들도 주문받으면서도 잠깐 중단하고는 휴대전화를 확인한다고 말하는 것이 주제문과 결부된다. 따라서 『stop + to-v』로 '~위해 멈춘다'가 적절하다.

[어휘] ruin v. 망치다, 엉망으로 만들다 drastic a. 과감한, 극단적인; 급격한 take aback ~를 깜짝 놀라게 하다 old-fashioned a. 구식의, 낡은, 진부한 out of touch 현실감이 없는, 세상 물정을 모르는

006 ④ .... 2019학년도 한국항공대학교 인문계 21번

❶ As the solar system condensed out of gas and dust, / ❷ Jupiter acquired most of the matter (that was not ejected into interstellar space) and did not fall inward / to form the Sun. ❸ [Had Jupiter been several dozen times more massive, the matter (in its interior) would have undergone thermonuclear reactions, ❹ and Jupiter would have begun to shine / by its own light]. ❺ The largest planet is a star (that failed). ❻ Even so, / its interior temperatures are sufficiently high / that it gives off about twice as much energy / as it receives from the Sun. ❼ In the infrared part of the spectrum, / it might even be correct / to consider Jupiter a star. ❽ [Had it become a star in visible light, ❾ we would today inhabit a binary system, ❿ and the night would come more rarely — / a commonplace, / (I believe), in countless solar systems / throughout the Milky Way Galaxy]. ⓫ We would doubtless think the circumstances natural and lovely.

Choose the most appropriate one for the blank.
빈칸에 들어가기에 가장 적절한 어구를 고르시오.

① a single-star system
   한 개의 태양이 있는 태양계
② a substantial human presence
   실질적인 인간 존재
③ a weaker magnetic field
   더 약한 자기장
✓④ a binary system
   두 개의 태양이 있는 태양계

[해석] ❶ 태양계가 가스와 먼지로부터 응축되면서, ❷ 목성은 성간 공간으로(태양계 밖으로) 분출되지도 않고 태양으로 끌려 들어가 태양을 형성하지도 않은 물질들 대부분을 갖게 되었다. ❸ 만약 목성이 지금보다 수십 배 더 컸다면, 내부의 물질이 핵융합 반응을 겪었을 것이고, ❹ 목성은 스스로 빛을 내기 시작했을 것이다. ❺ 태양계의 최대 행성인 목성은 실패한 항성(항성이 되려다 만 행성)이다. ❻ 그렇다 하더라도, 내부의 온도는 충분히 높으므로 태양으로부터 받아들이는 에너지의 약 두 배를 뿜어내고 있다. ❼ 가시파장역(스펙트럼)의 적외선 부분에서는, 목성을 하나의 항성으로 간주하는 것이 정확할 수도 있다. ❽ 만약 목성이 가시광선 부분에 있어서 하나의 항성이 되었다면, ❾ 우리는 오늘날 두 개의 태양이 있는 태양계에서 살고 있을 것이며, ❿ 밤은 더 드물게 올 것이다 — 나는 이것이 우리 은하 전체에 무수히 많은 태양계들에서 흔한 일이라고 생각한다. ⓫ 우리는 분명 그런 상황을 자연스럽고 사랑스럽다고 생각할 것이다.

[해설] 목성이 핵열반응을 통해 태양이 될 수도 있었음을 말하는 글이다. 따라서 빈칸에는 '두 개의 태양이 있는 태양계(a binary system)'가 가장 적절하다.

[어휘] condense v. 응축하다 eject v. 분출하다, 빠져나가다 interstellar space 성간 공간, 성간 우주(은하계 안에서 항성(별)과 항성 사이의 어두운 공간) massive a. 거대한 undergo v. 겪다 thermonuclear reaction 열핵반응, 원자핵 융합반응 give off 방출하다 infrared a. 적외선의 spectrum n. 스펙트럼, 분광, 가시광장역 visible light 가시광선 commonplace n. 흔히 있는[평범한] 일 the Milky Way Galaxy 우리은하(태양계가 속해 있는 은하), 은하계 binary a. 둘의, 2진

---

1) 가정법 과거완료 if S had p.p, S 조동사과거 have p.p (If 생략→주어동사도치)
   = If Jupiter had been ~
2) 혼합가정법 If S had p.p, S 조동사과거 동·원 : (과거에) ~했다면 (지금) ~일텐데
   (If 생략→주어동사도치) = If it had become ~

007 ④ 2019학년도 한국항공대학교 인문계 22번

글의 주제
❶ The only way (to really know / whether an idea is reasonable) is to test it. ❷ Build a quick prototype or mock-up of each potential solution. ❸ In the early stages of this process, / the mock-ups can be pencil sketches, foam and cardboard models, or simple images (made with simple drawing tools). ❹ I have made mock-ups / with spreadsheets, PowerPoint slides, and with sketches on index cards or sticky notes. ❺ Sometimes / ideas are best conveyed by skits, / especially / if you're developing services or automated systems (that are difficult to prototype). ❻ One popular prototype technique is called "Wizard of Oz," / after the wizard in L Frank Baum's classic book *The Wonderful Wizard of Oz*. ❼ The wizard was actually just an ordinary person / ❽ but, (through the use of smoke and mirrors), he managed to appear mysterious and omnipotent. ❾ In other words, it was all a fake: the wizard had no special powers. ❿ The Wizard of Oz method can be used to mimic a huge, powerful system before it can be built.

『be used to V』: ~하는데 사용되다
『be used to ~ing』: ~하는데 익숙해지다
『used to V』: ~하곤 했다

Choose the phrase that best fills in the blank.
빈칸에 들어가기에 가장 적절한 어구를 고르시오.

① as soon as it is built
  만들자마자
② without consideration of its building time
  만드는 시간을 고려하지 않고
③ after it is built
  만들어진 다음에
✓ before it can be built
  만들기 전에

해 석
❶ 어떤 아이디어가 합리적인지 정말로 알 수 있는 유일한 방법은 그것을 검증해보는 것이다. ❷ 각 잠재적 해결책에 대해서 즉석 원형이나 즉석 실물모형을 만들어라. ❸ 이 과정의 초기 단계에서는, 실물모형들이 연필 스케치이거나 발포 고무와 판지로 만든 모형(본)이거나 간단한 스케치 도구로 그린 단단한 그림일 수도 있다. ❹ 나는 스프레드시트와 파워포인트 슬라이드로, 그리고 색인 카드나 스티커 메모지 위에 스케치를 하여, 실물모형을 만들었다. ❺ 아이디어들은 때때로 짧은 모방풍자극으로 가장 잘 전달되는데, 특히 원형을 만들기 어려운 서비스 또는 자동화 시스템을 개발하고 있다면 그렇다. ❻ 인기 있는 원형 제작 기술의 이름은 "오즈의 마법사"로, 프랭크 바움(L. Frank Baum)의 고전적 동화『오즈의 마법사(The Wonderful Wizard of Oz)』에 나오는 마법사에서 따온 이름이다. ❼ 그 마법사는 실제로는 평범한 사람이었지만 ❽ 연기와 거울을 이용해 신비롭고 전지전능한 것처럼 보일 수 있었다. ❾ 다시 말해 그 마법사는 완전히 가짜였고, 특별한 힘을 전혀 갖지 않았다. ❿ "오즈의 마법사" 방법은 거대하고 강력한 시스템을 만들기 전에 그것을 모방해보는 데 사용된다.

해 설 아이디어의 검증을 위해 모형이나 모방을 주제로 하고 있다. 그 예시로 '오즈의 마법사'를 언급하고 있다. 따라서 거대하고 강력한 시스템을 만들기 전에 모방해보는 데 사용된다고 말하는 것이 가장 적절하다.

어 휘 resonable a. 합리적인, 이성적인 prototype n. 원형, 시제품 mock-up n. (실물 크기의) 모형 potential a. 잠재적인 foam n. 발포 고무 cardboard n. 판지, 미분지 spreadsheet n. 스프레드 시트(경리, 회계 등의 계산을 위해 사용되는 표 형식의 계산용지) index card 색인 카드 skit n. (모방을 통해 조롱하는) 촌극 wizard n. 마법사 ordinary a. 평범한, 보통의 omnipotent a. 전능한 mimic v. ~을 모방하다

008 ③   2019학년도 가톨릭대학교 인문계 A형 28번

❶ The Fertile Crescent's biological diversity (over small distances) contributed to the region's wealth in ancestors not only of valuable crops but also of domesticated big mammals. ❷ There were few or no wild mammal species (suitable for domestication in the other Mediterranean zones of California, Chile, southwestern Australia, and South Africa). ❸ Ⓐ In contrast four species of big mammals — the goat, sheep, pig, and cow — were domesticated very early in the Fertile Crescent, / possibly earlier than any other animal / except the dog anywhere else in the world. ❹ Those species remain today four of the world's five most important domesticated mammals. ❺ But their wild ancestors were commonest / in slightly different parts of the Fertile Crescent, / ❻ with the result (that the four species were domesticated in different places). ❼ Ⓑ Nevertheless, / even though the areas of abundance (of these four wild progenitors) thus differed, / ❽ all four lived / in sufficiently close proximity (that they were readily transferred / after domestication / from one part of the Fertile Crescent to another) ❾ and the whole region ended up with all four species.

Choose the most appropriate one for each blank.
각 빈칸에 들어가기에 가장 적절한 어구를 고르시오.

	Ⓐ	Ⓑ
①	In fact	… Instead
②	As a result	… However
③ ✓	In contrast	… Nevertheless
④	For example	… Consequently

해석

❶ 비옥한 초승달 지대는 좁은 지역의 생물학적 다양성 때문에, 그 지역에는 귀한 농작물들의 조상뿐 아니라 길들인 대형 포유동물들의 조상도 많았다. ❷ 캘리포니아, 칠레, 호주 남서부, 남아프리카 공화국 등의 다른 지중해성 기후 지역에는 가축으로 길들이기 적합한 야생 포유류가 거의 또는 전혀 없었다. ❸ Ⓐ이와 대조적으로, 비옥한 초승달 지대에서는 네 가지 종(種)의 대형 포유류 — 염소, 양, 돼지, 소 — 가 매우 일찍부터 길들여졌는데, 개를 제외한 세계 다른 그 어느 곳의 그 어떤 동물보다도 더 일찍 길들여졌을 것이다. ❹ 오늘날 이 종들은 세계에서 가장 중요한 다섯 개의 길들인 포유동물 중 네 개에 해당한다. ❺ 하지만 야생에 있던 이 동물들의 조상은 비옥한 초승달 지대 안에서도 약간씩 서로 다른 지역에서 매우 흔했고, ❻ 그 결과 그 네 가지 종들은 서로 다른 곳에서 길들여졌다. ❼ 그럼에도 불구하고, 야생에 있던 이 네 가지 종의 조상들이 많은 지역이 이렇게 서로 달랐지만, ❽ 네 종의 동물이 모두 충분히 가까운 곳에서 살고 있었기 때문에 길들여진 후에는 비옥한 초승달 지대의 한 지역에서 다른 지역으로 쉽게 옮겨갔으며, ❾ 결국에는 전 지역에 네 종류 모두가 있게 되었다.

해설

Ⓐ) ❷번 문장에서 길들이기 적합한 야생 포유류가 없다고 하지만 빈칸 다음에는 비옥한 초승달 지역에는 일찍부터 길들인 동물이 있다고 말한다. 그래서 'In contrast(이와 대조적으로)'가 에 가장 적절하다.

Ⓑ) ❻번 문장에서는 네 가지 종이 서로 다른 곳에서 길들여지게 되었다고 하지만, 빈칸 다음에는 그렇지만 가까운 곳에서 길들여져 차후에는 전 지역에 네 종류 모두가 있게 되었다고 말한다. 따라서 상반된 내용을 끌어내는 'Nevertheless(그럼에도 불구하고)'가 에 가장 적절하다.

어휘

Fertile Crescent 비옥한 초승달 지대(나일강과 티그리스강과 페르시아만을 연결하는 고대의 농업지대) **diversity** n. 차이; 변화, 다양성 **contribute** v. 기부하다, 기증하다; 기여하다 **ancestor** n. 선조, 조상 **domesticate** v. (동물 따위를) 길들이다 **mammal** n. 포유동물 **species** n. 종류; 종(種) **suitable** a. 적당한; 어울리는, 알맞은 **Mediterranean** a. 지중해의 **slightly** ad. 약간, 조금 **abundance** n. 풍부, 많음; 부유 **progenitor** n. 조상, 선조; 창시자 **sufficiently** ad. 충분히 **proximity** n. 근접, 가까움 **readily** ad. 손쉽게, 순조롭게 **transfer** v. 옮기다, 이동하다; 바꾸다, 변형시키다 **end up with** 결국 ~하게 되다

정답 및 해설

009 ①   2019학년도 건국대학교 인문·예체능계 A형 28번

글의 주제

❶ Optimists get the last laugh and their hearts stay healthy / longer than those of the grump. ❷ People (who described themselves a highly Ⓐ optimistic a decade ago) had lower rates of death from cardiovascular disease and lower overall death rates / than strong pessimists. ❸ Nine years ago / a study group — (999 men and women aged 65 to 85) — completed a questionnaire / on health, self-respect, morale, optimism and relationships. ❹ Since then, / 397 of them have died. ❺ Ⓑ Optimistic participants had a 55 percent lower risk of death / from all causes / ❻ and 23 percent lower risk of death / from heart failure. ❼ The study notes / that Ⓒ pessimistic people may be more prone to developing habits and problems (that cut life short, / such as smoking, obesity and hypertension). ❽ A predisposition (toward optimism) seemed to provide a survival benefit in subjects / with relatively short life expectancies / otherwise.

다음 글의 빈칸 Ⓐ, Ⓑ, Ⓒ에 들어갈 말로 가장 적절한 것은?

	Ⓐ	Ⓑ	Ⓒ
✓①	optimistic	Optimistic	pessimistic
②	optimistic	Pessimistic	pessimistic
③	pessimistic	Optimistic	optimistic
④	pessimistic	Optimistic	pessimistic
⑤	optimistic	Pessimistic	optimistic

해석

❶ 낙관론자들이 결국에는 웃으며 이들의 심장은 불평만 해대는 사람들의 심장보다 더 오랫동안 건강을 유지한다. ❷ 10년 전에 스스로를 매우 Ⓐ낙관적이라고 평가했던 사람들은 심한 비관론자들보다 심혈관계 질병으로 인한 사망률이 더 낮았고 전반적인 사망률도 더 낮았다. ❸ 9년 전, 65세에서 85세 사이의 999명의 남자와 여자로 구성된 한 연구 집단이 건강, 자존심, 사기, 낙관주의 그리고 인간관계 등에 관해 설문지조사를 완료했다. ❹ 그 이후로 그들 중 397명이 사망했다. ❺ Ⓑ낙관적인 참가자들은 모든 원인의 죽음에서 55% 더 낮은 사망률을 보였고, ❻ 심장마비로 인한 사망률은 23% 더 낮았다. ❼ 그 연구는 Ⓒ비관적인 사람들이 흡연, 비만, 고혈압과 같은 생명을 단축시키는 습관과 문제들을 발전시키는 경향이 더 높을수도 있다는 것에 주목했다. ❽ 낙관주의 성향은 그렇지 않으면 기대수명이 상대적으로 짧은 피험자들에게 생존에 이로운 점을 제공하는 것으로 보였다.

해설

빈칸반의어 문제이다. 주제문의 기조를 따라 논증하는 비교적 쉬운 내용이다. 주제는 낙관론자들은 불평하는 비관론자보다 더 오래 건강을 유지한다는 것이다. 따라서 긍정의 내용인 Ⓐ와 Ⓑ는 '낙관적' 그리고 부정적 내용인 Ⓒ에는 '비관적'이 적절하다.

어휘

optimist n. 낙관론자 get the last laugh 최후에[결국에는] 웃다[이기다, 성공하다] grump n. 성격이 나쁜 사람, 불평분자 cardiovascular disease 심장혈관계 질병 pessimist n. 비관주의자 questionnaire n. 설문지 morale n. 사기, 의욕 obesity n. 비만 hypertension n. 고혈압 predisposition n. 성향, 경향

010 ⑤ 2019학년도 숙명여자대학교 인문계 24번

❶ The effects of an earthquake are strongest in a broad zone (surrounding the epicenter). ❷ Surface ground cracking often occurs, / with horizontal and vertical displacements of several yards. ❸ Such movement does not usually occur / during a major earthquake: / ❹ slight periodic movements (called 'fault creep') can be accompanied / by microearthquakes, too small to be felt. ❺ The extent of earthquake vibration and subsequent damage to a region is partly dependent on characteristics of the ground. ❻ For example, earthquake vibrations last longer and are of greater wave amplitudes / in unconsolidated surface material, / Ⓐ such as poorly compacted fill or river deposits; / ❼ bedrock areas receive fewer effects. ❽ The worst damage occurs / in Ⓑ densely populated urban areas (where structures are not built / to withstand intense shaking).

Which would be the most appropriate pair for the blank Ⓐ and Ⓑ?
다음 중 빈칸 Ⓐ와 Ⓑ에 가장 적절한 짝은 무엇인가?

	Ⓐ		Ⓑ
①	such as (~와 같은)	…	clearly (깔끔하게)
②	such as (~와 같은)	…	rarely (드물게)
③	as for (~에 대해서 말하자면)	…	scarcely (거의 ~ 않다)
④	for instance (예를 들면)	…	scarcely (거의 ~ 않다)
✓⑤	such as (~와 같은)	…	densely (밀집하여)

해석

❶ 지진의 영향은 진원지를 중심으로 한 넓은 지역에서 가장 강력하다. ❷ 지면의 균열을 수 야드에 이르는 수평적이고 수직적인 방향의 이동(전위)과 함께 종종 발생한다. ❸ 그러한 움직임은 대규모의 지진이 일어나는 동안에는 대개 발생하지 않는다. ❹ '단층포행(지진을 일으키지 않으면서 단층이 미끄러지는 현상)'이라 불리는 미세한 주기적인 움직임은 너무 작아서 느낄 수 없는 미소(微小)지진을 동반할 수 있다. ❺ 지진 진동의 정도와 그에 따른 한 지역의 피해는 부분적으로 지면의 특성에 따라 달라진다. ❻ 예를 들어, 지진의 진동은 엉성하게 채워 넣은 흙(성토)과 강의 퇴적물 Ⓐ처럼 굳지 않은 표면 물질에서 더 오래 지속되고 파동의 진폭이 더 크다. ❼ 반면에 기반암 지역은 영향을 더 적게 받는다. ❽ 가장 큰 피해는 구조물이 극심한 흔들림을 견딜 수 있도록 지어지지 않은 인구가 Ⓑ밀집한 도시 지역에서 발생한다.

해설

Ⓐ) ❻번 문장에서 지진 진동의 정도가 지면의 특성에 따라 달라진다고 말한다. 그리고 빈칸 바로 앞에서 언급한 '굳지 않은 표면 물질(unconsolidated surface material)'의 예시가 언급되는 만큼 Ⓐ에는 'such as(예를 들어, ~처럼)'가 적절하다.

Ⓑ) Ⓑ는 통념적 논리가 요구되는데, 지진의 가장 큰 피해는 인구가 '밀집한 (densely)' 도시 지역에서 발생한다고 말하는 것이 가장 적절하다.

어휘

earthquake n. 지진 epicenter n. (지진의) 진원지(震源地), 진앙(震央) horizontal a. 수평의, 가로의 vertical a. 수직의, 세로의 displacement n. (단층의) 전위(轉位), 변위 periodic a. 주기적인 accompany v. 동반하다 vibration n. 떨림[흔들림], 진동 subsequent a. 그[이] 다음의, 차후의 unconsolidated a. 굳지 않은, 강화[통합]되지 않은 amplitude n. 진폭(振幅) compacted a. 꽉 찬, 탄탄한 fill n. 〈토목·건축〉 성토 deposit n. 침전물, 퇴적물 bedrock n. 기반암 withstand v. 견디다, 이겨내다

정답 및 해설

011 ③
2019학년도 상명대학교 인문·자연계 30번

❶ Why would people make an adventurous journey / across thousands of kilometers of ocean? ❷ Why did the pioneers cross the Great Plains, the Rocky Mountains, or the Mojave Desert / to reach the American West? ❸ Why do people continue to migrate / by the millions today? ❹ The hazards (that many migrants have faced) are a measure of the strong lure of new locations and the desperate conditions / in their former homelands. ❺ A permanent move to a new location disrupts traditional cultural ties and economic patterns / in one region. ❻ At the same time, when people migrate, / they take with them / to their new home their language, religion, ethnicity, and other cultural traits. ❼ Most people migrate for economic reasons. ❽ People think about emigrating from places (that have few job opportunities), ❾ and they immigrate to places (where jobs seem to be available). ❿ Because of economic restructuring, / job prospects often vary from one country to another and within regions of the same country. ⓫ The United States and Canada have been especially promising Ⓑ destinations for economic migrants. ⓬ Cultural factor can be especially a compelling push factor (that forces people to move / out of their present location).

문맥상 밑줄 친 Ⓑ에 들어갈 가장 적절한 것을 고르시오.

① stopovers 단기 체류
② storages 보관
✓ ③ destinations 목적지
④ refuge 피난
⑤ starting points 출발점

해석 ❶ 사람들은 왜 수천 킬로미터의 바다를 가로질러 위험한 여행을 할까? ❷ 개척자들은 왜 대평원, 로키 산맥, 또는 모하비 사막을 건너 미국 서부에 도달했을까? ❸ 사람들은 왜 오늘날 수백만 명씩 계속해서 이주하고 있을까? ❹ 많은 이주자들이 직면한 위험은 새로운 장소의 유혹이 얼마나 강한지와 옛 고향에서의 상태가 얼마나 절망적이었나를 나타내는 척도이다. ❺ 새로운 지역으로의 영구적인 이동은 한 지역의 전통적인 문화적 유대와 경제적 패턴을 파괴한다. ❻ 동시에, 사람들은 이주할 때 언어, 종교, 민족성, 그리고 다른 문화적 특징들을 가지고 그들의 새로운 고향으로 간다. ❼ 대부분 사람들은 경제적인 이유로 이주한다. ❽ 사람들은 취업 기회가 거의 없는 곳으로부터의 이주를 생각하고, ❾ 일자리를 구할 수 있는 것처럼 보이는 곳으로 이주한다. ❿ 경제적 구조조정 때문에, 일자리 전망은 종종 국가마다, 그리고 같은 국가 내에서도 지역에 따라 다양하다. ⓫ 미국과 캐나다는 특히 경제적 이주자들에게 유망한 Ⓑ목적지였다. ⓬ 문화적 요인은 특히 사람들이 현재 사는 곳에서 벗어나도록 하는 강력한 압박 요인이 될 수 있다.

해설 이주의 이유는 경제적인 이유라고 말하며 캐나다와 미국이 유망한 '목적지(destinations)'라고 말하는 것이 가장 적절하다.

어휘 adventurous a. 모험적인, 모험을 즐기는, 위험한 pioneer n. 개척자, 선구자 migrate v. 이주하다, 이동하다 hazard n. 위험 migrant n. 이주자 lure n. 유혹, 매력 desperate a. 자포자기의; 필사적인; 절망적인 permanent a. 영구적인, 영속적인 disrupt v. 방해하다, 혼란시키다, 붕괴시키다 ethnicity n. 민족성 emigrate v. 이민을 가다, (다른 나라로) 이주하다 immigrate v. (다른 나라로) 이주해[이민을] 오다 restructure v. 구조를 조정하다, 개혁하다 prospect n. 가망, 전망 promising a. 유망한, 촉망되는, 조짐이 좋은 destination n. 목적지, 도착지 compelling a. 강제적인, 강력한 stopover n. 머묾, 단기 체류 refuge n. 피난, 피난처, 도피처

012 ③
2019학년도 경기대학교 인문·예체능계 A형 35번

글의 주제

❶ Most of the electricity in the United States is produced / in steam turbines. ❷ There are many discrete steps / in this process. ❸ In a steam turbine, combustion of coal, petroleum, or natural gas heats water / to make steam. ❹ The steam rotates a shaft [that is connected to a generator (that produces electricity)]. ❺ Finally, / that electricity is converted / by a transformer / and conveyed / from the turbine to its place of use. ❻ Many sources can provide energy / to heat the water in a steam turbine. ❼ Coal is a Ⓐ primary source, producing 51 percent of the country's electricity. ❽ Another common way (to heat water for steam turbines) is through nuclear power. ❾ In nuclear fission, / atoms of uranium fuel are hit by neutrons, triggering a continuous chain of fission (that releases heat). ❿ In 2001, / nuclear power generated 21 percent of the electricity / in the United States. ⓫ Solar power meets less than 1 percent of the United States' electricity needs, because it is not regularly available and harnessing it is more expensive / than using fossil fuels. ⓬ Dependence on electricity permeates daily life / in the United States. ⓭ Still, few people are aware of the many components of electricity production.

Which of the following is most appropriate for blank Ⓐ?
빈칸 Ⓐ에 들어갈 가장 적절한 것은?

① cost-effective
비용 효율이 높은
✓③ primary
주요한, 주된, 제1의
② demanding
힘든, 벅찬
④ manageable
다루기 쉬운

해석

❶ 미국의 대부분 전기는 증기 터빈에서 생산된다. ❷ 이 과정에는 많은 개별적인 단계가 있다. ❸ 증기 터빈에서 석탄, 석유, 또는 천연가스의 연소가 물을 가열하여 증기를 만든다. ❹ 증기는 전기를 생산하는 발전기에 연결된 축을 회전시킨다. ❺ 마지막으로, 그 전기는 변압기에 의해 변환되어 터빈으로부터 사용 장소로 전달된다. ❻ 증기 터빈 속의 물을 가열하는 데 쓰이는 에너지원은 여러 가지다. ❼ 석탄은 미국 전체 전기의 51%를 생산하는 가장 Ⓐ주된 에너지원이다. ❽ 증기 터빈의 물을 가열하는 또 다른 일반적인 방법은 원자력을 이용하는 것이다. ❾ 핵분열에서는 우라늄 연료의 원자를 중성자에 부딪히게 하여 연속적인 분열이 일어나게 하는데, 이 과정에서 열이 발생한다. ❿ 2001년에, 원자력은 미국에서 21%의 전기를 생산했다. ⓫ 태양열 에너지는 정기적으로 사용할 수 없고 그것을 이용하는 것은 화석연료를 사용하는 것보다 비용이 더 많이 들기 때문에 미국 전기 수요의 1% 미만을 충족시킨다. ⓬ 미국에서 전기에 대한 의존은 일상생활에 널리 스며들어 있다. ⓭ 그럼에도 불구하고, 전기를 생산하는 많은 요소들에 대해 아는 것이 거의 없다.

해설

미국 대부분 전기는 증기 터빈에서 생산이 되며, 증기 터빈의 작동원리에 이어 작동 에너지원을 설명하고 있다. 에너지원으로 석탄이 51%를 생산하고 있기에 '주된(primary)' 에너지원이라고 말하는 것이 가장 적절하다.

어휘

steam turbine n. 증기 터빈 discrete a. 별개의, 분리된 combustion n. 연소 petroleum n. 석유 rotate v. 회전시키다, 순환시키다 shaft n. 샤프트, 굴대, 축(軸) generator n. 발전기 convert v. 전환하다, 바꾸다, 변환하다 transformer n. 변압기 convey v. 나르다, 운반하다; (소리·열·전류 따위를) 전하다 coal n. 석탄 nuclear fission 핵분열 atom n. 원자 uranium n. 우라늄 neutron n. 중성자 trigger v. (일련의 사건이나 반응 등을) 일으키다, 유발하다 release v. 풀어놓다, 떼어놓다; 방출하다; 해방하다 generate v. 산출하다, (전기·열 등을) 발생시키다 regularly ad. 정기적으로, 일정하게 available a. 이용할 수 있는; 입수할 수 있는 harness v. (자연력을) 동력화하다, 이용하다 expensive a. 값비싼 fossil fuel 화석연료 permeate v. 스며들다, 침투하다; 충만하다, 퍼지다 component n. 성분, 구성요소

정답 및 해설

013 ⑤ 2019학년도 광운대학교 인문계 A형 36번
글의 주제

① Ramadan is the ninth month of the Islamic calendar, and is observed by Muslims worldwide / as a month of fasting Ⓐ to commemorate the first revelation of the Quran to Muhammad / according to Islamic belief. ② This annual observance is regarded as one of the Five Pillars of Islam. ③ The month lasts 29-30 days / based on the visual sightings of the crescent moon, / according to numerous biographical accounts (compiled in the hadiths). ④ The word (Ramadan), means scorching heat or dryness. ⑤ Fasting is obligatory for adult Muslims, / except those (who are suffering from an illness, travelling, elderly, pregnant, breastfeeding, diabetic, chronically ill or menstruating). ⑥ Muslims (who live in regions / with a natural phenomenon / such as the midnight sun or polar night) should follow the timetable of Mecca, ⑦ but the more commonly accepted opinion is / that Muslims (in those areas) should follow the timetable of the closest country to them (in which night can be distinguished from day). ⑧ While fasting from dawn until sunset, / Muslims refrain from consuming food, drinking liquids, smoking, and engaging in sexual relations. ⑨ Muslims are also instructed Ⓑ to refrain from sinful behavior (that may negate the reward of fasting, / such as false speech (insulting, cursing, lying, etc.) and fighting / except in self-defense).

빈칸 Ⓐ와 Ⓑ에 들어가기에 가장 적절한 표현의 쌍은?

	Ⓐ		Ⓑ
①	to observe 지키다	…	to reflect on 반성하다
②	to overlook 간과하다	…	to leave off (습관 등을) 그만두다
③	to celebrate 기념하다	…	to stand for 나타나다
④	to disregard 무시하다	…	to get around 해결하다
✓⑤	to commemorate 기념하다	…	to refrain from 삼가다

해석
① 라마단은 이슬람 달력의 아홉 번째 달이며, 마호메트가 (신으로부터) 코란을 처음으로 계시받은 것을 Ⓐ 기념하기 위해 단식하는 달로, 전 세계 이슬람교도들이 이슬람 신앙에 따라 지키고 있다. ② 이 연례 의식은 '이슬람의 다섯 가지 기둥' 중 하나로 여겨진다. ③ 하디스(마호메트 언행록)에 편찬된 수많은 전기적(傳奇的) 이야기들에 따르면, 라마단이 있는 달은 육안으로 본 초승달에 근거해 29일 내지 30일 동안 지속된다. ④ 라마단이라는 단어는 타는 듯한 무더위나 메마름을 의미한다. ⑤ (라마단 기간 동안의) 단식은 성인 이슬람교도들에게 의무적이지만, 질병을 앓고 있거나, 여행 중이거나, 연세가 많거나, 임신, 모유 수유, 당뇨병, 만성 질병, 생리 중인 사람들은 예외이다. ⑥ 백야(白夜)나 극야(極夜) 같은 자연 현상이 나타나는 지역에 사는 이슬람교도들은 메카(Mecca)의 시간을 따라야 하지만, ⑦ 더 일반적으로 알려진 지침은 해당 지역(백야나 극야가 나타나는 지역)에 사는 이슬람교도들은 자신이 거주하는 곳과 가장 가까운, 낮과 밤이 구별되는 국가의 시간을 따를 것을 권장한다. ⑧ 새벽부터 일몰까지 단식하는 동안, 이슬람교도들은 음식 및 음료 섭취, 흡연, 그리고 성관계를 삼가야 한다. ⑨ 이슬람교도들은 모욕적인 말, 저주, 거짓말 등 정당방위를 제외한 옳지 않은 말과 싸움같이 단식에 대한 보상을 무효화 할 수도 있는 나쁜 행동들도 Ⓑ 삼가야 한다.

해설
마호메트가 신으로부터 코란을 받은 것을 Ⓐ '기념하기 위해(to commemorate)'라고 말하는 것이 신앙을 지키기 위한 단식을 설명하는 글에서 가장 적절하다. 'also(또한)'는 같은 기조의 내용을 끌어낸다. 따라서 라마단 기간 중 삼가야 하는 또 다른 내용이 나오는 만큼 Ⓑ '삼가다(to refrain from)'가 가장 적절하다.

어휘
observe v. (법률·규칙 등을) 지키다, 준수하다; (의식 등을) 거행하다 Muslim n. 이슬람교도 fasting n. 단식, 절식 revelation n. (신의) 계시 Quran n. 코란, 이슬람교의 경전 pillar n. 기둥; 지주(支柱) last v. 지속하다 crescent moon 초승달 biographical a. 전기의; 전기체의 account n. 설명, 이야기 compile v. 편집하다, 편찬하다 hadith n. 하디스(마호메트의 언행록) scorching heat 찌는 듯한 무더위, 폭염 obligatory a. 의무적인 pregnant a. 임신한 breastfeeding n. 모유수유 diabetic a. 당뇨병의, 당뇨병 환자의 chronically ad. 만성적으로 menstruate v. 생리하다 phenomenon n. 현상 midnight sun (극지에서 한여름에 볼 수 있는) 백야(白夜) polar night 극야(極夜) timetable n. 시간표, 일정표 refrain v. 자제하다, 삼가다 engage in ~에 관여[참여]하다 be instructed to do ~하도록 지시 받다 negate v. 효력이 없게 만들다, 무효화하다 insulting n. 모욕적인 언동 cursing n. 저주 self-defense n. 자기방어, 정당방위 commemorate v. (중요 인물, 사건을) 기념하다

014 A) ④ B) ② · · · · 2019학년도 가천대학교 인문계 1교시 C형 38,39번

❶ Recently / it has been claimed [that / the struggle (against childhood dependency / and for becoming oneself in fairy tales) is frequently described differently / for the girl than for the boy], and [that this is the result of sexual Ⓐ stereotyping.] ❷ Fairy tales do not render such one-sided pictures. ❸ Even when a girl is depicted as turning inward / in her struggle to become herself, / ❹ and a boy; as aggressively dealing with the external world, / these two together symbolize the two ways (in which one has to gain selfhood): through learning to understand and master the inner as well as the outer world. ❺ In this sense / the male and female heroes are again projections / onto two different figures of two (artificially) separated aspects of one and the same process (which everybody has to undergo in growing up). ❻ While some literal-minded parents do not realize it, / children know / that, (whatever the sex of the hero), the story Ⓑ pertains to their own problems.
❼ In "The Sleeping Beauty," / the harmonious meeting of prince and princess, their awakening to each other, is a symbol of what maturity implies: not just harmony within oneself, but also: with the other. ❽ It depends on the listener / whether the arrival of the prince at the right time is interpreted as the event (which causes sexual awakening or the birth of a higher ego): ❾ the child probably comprehends both these meanings.

A) Which of the following is most appropriate for the blank Ⓐ?
다음 중 빈칸 Ⓐ에 들어가기에 가장 적절한 것은?
① initiation 개시
② orientation 지향
③ reproduction 번식
✓ stereotyping 고정관념화

B) Which of the following is most appropriate for the blank Ⓑ?
다음 중 빈칸 Ⓑ에 들어가기에 가장 적절한 것은?
① contradicts 모순되다
✓ pertains to 관련 있다
③ subverts 뒤엎다
④ competes with 경쟁하다

해석

❶ 최근 어린 시절의 의존성을 버리고 자기 정체성을 찾으려는 노력은 동화에서 자주 남녀 아동 간에 다르게 묘사되며, 이것은 성적(性的) Ⓐ고정관념화의 결과라고 주장되고 있다. ❷ 동화는 그렇게 일방적인 모습을 그려 내지 않는다. ❸ 소녀는 자기 정체성을 찾으려고 노력하는 중에 내향적으로 변하는 것으로 묘사되고 ❹ 소년은 외부세계에 공격적으로 대처하는 것으로 묘사될 때조차도, 이 둘은 사람이 자아를 얻는 두 가지 방법, 즉 내면세계와 외부세계를 이해하고 숙달하는 법을 배우는 것을 통해서라는 두 가지 방식을 다 같이 상징한다. ❺ 이런 의미에서 남자 영웅과 여자 영웅 또한 모든 사람이 성장하며 겪어야 하는 사실 단 하나인 과정의 (인위적으로) 분리된 두 측면이 서로 다른 두 인물에 투영된 것이다. ❻ 일부 상상력이 부족한 부모들은 깨닫지 못하지만, 아이들은 주인공의 성별이 무엇이든지, 그 이야기가 자신의 문제와 Ⓑ연관이 있다는 것을 알고 있다.
❼ 『잠자는 숲속의 미녀(The Sleeping Beauty)』에서 왕자와 공주의 조화로운 만남, 서로를 향해 깨어나는(서로를 자각하는) 것은 성숙이 무엇을 의미하는지, 즉 성숙은 자기 내면의 조화뿐만 아니라 타인과의 조화도 의미한다는 것을 상징한다. ❽ 왕자가 적절한 시기에 도착한 것이 성적 자각을 일으키는 사건으로 해석되는지, 더 높은 자아의 탄생을 초래하는 사건으로 해석되는지는 듣는 사람에게 달려있지만, ❾ 아이는 아마도 이 두 가지 의미를 모두 이해할 것이다.

해설

A) 빈칸 앞 문장에서 '자주 남녀 아동 간에 다르게 묘사되며'라고 말하고 있다. 이 부분을 빈칸이 시작되는 문장에서 'this'가 지칭하는 것으로서 ④ 'stereotyping(고정관념)'이라고 할 수 있다. 참고로 ② orientation은 맥락상 성적(sexual) 지향성을 말하는 것이다.

B) 소녀와 소년이라는 인물의 묘사 시에도 두 사람의 자아를 얻는 두 가지 방법을 다 같이 상징한다고 말하는 부분, 그리고 이런 것이 단 하나인 과정의 분리된 두 측면이라는 부분, 마지막에서 아이는 두 가지 의미를 모두 이해한다는 부분까지 모두 빈칸 Ⓑ의 근거가 될 수 있다. 따라서 아이는 자신의 문제와 연관이 있다는 것을 알고 있다고 말하는 것이 가장 적절하다.

어휘

become oneself 자기 자신이 되다, 자기 모습에 충실해지다, 자기정체성을 찾다 frequently ad. 자주, 흔히 render v. 만들다, 주다, 제시하다 symbolize v. 상징하다 selfhood n. 자아, 개성, 이기심 projection n. 투사, 투영 one and the same 동일한, 사실은 단일한(=in fact, one single) undergo v. 겪다 literal-minded a. 문자 그대로 생각하는, 현실적인 생각을 가진 harmonious a. 조화로운, 사이좋은 maturity n. 성숙 imply v. 암시하다, 넌지시 던지다 interpret v. 해석하다, 설명하다 comprehend v. 이해하다, 깨닫다 initiation n. 시작, 개시, 가입 orientation n. 방향, 성향 reproduction n. 번식, 생식, 복제 stereotyping n. 고정관념 contradict v. 모순 pertain v. 존재하다, 관련하다 subvert v. 전복하다, 뒤엎다

정답 및 해설

015 A) ① B) ③ … 2019학년도 국민대학교 인문계 오후 A형 36, 37번

❶ By studying instinctive and learned fear / in people and in experimental animals, / ❷ we have gained much insight / into both the behavioral and the biological mechanisms of / instinctive and learned fear in people. ❸ One of the first behavioral insights was stimulated / by the theories of Freud and the American philosopher William James, ❹ who realized / that fear has both conscious and unconscious components. ❺ What was not clear was (how the two components interact).

❻ Traditionally, / fear in people was thought to begin with conscious perception of an important event, / such as seeing one's house on fire. ❼ This recognition produces / in the cerebral cortex / an emotional experience, / ❽ — fear — (that triggers signals to the heart, blood vessels, adrenal glands, and sweat glands / to mobilize the body / in preparation for defense or escape). ❾ Thus, according to this view, / a conscious, emotional event initiates the later Ⓐ_____ defensive responses in the body.

❿ James rejected this view. ⓫ In a highly influential article (published in 1884 and entitled "What is Emotion?") / he proposed that the cognitive experience of emotion is secondary / to the physiological expression of emotion. ⓬ He suggested / that when we encounter a potentially dangerous situation — for example, a bear (sitting in the middle of our path) — our evaluation of the bear's ferocity does not generate a consciously experienced emotional state. ⓭ We do not experience fear / Ⓑ_____ we have run away from the bear.

A) Which does NOT fit in the blank Ⓐ?
빈칸 Ⓐ에 적절하지 않은 것은?
✓① cognitive 의식적인
② reflexive 반사적인
③ biological 생물학적인
④ physiological 생리학적인

B) Which does NOT fit in the blank Ⓑ?
빈칸 Ⓑ에 적절하지 않은 것은?
① because 왜냐하면
② so that ~하기 위해서
✓③ until after 후까지
④ irrespective of ~와 관계없이 (= regardless of)

해석

❶ 사람과 실험용 동물의 본능적 두려움 및 학습된 두려움을 연구함으로써, ❷ 우리는 사람에게서 일어나는 본능적 두려움 및 학습된 공포의 행동 기제 및 생물학적 기제에 대한 많은 통찰을 얻었다. ❸ 행동에 관련된 첫 번째 통찰들 가운데 하나는 지그문트 프로이트(Sigmund Freud)와 미국의 철학자 윌리엄 제임스(William James)가 만들어낸 이론들에 자극받은 것이었는데, ❹ 이 두 사람은 두려움이 의식적인 구성요소와 무의식적인 구성요소를 둘 다 갖고 있다고 이해했다. ❺ (그러나) 명확하지 않은 점은 두 요소가 어떻게 상호작용하는가였다.

❻ 전통적으로, 사람들이 가지는 두려움은 자신의 집이 불에 타는 것을 보는 것처럼 중요한 사건에 대한 의식적인 인지에서 시작된다고 여겨졌다. ❼ 이러한 인지는 대뇌피질에서 감정적인 경험을 만들어내는데, ❽ 이 경험이 바로 두려움으로, 심장, 혈관, 부신, 그리고 땀샘에 신호를 보내 신체가 방어하거나 도망갈 대비를 하게 해준다. ❾ 따라서 이 견해에 따르면, 의식적이고 감정적인 사건은 나중에 신체에 반사적, 생물학적, 그리고 Ⓐ생리학적 방어반응을 일으킨다.

❿ 윌리엄 제임스는 이런 견해를 받아들이지 않았다. ⓫ 1884년에 발간된 매우 영향력 있는 『감정이란 무엇인가?(What is Emotion?)』라는 제목의 기사에서, 그는 감정의 인지경험이 감정의 생리적인 표현의 부차적인 것이라고 주장했다. ⓬ 그는 예를 들어 우리가 가는 길 한복판에 곰이 앉아 있는 것과 같이 잠재적으로 위험한 상황에 직면할 때, 곰의 흉포함에 대한 우리의 평가가 의식적으로 경험된 감정 상태를 만들어내지는 않는다고 주장했다. ⓭ Ⓑ즉, 우리는 곰으로부터 도망치고 나서야 두려움을 경험하게 된다는 것이다.

해설

A) 빈칸 앞에서는 의식적 인지가 두려움과 같은 감정적 경험을 만들어 내며, 신체가 방어하거나 도망갈 대비를 하게 해준다고 말한 만큼, 신체 반응에 관한 말이 오는 것이 적절하다. 따라서 '반사적인(reflexive)', '생물학적인(biological)', '생리학적인(physiological)'의 표현은 적절하나, ① 'cognitive(인식적인)'은 오히려 의식적인 뜻으로 적절하지 못하다.

B) 제임스는 의식적 감정 즉 공포를 느끼는 것은 부차적인 것으로 생리적 표현 이후에 일어난다는 것을 주장한다. 따라서 예시로 든 '곰과 마주쳤을 때는 도망치고 나서야 공포를 느낀다'고 말해야 옳다. 그러므로 ③ 'until after(이후까지)'는 '곰으로부터 도망친 이후까지 두려움을 경험하지 못한다'는 말이 되므로 정답이 된다.

어휘

instinctive a. 본능적인, 직감적인 **insight** n. 통찰력, 식견, 안식 **stimulate** v. 자극하다, 촉진시키다 **conscious** a. 의식하는, 지각하는 **component** n. 구성요소 **perception** n. 지각, 자각, 통찰력 **recognition** n. 인식, 알아봄 **cerebral cortex** 대뇌 피질 **trigger** v. 촉발하다, 일으키다 **adrenal gland** 부신 **sweat gland** 땀샘, 한선(汗腺) **mobilize** v. 동원하다, 결집시키다 **preparation** n. 준비, 대비, 조제품(약제) **influential** a. 영향력 있는 **entitled** a. 제목[표제]이 ~인 **cognitive** a. 지각하고 있는, 인식하고 있는 **secondary** a. 부차적인, 종속적인 **potentially** ad. 잠재적으로 **ferocity** n. 잔인, 흉포함 **reflexive** a. 재귀의, 반사성의, 반응하는

016 ① 2019학년도 단국대학교 자연계 A형 25번

❶ The scientific consensus (on global warming) comes from the Intergovernmental Panel on Climate Change (IPCC). ❷ It was established in 1988 by the World Meteorological Organization and the United Nations Environment Program to assess the science of climate change, determine its impacts on the environment and society, and formulate strategies (to respond). ❸ More than 900 scientists from 40 countries have participated as authors or expert reviewers in the IPCC's latest report, published in 1995.

❹ "It's a look at the state of the art — what we know about the climate system," says Gerald Meehl of the National Center for Atmospheric Research, (a lead author for one of the report's chapters). ❺ "Literally thousands of people wind up reading these things...." ❻ It's the consensus view of just about everyone (who's chosen to become involved.") ❼ In June, some 2,400 scientists signed a letter (saying they endorsed the findings).

❽ The basics of global warming are simple. ❾ So-called greenhouse gases — (including carbon dioxide and methane) — build up in the atmosphere. ❿ Carbon dioxide is the most important of the greenhouse gases (generated by human activity). ⓫ The gases trap the sun's heat, like a car (parked in the sun with the windows closed). ⓬ Couple that with a basic fact: The amount of carbon dioxide in the atmosphere has risen by 30% since pre-industrial times (about 1750). ⓭ The implication is that temperatures are rising, and that's what the IPCC was charged with studying.

Which is the most appropriate for the blank?
다음 중 빈칸에 가장 적절한 것은 무엇인가?

✓ ① endorsed 승인하다
② disputed 논쟁하다
③ rebuked 견책하다
④ denounced 비난하다

해석

❶ 지구 온난화에 대한 과학적인 합의는 기후 변화에 관한 정부간 패널(IPCC)에서 나온다. ❷ 이것은 1988년에 기후 변화의 과학을 평가하고, 기후 변화가 환경과 사회에 미치는 영향을 판단하고, 이에 대한 대응 전략을 수립하기 위해 세계기상기구와 UN 환경프로그램에 의해 설립되었다. ❸ 40개국에서 온 900명이 넘는 과학자들이 1995년에 출판된 IPCC의 최근 보고서에 저자 혹은 전문 검토자로 참여했다.

❹ "그것은 기술적 수준, 즉 기후에 대해 우리가 알고 있는 것을 살펴보는 것입니다"라고 그 보고서의 한 챕터를 담당한 주요 저자인 미국국립기상연구소(NCAR)의 제럴드 밀(Gerald Meehl)은 말한다. ❺ "말 그대로 수천 명의 사람들이 이것을 읽게 되었는데, ❻ 그것은 이 연구에 참여하기로 선택된 정말로 모든 사람들의 일치된 견해입니다." ❼ 6월에 약 2,400명의 과학자들이 그들이 연구 결과들을 승인한다는 내용의 문서에 서명했다.

❽ 지구 온난화의 기본은 간단하다. ❾ 이산화탄소와 메탄을 포함한 소위 온실가스라고 불리는 것이 대기에 축적되는 것이다. ❿ 이산화탄소는 인간의 활동으로 발생되는 온실가스 중 가장 중요하다. ⓫ 온실가스는 창문이 닫힌 채 햇빛 아래에 주차된 자동차처럼 태양의 열기를 가두어 놓는다. ⓬ 그것을 대기의 이산화탄소의 양이 산업혁명 이전 시기(약 1750년) 이후로 30% 증가했다는 기본적인 사실과 결부시켜 보면, ⓭ 그 의미는 기온이 상승하고 있다는 것이고, IPCC는 그것의 연구를 담당하게 된 것이다.

해설

빈칸 다음에는 the findings는 IPCC에서 수행한 연구 결과를 말하고 있으며, 빈칸 앞 문장에서 모든 사람의 일치된 견해라고 말하고 있다. 따라서 ① 'endorsed(승인하다)'가 가장 적절하다.

어휘

consensus n. 의견 일치, 합의 come from ~에서 나오다 meteorological a. 기상의, 기상학상의 assess v. 평가[사정]하다 formulate v. 공식화하다, 만들어 내다 participate v. 참여하다 wind up (연설·모임 등을) 마무리 짓다 carbon dioxide 이산화탄소 build up 늘다, 축적되다 trap v. 가두다 pre-industrial a. 산업화 이전의 implication n. 영향, 결과, 함축 endorse v. 지지하다, 보증하다, 승인하다 rebuke v. 질책하다, 꾸짖다

017 A) ② B) ②

······ 2019학년도 광운대학교 인문계 A형 38,39번

[글의 주제] (부분부정) 모두가 ~인 것은 아니다

❶ Not everyone consumes news. ❷ The time has come / to better understand the segment of people (who are not the news audience / but who are the news un-audience). ❸ Several years ago, / I estimated / that about 20 percent of the U.S. adults were what I described as "News Avoiders." ❹ More recently, / I found : the habit of news avoidance predates adulthood, / with 50 percent of U.S. teenagers (reporting very low exposure / to any type of news).

❺ Why is studying the news un-audience important? ❻ One answer is / that news organizations need news audiences. ❼ If half of U.S. teenagers are News Avoiders, / and that doesn't change / when they reach adulthood, ❽ it's problematic / for the long-term survival of the news industry. ❾ A second answer is / that democracy needs news consumers. ❿ News avoidance is related to several negative democratic outcomes. ⓫ I found / that it was News Avoiders (who) exhibited Ⓐ the lowest level of participation / across a variety of political and community-based activities. ⓬ It was their voices, their concerns, and their help (that was largely absent). ⓭ For all the important differences in the types of news (that people do consume), / ⓮ the fact remains / that being a news consumer is related to civic and political participation. ⓯ How can we better understand the un-audience? ⓰ It requires reframing the question. ⓱ In addition to asking "Why do people consume news?" / we need to ask Ⓑ "Why don't people consume news?" ⓲ These are different questions (that yield different insights). ⓳ What drives people / toward news is not the same as (what drives them away). ⓴ Understanding the un-audience requires going beyond demographics.

[해석]

❶ 모든 사람이 뉴스를 소비하는 것은 아니다. ❷ 뉴스 수용자가 아닌 뉴스 비수용자들을 더 잘 이해할 때가 왔다. ❸ 몇 년 전에, 나는 미국 성인 중 약 20%가 내가 '뉴스 기피자'라고 부르는 사람들이라고 추정했다. ❹ 보다 최근에, 나는 뉴스를 기피하는 습관이 성인기 이전에 형성된다는 것을 발견했는데, 50%의 미국 청소년이 어떤 유형의 뉴스에도 매우 적게 노출된다고 보고했다. ❺ 뉴스 비수용자를 연구하는 것이 왜 중요할까? ❻ 한 가지 대답은 언론사가 뉴스 수용자를 필요로 한다는 것이다. ❼ 만약 미국 청소년 중 절반이 뉴스 기피자이고, 어른이 되어서도 그대로 뉴스 기피자라면, ❽ 뉴스 산업의 장기적인 생존에 있어 문제가 된다. ❾ 두 번째 대답은 민주주의라는 정치가 뉴스 소비자들을 원하기 때문이다. ❿ 뉴스 기피는 여러 가지 부정적인 민주주의 결과와 연관이 있다. ⓫ 나는 다양한 정치 활동과 지역 사회활동에 Ⓐ 가장 저조한 수준의 참여를 보여준 사람이 바로 뉴스 기피자라는 것을 발견했다. ⓬ 대부분 빠져있는 것은 그들의 의견이었고, 그들의 관심이었으며, 그들의 도움이었다. ⓭ 사람들이 소비하는 뉴스의 종류에는 중요한 차이가 있지만, ⓮ 뉴스 소비자가 되는 것이 시민참여 및 정치참여와 관련 있다는 것은 여전히 변함없는 사실이다. ⓯ 우리가 어떻게 뉴스 비수용자를 보다 잘 이해할 수 있을까? ⓰ 이것은 질문의 재구성을 요구한다. ⓱ "왜 사람들이 뉴스를 소비하는가?" 라는 질문 외에도, 우리는 Ⓑ "왜 사람들이 뉴스를 소비하지 않는가?" 라는 질문도 던질 필요가 있다. ⓲ 이런 질문들은 다양한 식견을 만들어내는 다양한 질문들이다. ⓳ 사람들이 뉴스를 보게 만드는 것이 사람들이 뉴스에서 멀어지게 만드는 것과 같지 않다. ⓴ 비수용자를 이해하는 것은 인구통계자료를 분석하는 것 이상의 노력이 필요하다.

[어휘]

segment n. 부분, 영역 news audience 뉴스 수용자 news un-audience 뉴스 비수용자 voider n. 비우는[취소하는]사람 predate v. ~에 선행하다, 앞서서 발생하다 democracy n. 민주주의 community-based a. 지역사회에 기반한 absent a. 부재한, 결석한 for all ~에도 불구하고 the fact remains that ~이라는 사실에는 여전히 변함이 없다 civic a. 도시의; 시민의 reframe v. ~을 재구성하다 yield v. 생산하다, 산출하다 insight n. 통찰력, 식견 go beyond ~을 능가하다 demographics n. 인구 통계 (자료) have little to do with ~와 거의 관련이 없다

A) 빈칸 Ⓐ에 들어가기에 가장 적절한 것은?

① the importance of news organizations
   언론사의 중요성
✓② the lowest level of participation
   가장 저조한 수준의 참여
③ the absence of concerns about global issues
   국제 문제에 대한 걱정의 부재
④ the change in audience growth
   수용자 증가의 변화
⑤ the good understanding of current issues
   시사 문제에 대한 풍부한 이해

B) 빈칸 Ⓑ에 들어가기에 가장 적절한 것은?

① What drives people toward news?
   사람들이 뉴스를 보게 만드는 것은 무엇인가?
✓② Why don't people consume news?
   왜 사람들이 뉴스를 소비하지 않는가?
③ Why are teenagers different from adults?
   왜 청소년들은 어른들과 다른가?
④ What do people have to learn to reframe questions?
   질문을 재구성하기 위해 사람들이 배워야 하는 것은 무엇인가?
⑤ Why is demographics important to understand the news un-audience?
   뉴스 비수용자를 이해하기 위해 왜 인구통계자료가 중요한가?

해설

A) 빈칸 다음 문장에서 '대부분 빠져있는 것은 그들의 이었고~'에서 Ⓐ '참여의 가장 저조한 수준'을 추론할 수 있다.

B) 두 번째 빈칸 앞 문장에서 '질문의 재구성을 요구한다'라는 표현 이후 이어지는 또 다른 질문에서 Ⓑ를 추론할 수 있다.

정답 및 해설

018 ①   2019학년도 국민대학교 인문계 오전 A형 19번

❶ ⓐ Shedding kilos is harder than putting on, which is: (why the weight-loss industry is so big). ❷ Its latest manifestation is online weight-management sites: ❸ social networks for the plump (in which participants can set a target weight and monitor their progress towards it).

❹ As with other social networks, they can also get their help from friends — either real-life ones (who sign up to the same site), or else digital ones (whom they have befriended on the internet). ❺ Those friendships are likely to be important. ❻ Other studies of weight-loss programs have suggested that having the support or chivying of friends helps people stick to their diets and exercise regimes.

❼ Those studies, however, have all been done with groups of people (who knew each other in the real world). ❽ A team of researchers (led by Julia Poncela-Casanovas of Northwestern University, in Illinois), decided to check if the same was true of groups in cyberspace. ❾ Their results suggest that it is.

❿ But she and her colleagues are quick to point out that a study (like this) can establish only that two things — in this case, friends and weight-loss — are correlated. ⓫ It cannot show which causes which. Working this out requires controlled experiments.

⓬ Their results are, nonetheless, encouraging. ⓭ Weight-management websites have the potential to reach many more people / much more cheaply / than real-world support groups (do). ⓮ Moreover, if it turns out that friendship networks are a magic wand for weight loss, ⓯ then it may be easier to nudge people into such networks electronically than if they actually had to meet each other in a sweaty gym. ⓰ Given the medical consequences of rising levels of obesity, that would be well worth doing.

Which best fits in the blank Ⓐ?
다음 중 빈칸 Ⓐ에 들어가기에 가장 적절한 것은?

✓① Shedding
  없애다, 버리다
② Controlling
  통제하다, 관리하다
③ Increasing
  늘리다
④ Calculating
  계산하다

해석

❶ 몸무게를 Ⓐ줄이는 것은 늘리는 것보다 어려우며, 체중감량 관련 산업이 크게 성장한 것도 이런 이유 때문이다. ❷ 최근 들어 그것은 온라인 체중 관리 사이트로 모습을 드러냈는데, ❸ 이것은 살찐 사람들을 위한 소셜 네트워크로, 이 안에서 참여자들은 자신의 감량 목표를 설정하고 그 진행 상황을 관찰할 수 있다.

❹ 다른 소셜 네트워크와 마찬가지로, 이들은 친구 - 동일한 사이트에 가입하는 실제 친구, 또는 그렇지 않은 경우에는 인터넷상에서 사귄 온라인 친구 - 로부터도 도움을 받을 수 있다. ❺ 그런 우정은 중요할 것 같다. ❻ 체중감량 프로그램에 대한 다른 연구들에서는 친구들이 응원하거나 (살을 빼라고) 쫓아다니면서 귀찮게 하는 것이 식이요법과 운동요법을 지속하게 하는 데 도움이 된다고 주장했다.

❼ 하지만 그 연구들은 모두 현실 세계에서 서로 알고 있던 사람들을 대상으로 이루어졌다. ❽ 일리노이 주 노스웨스턴 대학의 줄리아 폰셀라-카사노바스(Julia Poncella-Casanovas)가 이끄는 연구팀은 사이버 공간 속의 사람들의 경우도 그러한지를 확인해보기로 했다. ❾ 그들의 연구 결과는 그 경우도 마찬가지라는 것을 보여준다.

❿ 하지만 그녀와 그녀의 동료들은 이와 같은 연구가 입증하는 것은 두 가지 - 이 경우에는 친구와 체중감량 - 가 서로 관련돼 있다는 사실뿐이라고 곧바로 지적한다. ⓫ 그런 연구는 둘 중 어떤 것이 원인인지를 보여주지 못하며, 이 문제를 해결하려면 대조군을 이용한 실험이 필요하다.

⓬ 그럼에도 불구하고, 그들의 연구 결과는 고무적이다. ⓭ 체중 관리 웹사이트는 현실 세계의 지원 그룹(공통의 고민을 가진 사람들이 모여 서로 정신적으로 지원하는 그룹)보다 훨씬 저렴하게 더 많은 사람에게 다가갈 수 있는 잠재력을 가지고 있다. ⓮ 더욱이, 만약 네트워크로 연결된 친구들이 체중감량을 위한 마법의 지팡이라는 것이 밝혀진다면, ⓯ 땀에 젖은 체육관에서 서로가 실제로 만나야 하는 것보다 온라인을 통해 사람들을 그러한 네트워크로 밀어 넣는 것이 더 쉬울지도 모른다. ⓰ 비만 수준의 증가로 인한 의학적 결과를 고려할 때, 그것은 충분히 할 가치가 있을 것이다.

해설

첫 번째 문장에서 이어지는 관계사의 계속적 용법인 which 이하에서 체중감량 관련 산업 성장을 말하고 있는 만큼 빈칸 정답 ① 'Shedding(버리다, 없애다)'를 통해 주어를 '살을 빼는 것'으로 추론할 수 있다.

어휘

manifestation n. 징후, 조짐, 명시 **plump** a. 살찐, 포동포동한, 통통한 **participant** n. 참여자, 관계자 **monitor** v. 감시하다, 관찰하다 **real-life** a. 현실의, 실재하는 **befriend** v. ~의 친구가 되다, 사귀다, 편들다 **regime** n. 제도, 체제, 정권 **correlate** v. 서로 관련시키다 **potential** n. 잠재력, 가능성 **wand** n. 막대기, (마술사의) 지팡이 **nudge** v. (~을 특정 방향으로) 조금씩 밀다[몰고 가다] **sweaty** a. 땀에 젖은; 땀을 빼게 만드는, 힘이 드는 **given** prep. ~라고 가정하면 **consequence** n. 결과; 중요성 **obesity** n. 비만 **shed** v. 없애다, 흘리다, (옷을)벗다

019 ② 2019학년도 단국대학교 자연계 A형 26번

글의 주제

❶ Ethics may be profoundly affected by / an adoption (of the scientific point of view); that is to say, / the attitude (that men of science, in their professional capacity, adopt / towards the world). ❷ This attitude includes a high (perhaps an unduly high) regard for the truth, ❸ and a refusal / to come to unjustifiable conclusions (which expresses itself / on the plane of religion / as agnosticism. ❹ [And along with this is found a deliberate suppression of emotion / until the last possible moment, / on the ground that emotion is stumbling-block / on the road to truth. ❺ So / a rose and a tape-worm must be studied / by the same methods / and viewed from the same angle, / even if the work is ultimately to lead to the killing of the tape-worms and the propagations of roses. ❻ Again, / the scientific point of view involves the cultivation of a scientific esthetic [which rejoices in / the peculiar forms of beauty (which characterize scientific esthetic theory)]. ❼ Those (who find an intimate relation between the good and the beautiful) will realize the importance of the fact (that a group of men so influential as scientific workers are pursuing a particular kind of beauty). ❽ Finally, since the scientist, (as such), is contributing to an intellectual structure (that belongs to humanity as a whole), his influence will inevitably fall in favour of ethical principles and practices (which transcend the limits of nation, colour, and class).

Which is the most appropriate for the blank?
다음 중 빈칸에 가장 적절한 것은 무엇인가?
① Instead 대신에
☑ Finally 결국
③ Nevertheless 그럼에도 불구하고
④ Intriguingly 흥미를 자아내어

해석 ❶ 윤리는 과학적인 관점, 즉 과학자들이 그들의 전문능력으로 세계를 향해 택하는 태도에 상당히 큰 영향을 받을지도 모른다. ❷ 이 태도에는 진리를 높이 (아마도 지나치게 높이) 존중하는 것과 정당성을 입증할 수 없는 결론에 이르기를 거부하는 것이 포함되는데, ❸ 이러한 거부는 종교의 관점에서는 불가지론으로 표현된다. ❹ 그리고 이와 함께 발견되는 것은 감정은 진리를 향한 길에 걸림돌이 된다는 이유로 가능한 마지막 순간까지 감정을 의도적으로 억압하는 것이다. ❺ 따라서 그 연구가 궁극적으로 촌충을 죽이고 장미를 번식시키는 결과로 이어진다 해도, 장미와 촌충은 같은 방법으로 연구되어야 하며 같은 각도에서 보아야 한다. ❻ 그 밖에도 과학적인 관점은 과학의 미학적 이론들을 특징짓는 특별한 형태의 아름다움을 즐기는 과학적 미학을 함양하는 것과 관련되어 있다. ❼ 선한 것과 아름다운 것 사이에서 친밀한 관계를 찾는 사람들은 과학자들만큼 영향력 있는 한 집단의 사람들이 특별한 종류의 아름다움을 추구하고 있다는 사실의 중요성을 깨닫게 될 것이다. ❽ 결국, 이처럼 과학자가 인류의 지적 구조에 기여하고 있으므로, 전체적으로 과학자의 영향력은 필연적으로 국가, 인종, 계급의 한계를 뛰어넘는 윤리 원칙과 관행을 위한 것이 될 것이다.

해설 두괄식 구조로서 과학자들의 관점과 능력의 영향과 역할이라는 주제로 글의 말미에는 결론을 끌어내고 있다. 따라서 ② 'Finally(결국)'의 가장 적절하다.

어휘 ethics n. 도덕 원리, 윤리 profoundly ad. 깊이, 완전히 adoption n. 채용, 채택 unduly ad. 지나치게, 과도하게 regard n. 고려, 존경, 존중 unjustifiable a. 정당화할 수 없는, 정당성 없는 plane n. 수준, 레벨, 정도; 면 agnosticism n. 불가지론 emancipation n. 해방, 이탈, 벗어남 on the ground that ~라는 근거로 stumbling block 방해물, 장애물, 고민거리 tape-worm n. 촌충 propagation n. 증식, 번식, 확대 cultivation n. 경작, 재배, 구축 rejoice v. 크게 기뻐하다 esthetic a. 미학의; 심미적인 peculiar a. 이상한, 특이한, 고유한 intimate a. 친밀한, 친한 inevitably ad. 필연적으로, 당연하게 in favour of ~에 찬성[지지]하여, ~을 위하여 transcend v. 초월하다

020 ①   2019학년도 한성대학교 인문계 A형 08번

❶ Egypt has recovered a stolen ancient artifact (that was listed for sale / at a London auction house, / the country's Ministry of Antiquities has confirmed). ❷ The section of tablet (— engraved with the cartouche, or royal symbol, of King Amenhotep I —) was stolen / from the Karnak Open Air Museum in Luxor, Egypt, in 1988. ❸ It was smuggled out of the country, / and ultimately put up for auction in London.

❹ Raed Khoury (director of repatriation at the Ministry of Antiquities), said / that the organization worked / to track down the stolen relief. ❺ They monitored the websites of international auction houses / before eventually finding the artifact for sale / in the UK. ❻ The ancient tablet was subsequently removed from sale / and delivered to the London embassy. ❼ The ministry officially announced its return to Egypt / on January 4.

❽ The tablet's recovery comes / as a dispute brews / around another ancient Egyptian artifact: / a casing stone / from the Great Pyramid of Giza. ❾ This block of limestone will go on display / at the National Museum of Scotland in Edinburgh / from February. ❿ However, Egypt's Ministry of Antiquities has contested the legitimacy of the stone's Ⓐ export, asking the museum to produce documents of ownership. ⓫ The museum says / the stone was extracted from Giza / in the 19th century / by engineer Waynman Dixon and given to Scotland's Astronomer Royal, Charles Smyth, who kept it in his Edinburgh home. ⓬ If it transpires that / the stone was Ⓒ illegally removed from Egypt, Khoury said, / the ministry will take "all the necessary steps" / to bring it back.

Choose the best word for Ⓐ and Ⓒ?
Ⓐ와 Ⓒ에 들어갈 가장 적절한 낱말은?

	Ⓐ		Ⓒ
✓ ①	export	…	illegally
②	imposter	…	illegally
③	export	…	lawfully
④	imposter	…	lawfully

해석

❶ 이집트는 런던의 한 경매장에서 경매 목록에 올라가 있던 도난당한 고대 유물 한 점을 되찾았다고 이집트 문화재 관리부가 밝혔다. ❷ 아멘호테프 1세(King Amenhotep Ⅰ)의 카르투슈, 즉 왕실의 상징이 새겨진 명판(名板) 조각이 1988년에 이집트 룩소르에 있는 카르나크 신전(야외 박물관)에서 도난을 당했다. ❸ 그 유물은 국외로 밀반출되었고, 결국 런던에서 경매에 부쳐졌다. ❹ 문화재 관리부의 유물 반환 담당 국장인 라에드 코우리(Raed Khoury)는 관리부가 도난당한 부조(浮彫) 작품을 찾아내기 위해 노력을 기울였다고 말했다. ❺ 그들은 국제 경매장의 웹사이트를 감시하여 결국 영국에서 경매에 나온 유물을 발견했다. ❻ 이어서 그 고대 명판은 경매 목록에서 제외되어 런던 주재 대사관에 배송되었다. ❼ 문화재 관리부는 1월 4일 그 명판이 이집트로 반환되었다고 공식적으로 밝혔다.

❽ 그 명판의 회수는 또 다른 고대 이집트 유물인 기자(Giza)의 대 피라미드에서 나온 케이싱 스톤(피라미드 표면의 돌)을 둘러싸고 논쟁이 일어나는 가운데 이루어진다. ❾ 이 석회암 조각은 2월에 에든버러에 있는 스코틀랜드 국립 박물관에 전시될 예정이다. ❿ 하지만 이집트의 문화재 관리부는 그 돌의 Ⓐ국외반출의 정당성에 이의를 제기했으며 박물관 측에 소유권 증빙 문서를 제시하라고 요청했다. ⓫ 박물관은 그 돌이 19세기에 공학자인 웨인먼 딕슨(Waynman Dixon)에 의해 기자에서 채굴되어 스코틀랜드의 왕립 천문대장인 찰스 스미스(Charles Smyth)에게 주어졌으며 그가 그 돌을 자신의 에든버러 집에 보관했다고 주장한다. ⓬ 만약 이 돌이 이집트에서 Ⓒ불법적으로 이전된 것으로 밝혀지면, 문화재 관리부는 그것을 다시 가져오기 위해 '필요한 모든 조치'를 취할 것이라고 코우리 국장은 말했다.

해설

이집트 유물이 어떻게 스코틀랜드에 전시되는 것인가에 대해 의문을 제시하는 만큼 Ⓐ에는 'export(국외반출)'가 적절하다. 두 번째 빈칸 다음 문장에 '필요한 모든 조치를 한다'는 문장에서 Ⓒ illegally(불법적으로)'가 추론이 가능하다.

어휘

artifact n. 인공 유물 auction house n. 경매장 antiquity n. (고대) 유물 engrave v. 새기다, 장식하다 cartouche n. 카르투슈(흔히 안에 국왕의 이름을 나타내는 이집트 상형 문자가 들어 있는 직사각형이나 타원형 물체) smuggle v. 밀수하다, 밀반입[출]하다 put up for auction 경매에 부치다 repatriation n. 본국 송환, 귀환 track down ~을 찾아내다 relief n. (조각·건축 등의) 돋을새김, 양각, 부조(浮彫); [가산] 양각 세공[작품] subsequently ad. 그 뒤에, 나중에 embassy n. 대사관 dispute n. 논쟁, 분쟁, 논란 brew v. [파란을] 일으키다, 양조하다 limestone n. 석회석, 석회암 contest v. 경쟁을 벌이다, 이의를 제기하다 legitimacy n. 적법, 합법성 extract v. 뽑다, 꺼내다, 발췌하다 transpire v. (일 따위가) 알려지다, 드러나다; (비밀 따위가) 새다, 누설되다 imposter n. 사기꾼

021 ①

2019학년도 한성대학교 인문계 A형 50번

❶ As you get older, little growths (called skin tags) might start popping up on your body. ❷ You'll recognize them because they're thinner at the base and get wider at the top. ❸ They aren't painful or dangerous like cancerous moles, ❹ but there's a very good reason you'll want them removed. ❺ People have used all kinds of crazy methods to try removing skin tags on their own, says Dr. Rossi, MD (dermatologic surgeon). ❻ He's heard of people tying strings around them, burning them, trying to pick them off with their fingers, and even slamming books against them. ❼ A dermatologist, on the other hand, can snip away skin tags quickly and cleanly.

❽ For one thing, dermatologists have sterile instruments, ❾ but using your own could lead to an infection. ❿ Plus, while dermatologists can use local anesthesia and have supplies to stop the blood, you could bleed uncontrollably with at-home methods. ⓫ Even hospital medications (claiming to dissolve the skin tags) could be bad news, says Dr. Rossi. ⓬ "You could burn the skin or make marks," he says. "There could be unintended consequences."

⓭ But there's an even bigger reason you should visit an expert. ⓮ After dermatologists remove a growth, they'll look at it under a microscope. ⓯ "There are things that look like skin tags but are cancerous," says Dr. Rossi. ⓰ That doesn't mean you should freak out if you do find a skin tag. ⓱ Most will just be benign, but you won't know for sure until you've asked. ⓲ Plus, checking a skin tag is a "Ⓔ good excuse to get your doctor to check the rest of your body for skin cancer and atypical or malignant growths," says Dr. Rossi.

Choose the best expression for Ⓔ.
Ⓔ에 가장 적절한 표현을 고르시오

✓ ① good excuse
  좋은 구실
② dangerous process
  위험한 과정
③ useless method
  쓸모없는 방법
④ necessary evil
  필요악

해석

❶ 당신이 나이가 들면서, 연성섬유종(쥐젖)이라고 불리는 작은 혹이 당신의 몸에 나타나기 시작할지도 모른다. ❷ 연성섬유종의 밑 부분은 얇고 위쪽으로 갈수록 넓어지기 때문에 연성섬유종을 알아볼 수 있을 것이다. ❸ 그것들은 암성(癌性) 사마귀처럼 아프거나 위험하지는 않지만, ❹ 당신이 연성섬유종을 제거하길 원하는 아주 좋은 이유가 있다. ❺ 사람들은 온갖 종류의 미친 방법을 사용하여 스스로 연성섬유종을 제거하려고 한다고 피부과 의사인 로시(Rossi) 박사는 말한다. ❻ 그는 사람들이 연성섬유종 주위를 실로 묶고, 태우고, 손가락으로 뽑으려고 하며, 심지어 연성섬유종을 책으로 세게 치기도 한다는 말을 들어왔다. ❼ 반면에, 피부과 의사는 연성섬유종을 빠르고 깨끗하게 잘라낼 수 있다.

❽ 우선 첫째로, 피부과 의사들은 살균 기기를 가지고 있지만, ❾ 당신이 갖고 있는 기기를 사용하는 것은 감염을 일으킬 수 있다. ❿ 또한, 피부과 의사들은 국소마취를 하고 지혈을 해주는 용품들이 있지만, 당신이 집에서 하는 방법으로는 제어하기 힘들 정도로 출혈이 일어날 수도 있다. ⓫ 심지어 연성섬유종을 녹여 없앤다고 하는 병원약도 좋은 것일 수 없다고 로시 박사는 말한다. ⓬ "당신은 피부에 화상을 입거나 상처를 남길 수 있으며 의도하지 않은 결과가 있을 수도 있습니다."라고 그는 말한다.

⓭ 하지만 당신이 전문가에게 진찰을 받아야 하는 더 중요한 이유가 있다. ⓮ 피부과 의사가 혹을 제거한 후에 그들은 그 혹을 현미경으로 자세히 살펴볼 것이다. ⓯ "연성섬유종처럼 보이지만, 암인 경우가 있습니다."라고 로시 박사는 말한다. ⓰ 그렇다고 연성섬유종을 발견했다고 해서 겁을 먹어야 한다는 뜻은 아니다. ⓱ 대부분의 연성섬유종은 양성(良姓)이지만, 당신이 물어보기 전까지는 확실히 알 수 없을 것이다. ⓲ 게다가, 연성섬유종을 검사하는 것은 의사로 하여금 당신의 몸의 나머지 부분을 검사하여 피부암과 비정상이거나 악성 종양이 있는지 확인하게 할 수 있는 Ⓔ'좋은 구실'이기도 하다고 로시 박사는 말한다.

해설

연성섬유종(skin tag)이 양성인지 악성인지 진단을 권유하며 이를 통해 몸의 다른 곳 이상이 있는지를 검진한다는 글이다. 따라서 ① 'good cause(좋은 구실)'가 가장 적절하다.

어휘

growth n. 종양, 혹 **skin tag** 연성 섬유종(쥐젖) **pop up** 튀어나오다[오르다], 불쑥 나타나다 **cancerous** a. 암의; 암에 걸린 **mole** n. (피부 위에 작게 돋은 진갈색) 점, 사마귀 **dermatologic** a. 피부(皮膚)의 **slam** v. 내동댕이치다, 쳐서 맞히다 **snip** v. 싹둑 자르다, 가위로 자르다 **sterile** a. 살균한, 소독한 **instrument** n. 기구, 도구 **anesthesia** n. 마취 **dissolve** v. 녹이다, 용해시키다, 사라지다 **under a microscope** 현미경으로, 꼼꼼하게 **freak out** 자제력을 잃다 **benign** a. 양성의, 상냥한, 유순한 **atypical** a. 이례적인 **malignant** a. 악성의, 악의에 찬

정답 및 해설

022 ②
2019학년도 한양대학교 에리카 인문계 A형 37번

❶ Dave Balter worked in advertising, and he knew that most people don't like ads. ❷ They avoid watching them, reading them, or listening to them. ❸ He also knew that people do pay attention when they hear about goods and services from people they know. ❹ So he said to himself, "If no one pays attention to advertising, but they do pay attention to the opinions of their friends and family, let's focus our attention there." ❺ What Balter came up with was a website where consumers could sign up to receive free products. ❻ In return, they promised that if they liked the products, they would tell their friends. ❼ In most cases, the volunteers also got coupons to give to their friends. ❽ All Balter asked was that they report back on two questions: what did you think of the product, and who did you talk to about it?
❾ After four years, Balter had 65,000 volunteers trying products and telling people about the ones they liked. ❿ Then a reporter heard about Balter's idea and wrote a story on it for a major magazine. ⓫ Free advertising! ⓬ Within a year after that story appeared, Balter had 130,000 volunteers. ⓭ Today, the company he started has over one million people spreading the word about a wide variety of products. ⓮ They are doing word-of-mouth advertising, perhaps the best kind of advertising there is.
⓯ There may be a risk to advertising by word of mouth, however, according to George Silverman, the author of The Secrets of Word-of-Mouth Marketing. ⓰ What's the danger? ⓱ Studies have shown that a customer who likes a product or service will tell an average of three people about it. ⓲ But when customers don't like it, on average they'll tell eleven.

1) 가정법과거 If S 동사의 과거시제, S 조동사과거 동사원형

빈칸에 들어갈 가장 알맞은 것을 고르시오.

① Similarly 마찬가지로
② **In return** 답례로, 보답으로 ✓
③ Consequently 결과적으로
④ In fact 사실은

해석
❶ 데이브 발터(Dave Balter)는 광고 분야에서 일했고, 대부분 사람들이 광고를 좋아하지 않는다는 것을 알았다. ❷ 사람들이 광고를 보거나, 읽거나, 듣는 것을 회피한다는 것이다. ❸ 그는 또한 사람들이 아는 사람들로부터 상품과 서비스에 대해 들을 때에는 주의를 기울인다는 것을 알았다. ❹ 그래서 그는 "아무도 광고에 주의를 기울이지 않고 친구들과 가족의 의견에 주의를 기울인다면, 우리의 관심을 거기에 집중시키자."라고 스스로에게 말했다. ❺ 발터가 생각해 낸 것은 소비자들이 가입하면 제품을 무료로 받을 수 있는 웹사이트였다. ❻ 그에 대한 보답으로, 그들은 그 제품이 마음에 들면 친구들에게 말해주겠다고 약속했다. ❼ 대부분의 경우, 지원자들은 친구들에게 줄 쿠폰도 받았다. ❽ 발터가 요청한 것은 '그 제품에 대해 어떻게 생각하는지, 그리고 제품에 대해 누구와 이야기했는지'라는 두 가지 질문에 대해 대답해 달라는 게 전부였다.
❾ 4년 후에, 제품을 써보고 마음에 든 제품에 대해 사람들에게 말하는 지원자의 수가 6만 5천 명에 이르렀다. ❿ 그 후에 한 기자가 발터의 아이디어에 관해 듣고 주요 잡지에 그에 관한 기사를 썼다. ⓫ 무료로 광고가 된 셈이었다! ⓬ 그 기사가 실리고 1년 안에, 발터는 13만 명의 지원자를 갖게 되었다. ⓭ 오늘날, 그가 시작한 회사는 100만 명 이상의 사람들이 다양한 제품에 대한 소문을 퍼뜨리고 있다. ⓮ 그들은 입소문 광고를 하고 있는데, 이것은 아마도 가장 좋은 종류의 광고일 것이다.
⓯ 하지만 『입소문 마케팅의 비밀(The Secrets of Word-of-Mouth Marketing)』의 저자인 조지 실버맨(Geroge Silverman)에 따르면, 입소문을 통한 광고에는 위험요소가 있을 수 있다. ⓰ 그 위험요소란 어떤 것일까? ⓱ 연구 결과, 제품이나 서비스를 마음에 들어 하는 고객은 평균 3명에게 그 사실을 알려준다. ⓲ 하지만 고객들이 그것을 좋아하지 않는다면, 그들은 평균적으로 11명에게 말을 할 것이다.

해설
빈칸 다음 문장에서 제품이 마음에 들면 친구들에게 말해주는 것을 약속한다. 따라서 ② 'In return(~보답으로)'이 가장 적절하다.

어휘
advertising n. 광고, 광고업 **attention** n. 주의, 주의력 **focus** v. 집중하다 **come up with** (해답·돈 등을) 찾아내다, ~을 생각해내다 **volunteer** n. 지원자; 자원봉사자 **spread** v. (소문·보도 따위를) 퍼뜨리다, 유포하다 **word-of-mouth** a. 구두의, 말로 전하는, 구전의

023 ④ 2019학년도 숭실대학교 인문계 A형 39번

❶ So / what's the right way / to be wrong? ❷ Are there techniques (that allow organizations and individuals to embrace the necessary connection (between small failures and big successes)? ❸ Smith College, (the all-women's school in western Massachusetts), has created a program (called "Falling Well") / to teach / its students / what all of us could stand to learn. ❹ "What we're trying to teach is / that failure is not a bug of learning; / ❺ it's the feature," / explained Rachel Simmons, (who runs the initiative), in a recent *New York Times* article. ❻ Indeed, when students enroll in her program, / they receive a Certificate of Failure [that declares / they are "hereby authorized" / to screw up, bomb, or fail" / at a relationship, a project, a test, or any other initiative (that seems hugely important) / and "still be a totally worthy, / utterly excellent human being." ❼ Students (who are prepared / to handle failure) are less fragile and more daring / than those (who expect perfection and flawless performance).

❽ That's a lesson (worth applying to business as well). ❾ Patrick Doyle, (CEO of Domino's Pizza since 2010), has had one of the most successful seven-year runs of any business leader in any field. ❿ But all of his company's triumphs, (he insists), are based on its willingness / to face up / to the likelihood of mistakes and missteps. ⓫ In a presentation to other CEOs, / Doyle described two great challenges [that stand Ⓐ in the way of companies and individuals (being more honest about failure)]. ⓬ The first challenge, (he says), is what he calls "omission bias" — / ⓭ the reality [that most people (with a new idea) choose not to pursue the idea / because if they try something and it doesn't work, / the setback might damage their career.] ⓮ The second challenge is to overcome what he calls "loss aversion" — / ⓯ the tendency for people / to play not to lose / rather than play to win, / because (for most of us), / "The pain of loss is double the pleasure of winning."

Which of the following best fits in Ⓐ?
Ⓐ에 들어갈 가장 적절한 말은?

① with ② for
③ on   ✓ in

해 석

❶ 그렇다면 잘못되는 올바른(제대로 잘못되는) 방법은 무엇인가? ❷ 조직과 개인에게 작은 실패와 큰 성공 사이의 필연적인 연관성을 깨닫고 받아들이게 해주는 기술은 있는 것인가? ❸ 서부 매사추세츠주의 스미스 여자대학교는 학생들에게 우리 모두가 배울 수 있는 것을 가르치기 위해 "Failing Well(잘 실패하는 법)"이라는 프로그램을 만들었다. ❹ "우리가 가르치려고 하는 것은 실패가 학습의 오류가 아니라 학습의 특징이라는 것입니다. ❺ (실패에서 배우는 학습)"라고 『뉴욕타임즈(New York Times)』의 최근 기사에서 그 프로그램을 담당하는 레이첼 시먼스(Rachel Simmons)는 설명했다. ❻ 실제로 그녀의 프로그램에 등록하는 학생들은 실패증서를 받는데, 이 문서는 학생들이 인간관계, 프로젝트, 시험, 그 외 다른 매우 중요하게 여겨지는 활동을 "망치거나, 실패하도록 허가되었다"라고 선언한다. 그래도 그들은 "여전히 완전히 가치 있고, 아주 훌륭한 존재"라는 것이 선언되는 것이다. ❼ 실패를 다룰 준비가 되어 있는 학생들은 완벽함과 흠잡을 데 없는 성취를 기대하는 학생들보다 덜 취약하고 더 대담하다.

❽ 그것은 사업에도 적용할 가치가 있는 교훈이다. ❾ 2010년부터 도미노피자의 최고경영자로 있는 패트릭 도일(Patrick Doyle)은 그 어떤 분야의 그 어떤 기업들보다 성공적인 7년을 경영한 사업가 가운데 한 명이었다. ❿ 하지만 그의 회사의 모든 승리는 실책과 실수의 가능성에 기꺼이 맞서려고 하는 것에 기초하고 있다고 그는 주장한다. ⓫ 도일은 다른 CEO들을 대상으로 한 발표에서 기업과 개인이 실패에 대해 좀 더 솔직해지는 것을 Ⓐ가로막는 두 가지 커다란 문제를 설명했다. ⓬ 첫 번째 문제는 그가 '부작위 편향'이라고 부르는 것이다. ⓭ 이것은 새로운 생각을 가지고 있는 대부분 사람들이 그들이 어떤 것을 시도해서 그것이 효과가 없으면 그 실패가 경력에 피해를 입힐 수도 있으므로 그 생각을 추구하지 않기로 선택하는 현실을 가리킨다. ⓮ 두 번째 문제는 그가 '손실 회피'라 부르는 것을 극복하는 것이다. ⓯ 이것은 사람들이 이기기 위해 경기를 하기보다는 지지 않으려고 경기를 하는 경향을 의미하는데, 대부분 사람들에게는 "손실이 주는 고통이 승리가 주는 기쁨의 두 배이기 때문이다."

해 설

빈칸 다음에는 2가지의 문제점을 제시하고 있으며 또한 이 글은 실패와 성공의 연관성에 대한 글이다. 따라서 빈칸에는 실패에 솔직해지는 것을 '가로막는' 두 가지 커다란 문제를 설명했다고 말하는 것이 가장 적절하다. 뿐만 아니라 정답 추론을 위해 『stand in the way of~』 즉 '~을 방해하다'라는 뜻의 이어동사를 숙지하고 있어야 한다.

어 휘

embrace v. 받아들이다, 수용하다 bug n. 결함, 오류 initiative n. 새로운 계획, 주도권, 조치 enroll v. 등록하다 declare v. 선언[포고]하다, 공표하다 hereby ad. 이에 의하여, 이로써 authorized a. 인가된 screw up 망치다, 엉망으로 만들다 bomb v. 실패하다 fragile a. 허약한, 연약한 daring a. 대담한, 용감한 flawless a. 흠 없는, 결점없는 triumph n. 대승리, 대성공 misstep n. 실수, 잘못된 조치 omission n. 생략, 누락 setback n. 방해, 좌절; 역전 aversion n. 아주 싫어함, 혐오감

정답 및 해설

024 ③
2019학년도 숭실대학교 인문계 A형 48번

❶ In 1923 / the *New York Times* published an article / about a Danish man (who had recently visited Germany). ❷ He had arrived sporting a large up-turned moustache, which he soon shaved off / upon discovering / that "the Kaiser Wilhelm brand of upper lip decoration is not popular / in the very modern commercial city of Hamburg." ❸ However, the Dane encountered a problem / when, (at the completion of his visit), he attempted to leave Germany. ❹ According to the article, / "The heavily moustached chap (on his passport photograph) did not in the least resemble the smooth-faced modern appearing Dane. ❺ Passport officials turned him back and detectives gave him the third degree. ❻ In his changed appearance / they found resemblance / to a famous international swindler." ❼ Apparently / "ashamed" of his failure / to resemble himself, / the unnamed Dane did not seek the assistance of Danish officials. ❽ Instead / he chose to grow a new moustache, which the article confidently predicted, / "[would] enable him to measure up to his passport photograph." ❾ This article, / (one of a handful from the period that recounts the problems shaving purportedly created for male passport bearers), reads today / as somewhat Ⓐ bizarre, / if not perhaps a little preposterous. ❿ While it may indeed be out of step / with our contemporary understanding of official identification practices, / and even if the events did not occur / exactly as reported, / ⓫ the article accurately captures some of the cultural and social tensions [that existed / around the documentation of individual identity / in the early decades of the twentieth century / (when travelers and immigrants first encountered universal demands for a passport]. ⓬ The informal introduction (of official attempts / to systematically use documents / to verify identity) pushes the beginnings of this history / back to the mid-nineteenth century; / ⓭ the apparent general acceptance of the necessity / and accuracy of the passport as an identification document / a

해석

❶ 1923년에 『뉴욕타임즈(New York Times)』는 최근 독일을 방문했던 덴마크인에 관한 기사를 실었다. ❷ 그는 끝이 위로 구부러진 커다란 콧수염을 자랑하며 독일에 도착했는데, 그는 곧 "카이저 빌헬름(Kaiser Wilhelm)과 같은 윗입술의 장식(끝이 올라간 콧수염)이 매우 현대적인 상업도시인 함부르크에서 인기가 별로 없다"라는 것을 발견하고는 바로 콧수염을 깎았다. ❸ 하지만 그 덴마크인이 방문을 마치고 독일을 떠나려고 했을 때 문제에 직면했다. ❹ 이 기사에 따르면, "그의 여권 사진에 있는 콧수염이 짙은 사람은 매끄러운 얼굴의 현대적인 모습을 한 그 덴마크인과 전혀 닮지 않았다. ❺ 출입국 관리 공무원은 그를 저지했으며 형사들은 그를 심하게 추궁했다. ❻ 그의 달라진 모습에서 그들은 (그가) 유명한 국제적인 사기꾼과 닮았다는 것을 발견했다."고 한다. ❼ 분명히 자신을 밝히는 것을 실패한 것에 대해 '부끄러웠던' 이름이 밝혀지지 않은 그 덴마크 사람은 덴마크 관리에게 도움을 구하지 않았다. ❽ 그 대신 그는 새로운 콧수염을 기르기로 결정했는데, 이 기사는 그 콧수염이 "여권 사진과 비슷한 모습을 하게 해주었다"라고 자신 있게 예측했다. ❾ 면도가 남성 여권 소지자에게 발생시켰다고 알려진 문제들을 자세히 이야기하는 당시 몇 안 되는 기사 중 하나인 이 기사는 어쩌면 다소 터무니없지는 않더라도 오늘날 읽어보면 약간 Ⓐ이상하게 여겨진다. ❿ 그 기사는 공식 신원 확인에 대한 현대적인 이해와 부합하지 않을지도 모르고, 그 사건이 실제로 보도된 대로 일어나지 않았을 수도 있지만, ⓫ 그 기사는 여행자들과 이민자들이 여권에 대한 일반적인 요구에 처음으로 맞닥뜨렸던 20세기 초에 개인의 신원을 입증할 문서를 둘러싸고 존재했던 문화적·사회적 긴장감의 일부를 정확히 포착했다. ⓬ 신원을 확인하기 위해 문서를 체계적으로 사용하려는 공식적 시도의 비공식적 도입은 이 역사의 시작을 19세기 중반으로 되돌린다. ⓭ 신분증명서로서 여권의 필요성과 정확성에 대한 명백한 일반적인 수용은 깨끗하게 면도한 덴마크인과 그의 여권 사진에 관한 이야기가 있고 10년 후에 이루어졌으며 그로 인해 이 역사는 1930년대에 끝맺는다.

어휘

danish n. 덴마크인, 덴마크어 **sport** v. 자랑스럽게 보이다[입다] **up-turned** a. 위로 향한, 끝이 위로 구부러진 **moustache** n. 콧수염 **shave off** (수염을) 면도해 [밀어] 버리다 **commercial** a. 상업의 **chap** n. 놈, 녀석, 사나이 **not in the least** 전혀, 조금도 **turn back** 돌려보내다, 저지하다 **third degree** (경찰의) 고문, 엄한 심문 **resemblance** n. 닮음, 비슷함, 유사함 **swindler** n. 사기꾼 **ashamed** a. 부끄러운, 창피한, 수치스러운 **unnamed** a. 익명의, 이름이 알려지지 않은 **confidently** ad. 확신을 갖고, 자신 있게, 대담하게 **measure up to** ~에 달하다, 필적하다 **recount** v. 자세히 말하다, 이야기하다; 하나하나 열거하다 **purportedly** ad. 소문에 의하면, 알려진 대로라면 **bearer** n. (여권 등의) 소지자 **preposterous** a. 말도 안 되는, 터무니없는, 가당찮은 **be out of step** 보조가 맞지 않다 **contemporary** a. 현대의, 당대의 **capture** v. 정확히 포착하다[담아내다] **encounter** v. 맞닥뜨리다[부딪히다] **verify** v. 확인하다, 입증하다 **apparent** a. 분명한, 외관상의 **reasonable** a. 합리적인, 합당한 **bizarre** a. 기이한, 특이한

decade after the story (of the clean-shaven Dane and his passport photograph) brings this history / to an end in the 1930s.

Which of the following best fits in Ⓐ?
다음 중 Ⓐ에 가장 적절한 것은 무엇인가?

① emotional
   감정적인
② reasonable
   분별력 있는
③ bizarre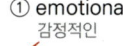
   별난
④ serious
   심각한

해 설 지문은 덴마크인의 신원을 확인하는 과정에서 다소 이상한 신분 확인 절차를 이야기하고 있는 글이다. 또한 빈칸 앞에 '다소 터무니없지는 않더라도'라고 말하는 만큼 약간 ③ '이상하게(bizarre)' 여겨진다고 말하는 것이 가장 적절하다.

정답 및 해설

025 ① 2019학년도 아주대학교 인문계 A형 44번

A ❶ In the global resource wars, / the environmentalism of the poor is frequently triggered / when an official landscape is forcibly imposed / on a vernacular one. ❷ A vernacular landscape is shaped / by the affective, historically textured maps (that communities have devised over generations), maps (replete with names and routes), / maps (alive to significant ecological and surface geological features). ❸ A vernacular landscape, (although (neither monolithic nor undisputed), is integral / to the socio-environmental dynamics of community / rather than being wholly externalized / — treated as out there, / as a separate nonrenewable resource.

B ❹ By contrast, an official landscape — (whether government, NGO, corporate or some combination of those) — is typically oblivious / to such earlier maps; / ❺ instead, it writes the land / in a bureaucratic, externalizing, and extraction-driven manner (that is often pitilessly instrumental). ❻ Lawrence Summers' scheme (to export rich nation garbage and toxicity to Africa), for example, stands / as a grandiose (though hardly exceptional) instance / of a highly rationalized official landscape (that, ❼ (whether in terms of elite capture of resources and toxic disposal), has often been projected onto ecosystems (inhabited by those "disposable citizens.")]

C ❽ The exponential upsurge / in indigenous resource rebellion / across the globe has resulted largely from a clash of temporal perspectives [between the short-termers (who arrive / with their Ⓐ official landscape maps to extract, despoil,) and depart ❾ and the long-termers (who must live inside the ecological aftermath and must therefore weigh wealth differently in time's scale.) ❿ More than material wealth is here at stake: ⓫ imposed Ⓑ official landscapers typically discount spiritualized Ⓒ vernacular

해석

A ❶ 글로벌 자원전쟁에서, 향토적인 경관에 공적인 경관을 억지로 강제하는 경우에 빈곤층의 환경보호운동이 빈번하게 촉발된다. ❷ 향토적인 경관은 공동체가 여러 세대에 걸쳐 만들어 온 역사가 묻어나는 정서적 지도, 이름과 길로 가득한 지도, 생태학적으로 중요한 지질학적 형태가 살아 있는 지도에 의해 형성된다. ❸ 획일적이지도 않고 모두가 받아들이는 것도 아니지만, 향토적인 경관은 저 바깥 세상에 있는 것으로 다루어지는, (인간사회와는) 별개의 재생불가능한 자원으로 취급되는, 전체적으로 외면화(外面化)된 것이라기보다 공동체 사회에 내포되어 그 사회·환경적 역동성을 완전히 이루는데 필수적인 것이다.

B ❹ 이와는 대조적으로, 공적인 경관 -정부, NGO, 기업 혹은 이들 가운데 일부가 조합된 것- 은 일반적으로 그러한 먼저 있던 지도들을 염두에 두지 않는다. ❺ 대신에, 그것은 관료적이고, 외면화하고, 기존의 것을 뽑아내는 방식으로, 종종 냉혹하게 수단을 앞세우는 방식으로, 그 땅을 그린다. ❻ 예를 들어, 부유한 국가의 유독성 폐기물을 아프리카에 수출하려는 로렌스 서머스(Lawrence Summers)의 계획은 고도로 합리화된 공적인 경관의 거창한 (그러나 이례적이라고는 할 수 없는) 사례인데, ❼ 이 공적인 경관은 일부 계층의 자원 독점과 유독성 폐기물 처분의 관점에서 보던 보지 않든, 저 "일회용 시민들"이 살고 있는 생태계에 종종 투영되어온 경관이다.

C ❽ 전 세계적으로 토착 자원 개발에 대한 반대가 급격하게 늘어난 것은 기존의 것을 뽑아내고 파괴하고 떠나기 위해 Ⓐ공적인 경관의 지도를 갖고 들어오는 단기적 관점을 가진 사람들과 그로 인한 생태적 영향 속에서 살아야 하고 ❾ 따라서 시간의 척도에서 부(富)를 다르게 평가할 수밖에 없는 장기적 관점을 가진 사람들 사이의 시간적 관점의 충돌에 대체로 기인했다. ❿ 여기에는 물질적인 부(富) 이상의 것이 걸려 있다. ⓫ Ⓑ공적인 경관을 강요하는 사람들은 일반적으로 정신적인 성격의 ⓒ향토적인 경관을 무시하고, 거미줄처럼 얽혀 있는 축적된 문화의 의미를 끊어 버리며, 그 경관을 마치 살아있는 사람들, 태어나지 않은 사람들, 그리고 살아있는 죽은 자들(영혼으로 떠돌고 있는 자들)이 살고 있지 않은 것처럼 대한다.

어휘 resource n. 자원 environmentalism n. 환경론, 환경보호주의 trigger v. (일련의 사건·반응 등을) 일으키다, 유발하다 landscape n. 풍경, 경치, 경관 forcibly ad. 강제적으로, 강력히 impose v. (의무·세금 따위를) 부과하다; 강요하다, 강제하다 vernacular a. 본국의, 지방의; 풍토의, 토착의 affective a. 감정적인, 정서적인 devise v. 궁리하다, 고안하다, 안출하다 replete a. 가득 찬, 충만한 significant a. 중요한, 상당한 ecological a. 생태학의, 생태적인 geological a. 지질학상의, 지질의 monolithic a. 하나의 단위를 이룬, 완전히 통제된, 획일적이고 자유가 없는 undisputed a. 반박[이론]의 여지가 없는, 명백한, 당연한 integral a. 완전한, 필수의, 필요불가결한 externalize v. 외면화하다, 객관화하다; 구체화하다 oblivious a. 염두에 두지 않는, 안중에 없는 bureaucratic a. 관료적인, 관료정치의 extraction n. 뽑아냄, 추출 pitilessly ad. 무자비하게, 냉혹하게 instrumental a. 중요한, 수단이 되는, 기구의 scheme n. 계획, 설계 toxicity n. 독성 grandiose a. 웅장한, 웅대한 exceptional a. 외적인, 이례의, 특별한 rationalize v. 합리화하다 disposal n. 처분, 매각 ecosystem n. 생태계 inhabit v. ~에 살다, 거주하다 exponential a. 기하급수적인, 급격한 upsurge n. 증가, 급증 indigenous a. 토착의, 원산의 rebellion n. 반란, 반대, 저항 temporal a. 사건의, 일시적인, 잠시의 perspective n. 시각, 견지 despoil v. 약탈하다, (자연환경 등을) 파괴하다 depart v. 떠나다 aftermath n. 결과, 여파, 영향 spiritualized a. 승화된, 영적인

landscape, severing webs of accumulated cultural meaning and treating the landscape / as if it were uninhabited / by the living, unborn, and the animate deceased.

Which of the following can best fill in the blanks Ⓐ,Ⓑ and Ⓒ in the paragraph Ⓒ?
Ⓒ단락에서 Ⓐ, Ⓑ, Ⓒ에 들어갈 가장 적절한 말은?

	Ⓐ		Ⓑ		Ⓒ
✓①	official	⋯	official	⋯	vernacular
②	vernacular	⋯	official	⋯	vernacular
③	vernacular	⋯	vernacular	⋯	official
④	official	⋯	vernacular	⋯	official
⑤	official	⋯	official	⋯	official

해설 향토적(vernacular) 경관은 옛것을 유지하는 것이고 공적인(official) 경관은 옛것을 지우고 새로운 것을 세우는 것이라고 간단하게 정리한다면 Ⓐ, Ⓑ에는 official, 그리고 Ⓒ에는 vernacular가 들어가는 것이 가장 적절하다.

어휘 **sever** v. 절단하다, 끊다 **accumulate** v. 축적하다 **uninhabited** a. 사람이 살지 않은, 무인의 **animate** a. 살아있는 **deceased** a. 사망한

026 ④　2019학년도 인하대학교 인문계 19번

❶ Ground beef has likely been served on some form of bread since time immemorial, ❷ but that does not make a hamburger. ❸ A hamburger is defined as much by the use of a purposefully baked bread — universally called a "hamburger bun" — as by the beef patty. ❹ You can add as many toppings as you like to this combination or cook the beef in a myriad of ways ❺ and you will still have a hamburger. ❻ But replace the bread or use a different type of meat and you have something other than a hamburger. ❼ The modern hamburger, (as we enjoy it today) was first conceived in 1916 in Wichita, Kansas when Walter A. Anderson combined a beef patty with a custom-made bun (designed to encapsulate it). ❽ In fact, it was just another type of sandwich until 1921 (when Anderson partnered with Edgar Waldo Ingram and founded White Castle.) ❾ In this restaurant, the hamburger was commoditized and standardized for a defined universally recognizable American dish. ❿ In addition to creating the modern hamburger, White Castle also set up the first fast food "system," creating the blueprint for all fast food chains to come. ⓫ The hamburger existed on restaurant menus before White Castle, ⓬ but it was listed within the sandwich section. ⓭ After White Castle, the hamburger became separate and distinct from other sandwiches, with its own section on the menu. ⓮ The first hamburgers were small in size — about two to three ounces of beef. ⓯ But it did not remain stagnant. ⓰ Innovations came quick and fast. ⓱ The first cheeseburger was reputedly created in 1926 at the Rite Spot in Pasadena, CA as a "cheese hamburger." ⓲ In the post World War II era, the nation enjoyed an explosion of cheap beef and cheap steel, as well as a burgeoning interstate

해석

❶ 다진 쇠고기는 아득한 옛날부터 이런저런 종류의 빵 위에 얹어 (식사에) 제공되어 왔겠지만, ❷ 그렇게 한다고 해서 햄버거가 되지는 않는다. ❸ 햄버거로 정의되려면, 쇠고기 패티를 사용해야 하는 만큼, 햄버거를 목적으로 구운 빵 -보편적으로 "햄버거 번"이라고 불리는-도 사용해야 한다. ❹ 당신은 이 조합에 당신이 좋아하는 토핑을 얼마든지 추가할 수 있으며 혹은 무수히 많은 방법으로 (햄버거에 들어갈) 쇠고기를 요리할 수 있다. ❺ 그래도 여전히 햄버거가 되는 것이다. ❻ 그러나 빵을 바꾸거나 다른 종류의 고기를 사용하면 햄버거가 아닌 다른 것이 된다. ❼ 오늘날 우리가 즐기고 있는 현대식 햄버거는 1916년 캔자스 주 위치타에서 월터 A. 앤더슨(Walter A. Anderson)이 쇠고기 패티와 그것을 감싸도록 주문 제작된 빵을 합쳤을 때 처음으로 고안되었다. ❽ 사실, 앤더슨이 1921년에 에드가 월도 인그램(Edger Waldo Ingram)과 제휴하여 화이트 캐슬(White Castle)을 설립할 때까지는 그것은 또 다른 종류의 샌드위치일 뿐이었다. ❾ 이 화이트 캐슬 레스토랑에서 햄버거가 상품화되었으며, 보편적으로 인식 가능한 미국 요리의 정의에 맞게 표준화되었다. ❿ 화이트 캐슬은 현대식 햄버거를 만들었을 뿐만 아니라, 최초의 패스트푸드 "시스템"을 세우고, 이후에 생겨난 모든 패스트푸드 체인들을 위한 청사진도 만들어냈다. ⓫ 햄버거는 화이트 캐슬 이전에도 레스토랑의 메뉴에 있었지만, ⓬ 그것은 샌드위치 섹션에 들어가 있었다. ⓭ 화이트 캐슬 이후에, 햄버거는 다른 샌드위치와 구별되고 떨어져 나오게 되어, 메뉴에서 그들만의 섹션을 갖게 되었다. ⓮ 최초의 햄버거는 크기가 작았고, 그래서 약 2~3온스의 쇠고기가 들어갔다. ⓯ 하지만 햄버거는 그 상태에 정체되어 있지 않았다. ⓰ 혁신은 매우 빠르게 이루어졌다. ⓱ 소문에 의하면, 1926년에 최초의 치즈버거가 캘리포니아 파사디나의 라이트 스폿(Rite Spot)에서 "치즈 햄버거"로 만들어졌다. ⓲ 2차 대전 후의 시기에, 미국에는 여러 주(州)를 잇는 고속도로망이 급속도로 생겨났을 뿐만 아니라 값싼 쇠고기와 값싼 강철도 폭발적으로 늘어났다.

어휘

ground beef 간 쇠고기, 다진 쇠고기 **time immemorial** 태고, 아득한 옛날 **purposefully** ad. 일부러, 의도적으로 **bake** v. (빵 따위를) 굽다 **universally** ad. 보편적으로, 일반적으로 **bun** v. 롤빵, 둥근 빵 **a myriad of** 무수한 **replace** v. 대신하다, 대체하다 **conceive** v. 마음에 품다, 이해하다 **custom-made** a. 주문제작된 **encapsulate** v. 캡슐에 싸다[넣다]; (캡슐에 싸듯이) 조심스럽게 보호하다 **commoditize** v. 상품화하다 **standardize** v. 표준화하다 **define** v. (성격·내용 따위를) 규정짓다, 한정하다 **recognizable** a. 인지할 수 있는, 알아볼 수 있는 **blueprint** n. 청사진 **separate** a. 분리된; 따로따로의 **distinct** a. 별개의, 다른 **stagnant** a. 정체된 **innovation** n. 기술혁신, 혁신 **reputedly** ad. 평판으로, 세평에 의하면 **explosion** n. 폭발; 급격한 증가 **burgeon** v. 급격히 성장[발전]하다 **interstate** a. (미국 등지에서) 주(州) 사이의

highway system). ⑲ This allowed the hamburger to move out of the industrial park and onto Main Street. ⑳ The hamburger (that emerged after the war) spoke to America's rapid rise — / ㉑ they became bigger and more diverse.

Which of the following is most appropriate for the blank?
다음 중 빈칸에 들어가기에 가장 적절한 것은?

① out of fashion
　유행이 지난
② more European
　보다 유럽적인
③ local and isolated
　일부 지역에 한정되고 격리된
✓ bigger and more diverse
　더 크고 더 다양한
⑤ something other than a hamburger
　햄버거가 아닌 다른 것

해석 ⑲ 이러한 상황은 햄버거가 공업 단지에서 벗어나 일반 대중에게 다가갈 수 있게 해주었다. ⑳ 2차 대전 후에 등장한 햄버거는 미국의 급속한 성장을 하도록 했다. ㉑ 햄버거는 점점 더 커지고 더 다양해졌다.

해설 마지막 부분에서 2차 대전 이후 경제 성장을 말하고 있으므로 햄버거의 발전을 말하는 ④가 정답으로 가장 적절하다.

어휘 **industrial park** 공업지대 **Main Street** (전통적·보수적인) 미국 중산층; 일반 대중, 서민 **emerge** v. 생겨나다, 나타나다 **speak to** 확증하다 **diverse** a. 다양한, 여러 가지의

027 A) ④   B) ①   2019학년도 숭실대학교 인문계 A형 30, 31번

❶ Nearly every night of our lives, / we undergo a startling metamorphosis. ❷ Our brain profoundly alters its behavior and purpose, dimming our consciousness. ❸ Around 350 BC, / Aristotle wrote an essay, "On Sleep and Sleeplessness," / wondering just what we were doing and why / during sleep. ❹ For the next 2,300 years / no one had a good answer. ❺ In 1924 / German psychiatrist Hans Berger invented the electroencephalograph, which records electrical activity / in the brain, / and the study of sleep shifted / from philosophy to ⒜ science. ❻ It's only in the past few decades, though, as imaging machines have allowed ever deeper glimpses of the brain's inner workings, / ❼ that we've approached a convincing answer to Aristotle.

❽ Everything : (we've learned about sleep) has emphasized its importance (to our mental and physical health). ❾ Our sleep-wake pattern is a central feature of human biology — / an adaptation to life on a spinning planet, / with its endless wheel of day and night. ❿ The 2017 Nobel Prize (in medicine) was awarded / to three scientists [who, (in the 1980s and 1990s), identified the molecular clock / inside our cells (that aims to keep us / in sync with the sun.)] ⓫ When this circadian rhythm breaks down, / (recent research has shown), we are at increased risk for illnesses / such as diabetes, heart disease, and dementia.

⓬ Yet an imbalance (between lifestyle and sun cycle) has become epidemic. ⓭ "It seems / as if we are now living / in a worldwide test (of the negative consequences of sleep deprivation,") says Robert Stickgold, (director of the Center for Sleep and Cognition at Harvard Medical School). ⓮ The average American today sleeps / less than seven hours a night, / about two hours less than a century ago. ⓯ This is chiefly due to the proliferation of electric lights, / followed by televisions, computers, and smartphones. ⓰ In our restless, floodlit

해 석

❶ 우리는 살면서 거의 매일 밤 매우 놀라운 변화를 겪는다. ❷ 우리의 뇌가 행동과 목적을 크게 바꾸며, 의식을 흐리게 하는 것이다. ❸ 기원전 350년경, 아리스토텔레스(Aristotle)는 우리가 자는 동안 우리가 무엇을 하는지 그리고 왜 그런 행동을 하는지를 궁금하게 여겨 『수면과 불면에 대하여(On sleep and Sleeplessness)』라는 에세이를 썼다. ❹ 그 후 2300년 동안 아무도 좋은 대답을 얻지 못했다. ❺ 1924년 독일의 정신과 의사인 한스 베르거(Hans Berger)는 뇌의 전기 활동을 기록하는 뇌파 전위 기록 장치를 발명하며, 수면에 관한 연구를 철학에서 ⒜과학으로 이동시켰다. ❻ 하지만 지난 수십 년 동안에야 비로소 영상 기구가 뇌의 내부 활동을 더 깊이 들여다보게 해주면서, ❼ 우리는 아리스토텔레스의 궁금증에 대한 설득력 있는 대답에 접근하게 되었다.

❽ 우리가 수면에 대해 배운 모든 것은 수면이 우리의 정신 및 신체 건강에 중요하다는 것을 강조해왔다. ❾ 자고 깨어나는 우리의 패턴은 인간 생태의 중심적인 특징이며, 이는 낮과 밤이 무한히 되풀이되는 상황을 만드는 자전하는 행성(지구)에서의 삶에 적응한 것이다. ❿ 2017년 노벨의학상이 세 명의 과학자들에게 수여되었는데, 이들은 1980년대와 1990년대에 우리를 태양과 (시간적으로) 계속 일치한 상태로 있게 하는 분자시계를 우리 세포 내부에서 발견했다. ⓫ 최근 연구는 이런 일주기 생체리듬이 깨지면 우리가 당뇨병, 심장질환, 치매와 같은 질병에 걸릴 위험이 높아진다는 사실을 보여주었다.

⓬ 하지만 생활방식과 태양 주기 사이의 불균형이 유행하게 되었다. ⓭ "마치 우리가 지금 수면 부족의 부정적인 결과라는 전 세계적인 시험 속에 살고 있는 것 같습니다."라고 하버드 의과대학의 수면 및 인지 센터의 소장인 로버트 스틱골드(Robert Stickgold)는 말한다. ⓮ 오늘날 일반적인 미국인은 하룻밤에 7시간 미만의 수면을 취하는데, 이것은 한 세기 전보다 약 두 시간 정도 줄어든 것이다. ⓯ 이는 주로 전등의 확산에 기인하며, 이어 텔레비전, 컴퓨터, 스마트폰의 확산에 기인한다. ⓰ 제대로 쉬지 못하고, 조명으로 빛나는 사회에서 우리는 종종 잠을 ⒝적으로, 즉 우리에게서 생산성과 활동을 앗아가는 상태로 생각한다.

어 휘

undergo v. 겪다, 경험하다 startling a. 깜짝 놀랄, 아주 놀라운 metamorphosis n. 탈바꿈, 변형, 변태 profoundly ad. 깊이, 완전히 dim v. 어둑하게 하다, 약해지다 psychiatrist n. 정신과 의사 electroencephalograph n. 뇌파 전위(電位) 기록 장치 glimpse n. 흘끗 봄[보임], 일견 convincing a. 설득력 있는, 그럴듯한 emphasize v. 강조하다 biology n. 생물학, 생태학 endless 무한한, 한없는 molecular a. 분자의, 분자로 된 in sync with ~의 추세에 따라, ~와 궤를 같이하여 circadian a. (24시간을 주기로 변하는 생물체의) 생물학적 주기의 diabetes n. 당뇨병 dementia n. 치매 epidemic a. 유행성의, 전염성의 deprivation n. 박탈, 부족 cognition n. 지각, 인지 chiefly ad. 주로 proliferation n. 급증, 확산 restless a. 제대로 쉬지[잠들지] 못하는, 부단히 활동하는 floodlight v. 투광 조명등을 밝히다

정답 및 해설

society, / we often think of sleep as an ⒷadversaryⒷ, a state depriving us of productivity and play. ⓱ Thomas Edison, (who gave us light bulbs), said / that "sleep is an absurdity, / a bad habit." ⓲ He believed / we'd eventually dispense with it entirely.

A) Which of the following best fits in Ⓐ?
다음 중 Ⓐ에 가장 적절한 것은 무엇인가?
① myth 신화
② art 예술
③ logic 논리
✓ ④ science 과학

B) Which of the following best fits in Ⓑ?
다음 중 Ⓑ에 가장 적절한 것은 무엇인가?
✓ ① adversary 적
② assistance 도움
③ equipment 장비
④ image 이미지

해석 ⓱ 우리에게 친구를 가져다준 토머스 에디슨(Thomas Edison)은 "수면은 불합리한 것이고, 나쁜 습관입니다."라고 말했다. ⓲ 그는 우리가 결국 완전히 수면 없이 살게 될 것이라고 믿었다.

해설 A) 빈칸 문장에서 1942년 독일의 정신과 의사가 뇌의 전기 활동을 기록하는 뇌파 전위 기록 장치 발명을 언급하는 만큼 Ⓐ에는 ④ science를 추론할 수 있다.

B) 빈칸 Ⓑ 다음 이어지는 동격 구문에서 '생산성과 활동을 앗아간다'라고 말하고 있다. 따라서 부정적 의미를 담고 있는 ① 'adversary(적)'가 가장 적절하다.

어휘 absurdity n. 부조리, 불합리, 모순 dispense v. 제공하다, 나누어주다, 내놓다, 면하다 adversary n. 상대방, 적

정답 및 해설

028 ① 2019학년도 아주대학교 인문계 24번

글의 주제

A ❶ The textbook genre, [irrespective of the discipline : (it is associated with)], serves a common purpose / in academic contexts, which is reflected / in a number of typical features of textbook genres. ❷ Textbooks disseminate discipline-based knowledge and, at the same time, display a somewhat unequal writer-reader relationship, with the writer as the specialist / and the reader as the non-initiated novice / in the discipline. ❸ However, this effort (to disseminate introductory uncontested knowledge) is sometimes compromised / by an attempt [to offer / (what is claimed to be the 'cutting edge' theories)]. ❹ Textbooks nevertheless are seen / as 'repositories of codified knowledge' (made accessible / to large audiences / by the frequent use of a variety of rhetorical devices / such as reporting, questioning, advance labelling and enumeration).

B ❺ However, Ⓐ in spite of these shared characteristics of textbooks across disciplines, disciplinary cultures differ / on several dimensions, / ❻ some of which include constraints / on patterns of membership, / variation (in knowledge structure and norms of inquiry), / typical patterns [of rhetorical intimacy (associated with typical modes of expressions, / specialist lexis and discourses)], and distinct approaches / (to the teaching of these disciplines).

C ❼ Let me begin / with two disciplines, / i.e. those of economics and law, / in an attempt to compare the way : (disciplinary knowledge is structured and communicated / in instructional contexts). ❽ On the face of it, / the two disciplines appear to be similar / in that both of them tend to reinforce the relationship / between rhetorical aspects, processes, and outcomes. ❾ Similarly, they may also create and formulate a complexity (of integrated concepts) and use grammatical metaphors / to pack

해석

A ❶ 교과서 장르는 그 교과서가 관련된 분야와 상관없이 학문적 맥락에서 공통된 목적을 수행하고 있는데, 이러한 점은 교과서 장르의 여러 전형적인 특징들에서 나타나고 있다. ❷ 교과서는 분야에 기초한 지식을 보급하고, 그와 동시에 저자는 그 분야에서 전문가지만 독자는 시작하지 못한 초보자이기 때문에 저자와 독자 사이의 다소 불평등한 관계를 보여준다. ❸ 하지만, 논쟁의 여지가 없는 기초적인 지식을 보급하려는 이러한 노력이 때때로 '최첨단' 이론이라고 주장되는 것들을 제공하려는 시도로 위태롭게 되기도 한다. ❹ 그럼에도 불구하고, 교과서는 보고, 질문, 진행 제시, 열거와 같은 다양한 수사적 장치를 빈번하게 사용함으로써 많은 독자들이 접할 수 있게 만든 '체계화된 지식의 저장소'로 간주되고 있다.

B ❺ 하지만, Ⓐ여러 분야에 걸쳐 교과서가 이러한 공통된 특성을 갖고 있음에도 불구하고 분야적 문화는 몇 가지 차원에서 서로 다른데, ❻ 그 몇 가지 차원에는 구성원 자격 양태에 대한 제약, 지식의 체계 및 연구 기준에서의 차이, 전형적인 표현 방식과 관련된 수사적 친밀성의 전형적인 양태, 전문적인 어휘와 담론, 그리고 이들 분야의 교육에 대한 독특한 접근법 등이 포함된다.

C ❼ 분야의 지식이 교육적 맥락에서 구성되고 전달되는 방식을 비교하기 위해, 경제학과 법학이라는 두 분야부터 시작해보자. ❽ 표면적으로는, 그 두 분야는 둘 모두 수사적 측면, 과정, 결과 간의 관계를 강화하는 경향이 있다는 점에서 서로 비슷해 보인다. ❾ 마찬가지로, 그 두 분야는 복잡한 통합 개념들을 만들어 공식화하고 분야마다 특정한 독자들을 위한 분야의 지식을 담아 넣기 위해 문법적인 은유를 사용할 수도 있다. ❿ 그 두 분야는 또한 사실과 수치를 언급함으로써 다양한 개념 사이의 상호관계를 설명하는 데 필요한 방법들을 공유할지도 모른다.

어휘

genre n. 장르 irrespective of ~에 관계[상관]없이 discipline n. 학과, 교과, 학문 분야 context n. (글의) 전후관계, 문맥; (사건 등에 대한) 경위, 배경, 상황 reflect v. 반영하다, 나타내다 typical a. 전형적인, 대표적인 feature n. 특징, 특색 disseminate v. 널리 퍼뜨리다, 선전하다; (사상 따위를) 유포하다, 보급시키다 display v. 보이다, 나타내다 novice n. 신참자, 초심자, 풋내기 introductory a. 서두의, 서문의; 예비적인, 초보의 uncontested a. 명백한, 논쟁의 여지가 없는 compromise v. (명예·평판·신용 따위를) 더럽히다, 손상시키다; 위태롭게 하다 cutting edge a. 최첨단의 repository n. 저장소 codify v. 법전으로 편찬하다; 성문화하다; (조별로) 요약하다 accessible a. 접근하기 쉬운, 이용할 수 있는 frequent a. 자주, 빈번한 rhetorical a. 수사학의, 수사적인, 화려한 device n. 장치, 설비 enumeration n. 열거, 목록 dimension n. 치수, 차원, (문제 등의) 일면, 양상 constraint n. 강제, 압박, 구속, 억제 variation n. 변화, 변동 norm n. 기준, 규범 inquiry n. 질문, 문의, 조사, 탐구 intimacy n. 친밀함, 친교; (사물에 관한) 자세한 지식, 잘 알고 있음 lexis n. (특정의 언어·작가 등의) 어휘, 용어집 discourse n. 담론, 강연, 설교, 논문 distinct a. 별개의, 뚜렷한, 명백한 instructional a. 교육의 on the face of it (겉으로) 보기에는, 표면적으로는 reinforce v. 강화하다, 보강하다, 강조하다 formulate v. 공식화하다 complexity n. 복잡성 integrated a. 통합된, 완전한 concept n. 개념, 생각 metaphor n. 은유 pack v. 채우다, 넣다

140 끝장편입 독해유형편 Top 20

disciplinary knowledge / for their specific audiences. ❿ They may also share the way (they need / to explain the interrelationship / between various concepts / by referring to facts and figures), / ⓫ though it is likely that / in business / such facts and figures have numerical values, whereas in law / they consist of human acts (entangled / in socio-legal relations).

D ⓬ In a number of other ways, / the two disciplines appear to be very different, / especially in terms of the rhetorical strategies (they employ) / to construct knowledge. ⓭ Business studies, (in general), depends on aggressive innovation / in the way (it constructs its discourses). ⓮ In fact, much of innovation (in communicative practices / in many other professional contexts), / (in the last few decades), has been inspired / by changes (in communicative patterns / in the field of business), / ⓯ which is also reflected / in economics textbooks. ⓰ Law, on the other hand, relies on extreme conservatism / in the way (it constructs its discourses). ⓱ This has also influenced other forms of expressions / in the field. Textbook writing (in law) is no exception / in this respect.

Which of the following best fits in the blank Ⓐ in paragraph Ⓑ.
다음 중 Ⓑ 단락의 빈칸 Ⓐ에 가장 적절한 것은?

✓① in spite of these shared characteristics of textbooks across disciplines
여러 분야에 걸쳐 교과서가 이러한 공통된 특성이 있음에도 불구하고
② regardless of definitions and clarifications of technical concepts
기술적인 개념의 정의와 설명에 관련 없이
③ with reference to a number of common disciplinary variations
분야의 여러 가지 일반적인 차이와 관련하여
④ by means of similar discursive practices in different disciplines
다른 분야에서 만연하고 있는 유사한 관행에 의해
⑤ apart from the universal relationship between genres and specialist disciplines
장르와 전문적인 분야의 보편적인 관계와는 별개로

해석
⓫ 그러나 경영에서는 그런 사실과 수치가 숫자로서의 가치를 가지지만, 법에서는 사실과 수치가 사회·법률적 관계로 얽혀 있는 인간의 행동으로 이루어져 있을 가능성이 높다.
D ⓬ 그 밖의 여러 가지 면에서, 특히 지식을 구성하기 위해 사용하는 수사적 전략의 측면에서, 그 두 분야는 매우 달라 보인다. ⓭ 대개, 경영학은 담론을 구성하는 방식에 있어서 적극적인 혁신에 의존한다. ⓮ 사실, 지난 수십 년 동안 많은 다른 전문적 맥락에서 의사 전달 방법에 일어난 많은 혁신은 경영학 분야의 의사 전달 방법의 변화에서 영감을 받았으며, ⓯ 이것은 경제학 교과서에도 반영돼 있다. ⓰ 반면에, 법은 그것의 담론을 구성하는 방법에서 극단적인 보수주의에 의존한다. ⓱ 이것은 또한 그 분야의 다른 형태의 표현에도 영향을 미쳤다. 이 점에서는 법률 교과서를 집필하는 것도 예외는 아니다.

해설 앞 Ⓐ 단락에서 교과서들의 공통된 특징을 말하고 있고, Ⓑ 시작에서 역접을 암시하는 'However' 이후 차이점을 말하는 단락이다. 그리고 빈칸에는 전치사 'in spite of(~에도 불구하고)'. 이후 위 단락의 내용을 포함하는 ①이 가장 적절하다.

어휘 numerical a. 숫자상의, 수를 나타내는 entangle v. 얽히게 하다, 휩쓸려들게 하다 strategy n. 계획, 전략 aggressive a. 적극적인, 공격적인 innovation n. 혁신, 쇄신 conservatism n. 보수주의, 보수적 경향, 보수성 influence v. ~에게 영향을 미치다 exception n. 예외 clarification n. 설명, 해명, 정화 discursive a. 두서없는, 산만한

정답 및 해설

029 ① 2019학년도 인하대학교 인문계 17번

❶ Many parents grew up with punishments, and it's understandable that they rely on them. ❷ But punishments tend to escalate conflict and shut down learning. ❸ They elicit a fight or flight response, ❹ which means that sophisticated thinking (in the frontal cortex) goes dark and basic defense mechanisms kick in. ❺ Punishments make us either rebel, feel shamed or angry, repress our feelings, or figure out how not to get caught. ❻ In this case, full-fledged 4-year-old resistance would be at its peak. ❼ So rewards are the positive choice then, right? ❽ Not so fast. ❾ Over decades, psychologists have suggested that rewards can decrease our natural motivation and enjoyment. ❿ For example, kids [who like to draw and are, (under experimental conditions), paid to do so], draw less than those (who aren't paid). ⓫ This is what psychologists call the "overjustification effect" — the external reward overshadows the child's internal motivation. ⓬ Rewards have also been associated with lowering creativity. ⓭ In one classic series of studies, people were given a set of materials (a box of pins, a candle, and a book of matches) and asked to figure out how to attach the candle to the wall. ⓮ The solution requires innovative thinking — [seeing the materials in a way (unrelated to their purpose (the box as a candle holder))]. ⓯ People (who were told they'd be rewarded to solve this dilemma) took longer, (on average), to figure it out. ⓰ Rewards narrow our field of view. ⓱ Our brains stop puzzling freely. ⓲ We stop thinking deeply and seeing the possibilities. ⓳ The whole concept of punishments and rewards is based on negative assumptions about children — ⓴ (that they need to be controlled and shaped by us), and (that they don't have good intentions). ㉑ But we can flip this around to see kids as capable, wired for empathy, cooperation, team spirit and hard work. ㉒ That

해석

❶ 많은 부모들이 벌(罰)을 받으면서 자랐기 때문에, 그들이 처벌에 의존하는 것은 이해할 만하다. ❷ 하지만 처벌은 갈등을 증폭시키고 (경험에 따른) 학습을 중단시키는 경향이 있다. ❸ 처벌은 '싸움 혹은 도망'이라는 반응을 이끌어내는데, ❹ 이는 전두엽에서 일어나는 정교한 사고(思考)가 작동을 멈추고 기본적인 방어 메커니즘이 작동하기 시작한다는 것을 의미한다. ❺ 처벌은 우리를 반항하게 만들고, 수치심이나 분노를 느끼게 하며, 감정을 억누르거나, 또는 들키지 않는 방법을 알아내게 만든다. ❻ 이 경우에, 어엿한 4살의 아이라면 격하게 반항할 것이다. ❼ 그렇다면 보상이 긍정적인 선택이다. 그런가? ❽ 속단하지 마라. ❾ 수십 년에 걸쳐, 심리학자들은 보상이 우리가 본래부터 가지고 있는 동기와 즐거움을 감소시킬 수 있다고 주장해왔다. ❿ 예를 들어, 그림 그리기를 좋아하는 아이들에게, 실험 조건에서, 돈을 주면서 그림을 그리도록 하면, 그 아이들은 돈을 받지 않은 아이들보다 그림을 덜 그린다. ⓫ 이는 심리학자들이 "과잉 정당화 효과"라고 부르는 것으로, 외부적인 보상이 아이의 내적 동기를 가린다는 것이다. ⓬ 보상은 또한 창의성을 저하하는 것과도 관련지어져 왔다. ⓭ 일련의 권위 있는 연구에서, 사람들에게 한 세트의 재료들(핀이 들어 있는 상자, 양초, 종이성냥)을 주고는, 양초를 벽에 붙이는 방법을 알아내도록 했다. ⓮ 그 문제는 해결하는 데에 혁신적인 사고를 요구한다. 즉, 재료들을 목적과 무관한 방식으로(상자를 양초의 받침대로) 봐야 하는 것이다. ⓯ 이 난제를 해결하면 보상을 받을 거라는 말을 들은 사람들은 해결방법을 알아내는 데 평균적으로 더 많은 시간이 걸렸다. ⓰ 보상은 우리의 시야를 좁힌다. ⓱ 우리의 뇌는 자유롭게 이리저리 생각해보는 것을 멈춘다. ⓲ 우리는 깊이 생각하고 여러 가능성을 살펴보는 것을 중단한다. ⓳ 처벌과 보상에 대한 전반적인 개념은 아이들에 대한 부정적인 가정을 바탕으로 두고 있다. ⓴ 아이들은 우리에 의해 통제되고 우리가 원하는 모습으로 형성돼야 하며 아이들은 좋은 의도를 가지고 있지 않다는 것이다. ㉑ 하지만 아이들이 공감, 협동, 팀 정신, 근면에 대한 역량을 갖추고 있음을 우리가 깨닫게 되면, 우리는 이 가정을 뒤집을 수 있다. ㉒ 그러한 관점은 우리가 아이들에게 말하는 방식을 크게 변화시킨다.

어휘

punishment n. 처벌, 체벌 **escalate** v. 단계적으로 확대시키다 **conflict** n. 갈등, 충돌, 대립 **elicit** v. (진리·사실 따위를 논리적으로) 이끌어 내다 **sophisticated** a. 정교한, 복잡한; 고도로 세련된 **frontal cortex** 전두엽 **go dark** (작동 등을) 정지하다, 멈추다 **mechanism** n. 구조, 매커니즘, 기제 **kick in** 효과가 나타나기 시작하다 **rebel** v. 배반하다; 반항하다, 반대하다 **sham** v. 창피주다, 모욕시키다 **repress** v. 억누르다, 제지하다 **full-fledged** a. 깃털이 다 난, 완전히 성장한, 자격을 제대로 갖춘 **resistance** n. 저항, 반항 **reward** n. 보수, 포상, 보상 **Not so fast** 서두르지 마라, 그렇게 덤비지 마라 **motivation** n. 자극, 동기부여 **overjustification** n. 과잉정당화 **external** a. 외부의, 외적인 **overshadow** v. 가리다, 어둡게 하다; (비교하여) ~보다 중요하다[낫다] **internal** a. 내부의, 내적인 **classic** a. 일류의, 권위 있는, 정평이 난, 전형적인, 대표적인 **a book of matches** (떼어 쓰는) 종이성냥 **unrelated** a. 관계없는 **dilemma** n. 궁지, 딜레마 **narrow** v. 좁게 하다, 좁히다 **field of view** 시야 **puzzle** v. 이리저리 생각하다, 머리를 짜내다 **concept** n. 개념 **assumption** n. 가정, 억측; 가설 **intention** n. 의도, 의향 **empathy** n. 공감, 감정이입 **cooperation** n. 협력, 협동, 제휴

perspective changes / how we talk to children / in powerful ways. ㉓
Rewards and punishments are conditional, / but our love and positive regard for our kids should be unconditional. ㉔ In fact, when we lead / with empathy / and truly listen to our kids, / they're more likely to listen to us.

Which of the following is most appropriate for the blank?
다음 중 빈칸에 들어가기에 가장 적절한 것은?

✓ ① Rewards have also been associated with lowering creativity
보상은 또한 창의력을 저하시키는 것과도 관련지어져 왔다

② However, rewards make kids more attentive to the parents
그러나, 보상은 아이들이 부모에게 더 주의를 기울이게 만든다

③ Rewards have also been associated with enhancing creativity
보상은 또한 창의력을 향상시키는 것과도 관련지어져 왔다

④ Rewards and punishments are vital to enhancing creativity
보상과 처벌은 창의성을 향상시키는 데 필수적이다

⑤ Rewards were more effective than punishments in enhancing creativity
창의력을 향상시키는 데는 보상이 처벌보다 효과적이었다

해석 ㉓ 보상과 처벌은 조건적이지만, 아이들에 대한 우리의 사랑과 긍정적인 관심은 무조건적이어야 한다. ㉔ 사실, 우리가 공감하면서 이끌고 아이들의 말에 진심으로 귀를 기울일 때, 아이들도 우리의 말에 더 귀를 기울일 것이다.

해설 해당 단락의 양초를 벽에 붙이는 방법을 알아내는 실험을 말하고 있고, 그에 대한 결과가 보상이 시야를 좁힌다는 결론을 내리고 있다. 따라서 빈칸에는 ① '보상은 또한 창의성을 저하하는 것과도 관련지어져 왔다'고 말하는 것이 가장 적절하다.

어휘 **perspective** n. 전망, 견지, 시각 **unconditional** a. 무조건적인 **attentive** a. 주의를 기울이는, 신경을 쓰는

정답 및 해설

030 ②   2019학년도 한국항공대학교 인문계 37번

❶ After running a plastic comb through your hair, / you will find / that the comb attracts bits of paper. ❷ The attractive force is often strong / enough to suspend the paper / from the comb, defying the gravitational pull of the entire Earth. ❸ The same effect occurs / with other rubbed materials, / such as glass and hard rubber. ❹ Another simple experiment is to rub an inflated balloon / against wool. ❺ On a dry day, / the rubbed balloon will then stick to the wall of a room, / often for hours. ❻ These materials have become electrically charged. ❼ You can give your body an electric charge / by vigorously rubbing your shoes / on a wool rug / or by sliding / across a car seat. ❽ You can then surprise and annoy a friend or co-worker / with a light touch on the arm, / delivering a slight shock / to both yourself and your victim.

❾ These experiments work best / on a dry day / because excessive moisture can facilitate a leaking away of the charge. ❿ Experiments also demonstrate / that there are two kinds of electric charge, which Benjamin Franklin named positive and negative. ⓫ A hard rubber or a plastic rod (that has been rubbed with fur) is suspended / by a piece of string. ⓬ When a glass rod (that has been rubbed with silk) is brought / near the rubber rod, / the rubber rod is attracted / toward the glass rod. ⓭ If two charged rubber rods or two charged glass rods are brought / near each other, the force (between them) is repulsive. ⓮ These observations may be explained / by assuming / that the rubber and glass rods have acquired different kinds of excess charge. ⓯ We use the convention (suggested by Franklin), / where the excess electric charge on the glass rod is called positive / and that (on the rubber rod) is called negative. ⓰ On the basis of observations / such as these, / we conclude / that like charges repel one another and unlike charges attract one another.

⓱ Objects usually contain equal amounts of positive and negative charge — / electrical forces (between objects) arise / when

해 석

❶ 플라스틱 빗으로 머리를 빗고 나면, 그 빗에 종잇조각들이 달라붙는다는 것을 알게 될 것이다. ❷ 그 인력(끌어당기는 힘)은 종종 충분히 강해서 종이가 지구 전체의 중력에 거슬러(반항하여) 빗에 매달려있게 된다. ❸ 유리나 딱딱한 고무와 같은 다른 물질들을 문지르더라도 동일한 효과가 발생한다. ❹ 부풀어 오른 풍선을 양모에 문지르는 또 다른 간단한 실험을 해볼 수 있다. ❺ 건조한 날이면, 그렇게 문지른 풍선은 몇 시간이고 방의 벽에 붙어 있을 것이다. ❻ 이 물질들은 전하(電荷)를 갖게 된 것이다. ❼ 당신이 신발을 양모 양탄자에 열심히 문지르거나, 차량 시트 위로 슬라이딩을 하면 당신의 몸에 전하가 발생할 수 있다. ❽ 그런 다음, 친구 혹은 동료의 팔을 가볍게 만져서, 당신과 그 사람 모두에게 가벼운 감전을 일으켜 상대를 깜짝 놀라게 하고 불쾌하게 만들 수도 있다.

❾ 이러한 실험은 건조한 날 가장 잘 되는데, 왜냐하면 과도한 습기가 전하의 유출을 촉진하기 때문이다. ❿ 전하에는 두 종류가 있음을 실험을 통해 알 수 있는데, 벤자민 프랭클린(Benjamin Franklin)은 이것을 각각 양전하와 음전하라고 이름 붙였다. ⓫ 모피에 문지른 딱딱한 고무 막대나 플라스틱 막대를 줄에 매달아 둔다. ⓬ (그런 다음) 비단에 문지른 유리 막대를 그 고무 막대에 가까이 대면, 고무 막대가 유리 막대 쪽으로 끌어당겨 진다. ⓭ 만약 전하를 가진 고무 막대 2개 또는 유리 막대 2개를 서로 가까이 가져가면, 그들 사이의 힘은 반발력이 있다. ⓮ 이러한 실험을 통해 고무 막대와 유리 막대가 서로 다른 과잉 전하를 갖게 된 것이라고 설명할 수 있다. ⓯ 우리는 프랭클린이 제안한 규칙대로, 유리 막대의 과잉 전하를 양전하, 고무 막대의 과잉 전하를 음전하라고 부른다. ⓰ 이와 같은 관찰에 기초하여, 우리는 같은 전하는 서로를 밀어내고 다른 전하는 서로를 끌어당긴다고 결론을 내린다.

⓱ 물체들에는 보통 같은 양의 양전하와 음전하가 있는데, 그 물체들이 순 음전하나 순 양전하를 갖게 될 때 그 물체들 사이에 전기력이 발생한다.

어 휘

comb n. 빗 **suspend** v. 매달리다 **defy** v. 반항하다, 거스르다, 무시하다 **gravitational** a. 중력의 **rub** v. 문지르다, 맞비벼다 **rubber** n. 고무 **inflate** v. 부풀리다, 팽창하다 **wool** n. 양모 **electric charge** 전하(물체가 갖고 있는 전기의 양) **vigorously** ad. 활발하게, 힘차게 **rug** n. 깔개, 무릎덮개 **shock** n. 감전(=electric shock) **victim** n. 희생자, 피해자 **excessive** a. 지나친, 과도한 **moisture** n. 수분, 습기 **facilitate** v. 가능하게 하다, 용이하게 하다 **leak** v. 누설되다, 새다 **demonstrate** v. 증명하다, 입증하다 **positive** n. 양성 **negative** n. 음성 **repulsive** a. 밀어내는, 반발하는 **convention** n. 관습, 관례, 조약 **repel** v. 반발하다, 밀어내다

those objects have net negative or positive charges. ⑱ Nature's basic carriers of positive charge are protons, [which, (along with neutrons), are located / in the nuclei of atoms]. ⑲ The nucleus is surrounded / by a cloud of negatively charged electrons / about ten thousand times larger / in extent. ⑳ An electron has the same magnitude charge / as a proton, / but the opposite sign. ㉑ In a gram of matter / there are approximately 10^{23} positively charged protons / and just as many negatively charged electrons, so the net charge is zero. ㉒ Because the nucleus of an atom is held firmly in place / inside a solid, / protons never move / from one material to another. ㉓ Electrons are far lighter than protons / and hence more easily accelerated / by forces. ㉔ Furthermore, they occupy the outer regions of the atom. ㉕ Consequently, objects become charged / by gaining or losing electrons. ㉖ Charge transfers readily / from one type of material to another. ㉗ Rubbing the two materials together serves to increase the area of contact, facilitating the transfer process. ㉘ An important characteristic of charge is / that electric charge is always conserved. ㉙ Charge isn't created / when two neutral objects are rubbed together; / ㉚ rather, the objects become charged / because negative charge is transferred / from one object to the other. ㉛ One object gains a negative charge / while the other loses an equal amount of negative charge and hence is left / with a net positive charge. ㉜ When a glass rod is rubbed with silk, / electrons are transferred / from the rod to the silk. As a result, the glass rod carries a net positive charge, / the silk a net negative charge. ㉝ Likewise, when rubber is rubbed with fur, / electrons are transferred / from the fur to the rubber.

Choose the most appropriate one for the blank.
빈칸에 들어가기에 가장 적절한 어구를 고르시오

① In contrast
이와 대조적으로
✓ Consequently
그 결과
③ However
그러나
④ Nevertheless
그럼에도 불구하고

해석 ⑱ 자연계의 기본적인 양전하 운반체는 양성자로, 중성자와 함께 원자핵 안에 위치해 있다. ⑲ 핵은 크기가 그보다 1만 배 큰 음전하의 전자구름에 둘러싸여 있다. ⑳ 하나의 전자는 양성자와 같은 양의 전하를 가지고 있지만, 그 부호는 반대이다. ㉑ 1그램의 물질에는 대략 1023개의 양전하를 가진 양성자들과 같은 수의 음전하를 가진 전자들이 있으므로 순 전하는 0이다. ㉒ 원자핵은 고체 안에 확고히 자리 잡고 있기에, 한 물질의 양성자가 다른 물질로 이동하는 일은 일어나지 않는다. ㉓ 양성자보다 훨씬 가벼운 전자는 힘이 가해지면 쉽사리 가속화된다. ㉔ 게다가, 전자는 원자의 바깥 영역을 차지하고 있다. ㉕ 그 결과, 물체는 전자를 얻거나 잃음으로써 전하를 갖게 된다. ㉖ 전하는 한 종류의 물질에서 다른 물질로 쉽게 옮겨간다. ㉗ 두 물질을 함께 문지르면 접촉면적이 늘어나게 되어 그 이동 과정을 촉진한다. ㉘ 전하의 중요한 특징은 그것이 항상 보존된다는 것이다. ㉙ 중성인 두 물체는 서로 마찰하더라도 전하가 생성되지 않는다. ㉚ 오히려, 음전하가 한 물체에서 다른 물체로 옮겨지기 때문에 두 물체는 전하를 갖게 되는 것이다. ㉛ 한 물체가 음전하를 얻지만 다른 물체는 같은 양의 음전하를 잃고, 그 결과 순 양전하 상태가 된다. ㉜ 유리 막대를 비단에 문지르면, 전자는 막대에서 비단 쪽으로 이동한다. ㉝ 그 결과 유리 막대는 순 양전하를 갖게 되고, 비단은 순 음전하를 갖게 된다. ㉞ 마찬가지로, 고무를 모피에 문지르면, 전자는 모피에서 고무 쪽으로 이동한다.

해설 빈칸 앞 단락에서 전하를 갖게 되는 원리를 설명하고 있으며 빈칸 다음 문장에서는 이러한 원리에 따른 논리적 결과를 말하고 있다. 따라서 ② 'Consequently(그 결과)'가 가장 적절하다.

어휘 **proton** n. 양성자 **neutron** n. 중성자 **nuclei** n. nucleus(핵)의 복수 **atom** n. 원자 **magnitude** n. 크기, 규모, 진도(지진) **firmly** a. 단호하게, 확고하게 **occupy** v. 차지하다, 점유하다

정답 및 해설

유형 06 내용이해 | 일치, 추론, 파악

001 ② — 2019학년도 인하대학교 인문계 05번

❶ Lee Child (the author of the perennially best-selling *Jack Reacher* series), sits down / to write each day unsure of what's about to happen. ❷ "I get the same shock (the reader gets)," Mr. Child says, / "at the end of a chapter. 'Wow, I definitely did not see that coming.' ❸ And the really funny thing (for me) is when, (afterward), a reader will say, / 'Oh, I had it all figured out by Page 50,' / and I think, 'Really? I didn't.'"

Which of the following is true about Mr. Child?
다음 중 차일드 씨에 관해 사실인 것은?

① He is famous for romance novels.
  그는 로맨스 소설로써 유명하다.
☑ He does not plan the ending in advance.
  그는 결말을 미리 세워두지 않는다.
③ He usually begins his chapter with a surprise.
  그는 보통 깜짝 놀랄 법한 내용으로 챕터를 시작한다.
④ He intends to shock readers as late as possible.
  그는 최대한 늦게 독자들에게 충격을 주려 한다.
⑤ He fails to solve the mystery in his own novel.
  그는 자신의 소설 속에 있는 미스터리를 풀지 못한다.

해석 ❶ 장기 베스트셀러 목록에 올라 있는 『잭 리처(Jack Reacher)』 시리즈의 작가인 리 차일드(Lee Child)는 무슨 일이 일어날지에 대해 확신하지 못하며 매일 앉아서 글을 쓴다. ❷ "챕터의 끝에서 독자가 받는 충격을 저도 똑같이 받습니다. '이런, 그렇게 될 거라고는 전혀 알지 못했어.' 라고 말이지요. ❸ 그리고 정말 재미있는 것은 나중에 어떤 독자가 '아, 나는 50페이지에서 이미 그 모든 걸 알아버렸네요.'라고 말하고, 그러면 나는 '정말? 나는 몰랐는데.' 라는 생각이 드는 순간입니다." 라고 차일드 씨는 말한다.

해설 '챕터의 끝에서 독자가 받는 충격을 저도 똑같이 받습니다.' 라고 말하는 부분에서 작가 ② 결말을 미리 세워두지 않는다는 것을 추론할 수 있다.

어휘 **author** n. 저자, 작가 **perennially** ad. 연중 계속되어; 지속되어, 영속적으로 **definitely** ad. 명확히, 명백히; 확실히 **afterward** ad. 뒤에, 나중에 **figure out** 이해하다, 해결하다 **in advance** 사전에, 미리

002 ②   2019학년도 숙명여자대학교 인문계 21번

❶ The 200 signatories (to the historic Paris climate accord) may have agreed / to a "rulebook" / on tracking efforts to curb emissions / at the COP24 meet / last week / in Poland. ❷ But there was little talk on countries / (actually ratcheting up emissions control). ❸ Global temperatures are headed / for a 3 degree Celsius rise / from pre-industrial levels / although scientists have warned / that anything (above 1.5 degrees) would be disastrous.

What can be inferred from the above passage?
윗글에서 추론할 수 있는 것은 무엇인가?

① All the signatories to the historic Paris climate accord had made actual policies for curbing emissions.
역사적인 파리 기후 협정에 합의한 모든 가맹국들은 온실가스 배출량을 줄이기 위한 실제적인 정책을 만들었다.

☑ All the signatories to the historic Paris climate accord did not make a practical policy for curbing emissions.
역사적인 파리 기후 협정에 합의한 모든 가맹국들이 온실가스 배출을 줄이기 위한 실제적인 정책을 만든 것은 아니었다.

③ Global temperatures rise for a 1.5 degree Celsius from pre-industrial levels.
지구 온도는 산업화 이전 수준에서 섭씨 1.5도 상승했다.

④ The 200 signatories took the warning of scientists very seriously.
200개의 가맹국들은 과학자들의 경고를 매우 심각하게 받아들였다.

⑤ Scientists warned that Global temperatures are going to be headed for a 3 degree Celsius rise.
과학자들은 지구 온도가 섭씨 3도 상승할 것이라고 경고했다.

해석 ❶ 역사적인 파리 기후 협정에 서명한 200개의 나라들은 지난주에 폴란드에서 열린 제 24차 유엔기후변화협약 당사국총회(COP24)에서 온실가스 배출 억제를 위한 노력을 추적하는 '규정'에 합의했을지도 모른다. ❷ 그러나 실제로 온실가스 배출 규제를 늘리는(강화하는) 나라들에 대한 이야기는 거의 하지 않았다. ❸ 과학자들은 지구 온도가 1.5도 이상 상승하게 되면 재앙이 될 것이라고 경고해왔지만, 지구의 온도는 산업화 이전의 수준보다 섭씨 3도 상승하고 있다.

해설 '실제로 온실가스 배출 규제를 강화하는 나라들에 대한 이야기는 거의 하지 않았다'고 말하는 만큼 ②이 정답이다.

어휘 signatory n. (공식 합의서의) 서명인, (조약) 가맹국 accord n. (기관·국가 간의 공식적인) 합의 rulebook n. 규정집 track v. 추적하다 curb v. 억제하다, 구속하다 emission n. (빛·열·가스 등의) 방출, 배출 ratchet up 조금씩 올리다, 증가시키다 disastrous a. 재앙의, 처참한

003 ① 2019학년도 한국산업기술대학교 인문계 28번

글의 주제

① Cubism was a modern art movement (that began in Paris around 1907). ② Its original founders were Pablo Picasso and Georges Braque. ③ Most of the early cubist art revolved around geometric shapes, planes, and fragmentation. ④ Cubists were more concerned with representing a complete or whole view of the subject matter. ⑤ Space and volume played important roles in their art. ⑥ Furthermore, cubists avoided realistic or accurate painting. ⑦ Instead, they focused on representing an object from multiple perspectives on the canvas. ⑧ Reducing the natural form into the abstract was also a trait of cubist artists. ⑨ The imitation of nature was no longer as important as it was in previous art movements. ⑩ Paul Cezanne is considered a major influence of the early cubists.

Which of the following is a characteristic of cubism?
다음 중 입체파의 특징인 것은 무엇인가?

① **the use of geometric shapes** ✓
기하학적 형태의 사용
② the details of the subject matter
제재의 세부적인 사항 (→ 전체적 모습)
③ the adoption of a single perspective
단일 시각의 채택 (→ 다양한 시각)
④ the depiction of natural objects
자연물의 묘사 (→ 자연 모방은 중요하지 않음)

해석 ① 입체파는 1907년경 파리에서부터 시작된 현대 미술 운동이었다. ② 입체파의 창시자는 파블로 피카소(Pablo Picasso)와 조르주 브라크(Georges Braque)였다. ③ 초창기의 입체파 미술의 대부분은 기하학적인 형태, 평면, 파편 등을 중점적으로 다루었다. ④ 입체파 화가들은 제재(그리는 대상)의 완전하거나 전체적인 모습을 표현하는 것에 더 관심이 많았다. ⑤ 공간과 부피는 입체파의 그림에서 중요한 역할을 했다. ⑥ 게다가, 입체파 화가들은 사실적이거나 정확한 그림을 피했다. ⑦ 대신, 그들은 사물을 여러 관점에서 보아 캔버스 위에 표현하는 데 중점을 두었다. ⑧ 자연적인 형태를 추상적인 형태로 환원(단순화)하는 것도 또한 입체파 화가들의 특징이었다. ⑨ 자연의 모방은 더이상 예전의 예술 운동에서만큼 중요하지 않았다. ⑩ 폴 세잔(paul Cezanne)은 초기 입체파 화가들에게 중대한 영향을 미친 인물로 여겨진다.

해설 '초창기 입체파 미술의 대부분은 기하학적인 형태, 평면, 파면 등을 중심적으로 다루었다'고 말하는 만큼 ①이 정답이다.

어휘 cubism n. 입체파, 큐비즘 revolve around ~을 중심으로 다루다 geometric a. 기하학의; 기하학적인 fragmentation n. 분열, 파쇄, 파편 subject matter 제재, 테마 accurate a. 정확한, 정밀한 reduce v. 줄이다, 환원하다, 단순화하다 abstract a. 추상적인 n. 추상화, 개요 trait n. 특성 imitation n. 모방

004 ④   2019학년도 건국대학교 인문·예체능계 A형 30번

❶ Gum disease is common / among adults. **❷** In fact, the loss of teeth (after forty) is attributed more often / to gum disease / than to cavities. **❸** Gum disease comes / as bacteria builds up in plaque, affecting the bone (that surrounds and supports teeth). **❹** Then the teeth become loose, / and sometimes fall out eventually. **❺** The gum becomes red and puffy and it sometimes bleeds. **❻** However, it is often not recognized / until it becomes too late. **❼** Tips (for healthy gum) are similar to those for healthy teeth. **❽** Brushing teeth well is the first (to be kept in mind). **❾** We have bacteria (that live on carbohydrates / in sugars and starches). **❿** And dentists advise to avoid sweet or starchy foods and to brush teeth right after meal or snack. **⓫** Flossing once a day / to remove plaque / from between teeth and below the gum line is also important, according to dentists.

잇몸병(gum disease)에 관한 다음 글의 내용과 일치하지 <u>않는</u> 것은?
① 성인들한테서 흔히 발생한다.
② 40세 이후의 치아 손실은 주로 잇몸병 때문에 생긴다.
③ 종종 너무 늦게 발견되기도 한다.
✓ 건강한 잇몸을 유지하는 방법과 건치를 유지하는 방법은 다르다. (→비슷하다)
⑤ 달고 딱딱한 음식은 피하는 것이 좋다.

해석
❶ 잇몸병은 성인들 사이에서 흔히 발생한다. ❷ 사실, 40살 이후에 치아가 빠지는 것은 충치보다는 잇몸질환에 의해 더 많이 발생한다. ❸ 잇몸병은 박테리아가 치석에 쌓이면서 치아를 둘러싸고 지탱해주는 뼈에 영향을 미치며 발생한다. ❹ 그러면 치아는 느슨해지면서 때때로 결국 빠지기도 한다. ❺ 잇몸이 붉게 되고 부으며 때때로 출혈이 일어난다. ❻ 그러나 종종 잇몸이 이런 상태인 것을 너무 늦게야 알게 된다. ❼ 건강한 잇몸을 유지하는 방법은 건강한 치아를 유지하는 방법과 비슷하다. ❽ 양치질을 잘하는 것을 가장 먼저 염두에 두어야 한다. ❾ 우리에게는 설탕과 녹말에 있는 탄수화물을 먹고 사는 박테리아가 있다. ❿ 그래서 치과의사들은 단 음식이나 딱딱한 음식을 되도록 피하고 음식 또는 간식을 먹은 후에 바로 양치질을 하라고 권한다. ⓫ 치아 사이에 그리고 잇몸선 밑에 있는 치석 제거를 위해 하루에 한 번 치실로 이를 깨끗이 닦는 것 또한 매우 중요한 것이라고 치과의사들은 말한다.

해설
윗글에서 '건강한 잇몸을 유지하는 방법은 건강한 치아를 유지하는 방법과 비슷하다.'라고 말하고 있기에 ④이 정답이다.

어휘
attribute v. (원인을) ~에 돌리다, (~의) 탓으로 하다 cavity n. 충치(구멍) plaque n. (치아에 끼는) 플라크, 치석 puffy a. 부푼, 부풀어 오른 keep in mind 명심하다, 유념하다 carbohydrate n. 탄수화물 starch n. 전분, 녹말 starchy a. 녹말의, 풀을 먹인, 딱딱한 floss v. (이 사이를) 치실로 깨끗이 하다

정답 및 해설

005 ⑤
2019학년도 아주대학교 인문계 A형 15번

❶ The transportation revolution and the market revolution would have come much more slowly / if the Americans of the early republic had followed the *laissez-faire* (non-interference) notions of political economy (that are often mistakenly ascribed to them).
❷ Instead, the people demanded / that their governments ally themselves with private enterprise / to speed the march of progress.

Ⓐ The most notable alliance of public and private enterprise was in the field of politics.
공기업과 민간기업의 가장 주목할 만한 제휴는 정치 분야에서 이루어졌다. (→ 정치경제 분야에서)

Ⓑ The Americans of the early republic are frequently misunderstood to have followed the policy of *laissez-faire*.
초기 공화정의 미국인들은 '자유 방임주의' 정책을 따랐다는 오해를 종종 받는다.

Ⓒ The people of the early republic asked their governments to work with private businesses.
공화국 초기의 사람들은 민간기업과 함께 일할 것을 정부에 요청했다.

Ⓓ Because the Americans of the early republic did not adopt the non-inference policy, the transportation and market revolutions were achieved more rapidly.
공화국 초기의 미국인들이 불간섭 정책을 채택하지 않았기에 운송과 시장 혁명이 더욱 빠르게 이루어졌다.

Choose the number with a correct set of statements that can be restated or inferred from the original text.
주어진 글에서 추론하거나 재진술 될 수 있는 올바른 문장을 고르시오.

① Ⓐ & Ⓑ　　② Ⓑ & Ⓒ　　③ Ⓑ & Ⓓ
④ Ⓐ,Ⓒ & Ⓓ　　 Ⓑ,Ⓒ & Ⓓ

해석
❶ 만약 공화국 초기의 미국인들이 종종 자신들의 탓이라고 오해를 받는 '자유 방임'(무간섭)의 정치경제 개념을 따랐다면, 운송과 시장의 혁명은 훨씬 더 느리게 이루어졌을 것이다. ❷ 그렇게 하는 (자유 방임을 따르는) 대신, 미국 국민들은 그들의 정부에게 민간기업과 제휴를 해서 진보를 향한 행진의 속도를 더 높일 것을 요구했다.

해설
첫 번째 문장에서 정치만의 분야를 말하지 않고 '정치경제 개념'이라고 말하고 있다. 따라서 Ⓐ는 위에서 언급한 내용과 다르며, 나머지는 모두 언급되고 있다.

어휘
transportation n. 운송, 수송　revolution n. 혁명, 변혁　laissez-faire n. 자유방임, 방종　non-interference n. 불간섭　notion n. 관념, 개념; 생각　ascribe v. (원인·동기 등을) ~에 돌리다; (결과 등을) ~의 탓으로 삼다　ally v. 동맹[결연, 연합, 제휴]하게 하다　enterprise n. 기획, 계획; 사업, 기업　speed v. 진척시키다, 추진[촉진]하다; 바르게 하다　notable a. 주목할 만한, 두드러진, 현저한　alliance n. 동맹, 맹약; 협력, 제휴　republic n. 공화국　frequently ad. 빈번히, 종종　misunderstand v. 오해하다　adopt v. 채택하다, 받아들이다

006 ③   2019학년도 숙명여자대학교 인문계 27번

글의 주제

❶ Macroeconomics is the study of the whole market economy.
❷ Like other parts of economics, / macroeconomics uses the central idea (that people make purposeful decisions / with scarce resources). ❸ However, instead of focusing on the workings of one market — / (whether the market for peanuts or the market for bicycles) — macroeconomics focuses on the economy as a whole. ❹ Macroeconomics looks at the big picture: Economic growth, recessions, unemployment, and inflation are / among its subject matter. ❺ Macroeconomics is important to you and your future / since you will have a much better chance (of finding a desirable job) / after you graduate from college / during a period of economic expansion / than a period of recession. ❻ Strong economic growth can help alleviate poverty, free up resources (to clean up the environment), and lead to a brighter future / for your generation.

Which of the following is TRUE for the above passage?
다음 중 윗글에서 옳은 것은 무엇인가?

① Macroeconomics uses the idea that people use enough data to reach decisions.
거시경제학은 사람들이 충분한 자료를 사용하여 결정한다는 개념을 사용한다.

② Macroeconomics is selective in the sense that it focuses on a critical area.
거시경제학은 중요한 하나의 영역에 초점을 맞춘다는 점에서 선별적이다.

✓③ Macroeconomics helps us to understand the future economic directions better.
거시경제학은 우리가 미래의 경제 방향을 더 잘 이해할 수 있도록 도와준다.

④ Macroeconomics could result in economic recession and poverty.
거시경제학은 경제 침체와 빈곤을 초래할 수 있다.

⑤ Macroeconomics always provides a blue print for the bright future.
거시경제학은 매번 밝은 미래를 위한 청사진(상세한 계획)을 제공한다.

해석

❶ 거시경제학은 시장경제 전체에 관한 학문이다. ❷ 다른 경제학 분야와 마찬가지로, 거시경제학은 사람들이 부족한 자원으로 목적에 부합하는 결정을 내린다는 중심 개념을 사용한다. ❸ 하지만 거시경제학은 땅콩 시장이든 자전거 시장이든 한 가지 시장의 작용에 초점을 맞추는 것 대신, 경제 전반에 초점을 맞추고 있다. ❹ 거시경제학은 큰 그림(전체적인 상황)을 보며, 경제 성장, 경기 후퇴, 실업률, 인플레이션 등이 거시경제학의 주된 주제이다. ❺ 경기가 침체되어 있을 때보다 경기가 확대되는 시기에 대학 졸업 후에 바람직한 직업을 찾을 수 있는 기회가 훨씬 더 많을 것이기 때문에, 거시경제학은 당신과 당신의 미래에 중요하다. ❻ 강력한 경제 성장은 빈곤을 완화하고, 자원을 원활히 확보하여 환경정화를 위해 쓸 수 있게 해주며, 여러분의 세대를 위한 보다 밝은 미래를 가져올 수 있다.

해설

거시경제학의 정의와 특징을 말하고 있으며 ❺, ❻번 문장에서 거시경제학이 미래에 어떻게 도움이 되는지를 말하고 있다.

어휘

macroeconomics n. 거시경제학 purposeful a. 목적이 있는, 합목적적인, 과단성 있는; 의미 있는 scarce a. 부족한, 드문 big picture 큰 그림, 전체적인 상황 recession n. 경기 후퇴, 불경기, 불황 inflation n. 팽창 desirable a. 바람직한, 탐나는, 호감이 가는 alleviate v. 완화하다 poverty n. 가난, 빈곤 free up ~을 해방하다, 풀어주다; 해소하다

007 ①

2019학년도 한성대학교 인문계 A형 26번

The nature of acquiring languages is still quite mysterious. Children seem to have a natural inclination toward learning to speak from birth, and they are capable of quickly speaking intelligently. Three theories have been developed by researchers as to why children are able to learn a language with ease. These theories attempt to clarify some of the unfamiliar aspects of language acquisition. Specifically, they examine the behavior children exhibit during the various stages of speech development. The conditioning theory, the imitation theory, and the innateness theory all concentrate on the distinctive characteristics of this development. No single theory is sufficient to completely explain the various characteristics of language acquisition, despite the fact that research on the subject is expanding. However, when taken together, the conditioning, imitation, and innateness theories can provide some assistance in comprehending the subtleties of language development in children.

Which one CANNOT be inferred from the passage?
다음 중 이 글에서 추론할 수 없는 것은 무엇인가?

✓ ① One theory is enough to expound the acquisition of languages.
언어 습득을 상세히 설명하는 데는 한 가지 이론으로 충분하다.

② Children learn languages effortlessly.
아이들은 노력하지 않고 언어를 배운다.

③ Researchers have not ceased studying language acquisition.
연구원들은 언어 습득에 관한 연구를 계속하고 있다.

④ The ability to acquire languages is still enigmatic.
언어를 습득하는 능력은 여전히 수수께끼다.

해석 ❶ 언어 습득의 본질은 여전히 매우 신비하다. ❷ 아이들은 태어날 때부터 말을 배우려는 타고난 성향이 있는 것 같으며, ❸ 곧 말을 지능적으로 할 수 있게 된다. ❹ 연구원들은 아이들이 왜 언어를 쉽게 배울 수 있는지에 대한 세 가지 이론을 개발했다. ❺ 이 이론들은 언어 습득에 대해 알려지지 않은 부분들을 명확하게 하려고 한다. ❻ 특히, 그들은 언어 발달의 다양한 단계에서 아이들이 보여주는 행동들을 조사한다. ❼ 조건화 이론, 모방 이론, 그리고 생득 이론은 모두 이런 언어 발달의 독특한 특징에 집중한다.
❽ 언어 발달에 대한 연구가 확대되고 있음에도 불구하고, 어떤 이론도 그 이론 하나만으로는 언어 습득에 대한 다양한 특징을 완전히 설명하기에 충분하지 않다. ❾ 그러나 조건화, 모방, 생득 이론을 종합해 본다면 아이들의 언어 발달의 중요한 세부 요소들을 이해하는 데 도움을 줄 수 있다.

해설 언어 습득의 본질을 소재로 아이들이 언어를 쉽게 배우는지에 대한 세 가지 이론을 말하는 글이다. 따라서 ①은 내용과 일치하지 않는다.

어휘 acquire v. 습득하다 inclination n. 의향[뜻]; 성향 be capable of ~할 수 있다 clarify v. 명확하게 하다, 분명하게 말하다 exhibit v. 나타내다, 보이다 innateness n. 타고남, 천부적임, 본질적임 concentrate v. 집중하다, 전념하다 distinctive a. 구별적인, 구별이 있는, 특수한 assistance n. 원조, 조력, 보조 comprehend v. 이해하다 subtlety n. 미묘함; 중요한 세부 요소[사항]들 expound v. 자세히 설명하다

008 ②
2019학년도 국민대학교 인문계 오전 A형 18번

❶ The movie ("Deadpool,") (which has so far taken more than $500 million in cinemas worldwide), is an atypical blockbuster (a foul-mouthed anti-hero film with a mature "R" audience rating). ❷ But in one important respect, it is typical of many of Hollywood's recent successful movies: ❸ it does not bank on a world-famous star to sell it. ❹ In contrast, two recent "star vehicle" films struggled in vain to attract audiences despite heavy promotion and high-profile openings. ❺ Much of the film industry's recent success, (at home and abroad), comes from the rise (of the big special-effects event film). ❻ Such productions are more likely to make stars than to be made by them. ❼ Yet there is one arena (where stars are as relevant as ever: the international market). ❽ Foreign cinemas like to exhibit films with known names in the lead roles. ❾ Some old-school stars are still big draws in the international market, even if the movies (in which they appear) are flops at home. ❿ Even if big names have lost some of their luster at home, abroad they can be "sort of like supernovas," a studio executive says. ⓫ "They have flamed out a long time ago, but the light shines on past their death."

According to the passage, which is NOT true?
위 글에 의하면, 다음 중 옳지 않은 것은?

① "Deadpool" is one of the "R"-rated movies.
"데드풀"은 "R" 등급 영화 중의 하나다.

✓② Many Hollywood's recent successful movies are "star vehicle" films.
최근에 흥행한 여러 할리우드 영화는 "흥행의 성공을 스타에 의존하는" 영화다.

③ There is no appearance of world-famous stars in "Deadpool."
"데드풀"에는 세계적으로 유명한 스타가 전혀 등장하지 않는다.

④ Big names still have influence in drawing audiences in the international market.
해외 시장에서는 여전히 관객을 끌어들이는 데 유명한 배우가 영향을 미치고 있다.

해석

❶ 지금까지 전 세계 극장에서 5억 달러 이상을 벌어들인 영화 "데드풀"은 기존의 틀에서 벗어난 블록버스터로, 욕설이 난무하는 반(反)영웅적인 성인용 "R" 관객 등급의 영화이다. ❷ 그러나 한 가지 중요한 측면에서 이 영화는 할리우드에서 최근 흥행한 여러 영화를 대표하는데, ❸ 즉 그것은 영화의 선전을 위해 세계적으로 유명한 스타에 의존하지 않는다는 것이다. ❹ 이와 대조적으로, 최근 개봉된 두 편의 "스타 비히클" 영화(출중난 스타를 중심으로 만들어진 영화)는 대대적인 홍보와 이목을 집중시키는 개봉행사에도 불구하고 관객을 끌어들이는 데 실패하고 말았다. ❺ 영화업계가 국내외에서 최근 거뒀던 성공의 많은 부분은 대형 특수효과 이벤트 영화의 부상에서 기인한 것이다. ❻ 그런 영화 제작은 스타에 의해 만들어지기보다는 스타를 만들어낼 가능성이 더 크다. ❼ 그러나 변함없이 스타의 존재가 의미 있는 무대가 하나 있는데, 그것은 바로 해외 시장이다. ❽ 외국의 극장에서는 유명 배우가 주연을 맡은 영화를 상영하는 것을 좋아한다. ❾ 일부 한물간 스타들이 출연하는 영화가 국내에서는 실패하더라도 해외 시장에서 이 스타들은 여전히 많은 관객을 끌어 모은다. ❿ 유명 배우들이 국내시장에서는 광채를 다소 잃었겠지만, 해외에서는 "어느 정도 초신성(超新星)과 같은 것" 일 수 있다고 한 영화 제작 관계자는 말한다. ⓫ "그들은 불꽃을 다 피우고 꺼져버린 지 오래됐지만, 그 빛은 죽은 뒤에도 빛나는 것입니다."

해설

본문 ❸ 문장에서 '영화의 선전을 위해 세계적으로 유명한 스타에 의존하지 않는다'라고 말하고 있다. 따라서 ②에서 말하는 '흥행의 성공을 스타에 의존하는 영화'라고 말하는 부분은 본문과 일치하지 않는다.

어휘

atypical a. 틀에 박히지 않은, 격식을 벗어난 foul-mouthed a. 입버릇이 상스러운, 상스러운 말을 많이 하는 mature a. 성숙한, (영화·연극 따위가) 성인용의 rating n. 등급 be typical of ~를 대표하다 bank on ~을 의지하다 sell v. 선전하다 star vehicle 스타 비히클(대중적으로 인기가 높은 스타의 매력을 중심으로 제작된 영화) in vain 헛되이 attract v. (주의·흥미 등을) 끌다, (사람을) 끌어들이다 high-profile a. 세간의 이목을 끄는, 눈에 띄는 arena n. (고대 로마의) 투기장; (일반적) 경기장; 활동 장소, 활약 무대 relevant a. (당연한 문제에) 관련된; 적절한, 타당한, 의미 있는 old-school a. 구식의, 전통적인 flop n. 툭 떨어뜨림, 픽 쓰러짐; (책·연극 등의) 실패작 luster n. 광택; 영광, 영예 supernova n. 초신성(超新星) executive n. 경영진, 경영 간부 flame out (제트 엔진이) 갑자기 멈추다, 갑자기 타오르다; 기운이 꺾이다, 힘을 전부 발휘하다

009 ②

2019학년도 한양대학교 에리카 인문계 A형 32번

❶ Doctors Without Borders (Medecins Sans Frontieres, or MSF) is an international medical humanitarian organization. ❷ The doctors, nurses, and other medical specialists who work with MSF are dedicated to helping people in crisis situations / regardless of their race, religion, or political affiliation. ❸ Since 1971, / MSF teams have been responsible for / providing quality medical care / in nearly 60 countries. ❹ The teams have well-qualified specialists who are familiar with working in difficult, even dangerous, circumstances and the majority of MSF's aid workers are / from the communities where the crises are occurring. ❺ The work of MSF teams is not limited / to offering direct medical care; ❻ they also share a commitment / about serving as witnesses / to the crises of the people (they assist). ❼ However, as an organization, / MSF is neutral. ❽ It has a reputation / for not taking sides / in armed conflicts and for being concerned with providing care / on the basis of need alone). ❾ This belief in operating independently of government or other parties and obtaining independent funding is the key to MSF's ability / to conduct its aid efforts.

위 글의 내용과 맞지 <u>않는</u> 것을 고르시오.

① MSF aims to provide qualified medical care to people in crisis.
  MSF는 위기상황에 놓인 사람들에게 훌륭한 의료 서비스를 제공하는 것을 목표로 한다.
✓ Most MSF members are volunteers from communities in peaceful situations.
  대부분의 MSF 회원들은 평화로운 상황에 있는 지역에서 온 자원봉사자들이다.
③ MSF aims to obtain funding independently of government or other parties.
  MSF는 정부나 다른 당사자들로부터 독립적으로 자금을 공급하는 것을 목표로 한다.
④ MSF offers direct medical care but stays away from political matters.
  MSF는 의료 서비스를 직접 제공하되 정치적인 문제에는 관여하지 않는다.

해 석 ❶ 국경없는 의사회(Médecins San Frontières, MSF)는 인도주의적 국제 의료 단체이다. ❷ MSF와 함께 일하는 의사, 간호사, 그리고 그 밖의 의료 전문가들은 위기 상황에 처한 사람들을 인종, 종교, 정치적인 소속과 상관없이 돕는 데 헌신하고 있다. ❸ 1971년부터 MSF는 거의 60개국에 양질의 의료 서비스를 제공하는 일을 맡아왔다. ❹ MSF에는 어렵고 심지어는 위험한 환경에서 일하는 것에 익숙한 뛰어난 전문가들이 있고 ❺ MSF에서 하는 일은 직접 의료 서비스를 제공하는 것에만 국한되지 않는다. ❻ 또한 그들이 돕고 있는 사람들이 처한 위기를 증언하는 역할도 맡고 있다. ❼ 하지만, 조직으로서의 MSF는 중립적이다. ❽ MSF는 무력분쟁에서 어느 쪽의 편도 들지 않으며 오직 도움이 필요한 것인지 만을 기준으로 의료 서비스를 제공하는 데 관여하는 것으로 잘 알려져 있다. ❾ 정부나 다른 당사자들로부터 독립적으로 운영되고 독자적으로 자금을 확보한다는 이러한 신념이 MSF가 구호활동을 수행할 수 있는 비결이다.

해 설 ❹ 문장에서 'MSF에는 어렵고 심지어는 위험한 환경에서 일하는~'이라고 말하고 있다. 따라서 ②은 일치하지 않는다.

어 휘 humanitarian a. 인도주의의, 박애의 organization n. 조직, 기구 specialist n. 전문가 dedicated a. 헌신적인 crisis n. 위기, 난국 regardless of ~에 관계없이, ~와 상관없이 affiliation n. (개인의 정치·종교적) 소속[가입]; 제휴 commitment n. 의무, 책무, 책임 witness n. 증인; 목격자 neutral a. 중립적인, 중립의 reputation n. 평판; 명성 take sides 편들다 armed conflict 무력분쟁 on the basis of ~을 기초로 하여 obtain v. 얻다, 획득하다 independent a. 독립적인, 독자적인 conduct v. (특정한 활동을) 하다, 지휘하다

010 ③   2019학년도 국민대학교 인문계 오전 A형 33번

❶ Stress is inevitable. ❷ No one can prevent it. ❸ But we can try to minimize its harmful effects / on our health. ❹ To understand (how some people keep their composure) / while others crumble / under the pressure, / it is useful / to examine the coping process and ask the question: ❺ What are some adaptive ways (to cope with stress)?
❻ Researchers distinguished two general types of coping strategies. ❼ The first is problem-focused coping, (designed to reduce stress / by overcoming the source of the problem). ❽ Difficulties in school? ❾ Study harder or hire a tutor. ❿ The goal is to attack the source of your stress. ⓫ A second-approach is emotion-focused coping, (in which one tries to manage the emotional turmoil), perhaps / by learning to live with the problem. ⓬ If you're struggling at school, at work, or in a relationship, / you can keep a stiff upper lip and ignore the situation or make the best of it. ⓭ People probably take an active problem-focused approach / when (they think) they can overcome a stressor / ⓮ but fall back on an emotion-focused approach / when they see the problem / as out of their control.

Which can be inferred as an example of emotion-focused coping?
다음 중 감정 중심인 대처법의 예로 추론할 수 있는 것은?

① Talking to parents when you have problems with them
부모님과의 관계에 문제가 있을 때 부모님과 대화하는 것

② Asking a stranger for a cell phone when you lost your phone
핸드폰을 분실했을 때 낯선 사람에게 핸드폰을 빌려달라고 청하는 것

✓ Trying to keep calm when you are in stressful situations
스트레스를 많이 받는 상황에 처해 있을 때 침착하려 노력하는 것

④ Studying extra time when you have academic difficulties at school
학교에서 학업에 어려움을 겪을 때 추가적으로 더 공부하는 것

해석
❶ 스트레스는 불가피하다. ❷ 아무도 스트레스를 막을 수 없다. ❸ 하지만 우리는 스트레스가 건강에 미치는 해로운 영향을 최소화하도록 노력할 수 있다. ❹ 어떤 사람들은 스트레스를 받고도 평정성을 유지하는 반면, 어떤 사람들은 (스트레스에) 무너지고 마는지를 이해하기 위해서는 스트레스에 대처하는 과정을 살펴보고 다음과 같은 질문을 던져보는 것이 유용하다. ❺ 스트레스에 대처하기 위한 적절한 방법들에는 어떤 것들이 있는가?
❻ 과학자들은 대처 전략을 일반적인 두 가지 유형으로 구분했다. ❼ 첫 번째로는 문제 중심의 대처 전략으로, 문제의 근원을 극복함으로써 스트레스를 줄일 수 있도록 하는 것이다. ❽ 학교생활에서 어려움을 겪는다고? ❾ 그렇다면 더 열심히 공부하거나 가정교사를 두도록 해라. ❿ 목표는 스트레스의 근원을 공격하는 것이다. ⓫ 두 번째 접근방법은 감정 중심의 대처 전략으로, 이 전략에서는 그 문제를 감수하는 방법을 배움으로써 감정적인 혼란을 다스리려고 노력하게 된다. ⓬ 만약 당신이 학교에서, 직장에서, 혹은 대인관계에서 어려움을 겪고 있다면, 당신은 꿋꿋하게 버텨내서 그 상황을 무시하거나 최대한 이용할 수 있다. ⓭ 사람들은 자신들이 스트레스 요인을 극복할 수 있다고 생각할 때 아마도 문제 중심의 접근법을 취하겠지만, ⓮ 그 문제를 자신이 통제할 수 없는 것으로 판단될 때에는 감정 중심적인 접근법에 의지할 것이다.

해설
지문에서 말하는 두 번째 스트레스 해결책은 '문제를 감수하는 방법을 배워 감정적인 혼란을 다스리려 노력한다'라는 것이다. 따라서 ③에서 말하는 '침착하려 노력하는 것'이 여기에 해당한다.

어휘
inevitable a. 피할 수 없는, 면할 수 없는, 필연적인 prevent v. 막다, 방해하다 minimize v. 최소화하다 composure n. 침착, 냉정, 평정, 자제 crumble v. 부서지다, 가루가 되다; 무너지다 cope v. 대처하다, 극복하다, 대항하다 adaptive a. 적합한, 적응하는; 적응을 돕는 distinguish v. 구별하다, 분별하다 strategy n. 계획, 전략 reduce v. 줄이다, 축소하다 overcome v. 극복하다 tutor n. 가정교사 turmoil n. 소란, 소동, 혼란 struggle v. 고군분투하다, 힘겹게 나아가다 keep a stiff upper lip 참다, 견디다 stressor n. 스트레스 요인 fall back on 의지하다, 의존하다

정답 및 해설

011 A) ③ **B)** ③ ··· 2019학년도 경기대학교 인문·예체능계 A형 31,34번

❶ Nature challenges humans / in many ways, / through disease, weather, and famine. ❷ For those living along the coast, / one unusual phenomenon (capable of catastrophic destruction) is the tsunami. ❸ A tsunami is a series of waves (generated in a body of water / by an impulsive disturbance). ❹ Earthquakes, landslides, volcanic eruptions, explosions, and even the impact of meteorites can generate tsunamis. ❺ Starting at sea, / a tsunami slowly approaches land, / growing in height and losing energy / through bottom friction and turbulence. ❻ Still, just like any other water waves, / tsunamis unleash tremendous energy / as they plunge onto the shore. ❼ They have great erosion potential, stripping beaches of sand, undermining trees, and flooding hundreds of meters inland. ❽ They can easily crush cars, homes, vegetation, and anything : (they collide with). ❾ To minimize the devastation of a tsunami, / scientists are constantly trying to anticipate them more accurately and more quickly. ❿ Because many factors come together / to produce a life-threatening tsunami, / foreseeing them is not easy. ⓫ Despite this, / researchers (in meteorology) persevere in studying / and : predicting tsunami behavior.

해석

❶ 자연은 질병, 날씨, 그리고 기근을 통해 여러 가지 방법으로 인간에게 도전한다. ❷ 해안 지역의 사람들에게는, 재앙적인 파괴를 가져올 수 있는 흔치 않은 현상이 쓰나미다. ❸ 쓰나미는 충격적인 동요에 의해 수역(바다)에서 생성되는 일련의 파도이다. ❹ 지진, 산사태, 화산 분출, 폭발, 그리고 심지어 운석의 충돌까지 쓰나미를 일으킬 수 있다. ❺ 바다에서 시작된 쓰나미는 서서히 육지로 접근하면서 바닥의 마찰과 물결의 거친 몰아침으로 인하여 높이는 높아지고 에너지를 잃게 된다. ❻ 그럼에도 불구하고, 다른 파도와 마찬가지로 쓰나미 또한 해안에서 밀려올 때 엄청난 에너지를 방출한다. ❼ 쓰나미는 침식하는 힘이 매우 강하여, 해변에서 모래를 쓸어내고, 나무들의 밑을 파서 훼손시키며, 내륙으로 수백 미터까지 물에 잠기게 한다. ❽ 쓰나미는 자동차, 집, 초목, 그리고 충돌하는 어떤 것이든 쉽게 파괴할 수 있다. ❾ 쓰나미에 의한 피해를 최소화하기 위해, 과학자들은 더 정확하고 빠르게 쓰나미를 예측하려고 끊임없이 노력하고 있다. ❿ 많은 요인들이 모여서 생명을 위협하는 쓰나미가 발생하기 때문에, 이것을 예측하기는 쉽지 않다. ⓫ 그럼에도 불구하고, 기상학자들은 쓰나미의 움직임을 연구하고 예측하는 일에 끈기 있게 임하고 있다.

어휘

famine n. 기근, 굶주림, 배고픔, 기아(饑餓) **phenomenon** n. 현상 **catastrophic** a. 큰 재앙의, 파멸의, 비극적인 **destruction** n. 파괴, 파멸 **generate** v. 산출하다; (전기·열 등을) 발생시키다, (결과·상태 등을) 야기하다, 초래하다 **impulsive** a. 충동적인, 추진적인 **disturbance** n. 소동, 방해, 교란, 외란(外亂; 상태를 혼란시키려는 외적 작용) **landslide** n. 산사태 **volcanic** a. 화산의, 화산성의, 화산작용에 의한 **eruption** n. (화산의) 폭발, 분화; (용암·간헐천의) 분출 **meteorite** n. 운석 **friction** n. 마찰 **turbulence** n. (바람·물결 등의) 거세게 몰아침; (사회·정치적인) 소란 **unleash** v. 촉발시키다, 자유롭게 하다 **tremendous** a. 무서운, 굉장한, 엄청난 **plunge** v. 뛰어들다, 몰입하다, 돌진하다 **shore** n. 해안, 호숫가, (해안을 낀) 나라 **erosion** n. 부식, 침식 **potential** n. 잠재력, 가능성 **strip** v. 벗기다, ~로부터 빼앗다[제거하다] **undermine** v. ~의 밑을 파다; (명성 따위를) 음험한 수단으로 훼손하다 **flood** v. 범람시키다, 물에 잠기게 하다 **collide with** ~와 충돌하다 **minimize** v. 최소화하다 **devastation** n. 황폐하게 함, 유린 **constantly** ad. 항상, 끊임없이 **accurately** ad. 정확하게 **foresee** v. 예견하다, 앞일을 내다보다 **meteorology** n. 기상학 **persevere** v. 인내하며 계속하다, 인내심을 갖고 하다 **predict** v. 예언하다, 예보하다

A) In the first sentence, why does the author mention weather?
첫 번째 문장에서, 저자가 날씨를 언급하는 이유는 무엇인가?
① because tsunamis are caused by bad weather
쓰나미는 악천후 때문에 발생하기 때문에
② because tsunamis are more destructive than weather phenomena
쓰나미는 기상 현상들보다 더욱 파괴적이기 때문에
✓③ as an example of a destructive natural force
파괴적인 자연력의 예시로서
④ as an introduction to the topic of coastal storms
해안 폭풍이라는 주제에 관한 도입부로서

B) Which sentence best expresses the essential information of this passage?
다음의 문장 중 위 글의 핵심 정보를 가장 잘 나타내는 것은?
① Tsunamis could become a new source of usable energy in the near future.
쓰나미는 가까운 미래에 사용할 수 있는 새로운 에너지원이 될 것이다.
② Tsunamis do more damage to the land than flooding.
쓰나미는 홍수보다 육지에 더 큰 피해를 준다.
✓③ Tsunamis can have an especially catastrophic impact on coastal communities.
쓰나미는 특히나 해안 지역에 파멸적인 영향을 미칠 수 있다.
④ Scientists can predict and track tsunamis with a fair degree of accuracy, reducing their potential impact.
과학자들은 쓰나미를 꽤 정확하게 예측하고 추적할 수 있어서 그 잠재적 영향을 줄일 수 있다.

해설

A) 첫 번째 문장에서 질병, 날씨, 기근 등 모두 인간에게 도전한다고 말하고 있으며, 이어지는 문장부터는 쓰나미의 위력을 말하는 글이다. 따라서 ③이 가장 적절하다.

B) 윗글의 요지를 묻는 유형이다. 따라서 글은 쓰나미의 위력을 말하는 만큼 ③이 가장 적절하다.

정답 및 해설

012 ⑤   2019학년도 인하대학교 인문계 16번

❶ Most of us are good at spotting overtly aggressive people. ❷ While it doesn't feel good / when someone insults, criticizes, or belittles you, / at least you know : why you are hurting. ❸ But sometimes / the people (around us), (including our close family, friends, and colleagues), make us feel uncomfortable, / but we cannot quite put a finger on why. ❹ For example, your friend may fail to greet you / in the hallway for the third time / in a week. ❺ You make yourself believe / that it is probably a slip, / yet you feel / that something is amiss. ❻ If this happens frequently / with one or more people / in your life, / ❼ you may be dealing with passive-aggressive behavior, which is much harder to detect / than overtly aggressive behavior. ❽ Passive aggression is a tendency [to engage in / implicit expression of hostility / through acts / such as subtle insults, sullen behavior, stubbornness, or a deliberate failure (to accomplish required tasks)]. ❾ Because passive-aggressive behavior is implicit, / it can be hard / to spot, / even when you're feeling the psychological consequences. ❿ To help you identify this type of behavior, / I describe five instances of it / below. ⓫ These are not all of the ways (a person can be passive-aggressive), / but they are the most common.

What will be discussed right after the passage?
위 글의 바로 뒤에서 논의될 것은?

① Comparison of aggressive behaviors
   공격적인 행동들의 비교
② Causes of passive aggression
   소극적인 공격성의 원인
③ Ways to deal with passive aggression
   소극적인 공격성을 다루는 방식
④ Effects of passive aggression
   소극적인 공격성의 영향
✓ Examples of passive-aggressive behavior
   소극적인 공격성 행동의 예시

해석
❶ 우리 대부분은 공공연하게 공격적인 사람들을 잘 알아차린다. ❷ 누군가가 당신을 모욕하거나 비판하고 혹은 얕보는 경우에 기분이 좋지 않지만, 적어도 당신은 왜 당신이 상처를 받고 있는지 알고 있다. ❸ 그러나 가까운 가족, 친구, 동료들을 비롯한 주변 사람들이 우리의 마음을 불편하게 만들 때도 있지만 그 이유를 콕 집어서 알 수 없는 경우가 때때로 있다. ❹ 예를 들어, 친구가 일주일에 세 번이나 복도에서 인사를 하지 않을 수도 있다. ❺ 당신은 친구가 당신을 못 보고 지나간 거라고 애써 믿기는 하지만, 뭔가가 잘못되었다고 느끼게 된다. ❻ 만약 살면서 이런 일이 여러 명의 사람들에게서 자주 일어난다면, ❼ 여러분은 소극적인 공격성 행동을 마주하고 있는 것일 수도 있는데, 이것은 공공연한 공격성 행동보다 알아채는 것이 훨씬 더 어렵다. ❽ 소극적인 공격성은 포착하기 어려운 모욕적 언행, 무뚝뚝한 행동, 완고함, 또는 시킨 일을 의도적으로 완수하지 않는 것 등과 같은 행동들을 통해 적개심을 암묵적으로 표출하려는 경향이다. ❾ 소극적인 공격성 행동은 암묵적이기 때문에, 그 심리적인 영향을 느낄 때조차도 발견하는 것이 어려울 수 있다. ❿ 이런 종류의 행동을 식별하는 것에 도움을 주기 위하여, 아래에서 그러한 행동의 다섯 가지 사례를 설명하겠다. ⓫ 이것들이 사람이 소극적인 공격성을 보일 수 있는 행동들 전부는 아니겠지만 가장 흔한 것들이다.

해설
이어질 유형을 물을 때는 마지막 문장에 유의해야 한다. 지문의 마지막 부분에서 '그러한 행동의 다섯 가지 사례를 설명한다'라고 한 만큼 ⑤이 가장 적절하다.

어휘
spot v. (누구인지) 알아맞히다, 발견하다, 탐지하다 overtly ad. 공공연히, 명백하게 aggressive a. 공격적인, 호전적인 insult v. 모욕하다 n. 모욕, 무례 criticize v. 비평하다, 비판하다 belittle v. 경시하다, 얕보다 colleague n. 동료, 동업자 cannot put a finger on ~에 대해 이유를 꼬집어 말할 수 없다 greet v. ~에게 인사하다 hallway n. 복도, 현관 slip n. 과실, 잘못; (못 보고) 빠뜨림 amiss a. 잘못된 frequently ad. 자주, 빈번하게 passive a. 수동적인, 소극적인 detect v. 간파하다, ~임을 알았다 tendency n. 경향, 성향 engage in ~에 종사하다, 관계하다 implicit a. 암시된, 내포하는 hostility n. 적개심, 적대행위 subtle a. 미묘한, 포착하기 힘든 sullen a. 무뚝뚝한; 음울한 stubbornness n. 완고, 완강 deliberate a. 계획적인, 고의의, 신중한 identify v. (본인·동일인물임을) 확인하다, (사랑의 성명·신원 따위를) 인지하다 instance n. 실례, 사례

013 ②

글의 주제

2019학년도 덕성여자대학교 사회·자연·예술대학 27번

① The variety of life on Earth, (its biological diversity), is commonly referred to as biodiversity. ② The number of species (of plants, animals, and microorganisms), (the enormous diversity of genes in these species, the different ecosystems on the planet, such as deserts, rainforests and coral reefs) are all part of a biologically diverse Earth. ③ Appropriate conservation and sustainable development strategies attempt to recognize this as being integral to any approach. ④ In some way or form, almost all cultures have recognized the importance of nature and its biological diversity (for their societies) and have therefore understood the need to maintain it. ⑥ Yet, power, greed and politics have affected the precarious balance.

⑦ Why is Biodiversity important? ⑧ Does it really matter if there aren't so many species? ⑨ Biodiversity boosts ecosystem productivity [where each species, (no matter how small), all have an important role (to play)]. ⑩ For example, a larger number of plant species means a greater variety of crops; greater species diversity ensures natural sustainability (for all life forms); ⑪ and healthy ecosystems can better withstand and recover from a variety of disasters. ⑫ And so, while we dominate this planet, we still need to preserve the diversity in wildlife.

According to the author of this passage, why is biodiversity so important?
위 글의 저자에 의하면, 생물 다양성이 그토록 중요한 까닭은 무엇인가?

① because all cultures have recognized its importance
모든 문화가 그것의 중요성을 인식했기 때문이다.

✓ ② because all species no matter how big or small play an important part in ecosystem productivity
모든 종은 크든 작든 생태계의 생산성에 중요한 역할을 하기 때문이다.

③ because a diverse wildlife means a more beautiful world
다양한 야생동물이 더 아름다운 세상을 의미하기 때문이다.

④ because a greater variety of crops means a larger number of animal species
농작물이 더 다양하다는 것은 동물 종의 수가 더 많다는 것을 의미하기 때문이다.

해석

① 지구상에 있는 생물의 다양성, 즉, 지구의 생물학적 다양성은 흔히 생물 다양성이라고 불린다. ② 식물, 동물, 미생물의 종별 수, 이들 종에서 나타나는 엄청난 유전자의 다양성, 사막, 열대우림, 산호초와 같은 지구상의 서로 다른 생태계들은 모두 생물학적으로 다양한 지구의 일부분이다. ③ 적절한 보존 및 지속 가능한 개발 전략은 생물 다양성을 모든 접근방법에 필수 불가결한 것으로 인식하려 하고 있다. ④ 어떤 형태로든, 방식으로든, 거의 모든 문화는 그들의 사회에 자연과 자연의 생물학적 다양성이 중요하다는 것을 인식해왔고, ⑤ 따라서 그것을 유지해야 할 필요성을 알고 있었다. ⑥ 그러나 권력, 탐욕, 정치는 그 불안정한 균형에 악영향을 끼쳐 왔다.

⑦ "생물 다양성"은 왜 중요한가? ⑧ 만약 그만큼 많은 종이 없다면, 그게 정말로 문제가 되는 것일까? ⑨ 각각의 종이 아무리 작은 것이라 하더라도 모두 중요한 역할을 하고 있는 경우에 생물 다양성은 생태계의 생산성을 높여준다. ⑩ 예를 들어, 식물 종의 수가 더 많다는 것은 작물의 종류가 더 많다는 것을 의미하고, 종의 다양성이 보다 더 클수록 모든 생명체가 자연적으로 지속 가능하게 되며, ⑪ 건강한 생태계는 여러 가지 재난을 더 잘 견디고 또한 재난에서도 더 잘 회복될 수 있다. ⑫ 그래서 우리가 지구를 지배하면서도, 우리는 여전히 야생동물의 다양성을 보존해야 할 필요가 있다.

해설

두 번째 단락 ⑦ 문장에서 생물 다양성의 중요성에 관한 질문에 답변을 ⑨ 문장에서 하고 있다. 즉, '크든 작든 생태계의 생산성에 중요한 역할을 한다'고 말하고 있는 만큼 정답은 ②이 된다.

어휘

variety n. 변화, 다양성 **biological** a. 생물학의, 생물학상의 **diversity** n. 차이, 상이; 변화, 다양성 **microorganism** n. 미생물 **enormous** a. 거대한, 막대한 **gene** n. 유전자 **ecosystem** n. 생태계 **planet** n. 행성 **rainforest** n. 다우림(多雨林) **coral reef** 산호초 **diverse** a. 다양한, 가지각색의 **appropriate** a. 적합한, 적절한 **conservation** n. (자원·자원의) 보호, 관리; 보존, 유지 **sustainable** a. 유지[계속]할 수 있는; (자원 이용이) 환경이 파괴되지 않고 계속될 수 있는 **strategy** n. 작전, 전략 **attempt** v. 시도하다, 꾀하다 **recognize** v. 알아보다; 인지하다, 인정하다 **integral** a. 완전한, 완전체의, 필수적인 **approach** n. 접근; 접근법, 해결방법 **maintain** v. 지속하다, 유지하다 **greed** n. 탐욕, 욕심 **affect** v. 영향을 미치다, 악영향을 끼치다 **precarious** a. 불확실한, 불안정한 **boost** v. 끌어올리다, 증가시키다; 후원하다 **productivity** n. 생산성 **ensure** v. 보장하다, 확실하게 하다 **sustainability** n. 지속가능성 **withstand** v. ~에 저항하다; 잘 견디다, 버티다 **disaster** n. 재해, 재난 **dominate** v. 지배하다, 통치하다; 위압하다 **preserve** v. 보전하다, 유지하다; 보존하다

정답 및 해설

014 ②
2019학년도 서울여자대학교 인문·자연계 30번

In 2006, researchers at Cornell University released results of a long-term study containing some hypotheses about the reorganization of television in the 1980s. The research project assembled data to suggest a correlation between television viewing by very young children and autism. One of the most urgent problems in autism studies has been to explain the extraordinary and anomalous rise in its frequency beginning in the mid to late 1980s. From the late 1970s, when autism occurred in one out of 2,500 children, the rate of incidence has risen so fast that, as of a few years ago, it affected approximately one in 150 children, and showed no sign of leveling off. Obviously, television had been pervasive in North American homes since the 1950s. Why then might it have markedly different consequences beginning in the 1980s? The study proposes that a new coalescence of factors occurred in that decade — in particular, the widespread availability of cable TV, the growth of dedicated children's channels and video cassettes, and the popularity of VCRs, as well as huge increases in households with two or more television sets. Thus conditions were, and continue to be, in place for the exposure of very young children to television for extended periods of time on a daily basis. Their specific conclusions were relatively cautious: that extended television viewing before the age of three can trigger the onset of the disorder in "at risk" children.

해석
❶ 2006년 코넬(Cornell)대학교 연구원들이 어떤 장기 연구 결과를 발표했는데, 거기에는 1980년대 TV 구성의 변화에 관한 몇 가지 가설들이 포함되어 있었다. ❷ 이 연구 프로젝트는 매우 어린 나이인 아이의 TV 시청과 자폐증 간의 상관관계를 시사해 줄 데이터를 수집했다. ❸ 자폐증 연구에서 가장 시급한 문제 중 하나는 1980년대 중후반부터 자폐증 발생빈도가 어마어마하게 이례적으로 증가한 것을 설명하는 것이었다. ❹ 자폐증이 2,500명의 아이들 중 1명꼴로 발생했던 1970년대 후반부터 자폐증 발생비율이 너무 급격하게 증가한 결과, 몇 년 전부터, 자폐증은 150명의 아이들 중 대략 1명꼴로 발병하였으며, 안정될 조짐이 전혀 보이지 않았다. ❺ 분명히 TV는 1950년대 이래로 북미의 가정에 이미 널리 보급되어 있었다. ❻ 그렇다면 왜 TV가 1980년대부터 (예전과) 현저히 다른 결과를 가져오게 되었을까? ❼ 연구결과는 1980년대에 새로운 여러 요인들이 복합적으로 나타났다는 의견을 내놓는다. ❽ 그 요인에는 널리 보급된 케이블 TV, 어린이 전용 TV 채널과 비디오카세트의 증가, 그리고 TV를 2대 이상 보유하고 있는 가정의 엄청난 증가 등이 있었다. ❾ 따라서 매우 어린 아이가 매일 장시간 TV에 노출될 여건이 마련되었고, 계속해서 마련되어오고 있는 셈이다. ❿ 이 연구의 구체적인 결론은 비교적 신중했다. ⓫ 즉 3세 이전에 장시간 TV를 시청하는 것은 '자폐증 위험군의' 아동에게 자폐증 발병을 촉발시킬 수 있다는 것이었다.

어휘
hypothesis n. 가설 **reorganization** n. 개혁, 개편 **assemble** v. ~을 모으다, 소집하다 **correlation** n. 상관관계 **autism** n. 자폐증 **urgent** a. 긴급한, 시급한 **extraordinary** a. 비범한, 보통이 아닌, 대단한 **anomalous** a. 비정상의, 불규칙의 **frequency** n. 빈도, 주파수 **incidence** n. (병·빈곤·사건 등의) 발생 **leveling off** 평등화, 수평화 **pervasive** a. 만연하는 **markedly** ad. 현저하게, 두드러지게 **coalescence** n. 합체, 융합 **dedicated** a. ~전용의 **household** n. 가정 **trigger** v. 유발하다, 일으키다 **onset** n. (보통 불쾌한 일의) 시작 **disorder** n. (신체 기능의) 장애[이상] **at risk children** 위험 아동(현재 지적, 사회적 정서 및 행동장애가 있는 것으로 진단되지는 않았으나, 환경 요인 등으로 장차 장애를 가질 가능성이 있는 아동)

According to the passage, which of the following is true?
위 글에 의하면, 다음 중 옳은 것은?

① In North America, dedicated children's channels were already popular in the 1950s.
북미에서, 어린이 전용 TV 채널들은 1950년대에 이미 인기를 끌었다. (→ 1980년대)

☑ ② In the late 1970s, the rate of child autism incidence was no higher than one in 2,500 children.
1970년대 후반에, 소아 자폐증 발병비율은 2,500명당 1명에 불과했다.

③ Watching TV for an extended period of time tends to cause autism in adults as well as in children.
장시간 TV 시청은 아이뿐 아니라 어른에게도 자폐증을 유발하는 경향이 있다. (→ 어른과의 관련성 언급 없음)

④ A few years ago, the rate of child autism incidence stabilized with approximately one in 150 children affected.
몇 년 전, 소아 자폐증 발병비율은 대략 150명당 1명 비율로 안정되었다. (→ 안정되지 않았다)

해설 윗글은 TV 시청과 자폐증 간의 상관관계에 대한 글로서 ④ 문장에서 정답 내용을 확인할 수 있다.

015 ④ 2019학년도 홍익대학교 인문계 A형 32번

❶ In the eighteenth century, Linnaeus classed human beings as primates, placing them in the same genus as apes, monkeys, and lemurs. ❷ Then in 1859 Charles Darwin proclaimed his theory of evolution in The Origin of Species, suggesting (at first, he did not dare say it outright) that humanity evolved from something like an ape. ❸ There were passionate debates and embarrassed snickers people joked about having gorillas for grandfathers. ❹ Racists depicted those from other cultures — Africans, Irish, Jews, and Japanese — as being like apes. ❺ The targeted people were drawn as slouched over with dangling arms and receding foreheads. ❻ But modern people have feared above all the "animal" in themselves. ❼ The metaphor of "the beast within" was used in the Victorian era to explain all sorts of vices, from lechery to gluttony. ❽ Physiognomists looked for animal features in the faces of human beings. ❾ Sigmund Freud and his disciples divided human character into the "id," which represented the beast (or instinct) in human beings, and the "ego," or self — the two of which were in constant conflict. ❿ Today anthropomorphic animals are everywhere we look: ⓫ tigers sell cornflakes and gasoline, talking cows sell milk; bulls and ducks represent sports teams. ⓬ Centerfolds of undressed women in Playboy are called "bunnies," while in Penthouse, a rival magazine, they are called "pets." ⓭ The cartoon character Joe Camel was so effective in selling cigarettes to teenagers that massive protests forced the tobacco company to discontinue ads with him in 1997.

해석

❶ 18세기에, 린네(Linnaeus)는 인간을 영장류로 분류하면서, 유인원, 원숭이, 여우원숭이와 같은 속(屬)에 인간을 배치하였다. ❷ 그러다가 1859년 찰스 다윈(Charles Darwin)은 『종의 기원(The Origin of Species)』에서 그의 진화론을 발표하였고, 인류가 유인원과 유사한 어떤 동물에서 진화했다고 주장하였다. (처음에, 그는 감히 이 주장을 노골적으로 하지는 못했다.) ❸ 격렬한 논쟁이 벌어졌고, 당혹함에 킬킬거리며 비웃기도 했다. 사람들은 고릴라를 할아버지로 뒀다고 농담을 했다. ❹ 인종 차별주의자들은 다른 문화권의 사람들, 즉 아프리칸인, 아일랜드인, 유대인, 일본인을 유인원처럼 묘사했다. ❺ 표적이 된 사람들은 양팔이 늘어뜨려져 있고 이마가 뒤로 들어가 있으며 몸은 구부정한 자세를 하고 있는 모습으로 그려졌다.

❻ 그러나 현대인들은 무엇보다도 자신들 속에 있는 '동물'을 두려워해 왔다. ❼ '내면의 짐승'이라는 은유가 빅토리아 여왕 시대에서는 음란에서부터 폭식에 이르기까지 온갖 종류의 악행을 설명하기 위해 사용되었다. ❽ 인상학자들은 인간의 얼굴에서 동물의 특징들을 찾았다. ❾ 지그문트 프로이트(Sigmund Freud)와 그의 제자들은 인간의 특성을 인간의 수성(獸性), 즉 인간의 본능을 나타내는 '이드(id)'와 자아를 나타내는 '에고(ego)'로 나누었는데, 이 이드와 에고가 끊임없는 충돌 속에 있다고 보았다.

❿ 오늘날의 의인화된 동물들은 우리가 어딜 보든 그곳에 존재한다. ⓫ 호랑이들은 콘플레이크(Kellogg's Cornfrost를 지칭)와 휘발유(Esso의 Tiger Gasoline을 지칭)를 팔고 있고, 말하는 젖소들은 우유(Real California Milk를 지칭)를 팔고 있으며, 황소들(Chidago Bulls를 지칭)과 오리들(Anaheim Mighty Ducks를 지칭)은 각각 스포츠 팀을 대표하고 있다. ⓬ 『플레이보이(Playboy)』에서 발가벗은 여성 모델들은 '토끼'라고 불리는 반면, 경쟁 잡지인 『펜트하우스(Penthouse)』에서는 발가벗은 여성 모델들은 '펫'이라고 불린다. ⓭ (낙타를 의인화한) 만화 속 등장인물인 조 카멜(Joe Camel)은 십대들에게 담배를 판매하는 데 매우 효과적이어서 1997년에 열린 대규모 시위집회에서 조 카멜이 나오는 광고를 담배회사가 강제로 중단하도록 만들었다.

어휘

class v. ~을 같은 부류에 넣다 **primate** n. 영장류 **place** v. ~을 놓다 **genus** n. 종류; 〈생물〉(분류상의) 속(屬) **ape** n. 유인원(꼬리 없는 원숭이, 오랑우탄, 침팬지, 고릴라 등) **lemur** n. 여우원숭이 **proclaim** v. 선언하다, 발표하다 **outright** ad. 노골적으로 **passionate** a. 열정적인, 열렬한 **debate** n 논의, 토론 v. 논의하다, 숙고하다 **snicker** n. (남을 얕보는) 킬킬 웃음, 숨죽여 웃는 웃음 **racist** n. 인종 차별주의자 **depict** v. 그리다, 묘사하다 **slouch** v. (어깨·머리 등을) 앞으로 수그리다, 몸을 웅크리다 **dangle** v. ~을 매달리다 **receding forehead** 벗겨져서 점점 넓어지는 이마 **in oneself** 그 자체로는 **metaphor** n. 은유 **vice** n. 악, 악행 **lechery** n. 호색, 음탕; 음탕한 행위 **gluttony** n. 폭식, 과음 **physiognomist** n. 인상(人相)학자, 관상가 **disciple** n. 제자 **anthropomorphic** a. 의인화된, 사람의 모습을 닮은 **bull** n. (거세하지 않은) 황소 **centerfold** n. 잡지의 한가운데에 접어 넣는 페이지(누드 사진 등); 누드모델 **cartoon character** 만화 속 등장인물 **protest** n. 항의, 시위 **discontinue** v. 중단하다 **missing link** 잃어버린 고리; (특히 유인원과 인간 사이에서) 생물 진화 계도(系圖) 중 결여된 종류

According to the passage, which of the following is NOT true?
본문에 따르면 다음 중 사실이 아닌 것은?

① Both Linnaeus and Darwin were concerned with the animal classification.
린네와 다윈 모두 동물을 분류하는 데 관심이 있었다.

② Animals have often been used for the purpose of profit motivation.
동물들은 수익 동기부여 목적으로 종종 이용되었다.

③ Negative sentiments toward animals have "humanized" them.
동물들에 대한 부정적 정서가 동물들을 '인간화' 시켰다.

④ It was Freud who discovered the missing link between humans and animals.
인간과 동물들 사이의 잃어버린 연결고리를 발견한 사람은 바로 프로이트였다.

해설 첫 단락에서 찰스 다윈의 '종의 기원'에 대한 언급이다. 여기서 인류가 유인원과 유사한 어떤 동물에서 진화했다고 주장하고 있다. 따라서 정답은 프로이트가 아니라 다윈으로 해야 한다.

016 ④ 2020학년도 숭실대학교 인문계 26번

❶ For Marxism, an ideology is a belief system, and all belief systems are products of cultural conditioning. ❷ For example, capitalism, communism, Marxism, patriotism, religion, ethical systems, humanism, environmentalism, astrology, and karate are all ideologies. ❸ Even our assumption that nature behaves according to the laws of science is an ideology. ❹ However, although almost any experience or field of study we can think of has an ideological component, ❺ not all ideologies are equally productive or desirable. ❻ Undesirable ideologies promote repressive political agendas and, ❼ in order to ensure their acceptance among the citizenry, pass themselves off as natural ways of seeing the world instead of acknowledging themselves as ideologies. ❽ "It's natural for men to hold leadership positions because their biological superiority renders them more physically, intellectually, and emotionally capable than women" is a sexist that sells itself as a function of nature, rather than as a product of cultural belief. ❾ "Every family wants to own its own home on its own land" is a capitalist ideology that sells itself as natural by pointing, ❿ for example, to the fact that almost all Americans want to own their own property, without acknowledging that this desire is created in us by the capitalist culture in which we live. ⓫ By posing as natural ways of seeing the world, repressive ideologies prevent us from understanding the material/historical conditions in which we live ⓬ because they refuse to acknowledge that those conditions have any bearing on the way we see the world.

해석

❶ 마르크스주의에서 이데올로기(이념)는 신념체계이며, 모든 신념체계는 문화적 조건 형성의 산물이다. ❷ 예를 들면, 자본주의, 공산주의, 마르크스주의, 애국주의, 종교, 윤리체계, 인도주의, 환경보호주의, 점성술, 가라테 등은 모두 이데올로기들이다. ❸ 자연은 과학의 법칙에 따라서 작용한다는 우리의 가정도 이데올로기이다. ❹ 그러나 우리가 생각할 수 있는 거의 모든 경험이나 학문 분야가 이데올로기적 요소를 가지고 있지만, ❺ 모든 이데올로기가 똑같이 생산적이고 바람직한 것은 아니다. ❻ 바람직하지 못한 이데올로기는 억압적인 정치적 의제를 조장하고, ❼ 시민들 사이에서 확실히 수용되기 위해 스스로를 이데올로기로 인정하기보다는 세상을 바라보는 자연스러운 방법인 양 행세한다. ❽ "남성들의 생물학적 우월성이 그들을 신체적, 지적, 정서적으로 여성들보다 유능하게 하므로 남성들이 주도권을 갖는 것이 자연스럽다."는 것은 성차별적인 이데올로기인데, 이러한 것은 스스로를 문화적 신념의 산물로가 아니라 자연의 결과로 선전하는 이데올로기이다. ❾ "모든 가족은 자기 땅 위에 자신의 집을 갖고 싶어한다."는 것은 자본주의적인 이데올로기인데, ❿ 이것은 예를 들면 이러한 욕망은 우리가 살고 있는 자본주의 문화에 의해 우리 안에서 만들어진다는 것을 인정하지 않고 모든 미국인들이 그들 자신의 사유재산을 소유하기 원한다는 사실을 지적함으로써 스스로를 자연스러운 것으로 선전하는 이데올로기이다. ⓫ 억압적인 이데올로기는 세상을 보는 자연스러운 방법으로 행세함으로써 우리로 하여금 우리가 살고 있는 세상의 물질적/역사적 조건을 이해하지 못하게 한다. ⓬ 왜냐하면, 억압적인 이데올로기는 그러한 조건들이 우리가 세상을 보는 방식과 어떠한 관계가 있다는 것을 인정하기를 거부하기 때문이다.

어휘

ideology n. 이데올로기, 이념 conditioning n. 훈련, 길들이기; 조건 형성 capitalism n. 자본주의 communism n. 공산주의 patriotism n. 애국주의 religion n. 종교 astrology n. 점성술 assumption n. 가정, 가설 component n. 요소 promote v. 장려하다, 홍보하다, 촉진하다 agenda n. 의제 citizenry n. (일반) 시민 pass oneself off as ~로 행세하다 superiority n. 우월성, 거만함 sell v. 팔다, 선전하다, 납득시키다, 속여 넘기다 function n. 기능, 함수, 결과 property n. 재산, 소유물, 특성 pose as ~인 체하다 render v. 만들다[하다], 주다, 제공하다

Which of the following is true?
다음 중 옳은 것은 무엇인가?

① Ideologies depend for their base on nature's operation.
이데올로기는 자연의 작용에 기반을 둔다.

② Repressive ideologies tend to reveal the material conditions people live in.
억압적인 이데올로기는 사람들이 살고 있는 물질적 조건을 드러내는 경향이 있다.

③ All ideologies are equally desirable.
모든 이데올로기는 똑같이 바람직하다.

✓ Human desires reflect certain aspects of cultures in which people live.
인간의 욕망은 사람들이 사는 문화의 특정한 측면을 반영한다.

해설 이데올로기에 대한 글로서 첫 문장에서 모든 신념은 문화적 조건 형성의 산물이라고 말한다. 그리고 ❾, ❿에서 욕망은 우리가 살고 있는 자본주의 문화에 의해 우리 안에서 만들어진다고 말하고 있다. 따라서 ④ '인간의 욕망은 사람들이 사는 문화의 특정한 측면'을 추론할 수 있다.

017 ③
2019학년도 홍익대학교 인문계 A형 39번

❶ The posthuman subject is an amalgam, / (a collection of heterogeneous components), a material-informational entity (whose boundaries undergo continuous construction and reconstruction).
❷ Consider the six-million-dollar man, (a paradigmatic citizen / of the posthuman regime). ❸ As his name implies, / the parts of the self are indeed owned, / ❹ but they are owned precisely because they were purchased, / not because ownership is a natural condition (preexisting market relations). ❺ Similarly, the presumption (that there is an agency, desire, or will belonging to the self / and clearly distinguished from the wills of others) is undercut / in the posthuman, / for the posthuman's collective heterogenous quality implies a distributed cognition (located in disparate parts). ❻ We have only to recall Robocop's memory flashes (that interfere with his programmed directives) / to understand how the distributed cognition of the posthuman complicates individual agency. ❼ If human essence is freedom / from the wills of others, / ❽ the posthuman is "post" / not because it is necessarily unfree but because there is no a priori way [to identify a self-will (that can be clearly distinguished from an other-will)]. ❾ Although these examples foreground the cybernetic aspect of the posthuman, / ❿ it is important to recognize / that the construction of the posthuman does not require the subject / to be a literal cyborg. ⓫ Whether or not interventions have been made on the body, / new models of subjectivity (emerging from such fields as cognitive science and artificial life) imply / that even a biologically unaltered Homo sapiens count as posthuman. ⓬ The defining characteristics involve the construction of subjectivity, / not the presence of nonbiological components.

해석

❶ 포스트휴먼 주체는 이질적인 구성요소들을 한데 모은 결합물이며, 그 경계가 지속적으로 구성되고 재구성되는 물질-정보적 실체이다. ❷ 포스트휴먼 정권의 전형적인 시민인 6백만 달러의 사나이를 예로 들어보자. ❸ 그의 이름이 암시하듯이, ❹ 자신의 신체 부분들은 정말로 자신이 소유하고 있다 해도, 엄밀하게 말해 그 부분들이 구입됐기 때문에 소유하고 있는 것이지, (사고 파는) 시장관계가 있기 전에 이미 자연적으로 소유한 상태에 있기 때문은 아니다. ❺ 마찬가지로, 자신에게 속하고 다른 사람들의 의지와 명확히 구별되는 작인(作因)이나 욕망이나 의지가 있다는 가정은 포스트휴먼에게는 힘을 잃게 되는데, 이것은 포스트휴먼의 집단적 이질적 속성이 인식이 각기 다른 여러 부분에 분산되어 일어남을 암시하기 때문이다. ❻ 포스트휴먼의 분산된 인식이 어떻게 개별적 작인(作因)을 복잡하게 만드는 것인지 이해하기 위해서는 프로그래밍 되어 있는 로보캅의 지령을 방해하는 로보캅의 메모리 플래시를 떠올려 보면 된다. ❼ 만일 인간의 본질이 다른 사람의 의지로부터 자유롭다면, ❽ 포스트휴먼은 '포스트'인데, 그 이유는 포스트휴먼이 반드시 자유롭지 않기 때문이 아니라 타인의 의지와 명확히 구분될 수 있는 자신의 의지를 확인할 수 있는 선험적인 방법이 없기 때문이다. ❾ 이러한 예들은 포스트휴먼의 인공두뇌학적 측면을 보여주지만, ❿ 포스트휴먼의 구성은 그 주체가 반드시 말 그대로 사이보그이기를 요구하지는 않는다는 것을 인식하는 것이 중요하다. ⓫ 개입이 신체에 이루어졌든 아니든, 인지 과학과 인공 생명과 같은 분야에서 등장하는 새로운 주체성 모델은 생물학적으로 바뀌지 않은 '호모 사피엔스'조차도 포스트휴먼으로 간주된다는 것을 암시한다. ⓬ 포스트휴먼을 정의하는 특징들은 주체성의 구성과 연관된 것이지 비생물학적인 구성요소의 존재와 연관된 것은 아니다.

어휘

posthuman n. 포스트휴먼(로봇 공학 및 다른 기술로 유전적 구조를 조작하고 자기의 몸을 확대·증대하여 인간에서 진화한 상상의 인류) subject n. 주제, 논제 amalgam n. 아말감(수온과 다른 금속과의 합금); 혼합물, 결합물 heterogeneous a. 이종의, 이질적인; 다른 부분[요소]으로 이루어진, 잡다한, 혼성의 entity n. 독립체, 본질, 실체 boundary n. 경계선, 경계 undergo v. 경험하다, 겪다 paradigmatic a. 모범의, 전형적인 regime n. 정권, 제도, 체제 preexisting a. 기존의 presumption n. 추정, 가정 agency n. 작용, 힘, 작인(作因) will n. 의지 distinguish v. 구별하다, 식별하다 undercut v. 효력을 약화시키다 distributed cognition 분산인식 disparate a. 이질적인, 서로 전혀 다른 recall v. 기억해내다, 상기하다 directive n. 지시, 지령 essence n. 본질 a priori a. (실험·경험이 아닌 가설·이론에 기초한) 선험적인 foreground v. ~을 중시하다 intervention n. 조정, 중재, 간섭 emerge v. 나타내다, 부각되다, 알려지다 cognitive a. 지각하는, 인지하는 artificial a. 인공의, 인위적인 unaltered a. 바뀌지 않은 count as ~이라 간주되다 represent v. 나타내다, 대표하다 altogether ad. 완전히, 전적으로

Which of the following can be inferred from the passage?
다음 중 본문에서 추론할 수 있는 것은?

① There is a humanist presumption that is never weakened in the posthuman.
포스트휴먼에서 결코 약해지지 않은 인본주의적 가정이 있다. (→ 휴먼주의에서)

② The posthuman is represented only through bodily interventions.
포스트휴먼은 신체적 개입을 통해서만 나타내진다. (→ 신체적 그리고 비신체적)

✓③ The construction of the posthuman subjectivity is not altogether artificial.
포스트휴먼의 주체성 구성이 전적으로 인공적이지는 않다.

④ The posthuman gives way to the biological aspect of *Homo sapiens*.
포스트휴먼은 '호모 사피엔스'의 생물학적 측면에 길을 내준다. (→ 생물학적 측면도 포함된다)

해설 포스트 휴먼의 구성은 그 주체가 반드시 말 그대로 사이보그이기를 요구하지 않는다는 글의 요지 그리고 휴먼인 호모 사피엔스 조차도 포스트 휴먼으로 간주 된다는 것에서 ③을 추론할 수 있다.

정답 및 해설

018 ④ 2019학년도 가톨릭대학교 인문계 A형 39번

글의 소재: 바이칼 호수

❶ Over millennia, / prolonged seasonal freezing (of Lake Baikal) has caused most of the lake's flora and fauna to adapt to life / on and under the ice. ❷ Phytoplankton, [microscopic organisms (that live in fresh- or saltwater environments)], are the basis of the lake's food web. ❸ Lake Baikal is the only lake in the world [in which both the dominant primary producers (phytoplankton) and the top predator (the Baikal seal) require ice (for reproduction)].

❹ Baikal's phytoplankton include green algae, which can grow explosively / in "blooms" (that may last days and weeks). ❺ Ice thickness and transparency determine the amount of light (reaching the water), a critical factor / for phytoplankton growth. ❻ Because these unique algae have adapted to specific under-ice conditions, / ❼ recent changes (in the ice), (which was caused / by warming air temperature), have decreased algae growth rates and slowed spring algal blooms. ❽ The effects of this decrease then move up the food chain, from the enormous quantities of tiny crustaceans (that eat the algae) / to the fish (that eat the crustaceans) to the seals (that depend on fish / as their main food source).

❾ The Baikal seal, [smallest of the world's seals / and the only species (exclusively living in freshwater)], mates and gives birth / on the lake ice. ❿ The seals require ice / in early spring for shelter. ⓫ If ice melt occurs early, / the seals are forced into the water, / and the extra energy expended affects female fertility and nurturing ability.

해석

❶ 수천 년 동안 이어진 바이칼 호수의 주기적인 결빙으로 인해, 그 호수의 동식물군 대부분이 얼음 위나 아래에서의 생활에 적응하게 되었다. ❷ 민물이나 바닷물 환경에서 서식하는 미생물인 식물성 플랑크톤은 바이칼 호수의 먹이사슬에서 근간을 이루고 있다. ❸ 바이칼 호수는 지배적 1차 생산자(식물성 플랑크톤)와 최상위 포식자(바이칼 물개)가 모두 번식을 하는 것에 있어 얼음을 필요로 하는 세계에서 유일한 호수이다.

❹ 바이칼 호수의 식물성 플랑크톤에는 녹색 조류(藻類)가 포함되는데, 이것은 며칠 혹은 몇 주에 걸쳐 폭발적으로 '만발하면서' 자랄 수 있다. ❺ 얼음의 두께와 투명도는 물에 도달하는 빛의 양을 결정하는데, 빛의 양은 식물성 플랑크톤의 성장에 매우 중요한 요소이다. ❻ 이들 독특한 조류들은 얼음 밑이라는 특정한 환경에 맞춰 적응했기 때문에, ❼ 최근에 기온 상승에 의해 발생된 얼음의 변화는 조류의 성장률을 감소시켰고 봄에 일어나는 조류의 대규모 증식을 더뎌지게 했다. ❽ 이러한 감소가 미치는 영향은 조류를 먹는 엄청난 양의 작은 갑각류에서 갑각류를 먹는 물고기와 물고기를 주로 먹고 사는 바다표범에 이른 먹이사슬을 따라 위로 파급된다.

❾ 세계에서 가장 작은 물개로, 담수(淡水)에서만 사는 유일한 종(種)인 바이칼 물개는 바이칼 호수의 얼음 위에서 짝짓기를 하고 새끼를 낳는다. ❿ 바이칼 물개는 이른 봄에 은신처로 얼음이 필요하다. ⓫ 만약 얼음이 일찍 녹아버린다면, 바이칼 물개는 물속으로 들어갈 수밖에 없고, (물속에 있게 되는 바람에) 추가적으로 쓰게 돼버린 에너지는 암컷의 번식력과 양육 능력에 악영향을 끼친다.

어휘

millennium n. 천년간, 천년기 **prolonged** a. 오래 계속되는, 장기적인 **seasonal** a. 계절의, 계절에 따른, 주기적인 **freeze** v. 얼다, 얼어붙다 **flora** n. (한 지방이나 한 시대 특유의) 식물군 **fauna** n. (일정한 지방 또는 시대의) 동물군 **adapt** v. 적합[적응]시키다; 순응하다 **microscopic** a. 극히 작은, 현미경적인 **organism** n. 유기체, 유기물 **dominant** a. 지배적인; 유력한, 우세한 **primary** a. 주된, 주요한, 기본적인 **producer** n. 생산자(무기물에서 유기물을 만드는 녹색 식물 따위 생물의 총칭) **predator** n. 포식자, 포식동물 **reproduction** n. 재생; 재생산, 복제; 번식, 생식 **phytoplankton** n. 식물 플랑크톤 **explosively** ad. 폭발적으로 **in bloom** 개화하여, 만발하여 **last** v. 지속하다, 존속하다 **transparency** n. 투명, 투명성 **determine** v. 결정하다, 확정하다 **critical** a. 결정적인, 중요한 **factor** n. 요인, 인자, 요소 **algae** n. 조류(藻類) **specific** a. 특유한, 독특한; 특정한 **rate** n. 비율, 속도 **enormous** a. 거대한, 막대한 **quantity** n. 양, 수량 **crustacean** n. 갑각류의 동물 **exclusively** ad. 독점적으로, 배타적으로, 오로지 **mate** v. 짝짓기하다 **shelter** n. 은신처, 피난장소, 보호, 옹호 **expend** v. (시간·노력 따위를) 들이다, 쓰다, 소비하다 **affect** v. 영향을 주다, 악영향을 끼치다 **fertility** n. 비옥함; 다산(多産), 풍부; 번식력 **nurture** v. 양육하다

끝장편입 독해유형편 Top 20

According to the passage above, what is the best expression for the blank in the following sentence?
위 글에 의하면, 다음 문장의 빈칸에 들어가기에 적절한 표현은?

> Recent changes in water temperature and ice over at Lake Baikal exemplify _____.
> 최근 바이칼 호수의 수온과 얼음의 변화는 _____의 예를 보여준다.

① that global warming may lead to beneficial changes in some areas around the globe
지구 온난화가 전 세계의 일부 지역에 유익한 변화를 가져올 수도 있다는 것

② that living things display remarkable resilience in the face of environmental changes
생물들은 환경 변화에 직면하여 놀랄 만한 회복력을 발휘한다는 것

③ how flora and fauna can protect the freshwater environment from climate change
동식물군이 어떻게 기후변화로부터 담수 환경을 보호 할 수 있는가

✓ ④ how changes in the atmosphere link to changes in the hydrosphere and biosphere
대기의 변화가 지구의 수계(水界)와 생물권의 변화에 어떻게 연결되는가

해설 두 번째 단락 ❼ 문장에서 최근 기온 상승 이후 조류에서 물고기와 바다표범까지 영향을 언급하고 있다. 따라서 ④이 가장 적절하다.

어휘 **exemplify** v. 전형적인 예가 되다, 예를 들다 **remarkable** a. 주목할 만한, 놀라운 **hydrosphere** n. 수권(지구상에서 물이 존재하는 영역) **biosphere** n. 생물권(지구상에서 생물이 생존할 수 있는 영역)

정답 및 해설

019 ① 2019학년도 국민대학교 인문계 오후 A형 16번

❶ If you ask any man in America, / or any man in business in England, / ❷ what it is / that most interferes with his enjoyment of existence, / he will say: "The struggle for life." ❸ He will say / this in all sincerity; / ❹ he will believe it. ❺ In a certain sense, / it is true; / ❻ yet in another very important sense, / it is profoundly false. ❼ The struggle (for life) is a thing [which does, (of course), occur]. ❽ It may occur / to any of us / if we are unfortunate. ❾ It occurred, for example, to Conrad's hero Falk, (who found himself / on a derelict ship), / one of the two men among the crew (who were possessed of firearms), / with nothing to eat / but the other men. ❿ When the two men had finished the meals / upon which they could agree, / a true struggle (for life) began. ⓫ Falk won, / but was ever after a vegetarian. ⓬ Now that is not what the businessman means / when he speaks of the "struggle for life." ⓭ It is an inaccurate phrase (which he has picked up / in order to give dignity to something essentially trivial). ⓮ Ask him how many men / he has known / in his class of life (who have died of hunger). ⓯ Ask him what happened to his friends / after they had been ruined. ⓰ Everybody knows / that a businessman (who has been ruined) is better off / far as material comforts are concerned than a man (who has never been rich / enough to have the chance of being ruined). ⓱ What people mean, therefore, by the struggle for life is really the struggle for success. ⓲ What people fear / when they engage in the struggle is not that they will fail to get their breakfast next morning, / but that they will fail to outshine their neighbors.

해석

❶ 만약 당신이 미국 사람이나 영국 사업가에게 그의 삶의 즐거움을 가장 방해하는 것이 무엇인지 물어본다면, ❷ 누구든지 "생존 경쟁"이라고 말할 것이다. ❸ 그 사람은 이 생존 경쟁이라는 말을 정말 진심을 담아 말할 것이다. ❹ 그는 그것이 사실이라고 믿을 것이다. ❺ 어떤 의미에서, 그 말은 사실이다. ❻ 하지만 매우 중요한 다른 의미에서, 그 말은 전혀 사실이 아니다. ❼ 생존 경쟁은 물론 일어나고 있다. ❽ 만일 우리가 불우하다면 우리들 중 누구에게나 생존 경쟁은 일어날 수 있다. ❾ 예를 들어, 생존 경쟁은 조셉 콘라드(Josheph Conrad)의 단편소설 『포크(Falk)』의 주인공인 포크에게 실제로 일어났다. 포크는 선원들 중에서 소형화기를 갖고 있던 두 명의 남자 중 한 명이었다. 포크는 자신이 타고 있던 배가 버려졌다는 것을 알게 되었는데, 먹을 거라고는 배에 탄 다른 선원들 외엔 아무것도 없다. ❿ 그 두 남자가 먹을 수 있다고 합의한 음식을 다 먹었을 때, 진정한 생존 경쟁이 시작되었다. ⓫ 포크가 그 생존 경쟁에서 이겼지만, 포크는 그 후 줄곧 채식주의자가 되었다. ⓬ 지금 포크가 겪은 생존 경쟁은 사업자가 말하는 '생존 경쟁'이 아니다. ⓭ 사업가의 생존 경쟁은 본질적으로 사소한 것에 품격을 부여하기 위해 사업가가 고른 부정확한 문구에 불과할 뿐이다. ⓮ 사업가에게 그가 속해 있는 계급에서 굶어 죽은 사람이 몇 명이나 되는지 한번 물어보라. ⓯ (또한) 망했다는 친구들이 실제로 어떻게 되었는지 사업가에게 한번 물어보라. ⓰ 망했다는 사업가는 물질적 안락함에 관한 한, 부자였던 적이 한 번도 없어서 망할 기회도 없었던 사람보다는 훨씬 더 유복하게 살고 있다는 사실을 우리는 모두 알고 있다. ⓱ 따라서 사람들이 생존 경쟁이라고 말할 때 실제로 의미하는 것은 성공 경쟁인 것이다. ⓲ 이러한 사람들이 경쟁할 때 두려워하는 것은 다음날 아침을 먹지 못하게 되는 것이 아니라, 그들의 이웃보다 더 잘 살지 못하는 것이다.

어휘

interfere with 방해하다 **sincerity** n. 성실, 정직 **profoundly** ad. 깊이, 완전히 **hero** n. 주인공 **derelict** a. 버림받은, 버려진 **crew** n. 선원 **possess** v. 소유하다, 지니다 **firearms** n. (라이플·권총 등의) 소형화기(火器) **struggle** v. 투쟁하다, 고군분투하다 **vegetarian** n. 채식주의자 **inaccurate** a. 부정확한 **dignity** n. 위엄, 품위, 존엄성 **essentially** ad. 근본적으로, 본질적으로 **trivial** a. 사소한, 하찮은 **class** n. 계급 **ruin** v. 망치다, 망하다, 몰락하다 **so far as ~ is concerned** ~에 관한 한 **material comforts** 물질적인 안락함[편안함] **engage in** ~에 관여하다, 참여하다 **deserted island** 무인도 **chase after** ~을 쫓다, 뒤쫓다 **calamity** n. 불행; 재난 **outshine** v. ~보다 밝게 빛나다; ~보다 훌륭하다

According to the passage, which is true of Conrad's hero Falk?
다음 중 조셉 콘래드의 단편소설 주인공인 포크에 대해 사실인 것은?

✓ ① He had a weapon on the derelict ship.
그는 버려진 배에서 무기를 가지고 있었다.

② He found himself on a deserted island.
그는 버려진 섬에 있다는 것을 깨닫게 되었다. (→ 버려진 배)

③ He and other crew members survived in the end.
그와 다른 선원들은 결국 살아남았다. (→ 살아남지 못했다)

④ He was chasing after a vegetarian who was on the ship.
그는 배에 타고 있는 채식주의자 한명을 뒤쫓고 있었다. (→ 그런 내용 없음)

해설 ❾ 문장에서 '포크는 소형화기를 갖고 있던 두 명의 남자 중 한 명이었다'고 말하고 있다. 따라서 ①이 사실이다.

020 ②   2019학년도 단국대학교 자연계 A형 15번

PRE-CONFERENCE EVENT
FIBERS FOR HIGH PERFORMANCE TEXTILES TUTORIAL
2:00–5:15pm Tuesday, March 6
Presenter: Dr. Seshardri Ramkumar, Professor of Advanced Materials, Nonwovens & Advanced Materials Laboratory, Texas Tech University

❶ High performance textiles are basically functional textiles that provide added value / to the textiles in addition to common attributes of clothing materials. ❷ The functionality is achieved / due to the starting material, / i.e., fibers, structural aspects and finishing imparted to the final product.
❸ This tutorial will focus on the first pillar, which is the raw material / for advanced textile products. ❹ The seminar is aimed at beginners / in this field as well as those who have the basic understanding of textiles and industrial textiles / in particular. ❺ Subject areas covered will include: / an outline of high performance textiles, classification of fibers, fibers (that provide different functionality), functionality (provided by 3-dimensional) and structural fibers / such as bi-component, sustainability aspects, micro and nano structural fibers, / and what's next?
❻ The tutorial is not included with the conference registration. ❼ A discounted tutorial registration fee will be available to individuals attending the conference.

해석
회의 전 행사
고성능 직물용 섬유에 관한 지도 강연
3월 6일 화요일 오후 2시 ~ 오후 5시 15분
발표자: 텍사스 테크 대학교 비조직 및 신소재 연구소 신소재학과 교수 Seshardri Ramkumar
❶ 고성능 직물은 기본적으로 직물에 의류 소재가 가진 공통된 특성 외에도 부가가치까지 함께 제공하는 기능성 직물이다. ❷ 이 직물의 기능성은 시초(始初)재료, 즉 섬유와 구조적인 측면과 최종 생산물에 가해지는 마무리 손질 등을 통해서 이루어진다.
❸ 이 지도 강연은 첨단직물제품의 원료인 첫 번째 핵심 요소에 초점을 맞출 것이다. ❹ 이 세미나는 직물, 특히 산업용 직물에 대한 기본적인 이해를 가지고 있는 사람들뿐만 아니라 이 분야의 초보자들도 대상으로 한다. ❺ 다뤄질 주제 영역에는 고성능 직물의 개요, 섬유의 분류, 서로 다른 기능성을 제공하는 섬유와 바이컴포넌트, 지속 가능한 측면, 마이크로 및 나노 구조 섬유 같은 3차원의 구조 섬유가 제공하는 기능성 등의 것들이 포함된다.
❻ 이 지도 강연은 회의 등록과는 별개의 것이다. ❼ (그러나) 회의에 참석하는 사람들에게는 지도 강연 등록비가 할인될 것이다.

어휘
conference n. 회의 **fiber** n. 섬유, 섬유질, 섬유 조직 **tutorial** n. 개별[그룹] 지도(시간), 사용 지침서, 취급설명서 **textile** n. 직물, 옷감 **attribute** n. 자질, 속성 **functionality** n. 기능성, 실용성 **impart** v. (특정한 특성을) 주다 **pillar** n. 기둥, 기본적인 부분[특징] **classification** n. 분류, 유형, 범주 **dimensional** a. 차원의 **sustainability** n. 지속[유지] 가능성; 환경 파괴 없이 지속될 수 있음 **registration** n. 등록, 신고 **accountant** n. 회계사

Who is most likely to have interest in this information?
이 정보에 가장 관심을 보일 사람은 누구인가?

① accountants of clothing companies
의류업체의 회계사

② researchers in fiber materials ✓
섬유소재 연구자

③ laborers working at energy plants
에너지 발전소에서 근무하는 노동자

④ teachers engaging in kindergartens
유치원 선생님

해 설 회의 전 행사로 진행될 '고성능 직물용 섬유에 대한 지도 강연'을 제목으로 하고 있으며, ❹ 문장에서도 직물에 대한 이해도를 가진 대상을 언급하고 있다.

021 ④ ……… 2020학년도 세종대학교 인문계 A형 49번

❶ Dr. Pickett, (a Canadian entomologist), and his associates struck out on a new road / instead of going along with other entomologists (who continued to pursue the will-o'-the-wisp of the ever more toxic chemical). ❷ Recognizing / that they had a strong ally in nature, / they devised a program (that makes maximum use of natural controls and minimum use of insecticides). ❸ Whenever insecticides are applied / only minimum dosages are used — (barely enough to control the pest / without avoidable harm to beneficial species). ❹ Proper timing also enters in. ❺ Thus, if nicotine sulphate is applied / before rather than after the apple blossoms turn pink / one of the important predators is spared, / ❻ probably because it is still in the egg stage.

❼ How well has this program worked? ❽ Nova Scotia orchardists (who are following Dr. Pickett's modified spray program) are producing as high a share proportion of first-grade fruit / as are those (who are using intense chemical applications). ❾ They are also getting / as good production. ❿ They are getting these results, moreover, at a substantially lower cost.

⓫ More important than even these excellent results is the fact (that Dr. Pickett's program is not doing violence / to nature's balance)]. ⓬ It is well on the way / to realizing the philosophy (stated by G. C. Ullyett a decade ago): ⓭ "We must change our philosophy, / abandon our attitude of human superiority / and admit that in many cases / in natural environments / we find ways of limiting populations of organisms / in a more economical way / than we can do it ourselves."

해석

❶ 캐나다의 곤충학자인 피켓(Pickett) 박사와 그의 동료들은 독성이 갈수록 더 강해지는 화학물질인 도깨비불을 계속 추구한 다른 곤충학자에 동조하는 대신 새로운 길을 개척했다. ❷ 자연에 강한 우군(友軍)이 있다고 인식한 그들은 자연이 가지고 있는 통제력을 최대한 활용하고 살충제를 최소한으로 사용하는 프로그램을 고안했다. ❸ 이 프로그램은 살충제를 살포할 때마다 최소량만을, 즉 유익한 종(種)에게 피할 수 있는 해를 입히지 않으면서 해충을 겨우 박멸할 수 있는 정도만, 사용하는 것이다. ❹ 적절한 타이밍 또한 고려된다. ❺ 그런 까닭에, 사과 꽃이 분홍색으로 변한 후가 아니라 그전에 니코틴 황산염을 살포하면 중요한 포식자(해충) 중의 하나를 살려주게 되는데, ❻ 이것은 그것이 아직 알 속에 있는 단계이기 때문일 것이다.

❼ 이 프로그램은 얼마나 효과가 있었는가? ❽ 피켓 박사의 완화된 (살충제) 살포 프로그램을 따르는 노바스코시아(Nova Scotia)의 과수 재배자들은 강한 화학약품을 살포하는 방법을 사용하고 있는 사람들만큼 높은 비율로 1등급 과일을 생산해내고 있고 ❾ 생산량 또한 마찬가지로 많다. ❿ 게다가, 그들은 상당히 더 저렴한 비용으로 이 같은 결과를 얻고 있다.

⓫ 이런 훌륭한 결과보다 더욱 중요한 것은 피켓 박사의 프로그램이 자연의 균형에 해를 끼치고 있지 않다는 사실이다. ⓬ 그것은 G. C. 울리에트(Ulyett)가 10년 전에 이야기했던 철학을 잘 실현해 나가는 중에 있다. ⓭ 울리에트는 "우리는 우리가 가진 철학을 바꿔야 하고, 인간이 우월하다는 태도를 버려야 하며, 우리 스스로 할 수 있는 것보다 더 경제적인 방법으로 유기체의 개체수를 제한하는 방법을 자연환경의 많은 경우에서 찾아볼 수 있다는 것을 인정해야 합니다."라고 말했다.

어휘

entomologist n. 곤충학자 associate n. 동료, 한패, 친구 strike out (방법을) 생각해 내다, (새로운 길을) 개척[밟기 시작]하다 pursue v. 추적하다, 추구하다 will-o'-the-wisp n. 유령, 도깨비불; 사람을 홀리는 것 toxic a. 독성의, 유독한 chemical n. 화학제품, 화학약품 recognize v. 알아보다; 인정하다, 인식하다 ally n. 동맹국, 연합국; 협력자 devise v. 고안하다, 궁리하다 insecticide n. 살충제 dosage n. 투약, 조제; (약의 1회분) 복용[투약]량 pest n. 해충 beneficial a. 유익한, 이익을 가져오는 proper a. 적당한, 타당한 nicotine sulphate 니코틴 황산염 predator n. 포식자 orchardist n. 과수 재배자, 과수원 경영자 modify v. 수정하다, 고치다 proportion n. 비율; 조합; 균형 intense a. 강렬한, 극심한 substantially ad. 실체상, 본질상; 충분히, 풍부히 do violence to ~를 해치다, 위반하다, 왜곡하다 abandon v. (계획·습관 등을) 단념하다, 그만두다 attitude n. 태도, 마음가짐 superiority n. 우월, 우위, 탁월 organism n. 유기체, 생물 economical a. 경제적인, 실속 있는

Which of the following can NOT be inferred from the passage?
다음 중 위 글로부터 추론할 수 없는 것은?

① Dr. Pickett and his associates believed that they had a strong ally in nature.
피켓 박사와 그의 동료들은 자연에 강력한 우군이 있다고 믿었다.

② One of the advantages of the Dr. Pickett's program was that it produced positive results at a lower cost.
피켓 박사의 프로그램이 가진 장점 중 하나는 더 낮은 비용으로 긍정적인 결과를 만들어냈다는 것이다.

③ G. C. Ullyett and Dr. Pickett saw eye to eye about ways to use nature.
G.C 울리에트와 피켓 박사는 자연을 이용하는 방법에 의견이 같았다.

✓ Dr. Pickett and his associates did not believe in the need to limit populations of organisms.
피켓 박사와 그의 동료들은 유기체의 개체 수를 제한할 필요성을 믿지 않았다. (→ 필요성을 믿었다)

해설 윗글은 피켓 박사가 살충제를 최소한으로 사용하여 해충을 박멸하는 프로그램 과정을 설명하는 글이다. 따라서 피켓 박사와 그의 동료는 유기체의 개체 수 제한의 필요성을 인정했다고 볼 수 있다.

022 ④ 2019학년도 한국항공대학교 인문계 32번

1) Strokes cause almost twice as many deaths as all accidents combined, / but 80% of respondents judged accidental death to be more likely.
2) Tornadoes were seen / as more frequent killers than asthma, / although the latter cause 20 times more deaths.
3) Death (by lightning) was judged / less likely than / death (from botulism) / even though it is 52 times more frequent.
4) Death (by disease) is 18 times as likely as accidental death, / but the two were judged / about equally likely.
5) Death (by accidents) was judged to be more than 300 times more likely / than death by diabetes, / but the true ratio is 4:1.

❶ The media do not just shape what the public is interested in, but also are shaped by it. ❷ Editors cannot ignore the public's demands / that certain topics and viewpoints receive extensive coverage. ❸ The world (in our heads) is not a precise replica of reality; ❹ our expectations (about the frequency of events) are distorted / by the prevalence and emotional intensity of the messages (to which we are exposed). ❺ The estimates of causes of death are an almost direct representation / of the activation of ideas / in associative memory, and are a good example of substitution. ❻ But Slovic and his colleagues were led to a deeper insight: ❼ they saw / that the ease (with which ideas of various risks) come to mind and the emotional reactions (to these risks) are inextricably linked. ❽ Frightening thoughts and images occur to us / with particular ease, and thoughts of danger (that are fluent and vivid) exacerbate fear.

해석

1) 뇌졸중은 모든 사고를 합친 것보다 거의 2배가 되는 사망자를 발생시키지만, 응답자의 80%는 사고로 인한 사망이 더 많을 것으로 판단했다.
2) 토네이도가 천식보다 더 빈번한 사망 원인으로 여겨졌지만, 후자(천식)가 20배 더 많은 사망자가 생기게 한다.
3) 번개에 의한 사망은 52배 더 빈번히 발생함에도 불구하고 보툴리누스 중독에 의한 사망보다 적은 것으로 판단되었다.
4) 질병에 의한 사망과 사고로 의한 사망이 거의 동일할 것으로 판단되었으나, 질병으로 인한 사망이 사고로 인한 사망의 18배에 이른다.
5) 사고로 인한 사망이 당뇨병으로 인한 사망보다 300배 이상 더 많을 것으로 판단되었지만, 실제 비율은 4:1에 불과하다.

❶ 대중 매체는 대중들의 관심사를 형성할 뿐만 아니라, 대중들의 관심사에 의해 형성되기도 한다. ❷ 편집 담당자들은 특정한 주제와 관점들이 광범위하게 보도되어야 한다는 대중들의 요구를 무시할 수 없다. ❸ 우리 머릿속의(우리가 생각하는) 세계는 현실의 정확한 복제가 아니다. ❹ 사건의 빈도에 대한 우리의 예상은 우리가 노출되는 메시지(보도내용)의 보급 정도와 정서적 강렬함에 의해서 왜곡된다. ❺ 사망 원인에 대한 추정은 연상적 기억 안에서 생각들이 활성화되는 것을 거의 직접적으로 보여주는 것이며 치환 작용의 좋은 예이다. ❻ 하지만 슬로빅(Slovic)과 그의 동료들은 한층 더 깊은 통찰에 이르렀다. ❼ 다양한 위험들이 마음속에 쉽게 떠오르는 정도와 이러한 위험에 대한 감정적 반응들은 불가분하게 연결되어 있다는 통찰을 얻은 것이다. ❽ 무서운 생각들과 이미지들은 특히나 쉽게 떠오르며, 거침없이 생생하게 떠오르는 위험에 대한 생각들은 두려움을 악화시킨다.

어휘

stroke n. 뇌졸중 **frequent** a. 자주, 빈번한 **asthma** n. 천식 **botulism** n. 보툴리누스 중독 **diabetes** n. 당뇨병 **viewpoint** n. 관점, 시각, 방향 **extensive** a. 넓은, 대규모의, 광범위한 **precise** a. 정확한, 정밀한 **replica** n. 복사, 복제품 **frequency** n. 빈도, 빈번, 주파수 **distort** v. 비틀다, 왜곡하다 **prevalence** n. 유행, 보급 **intensity** n. 강렬함, 강도, 세기 **estimate** n. 추정, 평가 v. 추정하다, 평가하다 **associative** a. 연상의, 결합의 **substitution** n. 대체, 치환(복잡한 판단을 내려야 할 때 마음에 더 쉽게 떠오르는 것으로 바꿔서 판단을 내리는 것으로, 많은 인지적 편견과 인식적 착각의 기저에 깔린 심리과정) **ease** n. 쉬움, 편의, 용이 **inextricably** ad. 불가분하게 **fluent** a. 유창한, 능수능란한 **exacerbate** v. 악화시키다 **perceive** v. 지각하다, 인지하다 **disproportionate** a. 불균형의

It can be inferred from the passage that _____.
이 글에서 _____ 라고 추론할 수 있다.

① unusual events get less attention and are consequently perceived as more unusual than they really are
특이한 사건들은 주목을 덜 받게 되어 결과적으로 실제보다 더 특이한 것으로 인식된다

② unusual events get less attention and are consequently perceived as less unusual than they really are
특이한 사건들은 주목을 덜 받게 되어 결과적으로 실제보다 덜 특이한 것으로 인식된다

③ unusual events attract disproportionate attention and are consequently perceived as more unusual than they really are
특이한 사건들은 불균형적인 (터무니없이 많은) 관심을 끌게 되어 결과적으로 실제보다 더 특이한 것으로 인식된다

④ **unusual events attract disproportionate attention and are consequently perceived as less unusual than they really are**
특이한 사건들은 불균형적인 (터무니없이 많은) 관심을 끌게 되어 결과적으로 실제보다 덜 특이한 것으로 인식된다
= 더 흔하게 발생하는 것으로 인식된다

해설 윗글은 특이한 사건들이 대중 매체들에 더 자주 보도되고, 그로 인해 대중들은 해당 사건이 더 자주 일어난다는 왜곡된 인식을 갖는다는 글이다. 따라서 ④이 가장 적절하다. ④에 'less unusual'은 '덜 특이하다'라는 말인데, 이를 '더 흔하게 발생한다는 것으로 여긴다'로 해석해야지 정답 근거가 분명해진다.

정답 및 해설

023 ②　　2019학년도 가톨릭대학교 인문계 A형 36번

❶ In a study / (by some social psychologists) / participants were asked / to take part in two tasks. ❷ In the first task, / they were asked / to make sentences / out of sets of provided words. ❸ Next, / as part of what was supposedly a different study, / ❹ participants played an economic game (in which they were given ten $1 coins and asked to divide them up / between themselves and the next participant). ❺ Only the next participant would know what they decided, and that participant wouldn't know who the givers were. ❻ Think for a moment / what you would do in this situation. ❼ Here's an opportunity (to make a quick 10 bucks), ❽ and there is a definite temptation (to pocket all the coins). ❾ But you might feel a little guilty / (hoarding all the money and leaving nothing for the next person). ❿ This is one of those situations (in which there is a devil / on one of our shoulders ("Don't be a fool, take it all!") and an angel on the other ("Do unto others as you would have them do unto you")). ⓫ In short, people want the money / but this conflicts with their goal (to be nice to others). ⓬ Which goal wins out? ⓭ It depends (in part) on / which goal has been recently primed. ⓮ Remember the sentence completion task people did first? ⓯ In the task, / half of the participants were given the words (that had to do with God) (spirit, divine, God, sacred, and prophet), which were designed / to set the goal of acting kindly to one's neighbor. ⓰ The other half got neutral words. ⓱ An important detail is / that the participants did not make a connection (between the sentence-making task / and the economic game) — ⓲ they thought the two tasks were completely unrelated. ⓳ Even so, / the people (who made sentences / out of words / having to do with God) left significantly more money / for the next participant ($4.56 on average) / than did people (who got the neutral words ($2.56 on average)).

해석

❶ 일부 사회심리학자들에 의해 실시된 연구에서, 참가자들은 두 가지 과제에 참여하도록 요청받았다. ❷ 첫 번째 과제에서, 그들은 제공된 단어들로 문장을 만들라는 요구를 받았다. ❸ 다음으로, 앞선 과제와 별개의 것으로 여겨진 연구의 일환으로, 참가자들은 경제 게임을 했다. ❹ 이 게임에서 참가자들은 1달러짜리 동전 10개를 받았고 그 돈을 자신들과 다음 참가자가 나누어 가지라는 요청을 받았다. ❺ 다음 참가자만이 그들이 무엇을 결정했는지 알 수 있고, 그 참가자는 돈을 준 사람들이 누구인지는 알지 못할 것이었다. ❻ 당신이라면 이 상황에서 어떻게 할지를 잠시 생각해보라. ❼ 여기에 10달러를 순식간에 벌 수 있는 기회가 있다. ❽ 그리고 모든 동전을 호주머니에 집어넣고 싶은 유혹이 분명히 존재한다. ❾ 하지만 당신은 모든 돈을 가지고 다음 사람에게 아무것도 남기지 않는 것에 약간의 죄책감을 느낄지도 모른다. ❿ 이것은 한쪽 어깨에는 악마가 있고 ("바보처럼 굴지 말고 모두 가져라!"), 다른 한쪽 어깨에는 천사가 있는 ("남에게 대접받고 싶은 대로 남을 대접하라.") 여러 상황 중의 하나이다. ⓫ 요컨대, 사람들은 돈을 원하지만, 이것은 다른 사람들에게 친절하게 대하려는 그들의 목표와 상충된다. ⓬ 어느 목표가 이길 것인가? ⓭ 그것은 부분적으로는 최근에 어느 목표가 자극을 받았는가에 달려 있다. ⓮ 사람들이 가장 처음에 했던 문장완성 과제를 기억하는가? ⓯ 이 과제에서, 참가자의 절반은 신(神) (영혼, 신성의, 신, 신성한, 예언자)과 관련이 있는 단어들을 받았는데, 이 단어들은 이웃에게 친절하게 행동하겠다는 목표를 세우게 하기 위해 고안된 것들이었다. ⓰ 나머지 절반은 중립적인 단어들을 받았다. ⓱ 한 가지 중요한 사항은 참가자들이 문장을 만드는 과제와 경제 게임 사이에 연관성을 만들지 않았다는 점이다. ⓲ 그들은 두 과제가 완전히 무관하다고 생각했다. ⓳ 그럼에도 불구하고, 신과 관련된 단어들로 문장을 만든 사람들은 (평균 4.56달러) 중립적인 단어들을 받았던 사람들보다 (평균 2.56달러) 다음 참가자에게 훨씬 더 많은 돈을 남겼다.

어휘

participant n. 관여자, 참여자　**take part in** ~에 참여[참가]하다　**supposedly** ad. 추정 상, 아마, 필경　**definite** a. 뚜렷한, 확실한, 한정된, 일정한　**temptation** n. 유혹, 마음을 끄는 것　**pocket** v. 포켓에 넣다; 감추다, 챙겨 넣다; 자기 것으로 하다　**hoard** v. 저장하다, 축적하다　**conflict** n. 대립, 불일치; 갈등　**win out** 성취하다, 이기다　**prime** v. (특정 목적·작업을 위해) 준비시키다; 미리 알려 주다; 자극하다　**divine** a. 신성한, 종교적인　**sacred** a. 신성한　**prophet** n. 예언자　**neighbor** n. 이웃, 이웃사람　**neutral** a. 중립의; 불편부당한; 중간의　**unrelated** a. 관계없는　**significantly** ad. 중대하게; 상당히

Which of the following is true according to the passage?
위 글에 의하면 다음 중 옳은 것은?

① All the participants were given the same set of words.
모든 참가자들에게 동일한 단어들이 주어졌다. (→ 절반은 신과 관련된 단어, 나머지 절반은 중립적인 단어)

② Who left money to the next participant remained unknown to the recipient.
다음 참가자에게 돈을 남긴 사람이 누구였는지는 받는 사람에게 알려지지 않았다.

③ The participants were well aware of the connection between the two given tasks.
참가자들은 주어진 두 과제 사이의 연관성에 대해 잘 알고 있었다. (→ 무관하다고 여겼다)

④ The participants were given two options — taking all the money or giving half of it to the next person.
참가자들에게는 두 가지 선택권 — 모든 돈을 가져가거나 절반을 다음 사람에게 주는 것 — 이 주어졌다. (→ 참가자 스스로가 결정했다)

해 설 ❷ 문장에서 정답과 같은 내용을 언급하고 있다.

어 휘 **recipient** n. 수령인, 받는 사람

정답 및 해설

024 ②   2019학년도 명지대학교 인문계 25번

① Medicine is as old as humankind. ② More than 50,000 years ago, stone-age, cave-dwelling humans first crushed and infused herbs for their curative properties. ③ Traditional forms of medicine [— few of which, (sadly), are known to written history] — ④ evolved on all continents, from the deserts and jungles of Africa to North American plains, South American rain forests, and balmy Pacific islands. ⑤ Earliest records (in West Asia, the Middle East, North Africa, China, and India) document myriad diseases, healing plants, and surgical procedures. ⑥ Ancient Egyptians had complex, hierarchical methods of medicine (integrated into their religious beliefs). ⑦ Gods and spirits were in charge of mortal disease, and priest-physicians — (Imhotep is one of the first great names in medical history) — ⑧ mediated with the supernatural realm to ease human suffering. ⑨ The civilizations (of Greece and Rome) had their respective medical giants (in Hippocrates and Galen). ⑩ Hippocrates set standards for patient care and the physician's attitudes and philosophy (that persist today). ⑪ Galen wrote so extensively and authoritatively that his theories and practices attained quasi-religious status and effectively stalled medical progress in Europe for 1,400 years. ⑫ After the Roman Empire ended, the murky arts of alchemy, sorcery, exorcism, and miracle cures flourished in Western Europe. ⑬ Ancient India and China also developed sophisticated medical systems with outstanding contributors. ⑭ In India, (in the centuries before and after Hippocrates), Susruta and Chakara produced encyclopedic (founding works of Ayurvedic medicine). ⑮ Chinese physician Zhang Zhongjing, (a contemporary of Galen), also compiled works (that described hundreds of diseases and prescribed thousands of remedies).

해석

① 의학은 인류의 역사만큼 오래되었다. ② 5만 년도 전에, 동굴에 살고 있던 석기시대의 사람들은 치료적 특성을 얻기 위하여 최초로 약초를 으깨고 달였다. ③ 전통적인 형태의 의학은 -안타깝게도 문자로 기록된 역사에 남아있는 것은 거의 없다.- ④ 아프리카 사막과 밀림에서부터 북미의 대평원, 남미의 열대우림, 그리고 온화한 기후의 태평양 섬에 이르기까지 모든 대륙에서 발전하였다. ⑤ 서아시아, 중동, 북아프리카, 중국 그리고 인도에서의 초기의 기록들은 수많은 질병, 치유 식물, 그리고 수술 과정을 기록하고 있다. ⑥ 고대 이집트인들에게는 그들의 신앙과 결합된 복잡하고 계층적인 의료 방법이 있었다. ⑦ 신들과 정령들은 불치병을 담당하였으며, 성직자이자 의사들이 — 대제사장이나 의사인 임호텝(Imhotep)은 의학사에서 유명한 인물 중 한 명이다. — ⑧ 인간의 고통을 덜어주기 위해 초자연적인 영역과의 중재 역할을 담당했다. ⑨ 그리스 문명과 로마 문명에는 각각 히포크라테스(Hippocrates)와 갈레노스(Galen)라는 의학의 거장이 있었다. ⑩ 히포크라테스는 환자 치료, 환자를 대하는 의사들의 태도 및 철학에 관한 기준을 정립했는데, 이 기준은 오늘날까지도 이어져 오고 있다. ⑪ 갈레노스는 너무나 광범위하고 권위적으로 저술해 그의 이론과 의술은 준종교적인 지위를 얻어, 그 후 1,400년 동안이나 유럽의 의학 발전을 사실상 정체시켰다. ⑫ 로마제국이 멸망한 이후에는, 이해하기 어려운 연금술, 주술, 퇴마의식, 특효약들이 서유럽에서 성행했다. ⑬ 고대 인도와 고대 중국에서는 의학사에 공헌한 인물들의 등장으로 수준 높은 의학 체계가 또한 발전했다. ⑭ 인도에서는 히포크라테스의 활동 시기 전후로 수백 년 동안 수스루타(Susruta)와 차카라(Chakara)가 아유르베다 의술에 관한 백과사전 같은 형태의 책들을 저술했다. ⑮ (그리고) 갈레노스와 같은 시대를 살았던 중국인 의사 장중경(Zhang Zhongjing)은 수백 개의 질병을 설명하고 수천 개의 치료법을 처방해 놓은 책들을 또한 편찬하였다.

어휘

cave-dwelling 동굴 생활 infuse v. (잎·뿌리 등을) (액체로) 달이다, 우리다 herb n. 약초, 허브 curative a. 치유력 있는 property n. 재산, 소유물, 특성 continent n. 대륙 balmy a. (날씨·바람 등이) 부드럽고 시원한, 온화한 myriad a. 수많은, 무수한 surgical procedure 수술 절차 hierarchical a. 계급[계층]에 따른 integrate v. 통합하다, 결합하다 mortal a. 필멸의, 치명적인 priest n. 성직자; 사제, 신부 mediate v. 중재하다, 중간에 위치하다 supernatural a. 초자연적인 realm n. (활동·관심·지식 등의) 영역 [범위] authoritatively ad. 위압적으로, 명령적으로 quasi-religious a. 준 종교적인 stall v. 교착 상태에 빠뜨리다, 지연시키다 murky a. 흐린, 어두컴컴한, 탁한 alchemy n. 연금술, 마력 sorcery n. 마법 exorcism n. 귀신 쫓기 flourish a. 번영하는, 번창하는 sophisticate a. 정교한, 복잡한 outstanding a. 두드러진, 뛰어난 encyclopedic a. 박식한, 해박한, 백과사전의 contemporary a. 현대의, 동시대의 prescribe v. 처방하다, 규정하다 remedy n. 치료약, 해결책

Choose the one that is not true according to the passage.
본문에 따르면 다음 중 일치하지 않는 것을 고르시오.

① Ancient Egyptian priest-physicians are recognized in medical history.
고대 이집트의 성직자이자 의사들은 의학사에서 인정받는다.

✓② Galen's practices advanced medicine after the fall of the Roman Empire.
갈레노스의 의술은 로마제국이 멸망하고 난 후 의학을 발전시켰다. (→ 정체시켰다)

③ In the past, medicine was thought to be tied to matters of faith.
과거에, 의학은 신앙의 문제와 관련되어 있는 것으로 여겨졌다.

④ Europe and China developed medical systems around the same time.
유럽과 중국은 거의 동시대에 의학을 발전시켰다.

해설 갈레노스는 너무 광범위하고 권위적으로 저술하여 거의 종교나 다름없는 지위를 얻었고 그 후 1,400년 동안이나 유럽 의학 발전을 사실상 정체시켰다고 말하고 있다.

정답 및 해설

025 ③ — 2019학년도 한국항공대학교 인문계 26번

① Human error is defined as any deviance from "appropriate" behavior. ② The word appropriate is in quotes because (in many circumstances), the appropriate behavior is not known or is only determined after the fact. ③ But still, error is defined as deviance from the generally accepted correct or appropriate behavior. ④ Error is the general term for all wrong actions. ⑤ There are two major classes of error: slips and mistakes. ⑥ Slips are further divided into two major classes and mistakes into three. ⑦ These categories of errors all have different implications for design. ⑧ I now turn to a more detailed look at these classes of errors and their design implications. ⑨ A slip occurs when a person intends to do one action and ends up doing something else. ⑩ With a slip, the action (performed) is not the same as the action (that was intended). ⑪ There are two major classes of slips: action-based and memory-lapse. ⑫ In action-based slips, the wrong action is performed. ⑬ In lapses, memory fails, so the intended action is not done or its results not evaluated. ⑭ Action-based slips and memory lapses can be further classified according to their causes. ⑮ A mistake occurs when the wrong goal is established or the wrong plan is formed. ⑯ From that point on, even if the actions are executed properly they are part of the error, because the actions (themselves) are inappropriate; they are part of the wrong plan. ⑰ With a mistake, the action (that is performed) matches the plan: it is the plan that is wrong. ⑱ Mistakes have three major classes: rule-based, knowledge-based, and memory-lapse. ⑲ In a rule-based mistake, the person has appropriately diagnosed the situation, ⑳ but then decided upon an erroneous course of action: the wrong rule is being followed. ㉑ In a knowledge-based mistake, the problem is misdiagnosed because of erroneous or incomplete knowledge.

[해석]

① 인간의 오류는 "적절한" 행동으로부터의 모든 일탈로 정의된다. ② '적절한'이라는 단어에 인용 부호를 붙인 것은 많은 경우에 '적절한' 행동은 알 수 없거나, 오직 사후(事後)에만 확인되기 때문이다. ③ 그러나 여전히, 오류는 일반적으로 인정되는 옳은 행동이나 적절한 행동으로부터의 일탈이라고 정의된다. ④ '오류'는 모든 틀린 행동을 가리키는 일반적인 용어이다. ⑤ 오류에는 크게 '착오'와 '실수'라는 두 부류가 있다. ⑥ 착오는 다시 두 가지로, 실수는 세 가지로 나뉜다. ⑦ 이러한 오류의 범주들은 모두 행동 설계에 대해 가지는 함의가 다르다. ⑧ 이제 이러한 부류의 오류들과 그것들의 행동 설계상의 함의를 좀 더 자세하게 살펴보겠다. ⑨ 착오는 어떤 행동을 의도하지만 결국 다른 행동을 해버리는 경우에 일어난다. ⑩ 착오의 경우, 수행된 행동은 의도된 행동과 같지 않다. ⑪ 착오에는 크게 '행동기반 착오'와 '기억소멸 착오'의 두 부류가 있다. ⑫ 행동기반 착오에서는, 틀린 행동이 수행된다. ⑬ 기억소멸 착오에서는, 기억이 나지 않아 의도된 행동이 수행되지 않거나 그 결과가 평가되지 않는다. ⑭ 행동기반 착오와 기억소멸 착오는 그 원인에 따라서 다시 세분화될 수 있다. ⑮ 실수는 틀린 목표가 설정되거나 틀린 계획이 세워질 때 발생한다. ⑯ 비록 행동들이 적절하게 실행된다고 하더라도, 그 목표설정이나 계획수립의 시점부터, 그 행동들 자체가 틀린 계획 일부이며 부적절하기 때문에, 그 행동들은 이미 오류의 일부인 것이다. ⑰ 실수의 경우, 수행되는 행동은 계획과 일치하지만, 계획 자체가 틀린 것이다. ⑱ 실수에는 크게 세 부류가 있는데, '규칙기반 실수', '지식기반 실수', '기억소멸 실수'이다. ⑲ 규칙기반 실수에서는, 사람이 상황을 적절하게 진단하였지만, ⑳ 그런 다음에 틀린 행동 과정을 택하기로 정한 셈인데, 이는 틀린 규칙을 따르고 있기 때문이다. ㉑ 지식기반 실수에서는, 틀린 지식이나 완전하지 못한 지식 때문에 문제를 잘못 진단하게 된다.

[어휘] deviance n. 일탈 appropriate a. 적합한, 적절한 quote n. 인용문구, 따옴표, 인용부호 circumstance n. 상황, 환경 after the fact 사후(事後)에 slip n. 작은 실수 implication n. 함의 lapse n. 착오, 소멸, 상실 classify v. 분류하다, 구분하다 diagnose v. 진단하다 erroneous a. 잘못된

㉒ Memory-lapse mistakes take place / when there is forgetting / at
　　　S　　　　　　　　　　일어나다, 발생하다
　　　　　　　　　　　　V
the stages of goals, plans, or evaluation.

It can be inferred from the passage that to pour some milk into coffee and then put the coffee cup into the refrigerator is an example of ____.
커피에 우유를 부은 다음 그 커피 잔을 냉장고에 두는 것은 ____의 사례라고 추론할 수 있다.

① knowledge-based mistake
　 지식기반의 실수
② memory-lapse mistake
　 기억소멸 실수
③ action-based slip ✓
　 행동기반의 착오
④ memory-lapse slip
　 기억소멸 착오

해석 ㉒ 기억소멸 실수는 목표, 계획 혹은 평가의 단계에서 망각이 발생해서 일어난다.

해설 본문에서 행동 기반 착오는 틀린 행동이 수반되는 것이라고 말하는데, 커피에 우유를 부은 다음 마시려는 행동이 요구되어야 하나 냉장고에 두었으므로 의도된 행동과 다른 행동이라고 볼 수 있다. 따라서 ③ 'action-based slip(행동 기반의 착오)'이 가장 적절하다.

026 ②

2019학년도 국민대학교 인문계 오전 A형 28번

글의 주제
① There are several pro tips (for long and healthy life). ② First, diet. Weight loss likely explains many of the positive changes, / such as lower blood pressure and better blood-sugar levels. ③ But some experts speculate / that fasting also makes the body more resistant to stress, which can have beneficial effects / at the cellular level. ④ One expert says, / "Diet is by far the most powerful intervention (to delay aging and age-related diseases)."

⑤ In the past couple of years, / scientists have shown / that sedentary behavior, (like sitting all day), is a risk factor / for earlier death. ⑥ They found / that hours (spent sitting) are linked to increased risks of Type 2 diabetes and nonalcoholic fatty liver disease. ⑦ You can't exercise away all the bad effects of sitting too much. ⑧ But the good news is / that doing anything but sitting still — (even fidgeting counts) — can add up. ⑨ People (who logged the least physical activity) had the highest risk of a heart event / in the next ten years, which isn't shocking. ⑩ But to the surprise of the researchers, / moving just a little bit / more during the day — (like doing chores around the house) — was enough to lower the risk of a heart event.

⑪ By now / it's clear to scientists / that our emotions affect our biology. ⑬ Studies have shown for years / that anger and stress can release stress hormones / like adrenaline into our blood, which trigger the heart / to beat faster and harder. ⑭ Stress may even have an effect on how well our brains hold up against Alzheimer's disease. ⑮ The researchers found / that people (who held more negative views of aging earlier in life) had greater loss / in the volume of their hippocampus, [a region of the brain (whose loss is linked to Alzheimer's disease)]. ⑯ This is not the first time / (research has suggested that how we feel about aging can affect how we age).

해석
① 건강하게 오래 사는 데 도움이 되는 몇 가지 팁이 있다. ② 가장 먼저, 다이어트를 들 수 있다. 체중 감량은 아마도 혈압을 낮추고 혈당 수치가 좋아지는 것과 같은 많은 긍정적인 변화를 가져올 것이다. ③ 그러나 일부 전문가들은 금식이 또한 우리 몸으로 하여금 스트레스에 내성을 많이 갖게 만들고, 이는 세포 수준에서 이로운 효과를 나타낼 수 있다고 추측한다. ④ 한 전문가는 "다이어트가 노화와 노화로 인한 질병을 지연시키기 위한 가장 강력한 개입"이라고 말한다. ⑤ 지난 2년 동안, 과학자들은 하루 종일 앉아 있는 것과 같이 몸을 많이 움직이지 않는 행동이 조기 사망의 위험 요소라는 것을 보여주었다. ⑥ 그들은 앉아서 보내는 시간이 제2형 당뇨병과 비알코올성 지방간 질환의 위험성 증가와 관련돼 있다는 사실을 발견했다. ⑦ 너무 많이 앉아 있는 것이 끼치는 온갖 안 좋은 영향들을 운동해서 모두 없앨 수는 없다. ⑧ 하지만 좋은 소식은 가만히 앉아 있는 것을 제외하고는 무엇을 하든 — 심지어 몸을 꼼지락대는 것도 가치 있다 — 보탬이 될 수 있다는 것이다. ⑨ 신체활동을 가장 적게 기록한 사람들은 향후 10년 안에 심장질환이 발생할 위험이 가장 컸는데, 이것은 충격적이지 않다. ⑩ 그러나 과학자들에게 놀라웠던 사실은 낮 동안 조금만 더 움직여도 - ⑪ 집안 여기저기서 허드렛일을 하는 것처럼 - 심장질환의 위험을 줄이기에 충분했다는 점이다. ⑫ 이제는 우리의 감정이 우리 몸의 상태에 영향을 미친다는 것을 과학자들은 분명하게 받아들이고 있다. ⑬ 연구결과들은 분노와 스트레스가 아드레날린과 같은 스트레스 호르몬을 우리 혈액에 방출시킬 수 있다는 것을 오랫동안 보여주었는데, 이렇게 되면 심장은 더 빠르고 강하게 뛰게 된다. ⑭ 스트레스는 심지어 우리 뇌가 알츠하이머병에 얼마나 잘 대항하는지에도 영향을 미칠지 모른다. ⑮ 과학자들은 젊었을 때 노화에 대해 더 부정적인 태도를 갖고 있던 사람들의 경우 해마의 크기가 더 작아져 있었다는 사실을 발견했는데, 해마는 뇌 일부분으로, 이것의 크기가 작아지는 것은 알츠하이머병과 관련이 있다. ⑯ 노화에 관해 우리가 어떻게 생각하는가가 우리가 어떻게 늙어가는가에 영향을 끼칠 수 있다는 연구결과가 나온 것은 이번이 처음이 아니다.

어휘
pro tip 유용한 팁 positive a. 확신하는; 단정적인, 확실한; 긍정적인 expert n. 전문가 speculate v. 추측하다, 억측하다, 투기하다 fasting n. 단식, 금식 resistant a. 저항하는, 견디는, 내성이 있는 beneficial a. 유익한, 이익을 가져오는 cellular a. 세포의 intervention n. 조정, 중재, 간섭, 개입 sedentary a. 주로 앉아서 하는, 한곳에 머무르는 risk factor 위험요인 diabetes n. 당뇨병 nonalcoholic a. 무알콜의 fatty liver 지방간 fidget v. 안절부절 못하다; 꼼지락거리다 add up 계산이 맞다; 이해되다, 조금씩 보태어 많아지다 log v. 일지에 기록하다; (특정 거리나 시간을) 항해[운항, 비행]하다 chore n. 지루한 일; (pl.) (일상의) 잡일, 허드렛일 lower v. 낮추다, 내리다, 낮게 하다 affect v. 영향을 미치다, 악영향을 끼치다 hormones n. 호르몬 adrenaline n. 아드레날린(부신수질에서 분비되는 호르몬) trigger v. (일련의 사건·반응 등을) 일으키다, 유발하다 negative a. 부정적인; 소극적인 hippocampus n. (대뇌 측두엽의) 해마 excessive a. 지나친, 과도한 regimen n. 식이 요법 optimistic a. 낙관적인, 낙관하는

According to the passage, which is NOT one of the pro tips for long and healthy life?
위 글에 의하면, 다음 중 건강하게 오래 살기 위해 도움이 되는 팁에 해당되지 않는 것은?

① not sitting still for long
긴 시간 동안 가만히 앉아 있지 않은 것
② doing excessive exercise ✓
과도한 운동을 하는 것
③ keeping to a regimen of diet
식이요법을 꾸준하게 하는 것
④ having an optimistic attitude
낙관적 태도를 가지는 것

해 설 운동하지 너무 않지 않는 것에 위험성은 언급되었으나 과도한 운동을 요구하는 언급은 없다.

정답 및 해설

027 A) ① B) ②   2019학년도 숭실대학교 인문계 A형 15, 16번

❶ *The New Negro: An Interpretation* (1925) is an anthology of fiction, poetry, and essays on African and African-American art / and literature [edited by Alain Locke, (who lived In Washington, DC and taught at Howard University during the Harlem Renaissance)]. ❷ As a collection of the creative efforts (coming out of the burgeoning New Negro Movement or Harlem Renaissance), the book is considered / by literary scholars and critics / to be the definitive text of the movement. ❸ This book included Locke's title essay "The New Negro," as well as nonfiction essays, poetry, and fiction by many of the African American writers.

❹ The New Negro dives into (how the African Americans sought social, political, and artistic change). ❺ Instead of accepting their position in society, / Locke saw the New Negro / as championing and demanding civil rights. ❻ In addition, his anthology sought to change old stereotypes and replaced them with new visions of black identity (that resisted simplification). ❼ The essays and poems (in the anthology) mirror real life events and experiences. ❽ The anthology reflects the voice of middle class African American citizens (that wanted to have equal civil rights / like the white, middle class counterparts).

❾ A theme (used by Locke commonly) is this idea of the Old vs the New Negro. ❿ The Old Negro (according to Locke) was a product of stereotypes and judgments (that were put on them), not ones (that they created). ⓫ They were forced / to live in a shadow of themselves / and others' actions. ⓬ The New Negro is a Negro (that now has an understanding of oneself). ⓭ They (at one point) lacked self-respect and self-dependence (which has created a new dynamic) and allowed the birth of the New Negro. ⓮ They have become the Negro of today (which is also the changed Negro). ⓯ Locke speaks about the migration (having an effect on the Negro /

해석

❶『신흑인에 대한 이해(The New Negro:An interpretation)』(1925)는 할렘 르네상스(Harlem Renaissance) 기간 동안 워싱턴 DC에 살며 하워드대학교에서 가르쳤던 알랭 로크(Alain Locke)가 편집한 아프리카와 아프리카계 미국 흑인의 예술과 문학에 대한 소설, 시, 에세이를 모은 문집이다. ❷ 급성장하는 신흑인 운동인 할렘 르네상스로부터 나온 창조적인 노력의 집합체인 그 책은 문학 연구가들과 비평가들에 의해서 이 운동의 완벽한 도서로 여겨진다. ❸ 이 책에는 로크의 에세이『신흑인』을 비롯하여 많은 아프리카계 미국인 작가들이 저술한 논픽션 에세이, 시, 소설 등이 실려 있다. ❹『신흑인』에서는 아프리카계 미국인들이 사회, 정치, 예술적 변화를 어떻게 추구했는지 깊게 파고든다. ❺ 그들의 사회적 지위를 받아들이는 대신에, 로크는 신흑인을 시민권을 지지하고 요구하는 것으로 생각했다. ❻ 게다가, 그의 문집은 낡은 고정관념을 바꾸기 위해 노력했고 그 고정관념들을 단순화에 저항하는 흑인 정체성의 새로운 시각으로 대체하고자 했다. ❼ 그 문집 속에 수록된 에세이와 시는 실제의 사건과 경험을 반영한다. ❽ 그 문집은 백인 중산층과 같은 동등한 시민권을 갖고 싶어 하는 중산층 아프리카계 미국인들의 목소리를 반영하고 있다. ❾ 로크가 일반적으로 사용한 주제는 구흑인 대 신흑인의 개념이다. ❿ 로크에 따르면 구흑인의 개념은 그들이 만들어낸 고정관념과 판단이 아니라 그들에게 부과된 고정관념과 견해의 산물이었다. ⓫ 그들은 어쩔 수 없이 자신과 타인들의 행동 그늘에서 살도록 강요되었다. ⓬ 신흑인은 현재 자신을 이해하는 흑인이다. ⓭ 한때 그들은 새로운 역동성을 창조하고 신흑인의 탄생을 가능하게 했던 자기 존중과 자기 신뢰가 부족했었다. ⓮ 그들은 변화된 흑인이기도 한 현재의 흑인이 되었다. ⓯ 로크는 흑인들이 공평한 경쟁의 장(場)을 만드는 데 영향을 미치고 흑인들에 대한 시각을 넓히는 데 영향을 주었던 이 주에 관해 이야기하는데, 흑인들이 미국 남부 주들을 떠나 그들이 새로 다시 출발할 수 있는 다른 지역으로 옮겼기 때문이다.

어휘

interpretation n. 해석, 설명 **anthology** n. (시)선집, 문집 **fiction** n. 소설, 허구 **literature** n. 문학 **edit** v. (책을) 편집하다 **Harlem Renaissance** n. 할렘 르네상스(1920년대에 New York시의 Harlem에서 개화한 흑인 문학 및 흑인 음악 문화의 부흥) **collection** n. (시·노래 등의) 모음집 **burgeoning** a. 급증하는, 급성장하는 **scholar** n. 학자, 장학생, 모범생 **critic** n. 비평가, 평론가 **definitive** a. 최고의, 거의 완벽한 **dive** v. (활동·일·문제 따위에) 몰두하다 **champion** v. 지지하다, 옹호하다 **stereotype** n. 고정관념 **identity** n. 정체성, 신원 **counterpart** n. 상대, 상대방 **shadow** n. 어둠, 그늘 **self-respect** n. 자기 존중, 자존심 **self-dependence** n. 자기 의존, 독립독행 **dynamic** n. 힘, 원동력 a. 역동적인

leveling the playing field and increasing the realm of how the Negro is viewed) / because they were moved / out of the southern parts of U.S. / and into other areas (where they could start over). ⓰ The migration (in a sense) transformed the Negro and fused them together / as they all came / from all over the world, all walks of life, and all different backgrounds.

A) Which of the following is NOT true about the book *The New Negro*?
다음 중 책 「The New Negro」에 대한 사실이 아닌 것은 무엇인가?
✓ ① It was written by Alain Locke alone.
그것은 알렌 로크가 혼자서 썼다. (→ 모아서 엮은 책이다)
② It includes works from a variety of literary genre.
그것은 다양한 문학 장르의 작품을 포함한다.
③ It deals with African Americans' effort for a new identity.
그것은 새로운 정체성을 위한 아프리카계 미국 흑인의 노력을 다루고 있다.
④ It reflects the real life experiences well.
그것은 실생활의 경험을 잘 반영한다.

B) Which of the following is NOT a feature of the New Negro?
다음 중 신흑인에 대한 특징이 아닌 것은 무엇인가?
① crave for a new identity
새로운 정체성에 대한 갈망
✓ ② quest for black supremacy
흑인 우월주의의 추구
③ knowledge of oneself
자기 스스로에 대한 지식
④ demand for civil rights
시민권의 요구

해석 ⓰ 어떤 의미에서 이주는 흑인들을 변화시키고 그들을 결합했는데, 그들 모두가 세계 모든 지역, 모든 계층, 서로 다른 모든 배경 출신이었기 때문이다.

해설 A) ❸ 문장에서 많은 아프리카계 미국인 작가들이 저술한 논픽션 에세이, 시, 소설 등이 실려 있다고 말하고 있으므로, 문집 즉 엮은 책이라고 해야 한다.

B) 흑인 우월성이 아닌 오히려 고정관념에서 탈피하여 새로운 정체성 그리고 기본적 권리를 요구하는 것을 특징으로 했다.

어휘 level the playing field 공평한 경쟁의 장을 만들다 realm n. 영역, 왕국 start over 다시 시작하다 fuse v. 융합[결합]되다[시키다] supremacy n. 패권, 우월주의, 주권, 최고

028 ③   2019학년도 인하대학교 인문계 39번

❶ For the past 48 hours / the 280-foot vessel *Knorr*, (temporary if not harmonious home to some 30 engineers, scientists, and academics, as well as a rotating roster of friends and financial supporters), has been lashed to a pier / in the northern Turkish city of Sinop, kept / from its appointed mission / by the lack of research visas. ❷ The American ship and crew have come to the Black Sea / to investigate ancient shipwrecks, / but the local media are skeptical. ❸ During the day / packs of journalists scramble up and down the stone dock, aiming their cameras and questions / at anyone / on the deck / within earshot.

❹ "Why are you really here? ❺ Are you searching for oil? ❻ Are you on a secret mission for the U.S. military? ❼ Are you looking for Noah's ark?"

❽ Hundreds of residents, (curious / to see for themselves), stroll arm in arm to the waterfront / in the lovely late July evenings / to marvel at the great ship (stuffed with high-tech wizardry / bobbing in the bay of their historic walled city).

❾ But for expedition leader Robert D. Ballard, / who is spending $40,000 a day on the project and is losing priceless research time — / having invested millions / in a state-of-the-art / remotely controlled submersible, deep-sea high-definition cameras, and a futuristic high-bandwidth satellite communications system — / ❿ there's nothing magical / about the nightly carnival on the dock.

⓫ "We're bleeding to death," he says. "We're hemorrhaging money." ⓬ Nor has this latest delay been the only setback of the summer. ⓭ Ballard's original itinerary called for testing his machines / on a series of Greek and Byzantine wrecks / off Bulgaria and Turkey / before moving on to a pair of 2,700-year-old Phoenician wrecks off Egypt.

해석

❶ 길이 280피트의 선박 노르(Knorr)호는 연구용 비자를 받지 못해 지시받은 임무를 수행하지 못한 채로 터키 북부의 도시 시노프(Sinop)의 부두에 지난 48시간 동안 발이 묶여 있었는데, 이 배는 교대로 배에 오른 친구들과 재정적 후원자들뿐만 아니라 약 30명의 기술자, 과학자, 교수들이 화목하게는 아니더라도 임시로 거주하기에는 적절한 처소의 역할을 하고 있었다. ❷ 미국에서 온 그 배와 선원들은 고대의 난파선들을 조사하기 위해 흑해에 왔지만, 현지의 언론은 의심의 눈초리를 보냈다. ❸ 낮 동안에는 여러 무리의 기자들이 돌로 된 선착장을 기어서 오르내리며, 부르면 들을 수 있는 가까운 거리에 있는 갑판원 아무에게나 카메라를 들이대며 질문을 해대었다.

❹ "여기에 온 진짜 이유가 뭡니까? ❺ 석유를 찾고 있는 겁니까? ❻ 미국의 비밀 임무를 수행 중인 겁니까? ❼ 노아의 방주를 찾고 있습니까?"

❽ 직접 보고 싶은 호기심이 생긴 수백 명의 주민이 아름다운 7월 말 저녁에 부두를 향해 서로 팔짱을 끼고 해안가를 거닌다. 그들은 성벽으로 둘러싸인 유서 깊은 도시의 만(灣)에 마법 같은 첨단기술로 가득 찬 거대한 배가 조금씩 잠겼다 떴다 하는 것을 보고서 감탄사를 늘어놓는다.

❾ 하지만 그 프로젝트에 매일 4만 달러를 쓰고 있고 값진 연구 시간을 허비하고 있는 탐험대 리더 로버트 발라드(Robert D. Ballard)에게는 -그는 물속에서 사용할 수 있는 최첨단 원격조종 심해 고화질 카메라와 초현대식 고대역 위성통신 시스템에 수백만 달러를 투자했다- ❿ 밤마다 갑판에서 벌어지는 축제에 마법 같은 게 전혀 없다.

⓫ "우리는 피를 흘리면서 죽어가고 있습니다. 우리는 걷잡을 수 없이 돈을 잃어가고 있어요."라고 그는 말한다.

⓬ 여름 들어 (연구 진행에) 차질을 겪은 일은 이번에 겪은 자연 사태뿐만은 아니었다. ⓭ 발라드가 계획했던 본래의 여정은 불가리아와 터키 앞바다에 있는 그리스와 비잔틴 난파선들을 대상으로 자신의 기계를 시험한 뒤 이집트 앞바다에 있는 2,700년 된 페니키아의 난파선 두 척으로 옮겨가는 것이었다.

어휘

vessel n. 용기, 그릇; 배; 항공기 **harmonious** a. 조화된; 화목한 **academic** n. 대학생, 대학교수 **rotate** v. 회전하다; 교대하다; 순회하다 **roster** n. 근무표, 명부, 등록부 **financial** a. 재정상의, 재무의 **supporter** n. 지지자; 원조자, 후원자 **lash** v. (밧줄·새끼줄 따위로) 묶다, 매다 **pier** n. 부두 **appoint** v. 지명하다, 임명하다, 정하다 **crew** n. (배·열차·비행기의) 탑승원, 승무원, 선원 **investigate** v. 조사하다 **shipwreck** n. 난파선 **skeptical** a. 의심 많은, 회의적인 **scramble** v. 기어오르다, 기어가다 **dock** n. 선창, 선착장, 부두 **deck** n. 갑판 **within earshot** 불러서 들리는 곳에 **ark** n. 방주(方舟) **resident** n. 거주자, 거류민 **curious** a. 호기심 있는 **stroll** v. 산책하다 **waterfront** n. 해안의 거리; 부두, 선창 **marvel** 놀라다 **stuff** v. ~에 채우다, 채워넣다 **wizardry** n. 마법, 마술, 묘기 **bob** v. (상하 좌우로) 홱홱[까닥까닥] 움직이다, 부동(浮動)하다 **bay** n. 만(灣) **expedition** n. (탐험·전투 등을 위한) 긴 여행[항해], 탐험(여행), 원정 **state-of-the-art** a. 최첨단의, 최신식의 **remotely** ad. 멀리서, 멀리 떨어져서 **submersible** a. 물속에 잠길 수 있는, 잠수할 수 있는 **high-definition** a. 고화질의 **futuristic** a. 초현대적인 **high-bandwidth** a. 고대역폭의 **bleed to death** 출혈이 심해서 죽다 **hemorrhage** v. (다량으로) 출혈하다; (거액의) 자산을 잃다, 큰 적자를 내다 **setback** n. (진행 따위의) 방해, 정지; 좌절, 차질 **itinerary** n. 여정(旅程); 여행 일정 계획

⓮ But weeks earlier, / just before the *Knorr* left its home port at Woods Hole, Massachusetts, / complications (in his negotiations with the Bulgarian Academy of Sciences) forced Ballard to cancel that part of the cruise for now. ⓯ Later, / after the expedition was under way, / Ballard also got words [that Egyptian security had denied him permission (to explore the Phoenician ships)].

According to the passage, why did the ship *Knorr* come to Turkey?
위 글에 의하면, 노르호는 왜 터키로 왔는가?

① To search for oil
  석유를 찾기 위해서
② To accomplish a military mission
  군사 임무를 완수하기 위해서
③ To investigate ancient shipwrecks
  고대 난파선들을 조사하기 위해서
④ To look for the remains of Noah's ark
  노아 방주의 잔해를 찾기 위해서
⑤ To rescue the crew from a sunken ship
  침몰한 선박에서 선원들을 구조하기 위해서

해석 ⓮ 그러나 출발을 몇 주 앞두고, 노르호가 매사추세츠 주의 우즈홀(Woods Hole)에 있는 모항(母港)을 떠나기 직전에, 불가리아 과학 학술원과의 교섭 과정에서 곤란한 문제가 발생하여 발라드는 항해 계획에서 그 부분을 당분간 취소해야 했다. ⓯ 뒤에, 탐험이 이미 진행되고 난 후에, 발라드는 또한 이집트 보안군이 페니키아 배를 탐험하는 것을 그에게 허가하지 않았다는 말을 전해 들었다.

해설 ❷ 문장에서 '고대의 난파선들을 조사하기 위해' 흑해에 왔음을 언급하고 있다.

어휘 **complication** n. 복잡, 복잡화; 곤란한 사정 **negotiation** n. 협상, 교섭, 절충 **cruise** n. 순항, 선박 여행 **for now** 우선은, 현재로는, 당분간 **deny** v. (권리·요구 등을) 인정하지 않다, 거부하다; 주지 않다 **permission** n. 허가; 허용 **explore** v. 탐험하다, 답사하다

정답 및 해설

029 ③   2019학년도 아주대학교 인문계 A형 42번

[A] ❶ *Cinderella* causes me a feeling of urgency. ❷ [What is unsettling about that fairy tale] is / that it is essentially the story of household — a world, (if you please) — of women gathered together and held together / in order to abuse another woman). ❸ There is a rather vague absent father and a nick-of-time prince / with a foot fetish. ❹ However, neither has much personality. ❺ There are also the surrogate "mothers," (of course (god- and step-)), who contribute both to Cinderella's grief (and) to her release and happiness. ❻ In fact, it is her step-sisters who interest me. ❼ How crippling it must be / for those girls / to grow up with a mother, to watch and imitate that mother, enslaving another girl.

[B] ❽ I am curious about their fortunes / after the story ends. ❾ For contrary to recent adaptations, / the step-sisters were not ugly, clumsy, stupid girls with outsize feet. ❿ The Grimm collection describes them / as "beautiful and fair / in appearance." ⓫ Having watched and participated in the violent dominion of another woman, / will they be any less cruel / when it comes their turn (to enslave other children), / or even when they are required / to take care of their own mother?

[C] ⓬ It is not a wholly medieval problem. ⓭ It is quite a contemporary one. ⓮ feminine power (when directed at other women) has historically been wielded / in (what has been described as a masculine manner). ⓯ I am alarmed / by the violence (that women do to each other): professional violence, competitive violence, and emotional violence. ⓰ I am alarmed / by the willingness of women / to enslave other women.

[D] ⓱ I want not to ask you / but to tell you not to participate in the oppression of your sisters. ⓲ I am suggesting / that we pay as much attention to our nurturing sensibilities / as to our ambition.

해석

[A] ❶ 『신데렐라(Cinderella)』는 나에게 절박감을 느끼게 한다. ❷ 그 동화의 심란한 점은 그것이 본질적으로 다른 여성을 학대하기 위해 함께 모여 똘똘 뭉쳐 있는 여성들의 가족 -괜찮다면 세상이라고 표현하고 싶다-에 대한 이야기라는 것이다. ❸ 막연하게 부재중인 아빠와 아슬아슬하게 때맞추어 등장하는 발에 집착하는 왕자가 있긴 하다. ❹ 그러나 둘 다 그다지 존재감이 없다. ❺ 물론, 당연히 대모(代母)와 계모인 대리 "엄마들"도 있으며, 신데렐라가 슬픔을 겪는 것도 해방되서 행복해지는 것도 모두 이들로 인한 것이다. ❻ 사실, 내 관심을 끄는 것은 그녀의 의붓언니들이다. ❼ 그 소녀들이 엄마와 함께 자라서, 엄마를 보고 흉내 내며, 다른 소녀를 노예로 만드는 것은 분명히 너무나도 파괴적인 일이다.

[B] ❽ 나는 이야기가 끝난 후의 그들의 운명이 궁금하다. ❾ 최근에 각색된 작품과는 다르게, 의붓언니들은 엄청나게 큰 발을 가진 못생기고, 볼품없고, 바보 같은 소녀들이 아니었다. ❿ 그림(Grimm)의 작품에서는 그들이 "아름답고 매력적인 외모"를 갖고 있던 것으로 묘사하고 있다. ⓫ 다른 여성에 대한 폭력적인 지배를 지켜보고 참여했던 그들이 다른 아이들을 노예로 삼을 차례가 왔을 때나 심지어 그들 자신의 엄마를 돌봐야 할 때는 과연 덜 잔인할까?

[C] ⓬ 그것은 전적으로 중세시대만의 문제는 아니다. ⓭ 그것은 현대에서도 분명히 일어나고 있는 문제이다. ⓮ 여성들의 권력이 다른 여성들을 향할 때, 그 권력은 역사적으로 소위 남성적인 방식으로 휘둘려왔다. ⓯ 나는 여성들이 서로에게 가하는 폭력에, 즉 직업적인 폭력, 경쟁에 따른 폭력, 감정적인 폭력에 경악을 금치 못한다. ⓰ 나는 여성들이 다른 여성들을 기꺼이 노예로 만들려 하는 것에 놀라움을 느낀다.

[D] ⓱ 나는 당신의 언니들이 하는 억압적인 행동에 동참하지 말라고 요청이 아닌 명령을 하고 싶다. ⓲ 나는 우리가 야망에 기울이는 주의만큼 많은 주의를 타인을 키워주는 감성에도 기울일 것을 제안한다.

어휘

urgency n. 긴급, 절박 **unsettling** a. 불안하게 만드는, 마음을 산란하게 만드는 **fairy tale** 동화 **household** n. 가족, 세대 **abuse** v. 남용하다, 오용하다, 학대하다 **vague** a. 막연한, 애매한 **absent** a. 결석한, 부재한, 없는 **nick-of-time** a. 아슬아슬하게 시간을 맞추는 **fetish** n. 집착; 페티시(특정 물건을 통해 성적 쾌감을 얻는 것) **surrogate** a. 대리의, 대용의 **contribute** v. 기부하다; 기여하다; ~의 원인이 되다 **grief** n. 슬픔, 비탄 **release** n. 해방, 석방, 면제 **crippling** a. (기능을 상실할 정도로) 큰 손해를[타격을] 주는 **imitate** v. 흉내내다, 모방하다 **enslave** v. 노예로 만들다, 예속시키다 **adaptation** n. 개작, 번안, 각색 **clumsy** a. 솜씨 없는, 서투른; 볼품없는 **outsize** a. 특대(特大)의 **fair** a. (여성이) 아름다운, 고운, 예쁜; 매력적인 **participate in** ~에 참여하다 **violent** a. 폭력적인 **dominion** n. 지배, 통치 **cruel** a. 잔인한, 잔혹한 **medieval** a. 중세의 **contemporary** a. 동시대의, 현대의, 당대의 **feminine** a. 여성의 **wield** v. (도구 따위를) 쓰다, 사용하다; (권력·무력 따위를) 휘두르다 **masculine** a. 남성의, 남자다운 **competitive** a. 경쟁적인, 경쟁에 의한 **emotional** a. 감정의, 정서의 **oppression** n. 억압, 압박, 압제 **nurture** v. 양육하다, 육성하다 **sensibility** n. 감각, 지각 **ambition** n. 야망, 포부

⓳ You are moving / in the direction of freedom / and the function of freedom is to free somebody else. ⓴ You are moving / toward self-fulfillment / and the consequences of that fulfillment should be to discover / that there is something / just as important as you are.

Which of the following CANNOT be inferred from the passage above?
다음 중 위 글에서 추론할 수 없는 것은?

① The surrogate "mothers" in *Cinderella* abused Cinderella.
『신데렐라』에 나오는 대리 "엄마들"이 신데렐라를 학대했다.

② The portrayal of Cinderella's step-sisters in our contemporary movies is different from that in the original story.
현대 영화에서 신데렐라의 의붓언니들에 대한 묘사는 원작과 다르다.

③ ✓ In a way, Cinderella's step-sisters are also victims, having been exposed to the abuse of another girl at a tender age.
어떤 면에서, 신데렐라의 의붓언니들 역시 어린 나이에 다른 소녀의 학대에 노출된 피해자들이다. (→ 가해자들이다)

④ Women shouldn't trade feminine sensibilities for success.
여성들이 성공을 위해 여성적인 감성을 버려서는 안 된다.

⑤ You cannot liberate yourself by enslaving others.
다른 사람들을 노예로 삼아서 자신을 해방시킬 수는 없다.

해석 ⓳ 당신은 자유를 향해 나아가고 있으며 자유의 역할은 다른 누군가를 자유롭게 하는 것이다. ⓴ 당신은 자기성취를 향해 나아가고 있고 그 성취의 결과는 당신만큼이나 중요한 무언가가 있다는 사실을 깨닫는 것이어야 한다.

해설 ❼ 문장에서 의붓언니들이 '엄마와 함께 자라서 엄마를 보고 흉내 내며, 다른 소녀를 노예로 만드는 것은 분명히 너무나 파괴적인 일이다'라고 말하고 있다. 따라서 같은 피해자가 아닌 오히려 가해자라고 하는 것이 맞다.

어휘 **self-fulfillment** 자아 실현 **victim** n. 피해자, 희생자 **tender** a. 부드러운, 연한, 예민한

정답 및 해설

030 ④   2019학년도 한국항공대학교 인문계 40번

❶ Kant rejects maximizing welfare and promoting virtue. ❷ Neither, (he thinks), respects human freedom. ❸ So Kant is a powerful advocate (for freedom). ❹ But the idea of freedom (he puts forth) is demanding — ❺ more demanding than the freedom of choice (we exercise / when buying and selling goods on the market). ❻ What we commonly think of as market freedom or consumer choice is not true freedom, (Kant argues), / because it simply involves satisfying desires (we haven't chosen / in the first place). ❼ So, if we're capable of freedom, / we must be capable of acting / (not according to a law (that is given or imposed on us), ❽ but according to a law (we give ourselves). But where could such a law come from?

❾ Kant's answer: from reason. ❿ We're not only sentient beings, [governed by the pleasure and pain (delivered by our senses)]; we are also rational beings, (capable of reason). ⓫ If reason determines my will, / then the will becomes the power (to choose independent of the dictates of nature or inclination). ⓬ (Notice that / Kant isn't asserting / that reason always does govern my will; / ⓭ he's only saying that, / insofar as I'm capable of acting freely, / according to a law (I give myself), then it must be the case (that reason can govern my will.))

⓮ Of course, / Kant isn't the first philosopher / to suggest / that human beings are capable of reason. ⓯ But his idea of reason, (like his conceptions of freedom and morality), is especially demanding. ⓰ Thomas Hobbes called reason the "scout for the desires." ⓱ David Hume called reason the "slave of the passions." ⓲ Reason's work, (for the utilitarians), is not to determine what ends are worth pursuing. ⓳ Its job is to figure out / how to maximize utility / (by satisfying the desires (we happen to have).

⓴ Kant rejects this subordinate role / for reason. ㉑ For him, / reason is not just the slave of the passions. ㉒ [If that were all reason amounted to, / (Kant says), we'd be better off with instinct].

해석

❶ 칸트(Kant)는 행복의 극대화와 미덕의 증진을 거부한다. ❷ 그 둘 중 어느 것도 인간의 자유를 존중하지 않는다고 그는 생각한다. ❸ 그러므로 칸트는 자유를 강력히 옹호하는 사람이다. ❹ 하지만 그가 제시하는 자유의 개념은 요구조건이 많다. ❺ 시장에서 물건을 사고팔면서 우리가 행사하는 선택의 자유보다 훨씬 더 많은 요구조건이 많다. ❻ 칸트에 따르면 우리가 흔히 시장의 자유 혹은 소비자의 선택이라고 생각하는 것은 단지 처음부터 우리가 선택하지 않은 욕망을 충족시키는 것과 관련이 있어서 진정한 자유가 아니다. ❼ 그러므로, 만약 우리가 자유를 행할 수 있으려면 우리에게 주어지거나 부과된 법칙에 따라서가 아니라, 우리가 스스로 부여한 법칙에 따라 행동할 수 있어야 한다. ❽ 하지만 그러한 법칙은 어디에서 나오는 것인가?

❾ 칸트의 답은 이성에서 나온다는 것이다. ❿ 우리는 감각이 전하는 쾌락과 고통에 지배를 받는 감각적 존재일 뿐만 아니라, 이성을 가질 수 있는 이성적 존재이기도 하다. ⓫ 만약 이성이 나의 의지를 결정한다면, 의지는 본성이나 성향이 명하는 바와 무관하게 선택할 수 있는 능력이 된다. ⓬ (칸트가 이성이 언제나 의지를 지배한다고 단언하지 않고 있음에 주목해야 한다. ⓭ 그는 단지 우리가 스스로 부여한 법칙에 따라 자유롭게 행동할 수 있는 한에서 이성이 의지를 지배할 수 있는 것이 틀림없다고 말하고 있을 뿐이다.)

⓮ 물론, 칸트가 인간이 이성을 사용할 수 있다고 주장하는 최초의 철학자는 아니다. ⓯ 하지만 그의 이성 개념은 그의 자유와 도덕 개념과 마찬가지로 특히 요구조건이 까다롭다. ⓰ 토머스 홉스(Thomas Hobbes)는 이성을 "욕망의 정찰병"이라고 불렀다. ⓱ 데이비드 흄(David Hume)은 이성을 "정념의 노예"라고 불렀다. ⓲ 공리주의자들에게 이성의 작용은 무슨 목적이 추구할 만한 가치가 있는지를 결정하는 것이 아니다. ⓳ 이성이 하는 일은 우리가 우연히 갖게 되는 욕망을 충족시킴으로써 효용을 극대화하는 방법을 알아내는 것이다.

⓴ 칸트는 이성의 이러한 종속적 역할을 거부한다. ㉑ 그에게 있어, 이성은 단순히 정념의 노예에 불과한 것이 아니다. ㉒ 만약 이성이 그 정도에 불과하다면, 우리는 차라리 본능에 따라 살게 될 때 더 행복해질 것이라고 칸트는 말한다.

어휘

welfare n. 안녕(행복), 복지 **promote** v. 촉진하다, 승진시키다 **virtue** n. 미덕, 선행, 장점 **advocate** n. 지지자, 옹호자 v. 지지하다, 옹호하다 **demanding** a. 부담이 큰, 힘든 **impose** v. 도입하다, 부과하다, 강요하다 **sentient** a. 지각이 있는 **rational** a. 합리적인, 이성적인 **dictate** n. 명령, 요구, 규칙 **inclination** n. 의향, 성향, 경사 **assert** v. 주장하다, 단언하다 **insofar as** ~하는 한에 있어서는 **philosopher** n. 철학자 **conception** n. 개념, 생각, 구상 **morality** n. 도덕, 도덕성 **scout** n. 정찰병, 척후병 **utilitarian** n. 공리주의자 **subordinate** a. 종속의

㉒ Kant's idea of reason — (of practical reason, the kind involved in morality) — is not instrumental reason / but "pure practical reason, which legislates a priori, / regardless of all empirical ends." ㉓ But how can reason do this? ㉔ Kant distinguishes two ways (that reason can command the will, / two different kinds of imperative). ㉕ One kind of imperative, (perhaps the most familiar kind), is a hypothetical imperative. ㉖ Hypothetical imperatives use instrumental reason: If you want X, / then do Y. ㉗ If you want a good business reputation, / then treat your customers honestly. ㉘ Kant contrasts hypothetical imperatives, which are always conditional, / with a kind of imperative (that is unconditional): a categorical imperative. ㉙ "If the action would be good / solely as a means to something else," (Kant writes), "the imperative is hypothetical. ㉚ If the action is represented / as good / in itself, ㉛ and therefore as necessary for a will (which of itself accords with reason), then the imperative is categorical." ㉜ The term categorical may seem like jargon, / ㉝ but it's not that distant / from our ordinary use of the term. ㉞ By "categorical," / Kant means unconditional. ㉟ So, for example, when a politician issues a categorical denial of an alleged scandal, / the denial is not merely emphatic; / ㊱ it's unconditional / — without any loophole or exception. ㊲ Similarly, a categorical duty or categorical right is one (that applies regardless of the circumstances).

Which of the following statement is true?
다음 중 본문의 내용과 일치하는 것은?

① Kant's exalted idea of freedom incorporates the principles of the greatest happiness.
칸트의 고귀한 자유 개념은 최대 행복의 원리를 통합한다.

② Kant's notion of practical reason is based upon a practical aspect of empirical truth.
칸트의 실천적 이성 개념은 경험적 진리의 실천적 측면에 바탕을 둔다.

③ Maximizing utility is the ultimate goal of both Kant and utilitarians, though they pursued it in different ways.
칸트와 공리주의자들이 추구하는 방법은 서로 다르지만, 효용성을 극대화하는 것이 그들의 궁극적인 목표이다.

④ A categorical imperative is founded upon the good itself rather than its consequences.
정언 명령은 선의 결과보다는 선 그 자체에 기초해 있다.

해석 ㉒ 칸트의 이성 개념은, 즉 도덕과 관련된 실천 이성 개념은 도구적 이성이 아니라 "모든 경험적 목적과 무관하게 선험적으로 규정하는 (법칙을 만드는) 순수 실천 이성"이다. ㉓ 하지만 이성은 어떻게 이렇게 할 수 있는가? ㉔ 칸트는 이성이 의지를 명령할 수 있는 두 가지 방식을, 즉 두 가지의 서로 다른 종류의 명령을 구별한다. ㉕ 한 종류의 명령은 아마 가장 익숙한 종류의 명령으로, 가언(假言) 명령이다. ㉖ 가언 명령은 도구적 이성을 사용한다. X를 원한다면 Y를 행하라는 식이다. ㉗ 기업의 좋은 평판을 원한다면 고객을 정직하게 대하십시오. ㉘ 칸트는 항상 조건적인 가상의 명령과 무조건적인 명령인, 정언(定言) 명령을 대조시킨다. ㉙ "만약 그 행위가 다른 어떤 것을 위한 수단으로서만 선한 것이라면," "그 (행동을 하라는) 명령은 가언적이다. ㉚ 만약 그 행위가 자체로 선한 것이라 한다면, ㉛ 그래서 이성과 저절로 일치하는 의지에 필연적인 것이라면, 그 명령은 정언적이다."라고 칸트는 썼다. ㉜ "정언적"이라는 용어가 어렵게 느껴질 수도 있지만, ㉝ 그것은 우리가 일상적으로 쓰는 그 용어의 용법에서 그리 멀지 않다. ㉞ 칸트는 "정언적"이라는 용어를 무조건적이라는 의미로 쓴다. ㉟ 그러므로 예를 들어, 어떤 정치인이 추문 혐의를 정언적으로 부인한다면, 그 부인은 단순히 단호한 것뿐 아니라, 무조건적이다. ㊱ 다시 말해 그 어떤 허점도, 예외도 없이 부인하는 것이다. ㊲ 마찬가지로, 정언적 의무 혹은 정언적 권리란 상황과 관계없이 적용되는 의무 혹은 권리이다.

해설 ㉛번 문장에서 만약 그 행위가 그 자체로 선한 것이라면, 그 명령은 정언적이라고 말하고 있다. ④ 정언 명령은 선의 결과보다는 선 그 자체에 기초해 있다고 할 수 있다.

어휘 instinct n. 본능, 직감 instrumental a. 중요한 legislate v. 제정하다 a priori n. 선험적 명제 empirical a. 경험적인 distinguish v. 구별하다 imperative n. 명령 hypothetical a. 가설적인, 가언적인 reputation n. 명성, 평판 categorical a. 절대적인, 무조건적인 categorical imperative 정언명령, 절대명령, 지상명령 jargon n. 뜻을 알 수 없는 어려운 말 ordinary a. 보통의, 일상적인, 평범한 alleged a. (혐의로) 주장되는 merely ad. 한낱, 그저, 단지 emphatic a. 단호한, 강한 loophole n. 빠져나갈 구멍, 허점 exalt v. 승격시키다, 고상하게 하다, 칭찬하다

유형 07 부분이해

001 ③ 2019학년도 강남대학교 인문·자연계 28번

❶ Who am I? ❷ I am your greatest helper or worst enemy. ❸ I will lift you up / or drag you down. ❹ You can control me 100%. ❺ Show me exactly how you want something, / and after a little practice, / I will do it every time. ❻ All great people, / I made great. ❼ All failures, / I made fail. ❽ Train and guide me, / and ⓐ I will put the world / at our feet. ❾ Be careless with me, / and I will destroy you. ❿ Who am I?

What do the underlined words ⓐ mean?
밑줄 친 문장 ⓐ의 의미는 무엇인가?

① I will make you very happy.
나는 당신을 매우 행복하게 만들 것이다.
② I will make you a great failure.
나는 당신을 커다란 실패자로 만들 것이다.
✓③ I will make you a great success.
나는 당신을 크게 성공한 사람으로 만들 것이다.
④ I will make you very comfortable.
나는 당신을 매우 편안하게 만들 것이다.

해석 ❶ 나는 누구일까? ❷ 나는 당신의 최고의 조력자 아니면 최악의 적이다. ❸ 나는 당신을 높일 수도 있고, 끌어내릴 수도 있다. ❹ 당신은 나를 100% 통제할 수 있다. ❺ 당신이 뭔가가 어떻게 되기를 원하는지 내게 정확하게 보여준다면, 약간의 연습 뒤에 나는 매번 그렇게 행할 것이다. ❻ 모든 위대한 사람들을 위대하게 만든 것이 바로 나다. ❼ 모든 실패자들을 실패하게 만든 것도 바로 나다. ❽ 나를 훈련시키고 지도하여라. 그러면 ⓐ나는 세상을 당신의 발아래에 가져다 놓겠다. ❾ 나를 아무렇게나 취급하라. 그러면 내가 당신을 파괴할 것이다. ❿ 나는 누구일까?

해설 첫 문장부터 나라는 존재의 잠재력을 말하고 있으므로 ③이 가장 적절하다.

어휘 lift up 끌어올리다 drag down 끌어내리다

002 ② 2019학년도 강남대학교 인문·자연계 30번

❶ House cats act like their wild ancestors / in several ways. ❷ Although most house cats do not have to catch their own food, / ❸ they show hunting behavior / such as being active / at dawn and dusk, / and chasing and jumping / on ⓐ pretend prey. ❹ Long legs, strong muscles and flexible joints give cats great jumping skill. ❺ Much of this behavior is inborn, and does not have to be trained. ❻ A cat (raised away from all other cats) still acts / this way.

What does the underlined part ⓐ mean?
밑줄 친 ⓐ가 의미하는 것은 무엇인가?

① canned food
통조림 식품
✓② cat toys
고양이 장난감
③ wild cats
야생 고양이들
④ mice
생쥐들

해석 ❶ 집고양이들은 몇 가지 면에서 그들의 야생 조상들처럼 행동한다. ❷ 대부분 집고양이들은 직접 먹이를 잡을 필요가 없지만, ❸ 이들은 동이 틀 무렵이나 황혼 무렵에는 활동적으로 되며 ⓐ가짜 사냥감을 쫓아다니고 점프하며 달려드는 것 같은 사냥 행동을 보여준다. ❹ 긴 다리와 강한 근육 및 유연한 관절은 고양이들에게 뛰어난 점프 실력을 부여하게 된다. ❺ 이러한 행동 대부분은 타고난 것으로, 학습할 필요가 없다. ❻ 다른 고양이들로부터 따로 떨어져 길러진 고양이도 여전히 이런 식으로 행동한다.

해설 글의 소재인 'House cat(집 고양이)' 이야기인 만큼 고양이 장난감을 추론할 수 있다.

어휘 ancestor n. 선조, 조상 dawn n. 동틀 녘, 새벽 dusk n. 어스름, 황혼 chase v. 쫓다, 추적하다 pretend a. 가짜의, 상상의 prey n. 먹이, 사냥감 flexible a. 유연한 joint n. 관절 inborn a. 타고난, 선천적인

003 ④   2019학년도 덕성여자대학교 오후 29번

❶ While many countries have endured the rise and fall of diverse forms of government, / few have changed as extensively, suddenly, and repeatedly as Japan. ❷ Once / an international trading destination / and home to hundreds of thousands of Christians, / Japan closed itself / to foreign commerce and religion / seemingly overnight. ❸ Ⓐ In doing so, / it may be argued / that it laid the thematic foundation for a significant degree of indigenous development / beyond the influence of the West.

Which of the following best summarizes the information in the underlined sentence Ⓐ?
다음 중 밑줄 친 문장 Ⓐ의 내용을 가장 잘 요약한 것은?

① Japanese culture developed over time without significant influences from the Western world.
일본의 문화는 시간이 지나며 서양 세계로부터 상당한 영향 없이 발전했다.

② Japan's modern culture is based on a combination of foreign Western influences and native traditional practices.
일본의 현대 문화는 외국 서양의 영향과 토착의 전통 관행의 조합에 기초한 것이다.

③ The cultural foundations of Japanese society are considered to be native rather than Western in nature.
일본 사회의 문화적 기반은 본질적으로 서양적인 것보다는 토착적인 것으로 간주한다.

④ By rejecting foreign institutions, Japan was able to develop on its own in several important ways without Western influences.
외국의 제도를 거부함으로써, 일본은 서양의 영향 없이 여러 중요한 면에서 스스로 발전할 수 있었다.

해석
❶ 많은 국가들이 다양한 형태의 정부의 흥망성쇠를 겪어온 반면, 일본처럼 광범위하게, 갑자기, 반복적으로 변한 국가는 거의 없었다. ❷ 한때 국제 무역의 목적지이자 수십만 명에 이르는 기독교인들의 본거지였던 일본은 대외통상과 종교에 대해 일견 하루아침에 문을 닫았다. ❸ Ⓐ그렇게 함으로써, 일본은 서양의 영향을 넘어 상당한 수준의 고유 발전을 이뤄낼 관련된 토대를 마련했다고 주장할 수 있다.

해설
In doing so'는 앞 문장에서 말하는 대외통상을 그만두는 것을 뜻하며, 그로 인해 일본 스스로 서양을 넘는 수준의 주요 토대를 마련했다는 뜻의 ④이 가장 적절하다.

어휘
endure v. 견디다, 참다 diverse a. 다양한 extensively ad. 광범위하게, 널리 repeatedly ad. 되풀이하여, 반복적으로 destination n. 목적지 home n. 발상지, 본고장 commerce n. 무역, 상업 religion n. 종교 seemingly ad. 겉보기에는, 외견상 overnight ad. 하룻밤 사이에, 갑자기, 별안간 thematic a. 주제의, 주제와 관련된 foundation n. 기초, 토대, 기반 lay the foundation for ~을 위한 토대를 놓다 significant a. 중대한, 중대한, 의미심장한, 상당한 indigenous a. 고유의, 토착의, 원산의 influence n. 영향, 영향력

004 ③

2019학년도 덕성여자대학교 오후 30번

❶ Karl Mannheim is one of the most important figures / in the history of society, founding a branch of the science (commonly known as the sociology of knowledge.) ❷ Ⓐ The field deals with the relationships (between ideas and societies,) exploring [how societal structures can affect the creation of new ideas] ❸ and [how ideas (themselves) can affect societies / in their own right.] ❹ The three phases of Mannheim's career each led to an increasingly sophisticated understanding of the complex interaction / between theoretical concepts and the communities (that produce them.)

Which of the following best summarizes the information in the underlined sentence Ⓐ?
다음 중 밑줄 친 문장 Ⓐ의 내용을 가장 잘 요약한 것은?

① The sociology of knowledge is primarily interested in how new ideas develop within societies.
지식사회학은 주로 사회 내에서 새로운 사상이 어떻게 발전하는가에 관심이 있다.

② The sociology of knowledge deals with the way social structure affects ideas present in the culture.
지식사회학은 사회 구조가 문화에 존재하는 사상에 어떻게 영향을 끼치는가에 대해 다룬다.

③ The sociology of knowledge looks at how ideas and societal structures affect each other.
지식사회학은 사상과 사회 구조가 서로 어떻게 영향을 미치는지에 대해 살펴본다.

④ The sociology of knowledge is mainly concerned with the way ideas affect and shape societies.
지식사회학은 주로 사상이 사회에 영향을 미치고 형성하는 방식과 관련이 있다.

해 석

❶ 카를 만하임(Karl Mannheim)은 사회 역사상 가장 중요한 인물들 중의 하나이며, 일반적으로 지식사회학으로 알려진 학문 분야를 창시했다. ❷ Ⓐ이 분야는 사상과 사회 둘 사이의 관계를 다루고, 사회 구조가 새로운 사상의 창조에 어떻게 영향을 미칠 수 있는지, ❸ 그리고 사상 그 자체가 사회에 어떻게 영향을 미칠 수 있는지에 대해 탐구한다. ❹ 만하임의 경력 세 단계 각각은 이론 개념과 그 개념을 만들어내는 사회 사이의 복잡한 상호 작용에 대한 이해를 점점 더 정교하게 했다.

해 설

카를 만하임(Karl Mannheim)은 지식사회학 분야 창시자로 사상과 사회 둘 사이 관계를 연구하고 사상과 사회 사이의 복잡한 상호 작용에 관해 연구했다고 말하는 만큼 ③이 가장 적절하다.

어 휘

found v. 설립하다, 창립하다 **branch** n. 분과, 부문 **sociology** n. 사회학 **explore** v. 탐구하다, 조사하다 **phase** n. (변화·발전의) 단계, 국면 **sophisticated** a. 세련된; 정교한, 복잡한 **complex** a. 복합적인, 복잡한 **interaction** n. 상호 작용, 상호 영향 **theoretical** a. 이론의, 이론상의 **primarily** ad. 주로

005 ①
2019학년도 숙명여자대학교 인문계 33번

글의 주제 신경다양성

① The idea of neurodiversity is really a paradigm shift / in (how we think about kids / in special education.) ② Instead of regarding these students / as suffering from deficit, disease, or dysfunction, neurodiversity suggests / that we speak about their strengths. ③ Neruodiversity urges us to discuss brain diversity / using the same kind of discourse (that we employ / when we talk about biodiversity and cultural diversity.) ④ We don't pathologize a colla lily / by saying / that it has a "petal deficit disorder." ⑤ We simply appreciate its unique beauty. ⑥ We don't diagnose individuals [who have skin color (that is different from our own)] as suffering from "pigmentation dysfunction." ⑦ That would be racist. ⑧ Similarly, we ought not to pathologize children (who have different kinds of brains / and different ways of thinking and learning.)

What does the underlined sentence mean best?
밑줄 친 문장을 가장 잘 의미하는 것은 무엇인가?

✓① The common principle that we use for biodiversity and cultural diversity should be applied to the area of brain diversity.
우리가 생물다양성과 문화적 다양성을 위해서 사용하는 공통적인 원칙이 뇌의 다양성 영역에 적용되어야 한다.

② Discourse analysis is a helpful tool that can be used in common in all those three areas.
담화 분석은 이 세 가지 영역에서 공통적으로 사용할 수 있는 유용한 도구다.

③ Neurodiversity brings our attention back to the areas of biodiversity and cultural diversity.
신경다양성은 생물의 다양성과 문화적 다양성의 영역으로 우리의 관심을 다시 집중시킨다.

④ Biodiversity and cultural diversity are more advanced areas of knowledge.
생물의 다양성과 문화적 다양성은 보다 진보된 지식의 영역이다.

⑤ Biodiversity and cultural diversity are used as models for a psychological treatment.
생물의 다양성과 문화적 다양성은 심리치료의 모델로 사용된다.

해석
① 신경 다양성의 개념은 우리가 특수교육을 받는 아이들에 대해 어떻게 생각하는가에 대한 패러다임의 대전환이다. ② 이런 학생들이 (심신의) 결함, 질병, 기능장애를 앓고 있다고 간주하는 대신에 신경 다양성은 우리가 이 학생들의 강점에 대해 말할 것을 제안한다. ③ 신경 다양성은 생물의 다양성과 문화적 다양성에 대해 말을 할 때 사용하는 것과 같은 종류의 담론을 사용하여 우리가 뇌의 다양성에 대한 토론 할 것을 권한다. ④ 우리는 콜라 백합이 '꽃잎 결핍 장애(꽃잎이 많이 안 붙어 있음)'가 있다고 말함으로써 이것이 병을 앓고 있는 것이라 여기지 않는다. ⑤ 우리는 그저 그 꽃의 독특한 아름다움을 감상한다. ⑥ 우리는 우리와 다른 피부색을 가진 사람들을 '색소 기능장애'로 진단하지 않는다. ⑦ 그렇게 하는 것은 인종차별주의적인 것이다. ⑧ 마찬가지로, 우리는 다른 종류의 두뇌와, 다른 방식으로 생각하고 학습하는 아이들을 병적인 상태로 간주하여서는 안 된다.

해설 윗글은 신경 다양성 개념을 통해 특수교육 받는 아이들을 병적 상태로 간주해서는 안 된다는 글이다. 따라서 ①이 이 뜻과 가장 적절하다.

어휘 neurodiversity n. 신경다양성(다양한 신경질환을 정상의 범주에 포함시키는 운동) paradigm shift 인식 체계[패러다임]의 대전환 deficit n. 부족, 결함 dysfunction n. 기능 장애 strength n. 힘, 강점, 장점 urge n. 충동 v. 주장하다, 강력히 권하다 diversity n. 다양성 discourse n. 담론, 담화 employ v. 쓰다, 이용하다 biodiversity n. (균형 잡힌 환경을 위한) 생물의 다양성 cultural diversity 문화적 다양성 pathologize v. 병을 앓고 있다(=to represent (something) as a disease) petal n. 꽃잎 disorder n. 장애, 무질서, 혼란 diagnose v. 진단하다 pigmentation n. (피부·머리카락·나뭇잎 등의) 색소

006 ②   2019학년도 한국산업기술대학교 인문계 34번

❶ The movie industry is obviously affected / by personal recommendations. ❷ Even though well over a billion dollars is spent every year / on promoting new movies, / people (talking to people) is what really counts. ❸ According to Marvin Antonowsky, (head of marketing for Universal Pictures,) "Word of mouth is like wildfire". ❹ This point is well illustrated by the number of low budget movies (that have succeeded with little or no advertising) — / and by the number of big budget flops. ❺ Like the movies, book publishing is another industry (where lots of money is traditionally spent on advertising) / but can't begin to compete with the power of friends (telling friends / about their discoveries.) ❻ Twenty five years ago, / The Road Less Traveled, (by psychiatrist M. Scott Peck,) was just another psychology book (lying unnoticed on bookstore shelves.) ❼ Then a few people read it, / told their friends, / and started a chain reaction (that is still going on.) ❽ Today, / there are well over two million copies / in print.

Which of the following is closest in meaning to the underlined part?
다음 중 밑줄 친 부분의 의미와 가장 가까운 것은 무엇인가?

① what people don't like
    사람들이 싫어하는 것
✓ what is really important
    정말로 중요한 것
③ what people can't trust
    사람들이 신뢰하지 않는 것
④ what is accounted for
    설명되는 것

해석 ❶ 영화 산업은 개인적인 추천의 영향을 분명하게 받는다. ❷ 새로운 영화를 홍보하는 데 매년 10억 달러 이상이 지출되고 있지만, 정말로 중요한 것은 사람들 사이의 입소문이다. ❸ 유니버셜 영화사의 마케팅 팀장인 마빈 안토노브스키(Marin Antonowsky)에 따르면, 입소문은 산불과 같다. ❹ 이 점은 광고를 거의 또는 전혀 하지 않고도 성공한 저예산 영화의 수와 많은 예산이 들고도 실패한 영화의 수에서 여지없이 드러난다. ❺ 영화와 마찬가지로, 책의 출판도 전통적으로 광고에 많은 돈이 소비되는 것에 반해 발견한 책에 대한 친구들 사이의 입소문의 영향력과는 경쟁이 되지 않는 또 다른 사업이다. ❻ 25년 전에 정신과 의사 M. 스콧 펙(Scott Peck)이 쓴 『아직도 가야할 길(The Road Less Traveled)』은 서점 진열대에서 주목받지 못한 상태로 놓여 있던 흔해 빠진 심리학 서적이었다. ❼ 그러다가 몇몇 사람들이 그 책을 읽고, 친구들에게 말했고, 그렇게 시작된 연쇄 반응은 아직까지도 계속되고 있다. ❽ 오늘날 출판된 부수는 200만 부가 훨씬 넘는다.

해설 count의 뜻은 '~을 세다'이외 '중요하다', '영향력 있다'의 뜻으로 사용될 수도 있다. 따라서 정답은 ②이 가장 적절하다.

어휘 recommendation n. 권고, 추천 affect v. 영향을 미치다, 작용하다 well over 훨씬 더 promote v. 촉진하다, 홍보하다 wildfire n. 산불, 들불 illustrate v. 분명히 보여주다 budget n. 예산 flop n. (책·연극·영화 등의) 실패작 just another 흔해 빠진, 그렇고 그런 unnoticed a. 눈에 띄지 않는 chain reaction n. 연쇄 반응

007 ④ 2019학년도 강남대학교 인문·자연계 33번

A ❶ The Taklimakan Desert, at Asia's heart, keeps an ancient secret. ❷ Here, long ago, two great civilizations — the East and the West — made forgotten contact. ❸ Here, hints of long-gone life raise the question: was early Chinese culture born alone, or was there a lost link with the West? ❹ Ⓐ Silent voices now speak: ❺ a woman, and others like her, up to 4,000 years old, amazingly preserved. ❻ Surprisingly, the mummies are clearly not Chinese. ❼ They help answer how distant cultures met and exchanged precious goods and ideas.

B ❽ The Silk Road, 6,000 kilometers long, crossed the whole known world. ❾ At one end were the great civilizations of Rome and Greece, and at the other, China's borderlands. ❿ It was thought that the ruins at the Silk Road's eastern end were Chinese. ⓫ Now, it seems the builders were a little-known people called Tocharians, who came over 4,000 years ago. ⓬ The mummies show that people of European origins lived on China's frontier as early as 2,000 B.C.

What does the underlined part Ⓐ mean?
밑줄 친 Ⓐ의 의미는 무엇인가?

① The desert people spoke no Chinese.
  그 사막에 사는 사람들은 중국어를 할 줄 몰랐다.
② Lost voices have been restored by modern technology.
  현대 기술에 의해 잃어버렸던 목소리를 복원하게 되었다.
③ The desert people used body language to communicate.
  그 사막 주민들은 의사소통하기 위해 몸짓 언어를 썼다.
✓ Archeological finds provide evidence of a long-forgotten culture.
  고고학 발굴 결과가 오랫동안 잊혀졌던 문화의 증거를 제공한다.

해석

A ❶ 아시아의 중심에 있는 타클라마칸 사막(Taklimakan Desert)은 고대의 비밀을 그대로 간직하고 있다. ❷ 오래전 이곳에서 동양과 서양이라는 두 위대한 문명은 지금은 아무도 기억하지 못하는 접촉을 했다. ❸ 오래 전에 사라진 삶의 모습을 보여주는 이곳의 흔적들은 고대 중국 문명이 홀로 탄생한 것인지 아니면 서양과의 잃어버린 연결고리가 있었던 것인가라는 질문을 던지게 한다. ❹ Ⓐ 침묵의 목소리가 지금 말한다. ❺ 거의 4천 년 된 한 여성과 또 다른 사람들이 놀라울 정도로 잘 보존돼 있다. ❻ 놀랍게도, 그 미라들은 분명히 중국인들이 아니다. ❼ 그것들은 멀리 떨어진 문화들이 어떻게 만나 귀중한 상품과 아이디어들을 교환했는지에 관한 답을 하는 데 도움을 준다.

B ❽ 6천 킬로미터에 달하는 실크로드(Silk Road)는 당시에 알려진 온 세상을 가로질렀다. ❾ 한쪽 끝에는 로마와 그리스라는 위대한 문명들이 있었고, 다른 쪽 끝에는 중국의 국경지대가 있었다. ❿ 실크로드의 동쪽 끝에 있는 유적지들은 중국의 것이라고 여겨졌다. ⓫ 그런데 지금은, 그곳을 건설했던 사람들이 4천 년 전에 온 토카라인(Tocharian)이라는 잘 알려지지 않은 사람이었던 것처럼 여겨진다. ⓬ 미라들은 유럽계 사람들이 일찍이 기원전 2천 년경에 중국 국경에 살았음을 보여준다.

해설 밑줄 친 앞 문장에서 고대 중국과 서양의 연결고리에 관한 질문을 던지고, 이어지는 문장에서는 떨어진 문화들이 어떻게 교류했는지를 언급하고 있다. 따라서 ④이 가장 적절하다.

어휘 ancient a. 고대의 contact n. 접촉 v. 접촉하다, 연락하다 long-gone 오래전에 없어진 silent a. 침묵의, 조용한 preserve v. 보존하다, 보호하다 mummy n. 미라 precious a. 귀중한 civilization n. 문명 borderland n. 국경 지역 ruin n. 폐허, 옛터 come over (어떠한) 기분이 들다 frontier n. 국경, 변경 restore v. 복원하다, 회복시키다 archeological a. 고고학의, 고고학적인

정답 및 해설

008 ⑤   2020학년도 광운대학교 인문계 A형 35번

❶ "Beauty is difficult," says Cacciari, (former mayor of Venice and professor of philosophy), sounding as if he were addressing a graduate seminar / in aesthetics rather than answering a question / about municipal regulations. ❷ The preceding day, / heavy rains had flooded Mestre in Venice again. Rain caused the flood, / not acqua alta, / Cacciari says, / "High tide is not a problem for me. ❸ It's a problem for foreigners. ❹ "End of discussion on flooding! No, he stresses, however, the problem lies elsewhere. ❺ There is tourism. ❻ Of that, Cacciari says, / "Venice is not a sentimental place of honeymoon. ❼ It's a strong, contradictory, overpowering place. ❽ It is not a city for tourists. ❾ Ⓐ It cannot be reduced / to a postcard." ❿ Tourism has been part of the Venetian landscape / since the 14th century, when pilgrims stopped / en route to the Holy Land. ⓫ So, what's so different about tourism now? "Now, Venice gets giant cruise ships. ⓬ The ship is ten stories high. ⓭ You can't understand Venice / from ten stories up. ⓮ You might as well be in a helicopter."

밑줄 친 Ⓐ의 의미는?

① Tourists should not use a postcard.
   관광객들은 우편엽서를 사용하지 말아야 한다.
② Venice has so many places to visit.
   베네치아는 방문할 곳이 매우 많다.
③ Honeymooners send many postcards.
   신혼여행 온 사람들은 우편엽서를 많이 보낸다.
④ Venice is a big place to fit into a postcard.
   베네치아는 우편엽서 안으로 들어가기에는 규모가 큰 장소이다.
⑤ Venice shouldn't be known only for tourism.
   베네치아가 관광으로만 알려져서는 안 된다.

해 석 ❶ "아름다움은 어렵습니다."라고 전 베네치아 시장이자 철학과 교수인 카치아리(Cacciari)가 말하는데, 그의 말은 시 정부의 규제에 대한 질문에 대답하기보다는 미학 관련 어느 대학원 세미나에서 연설하는 것처럼 들린다. ❷ 전날 폭우로 인해 베네치아의 메스트레(Mestre) 지역이 또다시 물에 잠기게 되었다. 만조(滿潮)가 아니라 폭우로 인하여 범람한 것이라며 카치아리는 "만조는 저에게 아무런 문제가 되지 않습니다. ❸ 만조는 외국인(관광객)에게 문제가 됩니다."라고 말했다. ❹ 범람에 관한 이야기는 그것으로 마쳤지만, 그게 아니라 문제는 다른 곳에 있다고 그는 강조한다. ❺ 문제는 관광이다. ❻ 그 내용에 대해, 카치아리는 "베네치아는 신혼여행으로 찾아오는 감상적인 곳이 아닙니다. ❼ 베네치아는 강력하고 모순적이면서 또한 굉장한 곳입니다. ❽ 베네치아는 관광객들을 위해 존재하는 도시가 아닙니다. ❾ Ⓐ베네치아가 우편엽서 한 장으로 전락할 수는 없습니다."라고 말한다. ❿ 관광은 14세기 이후 베네치아의 모습 일부가 되었는데, 14세기에 순례자들이 성지(聖地)로 가는 중간에 베네치아에 들리곤 했습니다. ⓫ 그래서 지금 관광은 (과거와) 무엇이 그렇게 다른가? "지금 베네치아에는 거대한 유람선이 다닙니다. ⓬ 유람선은 높이가 10층이나 됩니다. ⓭ 그 10층 높은 곳에서 보아서는 베네치아가 어떤 곳인지 알지 못합니다. ⓮ 차라리 헬리콥터에서 베네치아를 보는 편이 나을 겁니다.

해 설 앞 문장에서 베네치아는 관광객들을 위해 존재하는 도시가 아니라 강력하면서 굉장한 곳이라고 말하고 있다. 따라서 ⑤이 가장 적절하다.

어 휘 mayor n. 시장 address v. 연설하다 aesthetics n. 미학 municipal a. 지방자치체의; 시의 regulation n. 규정, 규제 preceding a. 이전의 flood v. 물에 잠기게 하다 acqua alta 아쿠아 알타(베네치아에 정기적으로 발생하는 이상 만조현상) high tide 만조(滿潮) stress n. 스트레스 v. 강조하다 sentimental a. 정서적인, 감상적인 honeymoon n. 신혼여행 v. 신혼여행을 하다 contradictory a. 모순되는 overpowering a. 강렬한, 굉장한 reduce v. (~로) 바꾸다; (~이) 되게 하다 landscape n. 풍경 pilgrim n. 순례자 en route to ~로 가는 도중에 story n. 층

009 ②
2019학년도 한성대학교 인문계 A형 16번

❶ Like other industries in 2008, / plastic surgery suffered a drop / in revenues / when the recession began to worsen. ❷ Recently, however, people have begun investing in cosmetic surgery / to increase their value / in the job market. ❸ For example, 56-year-old Max Seddon is aware / that the weakening music industry will likely force him to begin seeking work elsewhere. ❹ He spent $17,000 on a facelift / to make his appearance more youthful and to bolster his confidence / when he goes job-hunting. ❺ Other middle-aged men and women have found it necessary to turn to cosmetic surgery because they are competing with younger job applicants (who look young and fresh).

❻ Plastic surgeons have noted / that people now have cosmetic surgery done / not just so they can enjoy life more, / but also because they know / skills are often not enough / in a competitive job market. ❼ Surgeons are now offering cheaper face-lifts (that use only local anesthesia / to reduce the price and the recovery time). ❽ A plastic surgeon (in Manhattan) has considered the fact (that the older yet more qualified people ⓒ are being passed over / for their younger, better-looking counterparts) / ❾ and has offered a "job-fighter package" [that makes use of cosmetic surgery methods (that are less invasive and much cheaper)].

Which one can best replace ⓒ are being passed over for?
다음 중 ⓒ are being passed over for를 대체할 수 있는 것으로 가장 적절한 것은 무엇인가?

① are being preferred to
   ~보다 더 선호되고 있다
✓② are being less preferred to
   ~보다 덜 선호되고 있다
③ are getting closer to
   ~에 더 가까워지고 있다
④ are getting less close to
   ~에 덜 가까워지고 있다

해석

❶ 2008년에 불경기가 악화하기 시작하자, 성형수술 산업도 다른 산업들과 마찬가지로 수입 감소로 타격을 입었다. ❷ 하지만 최근에 사람들은 취업 시장에서 그들의 가치를 높이기 위해서 성형수술에 투자하기 시작했다. ❸ 예를 들면, 56세의 맥스 세든(Max Seddon)은 음반 업계의 악화로 인해 자신이 다른 일자리를 찾아 나서야 할 거라는 것을 알고 있다. ❹ 그는 구직 활동을 할 때 자신의 외모를 더 젊어 보이게 하고 자신감을 높이기 위해서 주름살 제거 수술을 받는 것에 1만 7천 달러를 썼다. ❺ 또 다른 중년의 남성과 여성들은 젊고 생기 있어 보이는 젊은 구직자들과 경쟁하고 있기 때문에 자신들이 성형 수술에 의지할 필요가 있다는 것을 느꼈다.

❻ 성형외과 의사들은 현재 사람들은 인생을 더 즐기기 위해서 뿐만 아니라 경쟁이 심한 취업 시장에서 기술만으로는 종종 충분하지 않다는 것을 알기에 성형수술을 받는다는 것에 주목했다. ❼ 성형외과 의사들은 현재 비용과 회복 시간을 줄이기 위해 국소 마취만 사용하는, 비용이 더 저렴한 주름 제거 수술을 제공하고 있다. ❽ 맨해튼의 한 성형외과 의사는 나이는 더 많지만, 더 실력 있는 사람들이 더 젊고 더 잘생긴 경쟁자들과 ⓒ비교하여 기피당하고 있다는 사실을 고려해서 ❾ 의사의 손이 덜 가고 훨씬 더 저렴한 성형수술 방법을 활용한 '구직용 성형 기획 상품'을 제공하고 있다.

해설

『pass over』는 '~을 무시하다', '피하다'는 의미로, overlook과 같은 뜻이다. 따라서 맥락상 더 실력있고 잘생긴 경쟁자들과 비교하여 기피당한다는 말임으로 ② 'are being less preferred to' 즉 '~보다 덜 선호되고 있다'가 가장 적절하다.

어휘

plastic surgery 성형 수술 revenue n. 수입 recession n. 경기 후퇴, 불경기, 불황 cosmetic surgery 미용 성형 수술 facelift n. 주름(살) 제거 수술 appearance n. (겉)모습, 외모 youthful a. 젊은, 젊은이다운 bolster v. 지지하다, 보강하다 job-hunting n. 구직 turn to ~에 의지하다 job applicant 구직자 anesthesia n. 마취, 무감각증 local anesthesia 국소 마취 pass over ~을 무시하다, 피하다 make use of ~을 이용[활용]하다 method n. 태도, 방법 invasive a. 몸에 칼을 대는, 외과적인

정답 및 해설

010 ③
2020학년도 서울여자대학교 인문·자연계 A형 32번

❶ The idea (that you can't buy happiness) has been exposed as a myth, / over and over. ❷ Richer countries are happier than poor countries. ❸ Richer people within richer countries are happier, too. ❹ The evidence is unequivocal: Money makes you happy. ❺ You just have to know what to do with it.

❻ Stop buying so much stuff, / psychologist Daniel Gilbert said / in an interview / a few years ago, and try to spend more money / on experiences. ❼ We think / that experiences can be fun / but leave us / with nothing (to show / for them). ❽ But that turns out to be a good thing. ❾ Happiness, (for most people), comes / from sharing experiences with other people; / experiences are usually shared — first when they happen / and then again and again / when we tell our friends.

❿ On the other hand, objects wear out their welcome. ⓫ If you really love a rug, / you might buy it. ⓬ The first few times you see, / you might admire it, / and feel happy. ⓭ But over time, / it will probably reveal itself to be just a rug. ⓮ Try to remember the last time : (an old piece of furniture made you ecstatic).

What does the underlined sentence imply?
밑줄 친 문장이 함축하는 것은 무엇인가?

① We can shop our way out of a bad mood.
   우리는 쇼핑을 하여 나쁜 기분에서 벗어날 수 있다.
② Objects are usually preferred to experiences.
   물건은 일반적으로 경험에서 선호된다.
✓ Our happiness from buying things declines with time.
   물건을 사서 얻는 행복은 시간이 지나면서 감소한다.
④ We usually buy what we want rather than what we need.
   우리는 일반적으로 우리에게 필요한 것보다 우리가 원하는 것을 산다.

해석
❶ 행복을 (돈으로) 살 수 없다는 생각은 근거 없는 이야기로 거듭해서 밝혀져 왔다. ❷ 부유한 나라들이 가난한 나라들보다 더 행복하다. ❸ 또한, 부유한 나라에서는 부유한 사람들이 더 행복하다. ❹ 돈이 당신을 행복하게 한다는 근거는 확실하다. ❺ 당신은 돈으로 무엇을 해야 할지 알고 있기만 하면 된다. ❻ 심리학자 다니엘 길버트(Daniel Gilbert)는 몇 년 전 인터뷰에서 너무 많은 물건을 사지 말고 경험에 더 많은 돈을 지출하도록 노력하라고 말했다. ❼ 우리는 경험이 재미있긴 하지만 경험했다고 하더라도 보여줄 것은 그 무엇도 남지 않는다고 생각한다. ❽ 하지만 경험은 유익한 것으로 드러났다. ❾ 대부분의 사람들의 경우 행복은 다른 사람들과 경험을 공유하는 것에서 나온다. 경험은 대개 공유되는데, 처음에는 경험이 발생할 때 공유되고, 그다음에는 우리가 친구들에게 이야기해줄 때 계속해서 공유된다. ❿ 다른 한편, 물건은 점점 환영을 받지 못할 것이다. ⓫ 당신이 어떤 양탄자를 정말 좋아한다면, 아마 그것을 구매할 것이다. ⓬ 처음 몇 번은 볼 때마다 그것에 감탄하며, 행복을 느낄 수도 있다. ⓭ 하지만 시간이 지나면 그것은 아마 그저 평범한 양탄자로 보일 것이다. ⓮ 오래된 가구 하나가 가장 최근에 당신을 황홀하게 만들었던 때를 기억해 보길 바란다.

해설
밑줄 다음 문장의 예시에서 양탄자 구매 후 행복을 느끼지만, 시간이 지나면 그것은 아마 그저 평범한 양탄자로 보일 것이라고 말한다. 따라서 주어진 문장 '물건들은 환영받지 못한다'는 뜻은 ③ 시간이 지나면서 그 행복이 감소한다고 말해야 가장 적절하다.

어휘
expose v. 드러내다, 노출시키다 myth n. 신화; 꾸며낸 이야기 over and over 반복해서 unequivocal a. 명백한, 분명한 stuff n. 물건 turn out 모습을 드러내다, ~으로 되어가다 wear out 점점 없어지다 wear out one's welcome 성가시게 방문하여 [너무 오래 머물러] 미움을 사다 rug n. 융단, 양탄자 admire v. 칭찬하다; 감탄하며 바라보다 furniture n. 가구 ecstatic a. 황홀해 하는, 열광하는

---

1) stop ~ing : ~하는 것을 멈춰라
   cf) stop to ~ : ~하기위해 멈추다

2) try to ~ : to~하려고 노력하다
   cf) try ~ing : ~ing 해보다

011 ③ 2019학년도 단국대학교 자연계 A형 20번

❶ Genus Homo's position in the food chain was, (until recently), solidly in the middle. ❷ For millions of years, / humans hunted smaller creatures and gathered what they could, / all the while being hunted by larger predators. ❸ It was only 400,000 years ago that several species of man began to hunt large game / on a regular basis, / ❹ and only In the last 100,000 years — (with the rise of Homo sapiens) — that man jumped / to the top of the food chain.

❺ That spectacular leap (from the middle to the top) had enormous consequences. ❻ Other animals (at the top of the pyramid), such as lions and sharks, / evolved into that position / very gradually, / over millions of years. ❼ This enabled the ecosystem to develop checks and balances (that prevent lions and sharks from wreaking too much havoc). ❽ As lions became deadlier, / so gazelles evolved to run faster, / hyenas to cooperate better, / and rhinoceroses to be more bad-tempered. ❾ In contrast, humankind ascended to the top so quickly that the ecosystem was not given enough time to adjust). ❿ Moreover, humans (themselves) failed to adjust. ⓫ Most top predators of the planet are majestic creatures. ⓬ Millions of years of domination have filled them with confidence. ⓭ Sapiens by contrast is more like a banana-republic dictator.

According to the passage, which best explains the underlined part?
이 글에 따르면, 밑줄 친 부분을 가장 잘 설명한 것은 무엇인가?

① Sapiens first evolved from the apes, being dependent on staple food crops, bananas.
사피엔스는 처음에 유인원으로부터 진화했고, 주식량인 바나나에 의존했다.

② Homo sapiens accomplished immense power based on unique political structures.
호모 사피엔스는 독특한 정치 구조를 기반으로 막강한 권력을 얻게 되었다.

✓ Humans are anxious about their position, which makes them brutal and dangerous.
인간은 그들의 위치에 대해 불안하고, 이는 그들을 잔인하고 위험하게 만든다.

④ Humankind accomplished agricultural revolution to make the original affluent society.
인류는 최초의 풍요로운 사회를 만들기 위해 농업 혁명을 이루었다.

해석

❶ 최근까지 먹이사슬에서 사람 속(屬)의 위치는 확실히 중간에 있었다. ❷ 수백만 년 동안, 인간은 계속해서 몸집이 더 큰 포식 동물에게 쫓기면서 더 작은 동물들을 사냥하고, 그들이 모을 수 있는 것을 모았다. ❸ 몇몇 인간 종(種)이 정기적으로 큰 사냥감을 사냥하기 시작한 것은 불과 40만 년 전의 일이었고, ❹ 호모 사피엔스 종의 등장과 동시에 인간이 먹이사슬의 꼭대기에 오른 것은 10만 년밖에 되지 않았다.

❺ 중간에서 꼭대기로 극적으로 뛰어오른 것은 엄청난 결과를 가져왔다. ❻ 사자와 상어와 같이 (먹이사슬) 피라미드의 꼭대기에 있는 다른 동물들은 수백만 년이 넘는 시간 동안 매우 점진적으로 그 위치로 진화했다. ❼ 이로 인해 생태계가 사자와 상어가 너무 큰 파괴를 일으키지 않게 막는 견제와 균형을 발전시킬 수 있게 해주었다. ❽ 사자가 점점 치명적으로 진화함에 따라, 가젤(영양(羚羊))은 더 빨리 달릴 수 있도록 진화했으며, 하이에나는 더 잘 협력하고, 코뿔소는 성미가 더 까다롭게 진화했다. ❾ 이와 반대로, 인류는 너무 빨리 먹이사슬의 꼭대기에 올라가게 되어서 생태계가 적응할 충분한 시간이 주어지지 않았다. ❿ 더욱이, 인간 스스로도 잘 적응하지 못했다. ⓫ 이 행성의 대다수 상위 포식자들은 위엄 있는 생명체들이다. ⓬ 수백만 년 동안의 지배가 그들을 자신감으로 가득하게 했다. ⓭ 반면에 사피엔스(현생(現生) 인류)는 바나나 공화국의 독재자에 더 가깝다.

해설

'바나나 공화국(banana-republic)'은 바나나 하나로만 수출해서 먹고사는 즉 불안정한 중남미 나라를 가리킨다. 따라서 인간의 불안정을 언급하는 ③이 가장 적절하다.

어휘

genus n. 속(屬)(과(family)와 종(species) 사이) food chain 먹이사슬 solidly ad. 튼튼[확고]하게 hunt v. 사냥하다 predator n. 포식자, 포식 동물 game n. 목적물; 사냥감 on a regular basis 정기적으로 spectacular a. 극적인, 장관을 이루는 leap n. 뜀, 도약 enormous a. 거대한, 막대한 evolve v. 발달하다, 진화하다 wreak v. (큰 피해 등을) 입히다[가하다] havoc n. 대파괴, 큰 혼란[피해] bad-tempered a. 곧장 성질을 내는; 화가 나 있는 majestic a. 장엄한, 위풍당당한 domination n. 지배, 통치, 제압 banana republic 바나나 공화국(해외 원조로 살아가는 가난한 나라) ape n. 유인원 staple a. 주된, 주요한 immense a. 엄청난 brutal a. 잔혹한, 악랄한 agricultural a. 농업의 affluent a. 부유한

012 A) ③ B) ④ ········ 2019학년도 광운대학교 인문계 34, 35번

❶ One key question (for the United States / in the 21st century) is whether noncoastal towns and rural communities will be able to participate in the digital revolution. ❷ We know / that almost all Americans are avid consumers of technology, but many lack the opportunity [to do the creative work (that fuels our digital economy)]. ❸ Ⓐ At stake is the dignity of millions of people. ❹ Within the next 10 years, / nearly 60 percent of jobs could have a third of their tasks (automated by artificial intelligence). ❺ Many traditional industries are becoming digital. ❻ Recently, / a senior hotel executive described his business / as essentially a digital one, / explaining / that his profit margins were contingent / on the effectiveness of his software architects. ❼ Today's hospitality vendors, precision farmers and electricians spend significant time / on digital work. ❽ Economists keep telling those (left / out of our digital future) to move / to the tech hubs. ❾ If they visit places like Lincoln, NE or Tacoma, WA, / ❿ they will realize / that many people (there) are not looking to move. ⓫ They are proud of their small-town values and enjoy being close to family. ⓬ They brag / that their town doesn't need many traffic lights. ⓭ Ⓑ The choice (facing small towns) should not be binary — / it should not be "adopt the Silicon name / or miss out on the tech future."

해석

❶ 21세기 미국의 한 가지 핵심적인 문제는 미국의 내륙지역과 농촌지역이 디지털 혁명에 참여할 수 있을 것인가 하는 것이다. ❷ 거의 모든 미국인들이 열정적으로 첨단 기술을 소비하는 것에 비해 많은 미국인들은 디지털 경제에 활력을 불어넣는 창의적인 일을 할 수 있는 기회가 부족하다는 것을 우리는 알고 있다. ❸ Ⓐ위기에 처한 것은 수백만 사람들의 존엄성이다. ❹ 향후 10년 안에, 일자리의 거의 60%는 업무의 1/3이 인공지능에 의해서 자동화될 수 있을 것이다. ❺ 수많은 전통 산업들이 디지털화되고 있다. ❻ 최근, 한 고위 호텔 경영진은 그의 사업이 본질적으로 디지털 사업이라고 묘사했으며, 사업의 이익은 그의 소프트웨어 설계자들의 능률에 달려있다고 설명했다. ❼ 오늘날 접객업 종사자, 정밀농업 종사자, 그리고 전기기술자들은 상당한 시간을 디지털 업무를 하며 보낸다. ❽ 경제학자들은 디지털 미래에서 소외된 사람들에게 첨단 기술 중심지역으로 이사를 가라고 계속해서 이야기한다. ❾ (그러나) 만일 그들이 뉴잉글랜드의 링컨(Lincoln)이나 워싱턴 주의 터코마(Tacoma) 같은 곳을 방문한다면, ❿ 그곳에 거주하는 많은 사람들이 첨단 기술 중심지역으로 이사 가는 것을 원치 않는다는 것을 그들은 깨닫게 될 것이다. ⓫ 그들은 시골 소도시의 가치관을 자랑스럽게 여기며, 가족과 함께 시간을 보내는 것을 즐긴다. ⓬ 그들은 그들이 사는 마을에 교통 신호등이 많이 있을 필요가 없다고 자랑한다. ⓭ Ⓑ시골 소도시가 직면한 선택은 양자택일이 되어서는 안 된다. 즉, (첨단 기술의) 실리콘 밸리 스타일을 채택할 것인지, 아니면 첨단 기술의 미래를 놓치느냐가 되어서는 안 된다는 것이다.

어휘

avid a. 열렬한, 열정적인 at stake (생명·안전 등이) 위기에 처한, 위태로운 dignity n. 위엄, 품위, 존엄성 artificial intelligence 인공지능 senior executive 사장, 고위 간부 margin n. 여백, 마진, 차이 contingent n. 분담액, 대표단 software architect 소프트웨어 아키텍트(기술적 관점에서 시스템을 바라보고, 설계와 구현 전체를 책임지며 개발팀을 이끄는 사람) hospitality n. 환대, 손님 접대 vendor n. 특정한 제품 판매 회사 precision farmer 정밀농업(각종 정보통신기술을 활용해 비료, 물, 노동력 등 투입 자원을 최소화 하면서 생산량을 최대화하는 생산방식) 종사자 significant a. 중요한, 상당한 be left out of ~에서 소외시키다[빼다] brag v. 자랑하다, 뽐내다 binary a. 2진법의, 양자택일의 adopt v. 채택하다, 받아들이다 miss out on ~을 놓치다

A) 밑줄 친 Ⓐ의 원인은?

① A great number of people in the rural areas have become unemployed although the economy started to recover.
경제가 회복되기 시작했음에도 불구하고, 시골지역에 거주하는 많은 사람들은 실직하게 되었다.

② Americans spend way too much money to purchase the latest technologies with artificial intelligence.
미국인들은 인공지능으로 무장한 최신 첨단 기술을 구입하기 위해 엄청 많은 돈을 소비한다.

✓③ Although America undergoes technological development, many people fail to be productive with such a change.
비록 미국이 첨단 기술의 발전을 경험하고 있다고 하지만, 많은 사람들은 그 변화에 생산적이지 못하고 있다.

④ Companies started to replace traditional human labors avidly with modern technologies with artificial intelligence.
기업들은 전통적인 인간의 노동을 인공지능으로 무장한 현대 기술로 열렬하게 대체하기 시작했다.

⑤ As companies in the United States relocate to other areas, many people who can't move may lose their jobs.
미국의 기업들이 다른 지역으로 이전하면서, 이사를 할 수 없는 많은 사람들은 일자리를 잃을지도 모른다.

S

① Small towns should adopt the Silicone name or miss out on the tech future.
시골 작은 도시는 실리콘 밸리 스타일을 받아들이거나 첨단 기술의 미래를 놓쳐야 한다.

② Small towns must delimit the growth to protect the populations to move out.
시골 작은 도시는 인구가 밖으로 나가는 것을 막기 위해 성장의 경계를 정해야 한다.

③ Small towns may move toward the digital future as changing to tech hubs.
시골 작은 도시는 첨단 기술 중심지역으로 바뀌면서 디지털 미래를 향해 가야 한다.

✓④ Small towns can protect their community value as creating various tech jobs there.
시골 작은 도시는 그곳에서 다양한 첨단 기술 일자리를 만들며 그들의 지역사회의 가치관을 보호할 수 있다.

⑤ Small towns need to encourage their people to be more aware of the digital economy.
시골 작은 도시는 주민들에게 디지털 경제를 좀 더 잘 인지하도록 장려해야 한다.

해설

A) 윗글의 시작부터 디지털 혁명에 도태되는 지역을 언급하는 것을 시작으로, 나아가 미국인들이 이런 경제에 창의적 일의 기회 부족 그리고 두 번째 단락부터는 자동화와 디지털화로 산업의 변화를 설명하고 있다. 따라서 이런 변화의 물결에 가담하지 못한 사람들은 생산적이지 못하다고 할 수 있는 ③이 가장 적절하다.

B) ⓫번 문장에서 '그들은 시골 소도시의 가치관을 자랑스럽게 여기며, 가족과 함께 시간을 보내는 것을 즐긴다'라고 말하고 있다. 따라서 그들의 지역 가치를 존중하면서 첨단 기술을 접목하자는 ④이 가장 적절하다.

어휘

delimit v. ~의 범위[한계]를 정하다

013 ② — 2019학년도 덕성여자대학교 사회·자연·예술대학 29번

❶ As globalization (in its current form) expands, / so too does the inequality that accompanies it. ❷ Rising inequality can result in an increase in racial bias (which advances xenophobic and isolationist tendencies). ❸ During the days of British and French Imperialism, / for example, racial bias was ingrained / within culture itself. ❹ However, an element of this is still seen / in today's period of globalization, / with the increasing "xenophobic culture of Globalization") seen / in some parts of the world.
❺ With expanding globalization, / the demand (for more skilled workers), (especially in North America), has led to increased efforts (to attract foreign workers) — / ❻ but filtered, based on skill.
❼ On the other hand, it is harder to immigrate to the wealthier nations / unless these citizens are part of the chosen few: highly-skilled computer wizards, doctors and nurses (trained at Third World expense). ❽ Global migration management strategy saps the Third World and the former Soviet bloc of its economic lifeblood, by creaming off their most skilled and educated workforces. ❾ From the perspective of globalization / the skills pool, (not the genes pool), is key.

Which phrase is closest in meaning to the phrase "xenophobic culture of globalization" in this passage?
다음 중 위 글의 "세계화의 외국인 혐오 문화"라는 표현과 의미가 가장 가까운 것은?
① isolation of foreign culture by globalization
    세계화에 의한 외국 문화의 고립
✓② excessive fear of foreign people within globalized societies
    세계화된 사회 속에서의 외국인에 대한 지나친 공포
③ cultures which resist globalization
    세계화에 저항하는 문화
④ imported cultures through globalization
    세계화를 통해 수입된 문화

해석
❶ 현재 형태의 세계화가 확대되면서 그에 따라 수반되는 불평등도 확대되고 있다. ❷ 불평등의 심화는 인종적인 편견을 심화시킬 수 있으며, 이는 외국인 혐오와 고립주의 경향의 심화를 부채질한다. ❸ 예를 들어, 영국과 프랑스 제국주의 시대에는 인종적 편견이 문화 그 자체에 스며들어 있었다. ❹ 하지만, 이러한 요소는 오늘날과 같은 세계화 시대에서도 여전히 나타나고 있으며, "세계화의 외국인 혐오 문화"는 세계 일부 지역에서 점차 늘어나고 있다. ❺ 세계화가 확대됨에 따라, 특히 북미 지역에서 더 많은 숙련 노동자에 대한 수요로 인해 외국인 노동자들을 끌어들이려는 노력이 커졌지만 — ❻ 이들은 기술을 바탕으로 선별적으로 받아들여졌다. ❼ 반면에, 이 시민들이 선택받은 소수, 즉 3세계에서 비용을 들여 훈련시킨 고도로 숙련된 컴퓨터 전문가, 의사, 간호사에 속하지 않으면, 부유한 국가로 이주하는 것은 더욱 어려운 일이다. ❽ 글로벌 이민 관리 전략은 제3세계와 구(舊) 소련으로부터 가장 숙련된 고학력의 인력을 뽑아감으로 인해 그 지역에서 경제적 활력소를 제거하게 된다. ❾ 세계화의 관점에서 본다면, 유전자 풀이 아닌 기술 풀이 핵심이다.

해설
'외국인 공포증의'이라는 뜻을 모른다면 전후 맥락에서 '인종적 편견' 그리고 '숙련된 노동자에 대한 수요' 등에서 추론할 수도 있다.

어휘
globalization n. 국제화, 세계화 expand v. 퍼지다, 넓어지다, 확대되다 inequality n. 불평등 accompany v. ~에 동반하다, ~에 수반하여 일어나다 result in ~을 초래하다 racial a. 인종의, 종족의, 민족의 bias n. 선입견, 편견 xenophobic a. 외국인 혐오의 isolationist a. 고립주의의 tendency n. 경향, 풍조, 추세 imperialism n. 제국주의 ingrain v. (습관 등을) 깊이 뿌리박히게 하다 element n. 요소, 성분 demand n. 수요 skilled a. 숙련된, 능숙한 filter v. 거르다, 여과하다 immigrate v. (타국에서) 이주해오다 wizard n. 마법사; 귀재, 천재 at one's expense ~의 비용으로, ~의 부담으로 migration n. 이주, 이전 strategy n. 전략, 작전 sap v. ~에서 수액을 짜내다; ~에서 활력을 없애다, 약화시키다 lifeblood n. 활력, 생명의 근원 cream off (자기 이익을 위해 가장 우수한 사람들이나 물건들을) 추려서 가다 perspective n. 전망, 시각, 견지 gene pool 어떤 생물집단 속에 있는 유전정보의 총량, 유전자 풀

014 ③ 2019학년도 서울여자대학교 인문·자연계 A형 31번

❶ These days / most people (around the world) dress in / much the same way: / ❷ the same jeans, the same sneakers, the same T-shirts. ❸ There are just a few places Ⓐ where people hold out against the giant sartorial* blending machine. ❹ One of them is rural Peru. ❺ In the mountains of the Andes, / the Quechua women still wear their brightly coloured dresses and shawls and their little felt hats, (pinned at jaunty angles / and decorated with their tribal insignia). ❻ Except that / these are not traditional Quechua clothes at all. ❼ The dresses, shawls and hats are in fact of Andalusian origin and were imposed by / the Spanish Viceroy Francisco de Toledo / in 1572, / in the wake of Tupac Amaru's defeat. ❽ Authentically traditional Andean female attire consisted of a tunic, / (secured at the waist by a sash), / over which was worn a mantle, / which was fastened with a tupu pin. ❾ What Quechua women wear nowadays is a combination of these earlier garments / with the clothes (they were ordered to wear / by their Spanish masters). ❿ The bowler hats (popular among Bolivian women) came later, / when British workers arrived / to build that country's first railways. ⓫ The current fashion (among Andean men / for American casual clothing) is thus merely the latest chapter / in a long history of sartorial Westernization.

* sartorial 의복의

What does the underlined Ⓐ imply?
밑줄 친 Ⓐ가 의미하는 것은?

① where people wear cheap clothes
사람들이 가격이 저렴한 옷을 입는
② where people dislike baggy clothes
사람들이 헐렁한 옷을 입는 것을 거부하는
✓③ where people refuse mass-produced clothes
사람들이 대량 생산된 옷을 거부하는
④ where people follow a current fashion trend
사람들이 현재 유행하는 패션 트렌드를 따르는

해석
❶ 오늘날 전 세계 대다수 사람들은 거의 동일한 방식으로 옷을 입는다. ❷ 똑같은 청바지, 똑같은 운동화, 똑같은 티셔츠로 말이다. ❸ Ⓐ이렇게 똑같은 의복이 나오는 거대한 믹서기에 사람들이 대항하는 몇 군데가 있는데, 그중 한 곳이 ❹ 바로 페루(Peru)의 시골 지역이다. ❺ 안데스(Andes) 산맥에 거주하는 케추아(Quechua)족 여인들은 여전히 밝은 색상의 드레스에 숄을 걸치고, 작은 펠트 모자를 멋있게 비스듬히 썼는데, 이 모자는 부족의 휘장으로 장식되어 있었다. ❻ 그런데 이러한 복장은 케추아족의 전통의상과는 거리가 멀다. ❼ 사실 (케추아족이 착용한) 드레스, 숄, 그리고 모자는 (스페인 남부지방인) 안달루시아가 원산지인데, 이 복장은 (잉카 제국의 마지막 황제인) 투팍 아마루(Túpac Amaru)의 (전쟁에서) 패배로 인해 1572년 스페인의 총독 프란시스코 드 톨레도(Francisco de Toledo)가 강요한 것이었다. ❽ 안데스 산맥에 거주하는 여성의 진짜 전통의상은 띠로 잡아맨 튜닉 위에 '투푸'라는 핀으로 고정시킨 망토로 이루어져 있다. ❾ 케추아족이 오늘날 입는 것은 이런 전통의상과 스페인 지배자들이 케추아족에게 입으라 명령한 옷들의 결합된 형태이다. ❿ 볼리비아(Bolivia) 여성들 사이에 인기 있는 중절모는 볼리비아 최초의 철도를 깔기 위해서 영국의 노동자들이 도착했을 시기에 볼리비아에 들어온 것이다. ⓫ 따라서 현재 안데스 산맥에 거주하는 남성들이 선호하는 미국식 캐주얼 의상은 의복 서구화의 오랜 역사에서 가장 최근의 형태일 뿐이다.

해설
『hold out against』의 뜻이 '~에 저항하다'는 의미를 가지고 있기에 ③ 추론이 가능하다. 뿐만 아니라 이어지는 문장에서 '안데스 산맥의 케추아(Quechua) 부족'의 예시를 활용하여 일반적이지 않은 독특한 의상을 입는 것을 설명하고 있기에 ③을 추론할 수도 있다.

어휘
sneaker n. 운동화(고무창을 댄 운동화) hold out against ~에 저항[대항]하다 sartorial a. 의류의, 재봉의 blending machine 믹서기 Quechua n. 케추아족(남미 페루 중부의 원주민족으로, 예전에는 잉카 제국의 지배층을 구성) shawl n. 숄 felt hat 펠트 모자, 중절 모자 at a jaunty angle 멋있게 비스듬히 insignia n. (관직·계급을 나타내는) 휘장, 배지 Andalusia n. 안달루시아(스페인의 남부지방) of origin ~출신의 impose v. 부과하다, 도입하다, 강요하다 viceroy n. (식민지의) 총독, 국왕 대리로서 통치하는 사람 in the wake of ~의 결과로 Túpac Amaru 투팍 아마루(잉카제국의 마지막 황제) defeat n. 패배 authentically ad. 확실하게 attire n. 의복, 복장 tunic n. 튜닉(고대 그리스나 로마인들이 입던, 소매가 없고 무릎까지 내려오는 헐렁한 웃옷) secure v. (단단히) 고정시키다 sash n. (특히 제복의 일부로 몸에 두르는) 띠 mantle n. 망토 garment n. 의복, 옷 bowler hat 중절모, 중산(中山)모자 baggy a. (옷이) 헐렁한

015 ④   2019학년도 단국대학교 자연계 A형 29번

❶ Democracy has another merit. ❷ It allows criticism, / and if there isn't public criticism / there are bound to be hushed-up scandals. ❸ That is why I believe in the press, despite all its lies and vulgarity, / and : why I believe in Parliament. ❹ The British Parliament is often sneered at / because it's a talking shop. ❺ Well, I believe in it because / it is a talking shop. ❻ I believe in the private member (who makes himself nuisance). ❼ He gets snubbed and is told / that he is cranky or ill-formed, ❽ but he exposes abuses (which would otherwise never have been mentioned), / and very often / an abuse gets put right just / by being mentioned. ❾ Occasionally, (too, / in my country), a well-meaning public official loses his head / in the cause of efficiency, / and thinks himself God Almighty. ❿ Such officials are particularly frequent / in the Home Office. ⓫ Well, / there will be questions (about them / in Parliament) / sooner or later, / and then they'll have to mend their steps. ⓬ (Whether Parliament is either a representative body or an efficient one) is very doubtful, / ⓭ but I value it / because it criticizes and talks, / and because its chatter get widely reported. ⓮ So two cheers for democracy: / one / because it admits variety / and two because it permits criticism. ⓯ Two cheers are quite enough: / there is no occasion to give three.

Which has the closest meaning to the underlined part?
다음 중 밑줄 친 부분과 가장 가까운 의미는 무엇인가?

① A space for diplomatic meetings
   외교 회의를 위한 공간
② A place for genuine and serious discussion
   진실하고 심각한 토론을 위한 공간
③ A space for healthy arguments
   건전한 토론을 위한 공간
✓ ④ A noisy and boisterous place
   시끄럽고 떠들썩한 공간

해석 ❶ 민주주의는 또 다른 장점이 있다. ❷ 민주주의는 비판을 허용한다는 것이다. 대중의 비판이 없다면 반드시 은폐된 추문이 있을 수밖에 없다. ❸ 이러한 점이 그 모든 거짓말과 저속성에도 불구하고 언론을 믿는 이유이고 국회를 믿는 이유이다. ❹ 영국 국회는 말만 무성한 곳이라는 이유에서 종종 조롱을 받는다. ❺ 그런데, 나는 의회가 말만 무성한 곳이기 때문에 의회를 믿는다. ❻ 나는 자기 스스로 성가신 존재가 되는 의회의 평의원을 믿는다. ❼ 그는 무시받고, 성미가 까다롭거나 부적격하다는 소리를 듣겠지만, ❽ 그는 그가 폭로하지 않았다면 절대 언급되지 않았을 (권력의) 남용을 폭로하고, 남용이 단지 언급되는 것만으로 바로 잡히는 일이 매우 자주 있다. ❾ 가끔 우리나라에서도 선의를 지닌 공직자가 능률을 위해 자제력을 잃고, 스스로를 전지전능한 신이라고 생각한다. ❿ 그런 공직자들은 특히나 내무부에 많이 있다. ⓫ 그런데, 조만간 의회에서 그들에 대한 질문이 있을 것이고, 그렇다면 그들은 자신들의 행동을 고쳐야 할 것이다. ⓬ 의회가 대의 기관인지 효율적인 기관인지 매우 의심스럽지만, ⓭ 의회가 비판하고 말을 하기에, 그리고 그 말이 널리 보도되기 때문에 나는 의회를 존중한다. ⓮ 그러므로 민주주의를 두 번 찬양하게 되는데, 한 번은 민주주의가 다양성을 인정하기 때문이며, 또 한 번은 민주주의가 비판을 허용하기 때문이다. ⓯ 두 번의 찬양이면 충분하며, 세 번 찬양할 이유는 없다.

해설 앞 문장에서 영국 의회가 'talking shop'으로 인해 조롱받는다고 했기에 부정적 뜻을 내포한 ④이 가장 적절하다.

어휘 democracy n. 민주주의 merit n. 장점 criticism n. 비평, 비난 be bound to 반드시 ~하다 hushed-up a. 은폐된, 숨겨진, 비밀의 vulgarity n. 무례함 언동 parliament n. 의회, 국회 sneer v. 비웃다, 조롱하다 private member (영국 정치에서 정부 각료가 아닌) 일반 의원 nuisance n. 성가신[귀찮은] 사람[것,일], 골칫거리 snub v. 모욕하다, 무시하다 cranky a. 성미가 까다로운, 짓궂은, 괴팍한 ill-formed a. 모양이 갖추어지지 않은, 부적격한 abuse n. 학대, 남용, 오용 put ~ right ~을 바로 잡다, 고치다 well-meaning a. 선의[호의]의, 악의가 없는 lose one's head 자제력을 잃다 frequent a. 자주, 빈번한 Home Office 내무부 mend v. 개선하다, 고치다 representative n. 대표, 대리인 a. 대표하는 doubtful a. 확신이 없는, 의심[의문]을 품은 chatter n. 수다 v. 수다를 떨다 diplomatic a. 외교의 genuine a. 진짜의, 진품의, 진실한 boisterous a. 활기가 넘치는

016 ①   2019학년도 서울여자대학교 인문·자연계 A형 33번

❶ We talk about food / in the negative: / What we shouldn't eat, / what we'll regret later, / what's evil, dangerously tempting, unhealthy. ❷ ⒶThe effects are more insidious / than any overindulgent amount of "bad food" can ever be. ❸ By fretting about food, / we turn occasions (for comfort and joy) into sources (of fear and anxiety). ❹ And when we avoid certain foods, / we usually compensate / by consuming too much of others. ❺ All of this happens / under the guise of science. ❻ But a closer look at the research / behind our food fears shows / that many of our most demonized foods are actually fine / for us. ❼ Consider salt. ❽ It's true that, / if people (with high blood pressure) consume a lot of salt, / ❾ it can lead to cardiovascular events / like heart attacks. ❿ It's also true / that salt is overused / in processed foods. ⓫ But the average American consumes / just over three grams of sodium per day, / which is actually in the sweet spot for health. ⓬ Eating too little salt may be just as dangerous as / eating too much. ⓭ This is especially true / for the majority of people (who don't have high blood pressure). ⓮ Regardless, experts continue to push / for lower recommendations. ⓯ Many of the doctors and nutritionists (who recommend avoiding certain foods) fail to properly explain the magnitude of their risks. ⓰ In some studies, / processed red meat (in large amounts) is associated with an increased relative risk (of developing cancer). ⓱ The absolute risk, however, is often quite small.

What does the underlined Ⓐ mean?
밑줄 친 Ⓐ가 의미하는 것은?

☑ ① The effects of food fears
  음식에 대한 공포감이 미치는 영향
② The effects of "bad food"
  '나쁜 음식'이 미치는 영향
③ The effects of eating too much
  과식이 미치는 영향
④ The effects of eating processed food
  가공식품 섭취가 미치는 영향

해석

❶ 우리는 무엇을 먹지 말아야 하며, 무엇을 먹으면 나중에 후회할 것이고, 해로운 음식, 구미가 당기지만 위험한 음식, 건강에 해로운 음식은 무엇인지 등, 음식에 대해 부정적으로 이야기한다. ❷ 그것은 '나쁜 음식'을 과도하게 탐닉하는 것이 끼칠 수 있는 영향보다 더 은밀하게 Ⓐ영향을 끼친다. ❸ 음식에 대해 전전긍긍함으로써, 우리는 (식사라는) 편안하고 즐거운 일을 두려움과 걱정의 원천으로 바꿔 버린다. ❹ 그리고 우리가 특정 음식을 피할 때, 우리는 보통 그것에 대한 보상으로 다른 음식들을 과도하게 섭취한다. ❺ 이 모든 일은 과학을 가정하여 일어난다. ❻ 하지만 음식 공포의 이면에 관한 연구를 좀 더 면밀히 살펴보면, 우리가 악마라고 취급한 음식들 중 많은 것이 실제로는 우리에게 좋은 것으로 드러난다. ❼ 소금을 예로 들어보자. ❽ 만일 고혈압이 있는 사람들이 많은 양의 소금을 섭취하게 되면, ❾ 소금이 심장마비 같은 심혈관 질환을 일으킬 수 있다는 것은 사실이다. ❿ 소금이 가공 음식에 과도하게 사용되는 것 또한 사실이다. ⓫ 하지만 평균적인 미국인은 하루에 나트륨을 불과 3그램 남짓 먹는데, 이 정도는 실제로 건강에 딱 좋은 수준이다. ⓬ 소금을 너무 적게 먹는 것은 소금을 너무 많이 먹는 것만큼 위험할지도 모른다. ⓭ 이것은 특히 고혈압이 아닌 대다수 사람들에게 사실이다. ⓮ 이런 사실에 개의치 않으며 전문가들은 소금을 보다 적게 먹을 것을 계속해서 권장하고 있다. ⓯ 특정 음식을 피할 것을 권장하는 많은 의사들과 영양사들 중에는 그 음식이 얼마나 위험한 것인지를 제대로 설명하지 못하는 사람이 많다. ⓰ 몇몇 연구에서는, 가공된 붉은 육류를 많이 섭취하는 것은 암 발병의 위험이 상대적으로 증가하는 것과 연관 있는 것으로 드러난다. ⓱ 하지만 절대적 위험은 종종 아주 미미한 수준이다.

해설

Ⓐ 다음에 이어지는 문장에서 '음식에 대한 전전긍긍함으로써, 우리는 식사를 두려움과 걱정의 원천으로 바꾼다'라고 말하고 있기에 ①을 추론할 수 있다.

어휘

tempting a. 솔깃한, 구미가 당기는 **insidious** a. 방심할 수 없는, 은밀히 퍼지는 **overindulgent** a. 지나치게 탐닉하는 **fret about** 전전긍긍하다 **occasion** n. 의식, 행사 **compensate** v. 보상하다 **under the guise of** ~을 가장하여; ~라는 명목으로 **demonize** v. 악마로 만들다[묘사하다], 악마취급을 하다 **cardiovascular** a. 심혈관의 **heart attack** 심장마비, 심근경색 **sodium** n. 나트륨 **sweet spot** (야구의 배트 등에서) 공이 가장 잘 맞는 장소; 안성맞춤인 상황 **nutritionist** n. 영양학자, 영양사 **magnitude** 규모, 진도(지진의 규모) **relative risk** 상대위험도 **absolute** a. 절대적인, 완전한

017 ④ 2019학년도 단국대학교 인문계 A형 36번

❶ Recently, / as the British doctor Lord Robert Winston took a train / from London to Manchester, / he found himself becoming steadily enraged. ❷ A woman had picked up the phone and begun a loud conversation, which would last an unbelievable hour. ❸ Furious, / Winston began to tweet about the woman, / taking her picture and sending it / to his more than 40,000 followers. ❹ When the train arrived at its destination, / Winston bolted. ❺ The press were waiting for the woman and showed her the Lord's messages. ❻ She used just one word / to describe Winston's actions: rude. ❼ Studies have shown / that rudeness spreads quickly and virally, almost like the common cold. ❽ Just witnessing rudeness makes it far more likely [that we, (in turn), will be rude later on]. ❾ Once infected, / we are more aggressive, less creative and worse at our jobs. ❿ The only way (to end a strain) is to make a ⓑ conscious decision / to do so. ⓫ We must have the guts (to call it out), face to face. ⓬ We must say, "Just stop." ⓭ For Winston, / that would have meant approaching the woman, / politely asking her to speak more quietly or make the call / at another time.

⓮ The rage and injustice (we feel at the rude behavior of a stranger) can drive us to do odd things. ⓯ In one research, / (surveying 2,000 adults), the acts of revenge people had taken ranged / from the ridiculous ("I rubbed fries on their windshield") to the disturbing ("I sabotaged them at work").

⓰ We must combat rudeness head on. ⓱ When we see it occur in a store, / we must step up and say something. ⓲ If it happens to a colleague, / we must point it out. ⓳ We must defend strangers / in the same way (we'd defend our best friends). ⓴ But we can do it with grace, / by handling it / without a trace of aggression / and without being rude ourselves. ㉑ Because once rude people can see their actions / through the eyes of others, / they are far more likely

해석

❶ 최근, 영국 의사인 로버트 윈스턴(Robert Winston) 경이 런던에서 맨체스터로 가는 열차를 탔을 때, 그는 계속해서 분노가 치밀어 오름을 느꼈다. ❷ 한 여인이 핸드폰을 집어 들고는 큰 목소리로 통화하기 시작했는데, 믿기 힘들 정도로 오랫동안 통화를 했던 것이다. ❸ 화가 난 윈스턴은 트위터에 그 여인에 대해 글을 남겼고, 그녀를 사진 찍어, 4만 명 이상 되는 팔로워들에게 그 사진을 보냈다. ❹ 기차가 목적지에 도착하자 윈스턴 경은 잽싸게 도망쳤다. ❺ 기자들이 그 여인을 기다리고 있었고, 그녀에게 윈스턴 경이 트위터에 남긴 글을 보여주었다. ❻ 그녀는 윈스턴 경의 이러한 행동을 표현하기 위해 단 하나의 단어만을 사용하였는데, 그 단어는 바로 '무례하다'였다. ❼ 무례함은 거의 감기처럼 빠르고 치명적으로 퍼진다는 것을 많은 연구 결과들이 보여준다. ❽ 무례함은 목격하는 것만으로도 우리가 그다음에 무례해질 가능성을 훨씬 높여준다. ❾ 일단 무례함에 물들게 되면, 우리는 훨씬 더 공격적으로 변하게 되고, 덜 창조적이게 되고, 우리가 하는 일을 전보다 못하게 된다. ❿ 기분 나쁜 상황을 끝낼 수 있는 유일한 방법은 그렇게 하기로 ⓑ 의식적인 결정을 내리는 것이다. ⓫ 우리는 그것을 얼굴을 마주 보며 큰소리로 외칠 배짱이 있어야 한다. ⓬ 즉, 우리는 "그만 좀 하세요."라고 말해야 한다. ⓭ 윈스턴 경에게 있어, 의식적인 결정은 그 여인에게 다가가서 좀 더 조용히 말하거나 나중에 통화해달라고 정중하게 요구하는 것을 의미했다.

⓮ 낯선 사람의 무례한 행동에 우리가 느끼는 분노와 부당함은 우리로 하여금 이상한 행동을 하게 만들 수도 있다. ⓯ 성인 남녀 2천 명을 설문 조사한 어떤 연구에서, (무례한 행동에 대해) 사람들이 행한 보복행위에는 우스꽝스러운 수준("내가 그들의 자동차 앞 유리창에 파리를 짓이겨놨어.")에서부터 마음을 불안하게 만드는 수준("직장에서 그들이 일을 못 하도록 내가 방해했어.")에 이르기까지 다양했다.

⓰ 우리는 무례함과 정면으로 싸워야 한다. ⓱ 무례함이 어떤 가게에서 일어나는 것을 우리가 볼 경우, 우리는 나서서 뭐라고 해야 한다. ⓲ 설령 동료가 무례한 행동을 하더라도, 우리는 그 무례함을 지적해야 한다. ⓳ 우리는 우리의 가장 친한 친구들을 변호하는 것과 똑같이 낯선 사람들도 변호해야 한다. ⓴ 하지만 우리는 공격 성향을 보이지 않고 스스로 무례해지지 않는 방식으로 무례함을 다룸으로써 예의 바르게 그렇게 할 수 있다. ㉑ 왜냐하면, 무례한 사람들이 그들의 행동을 다른 사람의 눈을 통해 볼 수 있고 나면, 그들이 기분 나쁜 상황을 끝낼 가능성이 더 높기 때문이다.

어휘

lord n. (영국에서 귀족을 칭하는) 경(卿) **steadily** ad. 착실하게, 끊임없이 **enraged** a. 격분한 **last** v. 지속되다 **tweet** n. 짹짹(새가 우는 소리) **destination** n. 목적지 **bolt** v. (사람이) 달아나다 **the press** 언론 **rudeness** n. 무례함 **virally** ad. 바이러스로 **common cold** 감기 **witness** n. 목격자 v. 목격하다 **in turn** 차례차례 **infect** v. 감염시키다; (특정한 감정을 갖도록) 물들이다 **strain** n. 부담, 중압[압박], 긴장 상태 **have the guts to do** ~하는 용기[배짱]가 있다, 감히 ~하다 **face to face** 마주 보고, 마주 앉아 **politely** ad. 공손하게 **rage** n. 격렬한 분노 **drive** v. (극단적이 되도록) 만들다[몰아붙이다] **odd** a. 이상한, 특이한 **revenge** n. 복수, 보복 **windshield** n. 방풍유리, 바람막이 창 **disturbing** a. 충격적인, 사람을 불안하게 하는 **sabotage** v. ~에 파괴 행위를 하다, (남의) 일을 은밀히 방해하다 **head on** 정면으로 **with grace** 기품 있게, 예의 바르게 **handle** v. 처리하다, 감당하다 **without a trace of aggression** 적대적인 기색도 없이

to end that strain (themselves). ㉒ As this tide of rudeness rises, / civilization needs civility.

Which is implied by the underlined Ⓑ?
다음 중 밑줄 친 Ⓑ가 함축하고 있는 것은?

① aggressive tweeting
  트위터에 공격적인 글 쓰기
② outrageous injustice
  터무니없는 부당함
③ ludicrous behavior
  우스꽝스러운 행동
✓④ decent appeal
  점잖은 호소

해석 ㉒ 이런 무례함의 경향이 증가할수록, 문명은 예의 바름을 필요로 한다.

해설 주인공 윈스턴 경이 말하는 의식적인 결정은 다음 이어지는 ⑬번 문장에서 '정중하게 요구 사항을 직접 요구하는 것'이라고 말하고 있다. 따라서 ④이 가장 적절하다.

어휘 **outrageous** a. 매우 모욕적인, 너무나 충격적인 **injustice** n. 불평등, 부당함 **ludicrous** a. 웃기는, 웃음을 자아내게 하는 **decent** a. 품위 있는, 예의 바른; 적절한 **tide** n. 경향 **civility** n. 정중함, 예의 바름

018 ③ 2019학년도 숭실대학교 인문계 A형 25번

❶ Environmentalists say / that clean coal is a myth. ❷ Of course it is. ❸ Just look at West Virginia, where whole Appalachian peaks have been knocked into valleys / to get at the coal underneath / and streams run orange / with acidic water. ❹ Or look at downtown Beijing, where the air (these days) is often thicker / than in an airport smoking lounge. ❺ Air pollution (in China), (much of it / from burning coal), is blamed / for more than a million premature deaths a year. ❻ That's on top of the thousands (who die in mining accidents, in China and elsewhere).

❼ These problems aren't new. ❽ In the late 17th century, / when coal (from Wales and Northumberland) was lighting the first fires of the industrial revolution in Britain, / the English writer (John Evelyn) was already complaining / about the "stink and darkness" of the smoke (that wreathed London). ❾ Three centuries later, / (in December 1952), a thick layer of coal-laden smog descended on London / and lingered / for a weekend, ❿ provoking an epidemic of respiratory ailments (that killed as many as 12,000 people / in the ensuing months).

⓫ Coal, (to use the economists' euphemism), is fraught with ⓑ "externalities" — / the heavy costs (it imposes on society). ⓬ It's the dirtiest, most lethal energy source (we have). ⓭ But by most measures / it's also the cheapest, and we depend on it. ⓮ So the big question (today) isn't whether coal can ever be "clean." It can't. ⓯ It's whether coal can ever be clean enough — / to prevent not only local disasters but also a radical change in global climate. ⓰ In 2012 / the world emitted a record 34.5 billion metric tons of carbon dioxide / from fossil fuels. ⓱ Coal was the largest contributor. ⓲ Cheap natural gas has lately reduced the demand (for coal in the U.S.), ⓳ but everywhere else, (especially in China), / demand is surging. ⓴ During the next two decades /

[해석]

❶ 환경보호론자들은 깨끗한 석탄은 근거 없는 믿음이라고 말한다. ❷ 물론 그럴 것이다. ❸ 지하에 매장되어있는 석탄을 캐기 위해서 애팔래치아 산맥 전체의 봉우리를 허물어 계곡으로 만들고, 겨울에는 주황빛을 띠는 산성수(酸性水)가 흐르는 웨스트버지니아를 한번 보라. ❹ 아니면 요즘 공항의 흡연실보다 종종 공기가 더 탁한 베이징 시내를 살펴보아라. ❺ 주로 석탄을 연소하는 것에서 비롯된 중국의 대기 오염은 매년 백만 명 이상 사람들의 조기 사망의 원인으로 간주되고 있다. ❻ 그것은 중국이나 다른 곳에서 광산 사고로 사망하는 그 수천 명의 사람들보다 더 많은 것이다.

❼ 이러한 문제들은 새로운 것이 아니다. ❽ 웨일스와 노섬벌랜드에서 나온 석탄이 영국에서 산업혁명의 첫 번째 불을 지피던 17세기 후반에, 영국의 작가인 존 이블린(John Evelyn)은 런던을 가득 메운 자욱한 연기의 '악취와 어둠'에 대해 이미 불평을 터뜨리고 있었다. ❾ 3세기가 지난 1952년 12월, 석탄으로 가득한 두꺼운 층을 이룬 스모그가 런던에 내려와 긴 주말 연휴 동안에 머물러 있었는데, ❿ 이로 인해 호흡기 질환이 급속하게 퍼지게 되었고 그 후 몇 달 사이에 무려 12,000명이나 되는 사람들이 사망했다.

⓫ 경제학자들의 완곡한 표현을 이용하자면, 석탄은 ⓑ외부적인 것들로 가득 차 있는 그것은 곧 석탄이 사회에 부과하는 막대한 비용들을 암시한다. ⓬ 석탄은 우리가 사용하는 가장 불순하고, 가장 치명적인 에너지원이다. ⓭ 하지만 대부분 기준에서 봤을 때 석탄은 또한 가장 저렴한 에너지원이며 우리는 석탄에 의존하고 있다. ⓮ 따라서 오늘날의 가장 큰 문제는 석탄이 과연 '깨끗해질 수' 있느냐가 아니다. ⓯ 석탄은 깨끗해질 수 없다. 문제는 석탄이 국지적 재난뿐만 아니라 지구의 급격한 기후변화를 막을 수 있을 만큼 충분히 깨끗해질 수 있느냐 하는 것이다.

⓰ 2012년에 세계는 기록적인 345억톤의 이산화탄소를 화석연료에서 배출하였다. ⓱ 석탄은 대기 오염에 가장 주요한 원인이었다. ⓲ 값싼 천연가스가 최근에 미국의 석탄 수요를 감소시키고 있지만, ⓳ 다른 곳, 특히 중국에서는 석탄의 수요가 급증하고 있다. ⓴ 향후 이십 년 동안 전 세계 수억 명의 사람들이 처음으로 전기를 공급받게 될 것이며 현재의 추세가 지속한다면 대부분은 석탄에서 생산되는 에너지를 사용할 것이다.

[어휘]

environmentalist n. 환경(보호)론자 coal n. 석탄 myth n. 신화 underneath ad. 아래에, 하부(下部)에 stream n. 개울, 시내 acidic a. 산성의 thick a. 탁한, 흐린, 투명하지 않은 premature death 조기 사망 stink n. 악취, 고약한 냄새 wreath v. 둘레[에워]싸다 -laden a. (형용사를 형성하여) ~이 가득한 linger v. 오래 머물다 long weekend 긴 주말 연휴(주말에 더해 금요일이나 월요일이 휴일이 되는 경우) provoke v. 유발하다, 짜증나게 하다 epidemic n. 유행병, 전염병 respiratory a. 호흡의, 호흡 기관의 ailment n. 질병 ensuing a. 다음의, 뒤이은 euphemism n. 완곡어 fraught with ~투성이의 externality n. 외부 효과 lethal a. 치명적인 radical a. 근본적인, 철저한, 과격한 emit v. (빛·열·가스·소리 등을) 내다[내뿜다] metric a. 미터(법)의 contributor n. 원인 제공자 surge v. 급등[급증]하다

several hundred million people worldwide will get electricity / for
the first time, / and if current trends continue, / most will use
power (produced by coal). ㉑ Even the most aggressive push (for
alternative energy sources and conservation) could not replace coal
— at least not right away.

Which of the following is closest in meaning to ⓑ "externalities"?
다음 중 ⓑ "externalities"와 의미가 가장 비슷한 것은 무엇인가?

① the direct costs in producing coal
　석탄을 생산하는 직접적인 비용
② the costs that coal miners pay to society
　석탄 광부들이 사회에 지불하는 비용
③ the indirect costs that society has to pay
　사회가 부담해야 하는 간접비용
④ the costs that consumers do not have to pay
　소비자들이 지불해야 할 필요가 없는 비용

해석 ㉑ 대체 에너지원과 환경보존에 대한 가장 강력한 압박마저도 석탄을 대체할 수는 없을 것이다. 적어도 지금 당장 대체할 수는 없을 것이다.

해설 대시로 이어지는 'the heavy costs it imposes on society(사회에 부과되는 막대한 비용)'에서 정답을 추론할 수 있다.

어휘 **aggressive** a. 공격적인, 대단히 적극적인 **alternative** a. 대안의

정답 및 해설

019 ②   2019학년도 숭실대학교 인문계 A형 12번

American football draws as much attention lately / for the knocks (that players take) as it does / for their drives down the field. ❷ The emergence of research (linking head collisions with behavioral and cognitive changes) (similar to those (seen in Alzheimer's patients)) puts the colliding / in a new context. ❸ Whether ramming opponents head-on or butting helmets, / athletes may face the risk of long-term brain injury / from hits (accumulated over time).
❹ Brain degeneration (from repeated blows to the head) had been known in boxers / since the 1920s / as dementia pugilistica, or punch-drunk syndrome. ❺ Recent research indicates / that small impacts can cause damage / as much as big ones, / ❻ widening the field of concern to young athletes, hockey players, and soldiers (subject to head-rattling blasts).
❼ At the University of North Carolina, (where football players receive an average of 950 hits to the head each season), neuroscientist Kevin Guskiewics and colleagues have spent (six years) analyzing impact data / from video recordings and helmets (equipped with accelerometers). ❽ They note / that there are plans [to test similar technologies / on various football teams (starting soon)]. ❾ Guskiewics believes / that on-field monitoring and education are paths (to progress). ❿ Already the spotlight (on football-related brain trauma) has resulted in new football practices, state laws, and congressional hearings on ways (to protect young athletes).
⓫ On the medical side, / there is hope (for advanced brain-imaging techniques, experimental blood or spinal fluid tests), ⓬ and even a genetic marker (that would enable doctors to identify chronic traumatic encephalopathy (CTE, the same as punch-drunk syndrome, but not limited to boxers) early on). ⓭ At the moment, / the definitive mark of the disease — (clumps of abnormal tau protein

해석

❶ 미식축구는 선수들이 운동장에서 질주할 때 받는 관심만큼 많은 관심을 최근에는 선수들이 받는 충격 때문에 끌고 있다. ❷ (선수 간의) 정면충돌을 알츠하이머 환자들에게서 볼 수 있는 변화와 비슷한 행동적·인지적 변화와 연관짓는 연구의 출현은 그 충돌을 새로운 상황에 놓이게 한다. ❸ 상대 선수를 정면에서 심하게 부딪치든 헬멧을 들이박든, 선수들은 시간이 지나며 점차 누적된 충격으로 장기적인 뇌 손상의 위험에 직면할 수도 있다.
❹ 머리에 가해지는 반복적인 타격으로 인한 뇌의 퇴화는 1920년대 이후로 권투선수들에게 권투선수 치매 혹은 펀치 드렁크 증후군으로 알려졌다. ❺ 최근 연구는 작은 충격 또한 큰 충격만큼이나 (뇌에) 손상을 입힐 수 있다는 것을 보여주며, ❻ 관심의 폭을 나이 어린 운동선수, 하키선수, 머리를 울리는 폭발을 겪기 쉬운 군인들에게까지 넓혀주었다.
❼ 미식축구 선수들이 매 시즌마다 머리에 평균 950번의 타격을 입는 노스캐롤라이나대학교에서, 신경과학자 케빈 거스큐이츠(Kevin Guskiewics)와 동료들은 동영상 녹화물과 가속도계 장착 헬멧에서 얻은 충격 자료를 분석하는 데 6년을 보냈다. ❽ 그들은 조만간 여러 미식 축구팀들을 대상으로 이와 유사한 기술들을 실험할 계획이 있다는 점에 주목한다. ❾ 현장 감시와 교육이 나아가야 하는 길이라고 거스큐이츠는 믿는다. ❿ 미식축구 관련 뇌 트라우마(외상)에 대한 관심은 이미 새로운 축구 연습, 주(州)의 법, 어린 선수들을 보호하는 방법에 대한 의회 청문회 등의 결과를 초래했다.
⓫ 의학적인 측면에서, 첨단 뇌 영상 기법과 실험적인 혈액검사나 척수액 검사에 대한 희망이 있으며 ⓬ 심지어 유전자 표지(유전적 해석에 지표가 되는 특정의 DNA 영역 또는 유전자)가 의사들이 만성외상성뇌병증(CTE, 펀치 드렁크 증후군과 같다. 하지만 권투선수들에게 한정되지 않은 질병)을 조기에 확인할 수 있게 해줄 것이라는 기대도 있다. ⓭ 현재로서는, 이 병의 확실한 징후인 뇌 속의 비정상적인 타우단백질 덩어리는 뇌를 잘라서 착색을 하여 현미경으로 관찰하는 경우에만 볼 수 있다.

어휘

draw attention 관심을 끌다 **knock** n. (단단한 것에 쾅 하고) 부딪침[찧기], 타격 **take a knock** (심한) 타격을 받다[손상을 입다] **collision** n. 충돌; 격돌 **cognitive** a. 지각하는, 인지하는 **ram** v. 심하게 부딪치다, 들이박다 **opponent** n. 상대, 상대편 **head-on** ad. 머리를 앞으로, 정면으로 **butt** v. (머리로) 들이받다[밀다] **accumulate** v. 모으다, 축적하다 **degeneration** n. 퇴보, 악화 **dementia pugilistica** 권투 선수 치매 **punch-drunk** a. (권투에서 펀치를 얻어맞고) 비틀거리는, 그로기 상태의 **syndrome** n. 증후군 **blast** n. 폭발, 폭파, 폭약 **neuroscientist** n. 신경과학자 **accelerometer** n. 가속도계 **spotlight** n. 주목, 관심 **spinal fluid** 척수액 **genetic** a. 유전의, 유전학의 **chronic** a. 만성적인 **encephalopathy** n. 뇌병, 뇌질환 **clump** n. 덩어리 **abnormal** a. 비정상적인 **protein** n. 단백질

in the brain) — can be seen / only when the brain is sliced, stained, and studied / under a microscope. ⓮ CTE typically appears / years after head traumas, / ⓯ and "we don't want to diagnose a disease / after death," / says Ann McKee, (co-director of Boston University's Center / for the Study of Traumatic Encephalopathy).
⓰ Gusklewics envisions databases [that track all the hits : (athletes take) / throughout their playing years / to help explain neurologic changes / later in life. ⓱ But, he says, / Ⓑ "it'll probably be my grandchildren (who are analyzing that data)."

Which of the following is closest in meaning to Ⓑ?
다음 중 Ⓑ의 의미와 가장 가까운 것은 무엇인가?

① Data collection was finished long ago.
데이터 수집이 오래전에 완료되었다.

② Analysis of data is not possible right now.
데이터 분석은 지금 당장은 불가능하다.

③ Guskiewics cannot have access to data now.
거스큐이츠 박사는 현재 데이터에 접근할 수 없다.

④ Accumulating data will be grandchildren's job.
데이터를 축적하는 것은 손자 손녀들의 일이 될 것이다.

해석 ⓮ 만성외상성뇌병증은 일반적으로 머리에 외상을 입고 몇 년 후에 증상이 나타난다. ⓯ 그리고 "우리는 사후에 병을 진단하기를 원치 않습니다."라고 보스턴대학교의 외상성 뇌병증 연구소의 공동 연구소장인 앤 맥키(Ann McKee)는 말한다.
⓰ 거스큐이츠 박사는 운동선수들이 선수 생활을 하는 내내 받는 모든 충격을 추적하여 만년에 나타나는 신경학적 변화를 설명하는 것에 도움을 줄 데이터베이스를 만들 구상을 하고 있다. ⓱ 하지만 그는 Ⓑ "그 데이터를 분석하고 있을 사람은 아마도 내 손자들이 될 것입니다."라고 말한다.

해설 앞 문장에서 거스큐이츠(Gusklewics) 박사가 해당 데이터베이스를 만들기 위한 구상을 하고 있다고 하는 만큼 밑줄 친 Ⓑ 의미는 지금 당장은 불가능하고 상당한 시간과 노력이 필요함을 함축한다고 볼 수 있다. 따라서 정답은 ②이 가장 적절하다.

어휘 stain v. (현미경으로 조사하기 위하여 조직의 일부에) 착색하다 diagnose v. 진단하다 envision v. 마음속에 그리다

020 ①   2020학년도 명지대학교 인문계 28번

❶ Even the zone of cultural memory / from the last century has relics (that feel like / they belong to a foreign country). ❷ Take the decline of martial culture. The older cities (in Europe) are dotted with public works (that flaunt the nation's military might). ❸ Pedestrians can behold statues of commanders on horseback and victory arches (crowned by chariots). ❹ Photos (from a century ago) show men (in gaudy military dress uniforms) parading on national holidays. ❺ But in the West today, / public places are no longer named after military victories. ❻ Our war memorials depict not proud commanders on horseback but weeping mothers, or weary soldiers. ❼ Military men are inconspicuous / in public life, with drab uniforms and little prestige / among the hoi polloi. ❽ Another major change (we have lived through in the 20th century) is an intolerance of displays of force / in everyday life. ❾ In earlier decades / a man's willingness (to use his fists / in response to an insult) was the sign of respectability. ❿ Today / it is the sign of a boor, (a symptom of impulse control disorder). ⓫ An incident (from 1950) illustrates the change. ⓬ President Harry Truman had seen an unkind review / in The Washington Post of a performance / by his daughter (Margaret, / an aspiring singer). ⓭ Truman wrote to the critic: / "Some day / I hope to meet you. ⓮ When that happens / you'll need a new nose and a lot of beefsteak / for black eyes." ⓯ Though every writer can sympathize with the impulse, / today / a public threat (to commit aggravated assault / against a critic) would seem buffoonish, / indeed sinister, / if it came from a person (in power). ⓰ But at the time / Truman was widely admired for his paternal chivalry. ⓱ [Even more revolutionary than the scorn (for violence between men) is the scorn (for violence / against women)]. ⓲ Many baby boomers are nostalgic / for The Honeymooners, a 1950s sitcom (featuring Jackie Gleason as Ralph, / a burly bus driver).

해석

❶ 심지어 지난 세기의 문화 기억을 갖고 있는 시대 구간조차 외국의 것인 것처럼 (낯설게) 느껴지는 유물들을 간직하고 있다. ❷ 군사 문화의 쇠퇴를 예로 들어보겠다. 유럽의 오래된 도시들에는 국가의 군사력을 과시하는 공공 작품들이 산재해 있다. ❸ 행인들은 말을 탄 지휘관 동상들과 여러 대의 전차들로 아치 윗부분을 장식한 개선문을 볼 수 있다. ❹ 100년 전에 찍은 사진들은 촌스럽게 화려한 군복을 입은 남자들이 국경일에 가두행진 하는 것을 보여준다. ❺ 하지만 오늘날 서양에서, 공공장소는 더 이상 군사적 승리에서 이름을 따서 지어지지 않는다. ❻ 우리의 전쟁 기념관은 말을 타고 있는 자랑스러운 지휘관이 아니라, 눈물을 흘리는 어머니나 지쳐있는 병사들을 표현하고 있다. ❼ 군인들은 단조로운 군복을 입고 대중들 사이에서 위엄도 거의 없이 눈에 띄지 않게 공중 생활을 하고 있다. ❽ 우리가 20세기를 살며 겪어온 또 다른 주요한 변화는 일상생활에서 힘을 과시하는 것을 용납하지 않는 것이다. ❾ 20세기 초 몇 십 년 동안에는 남자가 모욕에 대한 대응으로 기꺼이 주먹을 쓰려 하는 것이 존경할만한 행동이었다. ❿ (그러나) 오늘날에 그것은 천박한 남자나 하는 행동이며, 충동조절장애의 징후로 여겨진다. ⓫ 1950년에 있었던 한 사건이 이런 변화를 명확히 보여준다. ⓬ 해리 트루먼(Harry Truman) 대통령은 가수 지망생이었던 그의 딸 마가렛(Margaret)의 공연에 대한 『워싱턴포스트(The Washington Post)』의 혹평을 보았다. ⓭ 트루먼 대통령은 그 비평을 작성한 사람에게 이렇게 편지를 썼다. ⓮ "언젠가 자네를 만나길 바라네. 만나게 되면 자네는 새로운 코가 필요할 것이며 멍든 눈에 붙여야 할 비프스테이크가 많이 필요할 걸세." ⓯ 비록 모든 작가들이 (비평가에 대한) 그런 충동적인 언사에 공감할 수 있다 하더라도, ⓰ 비평가를 상대로 가중처벌이 될 만큼의 심한 폭행을 가하겠다는 공개적 위협이 만약 권력자에게서 나왔다면, 오늘날에는 우스꽝스럽다 못해 정말 사악하게 느껴질 것이다. ⓱ 하지만 당시에는 트루먼 대통령은 부모로서 할 도리를 한 것이라고 널리 존경받았다. ⓲ 남성들 간의 폭력에 대한 멸시보다 훨씬 더 혁명적인 것은 여성을 상대로 휘두르는 폭력에 대한 멸시이다. ⓳ 많은 베이비붐 세대들은 재키 글리슨(Jackie Gleason)이 건장한 버스 운전사 랄프(Ralph)로 나오는 1950년대 시트콤 『허니무너스(The Honeymooners)』에 그리워하고 있다.

어휘

relics n. 유물 take v. (예를) 들다 martial a. 호전적인 be dotted with ~이 산재해 있다 flaunt v. 과시하다 might n. 힘 pedestrian n. 보행자 behold v. 바라보다 statue n. 조각상 victory arch 개선문 chariot n. 전차 gaudy a. 촌스럽게 번지르르한 weeping a. 눈물을 흘리는 weary a. 지친, 피곤한 inconspicuous a. 눈에 띄지 않는 drab a. 담갈색의, 우중충한 prestige n. 명성 hoi polloi n. 대중, 서민 fist n. 주먹 insult n. 모욕, 모욕 v. 모욕하다, 모독하다 boor n. 무례한 남자 impulse n. 충동, 충격, 자극 disorder n. 무질서, 혼란, 장애 illustrate v. 분명히 보여주다 black eyes 멍든 눈 sympathize v. 동정하다, 지지하다 aggravated assault 가중 폭행 buffoonish a. 우스꽝스러운 sinister a. 사악한 chivalry n. 기사도 정신 scorn n. 경멸, 멸시 v. 경멸하다, 멸시하다 nostalgic a. 항수를 느끼는 burly a. (몸이) 건장한

㉑ In one of the show's recurring laugh lines, / an enraged Ralph
         └─되풀이해서 일어나는   S
shakes his fist / at his wife and bellows, / ㉑ "One of these days,
   V   O
Alice, POW, right in the kisser!" ㉒ Nowadays / our sensitivity
                             └─오늘날에는   └─민감성
(to violence / against women) makes this kind of comedy / in a
                              V   O
mainstream television program unthinkable.
                              O.C

Which of the following best explains the underlined the impulse?
다음 중 밑줄 친 the impulse를 가장 잘 설명한 것은?

✓ Truman's desire to physically attack the critic
   비평가에게 신체적인 공격을 하고자 하는 트루먼 대통령의 욕망
② Truman's desire to protest to the newspaper
   신문에 항의하려고 하는 트루먼 대통령의 욕망
③ Truman's desire to invite the critic to dinner
   비평가를 저녁 식사에 초대하고자 하는 트루먼 대통령의 욕망
④ Truman's desire to sue the critic
   그 비평가를 고소하려고 하는 트루먼 대통령의 욕망

해석 ㉑ 그 시트콤에서 반복적으로 등장하는 웃기는 대사에서, 화난 랄프는 그의 아내를 향하여 주먹을 흔들며 다음과 같이 소리 지른다. ㉑ "앨리스(Alice), 조만간, 내가 당신 얼굴을 뻥하고 날려버릴 거야!" ㉒ (그러나) 요즘에는 여성을 상대로 저지르는 폭력에 대한 우리의 민감성때문에, 주류 TV 프로그램에서 이런 부류의 코미디를 한다는 것은 상상조차 할 수가 없다.

해설 앞 문장에서 트루먼 대통령의 딸에 대해 혹평을 보였던 기자를 향한 폭행을 행사할 수 있는 위협을 하고 있음을 알 수 있다. 따라서 정답은 ①이 가장 적절하다.

어휘 recurring a. 되풀이해서 일어나는 enrage v. 격분하게 하다 kisser n. 키스하는 사람, 얼굴 mainstream n. 주류, 대세 unthinkable a. 상상 할 수 없는 protest n. 항의, 시위, 반대 . 항의하다, 이의를 제기하다 sue v. 고소하다, 청구하다

유형 08 지시대상

001 ④
2019학년도 가천대학교 인문계 2교시 A형 26번

❶ Since the advent of the automobile, / over 20 million fatalities have been recorded. ❷ Even as late as the 1950's, / car manufacturers stood by the claim (that it was impossible / to make vehicles any safer than they were) because the physical forces of a crash were too great to overcome. ❸ At the same time, / after testing with cadavers, / the first crash test dummy was unveiled. ❹ A crash test dummy is a full-scale anthropomorphic test device (ATD) (that resembles the body / in weight, proportions, and movement). ❺ Today's dummies are equipped with sensitive high-tech sensors (that provide vital crash test data). ❻ Thanks to these Ⓐ silent heroes, / humans have the greatest chances of surviving fatal accidents / than they have ever had.

Which of the following does the underlined Ⓐ silent heroes refer to?
다음 중 밑줄 친 Ⓐ말없는 영웅들이 가리키고 있는 것은?

① fatalities — 사망자 수
② manufactures — 제조업체
③ cadavers — 시체
✓④ dummies — 마네킹(모조품)

해석 ❶ 자동차의 출현 이래로 기록된 사망자의 수는 2천만 명이 넘는다. ❷ 1950년대만 해도, 자동차 제조업체들은 자동차 충돌 시에 발생하는 물리적 힘이 너무 커서 이겨낼 수 없기 때문에 차량을 지금보다 더 안전하게 만드는 것은 불가능하다는 주장을 고수했다. ❸ 동시에, 시체로 시험을 한 뒤에 최초의 자동차 충돌시험용 마네킹이 공개되었다. ❹ 충돌시험용 마네킹은 몸무게, 신체비율 및 움직임에서 인간의 신체를 닮은 실물 크기의 인체모형 시험장치(ATD)다. ❺ 오늘날의 마네킹은 충돌 테스트의 중요한 정보를 제공하는 고감도의 첨단 센서가 장착되어 있다. ❻ 이러한 Ⓐ말 없는 영웅들 덕분에, 인간은 그 어느 때보다도 치명적인 사고로부터 살아남을 수 있는 확률이 더 높아지게 되었다.

해설 Ⓐ 앞 문장에서 충돌 테스트를 위한 마네킹의 정의와 역할에 대해서 언급하고 있는 만큼 ④이 가장 적절하다.

어휘 advent n. 도래(到來), 출현 automobile n. 자동차 fatality n. (사고·전쟁 따위로 인한) 죽음; (pl.) 사망자수 manufacturer n. 제조업자, 제조업체, 생산자 stand by ~을 고수하다 claim n. 요구, 청구; 주장 vehicle n. (사람·물건의) 수송 수단, 탈것 physical a. 신체의; 물리적인 cadaver n. 송장, (해부용) 시체 dummy n. 인체모형; 마네킹 unveil v. 정체를 드러내다; (비밀 따위를) 밝히다 anthropomorphic a. 의인화된, 사람의 모습을 닮은 proportion n. 비율; 조화, 균형 equip v. (~에 필요물을) 갖추다, ~에 설비하다 sensitive a. 민감한, 예민한; 고감도의 vital a. 절대로 필요한, 지극히 중요한 survive v. ~의 후까지 생존하다 fatal a. 치명적인; 파멸적인

002 ①
2019학년도 인하대학교 인문계 31번

❶ We continue to test products rigorously / so you can make the best decision / for your family. ❷ Our New York City-based team methodically evaluates all the latest appliances, beauty essentials, clothing, and more for safety, quality, and value, / using state-of-the-art consumer testing methods. ❸ First, we put products / to the test in our labs / by evaluating safety and quality claims. ❹ We'll stretch, drop, pull, and even heat up products / to make sure / they can stand up / to any conditions (you and your family might put them through). ❺ Then, we send the items out / to select readers / to understand (how they actually work in the real world). ❻ Only after all that / do we deliver our recommendations to you).

What does the underlined they refer to?
밑줄 친 they가 가리키는 것은?

✓ ① products 제품
② select readers 엄선한 독자
③ consumers 소비자
④ testing methods 시험 방법
⑤ safety and quality claims 안전과 품질에 관한 요구사항

해석
❶ 우리는 여러분이 가족을 위한 최선의 결정을 내릴 수 있도록 엄격하게 제품에 대한 테스트를 지속적으로 실시합니다. ❷ 뉴욕시에 본부를 둔 우리 팀은 최신 기구, 미용 필수품, 의류 등에 관해 최신 소비자 테스트 방법을 사용하여 안전, 품질, 가치를 체계적으로 평가합니다. ❸ 첫 번째로, 우리는 안전과 품질에 관한 (우리의) 요구사항들을 평가하는 제품 시험을 실험실에서 진행합니다. ❹ 우리는 제품이 당신과 당신 가족이 사용할 수도 있는 어떠한 환경에서도 확실하게 견딜 수 있게 하려고 제품을 펴고, 떨어뜨리고, 당기며, 심지어 가열도 할 것입니다. ❺ 그다음, 우리는 실생활에서 어떻게 작동하는지 파악하기 위해 그 제품을 엄선한 독자들에게 보냅니다. ❻ 그 모든 과정을 거친 후에야 우리는 당신에게 우리의 추천서를 전달합니다.

해설
밑줄 친 they는 동일 문장에서 앞에서 언급한 products를 가리킨다.

어휘
rigorously ad. 가혹하게, 엄격하게, 혹독하게 methodically ad. 조직적으로, 질서정연하게 evaluate v. 평가하다 appliance n. 기구, 장치, 설비 essential n. 본질적인 요소, 필수적인 요소 state-of-the-art a. 최신의, 최첨단의 method n. 태도, 방법 claim n. 요구, 청구; 권리, 주장 stretch v. 늘이다, 펴다, 잡아당기다 drop v. 떨어뜨리다 stand up to (용감히) 맞서다, 대항하다; (물건이) ~에 견디다 select a. 가려낸, 정선한; 뽑은 deliver v. 배달하다, 송달하다 recommendation n. 추천; 추천장, 소개장

003 ④   2019학년도 인하대학교 인문계 08번

① Invasive plants are introduced species (that can thrive in areas / beyond Ⓐ their natural range of dispersal). ② These plants are characteristically adaptable, aggressive, and have a high capacity (to propagate). ③ Because Ⓑ they evolved / over long periods of time / in completely different habitats elsewhere in the world, / these exotics often have few natural enemies and contribute little / to the support of native wildlife. ④ Ⓒ Their vigor (combined with a lack of natural enemies) often leads to outbreaks / in populations. ⑤ Invasive plants can totally overwhelm and devastate established native plants and their habitats / by out-competing Ⓓ them / for nutrients, water, and light — / ⑥ and because they offer so little food value / to native wildlife, / Ⓔ they are destructive of biodiversity / on every level.

Which of the following refers to a different thing from the others?
다음 중 나머지와 다른 하나를 가리키는 것은?
① Ⓐ   ② Ⓑ   ③ Ⓒ   ✓ ④ Ⓓ   ⑤ Ⓔ

해석 ① 침입성 식물은 다른 지역에서 도입된 종(種)으로, Ⓐ그들의 자연적인 확산 범위를 넘어서는 지역에서도 잘 번성할 수 있다. ② Ⓑ이 식물들은 적응력이 뛰어나고, 공격적이며, 번식력이 강한 특징을 보인다. ③ 이 외래식물은 오랜 시간에 걸쳐 세계 여러 곳에서 완전히 다른 서식지들에서 진화해 왔기에, 종종 천적이 매우 적고 토착 생물에 거의 도움이 되지 않는다. ④ 이러한 번식력에 천적의 부족이 더해져, Ⓒ그 식물들은 종종 개체 수가 급격하게 증가하게 된다. ⑤ 침입성 식물은 영양분, 물, 빛을 얻는 데 있어 Ⓓ토착 식물보다 훨씬 월등하기 때문에 기존의 토착 식물과 그들의 서식지를 완전히 압도하여 황폐화시킬 수 있다. ⑥ 그리고 침입성 식물은 토착 야생 생물에게 식량으로서의 가치를 거의 제공하지 못하기 때문에, Ⓔ그것들은 모든 수준에서 생물 다양성을 파괴한다.

해설 Ⓓ는 '토착식물'을 가리킨다. 반면에 Ⓐ, Ⓑ, Ⓒ, Ⓔ는 '침입성 식물'을 가리키고 있다.

어휘 invasive a. 침입하는, 침략적인 species n. 종류, 종(種) thrive v. 번창하다, 번영하다 dispersal n. (개체의) 분산(分散), 전파 adaptable a. 적응할 수 있는, 순응할 수 있는 aggressive a. 침략적인, 공격적인 capacity n. 능력, 재능; 수용량 propagate v. 번식하다, 증식하다; 퍼지다 evolve v. 서서히 발전하다; 진화하다 habitat n. 서식지 exotic n. 이국적인 것; 외래종, 외래식물 contribute v. 기부하다; 기여하다, 공헌하다 wildlife n. 야생식물 vigor n. 활기, 활력 outbreak n. (소동·전쟁·유행병 따위의) 발발, 돌발, 창궐 overwhelm v. 압도하다, 제압하다, 궤멸시키다 devastate v. (국토·토지 따위를) 유린하다, 황폐시키다 established a. 확실한, 확립된; 제정된 out-compete v. 다른 경쟁자들을 압도하다, 다른 경쟁자보다 뛰어나다 nutrient n. 영양분, 자양분 destructive a. 파괴적인, 파멸적인 biodiversity n. 생물다양성

004 ①   2020학년도 국민대학교 인문계 오전 A형 27번

❶ What is consciousness? ❷ This may sound like a simple question / but it is not. ❸ Consciousness is at once the most obvious and the most difficult thing (we can investigate). ❹ We seem either to have to use consciousness / to investigate itself, which is Ⓐ a slightly weird idea, ❺ or to have to extricate ourselves / from Ⓑ the very thing (we want to study). ❻ No wonder (that philosophers and scientists have struggled / for millennia / with Ⓒ the concept), and (that scientists rejected Ⓓ the whole idea / for long periods / and refused even to study it). ❼ The good news is / that, at the start of the 21st century, 'consciousness studies' is thriving. ❽ Psychology, biology, and neuroscience have reached the point / (when they are ready to confront some tricky questions): / ❾ What does consciousness do? ❿ Could we have evolved without it? What is consciousness, anyway?

Which is different from the others in its meaning?
의미가 나머지와 다른 것은 무엇인가?
✓Ⓐ   ②Ⓑ   ③Ⓒ   ④Ⓓ

해 석 ❶ 의식이란 무엇인가? ❷ 이것은 간단한 질문처럼 들릴지도 모르지만 그렇지 않다. ❸ 의식은 우리가 연구할 수 있는 가장 명백하며 가장 어려운 것이다. ❹ 우리는 의식을 연구하기 위해 의식을 이용해야 할 것 같은데, 이것은 Ⓐ약간 이상한 생각이다. ❺ 또는 우리가 연구하려고 하는 Ⓑ바로 그것으로부터 우리 스스로를 해방시켜야 할 것처럼 보인다. ❻ 철학자와 과학자들이 Ⓒ그 개념과 수천 년 동안 씨름해 왔으며, 과학자들이 Ⓓ그 개념 전체를 오랜 기간 동안 거부한 것은 심지어는 연구하는 것조차 거부한 것은 그리 놀라운 일이 아니다. ❼ 21세기 초에 접어들면서, '의식 연구'가 번성하고 있다는 것은 좋은 소식이다. ❽ 심리학, 생물학 및 신경과학은 다음과 같은 까다로운 질문들에 직면할 준비가 되어 있는 수준에 도달했다. ❾ 의식은 무엇을 하는가? ❿ 의식이 없었다면 인간은 진화할 수 있었을까? 어쨌든 간에, 의식이란 무엇인가?

해 설 Ⓐ는 '의식을 사용해서 연구한다는 생각'을 가리킨다. 하지만 나머지는 '의식'을 가리키고 있다.

어 휘 consciousness n. 자각, 의식 at once A and B A하기도(하고) B하기도(하다) investigate v. 연구하다, 조사하다 weird a. 기묘한 extricate v. 해방시키다, 탈출시키다 struggle v. 투쟁하다, 고군분투하다 millennium n. 천 년(pl. millennia) thrive v. 번창하다, 잘 자라다 neuroscience n. 신경과학 confront v. 직면하다 tricky a. 까다로운, 곤란한

정답 및 해설

005 ④ ·············· 2020학년도 한국산업기술대학교 인문계 27번

❶ A large genetic study looked at nearly 1,000 people / in 51 places around the world / and found the most genetic diversity / in Africa / and less farther away from Africa. ❷ How could this happen? ❸ When small groups of people moved away, / they took only a small amount of all the possible genetic information / with them. ❹ People (in the small groups) reproduced. ❺ Their offspring inherited their parents' more limited set of genes. ❻ Therefore, their traits were very similar to those of their parents. ❼ This process continues / as small groups of people moved farther and farther / from Africa.

According to the passage, This process most likely refers to the fact that _____.
이 글에 따르면, 밑줄 친 This process는 _____는 사실을 지칭할 가능성이 가장 높다.

① children inherited their ancestors' traits
아이들이 그들 조상의 특성을 물려받았다
② transmittable genetic information grew bigger
유전되는 유전 정보는 더 커졌다
③ small groups survived when moving out of Africa
아프리카를 벗어났을 때 소규모 집단은 살아남았다
✓ offsprings have fewer sets of genes than their ancestors
후손들은 그들 선조보다 더 적은 유전자 세트를 지닌다

해석 ❶ 전 세계 51개 지역의 거의 1,000명의 사람들에 대해 대규모로 유전적 연구를 한 결과, 아프리카에서 가장 많은 유전적 다양성을 발견했으며, 아프리카에서 멀어질수록 유전적 다양성은 더 낮아졌다. ❷ 어떻게 이런 일이 일어난 걸까? ❸ 소규모의 사람들이 이주를 떠났을 때, 그들은 가능한 모든 유전적 정보 중에서 오직 소량만 가져갔다. ❹ 그 소규모의 집단 속에서 번식이 이루어졌다. ❺ 그들의 자손은 그들 부모의 더 제한된 유전자 세트를 물려받는다. ❻ 그러므로 그들의 특성은 부모의 특성과 매우 유사하다. ❼ 소규모의 사람들이 아프리카로부터 점점 더 멀리 이주함에 따라 이 과정은 계속된다.

해설 ❺번 문장에서 '이 과정'인 '그들의 자손은 그들 부모의 더 제한된 유전자 세트를 물려받는다'라고 말하고 있다.

어휘 genetic a. 유전의 diversity n. 다양성 inherit v. 물려받다 trait n. 특성 ancestor n. 조상 transmittable a. 전할 수 있는, 전염성의, 유전성의 offspring n. 자식, (동물의)새끼

006 ①

2020학년도 가천대학교 인문계 1교시 B형 26번

「It was not until … that~」: …하고 나서야 비로소 ~하다 (It ~ that 강조구문)

❶ It was not until the War of 1812 with Britain that US officials realized / the country was in desperate need of roads. ❷ Troops stationed in the West were needed / at the battlefront, / ❸ but because of the lack of adequate transportation networks, / military leaders found moving Ⓐ them to be a painfully slow process. ❹ A solution came / in the form of privately built roadways (called turnpikes), / ❺ Ⓑ which were maintained / by private companies / hoping to / earn big profits / by charging a toll / for Ⓒ their use. ❻ These early toll roads, (often established along stagecoach routes), were predecessors / to modern highways / and interstate systems, / ❼ and Ⓓ most were eventually taken over / by state highway departments / in the twentieth century.

Which of the following underlined Ⓐ, Ⓑ, Ⓒ and Ⓓ does NOT refer to the same thing?
다음 밑줄 친 Ⓐ, Ⓑ, Ⓒ, Ⓓ에서 같은 의미가 아닌 것은?
✓① Ⓐ　② Ⓑ　③ Ⓒ　④ Ⓓ

해석

❶ 영국과의 1812년 전쟁이 발발하고 나서야 비로소 미국의 공직자들은 미국에 도로가 절실히 필요하다는 것을 깨달았다. ❷ 서부에 주둔하고 있는 병력을 최전선에서 필요로 했지만, ❸ 적절한 수송망이 부족했기에 군 수뇌부는 Ⓐ그들을 이동시키는 것이 극도로 느린 과정임을 알게 되었다. ❹ 해결책은 턴파이크(유료도로)라고 불리는 민간 건설 도로의 형태로 나왔는데, ❺ Ⓑ이 도로들은 Ⓒ도로를 이용할 때 통행료를 부과함으로써 큰 이익을 얻기를 바라는 민간 기업들에 의해 유지 관리되었다. ❻ 종종 역마차 길을 따라서 나란히 세워진 이러한 초기 유료도로들은 현대 고속도로와 간선도로의 전신(前身)이었으며, ❼ 결국 Ⓓ이들 대부분은 20세기에 주(州)의 고속도로 담당 부서에 의해 인수되었다.

해설

Ⓐ는 앞에서 언급한 '서부에 주둔하고 있는 병력(Troops stationed in the West)'을 말한다. 하지만 나머지는 이들을 이동시키기 위한 '도로(privately built roadways)'를 말하고 있다.

어휘

desperate a. 자포자기의, 무모한; 필사적인　troop n. 무리; 군대, 병력　station v. 배치하다, 주재시키다　battlefront n. 전선, 제일선　adequate a. 적당한, 충분한　transportation n. 운송, 수송　painfully ad. 고통스럽게, 극도로　solution n. (문제 등의) 해결, 해법　turnpike n. 유료 고속도로, 유료 도로　maintain v. 유지하다; 주장하다　charge v. 청구하다; (요금, 부담을) 지우다　toll n. 통행료, 통행세　establish v. (학교·회사 따위를) 설립하다; (제도·법률 등을) 제정하다　stagecoach n. 역마차, 승합마차　predecessor n. 전임자, 선배; 전에 있던 것　interstate a. 주와 주 사이의, 주간의

정답 및 해설

007 ① — 2019학년도 상명대학교 인문·자연계 26번

❶ Asian Americans have been described in the media as "excessively, even provocatively" successful in gaining admission to universities. ❷ Asian American shopkeepers have been congratulated, as well as criticized, for their ubiquity and entrepreneurial effectiveness. ❸ If Asian Americans can make it, many politicians and pundits ask, why can't African Americans? ❹ Such comparisons pit minorities against each other and generate African American resentment toward Asian Americans. ❺ The ⓑ victims are blamed for their plight, rather than racism and an economy that has made many young African American workers superfluous. ❻ The celebration of Asian Americans has obscured reality. ❼ For example, figures (on the high earnings of Asian Americans / relative to Caucasians) are misleading. ❽ Most Asian Americans live in California, Hawaii, and New York — states with higher incomes and higher costs of living than the national average.

밑줄 친 ⓑ의 victims는 누구를 가리키는가?

✓ ① African Americans　　② Asian Americans
③ Minorities　　　　　　④ Unknown
⑤ Caucasians

해석
❶ 아시아계 미국인들은 대학 입학 허가를 받는 것에 있어 '지나치게, 심지어 도발적으로' 성공했다고 언론에서 묘사되어 왔다. ❷ 아시아계 미국인 가게 주인들은 그들이 곳곳에 있다는 것과 그들의 기업가적인 효율성 때문에 비난도 받고 축하도 받았다. ❸ 만약 아시아계 미국인들이 성공할 수 있다면, 왜 아프리카계 미국인들은 성공하지 못하냐고 많은 정치가들과 학자들은 묻는다. ❹ 그러한 비교는 소수민족들을 서로 대립시키고 아시아계 미국인에 대한 아프리카계 미국인의 분노를 불러일으킨다. ❺ 그 ⓑ피해자들(아프리카계 미국인들)은 그들의 곤경에 대한 책임이 인종차별이나 젊은 아프리카계 미국인 노동자들을 많이 남아돌게 만드는 경제에 있는 것이 아닌 그들 자신에게 있는 것으로 비난을 받고 있다. ❻ 아시아계 미국인들에 대한 칭송은 현실을 가려왔다. ❼ 예를 들어, 백인에 비해 아시아계 미국인들의 높은 소득에 대한 수치는 오해의 소지가 있다. ❽ 대부분의 아시아계 미국인들은 전국 평균보다 소득이 높고 생활비가 많이 들어가는 주(州)인 캘리포니아, 하와이, 뉴욕에 산다.

해설
윗글은 아시아 아메리칸들의 성공적 묘사로 인해 아프리카 아메리칸들의 피해를 말하는 글이다. 특히 ❸부터 ⓑ에서 말하는 피해자가 아프리카 아메리칸 임을 알 수 있다.T

어휘
excessively ad. 지나치게, 매우 provocatively ad. 도발적으로, 자극적으로 shopkeeper n. 가게 주인 criticize v. 비판하다, 비평하다 ubiquity n. 도처에 있음, 편재(遍在) entrepreneurial a. 기업가의, 기업가적인 effectiveness n. 유효성, 효과적임, 효율성 make it (자기 분야에서) 성공하다 pundit n. (인도의) 학자; 전문가, 권위자 pit v. (사람.지혜.힘 등을) 겨루게 하다, 경쟁시키다(against) minority n. (한 사회.국가 내의) 소수민족[집단] resentment n. 분개, 분노 victim n. 희생자, 피해자 plight n. 곤경, 역경 racism n. 인종차별, 인종차별주의 superfluous a. 여분의, 과잉의; 불필요한 celebration n. 축하; 축하 행사, 찬양, 칭송 obscure v. 어둡게 하다; 가리다; 모호하게 하다 relative to ~에 관하여, ~에 비례하여 Caucasian n. 백인 misleading a. 오도하는, 오해하게 하는

008 ③   2019학년도 한성대학교 인문계 A형 03번

❶ Thousands of years ago, / people used ancient types of wheat and other grains / to make flat bread on the hot rocks of their campfires. ❷ At some point in time, / early cooks started putting other kinds of food / on the bread — using the bread / as a plate. ❸ It was the world's first pizza crust! ❹ Over time, / pizza began to look more like the food (we know today). ❺ When European explorers arrived / in the Americas, / they saw Native American people eating tomatoes. ❻ When they brought Ⓑ them back to Europe, however, people (there) wouldn't eat Ⓒ them. ❼ They thought / eating tomatoes could make Ⓓ them ill. ❽ Slowly, however, / Europeans discovered / that tomatoes were delicious and safe (to eat). ❾ Cooks (in Naples), (an Italian city), began putting Ⓔ them / on their flat bread. ❿ The world's first true pizza shop opened / in Naples / in 1830. ⓫ People (there) ate / for lunch and dinner. They even ate it / for breakfast!

Which refers to a different one?
다른 것을 가리키는 것은?
① Ⓑ   ② Ⓒ   ✓③ Ⓓ   ④ Ⓔ

해석
❶ 수천 년 전, 사람들은 고대에 있던 종류의 밀과 또 다른 곡물들을 이용하여, 원판 형태의 납작한 빵을 모닥불로 뜨겁게 달군 바위 위에서 만들었다. ❷ 어느 순간 초창기 요리사들은 빵을 접시처럼 사용해서 빵 위에 다른 음식들을 올리기 시작했다. ❸ 이것이 세계 최초의 피자 크러스트였다. ❹ 시간이 지남에 따라, 피자는 오늘날 우리가 알고 있는 음식처럼 보이기 시작했다. ❺ 유럽의 탐험가들이 아메리카 대륙에 도착했을 때, 그들은 원주민들이 토마토를 먹는 모습을 보았다. ❻ 하지만 그들이 Ⓑ토마토를 유럽으로 가지고 돌아갔을 때, 유럽 사람들은 Ⓒ토마토를 먹지 않았다. ❼ 그들은 토마토를 먹는 것은 Ⓓ그들을 아프게 할 것이라고 생각했다. ❽ 하지만 서서히 유럽인들은 토마토가 맛있고 먹기에도 안전하다는 것을 알게 되었다. ❾ 이탈리아의 한 도시인 나폴리(Naples)의 요리사들은 납작한 빵 위에 Ⓔ토마토를 올려놓기 시작했다. ❿ 진정한 의미에서의 세계 최초의 피자 가게가 1830년에 나폴리에서 문을 열었다. ⓫ 사람들은 그곳에서 점심과 저녁 식사로 피자를 먹었다. 그들은 심지어 아침 식사로도 피자를 먹었다.

해설 정답인 Ⓓ는 people을 가리킨다. 하지만 Ⓑ, Ⓒ, Ⓔ는 tomatoes를 가리키고 있다.

어휘 ancient a. 고대의 wheat n. 밀; 소맥 grain n. 곡물; (곡식의) 낱알 flat bread n. 원판 모양의 빵 plate n. 접시, 그릇 crust n. 빵 껍질 explorer n. 답사자, 탐험가 ill a. 병든, 건강이 나쁜

정답 및 해설

009 ①   2020학년도 국민대학교 인문계 오후 A형 17번

❶ Sometime / in the nineteenth century, / philosophy was replaced / by literature / in the quest for national identity. ❷ For one thing, / after Immanuel Kant, / the sciences were philosophy's chief preoccupation, / and in the process of their incorporation, / philosophy, (excepting ethics), lost its taste / for speculation. ❸ Novels and poems came / to typify what Matthew Arnold called the "best (that has been thought and said,") / at least in the West. ❹ What the state and most educators wanted was to imbue the student's imagination / with Ⓐ what it was to be English, American, or French. ❺ Literature was best suited to this task / [because, (unlike philosophy and history), (which were international / in scope and were assimilated into the sciences), / literature was essentially national]. ❻ You can read the works of, (say), Dostoevsky, Flaubert, or Mann / in translation, / ❼ but as everyone knows, / something is always missing — chiefly, / the sense of place, / that is, the specificity of the vernacular (of which particular cultures are made).

Which does the underlined Ⓐ refer to?
다음 중 밑줄 친 Ⓐ가 가리키는 것은?

✓ ① **national identity**
    국가의 정체성
② taste for speculation
    성찰에 대한 감각
③ western perspectives
    서양인의 관점
④ philosophical preoccupation
    철학적 선입견

[해석] ❶ 19세기경 철학은 국가 정체성을 추구하는 과정 속에서 문학으로 대체되었다. ❷ 우선, 임마누엘 칸트(Immenuel Kant) 이후, 과학은 철학의 주요 관심사가 되었고, 이들이 통합되는 과정 속에서 윤리학을 제외한 철학은 성찰에 관한 감각을 잃어버렸다. ❸ 소설과 시는 적어도 서양에서 매슈 아놀드(Mathew Arnold)가 "생각되고 말해진 최고의 것"이라고 불렀던 것을 대표하게 되었다. ❹ 국가와 대부분 교육자들이 원했던 것은 학생들의 상상력이 Ⓐ영국적이거나 미국적이거나 또는 프랑스적인 것을 불어넣는 것이었다. ❺ 다루는 범위가 국제적이고 과학에 동화되었던 철학과 역사와는 다르게 문학은 이 과업에 가장 적합했는데, 문학은 본질적으로 국가적인 것이었기 때문이다. ❻ 즉 당신은 도스토예프스키(Dostoevsky), 플로베르(flaubert), 만(Mann)의 번역 작품을 읽을 수는 있지만, ❼ 모두 알다시피, 무언가가 언제나 결여되어 있는데, 그것은 주로 장소 감각, 즉 특정 문화를 만들어내는 토속어의 특별함이다.

[해설] 밑줄 친 빈칸 다음에서 한 번 더 '문학은 본질적으로 국가적인 것'이라고 말하고 있다. 따라서 ① 'national identity(국가의 정체성)'이 가장 적절하다.

[어휘] quest n. 탐색, 추구 identity n. 신원, 정체성 preoccupation n. 선입관, 편견 incorporation n. 결합, 합동 excepting prep. ~을 제외[생략]하고 ethics n. 윤리학, 도덕론 speculation n. 사색, 심사숙고, 성찰 typify v. 대표하다, 전형이 되다, 상징하다 imbue v. ~에게 (감정·사상·의견 등을) 불어넣다, 고취하다 assimilate v. 동화하다, 흡수하다, 이해하다 vernacular n. (특정 지역·집단이 쓰는) 말, 토착어, 방언

010 ②   2019학년도 서울여자대학교 인문·자연계 A형 40번

❶ Of all the horrors (Louis Zamperini endured / during World War II) — / a plane crash into the Pacific, / 47 days stranded at sea, / two years in a prisoner-of-war camp — / the one experience (that truly haunted him) was / : when a Japanese guard tortured and killed an injured duck. ❷ The episode, (recounted in Laura Hillenbrand's best-seller "Unbroken,") also traumatized many readers. ❸ So when she was writing a new edition (aimed at young adults), / she left that scene out. ❹ "I know / that ((if) I were 12 and reading it, / Ⓐ that would upset me)," Ms. Hillenbrand said. ❺ (Inspired by the booming market / for young adult novels, / a growing number of biographers and historians are retrofitting their works / to make them palatable / for younger readers). ❻ Prominent nonfiction writers (like Ms. Hillenbrand) are now grappling with how to handle / unsettling or controversial material in their books / as they try to win over this impressionable new audience. ❼ These slim-down, simplified and sometimes sanitized editions of popular nonfiction titles are fast becoming a vibrant, growing and lucrative niche.

What does the underlined Ⓐ refer to?
밑줄 친 Ⓐ가 가리키는 것은?

① A writer modifying her or his original works
자신의 원작을 수정하는 작가

☑ ② A guard torturing an injured animal to death
다친 동물을 고문해서 죽게 만든 교도관

③ A child being inspired by a novel at the age of 12
12세의 나이에 소설에 영감을 받은 아이

④ A man being in a prisoner-of-war camp for two years
2년 동안 전쟁포로 수용소 생활을 한 남자

해석

❶ 비행기가 태평양에 추락하여 47일 동안 바다에 좌초되었고 전쟁 포로수용소에서 2년을 보내는 등, 루이스 장페리니(Louis Zamperini)가 2차 세계대전 동안에 겪었던 온갖 공포 중에서 진정으로 그의 뇌리를 떠나지 않은 한 가지 경험은 한 일본 교도관이 다친 오리를 고문해서 죽이던 장면이었다. ❷ 이 일화는 로라 힐렌브랜드(Laura Hillenbrand)의 베스트셀러 『언브로큰(Unbroken)』에 자세하게 묘사되어 있는데, 많은 독자들에게도 엄청난 정신적 충격을 주었다. ❸ 그래서 그녀가 청소년을 대상으로 하는 책을 새로 썼을 때, 그녀는 이 장면을 제외하였다. ❹ "내가 만약 12살이고, 그 책을 읽고 있다면, Ⓐ그 장면에 몹시 당혹스러워할 거라는 것을 나는 압니다." 라고 힐렌브랜드가 말했다. ❺ 청소년 소설 시장이 급성장하는 것에 영감을 받아, 점점 더 많은 전기 작가들과 역사가들이 그들의 작품이 보다 어린 독자들의 입맛에 맞게 자신의 작품을 개조하고 있다. ❻ 힐렌브랜드 같은 유명한 논픽션 작가들은 감수성이 예민한 새로운 독자들의 마음을 사로잡기 위해 독자를 심란하게 하거나 논란의 여지가 있는 소재를 그들의 책에서 어떻게 다뤄야 할 것인지를 두고 현재 고심하고 있다. ❼ 인기 있는 논픽션 책에서 내용을 줄이고 단순화하며, 때로는 불쾌한 부분을 제거한 개정판 책들은 빠르게 활기 넘치고 성장세를 보이는 수익성 좋은 틈새시장이 되고 있다.

해설

Ⓐ 문장에서 '만약 내가 12살이라면, 그 책을 읽고 나를 몹시 당혹스럽게 할 것이다'라고 말하고 있는데, 이는 지문 첫 번째 문장에서 말하고는 일본 교도관이 다친 오리를 고문해 죽이는 장면을 말하고 있다.

어휘

the Pacific 태평양 strand v. ~을 오도 가도 못하게 하다, 좌초시키다 prisoner-of-war camp 전쟁포로 수용소 haunt v. (마음속에) 끊임없이 떠오르다, 괴롭히다 torture v. 고문하다 episode n. (사람의 인생·소설 등에서 중요하거나 재미있는) 사건[에피소드] recount v. 이야기하다, 묘사하다 traumatize v. 엄청난 정신적 충격을 주다 leave ~ out ~을 빼다[제외하다, 생략하다] booming a. 번창하는, 호황의, 급등하는 young adult novel 청소년 소설, 십대를 대상으로 하는 소설 biographer n. 전기 작가 historian n. 역사가, 사학자 retrofit v. 개조하다, 개선하다 palatable a. 맛있는; 마음에 드는, 구미에 맞는 prominent a. 중요한, 유명한 grapple with ~을 해결하려고 노력하다 unsettling a. 심란하게 하는 controversial a. 논란이 많은 win over ~의 지원이나 동정을 얻는 데 성공하다 impressionable a. 감수성이 예민한 slim down v. (규모를) 줄이다, 축소하다 sanitize v. 불쾌한 부분을 제거하다 edition n. (특정 인쇄소·편집자에 의한) 판(版) title n. 책, 서적, 출판물 vibrant a. 활력이 넘치는 lucrative a. 돈벌이가 되는 niche n. 틈새시장

정답 및 해설

011 ④ 2020학년도 세종대학교 인문계 A형 50번

❶ Every girl (I met) is amazing. ❷ I feel honored / to share their stories and images — and their strength — / with you: ❸ the look (on Alice's face / after she conquered the big hill / on her bike) / and Aris's proud smile / when she achieved her goal of becoming a pilot / at just 16. ❹ It is my goal (with these images) / to inspire girls and women to be their best selves, to challenge and test their limits. ❺ We (all) are constantly bombarded with Ⓐ societal messages / about (how women and girls should act, look, or be), / ❻ and processing Ⓑ them (in a healthy way) can be hard / even for a 40-year-old mother of two (who knows better). ❼ I worry about (what / my girls and their friends / are exposed to) and (how / their opinions of their bodies and selves / are being shaped) by the internet, TV, and magazines). ❽ I want these images / to combat Ⓒ those negative voices (that tell us / we are not good enough, thin enough, or whatever enough); ❾ because we are far more than enough! ❿ I want these girls to be able to hear their own voices / through these images, / and to inspire them to use Ⓓ them and continue to use them. Loudly.

The following refer to a similar idea except _____.
① Ⓐ   ② Ⓑ   ③ Ⓒ   ✓④ Ⓓ

해석 ❶ 내가 만난 모든 소녀들은 대단하다. ❷ 나는 그들의 이야기와 사진, 그리고 그들이 가진 힘을 여러분과 공유할 수 있게 되어 영광스럽게 생각한다. ❸ 자전거로 큰 언덕을 정복한 후에 앨리스(Alice)가 지었던 표정 그리고 겨우 16살에 조종사가 되겠다는 목표를 이루었을 때 아리스(Aris)가 보여줬던 자부심에 찬 미소를 말이다. ❹ 나의 목표는 이 사진들을 통해서 소녀들과 여성들이 자신의 최고의 모습이 되고 자신의 한계를 시험하고 도전하도록 격려해주는 것이다. ❺ 우리 모두는 여성들과 소녀들이 어떻게 행동해야 하고, 보여야 하며, 혹은 어떤 사람이 되어야 하는지에 대한 Ⓐ사회적 메시지를 계속해서 받고 있으며, ❻ Ⓑ그 메시지들을 건강하게 처리하는 것은 두 아이를 둔 40세의 분별력 있는 어머니에게도 어려운 일일 수 있다. ❼ 나는 나의 소녀들과 그들의 친구들이 어떤 것들에 노출되어 있는지와 자신의 몸과 자아에 관한 그들의 의견이 인터넷, TV, 잡지의 영향을 받아 어떻게 결정되는지에 대해 걱정하고 있다. ❽ 나는 이 사진들이 우리가 충분히 착하지 않고, 충분히 날씬하지 않으며, 또는 무엇이든 충분하지 않다고 말하는 Ⓒ부정적인 목소리들과 싸우길 바란다. ❾ 사실은 우리가 충분한 것 그 이상이기 때문에, ❿ 나는 이 소녀들이 이 사진들을 통해 그들 자신의 목소리를 들을 수 있기를 바라며, Ⓓ그것들을 이용하고 앞으로도 계속해서 이용하도록, 그것도 매우 '당당하게' 이용하도록, 그들을 격려하길 바란다.

해설 Ⓓ는 '자기 자신의 목소리(their own voices)'를 가리킨다. 반면에 Ⓐ,Ⓑ,Ⓒ는 '사회에서 규정하고 강요하는 여성상에 관한 메시지'를 가리키고 있다.

어휘 amazing a. 놀랄 정도의, 굉장한 conquer v. 정복하다, 공략하다 achieve v. 이루다, 달성하다, 성취하다 inspire v. 고무[격려]하다; 고무시켜 ~하게 하다 constantly ad. 변함없이; 항상 bombard v. 공격하다, 몰아세우다, (질문·탄원 등을) 퍼붓다 societal a. 사회의, 사회활동의 process v. 처리하다 expose v. (햇볕·바람·비 따위에) 노출시키다; (환경 따위에) 접하게 하다 negative a. 부정적인; 소극적인 loudly ad. 큰 소리로; 야단스럽게

228 끝장편입 독해유형편 Top 20

012 ② 2019학년도 인하대학교 인문계 32번

❶ People ask how I do it. ❷ Well, / I love clover: / ❸ the sweet smell, the common variant / with its cute trio of leaves. ❹ I look at it / more than most people do. ❺ I expect / that's the first reason (I find so many). ❻ I have a habit of dragging my fingers or toes / across a patch, / momentarily separating the individuals, / ❼ which brings irregularities into focus. ❽ That's part of finding them: / not a hardening of focus, / but a softening. ❾ The other reason is artful. ❿ Do you remember those posters / from the 1980s (made up of thick dots)? ⓫ If you looked too hard, / all (you'd see) was the pattern. ⓬ But if you let your eyes slip out of focus, / scenes would appear: / dinosaurs, landscapes, butterflies / — a trick of the eye. ⓭ It's the same / with four-leaf clovers. ⓮ If you try too hard, / you will only ever see the patch. ⓯ Instead, slip into a lazy, soft-focus, summer state of mind. ⓰ Drift your hand / across a thick patch, / letting the clovers reveal themselves. ⓱ Appreciate the ones (that have only three leaves). ⓲ Common things are beautiful too. ⓳ And a four-leaf clover may show itself / to you.

What does the underlined it refer to?
밑줄 친 it이 가리키는 것은?

① To soften the focus
부드럽게 집중하는 것

✓ To find four-leaf clovers
네잎 클로버를 발견하는 것

③ To savor the smell of clovers
클로버의 향기를 음미하는 것

④ To separate individual clovers quickly
개개의 클로버를 신속하게 서로 떼어놓는 것

⑤ To appreciate the beauty of three-leaf clovers
세잎 클로버의 아름다움을 감상하는 것

해석

❶ 사람들은 내가 그것을 어떻게 하는지 물어본다. ❷ 글쎄, 나는 클로버를 좋아한다. ❸ 향기로운 냄새와, 귀여운 잎이 세 개인 흔한 종류의 클로버 말이다. ❹ 나는 대부분의 사람들보다 그것을 더 많이 살펴본다. ❺ 그것이 내가 그렇게 많이 찾아내는 첫 번째 이유일 거라고 나는 생각한다. ❻ 나는 클로버 풀밭을 손가락이나 발가락으로 가로지르며 긁어서 각각의 클로버를 순간적으로 서로 떼어놓는 습관이 있는데, ❼ 이렇게 하면 특이한 것들이 명확히 눈에 들어오게 된다. ❽ 이것이 그것들을 찾는 방법 일부라 할 수 있다. 즉, 집중을 강하게 하는 것이 아니라 부드럽게 하는 것이다. ❾ 또 다른 이유는 기술적인 것이다. ❿ 굵은 점들로 이루어져 있던 1980년대의 광고 포스터를 기억하는가? ⓫ 너무 열심히 쳐다보면, 모두 무늬로만 보였다. ⓬ 하지만 눈에 힘을 풀어 초점을 흐리게 하면, 공룡, 풍경, 나비 등의 장면이 나타날 것이다. 일종의 눈속임인 것이다. ⓭ 네잎 클로버의 경우도 마찬가지다. ⓮ (찾으려고) 너무 열심히 노력하면, 클로버 풀밭만 보이게 된다. ⓯ 대신, 느긋하고 부드럽게 집중하고, 여름 같은 정신 상태가 되게 해라. ⓰ 클로버풀이 무성하게 나 있는 풀밭을 손으로 가로질러 쓸어, 클로버가 저절로 들어나도록 해라. ⓱ 잎이 세 개밖에 없는 클로버도 감상해라. ⓲ 흔한 것들도 아름답기는 마찬가지다. ⓳ 그러고 나면 네잎 클로버가 당신에게 모습을 드러낼지도 모른다.

해설 ❹번 문장부터 네 잎 클로버를 찾는 자기만의 방법을 설명하고 있다.

어휘 variant n. 변종, 이형(異形) trio n. 3인조, 세 개 한 벌 patch n. 작은 구획, 밭 momentarily ad. 순간적으로, 일시적으로 separate v. 분리하다, 가르다; 떼어놓다 irregularity n. 불규칙성, 가지런하지 않음 harden v. 굳히다, 단단하게 하다 soften v. 부드럽게 하다, 연하게 하다 artful a. 교묘한, 기교를 부린 be made up of ~로 구성돼 있다 dot n. 점, 작은 점 dinosaur n. 공룡 landscape n. 풍경, 경치, 전망 drift v. 떠내려 보내다, 표류시키다 reveal v. 드러내다; 알리다; 들추어내다 appreciate v. 평가하다; 진가를 인정하다; 감상하다

013 ②   2020학년도 상명대학교 인문·자연계 30번

❶ It now seems a curiously innocent time, though not that long ago, / when the lack of information appeared to be one of society's fundamental problems. ❷ Theorists talked about humanity's "bounded rationality" / and the difficulty (of making decisions / in conditions of limited or imperfect information). ❸ Chronic information shortages threatened work, education, research, innovation, and economic decision making — / whether at the level of government policy, business strategy, or household shopping. ❹ The one thing (we all apparently needed) was more information. ❺ So it's not surprising / that 'infoenthusiasts' exult / in the simple volume of information (that technology now makes available). ❻ They count the bits, bytes, and packets enthusiastically. ❼ They cheer the disaggregation of knowledge / into data ❽ (and provide a new word, datafication, to describe it). ❾ Ⓐ As Ⓐ the lumps break down and the bits pile up, words (like quadrillion, terabyte, and megaflop) have become the measure of value.

What does Ⓐthe lumps above refer to?
위의 Ⓐthe lumps는 무엇을 가리키는가?

① the 'infoenthusiasts' 정보광
✓② knowledge 지식
③ technology 기술
④ datafication 데이터화
⑤ measurements 치수

해석
❶ 정보의 부족이 사회의 근본적인 문제 중 하나로 여겨졌던 것이 그리 오래 전의 일이 아니지만, 지금은 이상할 정도로 (이를 무해하게 여기는) 순진한 시대처럼 보인다. ❷ (과거에) 이론가들은 인간의 "제한된 합리성"과 정보가 한정돼 있거나 불완전한 조건에서 결정을 내리는 것의 어려움에 관해 이야기했다. ❸ 만성적인 정보 부족은 정부 정책의 수준에서든, 사업 전략의 수준에서든, 또는 가정에서 하는 쇼핑의 수준에서든, 업무, 교육, 연구, 혁신 및 경제에 대한 의사결정을 위협했다. ❹ 우리 모두에게 분명하게 필요했던 한 가지는 더 많은 정보였다. ❺ 그러므로 (지금) '정보광(狂)'들이 현재의 기술로 인해 이용할 수 있게 된 얼마 되지 않는 양의 정보에도 매우 기뻐하는 것은 그리 놀랍지 않다. ❻ 그들은 비트, 바이트, 패킷을 열정적으로 세어본다. ❼ 그들은 지식을 데이터로 세분하는 것에 박수를 보내고 있다 ❽ (그리고 그것을 설명하기 위해 '데이터화'라는 새로운 단어를 제공한다). ❾ Ⓐ덩어리가 분해되고 비트가 쌓이며, '천조(千兆)', '테라바이트', '메가플롭' 같은 단어들이 가치의 척도가 되었다.

해설
앞 문장에서 'disaggregation of knowledge(지식의 분해)'를 말하고 있는 만큼 ②이 적절하다.

어휘
curiously ad. 기묘하게, 이상하게도 innocent a. 순결한, 순진한 fundamental a. 기본적인, 근본적인, 핵심적인 theorist n. 이론가 bounded a. 경계가 있는, 한계가 있는 rationality n. 합리성 chronic a. 만성적인 threaten v. 협박하다; 위협하다 innovation n. (기술) 혁신, 쇄신 policy n. 정책 strategy n. 전략 apparently ad. 명백히; 외관상으로는 infoenthusiast n. 정보광 exult v. 크게 기뻐하다, 기뻐 날뛰다 bit n. 〈컴퓨터〉 비트(정보량의 최소 단위) byte n. 〈컴퓨터〉 바이트(8비트에 해당하는 정보단위) packet n. 패킷(512 바이트) enthusiastically ad. 열광적으로, 열성적으로 cheer v. 갈채를 보내다, 성원하다 disaggregation n. 분해 datafication n. 데이터화 describe v. 묘사하다, 기술하다, 설명하다 lump n. 덩어리 pile up 쌓이다 quadrillion n. 1천조, 천의 5제곱 terabyte n. 테라바이트 megaflop n. 메가플롭(컴퓨터 속도 측정 단위, 초당 약 100만 번의 작동)

014 ⑤　2020학년도 건국대학교 인문·예체능계 A형 31번

❶ Prague Castle is not only a beautiful complex of historical monuments, but also a place that is closely connected with the political and legal developments of our country. ❷ Within these walls are reflected both great and tragic events. ❸ Since Ⓐ it was built, the castle has fulfilled a number of functions — ❹ Ⓑ it was the monarch's residence, a military fortification, a tribal sanctuary, a centre of Christianity, the seat of provincial councils and the hub of courts and administrative offices. ❺ Not least is Ⓒ its function as the burial place of Czech kings and the repository of the Czech Crown Jewels, which are still a symbol of Czech statehood. ❻ Since 1918, Ⓓ it has been the seat of the President of the Republic, (together with his office), and continues the tradition of Prague Castle as the seat of the head of the country, which has lasted for more than 1,000 years. ❼ The symbol of the presidential seat is the flag of the President of the Republic flying over Prague Castle, ❽ one of the state symbols of the Czech Republic with a great state coat of arms in Ⓔ its centre and the motto Pravda vitezi, which means "Truth prevails."

밑줄 친 Ⓐ~Ⓔ 가운데 가리키는 것이 다른 하나는?
① Ⓐ　② Ⓑ　③ Ⓒ　④ Ⓓ　✓⑤ Ⓔ

해석
❶ 프라하성은 역사적 기념비적인 건축물들의 아름다운 복합체일 뿐만 아니라 우리나라의 정치적, 법률적 발달과 밀접하게 연관된 장소이기도 하다. ❷ 프라하성의 성벽 안에는 크고 비극적인 사건들이 모두 반영되어 있다. ❸ Ⓐ프라하성이 지어진 이래로, 그 성은 많은 기능을 수행해왔다. ❹ Ⓑ그것은 군주의 거주지였고, 군사 요새였고, 부족의 안식처였고, 기독교의 중심지였고, 지방 의회의 소재지였으며, 법원과 행정청의 중심이었다. ❺ 특히 중요한 것은 체코 왕들의 매장지로서의 Ⓒ그것의 기능과 국가로서의 체코의 지위를 여전히 상징하고 있는 체코의 왕권 상징 보석이 보관되어 있는 곳으로서의 기능이다. ❻ 1918년부터 Ⓓ그것은 대통령의 집무실과 함께 체코 공화국 대통령이 있는 곳이었으며, 1천 년 이상 이어져 온 국가의 수장이 있는 곳으로서의 전통이 계속되는 곳이다. ❼ 대통령이 있는 곳의 상징은 프라하성의 꼭대기 위에서 휘날리고 있는 공화국 대통령의 깃발이며, ❽ 이 깃발은 체코 공화국의 상징 중 하나이며, Ⓔ깃발의 가운데에는 거대한 국가의 문장(紋章)과 'Pravda vitezi(진실은 승리한다.)' 라는 제명(題銘)이 있다.

해설
Ⓔ는 체코의 대통령 깃발을 가리키고 있으므로 ⑤가 정답이다. 나머지는 모두 프라하 성을 가리킨다.

어휘 monument n. 기념비적인[역사적인] 건축물 wall n. 벽, (pl.) 성벽 tragic a. 비극의, 비참한 fulfil v. (특정한 역할·기능을) 하다 function n. 기능, 구실 monarch n. 군주, 주권자 fortification n. 방어 시설, 요새화 tribal a. 부족의, 종족의 sanctuary a. 보호구역; 안식, 피난처 seat n. 위치, (활동의) 소재지, 중심지 provincial a. 주(州)[도(道)]의, 지방의 council n. 의회 administrative a. 관리[행정]상의 burial n. 매장, 장례식 repository n. 저장소; 진열장, 박물관 coat of arms (가문·도시 등의 상징인) 문장(紋章)

정답 및 해설

015 ③ 2020학년도 국민대학교 인문계 오전 A형 30번

❶ One morning, / after I had been hanging the washing out to dry, / something glistened / in front of me. ❷ With the morning sun shining in my eyes, / I squinted / to find the most glorious masterpiece / in our garden. ❸ ⒜ The mini architect had meticulously spun its web / across the path, / from the roof to the fence. ❹ I stared in awe / at the fine artistry (of ⒞ our garden resident). ❺ Sparming about two metres, / it was truly a magical sight. ❻ The web gently danced / in the morning breeze, reflecting light / from the sun. ❼ It was as if the spider had spun a fine web / from rays of sunlight (itself). ❽ How did it weave its web / from the roof to the fence? ❾ It's almost as if it built a house / while enjoying extreme sports at the same time. ❿ Very carefully, / I ducked my head / under the web, / taking great care not to ruin ⒟ the spider's creation. ⓫ Later that day / I went back to the web / to take another look. ⓬ My heart sank. ⓭ The beautiful web was now broken and swaying aimlessly / in the breeze. ⓮ It was nothing / more than a few pitiful strands (hanging loose). ⓯ I almost choked on emotion. ⓰ "Sorry, ⒠ little fella. It was such a splendid structure." ⓱ But the very next morning, / to my amazement, / there was another castle (floating in the air). ⓲ The mini architect had come back to work.

Which is different from the others in its meaning?
다른 의미를 가리키는 것은?
① Ⓐ ② Ⓒ ✓ ③ Ⓓ ④ Ⓔ

해석
❶ 어느 날 아침, 빨래를 말리기 위해 걸어 널고 있었던 내 앞에 무언가가 반짝거렸다. ❷ 아침 햇살이 내 눈을 비추면서 눈을 가늘게 뜬 나는 우리 정원에서 가장 찬란한 걸작을 발견했다. ❸ Ⓐ그 작은 건축가는 지붕에서 울타리까지 가로질러 꼼꼼하게 거미줄을 쳐서 거미집을 지었다. ❹ 나는 ⒞우리 정원 거주민의 훌륭한 예술성을 경외심을 가지고 바라보았다. ❺ 약 2미터에 걸쳐있는 그 거미집은 정말 환상적인 광경이었다. ❻ 거미집은 아침 산들바람에 부드럽게 춤을 추며 태양빛을 반사했다. ❼ 마치 그 거미가 햇빛으로 멋있는 거미집을 만든 것처럼 보였다. ❽ 어떻게 지붕에서 울타리까지 거미줄을 쳤을까? ❾ 거미는 마치 극한 스포츠를 즐기면서 집을 짓는 것 같다. ❿ 매우 조심스럽게, 나는 ⒟거미의 창작물을 훼손하지 않도록 조심하면서 거미집 아래로 머리를 숙여 지나갔다. ⓫ 그날 시간이 흐른 뒤에 나는 다시 거미집을 보러 갔다. ⓬ 내 가슴은 무너져 내렸다. ⓭ 그 아름다웠던 거미집은 부서져 바람에 정처 없이 흔들리고 있었다. ⓮ 그것은 단지 느슨하게 매달린 몇 줄의 가엾은 가닥들에 불과했다. ⓯ 나는 솟구쳐 오르는 감정에 거의 숨이 막힐 지경이었다. ⓰ "정말 안 됐구나, ⒠작은 친구여. 정말 빛나는 건축물이었는데." ⓱ 하지만 다음 날 아침 놀랍게도 또 다른 성이 공중에 떠 있었다. ⓲ 그 작은 건축가는 또 다시 작업했던 것이다.

해설
Ⓓ는 그 거미가 만든 '거미집'을 가리킨다. 하지만, 나머지 셋은 '거미'를 가리키고 있다.

어휘
glisten v. 반짝이다, 빛나다 squint v. 눈을 가늘게 뜨다 masterpiece n. 명작, 걸작 meticulously ad. 꼼꼼히 spin v. (실을) 짓다 awe n. 경외감 artistry n. 예술성, 예술적 기교 breeze n. 산들바람, 미풍 weave v. (직물을) 짜다; (거미가 집을) 얽다 duck v. (머리를) 수그리다 ruin v. 망치다, 폐허로 만들다 aimlessly ad. 정처 없이 pitiful a. 측은한, 가련한 strand n. 가닥 choke v. 질식하다 fella n. (남자) 친구 splendid a. 빛나는 architect n. 건축가, 설계자

016 ①   2019학년도 인하대학교 인문계 36번

❶ The Celts were the first Indo-European occupants of Britain. ❷ The southern British Celts had been first subdued and thereafter ruled and sheltered by the Romans. ❸ Julius Caesar's attempt at an early invasion in 55-54 BC did not result in occupation, unlike the results elsewhere in the Roman Empire, in particular Gaul (where the Latin spoken by Caesar's legions became, ultimately, Modern French). ❹ It was during the rule of the emperor Claudius (from AD 43) that the Roman invasion was followed by a more permanent occupation and military control. ❺ For about 400 years thereafter, Britain was a province of the Roman Empire. ❻ By the beginning of the fifth century, however, maintaining occupation forces in that outlying territory became too costly for the Romans, who were constantly subjected to the attacks of the Germanic tribes on the Continent. ❼ A highly simplified version of the events that followed is that when the Romans pulled out, with all of them gone by AD 410, the Celts in the south of the island were relatively defenseless. ❽ It was then that they invited Germanic mercenary soldiers to come over from northern Europe and protect them from invading Vikings, as well as from the Celts (from the north) and from Ireland (the Scots and the Picts).

What does the underlined that outlying territory refer to?
밑줄 친 '저 동떨어진 곳에 위치한 영토'가 가리키는 것은?

✓① Britain 영국
② Gaul 갈리아
③ Germany 독일
④ Europe 유럽
⑤ Ireland 아일랜드

해석
❶ 켈트족은 영국의 첫 인도-유럽 어족의 점령자들이었다. ❷ 영국 남부의 켈트족은 로마인들에게 처음으로 정복되었고, 그 후로는 그들의 지배와 보호를 받았다. ❸ 기원전 55-54년에 있었던 줄리어스 시저(Julius Caesar)의 초기 침략 시도는 로마 제국의 다른 곳, 특히나 갈리아(이곳에서는 시저의 군대가 사용하던 라틴어가 결국 현대의 프랑스어가 되었다.)에서의 결과와는 다르게 점령으로 이어지지 않았다. ❹ 로마인들의 침략이 보다 영구적인 점령과 군사적 통제로 이어진 것은 (서기 43년부터 시작된) 클라우디우스(Claudius) 황제의 통치 기간 동안이었다. ❺ 그 약 400년 동안 영국은 로마 제국의 속주(屬州)가 되었다. ❻ 하지만 5세기 초 무렵, 그 외곽지역에 있는 영토에 점령군을 유지하는 것이 로마인들에게 비용적인 측면에서 매우 부담스럽게 되었는데, 이는 로마인들이 유럽 대륙에서 게르만족의 공격에 계속해서 시달리고 있었기 때문이다. ❼ 뒤이어 일어난 사건들을 매우 간략하게 설명하자면, 로마인들이 철수하여 서기 410년에 모두 사라졌을 때, 영국 남부의 켈트족들은 상대적으로 무방비 상태에 있었다. ❽ 그때 그들은 북유럽으로부터 게르만 용병들을 끌어들여서 북유럽과 아일랜드의 켈트족(스코틀랜드족과 픽트족)의 침략뿐만 아니라 바이킹의 침략으로부터 그들을 보호하도록 했다.

해설 유럽 대륙에서 떨어진 섬 영국을 점령한 이야기인 만큼 'that outlying territory(그 외딴 영토)'는 영국을 가리킨다고 볼 수 있다.

어휘 occupant n. 점유자, 점거자 subdue v. 정복하다; 위압하다, 압도하다 thereafter ad. 그 후, 그 이래로 rule v. 다스리다, 통치하다 shelter v. 숨기다, 감추다, 비호하다, 보호하다 invasion n. 침입, 침략 occupation n. 점유, 점령; 직업 legion n. (고대 로마의) 군단, 군대 ultimately ad. 궁극적으로, 근본적으로 emperor n. 황제 permanent a. 영속적인, 불변의 province n. 지방, 지역, 속주(屬州, 고대 로마의 지배를 받던 국외의 토지) outlying a. 중심을 떠난, 동떨어진; 외진 territory n. 영토, 영지; 속령 costly a. 값이 비싼, 비용이 많이 드는 constantly ad. 항상, 변함없이 be subjected to ~을 당하다 tribe n. 부족, 종족 the Continent 〈영국 제도(諸島)와 구별하여〉 유럽 대륙 simplify v. 단순화하다, 간단하게 하다 pull out 철수하다, 빠져나가다 defenseless a. 무방비의, 방어할 수 없는 mercenary n. 용병 invade v. 침입하다, 침략하다

017 ③   2019학년도 상명대학교 인문·자연계 34번

❶ Five score years ago, / a great American, (in whose symbolic shadow / we stand), signed the Emancipation Proclamation. ❷ This momentous Ⓐ decree came (as) a great beacon light of hope / to millions of Negro slaves (who had been seared / in the flames of withering injustice). ❸ It came (as Ⓑ a joyous daybreak (to end the long night of captivity). ❹ But one hundred years later, / we must face the tragic fact (that the Negro is still not free). ❺ One hundred years later, / the life of the Negro is still sadly crippled / by the manacles of segregation and the chains of discrimination. ❻ One hundred years later, / the Negro lives / on a lonely island of poverty / in the midst of a vast ocean of material prosperity. ❼ One hundred years later, / the Negro is still languishing / in the corners of American society and finds himself an exile / in his own land. ❽ So we have come here today / to dramatize Ⓒ an appalling condition. ❾ In a sense / we have come to our nation's capital / to cash Ⓓ a check. ❿ When the architects of our republic wrote the magnificent words (of the Constitution and the Declaration of Independence), ⓫ they were signing Ⓔ a promissory note / (to which every American was to fall heir). ⓬ This note was a promise (that all men would be guaranteed the unalienable rights of life, liberty, and the pursuit of happiness).

밑줄 친 Ⓐ~Ⓔ 가운데 의미하는 바가 다른 것 하나를 고르시오.
① Ⓐ   ② Ⓑ   ✓③ Ⓒ   ④ Ⓓ   ⑤ Ⓔ

해석

❶ 100년 전에, 한 위대한 미국인이 노예해방선언에 서명했고, 우리는 현재 그의 상징적 그림자 속에 서 있습니다. ❷ 이 중대한 Ⓐ포고는 파멸적인 불의의 불길 속에 그을려 왔던 수백만 명의 흑인 노예들에게 큰 희망의 등불로 다가왔습니다. ❸ 이 포고는 기나긴 밤의 포로 생활에 종지부를 찍은 Ⓑ즐거운 여명으로 다가왔습니다. ❹ 하지만 100년 후에, 우리는 흑인이 여전히 자유롭지 않다는 비극적 사실에 직면해야 합니다. ❺ 100년 후에도 흑인의 삶은 인종차별의 수갑과 차별대우의 사슬에 의해 여전히 슬프게도 무기력합니다. ❻ 100년이 지나도 흑인은 광대한 물질적 풍요의 광대한 바다 한가운데에 있는 외딴 빈곤의 섬에서 살고 있습니다. ❼ 100년이 지난 지금도, 흑인은 여전히 미국 사회의 한구석에서 비참하게 살고 있으며 자신의 나라에서 추방된 자의 처지에 있습니다. ❽ 그래서 우리는 오늘 이 Ⓒ끔찍한 상황을 극적으로 알리기 위해서 여기에 왔습니다. ❾ 어떤 의미에서는, 우리는 Ⓓ수표를 현금으로 바꾸기 위해서 우리나라 수도에 왔습니다. ❿ 우리 공화국을 설립한 사람들이 헌법과 독립선언서의 웅장한 말들을 썼을 때, ⓫ 그들은 모든 미국인이 상속인이 될 Ⓔ하나의 약속어음에 서명하고 있었습니다. ⓬ 이 어음은 모든 사람들이 생명과 자유 그리고 행복 추구의 양도할 수 없는 권리를 보장받게 될 것이라는 약속이었습니다.

해설

Ⓒ는 흑인이 처한 끔찍한 상황을 의미한다. 하지만, Ⓐ,Ⓑ,Ⓓ,Ⓔ 모두 흑인의 자유와 권리를 보장하는 노예해방선언을 의미하고 있다.

어휘

score n. 20, 스무 사람[개] symbolic a. 상징하는, 상징적인 Emancipation Proclamation 노예해방선언 momentous a. 중요한, 중대한 decree n. 법령, 포고 beacon light 표지등, 등대 빛 sear v. 태우다, 그을리다 flame n. 불길, 불꽃, 화염 withering a. 파멸적인 injustice n. 부정, 불법, 불의 captivity n. 포로, 감금, 속박 daybreak n. 새벽, 동틀녘 tragic a. 비극의, 비극적인 cripple v. 불구가 되게 하다; 무능케 하다 manacle n. 수갑, 구속, 속박 segregation n. 분리, 격리, 인종차별 chain n. 사슬, (보통 pl.) 속박, 구속 discrimination n. 식별, 차별, 차별대우 poverty n. 가난, 빈곤, 부족 in the midst of ~의 한가운데에 prosperity n. 번영, 번창 languish v. 시들다, 쇠약해지다; 비참하게 살다 corner n. 구석, 모퉁이, 외딴[구석진] 곳 exile n. 망명자, 추방된 사람, 유랑자 dramatize v. 각색하다, 극적으로 표현하다 appalling a. 간담을 서늘케 하는, 끔찍한 capital n. 수도, 자본, 대문자 cash a check 수표를 현금으로 바꾸다 magnificent a. 장엄한; 훌륭한 promissory not 약속어음 fall heir to ~의 상속인이 되다 note n. 어음; 지폐 unalienable a. 양도할 수 없는, 빼앗을 수 없는(=inalienable) liberty n. 자유 overdue a. 기한이 지난, 오랫동안 기다려 온

018 ④   2019학년도 상명대학교 인문·지연계 38번

❶ The material culture (of the Paleo-Indians) differed little / from that of other Stone Age people (found in Asia, Africa, and Europe). ❷ In terms of human health, / however, something occured / on the Beringian tundra (that forever altered the history of Native Americans). ❸ For reasons (that remain obscure), the members of these small migrating groups stopped hosting a number of communicable diseases / — smallpox and measles (being the deadliest) — ❹ and although Native Americans experienced illnesses / such as tuberculosis, / ❺ they no longer suffered the major epidemics* [that (under normal conditions) / would have killed a large percentage of their population / every year]. ❻ The physical isolation of the various bands may have protected them from the spread of contagious diseases. ❼ Another theory notes / that epidemics* have frequently been associated with prolonged contact (with domestic animals) / such as cattle and pigs. ❽ Since the Paleo-Indians did not domesticate animals, / not even horses, / ❾ they may have avoided the microbes (that caused virulent European and African diseases). ❿ Whatever the explanation / for this curious epidemiological** record, / Native Americans lost inherited immunities (that later might have protected them from many contagious germs). ⓫ Thus, when they first came into contact with Europeans and Africans, / Native Americans had no defense / against Ⓐ the great killers of the Early Modern world.

*epidemics 전염병 **epidemiological 역학

밑줄 친 Ⓐ가 의미하는 바는 무엇인가?
① soldiers   ② immunities   ③ migrants
✓ microbes   ⑤ livestock

해석

❶ 고(古) 아메리카 인디언의 물질문화는 아시아, 아프리카, 그리고 유럽에서 발견되는 다른 석기 시대 사람들의 물질문화와 거의 차이가 없었다. ❷ 하지만 베링 툰드라에서 인간의 건강 측면에서 아메리카 원주민의 역사를 영원히 바꾼 어떤 일이 일어났다. ❸ 이유는 지금도 확실하지 않지만, 이 소규모 이주 집단의 구성원들은 치명적인 질병인 천연두나 홍역 같은 수 많은 전염병들의 균을 더 이상 몸속에 가지고 있지 않게 되었다. ❹ 그리고 아메리카 원주민들이 결핵 같은 질병에 걸리기는 했지만, ❺ 그들은 일반적인 경우에 매년 인구의 많은 부분을 죽였을 심각한 전염병을 더 이상 겪지 않았다. ❻ 다양한 무리들이 물리적으로 떨어져 살았던 것이 전염병의 확산으로부터 그들을 보호했을지도 모른다. ❼ 또 다른 이론에 의하면 전염병은 종종 소, 돼지와 같은 가축과의 오랜 기간 접촉과 연관 지어졌다. ❽ 고(古)아메리카 인디언들은 동물을, 심지어 말조차도, 가축으로 기르지 않았기 때문에 ❾ 그들은 유럽인과 아프리카인에게 치명적인 질병을 일으키는 미생물을 피했을지도 모른다. ❿ 이 기이한 역학 기록에 대한 설명이 무엇이든 간에, 아메리카 원주민은 나중에 많은 전염성 병원균으로부터 그들을 보호했을지도 모를 유전된 면역력을 잃어버렸다. ⓫ 그러므로 그들이 유럽인과 아프리카인과 처음 접촉했을 때, 아메리카 원주민은 초기 근대의 Ⓐ엄청난 살인자(사망원인)를 방어할 수 없었다.

해설

질병을 일으키는 눈에 보이지 않는 균 및 미생물을 말하는 만큼 ④ microbes (미생물)이 가장 적절하다.

어휘

material n. 물질, 재료 a. 물질의 in terms of ~면에서, ~에 관하여 tundra n. 툰드라 alter v. 바꾸다 obscure a. 불명료한, 모호한, 알기 어려운 migrating a. 이주하는, 이동하는 communicable a. (사람들 간에) 전달되는, 전염성의 smallpox n. 천연두 measles n. 홍역 tuberculosis n. 결핵, 폐결핵 contagious a. (접촉을 통해) 전염되는, 전염성의 spread n. 확산, 전파 frequently ad. 자주, 빈번하게 prolong v. 연장하다, 연장시키다 domesticate v. 길들이다, 사육하다 microbe n. 미생물, 병원균 virulent a. 악성의, 치명적인, 전염성이 강한 inherited a. 상속한, 계승한, 유전의 immunity n. 면역력 germ n. 세균, 미생물 come into contact with ~와 접촉하다, ~와 만나다 livestock n. 가축

정답 및 해설

019 ① 2020학년도 명지대학교 인문계 26번

글의 주제

❶ Diseases represent evolution in progress, / and microbes adapt by natural selection / to new hosts and vectors. ❷ But compared with cows' bodies, / ours offer different immune defenses, lice, feces, and chemistries. ❸ In that new environment, / a microbe must evolve new ways (to live / and to propagate itself). ❹ In several instructive cases / doctors or veterinarians have actually been able to observe microbes evolving / those new ways. ❺ The best-studied case involves what happened / when myxomatosis hit Australian rabbits. ❻ The myxo virus, (native to a wild species of Brazilian rabbit), had been observed / to cause a lethal infectious disease / in European domestic rabbits, which are a different species. ❼ Hence the virus was intentionally introduced to Australia / in 1950 / in the hopes of ridding the continent of its plague, / foolishly introduced / in the nineteenth century. ❽ In the first year, / myxo produced a gratifying 99.8 percent mortality rate / in infected rabbits. ❾ Unfortunately for the farmers, / the death rate then dropped / in the second year / to 90 percent and eventually to 25 percent, / frustrating hopes of eradicating rabbits / completely from Australia. ❿ The problem was that the myxo virus evolved / to serve its own interests, which differed from ours (as well as) from those of the rabbits. ⓫ The virus changed so as to kill fewer rabbits and : to permit lethally infected ones / to live longer / before dying. ⓬ As a result, a less lethal myxo virus spreads baby viruses / to more rabbits / than did the original, highly virulent myxo.

해석

❶ 질병은 (병원균의) 진화가 진행 중임을 나타내며, 병원균은 자연선택에 의해서 새로운 숙주와 질병 매개체에 적응한다. ❷ 하지만 젖소의 몸과 비교했을 때, 우리의 신체는 (젖소와는) 다른 면역방어수단, 기생충, 배설물, 화학반응을 내놓는다. ❸ 그 새로운 환경에서 미생물은 생존하고 번식하기 위해서 새로운 방식들을 진화시키고 있는 것이 틀림없다. ❹ 몇몇 교육적인 사례에서, 의사들이나 수의사들은 병원균이 그런 새로운 방식들을 진화시키고 있는 것을 실제로 관찰할 수 있었다. ❺ 가장 모범적으로 연구된 사례는 호주의 토끼가 점액종증에 걸렸을 때 일어난 일과 연관이 있다. ❻ 원래 야생종 브라질 토끼의 몸에 존재하던 믹소 바이러스는 유럽 집토끼에 치명적인 전염병을 유발하는 것으로 드러났는데, 이 유럽의 집토끼는 (야생종 브라질 토끼와는) 완전히 다른 종이다. ❼ 그래서 이 믹소 바이러스를 의도적으로 1950년에 호주에 들여왔는데, 19세기에 어리석게 (호주에) 들여왔던 유럽의 집토끼 무리를 호주 대륙에서 없애고자 하는 바람에서였다. ❽ 믹소 바이러스를 들여온 첫해에, 믹소 바이러스는 감염된 토끼에서 만족할만한 수준의 99.8%의 치사율을 보여주었다. ❾ (그러나) 농부들에게는 불행히도, 치사율이 이듬해에는 90%로 하락하다가 결국 25%로 주저앉아버려, 호주에서 유럽의 집토끼를 완전히 박멸하고자 하는 희망을 좌절시켰다. ❿ 문제는 믹소 바이러스가 자신에게 이익이 되도록 진화했다는 것인데, 이런 진화는 토끼의 이익뿐 아니라, 우리의 이익과도 거리가 멀었다. ⓫ 이 믹소 바이러스는 보다 적은 개체의 토끼를 죽이고 치명적으로 감염된 토끼들이 오래 살다가 죽도록 진화했다. ⓬ 그 결과, 덜 치명적인 믹소 바이러스는 원래의 매우 치명적인 믹소 바이러스가 새끼 바이러스를 토끼에게 전파했던 것보다 더 많은 토끼들에게 새끼 바이러스를 퍼뜨리고 있다.

어휘

microbe n. 미생물 **adapt** v. 적응시키다, 맞추다, 개작하다 **host** n. (기생동·식물의) 숙주 **vector** n. (질병의) 매개체 **immune** a. 면역의 **louse** n. 〈곤충〉 이; 기생충(pl. lice) **feces** n. 똥, 배설물 **propagate** v. 전파하다, 번식시키다 **instructive** a. 유익한 **veterinarian** n. 수의사 **myxomatosis** n. 점액종증(토끼에게 치명적인 병) **native to** ~가 원산지인 **lethal** a. 죽음에 이르는, 치명적인 **infectious** a. 전염성의, 전염되는 **domestic** a. 국내의, 자국의 **continent** n. 대륙 **plague** n. 전염병 **gratifying** a. 만족시키는, 즐거운 **mortality rate** 사망률 **frustrate** v. 좌절시키다, 좌절감을 주다 **eradicate** v. 근절하다 **serve one's own interests** ~에게 이익이 되다 **virulent** a. 유독한; 치명적인

What does the underlined its plague refer to?
밑줄 친 its plague가 가리키는 것은 무엇인가?
① European domestic rabbits
  유럽의 집토끼들
② infected rabbits
  감염된 토끼들
③ the myxo virus
  믹소 바이러스
④ a lethal infectious disease in European domestic rabbits
  유럽의 집토끼들에게 치명적인 전염병

해설 이 글은 병원균의 진화와 적응을 설명하는 글로서 두 번째 단락에서는 호주 토끼 박멸을 위한 병원균 활용 그리고 이에 따른 진화를 예시로 들고 있다. 또한 plague는 '전염병' 또는 '동물이나 곤충의 떼'을 말할 때 쓴다. 따라서 맥락상 its plague는 '유럽의 집토끼들'이 가장 적절하다.

020 ① 2020학년도 서울여자대학교 인문·자연계 A형 37번

❶ Originally, election days varied by state, but in 1845 a law was passed to set a single election day for the entire country. ❷ At first, it applied only to presidential elections, ❸ but it was later extended to congressional elections as well. ❹ At that time, the United States was still a largely agrarian society. ❺ For farmers, (who made up a majority of the labor force), much of the year was taken up by the planting, tending, and harvesting of crops. ❻ Early November was a good time to vote because the harvest was over but the weather was still relatively mild. ❼ Still, some days of the week were better than others. ❽ Two days were definitely out of the question. ❾ Most Americans were devout Christians and thus set aside Sunday as a day of rest and worship. ❿ Wednesday (in many areas) was a market day, when farmers sold their crops in town. ⓫ In addition, a travel day was sometimes required. ⓬ In rural areas, the nearest polling place might have been several miles away, and, in an era before automobiles, getting there could take a while. ⓭ If people couldn't use Sunday or Wednesday as their travel day, ⓮ then that meant election day couldn't be on Monday or Thursday, either. ⓯ And so Tuesday was perceived as the best option. ⓰ The reason (that election day was specified as the Tuesday "after the first Monday") was to prevent it from falling on November 1. ⓱ That day was considered unfavorable because some Christians observed it as All Saints' Day ⓲ and also because merchants typically took the first day of the month to settle their books for the previous month.

해석

❶ 원래 선거일은 주마다 달랐지만, 1845년 전국에서 단일 선거일을 정하는 법안이 통과되었다. ❷ 처음에 그 법은 대통령 선거에만 적용되었으나, ❸ 나중에는 의회의 선거에까지 확대되었다. ❹ 그 당시, 미국은 여전히 대체로 농경사회였다. ❺ 노동력 대다수를 차지하고 있는 농부들은 한 해의 대부분을 농작물을 심고, 가꾸고, 수확하는 것에 보냈다. ❻ 11월 초가 투표를 하기에 좋은 시기였는데, 추수가 끝났지만, 날씨는 여전히 비교적 온화했기 때문이다. ❼ 여전히 주중의 어떤 날들은 다른 날보다 더 좋았다. ❽ 이틀은 전혀 불가능했다. ❾ 대부분의 미국인들은 독실한 기독교인들이어서 일요일을 휴식과 예배를 보는 날로 챙겨두었다. ❿ 많은 지역에서 수요일은 장이 열리는 날이었는데, 농부들은 이때 그들이 기른 농작물을 도시에서 팔았다. ⓫ 그뿐만 아니라, 때로는 이동을 할 수 있는 날이 요구되었다. ⓬ 시골 지역에서는, 가장 가까운 투표소가 몇 마일 떨어져 있을 수도 있었고, 자동차가 나오기 전 시대에는 투표소까지 가는 데 많은 시간이 소요되었다. ⓭ 사람들이 일요일 또는 수요일을 이동일로 사용하지 못한다면, ⓮ 그것은 선거일이 월요일이나 목요일이 될 수 없다는 것을 의미했다. ⓯ 그래서 화요일이 최선의 선택으로 여겨졌다. ⓰ 선거일을 "첫 번째 월요일 이후" 화요일로 명시한 이유는 11월 1일을 선거일로 정하지 않기 위함이었다. ⓱ 이날을 적절하지 않은 것으로 여겨졌는데, 일부 기독교인들이 이날을 만성절(기독교에서 모든 성인을 기리는 날로 11월 1일)로 기념했으며 ⓲ 또한 상인들은 지난달의 장부를 정리하는 데 매월 첫째 날을 사용했기 때문이다.

어휘

election day 선거일 **entire** a. 전체의 **apply** v. (규칙을) 적용[발효]시키다 **extend** v. (사업·영향력 등을) 확대[확장]하다 **congressional** a. 의회의, 국회의 **agrarian** a. 농업의 **tend** v. (식물 등을) 기르다, 재배하다 **harvest** v. 수확하다; (성과 등을) 거두어들이다 **crop** n. 농작물 **out of the question** 불가능한, 의논해 봐야 소용없는 **devout** a. 독실한, 경건한, 믿음이 깊은 **set aside** 곁에 두다, 챙겨두다, 확보하다 **worship** n. 예배, 참배 **market day** 장날, 장이 서는 날 **rural** a. 시골의, 지방의 **unfavorable** a. 불리한, 알맞지[적합하지] 않은 **observe** v. 축하하다, 기념하다, 지키다 **merchant** n. 상인 **settle** v. (주어야 할 돈을) 지불[계산]하다, 정산하다, 정리하다

What does the underlined Two days refer to?
밑줄 친 Two days가 가리키는 것은 무엇인가?
① Sunday and Wednesday
일요일과 수요일
② Monday and Thursday
월요일과 목요일
③ Friday and Saturday
금요일과 토요일
④ Tuesday and Thursday
화요일과 목요일

해 설 밑줄 다음 문장에서 투표할 수 없는 교회 가는 일요일 그리고 시장이 열리는 수요일을 설명하고 있다.

정답 및 해설

유형 09 기타 | 태도, 분위기, 어조, 견해

001 ② 2020학년도 광운대학교 인문계 A형 01번

A: Our assignment is actually easier than I thought.
B: Really? Then, can you finish it on time, Peter?
A: Yes! You can count on me.
  └긍정답변 암시

빈칸에 들어가기에 가장 적절한 것은?

① I bet you will do that.
  틀림없이 너는 그것을 할 거야.
✓ You can count on me.
  나만 믿어.
③ Take your time, though.
  그래도 천천히 해.
④ Are you supposed to do that?
  네가 그것을 하기로 되어 있니?
⑤ What do you think I should do?
  너는 내가 무엇을 해야 한다고 생각하니?

해석
A: 우리가 맡은 과제가 사실은 내가 생각했던 것보다 쉬워.
B: 정말? 피터(Peter), 그렇다면 그 과제를 제시간에 끝낼 수 있니?
A: 당연하지! 나만 믿어.

해설 마지막 질문에 대한 긍정적 답변을 암시하는 'Yes!' 이후 ②이 가장 적절하다.

어휘 on time 정각에 bet v. 내기하다, 장담하다 I bet~ 확실히 ~이다 count on ~을 믿다 take one's time 천천히 하다 be supposed to do ~하기로 되어 있다

002 ③ 2020학년도 덕성여자대학교 오전 사회·자연·예술대학 26번

❶ Use your frequent flyer programs / to donate to charity. ❷ Your frequent flyer points may be used to help people (with life-threatening medical conditions) / travel by plane / to obtain the treatment (they need), ❸ or to transport emergency relief personnel / to the site of natural disasters, ❹ or simply to enable seriously ill children and their families to enjoy a trip to Jeju Island. ❺ You will be glad / you helped others.

Which adjective best describes the author's tone in this passage?
본문 필자의 어조를 가장 잘 기술하는 형용사는?

① Angry
  화가 난
② Sympathetic
  동정적인
✓ Persuasive
  설득력 있는
④ Impersonal
  인간미 없는

해석
❶ 자선단체에 기부하려면 당신의 항공사 우수여객 프로그램을 이용하십시오. ❷ 항공사의 우수여객 포인트를 사용하면, 생명을 위협하는 질병을 지닌 사람들이 필요한 치료를 받기 위해 비행기로 이동하는 것을 도와주거나, ❸ 자연재해 현장으로 달려가는 긴급 구호 요원들을 수송하거나, ❹ 중증 질환을 앓고 있는 아동들과 그 가족들이 제주 여행을 할 수 있게 해줄 수 있습니다. ❺ 여러분은 다른 사람들을 도움으로써 기쁨을 얻게 될 것입니다.

해설 자선단체 기부 방법과 참여 기쁨을 설득하는 글이다. 나머지 선택지는 글의 소재 및 주제와 연관성이 없다.

어휘 frequent a. 빈번한 donate v. 기부하다 charity n. 자선단체 obtain v. 얻다, 획득하다 relief personnel 구호 요원 sympathetic a. 동정적인, 동조적인 persuasive a. 설득력 있는 impersonal a. 비인격적인, 인간미 없는

003 ④ — 2019 덕성여자대학교 사회·자연·예술대학 25번

① The Ebola virus causes an acute, serious illness which is often fatal / if untreated). ② Ebola virus disease (EVD) first appeared / in 1976 / in 2 simultaneous outbreaks, / ③ one in Nzara, Sudan, / and the other in Yambuku, Democratic Republic of Congo. ④ The latter occurred / in a village / near the Ebola River, / from which the disease takes its name. ⑤ Ebola is introduced / into the human population / through close contact with the blood, secretions, organs or other bodily fluids of infected animals / such as fruit bats, monkeys and porcupines (found ill or dead).

⑥ Ebola then spreads / through human-to-human transmission / via direct contact with the blood, secretions, organs or other bodily fluids of infected people, / and with surfaces and materials (contaminated with these fluids). ⑦ Health-care workers have frequently been infected / while treating patients / with suspected or confirmed EVD. ⑧ This has occurred / through close contact with patients / when infection control precautions are not strictly practiced. ⑨ People remain infectious / as long as their blood and body fluids, (including semen and breast milk), contain the virus.

Which of the following best expresses the author's opinions about the Ebola virus in this passage?
다음 중 위 글의 에볼라 바이러스에 대한 저자의 견해를 가장 잘 나타내는 것은?

① Ebola is a disease which just started to appear in the past year.
에볼라는 지난해에 나타나기 시작한 질병이다. (→ 1976년 처음 발생)

② People contract the Ebola virus only with direct contact with other victims.
사람들은 다른 희생자들과의 직접적인 접촉을 통해서만 에볼라 바이러스에 감염된다. (→ 혈액 및 체액 등 접촉으로도 감염)

③ Few health-care workers are willing to take care of patients with the Ebola virus since Ebola is very contagious through human contact.
에볼라는 사람과의 접촉을 통한 전염성이 매우 강하기 때문에 에볼라 바이러스에 걸린 환자들을 기꺼이 돌보려는 의료 종사자는 거의 없다. (→ 의료 종사자 없다는 말 없음)

✓ Medical researchers have warned that close contact with people who have been infected by the Ebola virus is very dangerous, and therefore such people should take special precautions.
의학 연구원들은 에볼라 바이러스에 감염된 사람들과 가깝게 접촉하는 것은 매우 위험하므로, 그러한 사람들은 특별한 예방 조치를 받아야 한다고 경고했다.

해석
① 에볼라(Ebola) 바이러스는 치료하지 않는다면 종종 치명적일 정도로 심각한 급성 질병을 유발한다. ② 에볼라 출혈열(EVD)은 1976년에 2건의 동시 발병으로 처음으로 모습을 나타냈는데, ③ 하나는 수단의 은자라(Nzarz)에서, 나머지는 하나는 콩고민주공화국의 얌부쿠(Yambuku)에서 발생하였다. ④ 후자는 에볼라 강 근처에 있는 마을에서 발생했는데, 에볼라 출혈열이라는 이름은 여기에서 가져온 것이다. ⑤ 에볼라는 병들거나 죽은 채로 발견되는 과일박쥐, 원숭이, 호저(豪猪) 같은 감염된 동물의 혈액, 분비물, 장기 또는 기타 체액과 가까이 접촉하면서 사람들 속으로 들어오게 된다.

⑥ 그런 후에 에볼라는 감염된 사람들의 혈액, 분비물, 장기 또는 기타 체액과의 직접 접촉, 그리고 이러한 체액에 오염된 표면과 물질과의 직접적인 접촉을 거쳐서 사람과 사람 사이의 전염을 통해 퍼지게 된다. ⑦ 의료계 종사자들은 의심되거나 확인된 EVD 환자들을 치료하며 자주 감염되어 왔다. ⑧ 이는 감염 관리를 위한 예방 조치가 엄격하게 시행되지 않는 상황에서 환자와 긴밀히 접촉함으로써 발생한 것이다. ⑨ 사람들은 그들의 혈액, 그리고 정액과 모유를 포함한 체액에 바이러스가 들어 있는 한, 여전히 다른 사람에게 전염시킬 수 있다.

해설
저자의 견해를 묻고 있지만, 사실상 내용 일치 및 추론과 같은 접근이 요구되는 유형이다. 두 번째 단락에서 에볼라 바이러스의 감염 과정을 설명하는 만큼 예방 조치를 받아야 한다는 ④이 가장 적절하다.

어휘
acute a. 날카로운, 뾰족한; 빈틈없는; 급성의 fatal a. 치명적인, 죽음을 초래하는 simultaneous a. 동시의, 동시에 일어나는 outbreak n. (소동·쟁·유행병 따위의) 발발, 창궐 the latter (둘 중의) 후자(後者) introduce v. 안으로 들이다, 받아들이다; 소개하다 contact n. 접촉 secretion n. 분비, 분비물 organ n.(생물의) 기관, 장기(臟器) fluid n. 유동체, 유체 infect v. 감염시키다, 전염시키다 fruit bat 큰박쥐, 과일박쥐 porcupine n. 〈동물〉 호저(豪猪) spread 퍼지다, 번지다, 전해지다 transmission n. 전달, 매개, 전염 via prep. ~을 경유하여, ~을 거쳐 material n. 물질, 재료 a. 물질의, 재료의 contaminate v. (접촉하여) 더럽히다, 오염하다 suspect v. 의심하다 confirm v. 확증하다, 확인하다 precaution n. 조심, 경계; 예방책 strictly ad. 엄격하게 semen n. 정액 contain v. (속에) 담고 있다, 포함하다

004 ①
2020학년도 덕성여자대학교 오후 (인문·공과대학) 30번

❶ The American Revolution symbolized the connection (between the rights of the citizen and the rights of the state). ❷ The free citizen had a right (to govern himself); ❸ therefore the whole community (of the free citizens) had a right (to govern itself). ❹ This was not yet modern nationalism. ❺ The American people did not see themselves / as a national group / but as a community of free men (dedicated to a proposition). ❻ But within two decades, / the identification had been made. ❼ The French Revolution, (proclaiming the Rights of Man), formed the new style of nation. ❽ The levee-en-messe (which defeated the old dynastic armies of Europe) was the first expression of total nation unity / as the basis of the sovereign state. ❾ Men and nations had equally the right (to self-determination). ❿ Men could not be free / if their national community was not. ⓫ The same revolution quickly proved / that the reverse might not be true. ⓬ The nation could become completely unfettered / in its dealings with other states / while enslaving its own citizens. ⓭ In fact, over-glorification of the nation might lead inevitably / to the extinction of individual rights. ⓮ The citizen could become just a tool of the national will. ⓯ But in the first explosion of revolutionary ardour, / the idea (of the Rights of Man and of the Rights of the Nation) went together. ⓰ And, formally, that is where they have remained.

Which of the following can be the key words of the passage?
다음 중 이 글의 핵심어들은?

✓ ① Individualism and nationalism
　개인주의와 국가주의
② Individual rights and national prosperity
　개인의 권리와 국가의 번영
③ Revolution and free citizens
　혁명과 자유 시민
④ Sovereign states and nationalism
　주권국가 및 국가주의

해석
❶ 미국 독립혁명은 시민의 권리와 국가의 권리 사이의 연결성을 상징했다. ❷ 자유 시민은 스스로를 다스릴 권리가 있었고, ❸ 그러므로 자유 시민으로 구성된 공동체는 스스로 다스릴 권리가 있었다. ❹ 이것은 아직 현대적 국가주의는 아니었다. ❺ 미국인들은 그들 스스로를 하나의 국가적 집단이 아니라, 어떤 법안에 헌신하는 자유인의 공동체로 보았다. ❻ 하지만 그런 자기 정체의식은 20년 안에 이루어졌다.
❼ 인간(개인)의 권리를 선언하는 프랑스 혁명은 새로운 형태의 국가를 이루었다. ❽ 옛 유럽 왕조의 군대들을 격파했던 국민 총동원(levee-en-messe)은 주권국가의 기초가 되었던 완전한 국민통합의 첫 표현이었던 것이다. ❾ 인간과 국가는 동등하게 자기 결정권을 가지고 있었다. ❿ 만약 국가 공동체가 자유로울 수 없다면, 인간 역시도 그럴 수 없었을 것이다.
⓫ 똑같은 혁명은 그 반대가 사실이 아닐 수 있다는 것을 금세 증명했다. ⓬ 국가는 자국민들을 노예로 삼으면서 다른 국가들과의 관계에서 어떠한 제재도 받지 않게 될 수 있었다. ⓭ 사실, 국가의 영광을 지나치게 칭송하는 것은 불가피하게도 개인 권리의 소멸을 초래할 수 있다. ⓮ 시민은 단지 국가 의지의 도구가 될 수 있었다. ⓯ 하지만 혁명적 열정이 처음으로 폭발하였을 때, 인간의 권리와 국가의 권리에 대한 사상은 함께 나아갔다. ⓰ 그리고 공식적으로, 그곳이 그것들이 머물러 온 곳이다.

해설
윗글은 개인의 권리와 국가의 권리의 연결성, 또는 국가주의의 방향과 발전을 위한 개인주의의 권리 등을 주제로 하는 글이며, 마지막 문장에서 다시 한번 개인과 국가의 관계를 언급하고 있다. 따라서 글의 핵심어(소재)는 ①이 가장 적절하다. 또한 오답인 ②에서는 'national prosperity(국가의 번영)'는 글의 핵심어라고 볼 수 없다.

어휘
nationalism n. 민족주의, 국가주의; 애국심　dedicated to ~에 헌신하는　identification n. 신원확인　proclaim v. 선언하다　levee-en-messe n. (프랑스 혁명 당시의) 국민 총동원(=levy in mess)　dynastic a. 왕조의　sovereign n. 군주, 국왕, 통치자　self determination 자기 결정권, 민족 자결권　unfettered a. 제한받지 않는　glorification n. 칭송, 찬양　inevitably ad. 필연적으로　extinction n. 멸종, 절멸, 소멸　ardour n. 열정　prosperity n. 번영, 번성, 번창

005 ③ 2019학년도 단국대학교 인문계 A형 22번

❶ In Jamaica, / most British and American people encounter tourism / as consumers / — of culture, good weather, beautiful buildings, or any of the other things (that people travel in search of). ❷ During my year as a student (living in Jamaica and traveling around the Caribbean), / I have seen tourism / through the eyes of people (who live with it), ❸ and witnessed the corrupting effects of tourism / on the cultures (that depend on it / for economic survival). ❹ When I tell people / that I was living in Jamaica on scholarship, they roll their eyes and marvel at my luck, ❺ because they have seen the ads / for Jamaican tourism, / showing empty beaches, clear blue skies, and the occasional smiling black face. ❻ I don't know how to respond, / ❼ because the Jamaica (that I lived in), and (that only some tourists are privileged to see), is a poor, crowded, violent place ❽ [where most people, (from police officers to ganja (marijuana) peddlers), resent tourists / for their leisure and their money] — ❾ money (that goes almost exclusively / to a small elite of hotel owners and government officials). ❿ Among the rest, (who must bow, beg, sell, or steal to capture the visitors' money), tourism creates pickpockets and impostors. ⓫ It might be different / if the tourists weren't so obvious / in their appearance. ⓬ Many things — (dress, language, looks) — can distinguish tourists from the native population. ⓭ In Jamaica, / it is skin color that sets the tourists apart, / as 95 percent of Jamaicans are black, / and most tourists are white. ⓮ A white stranger (in the streets of Jamaica) is assumed to be a tourist, and therefore interested in buying trinkets, souvenirs, or drugs.

Which is the tone of the passage?
이 글의 어조는 무엇인가?
① excited 흥분한
② optimistic 긍정적인
③ analytic 분석적인
④ aesthetic 미학적인

해석
❶ 자메이카(Jamaica)에서, 대부분의 영국인과 미국인들은 관광을 문화, 화창한 날씨, 아름다운 건물, 그리고 사람들이 여행하며 찾는 다른 모든 것의 소비자로서 마주한다[경험한다]. ❷ 자메이카에서 거주하며 카리브(Caribbean) 해 일대를 여행하는 학생으로 보낸 1년 동안, 나는 관광으로 살아가는 사람들의 시선으로 관광을 보았으며, ❸ 관광이 경제적인 생존을 위해서 관광에 의존하는 문화에 끼치는 부정적인 영향을 목격하였다. ❹ 내가 사람들에게 자메이카에서 장학금을 받으며 살고 있다고 말하면, 그들은 눈을 두리번거리면서, 내가 운이 좋다고 감탄한다. ❺ 왜냐하면, 그들은 텅 빈 해변, 맑고 푸른 하늘, 그리고 가끔씩 웃는 흑인의 얼굴을 보여주는 자메이카 관광 광고를 본 적이 있기 때문이다. ❻ 나는 (그들의 반응에) 어떻게 반응해야 하는지 모르겠는데, ❼ 왜냐하면 내가 살고 있으며 오직 일부 관광객들만이 볼 수 있는 자메이카는 가난하고, 붐비고, 폭력이 난무하는 곳이기 때문이다. ❽ 이곳 자메이카는 경찰관에서부터 간자(대마초)를 파는 행상인에 이르기까지 대다수 사람들이 관광객들이 여가시간을 보내는 것과 관광객들이 소비하는 돈에 분노하는데, ❾ 이 돈은 호텔 소유주 및 정부 관리 같은 소수의 최상류층에게만 거의 독점적으로 돌아가기 때문이다. ❿ 관광객들의 돈을 얻기 위해서 허리를 굽혀 절하고, 구걸하며, 물건을 팔거나 훔쳐야 하는 나머지 사람들 사이에서는 관광이 소매치기들과 사기꾼들을 만들어내고 있는 것이다. ⓫ 관광객들이 그들의 외모에 있어서 그다지 뚜렷하게 눈에 띄지 않는다면, 상황이 다를지도 모른다. ⓬ 옷, 언어, 외모 등 많은 요소들로 인해 관광객은 원주민과 구별될 수 있다. ⓭ 자메이카에서는, 전체 인구 중 95%가 흑인이며, 관광객의 대부분이 백인이기 때문에 관광객들을 구별 지어주는 것은 바로 피부색이다. ⓮ 자메이카 거리의 백인 이방인은 관광객으로 추정되며, 따라서 자질구레한 장신구, 기념품, 그리고 마약을 사는 것에 관심이 있는 것으로 추정된다.

해설
윗글은 자메이카 관광의 이미지와 실제 모습을 묘사하고 설명하는 글인 만큼 글의 어조는 ③ 'analytic(분석적인)'이 가장 적절하다.

어휘
encounter v. 만나다, 마주치다 witness n. 목격자 v. 목격하다 corrupting a. 부패한; 순수성을 잃은 on scholarship 장학금을 받고 roll one's eyes 눈을 희번덕거리다 marvel at ~에 감탄하다 privileged a. 특권을 가진 ganja n. 간자, (흡연용으로 쓰는) 인도 대마(大麻) peddler n. 행상인, 판매원 exclusively ad. 예외적으로, 배타적으로 the rest 나머지 bow v. 허리를 굽혀 절하다 pickpocket n. 소매치기 imposter n. 사칭하는 사람, 사기꾼 distinguish v. 구별하다, 식별하다 native population 원주민 set ~ apart ~을 눈에 띄게 하다 trinket n. 값싼[자질구레한] 장신구 souvenir n. 기념품, 선물 optimistic a. 낙관적인, 낙관하는 analytic a. 분석적인 aesthetic a. 심미적인, 미학적인

006 ③

2020학년도 숭실대학교 인문계 37번

❶ Technical flaws can result in surprising and charming effects that you can only dream of achieving with Instagram filters. ❷ For example, some of our favorite analog photos are tinted green or purple from film used past its expiration date. ❸ In fact, many photographers actually seek out expired film to experience the excitement of not knowing what the shot will end up looking like. ❹ Sometimes a film photograph looks like it has a fabric overlay, a gritty surface, or even a dreamy smoothness. ❺ The depth of this texture is a delicate feature that is often overlooked. ❻ However, once you start paying attention it simply becomes a key factor in appreciating the true beauty of a photo. ❼ Film photography aims to grab all the color in your shot and paint it. ❽ The amazing variety of film choices available allows you to choose the best characteristics for each shooting — whether it's cooler or warmer tones, more or less light, or natural or vibrant colors. ❾ Monochromatic film is a classic. ❿ The deep blacks, contrast and dark shadows are any photographer's dream. ⓫ Some shots are just meant to be taken in black and white, and film manages to capture this in the moodiest of ways. ⓬ The feeling of holding an old film camera and carrying around rolls of film brings us back to a different era and reminds us of cherished memories. ⓭ This heartwarming feeling is believed to be one of the main reasons behind the growing trend of photographers going back to film over the last few years. ⓮ Yet it's about so much more than just reminiscing about past experiences. ⓯ Film also makes us miss a time when the world moved slower.

해석

❶ 기술적 결함은 당신이 인스타그램 필터로만 이뤄낼 수 있는 놀랍고 매력적인 효과를 가져다줄 수 있다. ❷ 예를 들면, 우리가 가장 좋아하는 아날로그 사진 중 일부는 유효기간이 지나서 사용된 필름으로 인하여 녹색이나 보라색으로 착색되어버린다. ❸ 사실 많은 사진작가들은 사진이 어떤 모습으로 보이게 될지 모른다는 흥분을 경험하기 위해 유효기간이 지난 필름을 실제로 찾는다. ❹ 때때로 필름 사진은 직물 겹침 효과, 거친 표면 또는 심지어 몽환적인 부드러움을 갖고 있는 것처럼 보인다. ❺ 이러한 질감의 깊이는 때때로 간과되는 미묘한 특징이다. ❻ 하지만 당신이 관심을 가지기 시작한다면 질감의 깊이는 사진의 진정한 아름다움을 감상하는 데 있어 핵심적인 요소가 된다. ❼ 필름 사진 촬영술은 사진 안에 있는 모든 색을 포함하여 그것을 생생하게 묘사하는 것을 목표로 한다. ❽ 사용할 수 있는 필름 선택이 놀라울 정도로 다양하기에 촬영할 때마다, 톤을 시원하게 할지 따뜻하게 할지, 빛을 많이 넣을지 적게 넣을지, 자연스러운 색으로 할지 강렬한 색으로 할지, 최선의 선택을 할 수 있다. ❾ 단색의 필름은 전형적인 예이다. ❿ 깊은 검은색 효과와 대조와 어두운 그림자는 사진작가의 꿈이다. ⓫ 어떤 촬영은 흑백으로 찍기로 의도된 것일 수 있는데, 필름이 이런 의도를 가장 분위기 있게 이루어낸다. ⓬ 오래된 필름 카메라를 들고 필름 한 통을 들고 다니는 느낌은 우리를 다른 시대로 되돌아가게 하고 소중한 추억을 떠올리게 한다. ⓭ 이 따뜻한 느낌은 지난 몇 년 동안 필름으로 돌아가는 사진작가들이 증가하는 추세의 이면에 있는 주요한 이유들 중 하나이다. ⓮ 하지만 그것은 단순하게 과거의 경험을 회상하는 것보다 훨씬 더 많은 것에 관한 것이다. ⓯ 필름은 또한 우리로 하여금 세상이 더 느리게 움직이던 시절을 그리워하게 만든다.

어휘

flaw n. 결함 **tint** v. (약간의) 색깔을 넣다[색조를 더하다] **expiration** n. 만료, 만기 **seek out** (특히 많은 노력을 기울여) ~을 찾아내다 **end up** 결국 ~이 되다 **fabric** n. 직물, 천, 기본 구조 **overlay** n. (다른 것 위에) 덮어씌우는[입히는] 것 **gritty** a. 자갈이 섞인, 모래투성이의 **smoothness** n. 매끄러움; 평온함 **texture** n. 감촉, 질감 **delicate** a. 섬세한, 연약한 **overlook** v. 못 보고 넘어가다, 간과하다 **vibrant** a. 활기찬, 생기 있는 **monochromatic** a. 단색의, 단차(單差)의, 단색성의 **era** n. 시대 **cherished** a. 소중한 **heartwarming** a. 마음이 따스해지는 **reminisce** v. (행복했던 시절에 대한) 추억[회상]에 잠기다 **render** v. 만들다, (서비스를) 제공하다

Which of the following best summarizes the first paragraph?
다음 중 첫 번째 단락을 가장 잘 요약한 것은 무엇인가?
① the flawless rendering of the analog world
　　아날로그 세계의 나무랄 데 없는 연출
② the use of recycled film
　　재활용된 필름의 사용
③ the unexpected imperfections
　　예상치 않은 불완전함(결함)
④ the vibrant character of creativity
　　창조성의 활기찬 특징

해 설　첫 단락 첫 번째 문장에서 기술적 결함은 인스타그램 필터처럼 매력적인 효과가 있음을 말하고 다음 문장부터는 이에 대한 예시를 활용하여 구체적으로 설명을 이어가고 있다. 따라서 예상치 않은 효과 즉 ③이 가장 적절하다.

정답 및 해설

007 ④ 2019학년도 명지대학교 인문계 29번

❶ My aunt Marti calls me / at home tonight / and asks (what I am doing). ❷ "Just hitting the books," I say. That doesn't go over / so well. ❸ She scolds me / for the violent metaphor — / ❹ no need to use the word "hit." ❺ "Okay, I'm performing gentle acupressure / on the books," / I say. ❻ She seems to like that better. ❼ I love Marti, but a conversation (with her) always includes a list of what I'm doing and saying wrong, and how it supports the phallocentric power structure. ❽ She's got some opinions, my aunt. ❾ There's liberal, / there's really liberal, / then there's Marti, / a few miles farther to the left. ❿ She lives out / near Berkeley, appropriately enough — / though even Berkeley is a bit too fascist for her. ⓫ I haven't talked to Marti / since Julie got pregnant. ⓬ I break the news / to her as gently as I can, and apologize to her / for contributing to the overpopulation problem. ⓭ "That's okay," she says. ⓮ She'll forgive me. But, she points out, I can help minimize the damage / to the environment / by raising the child vegan. ⓯ Marti (herself) is beyond vegan. ⓰ Animal rights are her passion (even if she thinks the concept of rights is too Western), ⓱ and she spends (a good part of the year) flying / around the country attending vegetarian conferences. ⓲ I could take up quite a bit of space / listing the things (that Marti doesn't eat meat), ⓳ of course, and chicken, fish, eggs, dairy (she likes to call ice cream "solidified mucus"), but also honey — ⓴ she won't eat honey / because the bees are oppressed, / not paid union scale or something). ㉑ You'd think / she'd like soy, / but she believes / the soy industry is corrupt. ㉒ She recently took her diet / to a new level / by becoming a raw foodist, meaning / she eats only food (that's uncooked), because it's more natural.

해석

❶ 나의 고모 마티(Marti)는 밤에 집으로 전화해서 내가 무엇을 하고 있는지 묻는다. ❷ 나는 "그냥 책을 쳐보고 있어요(열심히 공부하고 있다는 의미)."라고 말하지만, 그다지 좋은 말은 못 듣는다. ❸ 고모는 폭력적인 비유를 쓴다고 나를 꾸짖는다. ❹ '쳐보다(hit)'라는 단어를 굳이 쓸 필요가 없지 않느냐는 것이다. ❺ "알겠어요. 책에 부드러운 지압을 하고 있어요."라고 나는 바꿔서 말한다. ❻ 고모는 그 표현을 더 좋아하는 것 같다. ❼ 나는 마티 고모를 좋아하지만, 그녀와의 대화에선 매번 나의 잘못된 행동과 말에 대한 지적이 이어지며 그런 것이 어떻게 해서 남성 중심적 권력 구조를 강화시키는지에 관한 말도 나오게 된다. ❽ 아! 고모는 정말 자기 주관이 뚜렷한 사람이다. ❾ (세상에는) 진보성향을 가진 사람이 존재하고, 진짜 진보주의자도 존재하며, 그 다음 (이들보다) 훨씬 더 좌파적(급진적)인 마티 고모가 있다. ❿ 그녀는 버클리(Berkeley) 근처에 살고 있는데, 딱 적당한 곳이다. 비록 버클리도 고모에게는 약간 너무 독재적이겠지만 말이다. ⓫ 줄리(Julie)가 임신한 이후로 나는 마티 고모와 대화를 하지 못했다. ⓬ 나는 고모에게 되도록 상냥하게 임신 소식을 전하는 인구과잉문제에 기여하게 된 것에 대해 사과한다. ⓭ "괜찮아."라며 고모가 이야기한다. ⓮ 나를 기꺼이 용서해주시지만, 아이를 엄격한 채식주의자로 키움으로써 환경에 입히는 피해를 최소화하는 것에 힘을 보탤 수 있다는 지적도 해주신다. ⓯ 마티 고모는 엄격한 채식주의자 그 이상이다. ⓰ 동물의 권리는 그녀가 열정적으로 애착을 가지는 것이며(비록 고모는 동물의 권리에 관한 개념이 너무나 서구적이라고 여기지만 말이다.) ⓱ 그녀는 1년 중 많은 시간을 비행기를 타고 전국을 돌며 채식주의 회의에 참석하면서 보낸다. ⓲ 나는 마티 고모가 안 먹는 음식을 열거해서 꽤 많은 공간의 목록을 채울 수 있는데, ⓳ 그 목록에는 당연하게도 육류 고기와 닭, 어류, 계란, 유제품(고모는 아이스크림을 '응고된 점액'이라고 즐겨 부른다.)이 들어가 있으며, 꿀도 그 목록에 포함되어 있는데, ⓴ 그녀는 벌들이 노조에서 정한 최저 임금 조차도 받지 못한 채 억압받기 때문에, 꿀을 먹으려고 하지 않는다. ㉑ 그렇다면 당신은 '고모가 콩은 좋아하겠지'라고 생각할 것이다. 하지만 고모는 대두(콩) 산업이 부패했다고 믿고 있다. ㉒ 그녀는 최근 들어 생식가가 됨으로써 그녀의 식단을 새로운 수준으로 올렸는데, 생식가가 된다는 것은 그 음식이 더 자연스러운 것이라는 이유로, 날것의 음식만 먹는다는 것을 의미한다.

어휘

hit the books (열심히) 공부하다 **go over** 호평을 받다 **scold** v. 꾸짖다 **violent** a. 폭력적인 **metaphor** n. 은유적 표현, 비유적 표현 **acupressure** n. 지압(요법) **phallocentric** a. 남성 중심적인 **My (sainted) aunt!** (놀라움 등을 나타내어) 어머니!, 저런! **liberal** n. 진보주의자 **fascist** a. 극우적인, 극우파의 **corrupt** a. 부패한, 타락한, 사악한 **raw foodist** 생식을 하는 사람 **get pregnant** 임신하다 **break the news to** ~에게 (나쁜) 소식을 전하다 **point out** 지적하다, 가리키다 **vegan** n. 엄격한 채식주의자(고기는 물론 우유, 달걀도 먹지 않음. 어떤 이들은 실크나 가죽같이 동물에게서 원료를 얻는 제품도 사용하지 않음) **vegetarian** a. 채식의, 채식주의자의 **dairy** n. 유제품(乳製品) **solidified** a. 응고된 **mucus** n. (코 등에서 나오는) 점액 **union scale** (노조에서 정한) 최저 임금

| 정답 및 해설 |

Choose the one that best describes the author's demeanor.
저자의 태도를 가장 잘 묘사한 것을 고르시오.
① enraged and flabbergasted
　매우 화가 났으면서도 당황스러운
② calm and nonchalant
　침착하고 태연한
③ excited but critical
　신이 났지만 비판적인
✓ humorous but candid
　재미있지만 솔직한

해설 책을 읽는 것을 '쳐보고 있다' 대신 '부드러운 지압을 가하라'라는 표현, 출산 소식에 대해 '인구과잉문제에 이바지했다'는 표현, 꿀벌들에게 '노조에서 정한 최저 임금조차도 못 받는다'라는 표현 등에서 재미있으면서 솔직한 태도를 엿볼 수 있다.

어휘 **demeanor** n. 처신, 행실, 태도, 몸가짐 **enraged** a. 격분한, 화가 난 **flabbergasted** a. 놀란, 당황스러운 **nonchalant** a. 태연한, 냉담한 **candid** a. 솔직한, 진솔한

008 ①　2019학년도 숭실대학교 인문계 A형 38번

❶ Much of the criticism (leveled against globalization today) is related to the idea (that it enriches the few, / leaving the many behind). ❷ The people (making this argument) frequently advocate / for the wholesale abandonment of globalization.
❸ If the world takes the isolationist path, / three major shifts will happen. ❹ First, / a more isolated world will force businesses to adopt increasingly local and decreasingly global models. ❺ In essence, they will be more likely to rely on local and regional capital / — and less likely to be centrally run / from leading financial centers / such as New York City, Tokyo and London. ❻ This change will significantly alter (how businesses fund themselves), (how they structure costs) and (how they view the proposition of long-term growth). ❼ They will be less able to access to fund investments and grow companies — ❽ reducing their opportunities (to hire people and invest in communities).
❾ Second, there will be short-term deflation and then long-term inflation. ❿ We've already begun to observe the former. ⓫ Low energy costs, low wages and indeed the low price of money itself indicate a prevailing deflationary world, / though they all have notably risen recently. ⓬ As for the latter, / the persistence of low inflation has defied warnings of a sharp uptick (that date as far back as 2009, / right after the financial crisis). ⓭ Beyond that, / rising trade tariffs and protectionism will decrease rices of imported products. ⓮ This will undercut the actual value of wages' being forced higher by a relatively closed economy with reduced movement of labor.
⓯ The final shift is / that governments will likely favor national champions — ⓰ companies [that enjoy regulatory protections, tax breaks and subsidies (that offer an advantage in their home markets against foreign competitors)]. ⓱ What results are corporate

해석

❶ 오늘날 세계화에 대해 제기된 비판의 많은 부분은 세계화가 소수의 사람들만을 더 부유하게 하고, 많은 사람들을 뒤처지게 한다는 생각과 연관되어 있다. ❷ 이런 주장을 하는 사람들은 세계화를 전면적으로 포기하는 것을 종종 옹호한다. ❸ 만약 세계가 고립주의의 길을 간다면, 세 가지 주요한 변화가 일어날 것이다. ❹ 첫째, 보다 고립된 세계는 기업들이 지역적인 모델을 갈수록 더 많이, 그리고 글로벌 모델을 갈수록 더 적게, 채택하도록 강요할 것이다. ❺ 본질적으로, 기업들은 지역과 지역 자본에 더 많이 의존할 가능성이 있으며, 뉴욕, 도쿄, 런던 같은 주요 금융 센터를 중심으로 운영될 가능성이 더 적어지게 될 것이다. ❻ 이러한 변화는 기업들이 자금을 조달하며, 비용을 구조화하고, 장기적 성장의 과제를 바라보는 방식을 크게 바꾸어 놓을 것이다. ❼ 기업들은 자금을 투자하고 기업을 성장시키기 위해 필요한 국제 자본에 접근할 수 있는 기회가 줄어들게 되며, ❽ 이로 인해서 사람들을 고용하게 되고 지역 사회에 투자할 기회가 줄어들게 된다.
❾ 둘째, 단기적 디플레이션과 장기적 인플레이션이 있을 것이다. ❿ 우리는 이미 전자(단기적 디플레이션)를 목격하기 시작했다. ⓫ 비록 이 모든 것들이 최근에 눈에 띄게 나타났지만, 낮은 에너지 비용, 저임금, 실제로 낮은 금리는 널리 만연해있는 디플레이션 세계를 보여준다. ⓬ 후자의 경우에, 낮은 인플레이션의 지속이 금융위기 직후인 2009년까지 거슬러 올라간 급격한 증가에 대한 경고를 무시해 왔다. ⓭ 그 밖에, 상승하는 무역 관세와 보호주의는 수입품의 가격을 감소시킬 것이다. ⓮ 이것은 노동력 이동의 감소와 더불어 상대적으로 폐쇄적인 경제에 의해 더 높도록 강요받는 임금의 실제 가치를 약화할 것이다.
⓯ 마지막 변화는 정부가 국내의 대기업들만 편애할 가능성이 높다는 점이다. ⓰ 이 기업들은 국내 시장에서 외국 경쟁업체보다 우위를 가질 수 있도록 하는 규제 보호, 세제 혜택, 보조금 혜택을 누린다. ⓱ 이로 인한 결과는 경쟁적인 시장보다는 기업의 독점인데, 이러한 상황에서 정부는 누가 이기고 지는지에 대한 더 큰 결정권자가 된다.

어휘

level against ~을 비난하다 **enrich** v. (더) 부유하게 만들다 **leave behind** ~을 놓아 둔 채 잊고 오다, 뒤에 남기다 **advocate** v. 지지하다, 옹호하다 **wholesale** a. 도매의, 대량의, 전면적인 **abandonment** n. 포기, 버림, 유기, 자포자기 **isolationist** n. a. 고립주의자(적인) **adopt** v. 채택하다, 받아들이다 **capital** n. 수도, 대문자, 자본 **financial** a. 재정의, 재정적인 **significantly** ad. 중요하게, 상당하게 **proposition** n. 제의; (처리해야 할) 문제, 과제 **deflation** n. 디플레이션, 물가하락 **inflation** n. 인플레이션, 통화팽창 **prevailing** a. 널리 퍼져 있는, 유행하고 있는 **notably** ad. 특히, 현저히 **persistence** n. 버팀, 영속, 지속 **defy** v. 무시하다, 문제삼지 않다 **uptick** n. (경기·사업 등의) 상향, 상승, 개선 **trade tariff** 무역세 **protectionism** n. 보호무역주의 **undercut** v. (충격·효력 등을) 약화시키다, 꺾다 **favor** v. ~에 편들다, 장려하다 **regulatory** a. 조절[조정]하는; 규정하는 **tax break** 세금 우대[감세]조치 **subsidy** n. (국가·기관이 제공하는) 보조금[장려금] **monopoly** n. 독점, 전매

monopolies / rather than competitive markets, where the government becomes a bigger arbiter of who wins and who loses. ⑱ Ultimately, these companies gain outsize pricing power, which promotes larger and less efficient companies / while disadvantaging consumers.

What is the tone of the passage?
이 글의 어조는 무엇인가?
① persuasive 설득력 있는
② sympathetic 동조하는
③ humorous 재미있는
④ investigative 연구적인

해석 ⑱ 결국, 이러한 기업은 커다란 가격 결정력을 얻는데, 이는 소비자에게 불이익을 주는 동시에 더 크고 덜 효율적인 기업을 조성하게 된다.

해설 세계가 고립주의 길을 걸을 때 일어나는 세 가지 주요 변화를 설명하는 글인 만큼 ① persuasive(설득력있는)이 가장 적절하다.

어휘 arbiter n. 결정권자 outsize a. 특대(형)의 persuasive a. 설득력 있는 sympathetic a. 동정적인, 동조하는 humorous a. 재미있는, 유머러스한 investigative a. 조사의

009 ③ — 2020학년도 숭실대학교 인문계 20번

글의 요지 / 정답근거

❶ Americans are among the most ignorant people in the world / when it comes to history. ❷ Opinion surveys have shown / that large percentages of them do not know the difference (between World War I and World War II). ❸ Many believe / that Germany and the Soviet Union were allies (in the latter conflict). ❹ Many never heard of Hiroshima and have no idea / that the United States dropped an atomic bomb / on that city. ❺ Many could not tell you what issues were involved / in the Vietnam war or other armed conflicts (in which the United States has participated). ❻ Nor could they say much / about the history of aggression (perpetrated / against Native Americans) and the slavery (inflicted / upon Africans in America)].

❼ Americans (themselves) are not totally to blame for this. ❽ They are taught almost nothing of these things in primary and secondary school / nor even at the university level. ❾ And what they are taught is usually devoid of the urgent political economic realities (that allow both past and present to inform each other, making history meaningful to us). ❿ Nor do U.S. political leaders, news pundits, and other opinion makers find much reason (to place current developments in a historical context), especially one (that might raise troublesome questions / about the existing social order)]. ⓫ Popular ignorance is not / without its functions. ⓬ Those (at the top) prefer / that people know little / about history's potentially troublesome lessons / except those parts of history (that have been specially packaged with superpatriotic, system-supporting messages).

⓭ When portrayed in movies and television dramas, / history is usually stood on its head / or reduced / to personal heroics. ⓮ In this regard, the make-believe media reinforce the kind of history (taught in the schools, / mouthed by political leaders, /

해 석

❶ 역사에 관해서라면 미국인들은 세계에서 가장 무지한 사람들에 속한다. ❷ 여론 조사에 따르면 미국의 많은 사람들이 제1차 세계대전과 제2차 세계대전 사이의 차이점을 모르고 있다는 것을 보여주었다. ❸ 대다수의 사람들은 독일과 소련이 후자의 분쟁(제2차 세계대전)에서 동맹국이었다고 생각한다. ❹ 많은 사람들은 히로시마에 대해 들어본 적이 없고 미국이 히로시마에 원자폭탄을 투하했다는 사실을 전혀 알지 못한다. ❺ 많은 이들이 베트남 전쟁이나 미국이 참전한 다른 무력 충돌에 어떠한 문제가 관련되어 있었는지를 당신에게 설명하지 못할 것이다. ❻ 그들은 또한 인디언들에게 자행된 침략의 역사와 미국에서 아프리칸인들(미국 흑인들)에게 가해진 노예제에 대한 많은 것들을 설명할 수 없을 것이다.
❼ 이것에 대한 책임이 전적으로 미국인들 자신에게 있는 것은 아니다. ❽ 그들은 초·중·고등학교 혹은 심지어 대학교 수준에서도 이것들에 대해 거의 배우지 않는다. ❾ 그리고 미국인들이 학습하는 것에는 과거와 현재가 서로 영향을 미쳐 역사를 우리에게 의미 있게 하는 긴급한 정치·경제적 현실이 일반적으로 결여되어 있다. ❿ 미국의 정치 지도자, 뉴스 전문가, 다른 여론 형성자들도 또한 현재 상황 진전을, 역사적인 맥락에서 생각해야 할 근거를 많이 찾지 못하고 있다. ⓫ 대중의 무지는 그 기능이 없는 것이 아니다. ⓬ 고위층 인사들은 역사 중에 특히 광신적으로 애국주의 체제를 뒷받침하는 메시지가 들어있는 부분들을 제외하고는 역사가 가진 골칫거리가 될 가능성이 존재하는 교훈에 대해 사람들이 거의 알지 못하기를 원한다.
⓭ 영화와 텔레비전 드라마에서 묘사될 때, 역사는 일반적으로 반대로 뒤집어지거나 개인적인 영웅담으로 변형된다. ⓮ 이런 부분에서 가짜언론은 학교에서 배우고, 정치 지도자들이 이야기하며, 뉴스 매체가 기록하는 그런 종류의 역사를 강화한다.

어휘

ignorant a. 무지한, 무식한 when it comes to ~에 관한 한 ally n. 동맹국, 협력자 conflict n. 충돌, 갈등 atomic a. 원자의 participate v. 참가하다, 관여하다 aggression n. 공격성, 공격, 침략 perpetrate v. (나쁜 짓·죄를) 행하다, 범하다 inflict v. (괴로움 등을) 가하다 primary a. 주요한, 주된 devoid a. ~이 전혀 없는, 결여된 urgent a. 긴급한, 시급한 pundit n. 박식한 사람, 전문가 opinion maker 여론 형성자, 여론 주도자 troublesome a. 귀찮은; 다루기 힘든 potentially ad. 잠재적으로 superpatriotic a. (광적으로) 애국적인 portray v. 그리다, 묘사하다 stand ~ on its head ~를 뒤집어 놓다 make-believe a. 거짓의, 위장한 reinforce v. 강화하다 mouth v. 뽐내어[큰 소리로, 과장하여] 말하다, 연설조로 말하다

and recorded by the news media). ⓕ One can present almost any subject in the U.S. news and entertainment media : sex and scandal, / deviancy and depravity, / and sometimes even racial oppression and gender discrimination. ⓖ What cannot be touched is the taboo subject of class, / specifically the importance (of class power and class struggle).

Which of the following is the author's attitude toward Americans' ignorance of history?
다음 중 미국인들의 역사의 무지에 대한 필자의 태도는?
① nostalgic
  향수를 불러일으키는
② humorous
  재미있는
✓ critical
  비판적인
④ timid
  소심한

해석 ⓕ 미국의 뉴스와 예능 매체에서는 성(性)과 추문, 일탈과 타락, 그리고 때로는 심지어 인종적 억압과 성차별까지 거의 모든 주제가 다뤄질 수 있다. ⓖ 다루어질 수 없는 것은 계급과 관련한 금기시되는 주제, 특히나 계급 권력과 계급투쟁의 중요성이다.

해설 윗글은 미국인들이 역사에 무지함을 지적하고 원인을 설명하는 글이므로 ③이 가장 적절하다.

어휘 deviancy n. 일탈 (행동) depravity n. 타락, 부패; 사악함 discrimination n. 구별; 식별 struggle v. 고군분투하다

정답 및 해설

010 ②
2020학년도 숭실대학교 인문계 44번

① Rafael Nadal, (one of the world's top tennis players), now has twelve French Open championships. ② A bit of perspective: / until Roger Federer, Novak Djokovic, and Nadal came along, / Pete Sampras led the list of Grand Slam championship winners, / with an all-time total of fourteen. ③ On Sunday afternoon, / with the wind and rain (that had marred play / at Roland-Garros for days / yielding to comfortable Paris-in-springtime weather), / Nadal defeated Dominic Thiem 6-3, 5-7, 6-1, 6-1. ④ A bit more perspective: / it was not as lopsided / as the scoring line suggests. ⑤ The first hour or so was as good — / with lengthy rallies, barefooted scrambles, keen variations of pace and placement — / as clay-court tennis gets. ⑥ In the hour (that followed), Thiem managed to take a set / from Nadal, [something (he'd never before done at Roland-Garros)], despite being, (arguably), the second-best men's clay-surface player / at the moment. ⑦ Even in the final two sets, / Thiem reached balls and struck shots (that should have earned him points), but didn't — / not against Nadal. ⑧ Which is to say that / Thiem played championship-level tennis, / ⑨ but not Nadal-on-Chatrier-level tennis.

⑩ There are particular aspects of Thiem's game (that make it difficult for him to beat Nadal), though he had beaten him / four times on clay, / and lost eight times, / before this match. ⑪ Thiem requires time (to set up his groundstrokes) — he takes his racquet way back, / especially when getting ready to deliver his one-handed drive backhand. ⑫ He has to get his adjustment steps just right and his feet firmly planted. ⑬ This buys Nadal that extra second / to reestablish court position / after he's been yanked / to the corner by, (say), a deep, sharply angled shot. ⑭ A player (like Djokovic) can deny Nadal that time / by taking the ball early, / on the rise, / or by hitting big balance-defying / down-the-line shots

해석

❶ 세계 정상급 테니스 선수 중 한 명인 라파엘 니달(Rafael Nadal)은 현재 프랑스 오픈에서 12번의 우승을 하였다. ❷ 이에 관해 약간의 관점을 제시하자면, 로저 페더러(Roger Federer) 노박 조코비치(Novak Djokovic), 니달이 나오기 전까지 피트 샘프라스(Pete Sampras)가 전례 없던 기록으로 14번의 그랜드슬램 우승을 차지했다. ❸ 며칠 동안 롤랑가로스에서 개최되는 경기를 망쳤던 바람과 비가 따뜻한 파리의 봄 날씨로 바뀌었던 일요일 오후, 니달은 도미니크 팀(Dominic Thiem)을 6-3, 5-7, 6-1, 6-1로 물리쳤다. ❹ 여기서 좀 더 넓은 관점에서 보면, 그것은 점수 결과가 보여주는 것처럼 한쪽으로 치우친 경기는 아니었다. ❺ 첫 한 시간가량은 계속해서 서로 공을 쳐 넘기고, 발 빠르게 공을 쫓아다니며, 타구의 구속과 플레이스먼트(상대편 코트의 빈 곳으로 보낸 타구)가 예리하게 변화하는 등, 클레이 코트 경기에서 대개 그런 만큼이나 좋았다. ❻ 그 이후에 한 시간 동안 팀은 니달에게서 용케도 한 세트를 따냈는데, 틀림없이 그것은 그가 당시에 클레이 코트에서 2위에 올랐던 선수였음에도 불구하고 롤랑가로스에서 이전에는 해보지 못한 것이었다. ❼ 그리고 마지막 두 세트에도 팀은 공을 잡아내어 점수를 얻어내야 하는 샷을 날렸어야 했지만, 니달을 상대로는 그렇게 하지 못하였다. ❽ 즉, 팀은 우승할 수 있는 수준의 테니스를 했지만 ❾ 샤트리에 코트에서의 니달 수준의 테니스를 보여주지는 못했다.

❿ 비록 이 경기 전에 팀이 니달을 클레이 코트에서 4번 이기고, 8번 졌지만, 팀의 경기에는 그가 니달을 이기기 어렵게 만드는 특별한 점들이 있다. ⓫ 팀은 특히 한 손으로 백핸드 드라이브를 치려고 하는 순간, 그의 라켓을 뒤로 멀리 가져가다 보니, 그라운드스트로크(공이 땅에 닿고 튀어 오른 뒤에 치는 것)를 치는 데 시간이 소요된다. ⓬ 그는 자신의 적응 스텝(공의 낙하지점에 정확하게 스텝을 맞추기 위해서 잔걸음으로 거리를 조절하는 발동작)을 정확히 딱 맞게 밟아야 하고 그의 발을 단단히 땅에 고정해야 한다. ⓭ 이것은 예를 들어, 니달을 깊고 날카로운 앵글 샷으로 코너로 몰고 난 뒤에 니달에게 코트에서 자세를 다시 고쳐잡는데 여분의 시간을 벌어준다. ⓮ 조코비치 같은 선수는 떠오르는 공을 일찍 처리하거나 밸런스를 붕괴시키는 다운 더 라인 샷을 강하게 전력으로 때림으로써 니달에게 그 시간을 주지 않을 수 있다.

어휘

perspective n. 관점, 시각 **come along** 생기다, 나타나다 **lead the list** 으뜸을 차지하다 **all-time** a. 시대를 초월한, 전무후무한, 전대미문의 **mar** v. 손상시키다, 망치다 **yield to** ~으로 대체되다 **lopsided** a. 한쪽이 처진, 한쪽으로 치우친 **score line** (경기·대회 등에서) 최종 점수[결과] **rally** n. (배드민턴·테니스 등에서) 계속하여 서로 쳐 넘기기 **barefoot** a. 맨발의 **scramble** n. 서로 다투어 빼앗기, 쟁탈 **arguably** a. 거의 틀림없이, 어쩌면 **second-best** a. 차선(次善)의, 제 2위의 **groundstroke** n. 그라운드스트로크(공이 땅에 닿고 튀어 오른 뒤에 치는 것) **backhand** n. 백핸드(손등을 공쪽으로 향하게 해서 치는 것) **adjustment** n. 수정, 적응 **firmly** ad. 단호히, 확고히 **yank** v. 홱 끌다[잡아당기다] **down-the-line shot** 테니스에서 상대편 코트의 사이드 선과 평행하게 직선으로 공을 보내는 기술

/ at full stretch. ⓑ But that's not Thiem. ⓖ And Thiem, (like Federer in years past), struggles with Nadal's serve (to his backhand), / especially in the ad court. ⓗ The lefty's slice skids out wide on him; / more than once on Sunday, / Thiem's feet got tangled / in pursuit of it. ⓘ And Nadal kept showing him that serve, / unceasingly as the match wore on.

What is the tone of the passage?
이 글의 어조는 무엇인가?

① ironic
아이러니한

✓ analytic
분석적인

③ sarcastic
비꼬는

④ emphatic
단호한

해석
ⓑ 하지만 팀은 그럴 수 없다. ⓖ 지난 몇 년 동안 페더러처럼 팀은 특히나 어드밴티지 코트에서 나달의 서브를 백핸드로 받아내는 것을 힘들어한다. ⓗ 그 왼손잡이의 슬라이스는 팀에게서 먼 쪽으로 미끄러져 나가는데, 일요일 경기에서는 그 슬라이스 공을 쫓다가 팀의 발이 뒤얽혀버리는 일이 한 번 이상 있었다. ⓘ 그리고 나달은 경기가 흘러가는 동안 계속해서 그 서브를 그에게 계속 보여주었다.

해설
테니스 선수 나달과 롤랑가로스 대회(프랑스 오픈)에서 도미니크 팀이 나달을 상대로 어떻게 경기를 했는지에 대한 관점을 설명하는 글로서 ② 'analytic(분석적)'이라고 하는 것이 가장 적절하다.

어휘
at full stretch 전력을 기울여 **struggle** v. 노력하다, 고군분투하다 **ad court** n. 테니스에서 왼쪽 서비스 코트를 말함(어드밴티지 뒤에 서브를 하는 코트) **lefty** n. 왼손잡이 **slice** n. 슬라이스(공을 깎듯이 쳐서 한 쪽으로 휘어져 나아가게 하는 타법) **skid** v. 미끄러지다 **out wide** 측면 공격 **get tangled** 엉클어지다 **unceasingly** ad. 끊임없이 **ironic** a. 아이러니한 **analytic** a. 분석적인 **sarcastic** a. 빈정되는, 비꼬는 **emphatic** a. 강한, 강조하는, 단호한

memo